DIMENSION

Contemporary German Arts and Letters / Volume 13, No. 1, 1980

Department of Germanic Languages / THE UNIVERSITY OF TEXAS AT AUSTIN

DIMENSION

DIMENSION

Contemporary German Arts and Letters / Volume 13, No. 1, 1980

Department of Germanic Languages / THE UNIVERSITY OF TEXAS AT AUSTIN

A. LESLIE WILLSON, *Editor*
HANS BENDER, *Guest Editor*

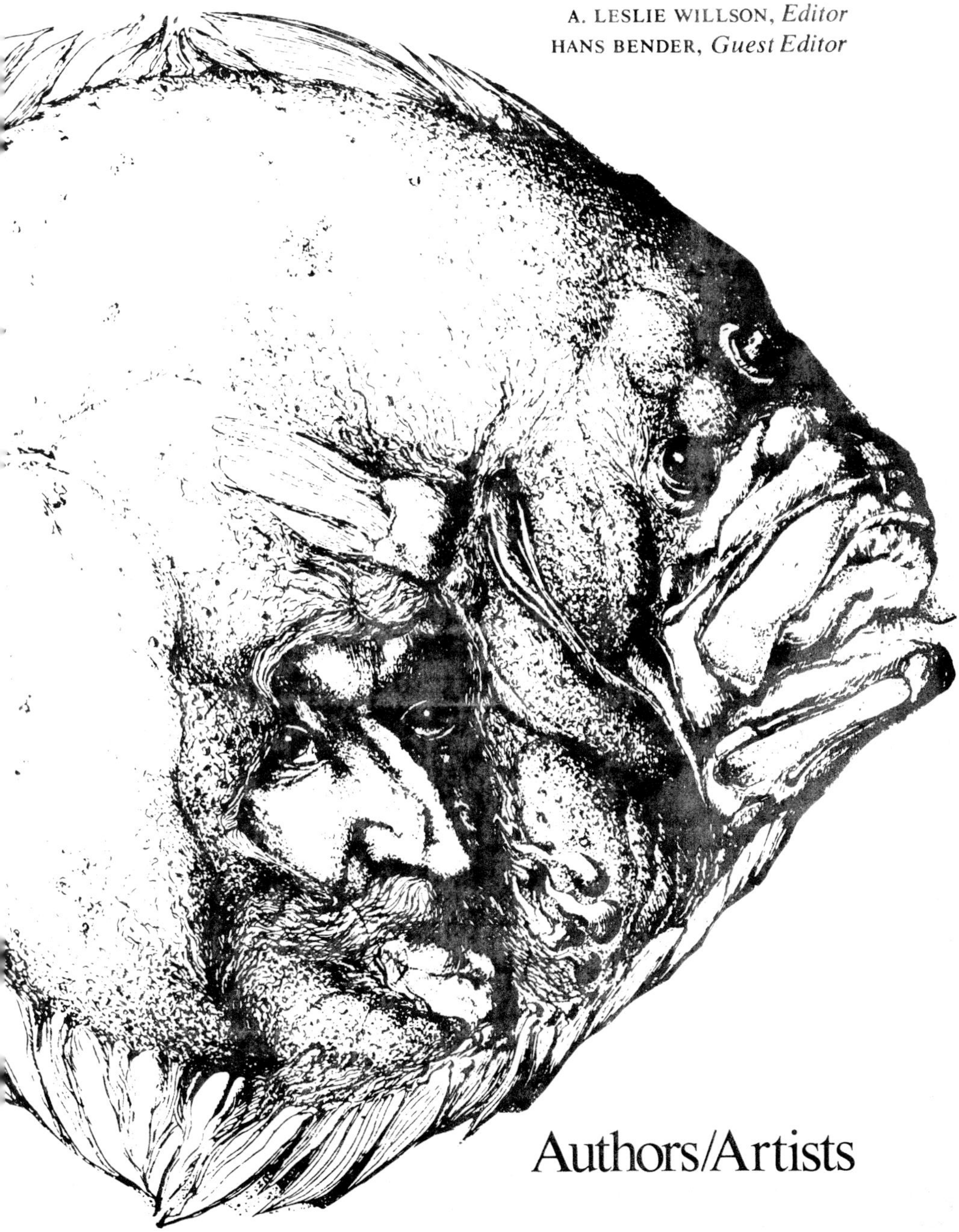

Authors/Artists

DIMENSION is published three times yearly at The University of Texas at Austin. Subscription: $12 per year for individuals, $15 per year for institutions in the United States, plus $2 postage and handling; $15 per year for individuals, $20 per year for institutions elsewhere, plus $4 postage and handling. Single copy $6 in the U.S., $8 elsewhere, plus postage and handling. All subscriptions should be sent to DIMENSION, The Department of Germanic Languages, P.O. Box 7939, Austin, TX 78712, USA. All contributions and editorial correspondence should be sent to: The Editor, DIMENSION, P. O. Box 26673, Austin, TX 78755, USA. Unsolicited manuscripts must be accompanied by a stamped, self-addressed envelope.

ISSN 0012–2882
DESIGN AND ART DIRECTION: DAVID PRICE

ACKNOWLEDGMENTS

"Persönliche Anmerkung" by Friedrich Dürrenmatt is the afterword from the volume *Bilder und Zeichnungen*, © 1978 by the Diogenes Verlag, Zurich, from which also the paintings reproduced in this issue are reprinted with the permission of the publisher. All rights reserved.

"Die Linkshänder," "Die Ballerina," and the drawings by Günter Grass are published with the kind permission of the author, who reserves all rights.

"An Interview with Günter Grass" is published with the permission of Mr. Grass.

"Leben und Tod von Sir Andrew Marbot" by Wolfgang Hildesheimer is published, with examples of his art, with the permission of the author/artist.

"Steinbruch-Morgenbuch" by Walter Höllerer is reprinted from *Akzente,* volume 26 (1979), with the permission of its editor, Hans Bender.

"Das Dings da" by Christoph Meckel is excerpted from the volume of the same title, © 1980 by the Verlag Eremiten-Presse, Düsseldorf, reprinted with examples of Meckel's drawings with the permission of Dieter Hülsmanns and Friedolin Reske.

"Einige Gedichte" by Ernst Meister are taken from *Wandloser Raum* and *Ausgewählte Gedichte, 1932–1979,* both © 1979 by Luchterhand Verlag, Darmstadt, and are republished with the permission of the publisher and Elsie Meister, who kindly sent samples of Meister's art.

"Depart" is published with the permission of the author, Erica Pedretti.

"Absteigende Gedichte" by Gerhard Rühm are published, along with examples of Rühm's graphic art, with the permission of the author/artist.

△ indicates original, previously unpublished contributions in German dialects. All contributions in English appear in print for the first time.

Subscribers to DIMENSION may order microfilm copies or photocopied duplicate issues through University Microfilms, Ann Arbor, Michigan 48106.

CONTENTS

Perspective — A. LESLIE WILLSON — 9

Letter from Germany — HANS BENDER — 11

Persönliche Anmerkung — FRIEDRICH DÜRRENMATT — 15
Personal Notes — *translated by Jeanne R. Willson*
Paintings

Syrakus und andere Gedichte — ERICH FITZBAUER — 40
Syrakus and other Poems — *translated by Herman Salinger*
Drawings

Die Linkshänder — GÜNTER GRASS — 52
The Left-Handers — *translated by A. Leslie Willson*

Die Ballerina — GÜNTER GRASS — 68
The Ballerina — *translated by A. Leslie Willson*

An Interview with Günter Grass — IRMGARD ELSNER HUNT — 84
Graphics

Leben und Tod von Sir Andrew Marbot — WOLFGANG HILDESHEIMER — 92
The Life and Death
of Sir Andrew Marbot — *translated by Allan Blunden*
Graphics

Steinbruch-Morgenbuch — WALTER HÖLLERER — 122
Stone-Quarry Morning Diary — *translated by Herman Salinger*
Drawing

Sechs Gedichte — ALDONA GUSTAS — 144
Six Poems — *translated by Julia Penn*
Graphics

from: *Shittelbecker's Holiday* (illustrated) — ERNEST JANDL — 154

Prosa, Gedichte, Kleine Essays — GÜNTER KUNERT — 158
Prose, Poems, Mini-Essays — *translated by A. Leslie Willson, Ulrich K. Goldsmith, and Stephen Zon*
Graphics

Ich brauche dieses Leben und andere Gedichte — WERNER LUTZ — 190
I Need This Life and other Poems
translated by Timothy A. Bonner-Saroff
Paintings

Triplet und andere Bild-Gedichte FRIEDERIKE-MAYRÖCKER 196
Triplet and other Picture-Poems
translated by Michael P. Elzay

Das Dings Da (illustrated) CHRISTOPH MECKEL 200
The Thingamajig *translated by Ralph R. Read III*

Bericht vom Handwerk CHRISTOPH MECKEL 208
Report on my Craft *translated by Ralph R. Read III*

Einige Gedichte ERNST MEISTER 218
Some Poems *translated by Georg M. Gugelberger*
Paintings

Der erste Regen und andere Gedichte KARL OPPERMANN 226
The First Rain *translated by Breon Mitchell*
and other Poems (with graphics)

Depart ERICA PEDRETTI 234
Departing *translated by Johannes Vazulik*
Graphics

Absteigende Gedichte GERHARD RÜHM 244
Descending Poems *translated by Allen H. Chappel*
Graphics

Liebeskummer (illustrated) ROBERT WOLFGANG SCHNELL 252
Pangs of Love *translated by Ken Fontenot*

Totsein in einem Winkel der Stadt und andere Gedichte GERD SONNTAG 268
To Be Dead in a Corner of the City
and other Poems *translated by George F. Peters*
Paintings

Zustände und andere Gedichte JOACHIM UHLMANN 274
Conditions and other Poems *translated by A. Leslie Willson*
Paintings

Aus dem Pariser Journal PETER WEISS 288
From the Paris Journal *translated by Ralph R. Read III*
Collages

Authors and Translators

PERSPECTIVE

AUTHOR/ARTISTS

WHEN, IN THE GERMAN MAGAZINE ART IN LATE 1979, GÜNTER GRASS PUBLISHED a two-column commentary on his own involvement with literature and graphic art under the title "Bin ich nun Schreiber oder Zeichner?" he made his first public pronouncements on the integral nature of his literary and his artistic impulses, impulses that distinguish not only his work but the work of other writers in Germany and throughout the world. Though Grass himself contributed drawings and cover designs of his own to his books of poetry and other literary works, the artistic side of the author has generally been ignored or little recognized. This is true not only in his case but in the cases of others for whom their graphic talents are inextricably bound to the literary works they have produced, authors such as Günter Kunert and Christoph Meckel, as well as the Austrian Erich Fitzbauer and the Swiss Wolfgang Hildesheimer, not to mention his compatriot Friedrich Dürrenmatt.

As guest-editor Hans Bender mentions in his "Letter from Germany," the artistic talents of writers have largely been overlooked, even by the sharpest-eyed critics and readers. However, to understand the work of an author/artist fully, attention must be paid to the concomitant activity of the creative author whose vision and impressions of the world about him and within him are precipitated onto drawing paper and canvas with the most varied kinds of artistic tools. Admittedly, the writer who also sculpts, draws, paints, or even doodles is not a new phenomenon. Generally, perhaps, attention is drawn to his adjunct creativity in the ratio to which he himself integrates it into his literary work, as Grass always has and as William Blake did. Few readers of Friedrich Dürrenmatt's stories and plays probably have realized to what a large extent his nighttime labors over drawing boards contributed to the firming up of themes elucidated in his writing, thanks in one instance—in regard to angels—to his encounter with the bat Mathilde.

It is quite possible that the almost indefinable creative essences of author/artists can be illuminated by critical attention to their works of art. That is certainly true of the work of Dürrenmatt, Grass, Hildesheimer, Kunert, Meckel, and Joachim Uhlmann. It may well be true of other authors represented in this issue of DIMENSION, whose artistic endeavors are less energetically, more marginally pursued. Pity the poor critic who brings to his literary analyses little knowledge of artistic media but who senses the intricate and indelible relationship between the written word and its sketched or painted transformation. A bit of self-education may be in order. Grass himself admits that the drawing at times precedes the literary variation or elucidation. But it may be true that the critic of literature must also take into account the artistic production of the author whose works he interprets; for strata of theme, symbol, and even aspects of style may have found expression—whether before or afterwards is of little consequence—in the art works of those authors, and certainly consideration of such expression of the creative minds at work can help probe meaning and signification.

This issue of DIMENSION began essentially with the first issue of 1968. Each issue has contained an example of art—drawings, collages, etchings, woodcuts, linoleum cuts, watercolors—from German-speaking lands, though not always by writers themselves. Even in that arena, however, issues have contained work by Fitzbauer, Grass, Hildesheimer, Gustas, Kunert, Friederike Mayröcker, Meckel, and Peter Weiss, all now represented here once again. Newly added to the roster of authors who also are artists, published by DIMENSION, are Dürrenmatt, Walter Höllerer, Ernst Jandl, Werner Lutz, Ernst Meister, Karl Oppermann, Gerhard Rühm, Gerd Sonntag, and Uhlmann. And this selective list by no means exhausts the ranks of contemporary artists who are also authors. The late Günter Bruno Fuchs, for example, is not represented in this issue, although he may be found in two previous issues of DIMENSION.

The editor owes a large debt of gratitude to guest editor Hans Bender for his unflagging efforts to obtain the contributions here presented and to the author/artists themselves for their cooperation. It is hoped that the issue will alert critics and readers alike to the fascinating phenomenon of the gifted author/artist, whose poetry and art may even be as entwined as that of Oppermann, who literally (and graphically) sets his poetry in an artistic frame. Despite problems of equipment and technology, it is to be hoped that photographic slides and printed illustrations will become part and parcel of the presentations of lecturers and critics from the academic and publishing world who make public comment and interpretation concerning the works of authors who also are artists.

A. LESLIE WILLSON

LETTER FROM GERMANY

ALTERNATELY

IF ONE PURSUES THE ALLURING AND DIVERSE PHENOMENON OF WRITER-artist, one encounters nothing but contradictions. For one writer art is a function on an equal with writing; to another it is, on the contrary, a matter of secondary importance, a hobby, a game, an amusement. To one, art and writing are really equivalent, entwined expressions; to another two contrary manifestations whose different means of presentation he is able to keep in balance. One writer-artist has attended an academy; his primary professional goal was to become an artist. Another has only his native talent; he is even proud that he is not a professional, but rather a bumbling, amateurish graphic artist or illustrator—and even that surprises him. Most writer-artists do not worry about such contradictions and classifications; they paint, draw, watercolor, make etchings and collages, scribble, paste, and daub to their heart's content—but the results are not without value, since their creators are not just ordinary *peintres naïfes* or weekend artists but also well-known writers.

One can begin with Goethe, if one wants to trace the subject and the diversity of the writer-artist. His drawings—landscapes were his favorites—taught him, he wrote, "how to look at artless things." Writers of the Romantic period might be mentioned: Clemens Brentano, Achim von Arnim, and E.T.A. Hoffmann (who was, in addition, a talented composer). Then the writer-artists of the next chapters in literary history: Adalbert von Chamisso, Wilhelm Hauff, August Kopisch, Wilhelm Waiblinger, Gottfried Keller, and Annette von Droste-Hülshoff; Wilhelm Busch and Wilhelm Raabe, Thomas and Heinrich Mann, Alfred Kubin, Ernst Barlach, Rainer Maria Rilke, Hermann Hesse, Hans Arp, and others. Each in his way a writer-artist; each with his own individual shading and character.

If Kurt Böttcher and Johannes Mittenzwei, the editors of the standard work *Dichter als Maler* (Writers as Artists), just published by the Kohlhammer Verlag in Stuttgart, have counted correctly, there have been or are 167 German writer-artists altogether. Of course, they exist in all lands and literatures. In the East Asian cultures they are ideally represented because there art and writing are by custom connected activities: Calligraphy is part of writing down a poem. In the concrete poetry of the fifties and sixties, internationally and in German and especially in the picture-poem, the writing itself and the text had equal function and meaning.

A double talent is, however, a problem for evaluation. *One* activity is usually taken less seriously than the *other*. The artist who also writes and the writer who also draws are seldom judged fairly in both activities. To call a picture "literary" is just as denigrating as to characterize a text as "picturesque." Art encyclopedias do not mention the poems of Paul Klee; dictionaries of literature do not mention the pictures of Friedrich Dürrenmatt. The literary histories speak of lyric poets, epic writers, dramatists—without mentioning their artistic sideline. A German characteristic is involved here: the lack of toleration of a bifurcated profession or a specialized division.

Since its beginning the magazine DIMENSION has interspersed and enlivened its printed pages with carefully selected pictures, drawings, graphics, collages, and so forth (that are, moreover, also commendably reproduced). They originate not just from clearly prominent graphic artists, illustrators, and caricaturists, such as HAP Grieshaber, Sascha Juritz, Alex Hertenstein, and Gerhard Grimm, among others, but repeatedly represent writer-artists of the German-speaking sphere. From Peter Weiss and Günter Grass; from Günter Bruno Fuchs and Günter Kunert; from Christoph Meckel and Ernst Jandl; from Friederike Mayröcker, Aldona Gustas, and sundry others. Here the love of the editor for double talents and for the artistic expression of poets and writers has been declared: A. Leslie Willson's esteem for the second activity of an author and for its importance in the whole of his figure and of his work. Now in this issue writer-artists of the German-speaking sphere are brought together in one group and on one palette. Some for the second or third time; others for the first time: Ernst Meister and Walter Höllerer, for example. They all demonstrated their double talent and its respective shadings.

From most of the writer-artists there are remarks about how they began to paint or write and how the second activity suddenly became more important than the first. Peter Weiss, Günter Grass, Günter Kunert, Günter Bruno Fuchs, and Christoph Meckel attended art academies in their youth. They began as painters, sketchers, graphic artists, or, as in the case of Günter Grass, as stonemason and sculptor. Wolfgang Hildesheimer started out as a technical draughtsman and stage designer. Friedrich Dürrenmatt wanted nothing more passionately than to become a painter and could not understand that the first people who viewed his pictures did not take them as seriously as he did. The circumstances of the times contributed to this—the story of his life and the fate that determined it.

Thus it was, also, that for Peter Weiss, beclouded in his youth by a foreign country and by the war, painting was an expression of life, a "performance," an "alternative." In the autobiographical novel *Fluchtpunkt* (*Vanishing Point*), Weiss communicated in retrospect what painting had meant to him then and how difficult the transition to the written word was for him, "that the things I wanted to say could not be said if the language lost its natural function as a means of expression. I took my quest back to the old language because I could control it completely in all details and because it was connected with my original impulses. And still in it something foreign, repellent, made itself felt, the words when written down stood soundless there, without any relation to the thought that I wanted to express." With the composition of the prose work *Der Schatten des Körpers des Kutschers* (*The Shadow of the Coachman's Body*) in 1952 Peter Weiss started on his way as an author without having given up his activity as a painter and illustrator. We still see in his visionary and metaphorical pictures, sketches, illustrations, and collages the experiences and the anguish of his youth, "when"—as the painter Erich Jansen wrote as a comment on them—"the life and death of mankind was on the line."

For Wolfgang Hildesheimer those periods in which he expresses himself as an artist or as a writer succeed each other as points in time momentarily separated. First he is busy painting or drawing, then writing. To him this is, more than just writing would be, "the principle of occupational therapy." "In this way," he writes, "I overcome fatigue, boredom, and depression; my thoughts are never on the finished work but often are involved with the activity—with pasting, with manual execution." Hildesheimer contrasts the advantages against his writing: "Work keeps me going, at almost any chosen moment. Nothing is planned for success, nothing can be repeated."

Günter Grass' double profession causes him no problems, no inconveniences. He writes and draws, as he expresses it, "alternately; but the writing of poems and the drawing of graphically objective realities do not exclude each other, rather they are simultaneously possible and necessary." Günter Kunert, too, sees no conflict between art and writing, but—in spite of his talent—writing is for him "by far the most important." When Kunert describes his drawings or paintings, his poetic texts could be meant, too. They have, he writes, "always something narrative, illustrative, sometimes drolly allegorical." Stories are told about Christoph Meckel that relate how his two equally significant talents coexist and do not interfere with one another: "I have to be my own referee," he writes, "either I write and put the etching tools away, or I draw and put the typewriter under the table."

Wolfdietrich Schnurre might be mentioned as one of that larger group of writers who devote less than half of their time—even much less—to working at painting or drawing. They are addicted to painting and drawing spontaneously, naively, moodily, frivolously. His art talent, Schnurre thinks, exists "on the level of childlike pavement painting on a scale from 'Ida is dumb' to stick figures." Fun is one motive, Schnurre writes; another is the unimpaired relationship of the artist to childhood: "For actually it seems in the drawings that the literary wish for emphatic consolidation joins with just that playful creative intent that can really be found in its pure state only in the heart of a child."

Certainly, the great or small "works of art" of the writer-artists—as we call them simply—would be intelligible and attractive even without this personal testimony. They are "art works" in and of themselves. Their themes are interesting—their technique, their style, their signature, their lines or strokes, their notions or wit. And they are all expressions of authors whose poems, tales, novels, and dramas we know and which we can perhaps understand even better in comparison to their artistic declarations. In this issue of DIMENSION the poetic texts are consciously contrasted with the great and small "art works." The exhibition complements the anthology. It should help to spread the reputation of the German double talents among American viewers and readers to begin with. But this DIMENSION issue might produce a surprise even for the German readers and viewers on the other side of the ocean.

HANS BENDER

translated by Jeanne R. Willson

Friedrich Dürrenmatt

Labyrinth I: Der entwürdigte Minotaurus (1958) Gouache

Labyrinth I: The Debased Minotaur

ortrait: Lotti Dürrenmatt (1959) Gouache

ortrait: Lotti Dürrenmatt

"Engel und Heilige stoben davon—Da setzte sich auf Gottes Thron / Der Täuferkönig Bockelson" (1966) Oil

"Angels and saints scattered away—Then there sat on the throne of God, the Baptist-King Beelzebub"

Die Astronomen (1952) Gouache

The Astronomers

PERSÖNLICHE ANMERKUNG

FRIEDRICH DÜRRENMATT

MEINE ZEICHNUNGEN SIND NICHT NEBENARBEITEN ZU MEINEN LITERARIschen Werken, sondern die gezeichneten und gemalten Schlachtfelder, auf denen sich meine schriftstellerischen Kämpfe, Abenteuer, Experimente und Niederlagen abspielen. Eine Einsicht, die mir erst beim Durchblättern dieses Buches bewußt geworden ist, auch wenn ich in meiner Jugend nur gezeichnet und erst später geschrieben habe. Ich war immer ein Zeichner. Doch ist die *Kreuzigung I* meine erste Zeichnung, die ich nachträglich noch zu akzeptieren vermag, aus dem einfachen Grunde, daß ich nicht ein kompositioneller, sondern ein "dramaturgischer" Zeichner bin. Ich kümmere mich nicht um die Schönheit des Bildes, sondern um dessen Möglichkeit. Um ein Beispiel aus der "großen" Kunst anzuführen: Michelangelos "David" ist eine Abstrusität, ein Koloß, 5,5 m hoch, während Goliath laut Bibel nur 2,9 m groß war. Aber der "David" ist deshalb eine bedeutende Plastik, weil Michelangelo ihn "dramaturgisch" in jenem Moment festhält, da er zur "Statue" wird. Es ist der Augenblick, in dem David Goliath zum erstenmal wahrnimmt und überlegt, wie er ihn besiegen könne: Wo muß ich den Stein hinschleudern? In diesem Moment verharrt der Mensch in der vollkommenen Ruhe des Nachdenkens und des Betrachtens. Er wird dramaturgisch zur Plastik. Ähnliches läßt sich von Michelangelos "Moses" sagen. Er ist in dem Augenblick dargestellt, da er realisiert, was er doch schon von Jahwe erfahren hat: daß das Volk um das Goldene Kalb tanzt. Noch staunt er, noch bereitet sich der Zorn in ihm erst vor, noch hat er die Gesetzestafeln in der Hand, aber im nächsten Augenblick wird er aufspringen und sie zerschmettern und dann befehlen, dreitausend Männer seines Volkes zu töten: Das ist dramaturgisches Denken in der Plastik. Dramaturgisch stellte sich daher in meinen *Kreuzigungen* die Frage: Wie gestalte ich *heute* eine Kreuzigung? Das Kreuz ist ein Symbol geworden und damit auch als Schmuck verwendbar, etwa als Kreuz zwischen Frauenbrüsten. Der Gedanke, das Kreuz sei einmal ein Marterinstrument gewesen, ist verlorengegangen. In meiner ersten *Kreuzigung* versuche ich durch den Tanz um das Kreuz, das Kreuz wieder zum Kreuz, zum Gegenstand des Skandals zu machen, den es einmal darstellte. In der zweiten *Kreuzigung* ist das Kreuz durch ein noch grausameres Marterinstrument, durch das Rad, ersetzt, auch ist nicht ein Mensch, sondern viele Menschen sind gerädert, nur ein Mensch ist gekreu-

PERSONAL NOTES

FRIEDRICH DÜRRENMATT
translated by Jeanne R. Willson

MY DRAWINGS ARE NOT OF SECONDARY IMPORTANCE TO MY LITERARY work but are rather the drawn and painted fields of battle on which my literary struggles, adventures, experiments, and defeats take place. An insight that I first became aware of when I leafed through this book [of my drawings], even though in my youth I only drew and did not write until later. I was always drawing. But the *Crucifixion I* was the first of my drawings that I could afterwards accept, for the simple reason that I am not a compositional but rather a "theatrical" artist. I do not bother about the beauty of a picture but about its feasibility. To use an example from "great" art: Michelangelo's *David* is an abstrusity, a colossus 5.5 meters tall, while Goliath according to the Bible was only 2.9 meters tall. But the *David* is an important piece of sculpture because Michelangelo arrests him "theatrically" in that moment when he becomes a statue. It is the moment in which David first perceives Goliath and considers how he can vanquish him: Where must I hurl the stone? At this moment the man pauses in the complete quiet of contemplation and consideration. He is turned theatrically into sculpture. Very much the same thing can be said about Michelangelo's *Moses*. He is represented in that moment when he realizes what he has already learned from Jahwe: that the people are dancing around the Golden Calf. He is still surprised, the anger is still building up within him, he still has the Tables of the Law in his hand, but in the next moment he will leap up and break them to pieces and then give commands to kill three thousand men from among his people: That is theatrical thought in sculpture. Theatrically, then, in my *Crucifixions* the question is put: How shall I picture a crucifixion *today*? The cross has become a symbol and thus suitable also as an adornment, for instance, as a cross between a woman's breasts. The thought that the Cross was once an instrument of torture has been lost. In my first *Crucifixion*, I attempt by means of the dance around the Cross to make the Cross into a cross again, into the shocking object that it once evoked. In the second *Crucifixion* the cross is replaced by the wheel, an even more horrible instrument of torture, also not one but many human beings are being broken on the wheel; only one person has been crucified, a beheaded, pregnant woman, out of whose abdomen, which has been cut open, a child hangs. On the zigt, eine geköpfte schwangere Frau, aus deren aufgeschnittenem Leib ein Kind hängt. An den Blutgerüsten klettern Ratten umher. In der dritten *Kreuzigung* wird ein dicker gekreuzigter Jude mit abgehackten Armen von Ratten beklettert. Nicht aus "Liebe zum Schrecklichen" sind diese Blätter entstanden, unzählige Menschen sind auf unvergleichlich schrecklichere Art gestorben als Jesus von Nazareth. Nicht der gekreuzigte Gott sollte unser Skandalon sein, sondern der gekreuzigte Mensch; vermag doch der Tod—und sei er noch so fürchterlich—für einen Gott nie so schrecklich wie für einen Mensch zu sein: Der Gott wird wieder auferstehen. So ist denn heute nicht mehr das Kreuz, sondern die Auferstehung das Skandalon des Christentums, und nur so ist Blatt Nr. 102 zu verstehen, entstanden 1978. Es ist nicht ein strahlender Gott, sondern eine Mumie, die ohne Zeugen aufersteht. Hier gibt es eine Parallele zu meinem dramatischen Schaffen: Im "Meteor" besteht der Skandal darin, daß ein Mensch immer wieder stirbt und immer wieder aufersteht. Er vermag, gerade weil er das Wunder am eigenen Leib erfährt, nicht daran zu glauben. Anders die *Engel* (Nr. 84, 85, 101): 1952 pumpte ich mir, ein Schriftsteller ohne Geld, in Neuenburg ein Haus zusammen. Es war ziemlich schwierig. Wer wollte auch damals einem Schriftsteller Geld leihen. Die Lebensversicherung "Pax", in deren Händen die erste Hypothek lag, kündigte mir denn auch gleich. Doch konnten wir das Haus beziehen. Es half, wer helfen konnte. Damals entstanden meine zwei Gouachen Nr. 11 (*Die Astronomen*) und Nr. 12 (*Ertrunkenes Liebespaar*) in einer Technik, die ich erst 1978 wieder aufgenommen habe (*Die Welt der Atlasse*, Nr. 100). Ich malte nachts und wurde beim Malen gegen 2 Uhr morgens stets von einer Fledermaus besucht, einem reizenden Tierchen, das ich Mathilde nannte. Einmal war ich unfair, ich schloß das Fenster und machte mich daran, Mathilde zu fangen. Als ich sie gefangen hatte, zeigte ich sie den Kindern und erklärte ihnen, Mathilde sei ein Mäuseengel, dann ließ ich sie wieder frei. Sie war sehr beleidigt und ließ sich nicht mehr blicken. Seitdem ließ mich das Motiv "Engel" nicht wieder los. Nicht aus Spott, mehr aus Übermut. Mathildens Rache: Ich zeichnete unzählige Menschenengel, auch eierlegende Cherubim, aus dem Handgelenk, als Karikaturen. Mein Humor verführte mich. Dieser Faktor—mein hauptsächlicher—ist nie zu unterschätzen; er ist überall wirksam. Erst nach und nach kam ich dahinter, daß die Engel doch eigentlich furchterregende Wesen sind, Wesen, zu denen sich Mathilde verhält wie eine Eidechse zum Tyrannosaurus-Rex. Es begann mich dramaturgisch zu interessieren, wie denn heute ein Engel zu gestalten wäre, gibt es doch auch in der Kunst kaum Engel, die mir einleuchten, vielleicht bloß die zustoßenden, zuschlagenden, zornigen Engel in der "Apokalypse" Dürers. So versuchte ich denn, Engel dramaturgisch darzustellen, die zwei *Todesengel* und den *Engel*, an welchem ich lange arbeitete: Auch Engel sind etwas Schreckliches. Wenn Elisabeth Brockscaffolds rats are scrambling around. In the third *Crucifixion* a fat, crucified Jew with arms cut off is covered with scrambling rats. These sheets did not originate in a "love of the horrible," countless men have died in incomparably more horrible ways than Jesus of Nazareth. Our shame should not be crucified God but rather crucified Man; for death could never—and be it ever so frightful—be as terrible for a god as for a human being: The god will rise again. So today not the Cross but the Resurrection is the shame of Christianity and only thus can my *Resurrection*, produced in 1978, be understood. It is not a shining god but a mummy that rises from the dead without witnesses. There is a parallel here to my dramatic work: In *Meteor* the ignominy is based on a human being who dies again and again and is resurrected again and again. And just because he experiences the miracle in his own body, he cannot believe in it. The *Angel* is different: In 1952 I, a writer without money, borrowed enough for a house in Neuenburg. It was rather difficult. Even then, who wanted to lend money to a writer? The insurance company Pax, which held the first mortgage, gave me notice right away. But we could still move into the house. Whoever could help helped. At that time my two gouaches, the *Astronomers* and the *Drowned Lovers*, were created in a technique that I did not take up again until 1978 in *The World of Atlases*. I painted at night, and as I painted, I was always visited around two o'clock in the morning by a bat, a charming little animal that I named Mathilde. One time I was mean, I closed the window and set about to catch Mathilde. When I had caught her, I showed her to the children and explained to them that she was a mouse angel, then I let her go free again. She was very insulted and never showed her face again. Since that time the motif "angel" will not let me go. Not out of spite, more out of playfulness. Mathilde's revenge: I drew untold numbers of "human" angels, also egg-laying cherubin, extemporaneously, as caricatures. My sense of humor led me astray. This factor—my main one—can never be underestimated; it is effective everywhere. Only little by little did I discover that angels are really frightening creatures, creatures to whom Mathilde relates as a lizard to a tyrannosaurus rex. It began to interest me then from a theatrical point of view how an angel should be represented today; there are, after all, scarcely any angels to enlighten me in the world of art, perhaps just the lunging, pounding, angry angels in the *Apocalypse* of Dürer. So I tried, then, to present angels theatrically, the two pictures called *Death's Angel* and the *Angel* on which I worked for a long time: Even angels are something dreadful. When in connection with

Sulzer im Zusammenhang mit meinen Federzeichnungen von einer "frühen Schabtechnik Dürrenmatts" schrieb und im späteren Zeichnen—etwa im schnellen Zeichnen nach der Natur mit dem Kugelschreiber—eine "Befreiung" sehen wollte, so kann ich ihr hier nicht beipflichten. Jene Zeichnungen sind nicht dramaturgisch, sondern konventionell. Jeder Maler macht sie besser. Sie waren eine Laune, Fingerübungen meinetwegen, so wie ich einmal einige Wochen lang Collagen verfertigte oder immer wieder karikiere. Die Technik, die ich bei meinen Federzeichnungen entwickelte, stellt das zeichnerisch "Durchgehende" bei mir dar: Hier besitze ich Erfahrung, läßt sich eine Entwicklung nachweisen. Persönlich ziehe ich das Malen vor. Aber Malen reißt mich aus der Arbeit, während meine Federzeichnungen auf meinem Schreibtisch entstehen, natürlich auch die Lavis. So ist die *Minotaurus-Serie* schnell entstanden—ich arbeitete oft am frühen Morgen daran, nach einer mit Schreiben durchplagten Nacht. Auch das erste *Selbstportrait* ist um fünf Uhr morgens gepinselt: Ich portraitierte mich in den Rasierspiegel starrend. An einer Federzeichnung dagegen arbeite ich durchschnittlich etwa vierzehn Tage. Viele nehme ich später wieder auf und bearbeite sie neu. Dramaturgisch und nicht blasphemisch sind auch die *Papst*-Szenen gemeint: Ist es doch etwas Skandalöses, daß jemand behauptet, er sei der Stellvertreter Christi auf Erden, unfehlbar usw. Ich erinnere mich an eine Fernsehdiskussion über den "Stellvertreter." Hochhuth wurde von einem Priester angepöbelt, ob er sich denn nicht schäme, mit seinem "Stellvertreter" Millionen von Gläubigen zu verletzen, denen der Papst etwas Heiliges sei. Man hätte den Priester fragen müssen, ob er sich denn nicht schäme, daß der Papst mit seinem Anspruch jene verletze, die nicht an ihn glauben. Ich glaube nicht an ihn. Das Christentum, das sich nicht als Skandalon begreift, hat keine Berechtigung mehr. Der Papst ist das Sinnbild des Theologischen und damit des Rechthaberischen, des Glaubens, im Besitze der Wahrheit zu sein. Wer diesen Glauben besitzt, streitet. Darum gibt es immer wieder viele Päpste—religiöse und politische—, und darum finden die Streitereien unter ihnen kein Ende: Immer wieder steht Wahrheit gegen Wahrheit, bis der letzte Papst auf dem Mammut seiner Macht in die Eiszeitnacht der Menschheit reitet und in ihr verschwindet (Nr. 30). Zu den *Turmbau*-Zeichnungen: Dramaturgisch ging es mir darum, die Höhe des Turms darzustellen. Der Turmbau zu Babel wurde oft dargestellt. Ich denke an die Bilder von Bruegel. Aber für mich war der Turm immer zu klein. Es war nie der Turm schlechthin; auf meinen Zeichnungen sieht man deutlich die Erdkrümmung—im Verhältnis zu ihr ist der Turm in der ersten Zeichnung, *Turmbau I*, 9000 km hoch. Die "Wolke", die hinuntergreift: kosmischer Staub, der die Erde beleckt. Im Hintergrund die Sonne, wie sie erscheint, wenn wir den Bereich der roten Wasserstofflinien ausblenden. Ich be-my pen drawings Elisabeth Brock-Sulzer wrote about "Dürrenmatt's early engraving technique" and claimed to see in the later drawings—for instance in the quick sketches done from life with a ballpoint pen—a "release," I cannot agree with her there. Those sketches are not theatrical but conventional. Any artist could do them better. They were done on impulse, finger exercises, if you like, just as when I once constructed collages for several weeks or constantly draw caricatures. The technique that I developed in my pen drawings represents the "absolute" in drawing for me: Here I have experience, some development can be detected. Personally, I prefer to paint. But painting takes me away from my work while pen drawings are produced on my desk, as, of course, the temperas are, too. Thus the *Minotaur* series was done quickly—I often worked on it early in the morning after a night spent toiling over my writing. My first *Self-Portrait* was also painted at five o'clock in the morning: I portrayed myself staring into the shaving mirror. On the other hand, I work on the average about two weeks on one pen drawing. Many of them I take up again and rework them. The *Pope* scenes also are meant to be theatrical and not blasphemous: It is, after all, rather shocking that someone should maintain he is the representative of Christ on earth, infallible, and so forth. I remember a television show about *The Deputy*. Hochhuth was vilified by a priest and told he should be ashamed to offend with his *Deputy* millions of believers to whom the Pope is something holy. The priest should have been asked whether he was not shamed that the Pope with his pretensions offended those who do not believe in him. I do not believe in him. A Christianity that does not comprehend itself as an ignominy has no justification any more. The Pope is the symbol of things theological and thereby of the dogmatic, of the belief that he possesses the truth. Whoever possesses this belief is going to engage in disputes. So there are over and over again many popes—religious and political—and so the quarrels amongst them have no end: Over and over again truth stands against truth until the last pope rides on the mammoth of his power into the nocturnal ice age of mankind and disappears into it. Concerning the *Tower* drawings: Theatrically I was concerned with presenting the height of the tower. The Tower of Babel has often been portrayed. I think of the pictures by Bruegel. But the tower was always too small for me. It was never quite *the* tower; in my drawings you can clearly see the curvature of the earth—in relation to it the tower in the *Tower I* is 9000 kilometers tall. The "cloud" that reaches down to it is cosmic dust that licks the earth. In the background the sun, as it appears when we screen out the range of red hydrogen lines. Since my childhood in the village I have schäftigte mich seit meiner Kindheit im Dorf mit der Astronomie, später trat die Physik in mein Denken, und heute amüsiert mich vor allem eines ihrer Teilgebiete, die Kosmologie. Hier führt die Moderne die Vorsokratier weiter. So zeigen denn alle meine *Turmbau*-Bilder die Unsinnigkeit des Unternehmens auf, einen Turm zu bauen, der bis in den Himmel reicht, und damit die Absurdität menschlichen Unterfangens schlechthin. Der Turm zu Babel ist das Sinnbild der menschlichen Hybris. Er bricht zusammen, und mit ihm stürzt die Menschenwelt zusammen. Was die Menschheit hinterlassen wird, sind ihre Ruinen. Die *Turmbau*-Zeichnungen *IV* und *V* zeigen diesen Zusammenbruch: Gleichzeitig ist das Ende der bewohnten Erde gekommen. Der Stern, der in *Turmbau IV* explodiert, ist eine Supernova. Zurück bleibt ein weißer Punkt, ein Neutronenstern, ein Stern mit unendlicher Dichte. Sichtbar werden Galaxien in verschiedenen Stadien ihres Werdens und Vergehens und ahnbar riesenhafte "schwarze Löcher." Sie deuten Endzustände von Sternen an, die wiederum (vielleicht) der Beginn neuer Welten sein können. Das Motiv des Weltuntergangs ist mit dem Motiv des Todes verbunden: Jeder Mensch, der stirbt, erlebt seinen Weltuntergang. Daß—wie in meinen Stücken—auch in meinen Zeichnungen der Henker eine Rolle spielt, ist nicht verwunderlich; verwunderlich wäre, wenn er fehlen würde. Der Mensch hat in unserem Zeitalter die Rolle des guten alten Sensenmannes übernommen. Der Mensch als Henker ist kein Gevatter Tod mehr, dafür leuchtet mir bisweilen der Gedanke Schopenhauers ein, das Leben des Einzelnen sei mit einer Meereswelle zu vergleichen: Sie vergeht, aber es entstehen neue Wellen. Ich kann mir nicht denken, daß ich einmal "nicht mehr" bin. Ich kann mir vorstellen, daß ich "immer" jemand bin. Immer ein anderer. Immer ein neues Bewußtsein, daß auch ich einmal den Weltuntergang erlebe. So ist denn der Weltuntergang von einer immerwährenden Aktualität. Dieses Motiv habe ich auf der Bühne im "Portrait eines Planeten" gestaltet. Ich konzipierte den Text als Schauspielerübung, um mit einem Minimum an dramaturgischen Mitteln möglichst viel auszusagen. Vor der Niederschrift habe ich das Motiv in einer Mischtechnik dargestellt (Nr. 42): Die Photographie eines Mannes mit je einem Kopf in der linken und rechten Hand erschien zur Zeit des Vietnam-Krieges in vielen Illustrierten. Unten links ist eine ausgebrannte Weltraumkapsel, in der zwei amerikanische Astronauten ums Leben kamen. *Der Weltmetzger* ist eine Gestalt aus der ersten Fassung des Stücks. So ist denn mein dramaturgisches Denken beim Schreiben, Zeichnen und Malen ein Versuch, immer endgültigere Gestalten zu finden, bildnerische Endformen. So stieß ich über den Weg des Sisyphos-Motivs zum Atlas-Motiv vor. Die erste *Sisyphos*-Gouache entstand im Jahre 1946, gleichzeitig mit dem *Pilatus*. Ich verließ die Universität und gab vor, Maler zu werden. Es wäre abenteuerlich occupied myself with astronomy, later on physics entered my thoughts, and today I amuse myself above all with one of their branches, cosmology. Here modern man carries on pre-Socratic thought. Thus all my *Tower* pictures show the senselessness of undertaking to build a tower that reaches into heaven and in this way the absurdity of any human enterprise. The Tower of Babel is the symbol of human hubris. It crumbles to the ground and with it the human world collapses. What mankind will leave behind is its ruins. The *Tower IV* and *V* show this collapse: The end of the inhabited earth has come at the same time. The star that is exploding in the *Tower IV* is a supernova. A white dot is left behind, a neutron star, a star with infinite density. Galaxies are visible at various stages of development and disintegration, and enormous "black holes" can be imagined. They indicate the last phases of stars that may (perhaps) in turn be the beginning of new worlds. The motif of the end of the world is joined to the death motif: Each man who dies experiences the end of his own world. The fact that in my drawings—as in my plays—the executioner plays a role is not surprising; it would be surprising if he were not there. In our era man has taken on the role of the good old grim reaper. Man as executioner is no longer kindly old Death; instead now and then Schopenhauer's idea becomes clear to me: that the life of an individual can be likened to the waves of the ocean: They vanish, but new waves arise. I cannot conceive that one day I will exist "no more." I can imagine that I will "always" be someone. Always someone else. Always a new consciousness, so that even I will someday experience the end of the world. Thus the end of the world becomes an eternal reality. I have given shape to this motif on the stage in *Portrait of a Planet*. I planned the text as an exercise for actors to use to say as much as possible with a minimum of theatrical means. Before writing it down I portrayed the motif with a mixed technique in *Portrait of a Planet II*: The photograph of a man with a head held in each of his hands appeared in many picture magazines at the time of the Vietnam War. Below at the left is the burned-out space capsule in which two American astronauts lost their lives. *The World Butcher* is a character from the first draft of this play. Thus my theatrical thought while writing, drawing, and painting is an attempt to find ever more conclusive characters, sculpted end forms. So then by way of the Sisyphos motif I happened on the Atlas motif. The first *Sisyphos* gouache was done in 1946 at the same time as the *Pilatus*. I left the university and pretended to be an artist. It would have been strange to announce that gewesen, die Schriftstellerei als mein Ziel anzugeben. Die beiden Bilder malte ich gleichsam als Alibi, um meinen Mitstudenten zu beweisen, daß es mir mit meiner Malerei ernst sei. Gleichzeitig schrieb ich die Erzählung "Pilatus" und "Das Bild des Sisyphos." Zum "Sisyphos" möchte ich nur bemerken, daß mich vor allem die Frage beschäftigte, was Sisyphos zwinge, den Fels immer wieder hochzustemmen. Vielleicht ist es seine Rache, die er an den Göttern nimmt: Er stellt ihre Ungerechtigkeit bloß. Während mich beim "Pilatus" die Idee nicht losließ, Pilatus habe vom ersten Augenblick an gewußt, daß ein Gott vor ihm stehe, und sei vom ersten Augenblick an überzeugt gewesen, dieser Gott sei gekommen, ihn zu töten. Atlas dagegen ist eine mythologische Figur, die erst heute wieder darstellbar ist, paradoxerweise; denn ein Mensch, der das Himmelsgewölbe trägt, scheint unserem Weltbild zu widersprechen. Aber wenn wir uns das Anfangsstadium der Welt als ungeheure kompakte Kugel von der Größe der Neptunbahn denken (March) oder als schwarzes Loch, das dann zum Urknall führt; oder wenn als Endstadium einer Welt, in ihrem In-sich-Zusammenstürzen, weil sie zu schwer geworden ist, wiederum die Vision einer Kugel von ungeheuer Schwere vor uns aufsteigt, wird in dieser Weltsicht Atlas mythologisch wieder möglich, gleichzeitig aber auch zum Endbild des Menschen, der die—seine—Welt trägt, tragen muß. Daß zur selben Zeit wie einige *Atlas*-Bilder mein letztes Stück entstanden ist, "Die Frist", ist nicht zufällig, handelt es doch auch von zwei Menschen in der Atlas-Situation: Der erste versucht, die Welt zu tragen, der zweite möchte sie nicht tragen, muß sie aber zum Schluß weiter tragen. Zugegeben, die erste Atlas-Darstellung geht auf das Jahr 1958 zurück, *Der versagende Atlas*. Das Wichtigste an diesem Weltuntergangsbild sind die Menschen. Sie tragen Inschriften: Atlas muß nicht versagen, Atlas darf nicht versagen, Atlas kann nicht versagen . . . , jenen, der schrieb, Atlas wird versagen, hat man geköpft: Die voraussehbare Katastrophe trifft ein, noch schärfer: voraussehbare Katastrophen treffen ein. Daß sich einmal alles rächen wird, drückt die Zeichnung Nr. 27 mit dem sonderbaren Titel aus "Die gläsernen Särge der Toten werden die Rammböcke sein." Dramaturgisch formuliert: die schlimmstmögliche Wendung trifft ein. Daß ich immer wieder die schlimmstmögliche Wendung darstelle, hat nichts mit Pessimismus zu tun, auch nichts mit einer fixen Idee. Die schlimmstmögliche Wendung ist das dramaturgisch Darstellbare, ist genau das auf der Bühne, was in der Plastik den "David" zur Statue und meine Bilder zu dramaturgischen Bildern macht. So etwa auch *Die Katastrophe*. Das Bild stellt mehr als ein Zugunglück mit anschließender Kettenreaktion dar: Oben stößt gleichzeitig die Sonne mit einem anderen Himmelskörper zusammen. Sechs Minuten später wird die Erde nicht mehr existieren. Auch hier: die schlimmstmögliche Wendung, der Versuch, nicht eine, sondern *die* Katawriting was my goal. I painted the two pictures as if to show my fellow students that I was serious about my painting. At the same time I wrote the story "Pilatus" and "The Image of Sisyphos." Let me remark about "Sisyphos" just that the question that mainly occupied me was what forces Sisyphos to press up the crag again and again. Perhaps it is the revenge that he is taking out on the gods: He reveals their injustice. While with "Pilatus" I could not escape the idea that Pilate knew from the very beginning that a god stood before him and was from the very beginning convinced this god had come to kill him. Atlas, on the other hand, is a mythological figure who only today can be represented again, paradoxically, since a human being who can carry the firmament seems to contradict our world image. But if we think of the beginning stage of the world as an extremely compact ball the size of the Neptune orbit (demarcation) or as a black hole that then results in the primal explosion, or of the end stage as a world collapsing into itself because it has become too heavy, then the vision of a ball of immense weight again rises before us, and in this world view Atlas is once more mythologically possible, but simultaneously also as the final image of man who must bear the world--his world. The fact that my last play *Days of Grace* was created at the same time as some of the Atlas pictures is not coincidental, since it is also concerned with two men in the Atlas position: The first is attempting to carry the world, the second does not want to carry it but in the end must continue to carry it. Granted, the first Atlas portrayal goes back to the year 1958, *The Failing Atlas*. The most important thing about this picture of the end of the world is the people. They carry placards: Atlas must not fail, Atlas may not fail, Atlas cannot fail . . . the one who wrote Atlas will fail was beheaded. The foreseeable catastrophe occurs, more exactly: Foreseeable catastrophes occur. That one day everything will take its toll is expressed by the drawing with the peculiar title, *The Glass Coffins of the Dead Will Become Pile Drivers*. Theatrically formulated: The worst possible turn of events takes place. That I am constantly portraying the worst possible turn of events has nothing to do with pessimism or with a fixed idea either. The worst possible turn of events is what is theatrically portrayable; on the stage it is exactly what in sculpture makes the *David* a statue and what makes my pictures theatrical pictures. *The Catastrophe* is about like that, too. The picture represents more than a train accident with the following chain reaction: At the same time the sun collides with another celestial body overhead. Six minutes later the earth will no longer exist. Here too: the worst possible turn of events, the attempt to portray not *a* but *the* catastrophe. Not the essence of the thing but the essence strophe zu schildern. Nicht das Ding an sich, sondern Bilder an sich sind darstellbar. Die letzte Gestaltung des *Atlas*-Motivs gehört zu meinen Lieblingsbildern. Es entstand aus einer Laune heraus. Ich heftete zwei Blätter meines für Gouachen bevorzugten Formats, 100 x 71, nebeneinander an die Wand meines Ateliers. Ich wollte eine flüchtige Skizze machen. Das war 1965. Seitdem arbeite ich an diesem Bild. Ich hätte es wissen müssen. Ich habe zu keinem meiner Bilder je eine Skizze gemacht. Reproduziert ist es im Zustand, den es am 10. Juni 1978 hatte. Zu sehen sind Atlasse, die mit Weltkugeln spielen. Je schwerer eine Welt, desto kleiner ihr Endzustand. Die Atlasse im Vordergrund keuchen unter ihren Kugeln. Daß auch der Eindruck einer Nachtlandung auf dem Flughafen von New York eine Rolle spielt, sei erwähnt, begriff ich doch damals zum erstenmal, wie höllisch es sein muß, auf einer von Menschen überfüllten Erde zu leben. Zu meinen Portraits: Sie sind schnell entstanden, außer den beiden ersten. Ich bin froh, daß mir von *Walter Mehring* wenigstens in der Malerei ein Portrait gelang, schriftstellerisch ist es mir bis jetzt nicht gelungen. Dieser sprachgewaltige Lyriker hat in vielen seiner späteren Gedichte nicht sich, sondern uns überlebt. Otto Riggenbach ist im Gespräch mit meiner Frau festgehalten. Er ist einer unserer wenigen Neuenburger Freunde und besitzt einige der schönsten Auberjonois (*Portrait eines Psychiaters*). Am spontansten entstand das Portrait meiner Frau, in kaum zehn Minuten, in Ste-Maxime an der Côte d'Azur (*Portrait Lotti Dürrenmatt*). Wir waren damals besonders glücklich. Wir glaubten, dort unten ein Haus erstanden zu haben, das unseren Vorstellungen entsprach und dessen Kauf später glücklicherweise dann doch scheiterte. In ihrem Übermut bemerkte meine Frau nicht, daß ich sie portraitierte. In Ste-Maxime entstand auch etwas früher die Federzeichnung mit Selbstportrait, *St. Tropez 1958*: Der Gedanke, daß damals jenseits des Mittelmeeres getötet und gefoltert wurde, bedrückte mich. Leider hat die Zeichnung ihre Aktualität nicht eingebüßt. Den Schauspieler *Leonard Steckel* malte ich 1965 aus dem Gedächtnis. Das Portrait von *Varlin* zeichnete ich am 22. Oktober 1977. Es war der letzte Tag, den ich mit Varlin verbrachte. Wir sprachen über Malerei. Varlin sagte mir, er halte Matisse für den größten Maler unserer Zeit. Er sagte: "Das Traurige an der Malerei: Man steht vor einer sauberen Leinwand, nimmt einen Pinsel, und schon ist die Leinwand versaut." Dann hat er mich gezeichnet, mehrmals, wieder durchgestrichen. Eine Zeichnung ließ er gelten und schenkte sie mir, dann sagte er, er wolle schlafen, und ich solle ihn zeichnen. Als er aufwachte, wollte er die Zeichnung sehen. Er fragte mich, ob er wirklich so aussehe. Ich antwortete nichts, und Varlin sagte, dann gehe es nicht mehr lange. Am 30. Oktober ist er gestorben. Das *Portrait eines Hoteliers* stellt meinen Freund Hans Liechti dar, Wirt und Bildersammler von of the pictures is portrayable. The last form of the Atlas motif (*The World of Atlases*) is one of my favorite pictures. It grew out of a mood. I fastened two sheets of paper of the size I preferred for gouaches, 100 x 71, next to each other on the wall of my studio. I was going to make a rough sketch. That was 1965. I have been continually working on this picture ever since. I should have known it. I have never made sketches for any of my pictures. It has been printed in the stage it was in on 10 June 1978. Visible are Atlases playing with earth spheres. The heavier a world is, the smaller is its end condition. The Atlases in the foreground groan under their spheres. Let me mention that the impression of a night landing at the airport in New York plays a role, too; I realized at that time for the first time how abominable it must be to live on an earth crammed full of people. As for my portraits: They were produced quickly, except for the first two. I am happy that I succeeded at least in painting a portrait of *Walter Mehring*; I have not succeeded yet in doing so in writing. This lyric poet, who had such immense power of language, outlived not just himself but us in many of his later poems. Otto Riggenbach is portrayed in conversation with my wife (*Portrait of a Psychiatrist*). He is one of our few Neuenburg friends and possesses some of the most beautiful Auberjonois. Most spontaneous was the creation of the portrait of my wife, in scarcely ten minutes, in St. Maximin on the Riviera (*Portrait of Lotti Dürrenmatt*). We were especially happy at that time. We thought we had bought a house down there that conformed to all our ideas and the purchase of which later fortunately fell through. In her high spirits my wife did not notice that I was doing her portrait. Also in St. Maximin somewhat earlier the pen sketch with self-portrait was created, *St. Tropez 1958*: The thought that at that time on the other side of the Mediterranean killing and torturing was going on oppressed me. Unfortunately, the drawing has not lost its topicality. I painted the actor Leonard Steckel in 1965 from memory (*Leonard Steckel as "Meteor"*). The portrait of *Varlin* I drew on 22 October 1977. It was the last day I spent with Varlin. We were talking about painting. Varlin said to me that he considered Matisse to be the greatest painter of our time. He said: "The sad thing about painting—you stand before a clean canvas, take a brush, and the canvas is straightaway a mess." Then he sketched me, a few times, scratched them out again. One drawing he allowed to pass and gave it to me, then he said he wanted to sleep and I should draw him. When he woke up, he wanted to see the drawing. He asked me if he really looked like that. I did not answer, and Varlin said then it wouldn't be much longer. On 30 October he died. The *Portrait of a Hotelkeeper* portrays my friend Hans Liechti,

Zäziwill, zu Fuß eine dreiviertel Stunde vom Dorfe entfernt, wo ich geboren wurde. Er ist wie ich nach Neuenburg verschlagen worden. Ich sitze nach dem Schreiben oft bis tief in die Nacht bei ihm, erzähle ihm, was ich schreibe, und zeichne, was man zeichnen könnte. Ich weiß nicht, ob ich ohne ihn noch zeichnen und malen würde. Seine Begeisterung für die Malerei wirkt produktiv. Sein Portrait entstand an einem Sonntagnachmittag. Er hatte gekocht, seine Beiz war zu Mittag überfüllt gewesen, dazu waren Verwandte gekommen, und am Abend hatte er im oberen Saal ein Bankett. Er kam im Arbeitsgewand in mein Atelier, um sich auszuruhen. Nach nicht ganz einer Stunde verließ er mich, um sich wieder hinter seinen Herd zu stellen, und ich malte das Bild zu Ende. Um zehn Uhr abends rief ich ihn an, er sollte kommen. Er kam, immer noch im Arbeitsgewand, und war mit mir zufrieden. Meine letzten Federzeichnungen sind ebenfalls Portraits: *Der zornige Gott*—wer begreift seinen Zorn nicht? (vollendet habe ich die Federzeichnung bei Liechti mit einem Küchenmesser). *Mazdak* war der Gründer einer kommunistischen Sekte. Ungefähr 530 n. Chr. wurden 3000 seiner Anhänger vom persischen Großkönig kopfvoran in die Erde gepfählt—und damit ihre Idee in den Boden gepflanzt. Man kann einen Menschen töten, aber die Idee lebt weiter. Das Kind, das die aussätzige und wahnsinnige *Ophelia* zur Welt bringt, wird weder aussätzig noch wahnsinnig sein. Geier entmannen den aufs Pferd gebundenen Kosaken. Er lebt in Gedichten weiter. *Chronos, Uranus entmannend*: Nur so war es möglich, daß die Zeit ihre Herrschaft begann; die mythologische Darstellung des Urknalls. Mit den *Labyrinthen* nehme ich ein Motiv auf, das mich auch schriftstellerisch fasziniert. Ich behandelte es zuerst in der Novelle "Die Stadt" und behandle es jetzt in der Erzählung "Der Winterkrieg in Tibet." Zum Labyrinth gehört der *Minotaurus*. Dieser ist eine Ungestalt, als solche ist er das Bild des Einzelnen, des Vereinzelten. Der Einzelne steht einer Welt gegenüber, die für ihn undurchschaubar ist: Das Labyrinth ist die Welt vom Minotaurus aus gesehen. Die *Minotaurus*-Blätter zeigen denn auch den Minotaurus ohne die Erfahrung des Andern, des Du. Er versteht nur zu vergewaltigen und zu töten. Er stirbt nicht durch Theseus, er verendet wie ein Stück Vieh. Theseus ist nicht imstande, ihn aufzuspüren (Nr. 60). Die Ermordung des Minotaurus ist eine Legende. Aus der Gestalt des Minotaurus ist als Assoziation das Blatt Nr. 88 (*Der Weltstier*) entstanden, in einer etwas anderen Technik, weil das Papier keine andere erlaubte. Der *Weltstier* ist das Sinnbild des amoklaufenden Ungeheuers, das wir "Weltgeschichte" nennen. Das Blatt Nr. 65, *Die beiden Tiere*, stellt eine Paraphrase zum Manichäismus dar, der heute ja wieder aufgekommen ist, zum Glauben, die Weltgeschichte sei ein Kampf zwischen zwei Prinzipien, einem guten und einem bösen. Die beiden Saurier, die sich im Hintergrund ineinander verbissen haben, sind innkeeper and art collector of Zäziwil, three-quarters of an hour away on foot from the town where I was born. He, like I, wound up in Neuenburg. After writing I often sit with him until late at night, tell him what I am writing, and draw what there is to draw. I do not know whether I would still draw and paint without him. His enthusiasm for painting has a productive effect. His portrait was done on a Sunday afternoon. He had been cooking. His barroom had been crowded at noon, besides that, relatives had come, and in the evening he had a banquet in the upper room. He came to my studio in his work clothes for a rest. He left me after not quite an hour to go back to his stove, and I finished painting the picture. At ten o'clock in the evening I called him up to say he should come over. He came, still in work clothes, and was satisfied with me. My latest pen drawings are likewise portraits: *The Angry God*—who is there who cannot understand his anger? (I finished the pen drawing at Liechti's with a kitchen knife.) Mazdak (*Mazdak, Impaled in the Earth*) was the founder of a communistic sect. About 530 A.D. three thousand of his followers were impaled in the earth headfirst by the Persian emperor—and in this way their ideas were implanted in the earth. A human being can be killed, but his ideas live on. The child born of the leprous and insane Ophelia (*Leprous Ophelia, Pregnant*) will be neither leprous nor insane. Vultures castrate the Cossack bound on a horse (*Mazeppa*). He lives on in poems. *Chronos, Castrating Uranus*: Only in this way was it possible for time to begin its dominion—the mythological representation of the primal explosion. With the *Labyrinth* I take up a motif that fascinates me as a writer also. I first used it in the novella "The City" and am using it just now in the story "The Winter War in Tibet." The *Minotaur* belongs to the Labyrinth. He is a monster; as such he is the picture of the individual, the solitary individual. The individual stands facing a world that is obscure for him: The Labyrinth is the world as seen by the minotaur. So the *Minotaur* sheets also show the Minotaur without the experience of the Other, of the You. He only knows how to rape and to kill. He does not die at Theseus' hand, he ends like a head of cattle. Theseus is in no condition to track him down. The murder of the Minotaur is a legend. *The World Steer* originated out of associations with the figure of the Minotaur, in a somewhat different technique because the paper would allow no other. *The World Steer* is a symbol of the monster that we call "universal history" running amok. *The Two Animals* represents a paraphrase of Manicheanism, which today has come into fashion again, of the belief that universal history is a battle between two principles, a good one and an evil one. Each of the two saurians who have sunk their teeth into each beide gleich stur. Natürlich gibt es auch nichtdramaturgische Blätter, Assoziationen zu literarischen Motiven, wie etwa *Flucht I* und *Flucht II*, die ich einst im "Tunnel" oder in der "Falle" gestaltet habe. *Der Kampf der beiden Alten* zeigt, daß der Haß auch dann weiterwütet, wenn er seine Motivation verloren hat. Ich lernte nie zeichnen oder malen. Ich weiß jetzt noch nicht, wie man Ölbilder malt. Der einzige Mensch, den ich fragte: "Wie malt man eigentlich Öl?" war Anna Keel. Und sie sagte mir: "Nimm Petrol." Die Ölbilder malte ich alle 1966. Daß auch meine *Bank*-Bilder mit Öl und Petrol gemalt sind, stellt keine Kritik am schweizerischen Bankwesen dar. Im Gegenteil, daß ich es würdig enden lasse (Nr. 56, *Letzte Generalversammlung der Eidgenössischen Bankanstalt*), sollte meine Kreditwürdigkeit bei unseren Banken erhöhen, wie ich hoffe, besonders jetzt, wo ich sie nötiger habe denn je, existiere ich doch—wie ich eben im "Bruckenbauer" lese—für die Kritik literarisch nicht mehr. Doch kehrte ich seitdem wieder zu den Wasserfarben zurück. Gerade meine *Bank*-Bilder machen deutlich, daß die Gründe meiner Zeichnungen und Malereien nicht nur in dramaturgischen Überlegungen liegen; meine *Bank*-Bilder sind der Nachhall meiner Komödie "Frank V", der Oper einer Privatbank. Ein Theaterstück, dessen bühnenmäßige Realisierung eigentlich nie glückte. Eine Neufassung liegt in meinem Schreibtisch. Aber auch *Der Turm zu Babel* oder die Blätter Nr. 31 (*Der gefangene Narses*), 32 (*Byzantinische Heilige*), mit den byzantinischen Motiven gehen auf ein vernichtetes Werk oder auf ein Fragment zurück. Zeichnen als Ersatzhandlung. Doch gibt es natürlich noch andere Zusammenhänge zwischen meinem literarischen und meinem zeichnerischen Schaffen. Jedes Darstellen, in welchen Medien auch immer, setzt einen Hintergrund voraus, der aus Eindrücken, Bildern und Denken besteht. Dieser Hintergrund ist heute nicht mehr allgemein; es sei denn, man gebe sich links engagiert, katholisch oder sei beides zusammen usw. Der heutige Schriftsteller, aber auch der heutige Maler, sucht im allgemeinen unbewußt eine Ideologie, etwas Allgemeines. Ich lehnte es seit jeher ab, mich auf einen allgemeinen Nenner bringen zu lassen. Ich bin deshalb notwendigerweise nur wenigen verständlich. Auf die Voraussetzungen meines literarischen Schaffens, aber auch meiner Bilder, die in meinem Denken liegen, das im wesentlichen erkenntnistheoretisch ist, und in meinem Humor, der an sich subjektiv ist, kommt man nicht von selber. Darum nimmt man mich lieber nicht ernst, sonst müßte man mitdenken. Ich bin bewußt ein Einzelgänger. Ich gehöre nicht zur Avantgarde. Wer heute dieser angehört, trampelt in einer Herde mit. So sind denn auch die Assoziationen, aus denen sich meine Bilder zusammenbauen, Resultate meines persönlichen Denkabenteuers, nicht die einer allgemeinen Denkmethode. Ich male nicht surrealistische Bilder—der Surrealismus ist eine Ideologie—, ich male für mich verständother in the background is equally stubborn. Naturally there are also pictures that are not theatrical, things associated with literary motifs as, for instance, *Flight I* and *Flight II* that I once fashioned in "The Tunnel" or in "The Trap." *The Fight of the Two Old Men* shows that hate continues to rage when it has lost its motivation. I never studied drawing or painting. I don't know yet how to paint with oil. The only person I asked: "How does one really paint with oil?" was Anna Keel. And she told me: "Use kerosene." I painted all the pictures done in oil in 1966. That my *Bank* pictures, too, are painted with oil and kerosene does not represent criticism of the Swiss banking establishment. On the contrary, that I allow it to end with dignity (*The Last Meeting of the Swiss Federal Bank*) should enhance my credit with our banks, as I hope, especially now, when I need them more than ever, since I do not exist literarily—as I have just read in Brückenbauer—for the critics any more. But since then I have gone back to watercolors again. My *Bank* pictures in particular make it clear that the foundation of my drawing and painting does not lie only in theatrical considerations; my *Bank* pictures are the echo of my comedy *Frank V*, the opera about a private bank. A stage play whose theatrical realization never truly succeeded. A new version is lying in my desk. But *The Tower of Babel*, too, and the drawings with the Byzantine motifs (*The Captive Narses, The Byzantine Saints*) have their origin in a destroyed work or a fragment. Drawing as substitute action. Still, there are naturally other connections between my literary and my artistic creation. Each presentation, in whatever media, presupposes a background that consists of impressions, images, and thoughts. Today this background is no longer universal, unless perhaps one acknowledges oneself to be involved with the Left or to be Catholic or both together, and so forth. The writer of today, but also the artist of today, is in general instinctively searching for an ideology, for something universal. I have refused all along to allow myself to be put under a common denominator. For that reason I am necessarily comprehensible to only a few. One does not automatically hit upon the presuppositions of my literary production nor of my pictures, which lie in my thought, which is basically cognitively theoretical, and in my sense of humor, which is in itself subjective. Thus people prefer not to take me seriously or else they would have to think along with me. I am consciously a loner. I do not belong to the avant-garde. Today those who do belong trample along with the herd. So the associations out of which my pictures are constructed are also the results of my personal adventures in thought, not those of a common method of thinking. I do not paint surrealistic pictures—surrealism is an ideology—I paint pictures that are liche Bilder: Ich male für mich. Darum bin ich kein Maler. Ich stelle mich der Zeit, und unserer Zeit kommt man nicht mit dem Wort allein bei. Das Denken in Begriffen, die Methode der Mathematik, die notwendige Abstraktheit des wissenschaftlichen Denkens sind in der bildenden Kunst abstrakt nicht darstellbar. Es gibt nichts Abstrakteres als die Formel. Sie ist die letztmögliche Abstraktion. $E = mc^2$, zum Beispiel. Die Mathematik hat eine Abstraktionsfähigkeit, die nicht mehr anschaulich ist, die das Anschauliche notwendigerweise durchstößt. Es ist unmöglich, die Relativitätstheorie nicht abstrakt darzustellen, außer man stellt sie in sinnlichen Gleichnissen dar. Sinnliche Gleichnisse jedoch sind nicht geometrische oder stereometrische Formen, sondern Mythen: unsere Mythen. Der ermöglichte Atlas. Vielleicht sind meine ersten Zeichnungen von Bosch beeinflußt, die grotesken Bilder des Beginns (Nr. 3, *Apokalyptische Reiter*, Nr. 4, *Die Welt als Theater*), noch bevor ich Schriftsteller wurde. Aber ich suche nicht die Symbolik, die Bosch fand. Was ich—in meinem Schreiben wie Zeichnen—suche, sind die Bilder und Gleichnisse, die im Zeitalter der Wissenschaft noch möglich sind, einem Zeitalter, dem etwas gelang, was der Philosophie mißlang: die Realität abstrakt zu beschreiben. Wenn wir vier oder n Dimensionen brauchen, benötigen wir sie, weil sich die Fakten der Realität nicht anders beschreiben lassen. Wir haben nicht die Möglichkeit, diese hochkomplizierten Zusammenhänge und Gegebenheiten zu vereinfachen. Die Kernphysik ist nicht volkstümlich darstellbar. Sie ist nur volkstümlich zu umschreiben. Sie muß gedacht werden, will sie erfaßt werden. Es gibt keinen Rückzug ins Einfache. Was seiner Natur nach nicht anschaulich ist, kann lediglich durch Gleichnisse dargestellt werden. Darum ist die abstrakte Kunst—dort, wo sie stimmt—bestensfalls poetisch, Schönheit der Linien. Sie ist reine Form und damit reine Ästhetik. Nie war die Malerei ästhetischer denn heute. Was sie als ihren Sinn ausgibt, ist nur behauptet, nicht integriert. Sie als "intellektuelle Aussage" darzustellen ist Unsinn. Immer wieder: ich bin kein Maler. Ich male technisch wie ein Kind, aber ich denke nicht wie ein Kind. Ich male aus dem gleichen Grund, wie ich schreibe: weil ich denke. Malerei als eine Kunst, "schöne Bilder" zu machen, interessiert mich nicht, ebenso wie mich die Kunst, "schönes Theater" zu machen, nicht interessiert. Ich könnte nicht hauptberuflich Maler sein, aus dem einfachen Grunde: ich wüßte die meiste Zeit nicht, was ich malen sollte. Ich bin ein zeichnerischer Dilettant. Als Student wohnte ich in Bern in einem Zimmer, das ich ausgemalt hatte. Über dem Bett war eine skurrile Kreuzigung, daneben Szenen aus meinem ersten, nie veröffentlichten Stück, zu dem noch eine Zeichnung existiert, eine meiner frühesten. So stellt denn mein Malen und Zeichnen eine Ergänzung meiner Schriftstellerei dar—für alles, das ich nur bildnerisch ausdrücken kann. So gibt es denn auch nur wenig rein intelligible to me: I paint for myself. For that reason I am not a painter. I place myself in our time, and our time is not to be gotten at with words alone. Thinking in concepts, the mode of mathematics, the necessary abstraction of scientific thought cannot be represented abstractly in the plastic and graphic arts. There is nothing more abstract than a formula. It is the last possible abstraction. $E = mc^2$, for example. Mathematics has a capability for abstraction that is no longer graphic, that of necessity penetrates the graphic. It is impossible to represent the theory of relativity in a way that is not abstract, unless one represents it by tangible similes. Tangible similes, however, are not plain or solid geometrical forms, but myths—our myths. Atlas made possible. Perhaps my first pictures were influenced by Bosch, the grotesque pictures of my beginning (*Riders of the Apocalypse, The World as Theater*), before I became a writer. But I do not look for the symbolism that Bosch found. What I look for—in my writing as in my drawing—are the pictures and similes that are still possible in the age of science, an age that succeeded in something at which philosophy was unsuccessful: the abstract portrayal of reality. When we use *4* or *n* dimensions, we need them, because the facts of reality cannot be described in any other way. We do not have the potential to simplify these highly complicated relationships and data. Nuclear physics cannot be presented in a popular way. It can only be paraphrased in a popular way. It must be intellectually perceived, if it is to be comprehended. There is no retreat possible into simplification. What is not by nature evident can be represented only by simile. For that reason abstract art—where it is fitting—is at best poetic, the beauty of lines. It is pure form and thus pure aesthetics. Painting was never more aesthetic than today. What it gives as its meaning is only a claim, not something integral. To present it as an "intellectual declaration" is foolish. Over and over: I am no painter. I paint like a child technically, but I do not think like a child. I paint for the same reason that I write: because I think. Painting as the art of making "pretty pictures" does not interest me, just as the art of making "pretty theater" does not interest me. I could not have painting as my primary profession for one simple reason: I would not know what to paint most of the time. I am an amateur in drawing. As a student I lived in Bern in a room that I had painted completely. Over the bed there was a ludicrous crucifixion, next to it scenes from my first play that was never published, of which one drawing still exists, one of my earliest. So my painting and drawing represents a supplement to my writing—for everything that I can express only graphically. Thus, too, there are only a few pure illustrations done by me.

"Illustratives" von mir. Auch beim Schreiben gehe ich nicht von einem Problem aus, sondern von Bildern, denn das Ursprüngliche ist stets das Bild, die Situation—die Welt. Im übrigen bin ich immer noch erstaunt über die Verrücktheit Daniel Keels, dieses Buch herauszubringen, und immer noch verlegen, daß Manuel Gasser, dem die Malerei so viel verdankt, gar das Vorwort dazu schrieb, und—ich muß es zugeben—nun doch etwas stolz darüber, daß er über meine Malerei und Zeichnerei kein "Donnerwort" gesprochen hat.

Even when writing I do not start with a problem but with images, for the initial impulse is always an image, a situation—the world. For the rest, I am still astonished at the craziness of Daniel Keel in bringing out a book of my pictures and still embarrassed that Manuel Gasser, to whom painting owes so much, even wrote the foreword to it, and now—I must admit—even a little proud about the fact that he did not use even one thunderous word about my painting and drawing.

Asklepion, Pergamon (1967)

Asclepion, Pergamon

Erich Fitzbauer

Rom (1968)

Rome

Kanoni, Corfu (1968)

Canoni, Corfu

Faraglioni, Capri (1968)

Faraglioni, Capri

SYRAKUS
UND ANDERE GEDICHTE

ERICH FITZBAUER

SYRAKUS

Gesang von des Aischylos Chören,
der für Jahrtausende schlief,
sickert mit den Düften der Erdey, des Unkrauts
zwischen den Steinen hervor,
steigt bis zum Rand der Orchestra,
löst sich auf wie Meerdunst im Wind,
wird verschluckt von den Tagesgeräuschen.

Aber er stirbt nicht. Wo immer du hingehst:
es wehen die Klänge dir nach. Als Geistermusik,
immer von neuem verloren, geboren, folgen sie dir,
schwellen im Grottenbezirk des Dionysios
an zu titanischer Stärke,
fallen von des Olympieions letzter, einsamer Säule
nieder auf dich wie das Zirpen von haarfeinen Saiten.

Aus den magischen Liedern vernimmst du
den Atem der Zeiten und Zeitlosigkeiten.
Anders duftet für dich das Grün, färbt sich morgens das Nachtgrau.
Öfter neigt sich ein heiterer Gott
dir zu aus dem Sommergewölk.
Und abends legt sich des Vollmonds schimmernde Scheibe
dir in die wartend geöffnete Hand.

SYRAKUS
AND OTHER POEMS

ERICH FITZBAUER
translated by Herman Salinger

SYRAKUS

Song of the choruses of Aeschylus,
that slept for thousands of years,
trickles with the smells of earth, of weeds,
up from between the stones,
rises to the edge of the dancers' platform,
dissolves like sea-mist in the wind,
is swallowed up by the noises of the day.

But it does not die. Wherever you go,
the echoes follow. Like spirit-music,
lost and reborn, they follow you,
swelling in the grotto-circle of Dionysus
into titanic strength,
falling from the final lonely pillar of the Olympieion
down upon you like the twitter of hair-fine strings.

From the magical songs you hear
the breath of sages and of timelessness.
For you the green smells different, the night's gray colors up in the morning.
Often a god, serene, bends down
towards you out of the summer clouds.
And in the evening the full moon's shimmering disc
places itself into your expectantly opened hand.

STÜRZENDE ENGEL

Jahrhunderte Wetter
und Wind
fressen an Statuen, Sockeln
und Simsen,
hoch oben, wohin
heute kaum ein Auge
sich hebt,
irgendwo tief
im ausgezehrten
Italien,
wo vom Kreuz des einstigen Glaubens
mehr Schatten
als Licht fällt.

Warten auf neue
Sterne.
Der Stein hat Zeit,
lebt länger
als die rasch- und doppelzüngigen
fetten Redner
mit den magern
Kulturprogrammen.

Wer dort vorbeikommt, gehorcht,
hält sich
in gemessener Entfernung:
Attenzione,
angeli cadenti.

Auch anderswo
stürzen die Engel
von morschen Gemäuern,
aus den zerstörten
Himmeln.

Die Wahrzeichen tragen heute
ein neues Gesicht,
das Angst macht,
und Fäuste schlagen gewandter,

FALLING ANGELS

For centuries weather
and wind
gnaw at the statues, pedestals
and cornices,
high up, toward which
hardly an eye today
is raised,
somewhere deep
in exhausted
Italy,
where, from the cross of one-time faith,
more shadow
than light falls.

They wait for new
stars.
Stone has time,
lives longer
than the quick-tongued, two-tongued
oily-fat orators
with their thin
cultural programs.

Whoever passes near there obeys,
stops
at a measured distance:
Watch out
for falling angels!

Elsewhere too
the angels are falling
from decaying walls,
out of the destroyed
heavens.

The omens today wear
a new face,
which brings fear,
and fists strike more tellingly,

Drähte spannen sich weiter
als die lange entwöhnten,
vergessenen
Flügel.

Manchmal rauscht noch
von ihrem Gefieder
nachts eine Stunde.
Doch wer hält sie fest,
und für wen?
Überall
weht schon der frostige Wind
von morgen
über erkaltende
Herzen.

Für Hans Fronius

MARCKS: KLEINER GEIGER

Eingewachsen
ins Spielzeug,
an dessen Singen
das Brausen der Welt
zerbricht.

Tremoli, Läufe, Arpeggi,
Perlenreihen aus Klang:
wiegen
alle Kronen und Schwerter
aller Jahrhunderte
auf.

Mitten im Dunkel der Zeit
steigen
aus zitternden Saiten
magische Funken

wires stretch farther
than the long disused,
forgotten
wings.

Now and then at night
there is a rustling
from their feathers.
But who can hold or keep them,
and for whom?
Everywhere
the freezing wind of tomorrow
blows already
over hearts
growing cold.

For Hans Fronius

MARCKS: LITTLE VIOLIN-PLAYER

Grown into
the toy,
against whose singing
the world's roaring
breaks to bits.

Tremolos, runs, arpeggios,
strings of pearls-of-sound:
outweigh
all crowns and swords
of all centuries
in value.

In the midst of the darkness of time
magic sparks
of joy
climb

der Freude.
Einige fallen
in offene Hände
und Herzen.

Und mancher verirrte
vollbringt das Wunder
Erweckung.
Dann hält
irgendwo eine Faust
inne, vergißt
auf den fällenden
Schlag.

ZUEIGUNG

Ich lese, doch fasse ich nicht
den Sinn. Aus verwirrenden Zeichen und Zeilen
steigt dein Gesicht.

Ich höre im Rauschen, im Fallen,
im Treiben des Laubs nur immer den Klang
deiner schwingenden Stimme.

Ich öffne die Nüstern dem Winde
vom Meer. Und herüber weht mir die Brise
den Duft deines Haars.

Ich greife nach Dingen, vergeblich.
Auf meine Hände setzen sich, kleine
Vögel, die deinen.

out of quivering strings.
A few fall
into open hands
and hearts.

And many a lost one
performs the miracle
of awakening.
Then somewhere
a fist holds back,
forgets
the falling
blow.

DEDICATION

I read, but I do not grasp
the sense. Out of confusing signs and lines
your face rises.

I hear in the rustling, in the falling,
in the budding of the leaves only the sound
of your voice vibrating.

I open my breathing to the wind
off the sea. And over to me the breeze
blows the perfume of your hair.

I reach out for things in vain.
On my hands settle yours,
two small birds.

DIE LINKSHÄNDER

GÜNTER GRASS

ERICH BEOBACHTET MICH. AUCH ICH LASSE KEIN AUGE VON IHM. BEIDE halten wir Waffen in der Hand, und beschlossen ist, daß wir diese Waffen gebrauchen, einander verletzen werden. Unsere Waffen sind geladen. In langen Übungen erprobte, gleich nach den Übungen sorgfältig gereinigte Pistolen halten wir vor uns, das kühle Metall langsam erwärmend. Auf die Länge nimmt sich solch ein Schießeisen harmlos aus. Kann man nicht einen Füllfederhalter, einen gewichtigen Schlüssel so halten und einer schreckhaften Tante mit dem gespreizten schwarzen Lederhandschuh einen Schrei abkaufen? Nie darf in mir der Gedanke reifen, Erichs Waffe könnte blind, harmlos, ein Spielzeug sein. Auch weiß ich, daß Erich keine Sekunde an der Ernsthaftigkeit meines Werkzeugs zweifelt. Zudem haben wir, etwa vor einer halben Stunde, die Pistolen auseinandergenommen, gereinigt, wieder zusammengesetzt, geladen und entsichert. Wir sind keine Träumer. Zum Ort unserer unvermeidlichen Aktion haben wir Erichs Wochenendhäuschen bestimmt. Da das einstöckige Gebäude mehr als eine Wegstunde von der nächsten Bahnstation, also recht einsam liegt, dürfen wir annehmen, daß jedes unerwünschte Ohr, in des Wortes wahrer Bedeutung, weitab vom Schuß sein wird. Das Wohnzimmer haben wir ausgeräumt und die Bilder, zumeist Jagdszenen und Wildbretstilleben, von den Wänden genommen. Die Schüsse sollen ja nicht den Stühlen, warmglänzenden Kommoden und reichgerahmten Gemälden gelten. Auch wollen wir nicht den Spiegel treffen oder ein Porzellan verletzen. Nur auf uns haben wir es abgesehen.

Wir sind beide Linkshänder. Wir kennen uns vom Verein her. Sie wissen, daß die Linkshänder dieser Stadt, wie alle, die ein verwandtes Gebrechen drückt, einen Verein gegründet haben. Wir treffen uns regelmäßig und versuchen unseren anderen, leider so ungeschickten Griff zu schulen. Eine Zeitlang gab uns ein gutwilliger Rechtshänder Unterricht. Leider kommt er jetzt nicht mehr. Die Herren im Vorstand kritisierten seine Lehrmethode und befanden, die Mitglieder des Vereins sollten aus eigener Kraft umlernen. So verbinden wir nun gemeinsam und zwanglos eigens für uns erfundene Gesellschaftsspiele mit Geschicklichkeitsproben wie: Rechts einfädeln, eingießen, aufmachen und zuknöpfen. In unseren Statuten heißt es: Wir wollen nicht ruhen, bis daß rechts wie links ist.

THE LEFT-HANDERS

GÜNTER GRASS
translated by A. Leslie Willson

ERICH IS WATCHING ME. AND I KEEP MY EYE ON HIM. WE BOTH HOLD weapons in our hands, and it has been decided that we will use these weapons, will wound each other. Our weapons are loaded. Slowly warming the cool metal we hold the pistols before us, tried out in long practice, carefully cleaned right after the practice. In the long run such a firearm looks harmless. Can't you hold a fountain pen, a heavy key that way, and with a spread-out black leather glove get a scream from an easily frightened aunt? Never may the thought arise in me that Erich's weapon could be a fake, harmless, a toy. I know, too, that Erich doesn't doubt for a moment in the seriousness of my implement. Besides, about a half hour ago we took the pistols apart, cleaned them, reassembled them, loaded them, and released their safety catches. We are no dreamers. We decided on Erich's weekend house as the place of our inevitable action. Since the one-story building is more than an hour's distance from the nearest train depot, thus is pretty solitary, we may assume that any unwanted ear, in the true sense of the word, will be far away from the shot. We have emptied the living room and have removed the pictures from the walls, mostly hunting scenes and game still lifes. The shots are not, of course, meant for the chairs, warmly gleaming chests, and richly framed paintings. And we don't want to hit the mirror or damage the porcelain. We plan to aim only at each other.

We are both left-handers. We know one another from the club. You know that the left-handers of this city, like all whom a similar handicap oppresses, have founded a club. We meet regularly and try to train our other handhold, so sadly inept. For a time an obliging right-hander gave us instruction. Unfortunately, he comes no more now. The gentlemen of the board criticized his teaching methods and concluded that the members of the club should retrain themselves through their own efforts. So, mutually and voluntarily, just for ourselves, we now combine made-up party games with tests for dexterity, such as threading a needle, pouring, unfastening, and buttoning up right-handed. In our bylaws it says: We will not rest until right is like left.

Wie schön und kraftvoll dieser Satz auch sein mag, ist er doch lautester Unsinn. So werden wir es nie schaffen. Und der extreme Flügel unserer Verbindung verlangt schon lange, daß diese Sentenz gestrichen wird und statt dessen geschrieben steht: Wir wollen auf unsere linke Hand stolz sein und uns nicht unseres angeborenen Griffes schämen.
Auch diese Parole stimmt sicher nicht, und nur ihr Pathos, wie auch eine gewisse Großzügigkeit des Gefühls, ließ uns diese Worte wählen. Erich und ich, die wir beide dem extremen Flügel zugezählt werden, wissen zu gut, wie tief verwurzelt unsere Scham ist. Elternhaus, Schule, später die Zeit beim Militär haben nicht dazu beigetragen, uns eine Haltung zu lehren, die diese geringfügige Absonderlichkeit—geringfügig im Vergleich mit anderen, weitverbreiteten Abnormitäten—mit Anstand ertrüge. Das begann mit dem kindlichen Händchengeben. Diese Tanten, Onkels, Freundinnen mütterlicherseits, Kollegen väterlicherseits, dieses nicht zu übersehende, den Horizont einer Kindheit verdunkelnde, schreckliche Familienfoto. Und allen mußte die Hand gegeben werden: "Nein, nicht das unartige Händchen, das brave. Wirst du wohl das richtige Händchen geben, das gute Händchen, das kluge, geschickte, das einzig wahre, das rechte Händchen!"
Sechzehn Jahre war ich alt und faßte zum erstenmal ein Mädchen an: "Ach, du bist ja Linkshänder!" sagte sie enttäuscht und zog mir die Hand aus der Bluse. Solche Erinnerungen bleiben, und wenn wir dennoch diesen Spruch—Erich und ich verfaßten ihn—in unser Buch schreiben wollen, so soll damit nur die Benennung eines sicher nie zu erreichenden Ideals versucht werden.
Nun hat Erich die Lippen aufeinandergepreßt und die Augen schmal gemacht. Ich tue das gleiche. Unsere Backenmuskeln spielen, die Stirnhaut spannt sich, schmal werden unsere Nasenrücken. Erich gleicht jetzt einem Filmschauspieler, dessen Züge mir aus vielen abenteuerlichen Szenen vertraut sind. Darf ich annehmen, daß auch mir diese fatale Ähnlichkeit mit einem dieser zweideutigen Leinwandhelden anhaftet? Wir mögen grimmig aussehen, und ich bin froh, daß uns niemand beobachtet. Würde er, der unerwünschte Augenzeuge, nicht annehmen, zwei junge Männer allzu romantischer Natur wollen sich duellieren? Sie haben die gleiche Räuberbraut, oder der eine hat wohl dem anderen Übles nachgesagt. Eine seit Generationen währende Familienfehde, ein Ehrenhandel, ein blutiges Spiel auf Gedeih und Verderb. So blicken sich nur Feinde an. Seht diese schmalen, farblosen Lippen, diese unversöhnlichen Nasenrücken. Wie sie den Haß kauen, diese Todessüchtigen.
Wir sind Freunde. Wenn unsere Berufe auch noch so verschieden sind—Erich ist Abteilungsleiter in einem Warenhaus, ich habe den gutbezahlten Beruf des Feinmechanikers gewählt—, können wir doch soviel gemeinsame

However beautiful and pithy this sentence may be, it is still the sheerest nonsense. We'll never manage it that way. And the extreme wing of our association has long demanded that this sentence be stricken and instead of it be written: We will be proud of our left hand and not be ashamed of our innate grip.

This motto, too, is certainly not correct, and only its pathos, as also a certain grandiosity of feeling, permitted us to choose these words. Erich and I, who both were included in the extreme wing, know too well how deeply our shame is rooted. Parental home, school, later our time in the military did not contribute to teaching us an attitude that would bear, with propriety, this slight peculiarity, slight in comparison with other, widespread abnormalities. It began with shaking hands as a child. Those aunts, uncles, women friends of my mother, colleagues of my father, this unavoidable, terrible family photograph that darkens the horizon of childhood. And all required a handshake: "No, not that naughty hand, the good one. Just give the correct hand, the good hand, the smart, dexterous, the one true one, the right hand!"

I was sixteen years old and for the first time grabbed a girl: "Oh, why you're left-handed!" she said with disappointment and pulled my hand out of her blouse. Such memories remain, and even though we choose to write this motto in our book anyway—Erich and I composed it—thereby we only aim to designate an ideal that can certainly never be achieved.

Now Erich has pressed his lips together tightly and narrowed his eyes. I do the same. The muscles of our cheeks play, our brows become tense, the bridges of our noses narrow. Erich now resembles a movie actor, whose visage is familiar to me from many adventurous scenes. May I assume that this unfortunate resemblance to one of those ambiguous movie heroes clings to me also? It may be we look ferocious, and I'm glad that no one is watching us. Would not he, the unwelcome witness, assume that two young men with a too romantic nature were about to duel? They have the same gang moll, or possibly one has said something nasty about the other. A family feud that has been going on for generations, an affair of honor, a bloody game for better or for worse. Only enemies glare at one another like that. Look at those narrow, colorless lips, the implacable bridges of those noses. How they chew on hate, these two craving for death.

We are friends. Even though our occupations are very different—Erich is the department head in a large store, I chose the well-paid occupation of precision mechanic—we still are able to count as many common

Interessen aufzählen, als nötig sind, einer Freundschaft Dauer zu verleihen. Erich gehört dem Verein länger an als ich. Gut erinnere ich mich des Tages, da ich schüchtern und viel zu feierlich gekleidet, im Stammlokal der Einseitigen eintrat, Erich mir entgegenkam, dem Unsicheren die Garderobe wies, mich klug, doch ohne lästige Neugierde betrachtete und dann mit seiner Stimme sagte: “Sie wollen sicher zu uns. Seien Sie ganz ohne Scham; wir sind hier, um uns zu helfen.”

Ich sagte soeben “die Einseitigen.” So nennen wir uns offiziell. Doch auch diese Namengebung scheint mir, wie ein Großteil der Statuten, mißlungen. Der Name spricht nicht deutlich genug aus, was uns verbinden und eigentlich auch stärken sollte. Gewiß wären wir besser genannt, würden wir kurz die Linken, oder klangvoller, die linken Brüder heißen. Sie werden erraten, warum wir verzichten mußten, uns unter diesen Titeln eintragen zu lassen. Nichts wäre unzutreffender und dazu beleidigender, als uns mit jenen, sicher bedauernswerten Menschen zu vergleichen, denen die Natur die einzig menschenwürdige Möglichkeit vorenthielt, der Liebe Genüge zu tun. Ganz im Gegenteil sind wir eine buntgewürfelte Gesellschaft, und ich darf sagen, daß unsere Damen es an Schönheit, Charme und gutem Benehmen mit manch einer Rechtshänderin aufnehmen, ja, würde man sorgfältig vergleichen, ergäbe sich ein Sittenbild, das manchen um das Seelenheil seiner Gemeinde besorgten Pfarrer von der Kanzel ausrufen ließe: “Ach, wäret Ihr doch alle Linkshänder!”

Dieser fatale Vereinsname. Selbst unser erster Vorsitzender, ein etwas zu patriarchalisch denkender und leider auch lenkender höherer Beamter der Stadtverwaltung, Katasteramt, muß dann und wann einräumen, daß wir nicht gutheißen, daß es am Links fehlen würde, daß wir weder die Einseitigen sind, noch einseitig denken, fühlen und handeln.

Gewiß sprachen auch politische Bedenken mit, als wir die besseren Vorschläge verwarfen und uns so nannten, wie wir eigentlich nie hätten heißen dürfen. Nachdem die Mitglieder des Parlamentes von der Mitte aus nach der einen oder anderen Seite tendieren und die Stühle ihres Hauses so gestellt sind, daß allein schon die Stuhlordnung die politische Situation unseres Vaterlandes verrät, ist es zur Sitte geworden, einem Schreiben, einer Rede, in der das Wörtchen links mehr als einmal vorkommt, eine gefährliche Radikalität anzudichten. Nun, hier mag man ruhig sein. Wenn ein Verein unserer Stadt ohne politische Ambitionen auskommt und nur der gegenseitigen Hilfe, der Geselligkeit lebt, dann ist es der unsrige. Um nun noch jedem Verdacht erotischer Abwegigkeit hier and für alle Zeit die Spitze abzubrechen, sei kurz erwähnt, daß ich unter den Mädchen unserer Jugendgruppe meine Verlobte gefunden habe. Sobald für uns eine Wohnung frei wird, wollen wir heiraten. Wenn eines Tages der Schatten schwinden wird, den jene erste Begegnung mit dem weiblichen Geschlecht interests as is necessary to lend our friendship durability. Erich has belonged to the club longer than I. I well remember the day when, timidly and much too solemnly dressed, I walked into the hangout of the Unilaterals, Erich came toward me, pointed out the cloakroom to this uncertain person, looked at me shrewdly but without irksome curiosity, and then with his voice said: "You're probably looking for us. Don't be ashamed; we're here to help one another."

I just said "the Unilaterals." That's what we call ourselves officially. But even this term seems to me inauspicious, like the greater part of our bylaws. The term does not state clearly enough what is supposed to tie us together and actually strengthen us, too. Of course, we would be better named if we called ourselves succinctly the Leftists, or more sonorously, the Left Brethren. You will guess why we had to forgo introducing ourselves with these titles. Nothing would be more inappropriate and, in addition, more insulting than to compare ourselves with those certainly deplorable people whom nature denies the only humanly dignified possibility of fulfilling love. Quite the contrary, we are a motley society, and I may say that our ladies are equal in beauty, charm, and proper behavior to many a right-handed woman; indeed, if one made a careful comparison, a model of propriety would emerge that would cause many a preacher, worried about the spiritual welfare of his congregation, to cry from the pulpit: "Oh, if only all of you were left-handers!"

This unfortunate club name. Even our first president, a rather high official of the city administration, the office of land registry, who both thinks and unfortunately also directs in a patriarchal manner, must now and then concede that we do not sanction that the Left might be lacking, that we are neither unilateral nor think, feel, and act unilaterally.

Of course, political considerations played a role when we rejected better suggestions and called ourselves what we actually should never have been called. Since the members of parliament, starting from the middle, lean to one side or the other and the chairs of their chamber are so set up that even the chair arrangement reveals the political situation of our homeland, it has become a practice to attribute a dangerous radicalism to a written statement, a speech, in which the little word "Left" occurs more than once. If there is any club in our city that gets by without political ambition and exists only for mutual assistance, for sociability, then it is ours. Now, in order to remove any suspicion at all of erotic deviation once and for all, just let it be mentioned that I met my fiancée among the girls of our youth group. As soon as we can find an apartment, we are going to get married. When one day the shadow disappears, which that first

auf mein Gemüt warf, werde ich diese Wohltat Monika verdanken können.
Unsere Liebe hat nicht nur mit den allbekannten und in vielen Büchern beschriebenen Problemen fertig werden müssen, auch unser manuelles Leiden mußte verwunden und fast verklärt werden, damit es zu unserem kleinen Glück kommen konnte. Nachdem wir in der ersten, begreiflichen Verwirrung versucht hatten, rechtshändig einander gut zu sein, und bemerken mußten, wie unempfindlich diese unsere taube Seite ist, streicheln wir nur noch geschickt, das heißt, wie uns der Herr geschaffen hat. Ich verrate nicht zuviel und hoffe auch, nicht indiskret zu sein, wenn ich hier andeute, daß es immer wieder Monikas liebe Hand ist, die mir die Kraft gibt, auszuharren und das Versprechen zu halten. Gleich nach dem ersten, gemeinsamen Kinobesuch habe ich ihr versichern müssen, daß ich ihr Mädchentum schonen werde, bis daß wir uns die Ringe—hier leider nachgebend und das Ungeschick einer Veranlagung bekräftigend—an die rechten Ringfinger stecken. Dabei wird in südlichen, katholischen Ländern das goldene Zeichen der Ehe links getragen, wie denn auch wohl in jenen sonnigen Zonen mehr das Herz als der unerbittliche Verstand regiert. Vielleicht um hier auf Mädchenart zu revoltieren und zu beweisen, in welch eindeutiger Form die Frauen argumentieren können, wenn ihre Belange gefährdet zu sein scheinen, haben die jüngeren Damen unseres Vereins in emsiger Nachtarbeit unserer grünen Fahne die Inschrift gestickt: Links schlägt das Herz.
Monika und ich haben diesen Augenblick des Ringewechselns nun schon so oft besprochen und sind doch immer wieder zu demselben Ergebnis gekommen: Wir können es uns nicht leisten, vor einer unwissenden, nicht selten böswilligen Welt, als Verlobte zu gelten, wenn wir schon lang ein getrautes Paar sind und alles, das Große und das Kleine, miteinander teilen. Oft weint Monika wegen dieser Ringgeschichte. Wie wir uns auch auf diesen unseren Tag freuen mögen, wird denn wohl doch ein leichter Trauerschimmer auf all den Geschenken, reichgedeckten Tischen und angemessenen Feierlichkeiten liegen.
Nun zeigt Erich wieder sein gutes, normales Gesicht. Auch ich gebe nach, verspüre aber dennoch eine Zeitlang diesen Krampf in der Kiefermuskulatur. Zudem zucken noch immer die Schläfen. Nein, ganz gewiß standen uns diese Grimassen nicht. Unsere Blicke treffen sich ruhiger und deshalb auch mutiger; wir zielen. Jeder meint die gewisse Hand des anderen. Ich bin ganz sicher, daß ich nicht fehlen werde; und auch auf Erich kann ich mich verlassen. Zu lange haben wir geübt, fast jede freie Minute in einer verlassenen Kiesgrube am Stadtrand zugebracht, um heute, da sich so vieles entscheiden soll, nicht zu versagen.

encounter with the female sex cast on my soul, I will be able to thank Monika for this good deed.

Our love has not only had to cope with the notorious problems described in many books, our manual affliction, too, had to be overcome and almost transfigured, so that it could become a part of our bit of bliss. After we had tried to love one another with our right hands, in our initial understandable confusion we were forced to realize how unfeeling this, our deficient side, is, and now we can caress one another adeptly, that is, like the Lord created us. I'm not revealing too much, and I hope not being indiscreet, when I point out here that it is Monika's sweet hand that again and again gives me the strength to endure and to keep my promise. Right after we went to the movies together for the first time, I had to promise her that I would respect her maidenhood until we had put the rings on our right ring fingers—in this respect surrendering, unfortunately, and confirming the clumsiness of a predisposition. Yet in the southerly Catholic countries the gold emblem of marriage is worn on the left, just as probably in those sunny zones the heart reigns more than relentless reason. Perhaps in order to revolt in a maidenly way here and to illustrate in what an unequivocal form women can argue when their interests seem to be threatened, the young ladies of our club, working assiduously at night, embroidered this inscription on our green banner: The heart beats left.

Monika and I have discussed the moment of exchanging rings so often and still have always arrived at the same conclusion: We cannot bring ourselves to be betrothed in the eyes of a world unknowing and not seldom malicious, even though we have been a trusting couple for a long time and share everything, large and small, with one another. Monika often weeps about this matter of rings. No matter how much we may rejoice about that day, our day, still a slight glimmer of sorrow will lie on all the gifts, richly set tables, and appropriate solemnities.

Now Erich again displays his good, normal face. I also relent, but still feel for a while the cramp in the muscles of my jaw. In addition, my temples still twitch. No, these grimaces were certainly not for us. Our glances meet more calmly and thus more courageously, too; we take aim. Each aims at that certain hand of the other. I am quite sure that I will not miss; and I can rely on Erich, too. We practiced too long, spending almost every spare minute in an abandoned gravel pit on the edge of town, to misfire today, when so much is to be decided.

Ihr werdet schreien, das grenzt an Sadismus, nein, das ist Selbstverstümmelung. Glaubt mir, all diese Argumente sind uns bekannt. Nichts, kein Verbrechen haben wir uns nicht vorgeworfen. Wir stehen nicht zum ersten Mal in diesem ausgeräumten Zimmer. Viermal sahen wir uns so bewaffnet, und viermal ließen wir, erschreckt durch unser Vorhaben, die Pistolen sinken. Erst heute haben wir Klarheit. Die letzten Vorkommnisse persönlicher Art und auch im Vereinsleben geben uns recht, wir müssen es tun. Nach langem Zweifel—wir haben den Verein, das Wollen des extremen Flügels in Frage gestellt—greifen wir nun endgültig zu den Waffen. So bedauerlich es ist, wir können nicht mehr mitmachen. Unser Gewissen verlangt, daß wir uns von den Gepflogenheiten der Vereinskameraden distanzieren. Hat sich doch da ein Sektierertum breitgemacht, und die Reihen der Vernünftigsten sind mit Schwärmern, sogar Fanatikern durchsetzt. Die einen himmeln nach rechts, die anderen schwören auf links. Was ich nie glauben wollte, politische Parolen werden von Tisch zu Tisch geschrien, der widerliche Kult des eidbedeutenden, linkshändigen Nägeleinschlagens wird so gepflegt, daß manche Vorstandssitzung einer Orgie gleicht, in der es gilt, durch heftiges und bessessenes Hämmern in Ekstase zu geraten. Wenn es auch niemand laut ausspricht und die offensichtlich dem Laster Verfallenen bislang kurzerhand ausgestoßen wurden, es läßt sich nicht leugnen: jene verfehlte und mir ganz unbegreifliche Liebe zwischen Geschlechtsgleichen hat auch bei uns Anhänger gefunden. Und um das Schlimmste zu sagen: Auch mein Verhältnis zu Monika hat gelitten. Zu oft ist sie mit ihrer Freundin, einem labilen und sprunghaften Geschöpf, zusammen. Zu oft wirft sie mir Nachgiebigkeit und mangelnden Mut in jener Ringgeschichte vor, als daß ich glauben könnte, es sei noch dasselbe Vertrauen zwischen uns, es sei noch dieselbe Monika, die ich, nun immer seltener, im Arm halte.

Erich und ich versuchen jetzt gleichmäßig zu atmen. Je mehr wir auch hierin übereinstimmen, um so sicherer werden wir, daß unser Handeln vom guten Gefühl gelenkt wird. Glaubt nicht, es ist das Bibelwort, welches da rät, das Ärgernis auszureißen. Vielmehr ist es der heiße, immerwährende Wunsch, Klarheit zu bekommen, noch mehr Klarheit, zu wissen, wie steht es um mich, ist dieses Schicksal unabänderlich oder haben wir es in der Hand, einzugreifen und unserm Leben eine normale Richtung zu weisen? Keine läppischen Verbote mehr, Bandagen und ähnliche Tricks. Rechtschaffen wollen wir in freier Wahl und durch nichts mehr vom Allgemeinen getrennt neu beginnen und eine glückliche Hand haben.

Jetzt stimmt unser Atem überein. Ohne uns ein Zeichen zu geben, haben wir gleichzeitig geschossen. Erich hat getroffen, und auch ich habe ihn nicht enttäuscht. Jeder hat, wie vorgesehen, die wichtige Sehne so unterbrochen, daß die Pistolen, nicht mehr kraftvoll genug gehalten, zu Boden

You all will cry out that it borders on sadism, no, that it is self-mutilation. Believe me, all these arguments are familiar to us. There is nothing, no crime, that we have not reproached one another with. We are not standing in this empty room for the first time. Four times we saw one another armed like this, and four times, horrified by what we were about to do, we let the pistols sink. Today, for the first time, we are lucid. The latest incidences of a personal nature and also in our life in the club justify us, we must do it. After long doubt—we questioned the club, the intentions of the extreme wing—now we finally take up our weapons. However regrettable it is, we can no longer go along. Our conscience demands that we remove ourselves from the practices of our comrades in the club. After all, a sectarian spirit has become dominant, and the ranks of the most sensible are saturated with visionaries, even fanatics. Some piously support the right, the others swear by the left. Something I never wanted to believe: Political slogans are shouted from table to table, the offensive cult of oath-enjoined, left-handed nail pounding is so customary that many a meeting of the board resembles an orgy in which the purpose is to fall into ecstasy through vehement and frenzied hammering. Even if no one says it out loud and those apparently fallen victim to the vice were expelled without hesitation in the past, it cannot be denied: That false love between members of the same sex, quite incomprehensible to me, has also found adherents among us. And, to mention the worst, my relationship with Monika has suffered, too. Too often she is with her girlfriend, an unstable and flighty creature. She reproaches me with being complaisant and lacking in fortitude in regard to the rings too often for me to be able to believe that there is the same trust between us, that it is still the same Monika whom, now more and more seldom, I hold in my arms.

Erich and I are trying now to breathe in unison. The more we coincide in this, the more certain we become that our actions are guided by a good feeling. Don't think it is the word of the Bible that advises you to cut off the offending member. Rather, it is the fervent, perpetual wish to achieve clarity, ever more clarity, to know how things are going for me, is this destiny unavoidable or do we have it within our grasp to intervene and point our lives in a normal direction? No more silly prohibitions, bandages, and similar tricks. Upright, with free choice and no longer separated by anything from what is universal, we want to begin anew and have a felicitous hand.

Now our breathing is in accord. Without giving one another a signal, we fired simultaneously. Erich hit the mark, and I, too, did not disappoint him. As planned, each of us cut the important tendon, so that our pistols, no longer held with enough strength, fell to the floor and, with that, any fielen und damit nun jeder weitere Schuß überflüssig ist. Wir lachen und beginnen unser großes Experiment damit, ungeschickt, weil nur auf die rechte Hand angewiesen, die Notverbände anzulegen.

further shot is superfluous. We laugh and begin our great experiment by putting the bandages on, clumsily, because we are dependent only on our right hands.

Koch Petri (1974) Dry-point etching on zinc

Petri the Cook

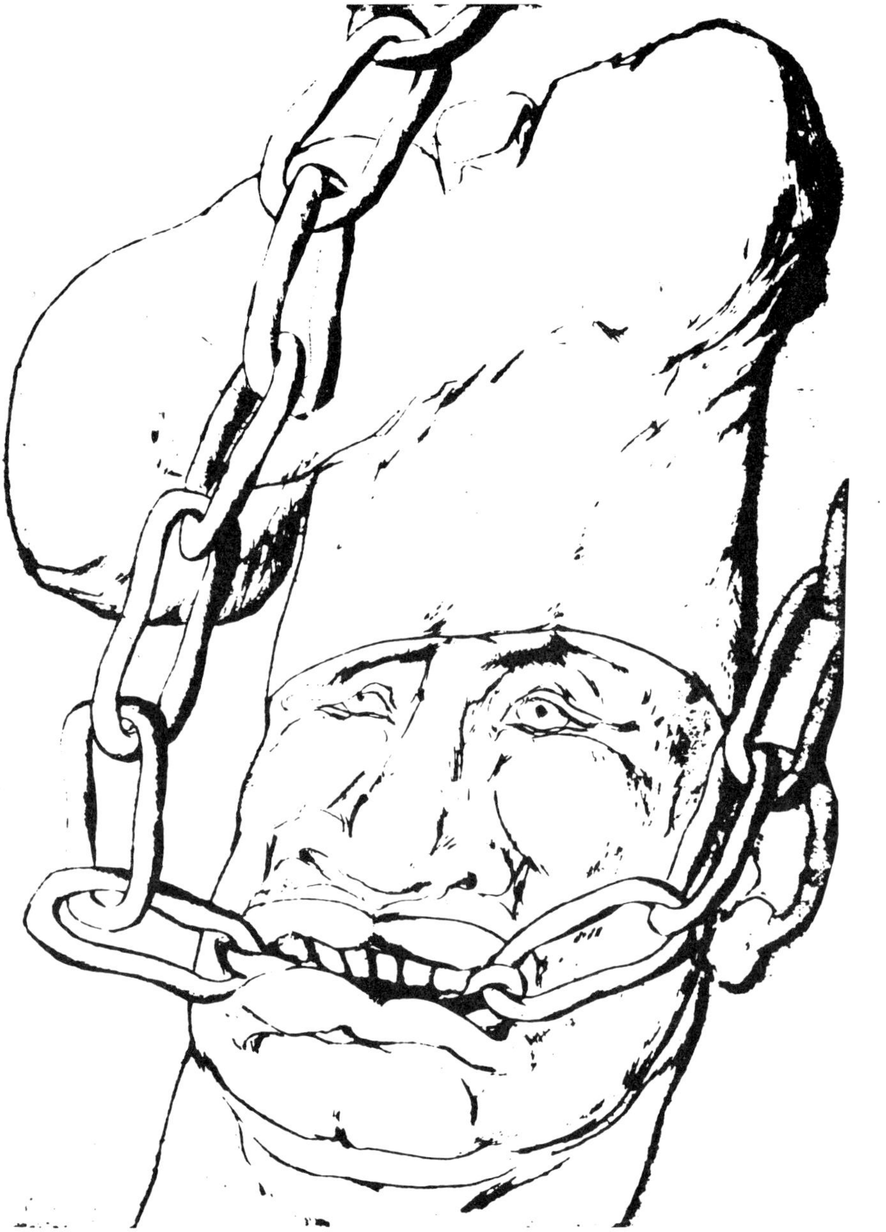

Koch Vasco (1974) zinc etching

Vasco the Cook

Günter Grass

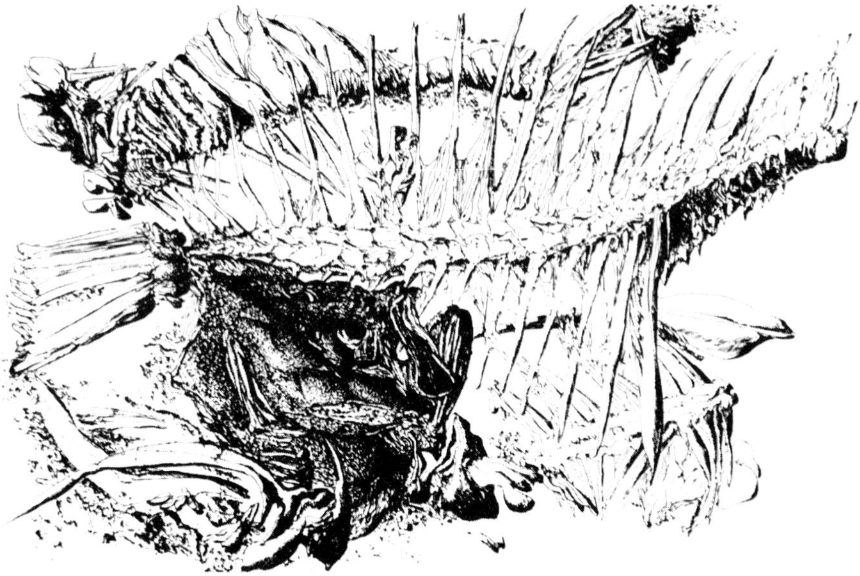

Kopf und Gräte (1977) copper etching

Head and Fishbones

Mann im Butt (1978) copper etching

Man in a Flounder

DIE BALLERINA

GÜNTER GRASS

IN DER WOHNUNG EINES RESTAURATEURS FAND ICH EINIGE STICHE, WELCHE Szenen in der Manier der Commedia dell'arte, pantomimische Schaustellungen, allerlei allegorischen Bühnenzauber illustrierten. Von einem dieser Bildchen soll hier die Rede sein.

Kleine, sichere, in der Tiefe des Zimmers, im offenen Dunkel des Fensters netzartig übereinandergelegte Stiche, ein hochbeiniges, zerwühltes Bett—als hätte ein Schlafloser es verlassen—, im Hintergrund der schmale Schrank, ein Bücherbord halb geahnt, zuvorderst mit kühner Hand entworfen, sorgsam den Ton des Papiers bewahrend, entwickelt sich die bewegteste Szene: auf seinem armen Stuhl, nachlässig mit Hemd, Tuch und Hose bekleidet, sitzt der Dichter. Er hat sich zurückgelehnt, läßt die Hand mit der Feder hängen, hat links das blanke Papier ergriffen. So, ungläubig noch, erblickt er die Ballerina. In spitzem Schuh steht sie auf seinem Tisch. Man sieht noch die gekreuzten Bänder über dem Knöchel, dann wölbt sich ein reicher, gewichtloser Rock, unter Perlen und durchbrochenem Besatz atmet die Büste. Schlank von der Taille aufwärts streckt sie sich mit erhobenen Armen bis in den letzten Finger. Unter dem leichten Schmerz in der Zeichnung der Brauen lächelt sie kaum und blickt den Beschauer des Blattes an, als tanze sie für ihn und nicht für den Dichter. Die ruhigen Konturen dieser Positionen lassen glauben, daß eine Folge ausgesuchter Bewegungen so abschließt. Vielleicht jedoch wird sie von neuem Beginnen, wird diesen mit Schrank, Tisch, Stuhl und zerwühltem Bett fast verstellten Raum nun auch mit Pirouetten füllen oder sie wird in zerbrechlicher Arabeske, einer Waage gleich, Harmonie bedeuten. Vielleicht aber wird sie ein Sprung, ein langsamer, bis ganz zum Schluß deutlicher Sprung in aufsteigender Linie durch das offene Fenster in den Nachthimmel tragen und den leeren Tisch zurücklassen. Er, Papier und Feder in den Händen, wird nach ihr greifen wollen, wird halten wollen, was nicht zu halten ist; gewiß nicht von einem, der mit gefüllten Händen greift. So wird er wieder zu seinem Stuhl finden, wird lange sitzen, hängend die Hand mit der Feder, links das jäh ergriffene Papier, wird auf dem Tisch die Stelle suchen, an welcher alles stattfand, und wird einen Kratzer finden—dumm wie alle Kratzer. Und dann wird er schreiben, der Dichter, auf jenem Stich.

THE BALLERINA

GÜNTER GRASS
translated by A. Leslie Willson

IN THE APARTMENT OF A RESTAURATEUR I FOUND SOME PRINTS THAT illustrated scenes in the manner of the commedia dell' arte, pantomimic performances, all kinds of allegorical stage magic. One of these pictures is the subject of this discourse.

Small, accomplished etchings, arrayed intricately one above the other deep in the room, in the open darkness of the window, a long-legged, rumpled bed—as though an insomniac had abandoned it—in the background a narrow wardrobe, a bookshelf half-imagined. Sketched first and foremost with a bold hand, carefully retaining the shade of the paper, the most exciting scene unfolds: The poet is sitting on his cheap chair, dressed carelessly in shirt, shawl, and trousers. He has leaned back, lets his hand droop with the pen, has seized the blank paper in his left hand. Thus, still incredulous, he catches sight of the ballerina. Wearing pointed shoes she is standing on his table. The crossed ribbons over her ankles can be seen, then a lavish, weightless skirt billows up, her breast breathes under pearls and an openwork flounce. Slender from her waist up, with arms raised she stretches to the ends of her fingers. Under the faint pain in the lines of her brow she scarcely smiles and looks at the observer of the print as though she were dancing for him and not for the poet. The quiet contour of these positions make us believe that a series of well-chosen movements conclude like this. Perhaps, however, she will begin anew, now will also fill this room, almost obstructed by wardrobe, table, chair, and rumpled bed, with pirouettes or, in a fragile arabesque, like a pair of scales, she will signify harmony. But perhaps a leap, a slow leap distinct to the very end, will carry her in an ascending line through the open window into the night sky and leave the empty table behind. He, paper and pen in his hands, will try to grab her, will want to keep what cannot be kept, least of all by one who grabs with filled hands. Then he will find his way back to his chair, will sit for a long time, the hand with the pen drooping, in his left the quickly grasped paper, will look for the place on the table where everything happened, and will find a scratch—stupid like all scratches. And then the poet in that etching will write.

Wir mögen lächeln bei der Betrachtung dieses naiven Bildchens und mit dem Finger die Stellen suchen und finden, welche uns gar zu peinlich den staubigen Porzellanschnörkeln in großmütterlichen Vitrinen gleichen. Die Intimität dieser Begegnung zwischen Poet und Muse werden wir in die Gartenlaube verbannen und derlei unbestellte Darbietungen auf unserer Schreibtischplatte nicht dulden. Und dennoch könnte es sein, daß heute, da wir Gartenzwerge und sehr zerbrechliche Schäferidylle gegen Bakelitaschenbecher und die Vitrine gegen den Nierentisch um einen fragwürdigen Gewinn eintauschen, der Dichter mit seiner Schreibmaschine dieses besondere Ereignis nötig hat. Auch heute entsteht kein Gedicht, wenn sich nicht hilfreich eine der Musen beugt.

Wenn es den Dichter ankommen sollte, die Ballerina zu beschreiben—Anlaß genug gab ihm ihr Tanz, der sprödkühle Raum aus ihrer Bewegung entworfen—wird er nähertreten, wird er dahinterblicken, entzaubern wollen. Er gleicht den Briefmarkensammler, welcher ein kleines, begehrtes Viereck prüfend ins Licht hält, um Zahnung und Wasserzeichen deutlich zu haben. Krone und Lächeln der bunten Königin, so wohlgelungen die Miniatur sein mag, beeinflussen niemals sein wertendes Auge.

Kehren wir zu unserem Stich zurück. Jenem Dichter hinterließ ein Augenblick künstlichster Darbietung nur die Spur der Ballettschuhe auf der Tischplatte. Davon wird er schreiben. Die Darbietung wird zur Erscheinung, der Kratzer zum Zeichen werden. Die Ballerina jedoch? Von dem Fenster, durch welches sie kam und ging, wird die Rede sein, und sollte ein guter Dichter dort an dem Tisch gesessen haben—nach dem Bildchen können wir es nicht beurteilen—wird er darauf verzichten, der Ballerina Augen gülden, ihr Antlitz hold und ihre Füßlein gar fein zu nennen. Dererlei Feststellungen über Augen, Gesicht und Füße machen sich nicht in so vagen Momenten. Dafür bedarf es der Erlaubnis, hinter der Kulisse zu stehn, in die Garderobe zu schauen.

Ihr Körper, ihr Requisit

Jeder Tenor, wenn es seine Stimme verlangt, wird hinter sich nach der Stuhllehne fassen—und immer wird ein Stuhl oder sonst Greifbares in seiner Nähe stehen—wird mit diesem Griff neue Kraft seinem Organ geben, gewinnender wird ihm die Arie gelingen. Nicht so die Ballerina. Ihr ist nicht viel erlaubt. Ihr Körper, dieser dem leicht hysterischen Weinen nahe Auswuch gequälter, auswärtsgedrehter Schönheit, bleibt, sobald sie mit winzigen pas de courus aus der Kulisse entlassen, ihr einziges Requisit. Einsam zeichnet sie ihre Figuren und erreicht zwischen der dritten und vierten Pirouette jenen Grad der Verlassenheit, den selbst

We may smile while observing this naive picture and with a finger seek and find the places that, much too distressing to us, resemble the dusty porcelain flourishes in grandmotherly glass cabinets. We will banish the intimacy of this encounter between poet and muse to the garden bower and not permit that kind of unasked-for offering on the surface of our desk. And still, it could be that today, when we exchange garden statuary and fragile shepherd idylls for bakelite ashtrays and glass cabinets for kidney-shaped tables—a questionable profit—the poet with his typewriter needs this specific event. Even today no poem comes into being without one of the muses bending down to help.

Should the poet be moved to describe the ballerina—her dance gave him reason enough, the primly indifferent space traced by her movement—he will wish to step closer, to look beyond it, to penetrate the illusion. He resembles the stamp collector, who, scrutinizing it, holds a small, coveted quadrangle to the light, in order to have a clear view of the perforations and the watermark. The crown and smile of the colorful queen, no matter how successful the miniature, will never influence his discriminating eye.

Let us return to our etching. A moment of the most artful performance left the poet with only the trace of a ballet shoe on the desk surface. He will write about that. The performance will become a vision, the scratch a sign. But the ballerina? He will speak of the window, through which she entered and departed, and should a fine poet have been sitting at the table—we cannot judge from the picture—he will refrain from calling the ballerina's eyes golden, her features winsome, and her tiny feet dainty. Such observations about eyes, face, and feet are not practicable in such vague moments. For that he would require permission to stand behind the scene, to peer into the dressing room.

Her Body, Her Accouterment

Any tenor, when his voice demands it, will reach around for the back of a chair—and a chair or something he can hold onto will always be standing nearby—with this grip he will give his voice new power, he will accomplish his aria more superlatively. But not the ballerina. She does not have much liberty. Her body, this excrescence of tortured, outwardly twisted beauty close to faintly hysterical weeping, as soon as she leaves the wings with tiny pas de courus, remains her only accouterment. Alone she draws her figures and between the third and fourth pirouette achieves that degree of das deutscheste Dichterlein nicht erreicht. Wird nun mit jeder beliebigen Drehung, wenn sie nur schwungvoll genug ist, dieser Ort der Verbannung bezogen? Ist es genau so, wenn Irmchen sich im Walzertakt dreht und die Augen selig dabei schließt? Wir werden sehen, daß mit der Pirouette, dieser geschraubten, gekünstelten Abstraktion, die letzmögliche Drehung geglückt scheint, daß hier das Kunststück gezeigt wird. Kunst weil nicht mehr Natur, weil hier die papierne Rose—wir kennen sie von den Schießbuden her—aller Vegetation voraus ist und niemals welken wird. Und nochmals Kunst, weil Gewaltsamkeit, Verleugnung der dummen, begrenzten Glieder, kleinliches Feilen an einer leeren Form hier und immer wieder zu gewichtsloser Schönheit ohne Vor- und Zunamen gereicht.

Der Garderobe bleibt es dann vorbehalten diesem nun schwitzenden siebenundzwanzig jährigen Geschöpf ein Vera oder Tascha zuzurufen, einen von harter Arbeit gezeichneten Körper aufzunehmen, welcher lispelt und keinen Blinddarm mehr hat. Nun zeigt es sich, wie harmlos and banal die Pause zwischen zwei anmutig anstrengenden Spitzenleistungen verbracht werden kann. Die Ballerina strickt Wollsocken für ihren kleinen Bruder, die Ballerina redet dummes Zeugs, die Ballerina hat sich kürzlich verlobt, jedoch ist es nicht ausgeschlossen, daß sie sich bald wieder entlobt. Die Ballerina setzt eine Brille auf, sie ist etwas kurzsichtig, und blättert in der Illustrierten, bis das Kreuzworträtsel gefunden und auch zur Hälfte gelöst wird. Nun weint die Ballerina ein bißchen. Sie hat heute eine schlechte Balance gehabt, sie hat "die Arabeske verwackelt" und ist während der dritten Pirouette "von der Spitze geknallt"—und das darf sie nicht.

Der Tenor darf hilfesuchend nach der Stuhllehne greifen, wenn er nur singt. Irmchen darf sogar mitten im Walzer ein wenig torkeln und tiefsinnig feststellen, daß sich ja alles dreht. Niemand wird ihr deshalb böse sein. Nur wenn die Ballerina "von der Spitze knallt", dann gefriert das Parkett, dann wird es heiß auf den Rängen, taghell und nüchtern dehnt sich die Bühne, Programme werden gefaltet, entfaltet, und alles Flüstern besagt, daß die Ballerina schon siebenundzwanzig ist, lispelt und keinen Blinddarm mehr hat.

Vom Barfußtanz

Feind und todernstes Gegenteil der Ballerina ist die Ausdruckstänzerin. Während die Ballerina ihren Körper nach festen Regeln bewegt und dabei lächelt, als sei ihr die Belanglosigkeit in die Mundwinkel gepinselt, tanzt die Ausdruckstänzerin mit ihrer schwierigen Seele and rührt ihre Glieder isolation that even the most German minor poet does not achieve. Will this place of banishment be occupied with every single whirl, if it is only spirited enough? Is it just like that when little Irma whirls in a waltz tempo and blissfully closes her eyes the while? We will see that with the pirouette, with this spiraling, affected abstraction, the last possible whirl seems to be accomplished, that the artistic feat is here revealed. Artistic because it is no longer nature, because here the paper rose—we know it from shooting galleries—is ahead of all garden growth and will never wither. And artistic, too, because force, the renunciation of foolish, limited limbs, trivial polishing on an empty form, suffices here and always for a weightless loveliness without first or last name.

It remains then for the dressing room to call this sweating, twenty-seven-year-old creature a Vera or a Tascha, to shelter a body marked by hard work, which lisps and no longer has an appendix. Now it becomes apparent how innocuously and banal the pause between two gracefully strenuous masterly performances can be spent. The ballerina knits woolen socks for her little brother, the ballerina talks nonsense, the ballerina recently became engaged, though it is not impossible that she will soon again break the engagement. The ballerina puts on glasses, she is somewhat nearsighted, and leafs through the illustrated until she finds the crossword puzzle and solves half of it. Now the ballerina weeps a bit. She had a bad balance today, she "blurred the arabesque" and during the third pirouette "thudded from the point"—and that's not allowed.

Seeking help, the tenor may reach for the back of the chair when he is only singing. Little Irma may even stagger a bit in the middle of the waltz and determine pensively that everything is whirling. No one will be mad at her for that. But when the ballerina "thuds from the point," then the parquet freezes, then it turns hot in the balconies, the stage stretches bright as day and dispassionately, programs are folded, unfolded, and all the whispering means that the ballerina is already twenty-seven, lisps, and no longer has an appendix.

On Dancing Barefoot

The enemy and deadly serious opposite to the ballerina is the modern dancer. While the ballerina moves her body according to firm rules and smiles the while, as though irrelevance had been painted in the corners of her mouth, the modern dancer dances with her troubled soul and moves dazu, als sei ihr privates und obendrein krummes Knie Anlaß genug, das achtel Parkett und halbvolle Ränge zwei lange Stunden zu fesseln. Die Ballerina wohnt bei ihrer Mutter, raucht nicht, ißt Joghurt und Bananen, füttert ein Hündchen and fühlt sich vor und nach dem Training müde, nichts als müde.

Die Ausdruckstänzerin ist gebildet. Sie weiß die Weise von Liebe und Tod auswendig herzusagen und hat Cocteaus "Orphée" schon fünfmal gesehen. In ihrem möblierten Zimmer hängt eine afrikanische Maske, eine Reproduktion nach Paul Klee und das Foto einer siamesischen Tempeltänzerin. Sie schneidert sich ihre Kleider selber und trägt ihre langen, wunderschönen Haare niemals zum Friseur. Da die Ballerina früh zu Bett geht, ist ihr Nachtleben, bis auf einige Kinobesuche, auf recht harmlose Art geregelt. Die Ausdruckstänzerin hat einen Pianisten zum Freund. Beide leben in ständiger Angst vor dem Kinde, wünschen sich aber ein Kind, sie sogar Kinder, Mutterschaft. Nun, wie zum Ersatz, tanzt sie mit aufgelöstem Haar—daher die Scheu vor dem Friseur—in sackähnlichem Gewand Wiegenlieder, Erwartungen, Erlösungen—ihre letzte Kreation hieß: Weinendes Embryo.

Die Ausdruckstänzerin tanzt barfuß, deshalb könnte man sie auch Barfußtänzerin nennen. Monotonem, preußischem Reglement gleich ist das Exercice der Ballerina. Ein zerquältes, zerdrücktes Fleisch versteckt sich in weißen, roten, gar silbernen Ballettschuhen. Die füße der Ballerina sind häßlich zu nennen. Geschundene, offene Zehen, ein übergroßer Spann. Sie scheinen die wahren Opfer all dieser gültig gezeigten Schönheit zu sein. Hier unten sammelt sich, was oben harmonisierte Geste und weiches Lächeln kaschiert. Das Maß dieser Schuhe bestimmt noch Mittelalter und Inquisition. So dürfen wir denn die erstrebenswerten zweiunddreißig Fouettês als ein Geständnis werten, und nichts, kein Barfußtanz, wird dieses Geständnis, diesen Schmerz ersetzen können.

Askese vor dem Spiegel

Die Ballerina lebt, einer Nonne gleich allen Verführungen ausgesetzt, im Zustand strengster Askese. Dieser Vergleich darf deshalb nicht überraschen, da alle auf uns gekommene Kunst stets Ergebnis konsequenter Beschränkung und nie genialischer Maßlosigkeit war. Auch wenn zeitweise Ausbrüche ins Unerlaubte zu Denken gaben und geben, der Kunst sei alles erlaubt, erfand sich immer, und gerade der beweglichste Geist, Regeln, Zäune, verbotene Zimmer. So ist auch der Raum unserer Ballerina beschränkt, übersehbar und erlaubt Veränderungen nur innerhalb der zur Verfügung stehenden Grundfläche. Die Erfordernisse der Zeit werden der her limbs as though her own personal and moreover bent knee were reason enough to rivet an eighth of the parquet and the half-filled balconies for two long hours. The ballerina lives with her mother, does not smoke, eats yoghurt and bananas, feeds a little dog, and before and after practicing feels tired, just tired.

The modern dancer is educated. She can recite the Lay of Life and Death by heart and has seen Cocteau's "Orphée" five times already. In her furnished room hangs an African mask, a reproduction of a picture by Paul Klee, and the photograph of a Siamese temple dancer. She makes all her own clothes herself and never goes to the hairdresser with her long, marvelous hair. Since the ballerina goes to bed early, any nightlife for her, except for a few movies, is regulated in a fairly innocuous way. The modern dancer has a friend who plays the piano. Both live in constant fear of having a child but want a child, she even wants children, motherhood. Now, as though to compensate, with flowing hair—thus her aversion to the hairdresser—in a sack-like robe she dances lullabies, expectations, deliverances—her last creation was called: Weeping Embryo.

The modern dancer dances barefoot, so she could be called a barefoot dancer, too. The practice of the ballerina is like a monotonous, Prussian regimen. Tortured, squeezed flesh hides in white, red, even silver ballet shoes. The feet of the ballerina may be called ugly. Flayed, open toes, an oversized instep. They seem to be the true victims of all this effectively displayed beauty. Here below is collected what harmonious gesture and mellow smile conceal above. The proportions of these shoes are still determined by the Middle Ages and the Inquisition. So we may appraise the desirable thirty-two fouettês as a confession, and nothing—no barefoot dance—will be able to replace this confession, this pain.

Asceticism before the Mirror

Like a nun, exposed to every kind of seduction, the ballerina lives in a condition of the most rigorous asceticism. This comparison should not be surprising, since all art that has come down to us was always the result of consistent restraint and never of genial excess. Even when at times outbursts into the illicit made it, and makes it, seem that art was permitted anything, even the most versatile spirit always devised rules, fences, forbidden rooms. So the space of our ballerina is also limited, visible at a glance, and permits alterations only within the floor space that is available. The exigencies of time will again and again demand of the ballerina a new

Ballerina immer wieder ein neues Gesicht abverlangen, werden ihr exotische und pseudoexotische Masken vorhalten wollen. Sie wird diese dekorativen Spielchen mitmachen, wissend, daß alle Mode ihr gut steht. Die wahre Revolution wird sich jedoch im eigenen Palast ereignen müssen.
Wie ähnlich verhält es sich in der Malerei. Wie sinnlos scheinen doch alle Versuche, grundlegende Entdeckungen im Erfinden neuer Materialien, im Austausch der Ölmalerei gegen ein Lackspritzverfahren auf Aluminium zu sehen. Niemals wird der Dilettantismus, an seinen Manieriertheiten leicht zu erkennen, das zähflüssige, selbst in der Revolution konservative Metier verdrängen können.
Der Spiegel wird durch die Ballerina zum unnachsichtigen Werkzeug der Askese. Hellwach trainiert sie vor seiner Fläche. Ihr Tanz ist nicht der Tanz mit geschlossenen Augen. Nichts anderes ist ihr der Spiegel als ein Glas, welches alles zurückwirft, überdeutlich, ein unerbittlicher Moralist, dem zu glauben ihr zum Gebot wird. Was tut der Dichter alles dem Spiegel an. Welch mystische, unleserliche Postkarten steckt er in seinen Barockrahmen. Ihm ist er Ausgang, Eingang, er sucht wie junge, noch unwissende Katzen hinter der Scheibe und findet dort allenfalls ein zerbrochenes, mit ungleichen Knöpfen gefülltes Kästchen, den Stoß alter Briefe, welchen er nie mehr zu finden hoffte, und einen Kamm voller Haare. Nur in den Augenblicken endgültiger Wandlung, da unser Körper bereichert oder verarmt scheint, stehen auch wir mit gleich wachen Augen wie sie vor dem Spiegel. Er zeigt den Mädchen die Pubertät an, ihm entgeht keine Schwangerschaft, kein fehlender Zahn—falls ihn ein Lachen provozieren will. Vielleicht daß der Friseur, der Taxichauffeur, der Schneider, der Maler beim Selbstporträt, die Prostituierte, welche ihr Zimmerchen mit einer Zahl solch deutlichmachender Scherben versehen hat, etwas Gemeinsames mit der Ballerina haben. Es ist der sorgenvolle Blick des Handwerkers, des Menschen, der mit dem Körper arbeitet, es ist der Blick in den Beichtspiegel.

Applaus und Vorhänge

Der Applaus ist das Kleingeld der Ballerina. Sie zählt es sehr sorgfältig, und hätten diese Münzen, wie anderes Hartgeld, die Eigenschaft, sich in einen Strumpf stecken zu lassen, sie würde sie sparen für spätere Zeiten, da es an Händen fehlen wird, da niemand mehr klatschen will, da das Klatschen weh tun könnte, da der Mann, der dem Vorhang befiehlt, keinen Grund mehr haben wird, auf einem Täfelchen Striche zu machen, bis daß es heißt: Sechzehn Vorhänge heute, zwei mehr als gestern.

face, will wish to hold up exotic and pseudoexotic masks before her. She will go along with this decorative little game, knowing that every fashion looks good on her. The true revolution will, however, have to take place in her own palace.

How similar it is with painting. How senseless do all attempts seem, to perceive fundamental discoveries in the invention of new materials, in the exchange of oil painting for a spray-paint procedure on aluminum. Dilletantism, easily recognized by its mannerisms, will never be able to oust the tenacious metier, conservative even in a revolution.

Through the ballerina the mirror becomes an unrelenting tool of asceticism. She trains before its surface wide-awake. Her dance is not a dance with closed eyes. The mirror is to her nothing more than a glass that reflects everything, ultra-bluntly, a merciless moralist, faith in whom becomes commandment to her. The things the poet inflicts on a mirror! What mystic, illegible postcards does he stick in its baroque frame. To him it is exit, entrance, like young, still ignorant cats he looks behind the pane and there finds, at best, a small broken box filled with assorted buttons, a bundle of old letters that he never expected to find again, and a comb full of hair. Only at moments of definite transformation, when our body seems enriched or impoverished, do we—like she—stand with wide-open eyes before a mirror. It shows girls their puberty, no pregnancy escapes it, no missing tooth—in the event a laugh provokes it. Perhaps the hairdresser, the taxi driver, the tailor, the painter at work on a self-portrait, the prostitute who has furnished her small room with a number of such plain-spoken shards, have something in common with the ballerina. It is the careworn look of the artisan, of the human being who works with his body, it is the examination in the confessional mirror of conscience.

Applause and Curtains

Applause is the small change of the ballerina. She counts it very carefully, and if these coins—like other hard cash—had the property of being able to be stuffed into a stocking, she would save them for later, for times when hands will be wanting, when no one will clap any more, when clapping could hurt, when the man who controls the curtain will no longer have a reason to make marks on a blackboard till it says: sixteen curtains today, two more than yesterday.

Dieselbe Gründlichkeit und Besorgnis, mit der wir die Rufe des Kuckucks während eines Sonntagsspazierganges im Stadtforst zählen, zeigt auch die Ballerina, wenn es gilt, der Dauer und Dichte des Beifalls die mögliche Zahl der Vorhänge zu entnehmen. Sie zählt und möchte Parkett und Ränge mit ihren präzisen und anmutigen Reverenzen versuchen, wie wir den Kuckuck versuchen, der unsere Jahre ausruft. —Dann, nach dem letzten Vorhang, fällt die Ballerina gleich einem Kartenhaus, das plötzlich der Zugluft ausgesetzt wird, in sich zusammen. Jedes ihrer sonst so gewogenen Glieder rutscht ins Beliebige. Die Ordnung in ihrem Gesicht, in diesem Teller voll kosmetischer Speisen, lockert sich. Ihren Augen gelingt kein Blick mehr, überspannt rutschen sie ab und erweitern sich schreckhaft. Desgleichen der Mund. Jederzeit bereit, in Hysterie laut zu werden, strengt ihn ein Lächeln, harmlos gemeint, derart an, daß ihm der Krampf in den Winkeln sitzt. Wozu dieses ständige Stirnrunzeln, dieses Heben der Brauen. Jedes Stück der mit viel Mühe und Können arrangierten Ausstellung verläßt seinen Platz. Die Ballerina scheint außer Rand und Band.

Das Pünktchen

Sie hebt den Arm in leichter Beugung. Oben ergibt sich die Hand, ein unnütz vielgliedriger Fortsatz. All das ohne Bedeutung, nur tauglich zum Ansehen, nicht mal ein Gruß oder die Einladung, näher zu treten. Halb auf dem Wege zum Ornament will es nur zeigen, was da ist, daß sich ein Arm da beugt und den Hintergrund einteilt, daß dort, wo der kleine Finger hindeutet, ein Pünktchen ist, welchem alle Schönheit gehorcht—und so auch die Ballerina. Nie käme ihr der Gedanke, man könne den Arm auch anders beugen, beugen, daß er nur Kraft, Verzweiflung oder gar häßlich geknickt einen Unfall bedeutet. Nie würde sie anderen Punkten den Finger hinschicken als jenem, welcher sinnlos ist wie ein Goldfisch und doch so geräumig, so unersättlich, daß all unser Ballast sich in ihm verlieren könnte. Denn sagten wir zu unserer Ballerina: “Ach, tanzen Sie uns doch einmal die Atombombe!”, sie würde sieben Pirouetten drehen und hernach lächelnd zum Stand kommen. Und käme einer und wünschte das Verkehrsproblem oder die Wiedervereinigung getanzt zu sehen, sie zeigte ihm sofort jene Kombination ästhetischer Figuren, an deren Ende dann eine Arabeske die Wiedervereinigung vollzieht und das Verkehrsproblem löst, indem sie aufs Pünktchen weist.

Zu all diesen Demonstrationen erklingt der “Türkische Marsch” oder ein Stückchen aus der Nußknackersuite, es bleibt sich gleich, die Ballerina ist nicht unbedingt musikalisch zu nennen. Sie läßt sich vom Pianisten den Takt ansagen, erklären, vorzählen and übergibt sich in schöner Gläubig-

The same thoroughness and care with which we count the calls of the cuckoo during a Sunday stroll in the municipal woods is shown by the ballerina, when it is a matter of inferring the potential number of curtains from the length and intensity of applause. She counts and would like to tempt the parquet and the balconies with her precise and charming curtsies, like we tempt the cuckoo who calls out the years left to us. —Then, after the last curtain, the ballerina collapses like a house of cards suddenly exposed to a draft. Each of her otherwise poised limbs slips into whatever. The order of her face, in that plate full of cosmetic fare, gives way. Her eyes are capable of no glance; overstrained they slip away and widen horribly. The same with her mouth. At all times ready to break out into hysteria, a smile—meant harmlessly—strains so much that a cramp sits in its corners. Why this constant wrinkling of the brow, this raising of the eyebrows? Every piece of the exhibition arranged with much effort and ability leaves its place. The ballerina seems completely out of hand.

The Dot

She raises her arm in effortless flexion. The hand rises above, a superfluously many-membered projection. All of that without significance, merely nice to look at, not even a greeting or an invitation to step nearer. Halfway to becoming an ornament it only wishes to show what is there, that an arm bends and subdivides the background, that there where the little finger points is a dot that all beauty obeys—and so too does the ballerina. The thought would never occur to her that she could flex her arm differently, flex it so that it could signify only strength, desperation, or even, horribly bent, mean an accident. Never would she send her finger toward any dot other than that which is absurd as a goldfish and still so spacious, so insatiable, that all our ballast could be lost in it. For were we to say to our ballerina: "Oh, dance the atom bomb for us!" she would spin seven pirouettes and afterwards come smiling to a standstill. And were someone to come and wish to see the traffic problem or reunification danced, she would at once show him that combination of aesthetic figures at the end of which then an arabesque would complete the reunification and solve the traffic problem, as she points to the dot.

Accompanying all these demonstrations sounds the "Turkish March" or a piece of the "Nutcracker Suite," it does not matter, the ballerina cannot be called especially musical. She lets the pianist set the tempo, define it, and count it out, and surrenders herself in exquisite devotion to the ballet

keit dem Ballettmeister, damit er Zahl und Reihenfolge der Attituden, Touren, Rélevés bestimmt und ihren Auftritt insgesamt formuliert.
Es darf auch der Radetzky-Marsch sein, dessen unüberhörbare Klänge in verblüffender Abwegigkeit ihren Weg auf der Bühne begleiten, wenn nur am Ende, mit dem letzten Ton und Paukenschlag, der Finger wieder aufs Pünktchen weist, dann ist es schon recht.

Natur und Kunst

Noch einmal zurück zu dem Bildchen. Die Ballerina, in steifen, leicht knüllenden Stoffen, tanzte auf dem Tisch. Das geöffnete Fenster ließ ahnen, daß Auftritt und Abgang keiner Tür bedurften. Leicht läßt sich Zimmer, Tisch und Fenster mit einer Bühne, Podest, Kulissen vertauschen. Der Dichter, auf dem Stich etwas schmalbrüstig, wandelt sich gleichfalls, wird zum springenden, tanzenden Troubadour. In einem pas de deux nimmt die Geschichte ihren weiteren Verlauf. Liebe, Trennung, Versuchung, Eifersucht und Tod. Einfach ist diese Handlung, bloßer Vorwand, die Ballerina in ihrer schwierigen Existenz, auf Spitzen tanzend, zu zeigen. Im reichsten Décor erfüllt sich hier, was tägliches Exercice zu den Klängen eines verstimmten Klaviers dem Körper und nur dem Körper vorschreibt.
Wer zwingt die Ballerina, dieses empfindliche, im Alltag fast ein wenig fade Wesen, sich an die Stange zu stellen und unter der Aufsicht einer ältlichen, oftmals recht zynischen Ballettmeisterin Jahr um Jahr zu trainieren? Ist es nur Ehrgeiz, nur Sucht zum Erfolg hin? —Widerstrebend betritt sie den Übungssaal, sucht ihren Platz auf. Widerstrebend kommt sie den ersten Bewegungen nach. Und dann packt es sie. Plötzlich ist ihr dieser Kampf gegen den Körper auf ähnliche Art faszinierend, wie einem erklärten Pazifisten ein todernster Vorbeimarsch im Stechschritt.
Ist es schon ein hausbackener Witz, dem Dichter den allzu gut gemeinten Rat auf den Weg zu geben, immer recht natürlich zu schreiben, um wieviel unerträglicher wäre dem feinen Auge die Tänzerin, welche es wagte—weiß ich, welchem Drang immer folgend—natürlich, das heißt ohne jeden Anstand, geschwätzig und maßlos wie die Vegetation eines Urwaldes oder auch Treibhauses über die Bühne zu hüpfen.
Es ist uns zur Selbstverständlichkeit geworden, ein Stück Hammel nicht in rohem, noch blutigem Zustand barbarisch zu verschlingen. Nein, wir braten, kochen oder dünsten es, tun immer wieder noch ein Gewürz in den Topf, nennen es am Ende gar und schmackhaft, essen es manierlich mit Messer und Gabel, binden uns eine Serviette um. So sollte nun endlich den anderen Künsten dieselbe Ehre wie der Kochkunst zuteil werden und—

master, so that he determines the number and sequence of the attitudes, figures, rélevées, and altogether formulates her appearance.

It may also be the "Radetsky March," whose inescapable sounds accompany her way on the stage in bewildering irrelevancy, if only at the end, with the last chord and drum beat, the finger again points at the dot, then it is all right.

Nature and Art

Back to the picture again. The ballerina, in stiff, lightly crumpled fabrics, was dancing on the table. The open window presaged that her entrance and exit required no door. The room, table, and window can easily be exchanged for a stage, a platform, wings. The poet, narrow-chested in the etching, is likewise transformed, becomes a leaping, dancing troubadour. The tale takes its further development with a pas de deux. Love, separation, temptation, jealousy, and death. This action is simple, just a pretext to show the ballerina in her difficult existence, dancing on tiptoes. Here is fulfilled in the richest decor what the daily drill to the sounds of a piano out of tune prescribes for the body and only the body.

Who forces the ballerina, this sensitive creature, almost insipid in daily life, to take her position at the barre and under the supervision of an elderly, often somewhat cynical ballet mistress to train year after year? Is it only ambition, only the drive for success? —Reluctantly she enters the rehearsal hall, locates her position. Reluctantly she performs her first movements. And then it seizes her. Suddenly this battle against her body is as fascinating to her as a deadly serious marching review in goose-step is to a pacifist.

After all, if it is just a pedestrian joke to give the poet on his way the all-too-well-meant advice always to write naturally, how much more intolerable to the practiced eye would be the dancer who dared—always following some unknown impulse—to hop about the stage naturally, that is, without any sort of decorum, babbling, and extravagant as the vegetation of a primeval forest or even a greenhouse.

It has become matter-of-course for us not to gobble up a piece of mutton barbarically in a raw, still bloody state. No, we fry, boil, or stew it, always add a spice to the pot, say finally that it is done and tasty, eat it politely with knife and fork, tie a napkin around our neck. The other arts ought, in the final analysis, to be treated like the art of cooking and—if wenn dann und wann Stimmen laut werden und das klassische Ballett totsagen wollen—bewundernd festgestellt werden, daß bislang diese Kunst, mehr noch als Kochkunst und Malerei, eine der unnatürlichsten und damit formvollendetsten aller Künste zu nennen ist.

Erst wenn es gelingen sollte, aus all den Experimenten—und bisher wurden nur Experimente gezeigt—gleichstarke Formeln der tänzerischen Bewegung zu kristallisieren, welchen gleich dem Ballett alle Zufälligkeit abgeht, wird sich die Ballerina zum letztenmal verbeugen.

Vielleicht zeigt sich dann die große, ganz und gar künstliche Puppe. In seinem Traktätchen über das Marionettentheater weist Kleist auf sie hin, Kokoschka ließ sich solch ein unempfindliches Mädchen schneidern, in Schlemmers Triadischem Ballett machten kühn entworfene Figurinen den ersten, wichtigen Schritt. Vielleicht werden sich beide vertragen und eine Ehe eingehen, die Marionette und die Ballerina. —

now and then voices make themselves heard and want to pronounce classical ballet dead—it ought to be declared with admiration that up to now this art, even more than the arts of cooking and of painting, may be called one of the most unnatural and thus most perfected in form of all arts.

Only when all the experiments—and until now only experiments have been shown—have succeeded in crystalizing equally strong formulas of choreographic movement, which like ballet lacks all fortuitousness, will the ballerina bow for the last time.

Perhaps then the immense, wholly artificial doll will be revealed. In his little treatise about the marionette theater Kleist refers to her, Kokoschka had such an insensitive girl tailored for himself, in Schlemmer's triadic ballet boldly sketched figures took the first, important step. Perhaps the two will become compatible and enter upon a marriage—the marionette and the ballerina.

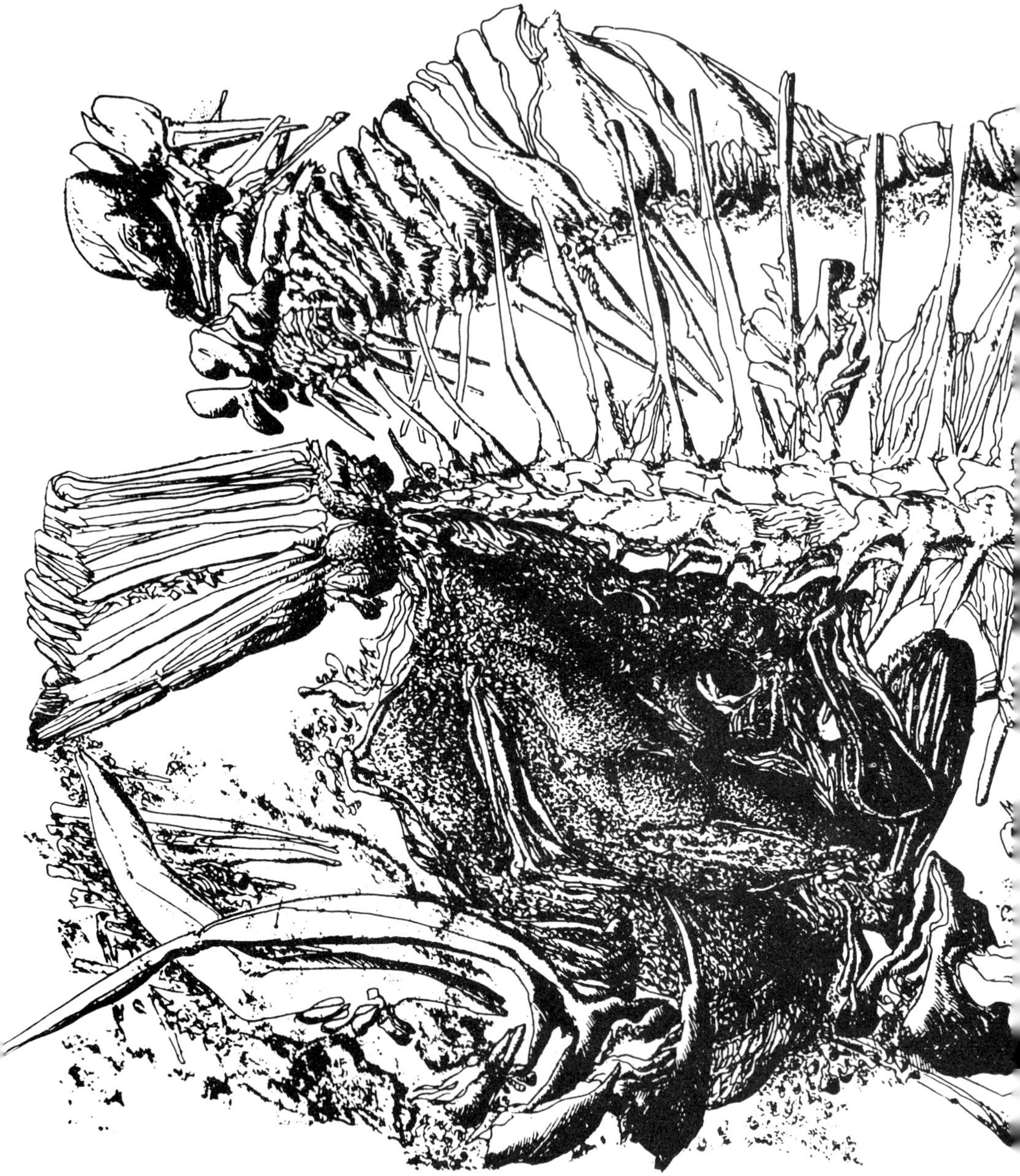

AN INTERVIEW WITH GÜNTER GRASS

IRMGARD ELSNER HUNT

[*The interview was conducted in Berlin on 7 July 1980.*]

Hunt: Günter Grass, what led to the idea of your newest book, *Headbirths*?
Grass: Well, there are several ideas in this book. At first, long before I began writing *Headbirths*, I had an idea for an essay, an attempt to investigate the relationship of the two German literatures to one another. This last area of a German union that is left to us indicates the inability of the Germans to define themselves as a nation. Besides that essay there was nothing but a few sketches and a short lecture, which I took along on the Asian trip last year. Then I gave this lecture about the two German literatures, among other places, in the Republic of China, in the Philippines, and elsewhere in Asia, and thus it naturally acquired an absurd frame of reference: this inner-German topic carried off to Asia, the impressions in China, and the return to the Federal Republic of Germany, where shortly after our return there was again a debate in the Bundestag about whether the Germans might possibly become extinct, a question posed by the opposition, the Christian Democratic Party, about the decline in population, inflamed alarmingly—all that in combination with a crazy notion I had in Shanghai, the notion that there were 950 million Germans instead of 950 million Chinese. These two extremes, nearly one billion Germans on the one hand and the fear of extinction on the other—that was the starting point. Suddenly there was an overall concept in which this reflection, too, this essay on the two German literatures, could find a place. And even in the first draft this was personified and became the plan for a film script, surely inspired in part by the previous good collaboration with Volker Schlöndorff in the period during which the *Tin Drum* was to be filmed. Accordingly, the three strands of the book emerged: essay, travel report, and the plan for a film script.
Hunt: Could this book be seen as a prelude to the election campaign?
Grass: Surely not as a prelude, yet it is a book written in the last part of the seventies; it ends with New Year's Eve; the last catastrophe in the news is the invasion of Kabul by Soviet troops, the exaggerated reactions to it in the West as in the East; the danger of a possible World War III rises—that is the end of the book; and because I believe that the eighties will present us with comparable catastrophes and crises at shorter and shorter intervals, and because this is an election year in both the United States and

the Federal Republic, the political aspect of this election year naturally is a part of the general state of affairs in the eighties. Therefore this book fits in well with the election campaign. Only on the fringes would it have received another form, and other accents, had it materialized at a different time. The topic of the two German literatures in relation to one another, the topic of world population, the theme of statistical knowledge here in the industrial states and impotence there when confronted with reality—all that is independent of election year and election campaign.

Hunt: In the subtitle of the book, and repeated in the text, "the Germans" are mentioned. Who are "the Germans"?

Grass: That is a question raised anew in this book. They are first of all people who have a hard time defining themselves. Certainly, compared to other European nations, Germany began the historical process of becoming a nation very late, very inadequately, and poorly defined, then welded together through force by Bismarck—accordingly it all came to a bad end. What began in that shaky manner in the nineteenth century erupted in the twentieth century in two world wars, among other things; but this national vacuum remains with us to this day: What does the relationship between the two German states look like? How do the Germans define themselves? It began already with the founding of the empire in the nineteenth century: Should it be a greater Germany, with Austria included? Should it be a small Germany according to Bismarck's concept, because that suited his calculations of power better? These things were never well thought through; they were seemingly solved prematurely by force and are still exploding in our time. Today they actually explode by not doing so—by creating a vacuum. One simply excludes this question. Now I am attempting to take up what, to start with, is nothing new and what has been proposed by German writers again and again: to establish the question of the nation not primarily from the political, not from the geographical point of view, nor from the constellation of power, but from the German culture within the European culture—culture in the widest sense, so that the burden of our history, and the grandeur of that history too, belong together there in that concept as a basis, as an offer to our neighbors, too, an offer they do not have to fear; for a national concept that would strive towards political reunification would be something that our neighbors would again fear, and that they do not want, neither in the East nor in the West. Nobody wants a concentration of power in the middle of Europe, where two world wars began. Therefore, the alternative of a cultural German union could be offered; it is one topic of the book *Headbirths*.

Hunt: What could a national foundation mean for a cultural German union?

Grass: During his time as chancellor, Willy Brandt, in his governmental declaration in January, 1973, announced a National Foundation, surely out of the wish that I can understand, to define the nation as a culture, a national foundation that would be a kind of central focus. Germany actually has no capital in that sense. Berlin was the capital only for a short time; that, meanwhile, has all changed. But it very quickly turned out that the proposal got nowhere. The various federal states began immediately to argue about who should administer the Foundation; the opposition, the Christian Democrats, played up the question of the location, wanted Berlin as the seat of the National Foundation, which failed because of the justified objection of the occupation powers, and so it was postponed indefinitely. But I think the main reason for this is—and I came to see it relatively late myself—that no single state, neither the FRG nor the GDR, can be in a position to call forth a national foundation. This can be accomplished only by the two states in relation to one another, and that means in dispute. With that, the conflict arises, but this conflict cannot be avoided. It will be the task of a decade, if one intends to take it up, and this presupposes that the GDR participates with equal rights in these negotiations between the two German states, so that finally for the first time we would have a unified German office, namely, that National Foundation, that would have to be supported by both German states.
Hunt: Has this National Foundation been discussed by writers, and would they still support it?
Grass: Yes, it has been discussed but never really took enough shape for them to really make a start. Several million marks accumulated that were collected from the budget but that could not be paid out because the Foundation did not yet exist, and now cultural associations, musicians, sculptors, architects, and so forth, have been asked to make use of these funds, and now they are being sprinkled around. I am afraid that with the expenditure of these fifteen million marks that were accumulated the view could now set in: Well, we have paid it out now; let's forget about the National Foundation. This would be payment in the wrong way. I want to warn against it.
Hunt: You have called the eighties "Orwell's decade." Something like "1984" will probably not occur?
Grass: No. On the one hand Orwell is disproven in his details, if you will, though not in his basic tenets. With regard to military technology things are even far worse than with Orwell, worse than he could have foreseen. Judging by the trend, his insight, which became the propositon "Big Brother is watching you" has also come true, in that we are more and more watched and checked, that our data can be retrieved without our knowing anything about it, not to mention suspecting it, and technology

has been developed that meanwhile produces what people dream about: self-realization. But it is a technology that has become independent, that evades all democratic control, and that therefore has become dangerous. I am afraid that our quickly-passed data protection laws limp along behind the developments.

Hunt: In *Headbirths*, as well as in your Döblin essay, you have occupied yourself very much with the future. In the new book we find the marvelous word *paspresenture* [Vergegenkunft]. Time cannot be separated?

Grass: No. I regard our chronological measure of time, which we use for everything and clap over everything, as a mere fiction. In our imagination, in our inner thought process, in that chaos that permanently exists in each human head, time is mixed, too. There what is past shows itself as strongly present, often crowds out what is present, and anticipated future is frequently so vivid and so much now in our imaginings—be it in the form of fear or wishful thinking—that the other times, present and past, are thoroughly mixed with it and are no longer neatly separable from one another. One can do that as in grammar, a helpful means of weeding out the tenses, but my understanding of reality, if I apply it to our concept of time, allows for a fourth time, a *paspresenture*.

Hunt: Have you thought of one day writing a purely futuristic work?

Grass: I don't want to exclude the possibility. Only—I know the difficulties. We can see in all futuristic novels, be they ever so interesting, that language, as soon as it presumes to express the future, is always only the language of the past or of the present, applied to the future. Or the very desperate attempt is made to develop a future language. But that will always remain speculative and accidental, because it lacks all the components of experience through which language comes alive. This is a flaw in every futuristic novel, and it is a problem I would have to deal with, if I were to propose to write a futuristic book. I am tempted, but I cannot say whether it will happen in the foreseeable future.

Hunt: *Headbirths* ends in August, 1980. How does it feel to have written ahead of the times?

Grass: Even this limited preview shows how many coincidences and misdoubts such speculations about the future are prone to, but what should be gathered in a paspresenture, for me, are the real anxieties that we have today and that involve the future. I believe that shows in *Headbirths*.

Hunt: In your book the couple talk together over the problem of having children—their own actual problem about having a child—as well as the "headbirths," that is, ideas.

Grass: Yes, they do this together about both. It is a so-called modern couple who have made the old-fashioned problem of love—so out of fashion as they see it—into an objective partnership, no isolated case, as

we know; this leads, if you will, to the point where the role division—here man, here woman—no longer happens in the traditional way, which surely is good. But it also leads to confusion, to a leveling of feeling and rapture, namely, to an objectification and to a limitation of the old concept of existence. Therefore, with their interchangeable arguments neither of them is capable any more of giving priority to their true and, as both would certainly agree, irrational wish for a child, because any number of reasons—only name them—speak against it: the population explosion, nuclear power, the general political situation, the lack of perspective with regard to the future—all of these are important to both of them alternately, now to him, now to her, and constantly serve to impede the real desire that both also alternately have.
Hunt: The book has a very sobering effect for this reason. All eroticism is eliminated. Do you think very many young couples start out their partnership with that much calculation?
Grass: Whether they stick to it is another question. Certainly Harm and Dörte don't always stick to it. But it has become conventional in the meantime. What was thought of ten or twelve years ago as a sudden outburst and also as a protest against middle-class standards of behavor has in the meantime degenerated, one can say, into conventional practice. From these modes of behavior you can even deduce a new middle-class Left, leftist behavior of the common man, which distinguishes itself by as much verbal generosity as possible.
Hunt: Must Dörte first become romantic by reading Vicki Baum's book *Love and Death on Bali*, because one cannot get at the problem rationally and realistically?
Grass: Surely this book, purposely given to her by the tour leader, plays a role, but there is also the confrontation of two rational and enlightened people with something they perceive as irrational—with Indic mysticism, with the world of Indonesia, especially of Bali. These are things that are not comprehensible to either. They compare their statistical knowledge with reality. This begins with the terrifying recognition that, for example, the undernourished children in the slums are more cheerful and happier than our overfed children in the West. Harm and Dörte have to deal with this; it bewilders them, it brings them into confusion and leads, with regard to their main problem—the child "Yes," the child "No"—to new complexities.
Hunt: What is the meaning of the bat or perhaps the snake—are these symbols of some kind?
Grass: I play a game with these things that at most needs only the explanation that a bat in the hair of a woman is a natural occurrence in Indonesia, just as, for example, a liverwurst is something natural in northern

Germany, while a liverwurst brought along on a trip to Indonesia means about the same thing that a bat in the hair of a woman would mean in the North—something incomprehensible.

Hunt: Imagine you are a dictator: Would you abolish compulsory education?

Grass: Abolishing compulsory education—if I may omit the pretense of dictator—means that I see we carry on a chaotic action of pupil-teacher-parent with mere school reforms that never are fully realized, and this at the cost of all three groups involved. One sometimes has the feeling that the Germans are a nation of Pestalozzis who pursue the concept of European enlightenment—which came to Germany very late—with super-industriousness and super-obligatory vigor: the child as the product of education. But in this way everything accidental, everything humanly impossible is rationalized as something humanly possible, that is, explained away. Our school system is characterized by that. As always it strives for performance; it is decided by practicability; all subjects in which there was still anything nonutilitarian—learning anything that later might not turn into profits and losses—were also rationalized away. School seems to be only a preparation for vocational and social life—I see this as a process of impoverishment. If there were a school that allowed for leisure and taught creative idleness, I would be reconciled with this school again, although I am afraid that the Germans, if they initiated this subject called "creative idleness," would immediately burden it again with grades.

Hunt: We have to call up the immortal Flounder one more time—he might still come swimming. If he were still talking to men and if he would grant you, for instance, some political wishes, what would they be?

Grass: The Flounder has turned away from men. Since he did that—and as far as I, as a writer, have been able to determine—nothing decisive has happened on the part of men that would move him ever to give a man a chance again. For already at the first consideration of what I might wish from the Flounder—however carefully I might word my wishes—I would only formulate the old masculine concept that has led to well-known results with regard to power.

Hunt: Does that mean a man still cannot have a wish that would not aspire after power?

Grass: It has been said in *The Flounder*. I would be for an exoneration of men. But that presupposes that women commit themselves to being women. And here a man begins again to tell women what they should do—that they should change to a different concept of power and the use of power. What we are experiencing now is that women, when they reach, for example, positions of political power, use power in the same fashion men have been using it: So they assume the male role. They do not intro-

duce unmistakably feminine accents into the picture—accents that I would for once somewhat sentimentally characterize as life-sustaining.
Hunt: If the Flounder can no longer be approached and will not aid us anymore in our present political situation, what can we hope for at all? Do you look with confidence into the future?
Grass: I do. I think that the social-liberal coalition will win this election. But an election victory, however it turns out in the fall, is still no answer to the problems. I am convinced only that the cooperation of these parties under a Chancellor Helmut Schmidt will be more capable of recognizing the problems and crises that confront us, not of evading them but of accepting them—but today no single country can do that by itself. Actually, Willy Brandt drew a line in his North-South Report, which he submitted. But these are decisions that have to be made by many countries and governments together. All these decisions concerning the Western industrial nations will mean renunciation—renunciation in the face of the demands of the countries of the Third World, but also renunciation of things that can be done but that do not absolutely have to be done because they do not correspond to our needs, because they meet, at most, artificially invoked needs. But whether or not people are capable of leaving something doable undone, just because it is not necessary, that question remains open.

translated by Irmgard Elsner Hunt

Vorzeitliches (1973) Pen and Ink

Prehistoric Image

Bedroom (1965) Pen and Ink

Bedroom

Wolfgang Hildesheimer

Vogelmoden (1973) Pencil

Bird Fashions

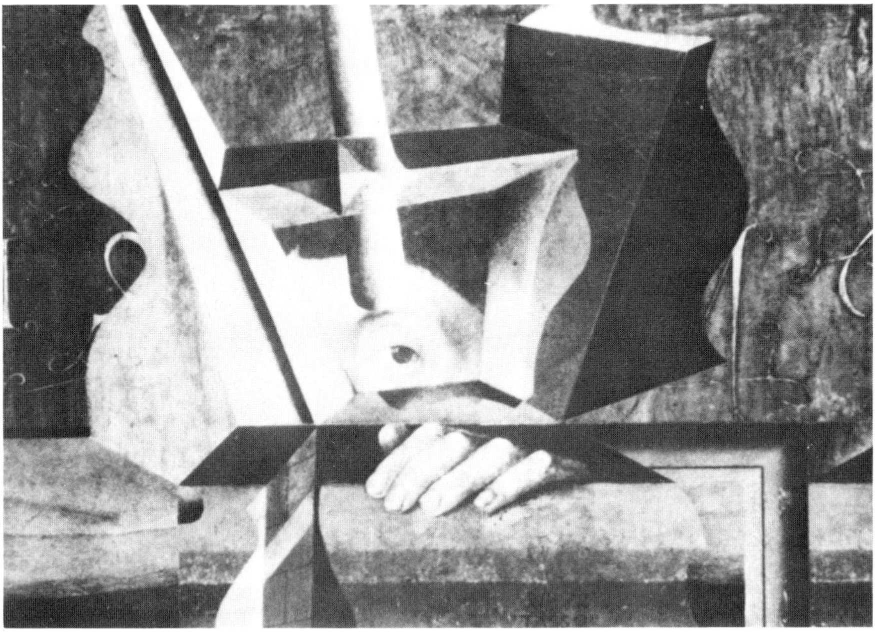

"*Tasso*" (1972) Collage

"*Tasso*"

Blitzableiter (1973) Pen and Ink

Lightning Rod

Neapolitanisches (1971) Collage

Neapolitan Scene

LEBEN UND TOD VON SIR ANDREW MARBOT

WOLFGANG HILDESHEIMER

VOR HUNDERTFÜNFZIG JAHREN, IM FEBRUAR 1830, DER TAG IST NICHT bekannt, nahm sich Andrew Marbot, noch nicht neunundzwanzigjährig, bei Urbino das Leben. Das Wort "Selbstmord", das diesen Akt selten sinngetreu wiedergibt, wäre, für ihn angewandt, besonders inadäquat. Weder Verzweiflung noch Auswegslosigkeit befahlen ihm die Tat. Sie war vielmehr der finale Programmpunkt eines Lebensplanes, zwar nicht von Beginn an einbezogen, doch allmählich zum notwendigen Ziel angewachsen. Marbot tötete nicht jemanden, den er verachtete oder dessen er überdrüssig war, sondern jemanden, dem er die Routine sich wiederholender Erfahrungen ersparen wollte; der neues nicht ersehnte und besseres nicht erwartete. Ein Jahr vor seinem Tod hatte er, nach einem Besuch bei Leopardi, in sein Journal eingetragen: "Ein denkender Mensch sollte wissen, wann seine Zeit abgelaufen ist. Die Unwürdigkeit, darüber hinauszuleben, wird ihm bestraft, indem er sich mit jedem Tag unerträglicher wird. Rücksicht auf Mitmenschen darf ihn nicht hindern. Wer sich selbst nicht erträgt, wird auch von anderen nicht ertragen." Marbot war nicht gewillt, den Beweis dieser These anzutreten. Sein Außenseitertum hatte er mit Würde getragen. Sein Leben war das eines vom äußeren Schicksal Privilegierten. Doch wahrhaft von Freiheit beflügelt war erst sein Tod.

Der Tod bleibt zunächst unbekannt. Seine Geliebte Anna Maria Baiardi wähnte ihn auf einem improvisierten Ausflug, ließ daher seine Familie in England ohne Nachricht. Beunruhigung breitete sich erst nach einigen Tagen aus, und nach einigen Monaten wurde der Vermißte zum Verschollenen erklärt, der er geblieben ist, bis sich, ab 1904, jene fehlenden Blätter seiner Aufzeichnungen fanden, die nicht nur manches Rätsel seines Lebens klären, manche Vermutung bestätigen, sondern auch Todesort und Todesart belegen: Marbot hat sich erschossen, und zwar im Gebirge des Montefeltro, das er liebte, und in das er seine Hausgäste zur Jagd schickte, wenn er ihrer Gegenwart überdrüssig war.

Nicht etwa, daß er sich aktiv bemüht hätte, seine Spuren zu verwischen. Gewiß, er war ein Exzentriker, aber ein tiefer, einsamer und geheimer;

THE LIFE AND DEATH OF SIR ANDREW MARBOT*

WOLFGANG HILDESHEIMER
translated by Allan Blunden

A HUNDRED AND FIFTY YEARS AGO, IN FEBRUARY OF 1830 (THE EXACT date is unknown), Andrew Marbot took his own life not far from Urbino. He was not yet twenty-nine. The conventional term "suicide," which rarely conveys the true nature of such an act, would be particularly inadequate in his case. Neither despair nor hopelessness impelled him to the fatal deed. It was, rather, the culmination of a design, a life's plan; and though not initially contemplated, it came gradually to appear as the final goal towards which all else must tend. Marbot did not kill one whom he despised, nor one of whom he had grown weary, but one whom he wished to spare the tedium of experience ever repeating itself—one who longed for nothing new and expected nothing better. A year before his death, on the occasion of a visit to Leopardi, he had written these words in his journal: "A man of sensibility must know when his appointed time has come. Unworthy the man who outlives his season; his punishment shall be to despise himself the more with each day that passes. No concern for his fellow men must stay his hand. He who is intolerable in his own eyes will find no favour in the eyes of others." Marbot was not disposed to put this thesis to the proof. Different from other men, he had borne his difference with dignity. His life was the life of one on whom destiny had outwardly smiled. But freedom—true freedom—attended him only at his death.

His death was not immediately discovered. His mistress, Anna Maria Baiardi, supposed him to be absent on some impromptu excursion and consequently saw no reason to inform his family in England. But when several days had passed without news, people grew alarmed; and when several months had passed, the absent lord was pronounced "missing, presumed dead." This state of affairs persisted until 1904, when the missing pages from his journal began to come to light, solving many a riddle in his life, confirming many a theory—and also establishing both the place and the manner of his death. Marbot shot himself, choosing to die in the mountains of Montefeltro that he loved so dearly, and where he had been wont to send his house guests hunting when he tired of their company.

Not that he had consciously striven to cover over his traces. True, he was an eccentric by nature, but a brooding, solitary, and secretive eccennicht einer, der die Wirkung seines Gebarens berechnet und die Reaktion der Öffentlichkeit erheischt, weder Dandy noch demonstrativer Sonderling. Er wußte, daß es wenige waren, die sein Tod ins Herz treffen würde, hielt es für unangemessen, ihn zu inszenieren, und befand es für würdiger, in Nacht und Wind spurlos zu verschwinden als Hinterbliebene mit einem selbstzerstörten Leichnam zu belasten. Man hat ihn niemals gefunden.

Seine Schriften erschienen postum 1834 unter dem summarischen Titel "*Art and Life*", herausgegeben von Gerard Ross. Thomas de Quincey und, unabhängig von ihm, Karl von Rumohr waren die ersten, die Gedanken und Diktion des Werkes zwar hoch priesen, jedoch Befugnis und Objekttreue des Herausgebers in Frage stellten und konstatierten, daß der Text beschnitten und gereinigt worden sei. In der Tat handelt es sich um eine Auseinanderreihung von Tagebuchaufzeichnungen und Briefpassagen, thematisch zwar geordnet, doch meist auf artifizielle Weise in Kontext gebracht. Was hier als kategorische Feststellung eines beinah unfehlbaren *arbiter artium* erscheint, ist in Wirklichkeit Arbeitsthese, sind Stadien im Prozeß der Erforschung dessen, was den Künstler bewegt und antreibt. Die Grenzen des Empirischen hätte Marbot niemals zu überschreiten gedacht, angestrebt war normative Erkenntnis, nicht Wissenschaftlichkeit.

Dennoch hat dieses manipulierte Stückwerk seine erhebliche Bedeutung für die psychoanalytisch ausgerichtete Ästhetik begründet. Das schiefe Licht, in das es seinen Autor setzt, hat bis heute nicht aufgehört, die behandelte Materie dennoch zu beleuchten. Überdies ist der editorische Fehlgriff subjektiv nur allzu leicht zu entschuldigen. Denn der Verantwortliche war "kein anderer als" Pater Gerardus van Rossum, Kaplan der Familie Marbot and ihrer Pächter, der als Herausgeber weltlicher Betrachtungen nicht in Erscheinung treten durfte. Er war denn auch der Empfänger des überwiegenden Teiles der Briefe. Der Rest ist an die Mutter gerichtet, die ferne und ewig nahe Geliebte seines Lebens, die dem Pater die sachbezogenen Textseiten ihres Konvoluts überließ, nachdem sie die intimen vernichtet und die inkriminierenden Übergänge vom Persönlichen ins Betrachtende unlesbar gemacht hatte. Doch auch hier wie in den Tagebuchseiten, die ihm die Baiardi 1831 überließ, hat van Rossum expurgiert, sonst hätte er vielleicht einen schwelenden Skandal zum Ausbruch gebracht. Zudem aber wollte er gewiß durch Elimination alles Ichbezogenen seinem Freund und Schüler jene Objektivität der Sicht attestieren tric, not one who contrives his conduct for the sake of effect and seeks popular acclaim, neither a dandy nor an exhibitionist. He knew that few people would be deeply touched by his demise, thought it unfitting to die with a theatrical flourish, and considered it more seemly to vanish discreetly from the face of the earth, rather than burden friends and family with the body on which he himself had laid hands. His corpse has never been found.

His writings appeared posthumously in 1834 under the general title of *Art and Life*, edited by Gerard Ross. The first critical responses came from Thomas de Quincey and Karl von Rumohr, both of whom—quite independently of one another—praised the work highly for its ideas and language but at the same time cast doubt on the authority and objectivity of its editor, claiming that the text had been cut and amended. And indeed, the work consists of a series of diary entries and passages taken from letters, grouped together according to subject matter, but for the most part forced into context in the most contrived manner. What here appears as a categorical statement issued by a virtually infallible arbiter of the arts is in point of fact a kind of working hypothesis, a series of stages in that inquiry which Marbot conducted into the roots of artistic motivation. He never aspired to move beyond the bounds of empirical reality; practical insights were his aim, not some abstract scheme of knowledge.

Yet it is on this collection of fragments, doctored by the hand of another, that his considerable importance for the psychoanalytical school of aesthetics is founded. The unfavorable light in which these writings place their author nonetheless continues to illuminate those subjects to which he addressed himself. And as for the misguided editorial intervention, it is not hard to excuse it in human terms, for it was the work of "none other than" Father Gerardus van Rossum, chaplain to the Marbot family and their tenants, whose position would not allow him to stand revealed as the editor of wordly reflections. He was also the recipient of the major portion of the letters. The remainder were addressed to Marbot's mother, the distant yet ever present object of his life's love, who entrusted to Father van Rossum's care those pages from her collected papers that treated of general matters, after first destroying those of a more intimate nature and rendering illegible all those incriminating passages in which the writer passed from private thoughts to general contemplation. Yet here too van Rossum has expurgated the text, as he did the diaries that Anna Maria Baiardi left to him in 1831; had he not done so he might well have precipitated public knowledge of the scandal that smoldered as yet beneath the surface. At the same time it was doubtless his intention, by the elimination of all private references, to attest that objectivity of vision in his friend dürfen, die, wie er wohl meinte, den Inhalt in den Bereich des, vom Willen nicht getrübten, reinen geistigen Wertes erheben sollte. Ihm dies zu verübeln wäre ungerecht. Die Rekonstruktion einer Ideenwelt wird hier also durch eben jene Mystifikation erschwert, der wir verdanken, daß sie überhaupt auf uns gekommen ist.

Marbot Hall, wo Andrew Gregory am 4. April 1801 geboren wurde, eine weitläufige Villa aus der Restaurationszeit, steht, wie sie damals stand —sie gehört heute dem National Trust—in Northumberland, fern den Zentren des Weltgeschehens. Bis zum Antritt seiner *grand tour* 1820 hat Andrew den Norden Englands nicht verlassen, die Erfahrungswelt seiner frühen Jahre setzt sich aus wenigen Schauplätzen und Figuren zusammen. Der Vater, Sir Francis, der einzige katholische Lehnsherr der Grafschaft, ein rechtschaffener Philister, dessen Großspurigkeit dem Sohn peinlich war; die schöne, leidenschaftlich veranlagte Mutter, Lady Catherine, die er über die Maßen des Erlaubten liebte; und der Erzieher, Pater Gerardus, der wahrscheinlich ihn über die Maßen des Erlaubten liebte, sich aber jedwede entsprechende Annäherung versagt hat: dies waren Andrews Partner im Vaterhaus. Die jüngeren Geschwister Matthew und Jane blieben seinem Geist so fern wie die rudelweise auftretenden Jagd- und Festgäste mit ihren Gesprächen über "Wild und Fisch, Weide und Vieh, also den nützlichen Teil der Natur, während mich nur ihr unnützer Teil ansprach, die Metamorphosen ihrer ungezähmten Selbstverwirklichung." (In solchen Nebensätzen spricht der Romantiker, der in Hauptsätzen kaum zu Worte kommt.)

Der Alltag war Unterricht. Van Rossum, Jesuit, Holländer aus Zwolle, der an den Kollegien von Köln, Innsbruck und Rom studiert hatte, daher Deutsch und Italienisch vollkommen beherrschte, war ein ungewöhnlicher geistiger Vermittler, der seinen Gott zwar liebte, Ihn aber nicht dort aufzuspüren suchte, wo Er sich entzieht oder verweigert. Mit ihm las Andrew, der mit Hingabe und Leichtigkeit lernte, die griechischen und lateinischen Klassiker, er las Lessing und Goethe, Dante und Petrarca. Die englischen Klassiker las er allein, vor allem Shakespeare, der ihn sein Leben lang begleitete, als Norm und Korrektiv bei der Auswertung seiner Erfahrungen mit anderen und mit sich selbst. "Bei Shakespeare lernen wir, uns als Rätsel zu betrachten und uns gleichzeitig von der Unlösbarkeit des Rätsels zu überzeugen, nicht aber uns damit abzufinden." Ein Meister im Sich-Abfinden ist er denn auch niemals geworden.

Der andere Ort seiner Jugend war Redmond Manor in Westmoreland, der Landsitz seines Großvaters mütterlicherseits, Viscount Claverton, eines weltläufigen Epikureers, der bis 1797 englischer Gesandter in Venedig and pupil which, so he must have felt, lifted his work into the realm of pure intellect, unsullied by selfish desire. It would be unjust to think the worse of him for that. Here, then, the task of reconstructing a world of ideas is rendered more difficult by the very process of mystification to which we owe all knowledge of that world's existence.

Marbot Hall, the rambling Restoration mansion where Andrew Gregory was born on 4 April 1801 (now the property of the National Trust), is situated in Northumberland, then as now remote from the main scenes of world events. Until he embarked upon the Grand Tour in 1820 Andrew had never ventured beyond the confines of the North of England, and the range of his early experiences is circumscribed by a small handful of places and figures. His father, Sir Francis, the only Catholic among the lords of the county, a worthy philistine whose grandiose pretentions were a source of embarrassment to his son; his mother, Lady Catherine, beautiful and passionate, whom he loved with a devotion more than filial; and his tutor, Father Gerardus, who probably loved him with an affection more than tutelary, though he refrained from any overt declarations; such were Andrew's companions in the house of his birth. His younger brother and sister, Matthew and Jane, were alien spirits, as alien indeed as those hordes of house guests who came to hunt and carouse and spoke of "game and fish, pasture and cattle, Nature's useful portion, whilst I was drawn to that which lacked utility in Nature, the transformations wrought by her unbridled appetite for self-realization." (In subordinate clauses such as these we hear the true voice of the Romantic, who seldom expresses his thoughts in finished utterances.)

Andrew's days were given over to instruction and study. Van Rossum, a Dutch Jesuit from Zwolle, who had studied at the colleges of Cologne, Innsbruck, and Rome, whence he had acquired a thorough mastery of German and Italian, was a remarkably accomplished teacher, who loved his God but did not seek to find Him in places where He eludes discovery. His pupil learned with dedication and alacrity, and together they read the Greek and Latin classics, Lessing and Goethe, Dante and Petrarch. The English classics he read alone, above all Shakespeare, who became his lifelong companion and the yardstick by which he measured and interpreted his experiences, both social and private. "In Shakespeare we learn to view ourselves as a riddle and, at the same time, to know that the riddle is insoluble; but we never learn to resign ourselves to the fact." So it was that resigning himself to facts was never one of Andrew's leading accomplishments.

The other scene of his youth was Redmond Manor in Westmoreland, the country home of his maternal grandfather, Viscount Claverton, a conventional epicurean who until 1797 had been the English ambassador to gewesen war, und den die Gelegenheit zum Kunstsammler gemacht hatte. Hier traf Andrew eine ihm gemäßere Art von Gästen, unter anderen de Quincey, den Physiker Sir David Brewster und die Mathematikerin Mary Sommerville.

Die Someraufenthalte in Redmond haben den aktiven Teil seiner Persönlichkeit—denn wir müssen bei ihm zwischen dem aktiven und dem vegetativen Teil unterscheiden—definitiv vorgezeichnet. Er verbrachte Stunden in Betrachtung der Bilder, dazu las er, vom Großvater dazu angehalten, Vasari und später Alberti. In den Aufzeichnungen heißt es: "Das Lebensprojekt des phantasiebegabten (*imaginative*) Kindes wird durch Bilder in die Bahn seiner Verwirklichung geleitet. Auf ihnen sieht es nackte oder seltsam bekleidete Erwachsene, (. . .) in Geschehen verwickelt oder Geschehen auslösend, die es nicht versteht und alsbald dem Leben abverlangt. Die Ernüchterung tritt ein, wenn es feststellt, daß diese Geschehen, und damit die Inhalte der Kunst, dem Leben nicht entsprechen; daß sie vielmehr Resultat der Wunschvorstellung (*wishful thinking*) der Künstler sind, nämlich jener Privilegierten, die solche Vorstellungen auszudrücken und sich damit des Wunsches zu entledigen vermögen."

Diese These wurde der Grundsatz seiner Forschungen. Darüber hinaus enthüllt sie die Verarbeitung eines Schlüsselerlebnisses: unter den Bildern in Redmond befand sich Tintorettos "Entstehung der Milchstraße" (heute London, National Gallery). Der Fünfjährige forderte seine fünfundzwanzigjährige Mutter auf, ihm das Bild zu erklären und, da sie offensichtlich desselben Geschlechts sei wie die dargestellte Juno, aus deren Brüsten die Milch verspritzt, ihm die entsprechenden Teile an ihrem Körper zu entdecken. Die Mutter wies den Wunsch zwar zurück, doch nicht etwa in Entrüstung; sie schloß das Kind lachend in die Arme, so daß es das geheimnisvolle Gebiet zumindest körperlich aufnehmen konnte. Dies war Andrews früheste Erinnerung, und die schönste. "*There I was, in beauty softly embedded.*"

Hier also, wenn nicht gar früher und unerinnert, fand die Mutter-Sohn-Beziehung einen schulbeispielhaften symbolischen Ausdruck. Wann die volle Macht der gegenseitigen Anziehung manifest wurde, wissen wir nicht, denn bis zum Ausbruch des Ungeheuerlichen, dem Vollzug des Inzest, sollten fünfzehn Jahre vergehen, in denen das bestürzende Schicksal sich bekämpfen ließ, um schließlich seine beiden nur allzu willigen Opfer zu fordern. Der Ort des Geschehens war das Londoner Stadthaus der Clavertons, wo Andrew, begleitet von der Mutter, die Monate vor seiner *grand tour* verbrachte.

Wir stellen uns vor: die Nacht nach einer Party, vielleicht der letzten der Saison, die Gäste verlassen die Halle, Gespräche verklingen, in Sälen

Venice and had been led by this circumstance to become a collector of art. Here Andrew made the acquaintance of visitors who were more to his taste, including de Quincey, the physicist Sir David Brewster, and the mathematician Mary Sommerville.

The summer sojourns in Redmond had a decisive influence on the development of the active portion of his personality (for we must distinguish, in his case, between an active and a vegetative portion). He spent many hours studying paintings, and at the urging of his grandfather he read Vasari and later Alberti. In his journal we read: "The life's work of the imaginative young child first begins to assume form and reality under the influence of paintings. In them he sees adults naked or strangely clad, (. . .) engaged in events, or initiating events, which he cannot comprehend, and which he forthwith looks to discover in his own experience. Great is his disappointment when he learns that these events—and consequently the subjects treated by art—do not correspond to the realities of life; that they are the products, rather, of wishful thinking on the part of artists, those privileged individuals who, by giving expression to the objects of their thought, are able to rid themselves of wishfulness."

This proposition furnished the basis for his subsequent investigations. In it we may also discern the imprint of a key experience: Among the paintings at Redmond was Tintoretto's *Origin of the Milky Way* (now in the National Gallery in London). The five-year-old boy asked his twenty-five-year-old mother to explain the painting to him; and since she was manifestly of the same sex as the Juno depicted on the canvas, from whose breasts the milk is spurting forth, he asked her to show him the corresponding portions of her own anatomy. His mother declined, though not in any spirit of dismay or anger; instead she laughed and clasped the child to her bosom, so that he was able, at least, to experience immediate physical contact with that mysterious region. This was Andrew's earliest recollection, and the most beautiful. "There I was, in beauty softly embedded."

Here then, if not indeed at some earlier and forgotten period, the mother-son relationship found its archetypal symbolic expression. We do not know when the mutual attraction first declared itself in full force; for until their relationship reached its outrageous climax in the incestuous act, fifteen years were to pass, fifteen years in which they struggled against their bewildering destiny, only to succumb at the last, all too willing victims both. The act itself took place at the London residence of the Clavertons, where Andrew had come with his mother to spend his final months in England prior to embarking on the Grand Tour.

We may picture the scene thus: It is late in the night, after a party, perhaps the last of the season, and the guests are leaving by the front und Gängen werden die Lichter gelöscht, Andrew und Lady Catherine steigen die Treppe empor, die Trennung steht kurz bevor, sie flüstern vom nahen Abschied, der übliche Kuß zur Nacht wird unüblich und mündet in einen heißen Atemtausch, die reale Welt versinkt mitsamt ihren Regeln des Anstands und der Vernunft, alle Vorsicht ist weggewischt, wer wen ins Schlafzimmer zieht, ist ungewiß, das Unerhörte nimmt seinen Lauf,

und eine neue Dimension ist in Andrews Bewußtsein jäh erwacht, ein Empfindungszentrum entstanden, das ihn von Stund an leitet und beherrscht; das ihn zukünftig bei all seinen Begegnungen nach verborgenen oder unterdrückten Kräften unter der Oberfläche suchen läßt: weniger also die Leistung des Menschen oder ihr Maß, als das Motiv und die Psyche, der sie entspringen; weniger die Wirkung als ihr Ursprung. Sein eigenes Erlebnis wurde ihm so zum Anlaß, den Wegen und Irrwegen menschlichen Verhaltens nachzudenken und in Bildwerken nach den Spuren der für ihre Schöpfer erträglichen oder unerträglichen Lebensumstände zu forschen: die Suche nach dem Tabu, seiner Quelle in der Seele und seiner Rechtfertigung in der Kunst.

Das Haus der Clavertons war nicht einer der fashionablen Treffpunkte Londons. Die Gesellschaft der Regency-Epoche wurde vom Dandy beherrscht, den Lord Claverton nicht hofierte und Andrew nicht zur Kenntnis nahm. Er hatte anderes zu tun, nämlich Kunst und Künstler zu entdecken. Van Eyck, Rembrandt und Vermeer hingen in Häusern, die ihm offenstanden. Andrew, an Venezianern geschult, machte eine weitere Entdeckung: "Große Kunst dient nicht der Interpretation von Geschehen, sondern macht eine Art von Wahrheit sichtbar, die sich anderen Medien entzieht." Daß große Kunst beides tun kann, ist ihm erst später in Italien aufgegangen, doch hat er in seiner Theorie die Trennung streng beibehalten.

Die *grand tour* dauerte zwei Jahre. Ihre erste Station war Paris, wo er den Bestand des damals noch jungen und überblickbaren Louvre wahrscheinlich Bild für Bild registrierte und sich in den Ateliers mit dem französischen Klassizismus konfrontierte, ohne sich je über ein Werk zu äußern. In Gérards Atelier traf er Sulpiz Boisserée. Boisserée über Marbot: "Ein schöner junger Mensch, groß und dunkel, aber verschlossen und überheblich." Marbot über Boisserée: "Aufrecht und beflissen, weder inspiriert noch inspirierend." Also beiderseits keine Zuneigung.

Über die Zwischenstationen der Reise liegen wenige datierte Eintragungen vor. Wir vermuten, daß sein Sinn für das Maß des Mitteilswerten ihm door; the sounds of conversation grow faint, the lights are extinguished in the rooms and passageways of the house, Andrew and Lady Catherine mount the stairs, the moment of separation is at hand, they whisper of the parting soon to come, the accustomed goodnight kiss assumes an unaccustomed intensity, their breathing grows hot and heavy, the real world ceases to exist along with all the claims of decency and reason, all caution is cast to the winds; who pulled whom into the bedroom we shall never know, the scandalous deed is consummated—

—and a new dimension suddenly enters Andrew's awareness, a new seat of consciousness that will direct and rule him from this moment forth; that in all future encounters will cause him to seek out forces hidden or suppressed beneath the surface; to pay less heed to the accomplishments of a man and the measure thereof and to attend instead to a man's motives and the mind from which they spring; to regard the effect as of less significance than its cause. Thus his own experience became the means whereby he was prompted to ponder the ways and vagaries of human behavior and to study the images of art in order to discover there the imprint of those circumstances, tolerable or intolerable, in which their authors lived out their lives: The object of his quest was the taboo, its origins in the human soul and its vindication in art.

The Claverton residence was not one of London's fashionable meeting places. Regency society was dominated by the dandy, whom Lord Claverton would not court and whom Andrew ignored. He was otherwise occupied: with the discovery of art and artists. He came and went in houses whose walls were hung with Van Eycks, Rembrandts, and Vermeers. Schooled as he was in the works of the Venetian painters, Andrew made this further discovery: "The purpose of great art is not to interpret occurrences, but to render a kind of truth which is beyond the grasp of other media." That great art can achieve both these ends became clear to him only later, when he was in Italy; but in his theory he continued to maintain this strict distinction.

The Grand Tour lasted two years. His first destination was Paris, where he very likely catalogued the entire holdings of the Louvre picture by picture, at a time when it was still relatively young and relatively small; and where he also encountered French Classicism in the studios. He passed no comment on any of the works he saw. In Gérard's studio he met Sulpiz Boisserée, who observed of Marbot: "A handsome young man, tall and dark, but withdrawn and haughty." Marbot noted of Boisserée: "Worthy and assiduous, neither inspired nor inspiring." A marked absence of warmth on both sides, it seems.

His journal contains little in the way of dated entries on the various places he visited en route. One supposes that his acute sense of literary nicht gestattete, vegetatives Wohlsein oder Unwohlsein zu verzeichnen, sein Ich erscheint beinah immer objektiviert. Als echter Melancholiker gebraucht er das Wort "Melancholie" niemals. Zudem lag es ihm fern, Inhaltsverzeichnisse seiner Tagesläufe anzufertigen, seine Notate stehen selten im Imperfekt oder Perfekt. Gedächtnisstützen benötigte er nicht. "*A thought which escapes the mind never does so without good reason.*" Bekannt ist jedoch, daß er die Fahrten oft tagelang unterbrach, um "am scheinbaren Frieden der Natur teilzuhaben, dieser großen verschwiegenen Macht, der wir auf wunderbar-unheimliche Weise gleichgültig sind." Mit "Natur" meinte er aber nicht nur die "ungezähmte Selbstverwirklichung", nicht nur das Grandiose oder Idyllische, also nicht nur jene Landschaften der Bildhintergründe, die er auf unübertroffene Weise analysiert hat, sondern auch das scheinbar Unscheinbare, das Undarstellbare oder zumindest bis dahin noch nicht Dargestellte, das "Sehnsüchte nach nichts bestimmtem erweckt, außer vielleicht danach, alle Erfahrung abstreifend, rückwärts zu leben"—und hier dürfen wir wohl ergänzen: um schließlich in den Mutterschoß zurückzukehren. Denn "*longing is retroverted curiosity.*"

Aus späteren Aufzeichnungen erfahren wir, welche Landschaften er gemeint hat, nämlich die Po-Ebene, und zwar zwischen Piacenza und Cremona. "Der Po, ein gebieterischer Strom und doch von souveräner Ruhe (. . .) schafft Fluchten von Kammern an seinen Ufern, still und intim, so daß der Geist sie mit Muße auslotet, während die Seele sich ausruht." Wir sehen ihn dort sitzen, im milden, von Pappelreihen gefilterten Licht, auf einer von Schilf zerfaserten Sandbank—vielleicht sieht er einem Fischer zu—in jenem Panorama der Schwermut also, das für weniger differenzierende Reisende nichts als eine Durststrecke zwischen Alpen und Appenin war.

Nach Rom ist Marbot auf seiner ersten Reise nicht gekommen. Ohne Zielzwang und nur der Laune gehorchend durchstreifte er die Lombardei, die Marken, Venezien und die Toskana, nicht im Verfolgen von Bildung, sondern im Verlangen nach Bildern und ihren Motiven, nach Landschaften und Seelenlandschaften, auf der Suche und, zunehmend, auf der Spur seiner These, die er nicht darlegen werde, bis sie sich ihm von selbst als Erkenntnis offenbare. Im Herbst 1821 schreibt er an van Rossum: "Zwischen den Bilderrahmen verbergen sich Geheimnisse, die nicht nur bisher von niemandem gelöst, sondern auch von niemandem als solche erkannt wurden. Vielleicht werde auch ich sie nicht lösen, aber ich werde sie erkennen."

Im Winter 1821 verbrachte Marbot einen Monat bei Byron und dessen Kreis in Pisa. "Ein exotischer Hofstaat. Mylord ein Apollo mit Faunsfuß discrimination would not permit him to record states of vegetative well-being or discomfort, and his own person is nearly always viewed objectively, from without. True melancholic that he was, the word "melancholy" is totally absent from his writings. Nor was it his manner merely to list his daily doings, and his journal entries are rarely formulated in the imperfect or perfect tense. He had no need of aids to memory: "A thought which escapes the mind never does so without good reason." But we do know that he frequently interrupted his travels for days at a time in order "to partake of the seeming tranquillity of Nature, that vast, mysterious power which looks upon us with an indifference at once marvellous and disquieting." What he meant by "Nature," however, was not merely that "unbridled appetite for self-realization," not merely those elements of the grandiose or the idyllic that, in the landscapes that form the background to so many paintings, he has analyzed with unparalleled mastery, but also the seemingly ordinary, the unreproducible, or at least that which had not previously been reproduced, and which "excites longings directed at no specific goals, except perhaps to live one's life in reverse, discarding all experience"—and here we may doubtless add: in order to revert finally to the mother's womb. For "longing is retroverted curiosity."

From some later notes we learn that these reflections were prompted by the landscape of the Po Valley as it appears between Piacenza and Cremona. "The Po, an imperious stream, yet full of majestic repose (. . .) has disposed along its banks as it were a succession of chambers, tranquil and intimate, which the mind may explore at its leisure while the soul takes its rest." We may picture him sitting there, bathed in the gentle sunlight that filters through the rows of poplars, disporting himself on some reedy sandbank—intent perhaps on the figure of a fisherman—lost in that vista of melancholy that for travelers less discerning than he was no more than a dull interlude between the Alps and the Apennines.

Marbot failed to reach Rome on his first journey. Having no strict itinerary to follow he yielded to the dictates of fancy, wandering at will through Lombardy, the Marches, the Veneto and Tuscany, in search not of culture but of pictures and their motifs, Nature's landscapes and the inner landscapes of the mind, seeking and increasingly pursuing his thesis, which he would not lay before the world until it had manifested itself to him as certain knowledge. In the autumn of 1821 he writes to van Rossum: "Within the frames of pictures lie hidden mysteries which no man has solved—nay, which no man has even recognized as such. Perhaps I too shall not solve them; but at least I shall have the recognition of them."

In the winter of 1821 Marbot spent a month in the company of Byron and his circle in Pisa. "An exotic household. Mylord is an Apollo en-als Gegengewicht. Dieser Makel ist das Menschlichste an ihm, denn seine Schönheit ist böse (*wicked*). Er hält sich einen Hofnarren namens Trelawny, einen Hofrivalen namens Shelley, der besser dichtet als er, was er weiß, und eine Mätresse namens Teresa Guiccioli, die so schön wie töricht (*silly*) ist." Das letztere Urteil hat er nicht revidiert als, sechs Jahre später, die Gräfin Guiccioli für eine kurze aber bewegte Zeit seine eigene Geliebte wurde. Menschliche Wärme gehörte nicht zu seinen Eigenschaften.

Im Frühjahr 1822 war er in Siena, im Sommer in Florenz, wo er Schopenhauer begegnete. (Schopenhauer an Osann: "... ein äußerst angenehmer junger Engländer von remarkablem Verstand...") Hier erreichte ihn im November die Nachricht vom Tode seines Vaters. Andrew, nunmehr Sir Andrew, Herr über Marbot Hall und beträchtliche Ländereien kehrte heim, seinem Schicksal entgegen, in den Schoß der Mutter, im bestürzend wahren Sinne des Wortes.

Ein seltener, wahrscheinlich einmaliger Fall: ein Mann von höchster Sensibilität und kontrollierte Sexualität, dessen Libido dem Liebesobjekt der ödipalen Phase sein Leben lang nicht entwachsen ist; eine Frau von lebhaftem Geist, mit einem intensiven, vielleicht ausschweifenden, Gefühlsleben, ihrem Sohn bis ins letzte verfallen, so daß weder Inzest- noch Religionsschranke wirksam wurden. Genuß des Sexus als Sünde, "*sweet sin*," "*sinful bliss*" als Anreiz und Erfüllung, als Sehnsucht, die sich nach zweijähriger Trennung nicht hatte stillen lassen und nun erschöpfende Befriedigung verlangte, beiderseits in wachem Bewußtsein vollzogen und bis zur Neige ausgekostet. Denn die Beziehung durfte nicht von Dauer sein. Das Handeln wider alle Gesetze—deren Gültigkeit anzuerkennen sich Andrew bis an sein Ende geweigert hat—mußte sich an der Entdekkungsgefahr, an den dauernden Vorkehrungen der Heimlichkeit aufreiben. Skandal drohte. Seltsamerweise brach er nicht aus.

Lady Catherine beichtete, Pater Gerardus sprach das Machtwort, das ihm gewiß schwer wurde, die Trennung erfolgte im Mai 1825. Beide wußten, daß sie endgültig sei. Lady Catherine starb zwei Jahre nach ihrem Sohn. Wenn wir den Fall als romantisches Drama von höherer—oder, wie mancher es lieber hätte, von niedriger—Gewalt zu betrachten belieben, so könnten wir sagen: Lady Catherine starb an gebrochenem Herzen.

Den Sommer 1825 verbrachte Marbot in London, wo er Turner, Bonington und Delacroix begegnete. Delacroix lobte seine "unabhängige Urteilskraft" (deren Opfer er werden sollte). Ende June schiffte er sich nach Hamburg ein und begann seine diesmal gezielte Reise, in deren anfangs gedrängtem Programm wir einen ablenkungstherapeutischen Zug vermuten. Anstrengung scheint eingeplant, ein Verlangen nach Abschluß seiner cumbered with the foot of a faun. This physical blemish is the most human thing about him, for his beauty is a wicked beauty. He keeps a court jester by the name of Trelawny, a court rival by the name of Shelley, who writes better poetry than he—as he knows full well—and a mistress by the name of Teresa Guiccioli, who is no less beautiful than she is silly." Nor did he revise this last verdict six years later, when the Countess Guiccioli became his own mistress for a brief but stormy season. Human warmth was not one of his characteristics.

In the spring of 1822 he was in Siena, while the summer found him in Florence, where he met Schopenhauer. (Schopenhauer to Osann: ". . . an extremely agreeable young Englishman of remarkable intellect . . .") It was here, in November, that he received news of his father's death. Andrew, now Sir Andrew, master of Marbot Hall and a landowner of considerable substance, returned home to England, to his destiny, and to the bosom of his mother—in the most startlingly literal sense.

A rare, if not indeed a unique, case: a man of the loftiest sensibility and controlled sexuality, whose libido never outgrew the love-object of the Oedipal phase; and a woman of lively intellect and intense, perhaps even dissolute, emotions, so utterly infatuated with her son that neither the incest taboo nor the prohibitions of religion had any power over her. Sexual experience was embraced as "sweet sin," and the pattern of arousal and gratification was "sinful bliss" to them both, a longing that two years of separation had done nothing to alleviate, and that now cried out for satisfaction. In the full light of awareness mother and son drank the cup of pleasure to the dregs. For their union was not to be a lasting one. Their conduct flouted every law of mankind—though Andrew steadfastly refused to acknowledge the legitimacy of such laws—and the fear of discovery, coupled with the constant need for subterfuge to maintain the secrecy of their relations, gradually took its toll. A scandal seemed inevitable. Yet somehow it was averted.

Lady Catherine confessed, Father Gerardus commanded (though doubtless with a heavy heart), and the parting took place in May 1825. They both knew that it was final. Lady Catherine died two years after her son. If one were disposed to view the affair as a Romantic drama impelled by higher forces—or lower forces, as some would rather have it—then one might say that Lady Catherine died of a broken heart.

Marbot spent the summer of 1825 in London, where he met Turner, Bonington, and Delacroix. Delacroix praised his "independence of judgement" (of which he himself was later to become a victim). At the end of June he took ship for Hamburg and set out upon his travels again, this time with a more definite end in view. The very full itinerary on which he embarked was no doubt conceived with the object of distracting his mind

Suche, nach Zusammenfassung des Entdeckten und noch zu Entdeckenden: die Psyche des Künstlers und deren Anomalie, die, wie er meinte, jeder wahren künstlerischen Tätigkeit zugrunde liegen müsse. In Braunschweig wurde ihm Giorgiones Selbstporträt zum Erlebnis. "Dieser Blick von geradezu stechender Unbestimmtheit (*vagueness*), von aufgerührter, leidender weil zweifelnder Selbstliebe. Denn der wahre Künstler, ob er es weiß oder nicht, liebt nur sich selbst."

Der Besuch bei Goethe im Juli schien ihm die These zu bestätigen. "Goethe nährt ein Feur in seinem Busen, das ihn selbst wunderbar erwärmt, sein Gegenüber jedoch seltsam kalt läßt." Dennoch hat der Dichter den "geheimnisvollen jungen Engländer" wiederholt eingeladen; Ottilie hätte ihn am liebsten ganz behalten. Nach vier Tagen riß er sich los und fuhr über Kassel (Rembrandt, späte Niederländer) durch die Röhn nach Würzburg, wo ihn die Tiepolo-Fresken so überwältigten, daß er seine entstehende Theorie über "diktierte Kunst"—"das Primat des inneren Auftrags über den äußeren Auftrag"—revidierte (" . . . ein Panorama des Göttlichen . . . ein Schweben zwischen Schichten eines von Luftgeistern belebten Himmels.") Weiter über den Bodensee, Chur, Splügen—wo er einen Monat krank verbrachte und von einer alteingesessenen Walserfamilie gesundgepflegt wurde—und kurz vor Winteranbruch bei Schneefall über den Paß hinunter nach Chiavenna, über den Comersee in die Brianza und die Po-Ebene, "*breathing the damp, the fog and the foul air of swamp*." Er muß von robuster Konstitution gewesen sein, einer jener resisten Astheniker, deren Körper fälschlich auf eine unverletzliche Seele schließen lassen.

In Cremona begegnete er einem kunstsinnigen österreichischen Offizier, der in Mantua stationiert war und ihn dorthin mitnahm, um ihm die 1790 von Knoller restaurierten Mantegna-Fresken zu zeigen. Damit war Marbot der erste und für einige Jahrzehnte der letzte Kunstreisende des neunzehnten Jahrhunderts, der die *Camera degli sposi* gesehen hat. "Ein Familientreffen der Gonzaga, inszeniert (*put on the stage*) von Andrea Mantegna, (. . .) alle verharren in steinerner Stille, völlig ratlos (*completely at a loss*). Der Herzog neigt sich zu seinem Sekretär, um ihm etwas Wichtiges ins Ohr zu schweigen. Doch sind die Figuren wunderbar gemalt und gemeißelt, nichts gegen den Künstler, dessen Aufgabe es war, eine berüchtigt häßliche Familie zu verewigen."

Das Frühjahr 1826 verbrachte er in Urbino, wo er ein Haus mietete, die Casa Baiardi an der Piazza Pompeo Gherardi (heute Palazzo di Giustizia), deren Besitzer, ein Urbinater Patrizier, kurz zuvor gestorben war. Die zweiunddreißigjährige Witwe, Anna Maria, Mutter von zwei Kindern, from grief, for he seems to have spared himself no exertion in the effort to end his quest, to summarize his past discoveries along with what was still to be discovered: the psyche of the artist and its abnormal character, which, as he supposed, were the source and origin of all true artistic creation. In Brunswick the sight of Giorgione's self-portrait made a deep impression upon him. "That look of virtually piercing vagueness, of agitated self-love, afflicted with doubt. For whether he knows it or not, the true artist loves only himself."

His visit to Goethe in July evidently served to confirm this view. "Goethe nourishes in his bosom a flame that affords to him a most excellent warmth, but leaves the visitor strangely cold." Nevertheless the poet repeatedly invited the "enigmatic young Englishman" to his house, and Ottilie would gladly have kept him forever. But after four days he tore himself away and journeyed via Cassel (Rembrandt and the Late Dutch School) through the Rhön mountains to Würzburg, where the Tiepolo frescoes so overwhelmed him that he revised his emergent theory of "dictated art"—"the supremacy of inward mission over outward commission." He noted in his journal: ". . . a panorama of the divine . . . suspended between the layers of a sky peopled by spirits of the air." He traveled on, across Lake Constance, to Chur, then Splügen, where he lay ill for a month until he was nursed back to health by an old-established Walser family. As winter approached he traversed the pass in falling snow, descended to Chiavenna, crossed Lake Como, and entered the Brianza and the Po Valley, "breathing the damp, the fog and the foul air of swamp." He must have been robust of constitution, one of those hardy asthenics whose body misleads observers into thinking that the soul is invulnerable.

In Cremona he made the acquaintance of an Austrian officer well-versed in the arts, who took him to Mantua (where he was stationed) to show him the Mantegna frescoes restored by Knoller in 1790. Thus Marbot became the first, and for many decades the only, visiting connoisseur of art in the nineteenth century to view the *Camera degli sposi*. "A gathering of the Gonzaga family, put on the stage by Andrea Mantegna, (. . .) all the actors are frozen in stony silence, completely at a loss. The Duke is inclined towards his secretary, to whisper in his ear some important piece —of silence. Yet the figures themselves are marvellously painted and carved, and it is no fault of the artist that he was commissioned to immortalize a family celebrated for its ugliness."

He spent the spring of 1826 in Urbino, where he rented a house, the Casa Baiardi on the Piazza Pompeo Gherardi (now the Palazzo di Giustizia), whose owner, a patrician of the city, had recently died. The thirty-two-year-old widow of the former owner, Anna Maria, mother of two behielt er bei sich, zuerst als Hausdame, später als Dame des Hauses, in welcher Eigenschaft sie bei der zwar provinziellen aber nicht prüden Urbinater Gesellschaft Mißfallen nicht zu befürchten hatte, zumal da Andrew, obgleich distanziert und eher höflich als herzlich, ein begehrter Gast in ihren Häusern war.

Im April 1826 ist er endlich in Rom. Seiner Mutter schreibt er: "Rom lebt von seiner Vergangenheit und stirbt an ihren Gewicht. Jedermann scheint damit beschäftigt zu sein, den Mythos der Ewigen Stadt zu zerstören." Wen er mit "Jedermann" meint, erhellt das Journal: die nachnapoleonischen Klassizisten und die deutschen Spätromantiker, zumal die Nazarener, die "Musterknabentum für heiligmäßiges Leben und Mission für Botschaft halten (*who mistake priggery for saintliness and mission for message*)." Einige Künstler traf er im Haus des preußischen Gesandten Karl Josias von Bunsen: die Namen bleiben unerwähnt: eine Demonstration, nicht völlig gerecht vielleicht, doch verständlich.

Bunsen, Freund und Bewunderer Leopardis war es, der ihm dessen im Jahr zuvor erschienene "Canzoni" zu lesen gab, zehn Gedichte, die ihn sofort merkwürdig tief berührten, und aus denen er auf eine konstitutionelle Affinität schloß; zu Recht und zu Unrecht, wie sich heraustellen sollte.

Im Haus der Marchesa Sacrati hoffte er den Dichter anzutreffen, traf aber statt dessen die Großnichte der Marchesa: Teresa Guiccioli, die sich nach Byrons Tod mit diesem und jenem hochgestellten jungen Engländer tröstete und sich sogleich dem "enimmatico Andrea" zuwandte. Die Affäre war heftig und gedrängt; Teresas Temperament, das selbst ein Byron nicht hatte bändigen können, muß sich an Andrews gewiß nicht ungefügigem, doch letztlich detachiertem Verhalten aufgerieben haben. Sein Herz war anderswo. Er notiert: "*He whose innocence is raped by an angel loses by every novel experience.*" Weder Ottilie noch Teresa noch Anna Maria—alle bezeichnenderweise älter als er—haben ihm die Mutter ersetzen können.

Die letzten zweieinhalb Jahre seines Lebens verbrachte er meist in Urbino. Die einzige längere Unterbrechung war seine dreimonatige Reise nach Frankreich im Herbst 1827. Ihr Anlaß war der Besuch bei Delacroix, der ihm zur abschließenden Bestätigung seiner These der "seelisch bedingten Wahl der Bildthemen" und damit seiner rigiden Trennung zwischen "deskriptiver" und "reflektierter" Malerei wurde. Indem die "deskriptive Malerei" primär dem aus der Kindheit übernommenen, unbewußten Wunsch entspringe, Seltsames und Wunderbares wiederzugeben, sei ihr Impuls nur sekundär und über den Umweg der dramatisierenden Ver-children, stayed on with him, initially as his housekeeper and later as the lady of the house—a situation in which she had no cause to fear the censure of Urbino society, which was provincial but not prudish, especially since Andrew himself was much sought after as a guest in their houses, despite a manner that was distant and polite rather than cordial.

In April of 1826 he finally reached Rome. To his mother he writes: "Rome is living on its past—and perishing under the weight of it. Everyone seems to be labouring to destroy the myth of the Eternal City." His journal reveals the identity of that "everyone": the post-Napoleonic Classicists and the German Late Romantics, especially the Nazarenes, "who mistake priggery for saintliness and mission for message." He met various artists at the house of the Prussian ambassador, Karl Josias von Bunsen, but he does not mention them by name: a telling omission, not entirely just, perhaps, but understandable.

It was Bunsen, friend and admirer of Leopardi, who introduced Marbot to the latter's *Canzoni* in the year following their publication. These ten poems had an immediate and profoundly moving effect on him, leading him to infer the existence of some constitutional affinity between himself and their author—rightly *and* wrongly, as subsequent events were to show.

He hoped to encounter the poet at the house of the Marchesa Sacrati, where instead he met the Marchesa's great-niece—none other than Teresa Guiccioli, who had consoled herself after the death of Byron with a series of young English aristocrats, and who now swiftly transferred her affections to the "enimmatico Andrea." The affair was passionate and short-lived; Teresa's temperament, too much even for Byron to tame, must have been sorely tried by Andrew's behavior, for though far from uncompliant he remained ultimately aloof. His heart was elsewhere. An entry in his journal reads: "He whose innocence is raped by an angel loses by every novel experience." Neither Ottilie nor Teresa nor Anna Maria—all of them, significantly enough, older than he—were able to take the place of his mother.

The last two and a half years of his life he spent for the most part in Urbino. His only extended absence was in the autumn of 1827, when he traveled to France for three months. This was the occasion of his visit to Delacroix, which brought him final confirmation of his thesis that "the painter's choice of subject is psychologically determined," and that there is a fundamental distinction to be made between "descriptive" and "reflective" painting. Because "descriptive painting" (he argues) springs primarily from the unconscious desire, nurtured in childhood, to render the strange and the wonderful, its stimulus is pictorial only in a secondary, derived bildlichung malerisch, das Visuelle diene dem Erzählen. Zwar erkennt er ihr die Funktion zu, Mythos und Geschichte für jedermann erstehen zu lassen, der bildlicher Vergegenwärtigung bedürfe, um sein Vorstellungsvermögen zu aktivieren, doch bevormunde sie die latente Einbildungskraft des tieferblickenden Betrachters durch die implizierte Aussage: so war es, denn so sehe ich es. "Reflektierte Malerei" dagegen, ein primär bildnerischer Vollzug, subjektiv sogar meist ein Zwang, wirke durch die Verwandlung dessen, was scheinbar jedermann sehe, in ein metaphysisches Abbild, das erst der Maler sichtbar mache, doch auch nur für jenen, der den Akt der Sichtbarmachung in seinem eigenen, potentiell schöpferischen, Inneren nachzuerleben imstande sei. "Jupiter und Juno"—ein Beispiel nicht von ungefähr!—"sind ein Teil von uns, sie leben in der Luft, die wir atmen, und jeder von uns gibt ihnen seine eigene Gestalt. Aber ein unbekannter alter Mann oder eine Frau, die einen Brief liest, oder das Spiel der Sonne in einem Wohnzimmer, all dies lebt, als unaussprechliches Geheimnis, nur durch die sublime Kunst eines großen Schöpfers." Eine überschwengliche Aussage, gewiß, aber bedenken wir, daß sie zur Zeit der Romantik gemacht wurde! "Allegorie wirkt, wenn überhaupt, durch ihre malerische Qualität der Darstellung, niemals aber durch die Evidenz ihrer Bedeutung. Heute ist sie zum Handwerk einfältiger Moralisten verkommen." Ein Hieb gegen Lukasbrüder und Nazarener; nicht der einzige.

Diese Aufzeichnungen, anfangs gewiß als Mitteilung an andere konzipiert und gesammelt—dafür sprechen verstreute Entwürfe zu essayistischen Exkurzen—wurden zunehmend zur Selbstregistration, an sich gerichtet und vielleicht an wenige Auserwählte: *to whom it may concern.* Wir sehen Marbot nicht bei systematischer Arbeit, seine vegetative Seite forderte ihr Teil. Sofern er gern lebte, lebte er gern in Urbino, von wo er, meist allein, Ausflüge in die Umgebung machte, und wo er bis zuletzt gewichtige Besucher empfing: im Januar 1829 den durchreisenden William Turner, im Spätsommer Karl Blechen auf einem Abstecher von Florenz, und kurz darauf August von Platen, dessen gegenwart er als quälend empfand. Dem Engländer Marbot, der sein Außenseitertum bewältigt hatte, mangelte es an Nachsicht jenen gegenüber, die das ihre nicht zu tragen verstanden. "Graf Platen lebt von seiner Trauer. Er hat nichts zu sagen, aber er sagt es mit außerordentlicher Schönheit. Aus Schmerz macht er eine Form, die sense, in so far as it serves to illustrate a sequence of events—the visual in the service of a narrative purpose. He concedes its function as a means of creating myth and history for the benefit of those whose imagination needs to be stimulated by pictorial representations; but to the observer capable of more profound imaginative insight such painting appears merely to condescend and patronize, with its implicit claim that "thus it was, for thus do I perceive it." "Reflective painting," on the other hand, is first and foremost a pictorial undertaking, which generally imposes itself upon the artist as a kind of compulsion; it achieves its effects by transforming that which all appear to see into a metaphysical image that only the artist has succeeded in making visible—but visible only to him who is endowed with sufficient creative potential of his own to experience vicariously the act whereby the artist has rendered that image. "Jupiter and Juno"—a revealing choice of an example—"are a part of us, they inhabit the air we breathe, and each of us clothes them in forms of our own devising. But an unknown old man, or a woman reading a letter, or the play of sunlight within a room—all this lives, an unspeakable mystery, only through the sublime art of a great creative genius." An extravagant claim, no doubt; but then we must remember that it was made in the age of Romanticism! "Allegory achieves its effects, such as they are, through the purely pictorial qualities of the representation, not through the successful communication of its meaning. Today it has degenerated into an occupation for simple-minded moralists." A barbed allusion (and not the last) to the Lucas Brotherhood and the Nazarenes.

These observations, which were originally conceived and collected, no doubt, for communication to others (as we may infer from the various sketches for longer pieces in essay form), became increasingly a record of the self, addressed to the self, and perhaps to a few select friends: to whom it may concern. We cannot visualize Marbot pursuing his enterprise in any systematic fashion, for here the vegetative side of his character claimed its due. In so far as he enjoyed living at all, he enjoyed living in Urbino: from here he undertook excursions into the surrounding country, unaccompanied for the most part, and here he received important visitors up until the last. These included William Turner, who was passing through in January of 1829; Karl Blechen, who came out from Florence in the late summer of that year; and shortly thereafter August von Platen, whose presence he found trying to the point of torment. As one who had come to accept that he was different from other men, the Englishman Marbot had little patience with other outsiders who remained troubled in their minds. "Count von Platen thrives on sorrow. He has nothing to say, but he says it with extraordinary beauty. Out of pain he constructs a form man anfassen kann, Leopardi dagegen eine Welt, die man sehen und bewundern kann."

Leopardis Dialoge waren 1827 erschienen. Marbot hatte sie sofort gelesen und kritisch kommentiert. Im Januar 1829 erfuhr er, daß sich der Dichter in seinem Elternhaus in Recanati aufhalte, und fuhr zu ihm. Über den Besuch hat er ausführlich berichtet. Einen vollen Tag saß er in der spärlich geheizten Bibliothek dem in einem Sessel kauernden, in eine schmuddelige Decke gehüllten Leopardi gegenüber. Sie sprachen über "Lebens- und Todesarten." Leopardi war "unentschieden und ausflüchtig." "*Deep down in his heart he loves life. Why? I do not know. For, indeed, this misshapen minstrel is not loved by God.*" Eine Anklage gegen Gott, ein Vorwurf gegen Leopardi.

Er selbst hatte sich zu dieser Zeit schon zu seiner Tat entschlossen. Von Recanati zurückgekehrt, von Leopardis Schwäche und Unentschlossenheit zum Gegenteil ermutigt, gab er sich noch ein Jahr Leben.

Marbot war der erste, der zum einzelnen Kunstwerk die Frage nach seiner unbewußten Motivation gestellt hat. Er hat dazu vornehmlich die Malerei gewählt, nicht nur weil sie ihm von den Künsten am meisten bedeutete, sondern auch weil die Betrachtung des Bildes uns "auf ein Gebiet nötigt, das nicht mehr in Bewegung ist, außerhalb der Zeit liegt, daher dem Geist Raum zu freiem Nacherleben (*reconstruction*) schafft." In der Malerei suchte er den Künstler als Individuum, als Objekt und Subjekt, seinen Willen und sein Scheitern, Drang und Verdrängung. Daß seinem Forschen Endgültigkeit versagt bliebe, wußte er. An eine Veröffentlichung in der Form von 1832 hätte er niemals gedacht. Daß also aus einem Diaristen und Briefschreiber ein Essayist und Ästhetiker würde, hätte weder seinem Erwarten noch seinem Verlangen entsprochen.

Inzwischen liegen die später aufgefundenen Tagebuchseiten beinah vollständig vor. Das von van Rossum Gestrichene ist eingeordnet. Die Übergangspassagen der Briefe an die Mutter sind heute mit Quarzlampen lesbar. Eine kommentierte kritische Ausgabe der erhaltenen Texte steht bevor. Ein wichtiger Seitenweg deskriptiver Ästhetik wird damit erschlossen. Die Gestalt Marbot, die Flucht vor dem Leben in die Kunst, Stigma und Charisma des Flüchtigen, lassen sich erschöpfend zwar nicht mehr interpretieren, doch beleuchtet dieses fragmentarische Werk die wesentlichen Aspekte einer einzigartigen Persönlichkeit: ein vehementes Engagement in der Erforschung von Beziehungen zwischen Movens und Agens, eine mitunter quälende Spannung zwischen der Intensität äesthetischer Erfahrung und der angestrebten Zurückhaltung im emotionalen Erleben; den unbedingten Willen zur Objektivität und die Einsicht der Gefanthat one can touch and grasp, while Leopardi constructs a world that one can see and admire."

Leopardi's *Dialogues* had appeared in 1827. Marbot had read them immediately and written a critical commentary. In January of 1829 he learned that the poet was staying at the home of his parents in Recanati, and he journeyed to meet him. He has left us a detailed account of the visit. For an entire day they sat together in the poorly heated library; Leopardi was hunched in an armchair, wrapped up in a dirty blanket. They spoke of "forms of life and death." Leopardi was "undecided and evasive." "Deep down in his heart he loves life. Why? I do not know. For, indeed, this misshapen minstrel is not loved by God." An indictment of God: a reproach against Leopardi.

For his own part he was already resolved to act. Returning home from Recanati, and spurred on to decision by Leopardi's weakness and lack of resolution, he gave himself one more year of life.

Marbot was the first to inquire into the unconscious motivation underlying the individual work of art. He chose to concentrate principally on painting, not only because it meant more to him than other art forms, but also because the contemplation of a picture "compels us into a region which is no longer in motion, which lies beyond Time, and thus gives the mind room to indulge freely in reconstruction." What he sought in painting was the artist as individual, as object *and* subject, his force of will and his failures, his deepest drives and repressions. That his studies would result in no definitive conclusions, he knew full well. Nor would he ever have contemplated publishing his researches in the form in which they existed in 1832. So the transformation from diarist and correspondent to essayist and aesthetic theorist would have been contrary both to his expectations and his wishes.

Most of the missing pages from his journal have now been found. The passages deleted by van Rossum have been restored to their rightful place in the text. The transitional passages in the letters to his mother can now be deciphered with the aid of modern quartz lamps. An annotated critical edition of the surviving texts is in preparation. Its publication will shed valuable light on an important by-way of descriptive aesthetics. The figure of Marbot, the flight from life into art, the stigma and the charisma of the fugitive—these things are no longer accessible to definitive interpretation. But this fragmentary work succeeds in illuminating the major aspects of a unique personality: a passionate commitment to the study of the relationship between motive and agent; a tension, often agonizing to bear, between the intensity of aesthetic experience and the reserve he strove to maintain in his own emotional life; the absolute will to objectivity, and the percepgenschaft im Subjektiven. “Die Antwort des Kunstwerks richtet sich nach der Frage des Betrachters. Mit allerletzter Gewißheit werden wir nichts von dem erfahren, was im Künstler vorgegangen ist, außer seinem Gebot dessen, was in uns vorzugehen habe.”

tion that we are ultimately the prisoners of our own subjectivity. "The answer vouchsafed by a work of art depends on the question put to it by the observer. We shall never know, with absolute certainty, the things that have been enacted in the mind of the artist—only the things that are to be enacted, at his command, in our own."

*This commemorative essay heralds the publication in 1982 of a definitive biography of the English art critic and aesthetic theorist, Andrew Marbot, whose place in the history of art is assured. Although he never in fact existed, it would be misleading to call him a "fictional" figure. He could have existed; and many indeed would argue that he should have.

Streit um Gene

Battle for Genes

Walter Höllerer

STEINBRUCH-MORGENBUCH
Ein Evolutions-Liebesgedicht von Urvogel bis Floh

WALTER HÖLLERER

1

ARCHÄOPTERYX-TRAUM

Archäopteryx, griech. Urvogel, wurde in einem Steinbruch im Altmühltal gefunden; reptilähnlich, mit Zähnen und mit Krallen an den Flügeln.

Ich kenne dich lange Zeit,
wenn ich hinter dir, deinem Rücken zugekehrt,
liege,
die Echsenhaut, Flugsaurierhaut
vor meiner Nase,—
Diluvium, sage ich, ich bin
in einem Kalksteinbruch gefunden worden, mit dir,
wir lagen, dicht beieinander,
jahrtausendelang. —Versteint
sind wir nicht.
Wir sind feucht, moosartig, moorig, eine
feuchte Erinnerung—zurückdenkend und
vorfühlend.—

Meine Haut fühlt sich wohl, sage ich, seit
die Flugechsen aus dem Wasser sich wagten,
aufzufliegen versuchten, und dann
mit dem Bauch in die Pfütze plumpsten,—
und als du, plamm, mit dem Bauch

STONE-QUARRY MORNING DIARY
An Evolutionary Love Poem from Prehistoric Bird to Flea

WALTER HÖLLERER
translated by Herman Salinger

1

ARCHAEOPTERYX-DREAM

Archaeopteryx, Gr. prehistoric bird, was discovered in a stone quarry in the Altmühl Valley; reptilian, with teeth and with claws on the wings.

I have known you for a long time,
when, behind you, turned toward your back,
I lie,
with your lizard skin, flying-saurian hide,
in front of my nose,—
Diluvium, I say, I was
found in a limestone pit with you;
we lay close to one another
for thousands of years. —We never
were petrified.
We are damp, mossy, moor-soaked,
a wet memory—thinking back and
feeling forwards.—

My skin feels fine, I say, since
the flying lizards ventured out of the water,
tried to fly up, and then
plumped bellywise into the puddles,—
and when you, wham, on your belly

in die Pfütze fielst,
du neben mir, ich dann auf dir,
lachten wir unser Steinbruchlachen!

Es macht uns nichts aus, in diesem Augenblick,
nicht einmal, wenn wir um uns schauen,
aus der Pfütze über den flachen Platz,
und wir sehen, rings um uns ist,
inzwischen,
alles saniert, asphaltiert.—

Ich kenne dich lange Zeit.
Jahrtausende.
Moorig, moosartig.
Lachend.
Zurückdenkend.
Vorfühlend.

fell into the puddle,
you next to me, then I on top of you,
we laughed our limestone-pit laugh!

It makes no difference to us, at this moment,
not even when we look around us,
out of the puddle across the flat place,
and we see, all around us,
meanwhile,
everything is sanitized, asphaltized.—

I have known you for a long time,
thousands of years.
Moor-soaked, mosslike.
Laughing.
Thinking back.
Feeling forwards.—

2

ÜBER DAS SCHLAGEN VON PURZELBÄUMEN IM SCHNEEGESTÖBER

Ich sehe dich im Schneegestöber Purzelbäume,
so schöne, flitzig-schnelle schlagen, daß
das Schneegestöber in die Morgenträume
zu mir hereinfliegt, in mein Morgenfaß—

Die Flocken sausen jetzt
zentrifugal
im Wirbel, kommandiert
durch deinen Drall:

Kopfunter seh ich dich
mit Müllern, Bäckern drehn!
Durchs Faß, das keinen Boden hat,
hab ichs gesehn!

So pudelnackt den Purzelbaum
im Traum,
am Morgen seh ich ihn,
die Bäcker schaun

sich fragend an in ihrer
Morgenschicht,
sie sind auf Tanz mit dir,
auf Torten nicht erpicht.

Und ich, ich seh
in meinem Morgentraum,
kopfunter dich, mit Bäckern, dich
als Purzelbaum,

dein runder Rücken ist
des Müllers Lust,
doch mehr die meine,
was du wissen mußt.

2

ON DOING SOMERSAULTS IN A SNOW FLURRY

I see you in the snowy flurries quickly turning
such pretty flitting somersaults, so that
the snowy flurries in my dreams that morning
fly into me there in my morning vat.

The flakes whirr now
in centrifugal whirl,
in that whirl, commanded
by your tight twirl:

Head-over-heels I see you,
amidst millers and bakers you turn!
Through my barrel without any bottom
this I can clearly discern!

So stark naked the somersault
on my dream's white acres,
I watch it at morning;
so do the bakers,

looking in astonishment
as their morning shift starts,
they are bent to dance with you,
not on baking tarts.

In my dream I see you
without flaw or fault,
upside-down with the bakers:
you as somersault;

your rounded back is
the miller's delight,
but mine the more,
as well know you might.

3

BASEL, RHEINBRÜCKE

Auf der Brücke übern Rhein,
wo die Emma-Möven schrein,
auf die Mitte von der Brücke
setzt der Rhein ein Bein.

Hört den Rhein: ‘Bitte sehr,
von dort hinten komm ich her,
dort hinunter komm ich hin,
und mein Bein ist, wo ich bin.

Wo ich bin, in Basel bin,
ist es närrisch. Komm ich hin?
Oder komm ich lieber her?
Oder tu ichs um-verquer?

Basel schwappt in mir, dem Rhein.
Möven flitzen in mich rein.
Flöten schwirrn auf meiner Brücke,
und inmitten von der Brücke,
steht mein Bein.’

‘Siehst du dort vom Rhein das Bein?’
sagst du in mein Ohr hinein,
‘auf der Mitte von der Brücke,
und es winkt mir insgeheim?

Winkt zu mir, mit einem Zeh.
Geh ich hin, damit ichs seh.
Komm mit mir, es muß was los sein,

denn jetzt weht ein heller, grauer,
und er will besonders groß sein,
Rüssel von der Brückenmauer

von der Mitte unserer Brücke
schräg herüber
zu uns rein.’

3

BASEL, RHINE BRIDGE

On the bridge across the Rhine,
where the Emma-gulls wheel and whine,
on the middle of the bridge,
the Rhine extends a leg-like ridge.

Hark to the Rhine: "Just let me say,
I come down from mountains far away,
down below is where I go
and my leg's wherever I am, you know.

When past Basel I am flowing
(it's foolish!) am I coming or going?
Going or coming? Which is worse?
Or am I doing the reverse?

Basel trembles in my waves of Rhine.
Sea gulls flit across my spine.
Flutes go twittering on my bridge
and in the middle of the bridge
stands my leg-like ridge.

"Can you see the leg of the Rhine from here?"
You whisper it into my ear.
"On the middle of the bridge,
it beckons secretly but clear?

"Beckons me with one big toe.
To see it, I must closer go.
Come with me; some must arise,

for now suddenly a bright light-gray
elephantine, huge in size,
a trunk wafts from the wall this way

from the middle of our bridge
right to us across
in diagonal wise."

4

ZETTEL ZU EHREN DER EULENKOPFMEERKATZE IM ZOO ZU BASEL

O Eulenkopf
o Meerkatzschopf,
wo Mann und Frau
so lila-blau,

wo grün im Dunkeln,
rückengrün,
die Eulenaugen
grünlich glühn,

wo lila-blau
signalisiert,
daß Mann und Frau
sich finden wird,

es glänzt das Haar
am Eulenschopf,
das Augenpaar
im Meerkatzkopf,

und wer im Trommeln
Tag und Nacht
dahinläuft und
im Zoo erwacht,

dem glänzt der Rücken,
glänzt das Haar,
weil er in Basel
fündig war.

4

NOTE IN HONOR OF THE OWL-FACED MONKEY
IN THE BASEL ZOO

O owl face
o monkey grace,
male, female too
both lilac-blue,

where green in darkness,
green as your back,
your owlish eyes
glow green and black,

where lilac-blue
is a signal (no other)
that male and female
will find each other,

that gleaming fur
on the head of an owl,
those piercing eyes
and monkey's cowl;

whoever drumming
night and day
wakes up in the zoo
after running away,

his back will glisten,
hair gleam forever,
because in Basel
he was so clever.

5

VOGELKOPF, MORGENS

Straußenfedern, fast erschreckt,
fühl ich gegen Morgen, seh
weiter oben Augen, eh
ich erwache, und versteckt

neben mir am langen Hals
hoch gewunden, hoch da droben,
wo die Augen eingeschoben,
kleines Köpfchen, ebenfalls.

Straußenfedern, Straußenei
zieht die Dämmerung vorbei
lang an Schnüren, Traumgetier,—
bis ich Augen neben mir,

andere, vor Augen seh,
nahe,—und ich schieb den Strauß
in die Maskenwelt hinaus.

5

BIRD'S HEAD IN THE MORNING

Ostrich feathers, frightened nearly,
I feel toward morning and I descry,
opening wider sleepy eye,
waking up, all unclearly

lying before me, neck so rough
twisting there, high, averted,
where the eyes appear inserted,
tiny bird-head, that's enough.

Ostrich feathers, ostrich eggs,
pass in the dusk on ostrich legs
like long strings, a dream-beast she,
till other eyes I by me see,

other eyes before my gaze,
close—the ostrich I push away
into the world where false masks play.

6

ERSTE BEWEGUNG

Ach gib acht
so neugeborn!
Ohne Ohrn
wärst du verlorn!
Gib acht, Nashorn-
kind im Schnee,
fall nicht in den
See.

Sitzt du im
Lawinenball,
rollst mit im
Lawinendrall,
Zungen, schmeckt,
und Lippen, lacht,
Augen laßt
euch nichts entgehn,

Auge, laß
vorm Aug dich sehn,
Ohr, gib acht,
wenns knacht und kracht,
wenn die Nasen
sich im Schnee,
Nasenaffen,
um sich drehn!

Nasen, riecht
und laßt euch spüren,
Finger, laßt euch
leicht verführen,
Ohren, alles
laßt verstehn!
Augen, die wie
Flocken wehn,

6

FIRST MOTIONS

Oh, watch out,
so young in years!
without ears
you'd be lost, I fear.
Watch out, rhino-
ceros child in the snow,
do not fall in the lake
below.

Once inside
the avalanche ball,
you will roll along
with it all;
tongues, taste
and laugh, lips;
eyes won't waste
nor one moment skip.

Eye, let by
eye now be seen;
ear, attend
each knock and crack
when the noses
in the snow,
apes' noses,
turn and go.

Noses, smell;
make your presence known;
fingers, let
yourselves be shown;
ears, let all be
understood and known,
eyes that like
snowflakes are blown,

wenn wir im
Lawinenknall,—
ohne uns wärn
wir verloren—,
schnell uns, immer
schneller drehn!
Komm ganz nah und
laß dich sehn!

when we,
in avalanches tossed,
without ourselves
we should be lost—
fast and ever
faster turn!
Come quite near till
I discern!

7

TAGESFAHRT

Das Fell ist weich, und sonnenwarm das Fell.
Wir kriechen durch das Fell.
Es geht bergab, bergauf im weichen Fell.
Es geht den Rücken des Kamels entlang.
Wir schalten, und es bockt
der Rückwärtsgang.

Wir fühln uns wohl im warmen Fell,
o wohl, so wohl im Morgenfell,
wir wandern lang

und schwimmen dann im Abendfell
in Vollmondgassen, sitzen lang
an Tischen zwischen Stimmen und Gesichtern,
finden dann

hinter den weißen hohen Wall
in unseren Stall.

Es glänzen hell
zwei Bäuche in den vollen Mond,
in Flechten-Bärten, ungewohnt,
die man befühlen kann.

Es glänzen dann
zwei Rücken, rund, als kämen sie weit her,
aus einem Frösche-Land.

So fing es an:
wir, äußerst schnell,
versteckten uns in einem Fell.
Das Fell war weich und hell,
und weiß und sonnenhell
sahn wir die Dörfer in den Tälern
in dem Fell.

Mit Siebenmeilenstiefeln springen wir
im Wollgestöber, und da fühlen wir
mit Zehenspitzen uns dahin, daher,
und streicheln Kuh und Katze, Meerkatz, Bär,
und finden Wiesen, Inseln, Sumpfgestrüpp
mit Elephantengras wie Ritter Serendip.

7

DAY'S JOURNEY

The fur is soft, the fur is warm as sun.
We are creeping through the fur.
We go downhill, uphill in the soft fur.
We go along the camel's back.
We shift our speed and the
reverse jerks.

We feel well in the warm fur,
oh, so well in the morning fur,
we walk for a long time

and then swim in the evening fur
in full-moon lanes, sitting long
at tables between voices and faces,
then find our way

behind the high white wall
into our stall.

Shining brightly
two bellies gleam in the full moon,
in braided beards, unusual,
that one can touch.

Gleaming, too,
two backs, round, as though from far away
from a land of frogs.

Thus it began:
we, extremely fast,
hid ourselves in a fur.
The fur was soft and light
and white and sun-bright
we saw the villages in valleys
in the fur.

With seven-league boots we jump
in the wool-flurry and we feel
our way with toe-tips, here and there,
and stroke cow and cat, monkey and bear,
and find meadows, islands, a swampy tip
with elephant-grass like Sir Serendip.

Das alles finden wir, wir reisen
leicht und schnell
im hellen Fell,

und kommen über Treppen
aus dem Morgentraum,
und knüpfen Hängematten
in den Steinbruchbaum—

ein Wort gibt hier dem
anderen die Hand,
so geht es fort, gebannt
verfolgen wir die Spur
von uns im
Baumbestand.

Das ist der Samt,
von Lippen und
von Zungen Samt.

Der Hauch von Feigen kommt aus einem Land,
wo Blätter rascheln, die mit uns verwandt,
du kannst sie hören, kannst sie vor dir sehn,
von weit her kommen, weit hin mit uns gehn.

All this we find, we travel
quickly and light
in that fur so bright,

and come across steps
from morning's dream free,
and tie our hammocks
in the stone-pit tree—

one word gives here
the other its hand,
so on it goes, spellbound we stand,
then follow our tracks
(our own)
in tree-covered land.

That is the velvet
of lips and
the tongue's velvet.

The breath of figs blows up from a land
where leaves rustle (how like us!) near at hand;
you can hear them, see them with your own eyes,
come from afar, going with us comradewise.

Schneckenprinzessinnen

Snail Princesses

Perlenprinzessinnen

Pearl Princesses

Aldona Gustas

Vexiermärchen

Fairy Tale Puzzle

xiermärchen II

airy Tale Puzzle II

Vexiermärchen III

Fairy Tale Puzzle III

SECHS GEDICHTE

ALDONA GUSTAS

obwohl
wir grundverschieden sind
unsere Zuneigung
wie Zierklee
der noch gezüchtet
werden muß
anmutet
gebe ich vor
dir schon heute nacht
schwer zu Sagendes
zu flüstern

ich liebe dich
mit einer Menge
von Gefühlen
auf meine Weise
sagst du
nach Berührungen aller Art

was mich angeht
so habe ich
heute nacht
Dank deiner Zuneigung
mehr Identität
als sonst in vielen Jahren

SIX POEMS

ALDONA GUSTAS
translated by Julia Penn

although
we're thoroughly different
our attraction
seems
like ornamental clover
that must be pampered to grow
I pretend
already tonight
to whisper
difficult things
to you

I love you
with a whole lot of
feelings
in my own way
you say
after touchings of all kinds

as for me
tonight
I have
because of your affection
more identity
than I've had in several years

der Himmel war
regensatt

du
ein Geschöpf
aus Schatten Knochen Fleisch
und salzigen Träumen
hast mich
verletzlicher als sonst
zurückgelassen

mein Wort
wie gern hätte ich
dich überredet
zu bleiben

weil ich
aber schwieg
war mir
nicht zu helfen

auch mein Alleinsein später
führte zu nichts

the sky
was rain-soaked

you
a creature
of shadows bones flesh
and salty dreams
left me
more vulnerable
than before

my words
how I would have loved
to persuade you
to stay

but since I
said nothing
I was
beyond help

even my solitude later
came to nothing

um mir
zu genügen
wickelte ich mich
in Segeltücher
flog
ins Land der Käfer
die sich im Gras totstellen

Gras meine zweite Haut

passabel
ist das Gras
hier
es gleicht Gräsern
die Whitman einst besang

laß uns
woanders hingehen
vielleicht zurück
in unsere Asphaltgegend
an die wir uns
gewöhnt haben

to satisfy
myself
I wrapped myself up
in sailcloth
flew
into the land of the beetles
that play dead in the grass

grass my second skin

the grass
is all right
here
it's like the grass that
Whitman sang about

let us
go somewhere else
maybe back
to our own paved-over region
that we have
gotten used to

from: SHITTELBECKER'S HOLIDAY
A Work without Progress

ERNST JANDL

the head, the hand, the elephant, and the shoe
4 poems after 4 drawings

1

the head is just
prettily stuffed
with bars and stripes
and gloomy shapes
like any old prison
it is indeed the oldest
prison of all

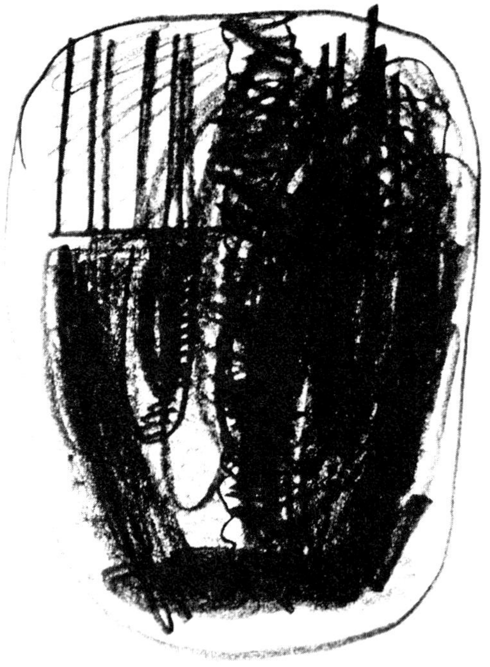

2

the hand will full of fingers be
and it was canned with all of them
shorty was one of them called
and none of them was longer
a lot of darkness in the can
no wonder they all said good night

3 (for friederike mayröcker)

if the elephant
were not elegant
he would not look
that sad
that old snob

4

little drops of water
little drops of wine
are collected in the shoe
of the little old lady who knew
all about tears
yours, hers, and mine

epilogue:
badly drawn and badly rhymed
makes a man healthy, wealthy, and kind
(of crazy)

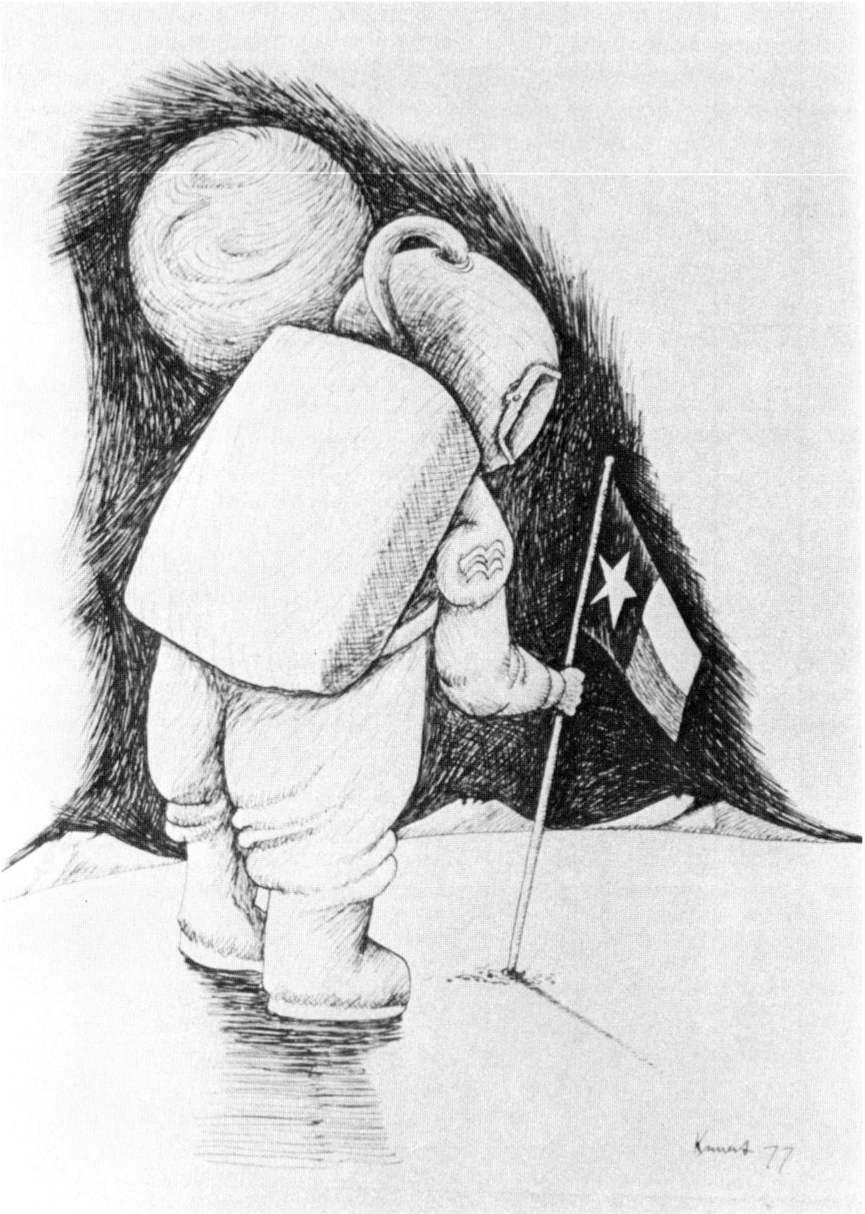

USA (1977) Ink

USA

Günter Kunert

Gewidmet der fröhlichen Gärtnerin in ihrem Garten (1977) Pencil

Dedicated to the happy gardener in her garden

GÜNTER KUNERT

FLASCHENPOST

Trotz anhaltenden Suchens ließ sich die Quelle nicht wiederfinden, obwohl sie, wenn auch nicht besonders genau—wegen der vormals schwächeren Radioteleskope—, im Sternbild des Schwans geortet worden war. Seitdem das neue Programm zur Erforschung elektromagnetischer Erscheinungen unbekannter kosmischer Herkunft lief, wurden auch die bereits bekannten Strahlungen, welche die Erde trafen, erneut untersucht, zwecks genauerer Meßergebnisse, aber als die verbesserten Antennen sich auf jene schon früher abgetastete Stelle am Rande der Galaxis richteten, wo man noch vor wenigen Jahren eine schwache, dort deutliche Emission festgestellt hatte, gab es nun für die Geräte nichts zum Registrieren.

Das Universum, mit seinem vielfältigen, durch Verstärker und Lautsprecher ins Hörbare transformierten Lärmen den ahnungsvoll-altertümlichen Begriff der "Sphärenklänge" bestätigend und zugleich verhöhnend, blieb am anvisierten Punkt stumm. Ungewöhnlich, weil Strahlung niemals abrupt zu erlöschen pflegt, zumindest vor einem Schwächerwerden ansteigt, und noch einmal im Stadium der Letalität sich maßlos verstärkt, was auf eine unsichtbare Katastrophe schließen läßt. Erst dann der Abgesang, die Ermüdung, diagnostizierbar an der geringeren Ausschüttung von Elektronen durch Raum und Zeit, so daß die gegenwärtige Stille und Reglosigkeit anstelle orgiastischer oder moribunder Materie Verwunderung, sogar Verdacht hervorrufen mußte.

Man schloß anfänglich auf einen Defekt des einst verwendeten Gerätes, Aufnahme ungefilterten Eigenrauschens, bis man das seit langem archivierte Magnetband vorholte und die aufgezeichneten Signale abhörte. So arhythmisch und von gewöhnlichen Aufnahmen abweichend erwiesen sie sich, daß sofort die Frage auftauchte, warum eigentlich damals keine exakte Analyse stattgefunden habe. Als sei das Krachen und Prasseln moduliert, etwas wie eine Stimme, zerlegt in unverbundene, zu mechanischen Geräuschen verwandelte Vokale. Nach mehrfachen Abhören entschied man, diese Geräusche, die Art ihres Entstehens durch Vergleichstests identifizieren zu wollen sowie durch statistische Berechnungen ähnlicher elektronischer Entladungen Analogieschlüsse anzustreben, um

PROSE, POEMS, MINI-ESSAYS

GÜNTER KUNERT
translated by A. Leslie Willson
Ulrich K. Goldsmith
Stephen Zon

MESSAGE IN A BOTTLE

In spite of a persistent search the source could not be located again, although it had been fixed, even if not with particular accuracy—because of the formerly weaker radio telescope—in the constellation of the Swan. Since the new program was engaged in the research of electromagnetic phenomena of unknown cosmic origin, the already known rays that struck the earth were also investigated anew for the purpose of more exact measurements; but when the improved antennas were directed toward that spot at the edge of the galaxy that had earlier been scanned, where a few years before a weak, distinct emission there had been detected, now there was nothing for the instruments to register.

The universe, confirming and at the same time ridiculing the portentous archaic concept of the "music of the spheres," with its manifold noise that had been transformed into audibility by means of amplifiers and loudspeakers, remained mute at the point on which a bearing had been taken. Unusual, because radiation customarily never ceases abruptly, at the very least rises before becoming weaker, and at the stage of extinction increases more and more extravagantly, which allows the inference of an invisible catastrophe. Only then the hymnic conclusion, the exhaustion, diagnosable by the lesser fallout of electrons through space and time, so that the present quiet and lack of activity in place of unrestrained or moribund elements was bound to provoke amazement, even suspicion.

It was determined at first that there was a defect in the instrument used previously, the reception of unfiltered background noise, until the magnetic recording long since stored in the archives was brought forth and the signals recorded were monitored. They proved to be so arhythmical and divergent from the customary receptions that the question arose at once: Why had an exact analysis actually not taken place at the time? As though the crackling and rattling were modulated, something like a voice disassembled into unconnected vocables transformed into mechanical noises. After repeated monitoring it was decided to try to identify these noises, the manner of their origin, through comparative tests as well as to attempt to achieve analogical conclusions through statistical calculations of similar die eventuelle Verwandtschaft mit bestimmten kernphysikalischen Abläufen festzustellen. Aber obschon alle beteiligten Radioastronomen mit Hilfe des Institutscomputers die Geräusche angingen, als gelte es, eine fremde, extrem exotische Sprache in die eigene zu übersetzen, scheiterte das Unternehmen, weil—wie der Institutsdirektor während einer Beratung feststellte—ihr Rechner ausschließlich für Astronomie eingerichtet sei, indessen die Enträtselung der Geräusche auf dem Band eine andere Programmierung zu verlangen schien. Er habe, meinte er und schaute dabei bedeutungsvoll in die Runde, einen Verdacht, von dem er annehme, daß ihn auch andere Institutsmitarbeiter hegten, wolle diesen jedoch nicht näher und leichtfertig definieren, weil man sich in Fachkreisen damit rasch lächerlich machen und dem guten Ruf des Instituts schaden könne. Er jedenfalls wolle nicht für einen Spinner gehalten werden. Aber, und erneut versuchte er das Unmögliche, nämlich die Versammelten mit einem Blick so zu umfassen, daß jeder einzelne gerade sich ganz besonders eindringlich angesprochen vorkomme, aber falls dieses Magnetband enthalte, was man argwöhne, dann könnten nur Spezialisten besonderer Sorte etwas damit anfangen. Durch einen Zwischenruf: "Was denn für Spezialisten?" aus dem Konzept gebracht, erwiderte er reflexartig und unbedacht: "Spionageabwehr . . .", was ein allgemeines Murren zur Folge hatte. Wie entschuldigend fuhr er fort, daß doch niemand sonst in der Lage wäre, möglicherweise rational Codiertes in den Geräuschen zu entschlüsseln—dazu bedürfe es doch eines entsprechend fachmännischen Ansatzes, der ja hier im Institut fehle.

Nachdem er die anwesenden Mitarbeiter fast pathetisch zum Schweigen verpflichtet hatte, aktivierte er seine Beziehungen, deren Existenz jeder seiner Untergebenen ohnehin ahnte: Wer wußte nicht, daß zwischen der Radioastronomie und dem militärischen Bereich durch beiderseitigen Bezug zur Raumfahrt, durch gewisse Aufträge im Satellitenprogramm Berührungspunkte bestanden. Der einzige schwache Trost dabei war, daß überhaupt keine naturwissenschaftliche Disziplin sich von den Sonderinteressen der Strategen moderner Kriegsführung freizuhalten vermochte. Künftig konnte keiner mehr sagen: Ich habe nichts von den Folgen meiner Forschung gewußt. Aber verhindern konnte man sie auch nicht. Eine Illusion, zu forschen, zu entdecken, und gleichzeitig sich den praktischen Konsequenzen entziehen. Hinter jedem von ihnen, so sie den Mut fanden, ihre Tätigkeit genauer ins Auge zu fassen, stand ein Gespenst mit wirren weißem Haar und herausgestreckter Zunge, dieses Musterbeispiel eines "reinen" Forschers, Denkmal expliziter Ethik, unwillentlich und unbewußt zum Helfershelfer hunderttausendfachen Tötens geworden und zum Spuk, vor dem jeder denkende Wissenschaftler gefälligst zu erschrekken hatte. Jeder ein Parzival, aber das entschuldigte trotzdem nichts.

electronic discharges, in order to determine the possible relationship with specific nuclear physical processes. But although all the participating radio astronomers attacked the noises with the help of the Institute's computer, as though it were a matter of translating a foreign, extremely exotic language into their own, the undertaking came to naught because—as the director of the Institute concluded during a discussion—their computer was programed exclusively for astronomy while the decipherment of the sounds on the tape seemed to require a different program. He had a suspicion, he said, and at this looked meaningfully around the circle, which he assumed was held by other colleagues in the Institute, but he did not want to state it more specifically or flippantly, because among experts he could quickly make himself ridiculous and could damage the fine reputation of the Institute. Anyway, he did not want to be considered a screwball. However—and again he tried the impossible, namely, to embrace the gathering with one glance, in such a way that each individual would feel himself addressed with special intensity—however, in the event that this magnetic tape should contain what was suspected, then only specialists of a particular kind could get anywhere with it. Losing his thread at the interrupting cry of "What kind of specialists?" he replied as a reflex and rashly: "Counterespionage . . ." which resulted in a general grumbling. As though apologizing he continued that no one else would be in the position to decipher something possibly rationally encoded in the noises—for that, certainly, an appropriately expert effort would be required, which admittedly was lacking here in the Institute.

After he had pledged those of his colleagues who were present almost solemnly to silence, he activated his connections, the existence of which each of his subordinates suspected anyway. Who was not aware that points of contact existed between radio astronomy and the military realm through a mutual involvement with space travel, through certain missions in the satellite program. The single slight consolation in this was that absolutely no discipline of the natural sciences was able to stay uninvolved with the special interests of the strategists of modern warfare. No one could say in the future: I knew nothing about the consequences of my research. But neither could they be prevented. It was an illusion to conduct research, to discover, and simultaneously to disassociate oneself from the practical consequences. Behind each of them, if they found the courage to observe their activity more precisely, stood a specter with tangled white hair and protruding tongue, this epitome of the "pure" research scientist, monument of manifest ethics, involuntarily and unconsciously become the accessory of a hundredthousandfold death and the specter before which any thinking scientist was obliged to be horrified. Each one a Parzifal, but that excused nothing nevertheless.

Wie in fernen, fast vergessenen Kindermärchen war ihm "das Herz schwer", angefüllt mit ambivalentem Empfinden, als er eine Kopie des Bandes dem zuständigen Offizier in der entsprechenden Abteilung übergab und zum ersten Male seinen Verdacht äußerte und ihr technisches Unvermögen bekannte, die Geräusche, vielleicht bedeuten sie gar nichts, auf ihren vermuteten Inhalt zu überprüfen. Verlegenheit, wie seit langem nicht. Obgleich die Astronomie mit der Vorstellung lebte, einmal doch auf Zeichen fremder Vernunft zu stoßen, geriet sie, da der Moment nahe schien, in Selbstzweifel, in Furcht, durch einen Irrtum ihre Reputation einzubüßen. Zumindest deutete der Direktor diese Besorgnis als weiteren Grund des Kontaktes und der Bitte um Hilfe an und war erleichtert, als der Offizier Verständnis zeigte und versprach, die Angelegenheit diskret zu behandeln. Und er meinte sogar mit einem fragwürdigen Lächeln, er unterstütze die Ansicht, daß die Wissenschaft nicht ins Licht des Zweifels gerückt werden dürfe. "Diese letzte Säule müssen wir erhalten", sagte er ernst, "das ist auch unsere Aufgabe. Darin stimmen wir mit dem Feind überein . . ."

Kaum zwei Wochen später der Anruf im Institut, die dringliche Einladung zur Dienststelle, doch als der Direktor, sein Pulsschlag beschleunigte sich plötzlich, nach dem Grund für die Eile fragte, ob denn positive Ergebnisse zu begrüßen wären, erfuhr er nur, jedes weitere Wort am Telefon sei sträflicher Leichtsinn. Vergleicht man die Psyche mit einer chemischen Substanz, was sie ja mittelbar auch ist, deren wechselnde Zusammensetzung alle Reaktionen und Stimmungen steuert, so war diese im Falle des Direktors und wie er es selber empfand, noch zusätzlich "aufgewühlt." Was sonst als die Bestätigung des Verdachts konnte diese Art der Einladung heißen? Warum aber jetzt dieses innere Vibrieren, diese Aufgeregtheit, kenntlich am Zittern der Finger, das immer wieder zu bestaunen er Arme und Hände ausstreckte: Sie hatten doch immer damit gerechnet. Um eine der zahllosen Milliarden Sonnen, soviel versprach die Wahrscheinlichkeitsrechnung, mußte ja ein Planet kreisen, auf dem die Lebensbedingungen ähnlich waren—Nein: nicht einer! Eine Vielzahl solcher von Eiweiß bewohnter Kugeln schoß in unvorstellbarer Entfernung auf den sie bindenden Bahnen dahin, und bedachte man es recht, so galt es eher als Wunder, daß man bis dato noch zu keiner Kontakt hatte. Jetzt—endlich!

Seine Hände, um keine Spur ruhiger, empfingen aus denen des Offiziers einen dünnen Schnellhefter ohne Aufschrift, nur mit dem Stempel "Höchst geheim" versehen, halbverwischt, Indiz nervöser Hast, dazu die Aufforderung, eher: den Befehl: "Lesen Sie es und vergessen Sie es sofort wieder!" Das rief Verwirrung hervor, die, als der Offizier sie erkannte, ihn zu einigen Erklärungen veranlaßte:

As in distant, almost forgotten, children's fairy tales "his heart was heavy," filled with ambivalent sensations, as he handed over a copy of the tape to the appropriate officer in the corresponding agency and for the first time expressed his suspicion and admitted their technical inability to check the noises—maybe they had no significance at all—for their presumed contents. More embarrassment than in a long time. Although astronomy dwelled with the idea of sometime stumbling upon signs of an alien intelligence, now that the moment seemed near, it fell into self-doubt, into the fear of losing its reputation through an error. At least the director cited this concern as a further reason for the contact and the plea for assistance and was relieved when the officer indicated his understanding and promised to treat the matter with discretion. And he even said, with a quizzical smile, that he supported the view that science ought not to be shoved into the light of doubt. "We must maintain this last pillar," he said earnestly. "That is also our task. In this we agree with our foe . . ."

Hardly two weeks later the call at the Institute, the urgent invitation to the agency, but when the director—his pulse rate increased suddenly—inquired about the reason for the hurry, whether he might receive positive results, he learned only that any further word by telephone would be reprehensible recklessness. If the psyche is compared to a chemical substance—which, of course, it is indirectly—whose variable composition directs all reactions and moods, then in the case of the director, and as he himself felt it, it was additionally "agitated." What else besides the confirmation of his suspicion could this kind of invitation mean? But why now this inner vibration, this excitement, recognizable by the trembling of his fingers that he again and again held out his arms and hands to wonder at: They had always counted on it. Around one of the countless billions of suns—the law of probability promised that much—had to circle at least one planet on which the conditions for life were similar—No: not one! A myriad of such protein-laden spheres soared at inconceivable distances on orbits that held them, and if one really thought about it, then it was more a miracle that no contact had occurred until today. Now—finally!

His hands, not a whit more calm, received from those of the officer a thin folder without a label, furnished only with the stamp "Top Secret," half-smeared, an indication of nervous haste, with the request, or rather, the command: "Read it and then forget it immediately!" That produced bewilderment which, when the officer noticed it, prompted him to make some explanatory remarks:

"Es handelte sich um eine doppelte Verschlüsselung in zwei unterschiedliche Systeme, nacheinander zuerst in die einfache genetische Struktur der Coli-Bakterie, danach wurde diese, sagen wir mal, biologische Übersetzung noch einmal in die Sprache der Mathematik übertragen—eine knifflige Aufgabe! Wir haben die Decodierung der Einfachheit halber ausschreiben lassen, sie liegt vor Ihnen. Ich muß Sie aber darauf aufmerksam machen, daß Sie der militärischen Geheimhaltepflicht unterliegen, sowie dem Paragraphen achtzehn des Militärstrafrechts: Jede Weitergabe dieser Information wird kriegsgerichtlicher geahndet. Privat möchte ich hinzufügen: Ich habe mich dafür eingesetzt, daß Sie das überhaupt erfahren, man wollte Ihnen gegenüber die Aufzeichnung als durch die Enträtselungsversuche vernichtet ausgeben, aber Sie besitzen ja das Original. Ich habe es auf meine Kappe genommen, daß Sie es uns ausliefern werden, nachdem wir Sie eingeweiht haben. Enttäuschen Sie mich nicht, zwingen Sie mich nicht zu Maßnahmen, die . . ." Er machte eine verzichtende Geste mit der Hand: "Lesen Sie es doch erst einmal!" So glücklich und freudig, wie er in seinen Fantasien den Augenblick sich immer vorgestellt hatte, fand der Direktor ihn nun nicht mehr. Ob das Ergebnis möglicherweise die negativen Utopien von Science-fiction-Autoren bestätigten? Gegner weit draußen im All, ihre Todesstrahlengeschütze auf uns gerichtet, bösartige Geschöpfe, unsere Vernichtung planend?

"Lesen Sie's endlich!" Ungeduldige Aufforderung ohne Alternative. Raschelndes Deckelöffnen: Der maschinengeschriebene Text setzte mitten auf der Seite und mitten im Satz ein, und erwies sich wirklich als alles andere als die Lautwerdung molekularer Mechanismen.

". . . sagen die einen", las der Direktor, und Wort für Wort langsam weiter: "Die anderen sagen, das wäre zwecklos. Angeblich sollen damals alle historisch-politischen Landkarten eingezogen und vernichtet worden sein, um Nationalismus und Völkerhaß endgültig abzuschaffen, so daß man heute nicht mehr weiß natürlich, daß ich im Planquadrat HB Einhundertelf angesiedelt bin, aber da alle Planetarier in Planquadraten gleicher Größe wohnen, besteht unter ihnen weder Neid noch Mißgunst—zumindest nicht, was die räumliche Ausdehnung ihres Umfeldes betrifft. Die großen Städte wurden verähnlicht, indem zur Zeit der Planquadratreform hier und dort vorhandene historische Bauwerke abgetragen worden sind, weil sie Planquadratbewohner zur Identifizierung ihres Territoriums und damit zu neuen Suprematieansprüchen hätten verleiten können. Aber wir sind alle gleich. Und ich selber wohne eher mehr nördlich als südlich, ohne je mein Planquadrat zu verlassen, was auch mit enormen Schwierigkeiten verbunden, falls nicht ganz unmöglich wäre. Die Seitenlinien sind praktisch unüberwindlich. Was in benachbarten Quadraten geschieht, erfährt man durch Umdruck. Täglich kann man nachlesen, ob und was

"It was a matter of a double encipherment in two different systems, sequential first in the simple genetic structure of the coli bacterium, then this, let's call it a biological translation, again transcribed in the language of mathematics—a tricky job! For the sake of simplicity we had the decoding written out—it lies before you. But I must call to your attention that you are subject to the military code of secrecy as well as to Paragraph 18 of the military penal code: Any further transmission of this information will be punished by court martial. I would like to add, confidentially: I used my influence for you even to find this out. As far as you were concerned, they wanted to pretend that the recording had been destroyed during the effort to decipher it; but of course, you possess the original. I took the responsibility that you would deliver it to us after we let you in on the secret. Don't disappoint me, don't force me to take measures that . . ." He made a resigned gesture with his hand: "Just read it first!" The director no longer found this moment as happy and joyous as he had always supposed it would be in his imagination. Did the result possibly confirm the negative utopias of science fiction authors? Opponents far out in space, their death-ray weapons aimed at us, malicious creatures planning our destruction?

"Just read it!" Impatient request with no choice. Rustling as he opened the cover: The machine-written text began in the middle of the page in midsentence and proved to be anything but the utterance of molecular mechanisms.

". . . some say," the director read, and word by word slowly read on: "Others say that would be pointless. Supposedly at that time all historico-political maps were said to have been confiscated and destroyed, in order once and for all to get rid of nationalism and genophobia, so that it is today no longer known, naturally, that I am settled in grid square HB One Hundred and Eleven. But since all planetarians live in grid squares of equal size, there exists among them neither envy nor ill-will—at least not insofar as the spatial extent of their environs is concerned. The large cities were homogenized in that, at the time of the grid-square reform, existing historical structures here and there were pulled down because they could have induced residents of grid squares to identify their territory and to claim supremacy. But we are all equal. And I myself live more northerly than southerly, without ever leaving my grid square, which would involve enormous difficulties, supposing that it were not entirely impossible. The lines on the sides are practically insurmountable. What happens in neighboring squares is learned through circuprint. One can read up daily on sich jenseits der begrenzenden Grade ereignet hat. Aber—sagen die einen—nichts davon sei faktisch; und die anderen: Man müsse es nur richtig lesen, von hinten nach vorne und manchmal von unten nach oben, dann erführe man schon ungefähr die Wahrheit. Doch das berührt das Gebiet der Philosophie, von der ich nichts verstehe, da es zwei Richtungen gibt, die einander widersprechen, obwohl die eine gar nicht geduldet ist: sie lehrt, wie man hört, daß der Zweifel Grundlage jeglichen Denkens sei; ferner bestreitet sie die Existenz von Planetariern außerhalb unseres Quadrates und weist syllogistisch nach, daß das Sein unseres Gesamtplaneten vorgetäuscht wäre, ohne daß man den Zweck dieser Täuschung durchschaute—diesen zu erkennen und gleichzeitig zu konstituieren habe sich diese Philosophie zur Aufgabe gesetzt. Die andere, die erlaubte Richtung, erklärt, nichts sei Täuschung, sondern alles unwiderleglich und von begrüßenswerter Evidenz: Daraus resultiere unsere Pflicht, uns den Anforderungen des Quadrats zu unterwerfen, weil nur aus diesem die Sinngebung unseres Daseins herrühren könne. Die menschliche Gleichheit wird bestimmt von der ungleich höheren Wertigkeit des Quadrats, das den einzigen Bezugspunkt aller Moralität bildet. Doch das sind Probleme, denen unsereins nicht gewachsen ist. Ich bin nur ein einfacher Mann, der einen Wellenmodulator bedient, um die Nachbarquadrate über unser Quadrat zu informieren. Meine Aufgabe ist die reibungslose Übermittlung, nicht die Kontrolle der übermittelten Inhalte. Dafür bin ich nicht zuständig. Ich halte mich an meine Zahlenkolonnen, welche im Aggregat sich in unterschiedliche Quanten verwandeln, um abgesandt zu werden. Mit meiner Arbeit bin ich zufrieden. Sie ist besser als die am Anihilator, weil dort, wie es heißt, oftmals die zur Entzeitlichung Beorderten plötzlich gegen den Endzweck Widerstand leisten und ihre Freiwilligkeit abstreiten. Aber früher oder später gehen wir alle diesen Weg. Ich bin jedoch nicht ehrgeizig und habe mich erst für mein vierzigstes Lebensjahr zur Anihilation verpflichtet; das ist wenig vorteilhaft, wie man weiß. Es sind unter uns Auserwählte, die in ihrer Liebe zum Planquadrat und im Hinblick auf das allgemeine Wohlergehen sich beizeiten zu einer frühen Extermination melden, manchmal sogar das zwanzigste Lebensjahr als Schlußtermin eintragen lassen, um in Saus und Braus die Tage zu verbringen und überall Vorteile einzuheimsen, die ihnen gewährt werden müssen, sobald sie ihre Selbstverpflichtungskarte vorweisen. Trotzdem: Um einmal in der Woche baden zu dürfen, jeden Samstag tierisches Fleisch zu genießen, um einiger weiterer Bevorzugungen willen nach kurzer Frist den persönlichen Energiespeicher hingeben—dazu konnte ich mich nicht durchringen! Meine Moral ist eben nicht hoch. Obwohl ich einsehe, daß wir in unserem Quadrat keine anderen Möglichkeiten der Energiegewinnung besitzen, da die Generationen vor uns alles verbraucht haben. Im täglichen Umdruck whether anything and what has occurred beyond the bordering square. But —some say—none of that is factual, and others: You just have to read it right, from back to front and sometimes from bottom to top, then you would indeed find out the approximate truth. But that touches the realm of philosophy, of which I understand nothing, since there are two schools that contradict one another, although the one is not at all tolerated: It teaches, as one hears, that skepticism is the foundation of all thought; further, it disputes the existence of planetarians outside of our square and demonstrates syllogistically that the existence of our entire planet is simulated without our finding out the purpose of this simulation—to recognize this and at the same time to establish it is the task taken on by this philosophy. The other, the permitted school, declares that nothing is illusion, rather everything is irrefutable and of a welcome certainty. From this comes our obligation to submit to the requirements of the square because the meaning of our existence can proceed only from that. Human equality is determined by the much higher valence of the square, which forms the only reference point of all morality. But those are problems people like us are not equipped to handle. I am only a simple man who operates a wave modulator to inform neighboring squares about our square. My task is smooth transmission, not checking the material transmitted. I am not responsible for that. I stick to my columns of numbers, which in the aggregate are transformed into variable quanta to be broadcast. I am content with my work. It is better than the annihilator because there, as they say, those ordered to be detemporalized often suddenly resist the final purpose and deny their voluntariness. But sooner or later we all take that path. However, I am not ambitious and I have not obligated myself for annihilation until my fortieth year; that has few advantages, as you know. There are among us some chosen ones who, in their love for the square and with regard for the common good, volunteer in good time for early extermination, even sometimes have their twentieth year entered as their final date, so they can spend their days in riotous living and everywhere rake in advantages that must be granted them whenever they show their self-commitment card. Still, to be allowed to bathe once a week, to enjoy meat every Saturday, for the sake of a few more privileges to surrender one's personal energy accumulator after a short term—I couldn't force myself to do that! My morals are just not high. Even though I realize that in our square we have no other possibility of energy-gain, since the generations preceding us used everything up. In the daily circuprint you read again and again how liest man immer wieder, wie viele Anihilationen nötig sind, um unter anderem eine winzige Menge Eisen zu gewinnen! Glücklicherweise haben wir einen bedeutenden Populationsgrad, so daß wir vorerst an Human-Rohstoff keinen Mangel leiden. Neben jenen, die ehrlich der Gesellschaft nutzen wollen, treiben auch ethische Nichtse, Kriminelle geradezu, ihr Unwesen, indem sie wegen der erwähnten Privilegien die Verpflichtungskarten fälschen und wie die Made im Grünkohl leben. Die Umdrucke warnen ständig vor ihnen und bieten Prämien, falls man hilft, sie dem verdienten Abbau zuzuführen. Man wird mit zwei Vollbädern ausgezeichnet. Leider ist mir bisher nie einer untergekommen, so daß ich über die besondere Errungenschaft des Vollbades nichts mitzuteilen vermag. Meine eigene Limitierung schließt derartige Bevorzugungen aus. Aber herrlich muß es schon sein, staunenswert und ganz einmalig!

An einem anderen Körper jedenfalls durfte ich das Ergebnis wenigstens theoretisch bewundern, und diese Bewunderung verursachte mein Motiv, den Wellenmodulator zu privatem Zweck zu mißbrauchen. Über die Schändlichkeit meiner Tat bin ich mir im klaren. Aber ich will nicht, daß vergessen wird und untergeht, was ich erfahren mußte. Wen immer diese Botschaft erreicht, der möge wissen, daß es eine tiefere Treue gibt als die gegenüber einem Apparat, den redlich zu bedienen ich einstmals schwor. Den Schwur habe ich gebrochen, zu allen Konsequenzen bereit.

Vor Wochen, jedoch wenigen, und zwar im zentralen Reflektionspalast, wo man sich an arbeitsfreien Tagen damit unterhält, die eigene Gestalt verzerrt widergespiegelt zu sehen, begegnete mir eine weibliche Person. Anfangs gleichgültig, stellte sich bald Aufmerksamkeit ein, da wir wiederholt und zufällig uns in denselben Reflektoren zugleich betrachteten. Unsere ballongroßen Köpfe, die Rümpfe zu Anhängseln gesschrumpft oder zu Strichen verdünnt, verbuckelt, blasig aufgeschwollen, Albtraumgeschöpfen gleich, amüsierten uns herzlich. So gerieten wir ins Gespräch. Aus diesem, von dem ich jede Wendung, jeden Tonfallwechsel erinnere, entstand etwas mir bisher Ungekanntes zwischen uns, eine chemische Umwandlung der Ganglien, ungesteuert und beängstigend. Später, nachdem wir gemeinsam meine Unterkunft betreten, schien mir, unterwegs sei ich ein anderer geworden. Gleich darauf ruhte ich im Dämmerlicht und im Duft von Jugend, umarmt und umarmend, schweigend oder vielmehr wortlos miteinander sprechend, doch völlig verständlich für den jeweils anderen. Danach dann, wenn eins von uns beiden einen Satz gebar, etwa "Warum erst jetzt?" oder "Hast du vor einer Stunde daran gedacht?" und die Feststellung folgte, genau das gleiche habe der Zuhörende eben gedacht, zeigte sich wie weit die Übereinstimmung ging. Doch trotz meiner redseligen Einwände, daß der Gesichtssinn dem Tastsinn gleichwertig, wenn nicht gar überlegen wäre, scheute sie das Licht und kleidete sich vor dem Anschalten der Beleuchtung an.

many annihilations are necessary in order to obtain, among other things, a tiny amount of iron! Fortunately, we have a significant population level, so that for now we have no dearth of human raw material. Along with those who honestly want to be useful to society, there are ethical zeros, actually criminals, who do their mischief by counterfeiting commitment cards for the privileges mentioned and live like worms in cabbage. The circuprints warn about them constantly and offer premiums to those who help lead them to their deserved deconstruction. You are awarded two complete baths. Unfortunately, up to now not one has ever come to me, so that I am not able to furnish information about the salutary innovation of a complete bath. My own limitations preclude those kinds of privileges. But it must be splendid nonetheless, astonishing and quite unique!

"In another body, at any rate, I could at least theoretically admire the result, and this admiration formed my motive to misuse the wave modulator for a private purpose. I realize full well the dishonor of my deed. But I don't want what I had to experience to be forgotten, to perish. Whoever this message reaches should know that there is a deeper loyalty than that given to a machine that I once swore to operate honestly. I have broken that oath, am ready for any consequences.

"Weeks ago, though only a few, and in the central Palace of Mirrors, where on workfree days one can amuse oneself by looking at the distorted reflections of one's own figure, I encountered a female person. At first indifferently, but soon an attentiveness set in, since we repeatedly and by chance watched ourselves in the same reflectors at the same time. Our heads as big as balloons, our torsos shrunken to appendages or thinned into streaks, bent, swollen like blisters, like creatures from nightmares, we were heartily amused. So we happened to start a conversation. From the conversation, of which I remember every phrase, every change of intonation, there arose between us something I had hitherto not known, a chemical transformation of the ganglia, undirected and alarming. Later, after we entered my shelter together, it seemed to me that I had become someone else along the way. Immediately afterwards I rested in twilight in the aroma of youth, embraced and embracing, silent or rather talking together wordlessly but completely comprehensibly to the other one in question. After that, then—when one of the two us brought forth a sentence, something like 'Why just now?' or 'Did you imagine this an hour ago?' and the realization followed that the listener had just thought of exactly the same thing—it was clear how far our harmony went. But in spite of my voluble protestations that the sense of sight was equal to the sense of touch, if not superior to it, she avoided the light and dressed before the illumination was turned on.

Jedesmal sobald wir uns sahen, oder eben nicht sahen, nur blind spürten, stieg das Verlangen in mir, auch optisch überwältigt zu werden. Schließlich war der Drang derart unwiderstehlich, daß ich eines Abends, kaum daß sie sich vom Bett erhoben, den Schalter drehte. Gekränkt wandte sie sich von meiner Emphase ab, die gleich darauf erlosch, da mir der Grund ihrer bisherigen Heimlichkeit kenntlich wurde. Sie war frisch gebadet.

Der Unterschied zwischen einem gebadeten Körper und einem mittels regenerierter Flüssigkeit oberflächlich gereinigten, hatte mir die Finsternis verborgen—jetzt war er offenkundig! Glätte und Geschmeidigkeit der Haut, stärker durchpulst von vordem durchtränkender Wärme, als stünden alle Poren genießerisch offen, ein besonderer leiblicher Geruch, dazu die Lockerheit ihres Haares, alles, was ich ihrer Jugend zugeschrieben, einer in ihrem Falle großzügigeren Natur, mußte zum Teil auf das besagte Privileg zurückgeführt werden. Als mir nach meiner ersten Begeisterung und Verblüffung die Wahrheit aufging, nämlich daß sie sich für eine extrem frühe Anihilation entschieden hatte, begann mein Sensorium sich sofort gegen die Tatsache zu wehren, vor allem die Coronargefäße protestierten dagegen durch schmerzhafte Verkrampfung.

Während sie ihr Kleid überstreifte, ohne weitere Scheu vor der Helligkeit, meinte sie mit echter oder gespielter Gleichgültigkeit: So, nun weißt du es!

Mein Mund benötigte eine Weile, um ein einziges Wort hervorzubringen:

"Wann?"

Sie wenigstens hob erneut zu lächeln an, doch das Lächeln unterschied sich von den vorangegangen, vermutlich weil es eine keineswegs heitere Erklärung zu begleiten bezwungen wurde; an ihren einundzwanzigsten Geburtstag, hieß es dann, und um dialogische Weiterungen zu blockieren:

"Wir wollen nicht mehr davon reden!"

Meine Schätzung erlaubte ihr allerhöchstens siebzehn Jahre. Freilich war meine Kenntnis biologischer Entwicklungsstadien des anderen Geschlechts sehr mangelhaft. So versuchte ich, meine fragwürdige Vermutung zu verifizieren, was mir jedoch nicht gelingen wollte. Allen Fangfragen wich sie geschickt aus, selbst scheinbar nebensächlichen Erkundigungen nach ihrer Teilnahme an bekannten planquadratischen Ereignissen der letzten Jahre, von denen ausgehend ich genauere Berechnungen hätte anstellen können. Ihre Tasche zu untersuchen verlockte mich zwar, doch ein derartiger Vertrauensbruch wäre vielleicht unheilbar gewesen. Darum lebte ich mit ihr dahin in der peinigenden Gleichzeitigkeit von Glück und Unglück. Die Vorstellung, ihr Leib, der meinen überhaupt erst vervollständigte, würde in Kürze in Energie aufgehen, indessen ich als lebender

"Each time we saw one another, or didn't see one another, only blindly felt one another, the longing grew in me to be optically overwhelmed as well. Finally the urge was so irresistible that one evening, when she had scarcely gotten out of bed, I turned the switch. Offended, she turned away from my passion, which then immediately was extinguished, as I became aware of the reason for her previous secrecy. She was freshly bathed.

"The difference between a bathed body and one superficially cleaned by means of regenerated liquid had been hidden from me by the darkness—now it was obvious! Smoothness and suppleness of the skin, more strongly pulsating from the previous soaking warmth, as though all pores were hedonistically open, a special body odor, and in addition the looseness of her hair, everything that I had attributed to her youth, in her case to a more generous nature, had in part to be traced back to the aforementioned privilege. When I realized the truth, after my first enthusiasm and stupefaction, namely, that she had decided on an extremely early annihilation, my sensory faculties began at once to resist the fact, above all my coronary vessels protested with painful cramps.

"While she pulled on her dress, without further timidity because of the brightness, she said, with genuine or pretended indifference: So, now you know!

"It took my mouth a while to produce a single word:

" 'When?'

"She, at least, began to smile anew, but this smile was different from those before, presumably because it was forced to accompany a by-no-means pleasant explanation: on her twenty-first birthday, she said, and to block further dialogue:

" 'Let's not talk about it any more!'

"I estimated that she was no more than seventeen. Admittedly, my knowledge of the biological stages of development of the other sex was very deficient. So I tried to verify my questionable supposition, in which however I did not succeed. She adeptly dodged all leading questions, even apparently incidental queries about her participation in well-known grid-square events of recent years, proceeding from which I could have made more exact calculations. I was tempted to search her bag, of course, but such a breach of trust would perhaps have been irreparable. So I lived on with her in the painful coexistence of happiness and unhappiness. The idea that her body, which really for the first time made mine complete, would in a short while be turned into energy, when I remained behind as a living

Torso zurückbliebe, ohne Hoffnung auf Gewöhnung an die Amputation, verdrängte ich immer mühsamer, so daß es unser Zusammensein mehr und mehr vergiftete. Bis es eines Tages nach dem Aufstehen und Anziehen hieß:

"Ab morgen komme ich nicht mehr . . ."

Was besagte, daß der befürchtete Geburtstag bevorstand. Und als ob sie auf meine Weigerung, ein solches Ende zu akzeptieren, nur gewartet hätte, entkleidete sie sich erneut, keiner sie überredenden Argumente bedürftig und obwohl wir das Verbot nur zu genau kannten. Meine Nahrungsration reichte für uns beide, ich war kein Vielfraß, und ein besonderes Versteck war nicht aktuell: keiner würde den Ort ihres Verschwindens erraten, da wir immer erst am Abend zu mir gegangen waren. Das schützte auch meine Person, die bei Entdeckung unseres Vergehens ebenfalls der Entzeitlichung anheimfiele. Warum sollte sich nicht später irgendwann die Chance ergeben, unser Quadrat zu verlassen und in einem andern unterzuschlüpfen? Meine Anhänglichkeit an dieses hier hatte ohnehin eine starke Reduktion erlitten, und mir wäre jedes Quadrat recht, meinetwegen sogar keines, könnten wir nur zusammenbleiben. Als ich am nächsten Nachmittag vom Wellenmodulator heimkam, ruhte sie unter der Bettdecke, blaß, fiebrig, aus den Kissen klagend, daß sie noch niemals krank gewesen wäre. Wir hofften, ihr Unwohlsein stamme von der Aufregung, sich für eine eigene Zukunft entschieden zu haben, denn den öffentlichen medizinischen Dienst in Anspruch zu nehmen, verhinderte ja unsere Lage. Am darauffolgenden Morgen fühlte sie sich besser, ich ließ sie beruhigt allein, brach aber meine Arbeit vorfristig ab, Kopfschmerzen vortäuschend, und beeilte mich nach Hause, um dort eine Tote vorzufinden. Der Schock verweigert sich immer noch dem Berichtwerden. Ein gesundes Geschöpf, ohne besonders bedrohliche Symptome, und plötzlich verschieden. Nachdem mein Denken sich zu ordnen begann, schlußfolgerte es und wahrscheinlich zutreffend auf die Todesursache: Das unaufhörliche intensive Bewußtsein vom letzten Lebenstag muß eine Sperre herangezüchtet haben, die es verhinderte, das Datum zu überleben.

Wenigstens gelang es mir, ihre Gestalt unversehrt und somit unverarbeitet in eine natürliche Ewigkeit zu überführen. Nachts um zwei und in absoluter Finsternis bettete ich sie zwischen Rasenflächen und Gebüsch, wo die Erde locker ist und kein Blockbewohner den Fuß auf ihre Vergänglichkeit setzt. Nur den Spaten hatte ich vordem von Gartenarbeitern im Park stehlen müssen, um durch den Erwerb solchen Produktionsinstrumentes, der schriftlich zu begründen ist, nicht aufzufallen. Mit ihrem Verschwinden verließ mich fast zugleich die Fähigkeit, noch irgendetwas zu empfinden. Als seien alle feineren Nervenstränge sorgfältig aus meiner Physis herauspräpariert worden. Seitdem spiele ich manchmal mit dem torso, without any hope of becoming used to the amputation, I repressed with more and more effort, so that it more and more poisoned our being together. Until one day, after rising and dressing, she said:

" 'After tomorrow I won't be coming anymore . . .'

"Which was to say that the feared birthday was at hand. And as though she had only been waiting for my refusal to accept such an end, she undressed again, requiring no persuasive arguments and although we knew the prohibition only too well. My food ration was sufficient for both of us, I was no glutton, and a special hideout was not acute: No one would guess the place of her disappearance, since we had always gone to my place only at evening. That protected my own person also, which would also be subject to detemporalization on the discovery of our offense. Why shouldn't later, at one time or another, the chance come to leave our square and to seek refuge in another? My attachment to this one here had, in any event, suffered a heavy reduction, and any square would have been all right with me, for all I cared, none at all, if only we could remain together. When I returned home the next afternoon from the wave modulator, she was resting under the bedcovers, pale, feverish, complaining from the pillows that she had never ever been ill. We hoped that her indisposition came from the excitement of her having decided on her own future, since calling on public medical services was prevented by our situation. She felt better the following morning; reassured, I left her alone, but quit work early, pretending to have a headache, and hurried home to find a dead woman. The shock still refuses to allow description. A healthy creature, without especially threatening symptoms, and suddenly gone. After my thoughts began to collect themselves, I came to a decision—and probably an accurate one—about the cause of death: The incessant, intensive consciousness of the last day of life must have cultivated a barrier that prevented living beyond that date.

"At least I was successful in transfering her form intact and thus unprocessed into a natural eternity. At two o'clock in the morning and in absolute darkness I bedded her down between expanses of lawn and bushes, where the earth is light and no apartment block resident will set foot on her mortal remains. Only I had to steal the spade ahead of time from garden laborers in the park, in order not to attract attention by acquiring such a production implement, which must be justified in writing. With her disappearance I lost almost simultaneously the ability to feel anything at all: As though all the finer nerve centers had been carefully excised from my physique. Since then I play sometimes with the thought of

Gedanken, meinen Exterminationszeitpunkt vorverlegen zu lassen. Niemand existiert, dem ich mich eröffnen könnte. Es gibt keine Ermutigung, keinen Trost. Nur die abweisenden Gesichter rundum, ebenfalls geprägt, wie mir jetzt scheinen will, von verborgenen Leid, das nach Außen drängt und sich doch nicht zu äußern wagt. So bleibt es bei sachlichen Gesprächen. Über funktionale Vorgänge. Über anderes, meinen sowieso die meisten, lohne kein Diskurs, da eben nichts veränderbar wäre, denn es sei . . ."

Wie begonnen, so hörte mitten im Satz der Text auch auf, doch weil zugleich mit der Seite, wendete der Direktor sie um, stieß aber auf nichts weiter als den rückwärtigen Deckel aus schwarz-weiß marmoriertem Karton, der alles beendete. Für längere Dauer, wie lange, merkte er nicht, hielt er die Botschaft unbeweglich auf seinen Knien, leicht darüber gebeugt, als müsse doch noch etwas folgen, bis der Offizier hinter dem Schreibtisch sich ungeduldig räusperte, und der Direktor langsam den Blick hob. Bevor er zum Sprechen ansetzte, hüstelte auch er, und sagte dann:

"Ein erschüterndes Dokument kreatürlichen Leides . . ." war aber, ehe er verstummte, von der eigenen Banalität peinlich berührt. Besser man schwieg. Jedes emotional gefärbte Wort mußte in diesem kahlen Büro mit dem Bildnis des Staatspräsidenten an der Wand ironisch klingen, falsch, verlogen, wie in Anführungsstrichen. Und außerdem: Was eigentlich sollte man noch dazu sagen?!

Rasch entzog ihm der Offizier den Schnellhefter:

"Jede Mitteilung darüber an Dritte ist untersagt. Ich erwarte also, daß Sie so schnell wie möglich das Original ausliefern, damit es vernichtet werden kann . . ." Und weil der Direktor nur sprachloses Unverständnis darbot, ging er in seiner Erklärung weiter, als ursprünglich beabsichtigt:

"Ich brauchte es nicht, aber ich will Ihnen doch den Grund der Anordnung andeuten. Zwar sind wir keine wissenschaftlichen Koryphäen, trotzdem stellten wir fest, daß diese sogenannte Botschaft aus dem Universum keinesfalls von einem andern Planeten herrührt. Und wissen Sie warum? Weil der Absender seinen Senderstandort exakt angibt: Planquadrat HB Einhundertelf. Und genau das liegt dem neuesten Generalstabsplan nach in Mitteleuropa. Ja—es ist Mitteleuropa! Doch die Kenntnis soeben vollzogener globaler Planquadratierung kann niemand außer uns besitzen. Was schließen Sie daraus?"

Unmittelbarer Blick in die Augen des anderen, die Bestätigung der eigenen Hypothese abzulesen, was, nachdem es ohne Schwierigkeit gelungen, noch einmal wörtlich besiegelt werden sollte. Komplizenschaft war angestrebt, weil notwendig:

"Genau so ist es", sagte der Offizier, "ein bisher unkalkuliertes Phänomen der Relativitätstheorie, etwas wie ein Rückkopplungseffekt aus advancing the date of my extermination. There is no one to whom I can confide. There is no encouragement, no consolation. Only unfriendly faces all around, likewise marked—as it seems to me now—by concealed suffering that forces its way out and still does not dare to express itself. So we stick to technical conversations. About functional procedures. About anything else, in the opinion of most people anyway, no discourse is worthwhile, since nothing can be changed, for it is . . ."

Just as it began, the text also stopped in midsentence, but because it was the end of the page, the director turned it over, but found nothing more than the back cover of black-and-white marbled cardboard, which ended everything. For a rather long time, how long he did not notice, he held the message motionless on his knees, slightly bent over it, as though something still had to follow, until the officer behind the desk cleared his throat impatiently, and the director slowly raised his glance. Before he started to speak he, too, coughed and then said:

"A shocking document of creature suffering . . ." but, before he fell silent, he was painfully touched by his own banality. Better to keep silent. Any emotionally colored word in this bare office with the likeness of the state president on the wall had to sound ironic, false, untruthful, as though in quotation marks. And besides: What could one actually say to all that?

Quickly the officer took the folder away from him.

"Any communication about this to a third person is prohibited. So I expect you to deliver the original as fast possible, so that it can be destroyed." And because the director showed only speechless puzzlement, he continued his explanation farther than he had originally intended:

"I wouldn't have to, but I want to point out to you the reason for this order. Of course, we are not scientific big shots, but we nevertheless found out that this so-called message from the universe by no means originates from another planet. And do you know why? Because the sender gives his point of broadcast exactly: The grid square HB One Hundred and Eleven. And that, according to the most recent plan of the general staff, lies in Central Europe. Yes—it is Central Europe! But the knowledge of the global grid-square arrangement just completed can be possessed by no one but us. What do you conclude from that?"

A direct stare into the other's eyes to read the confirmation of one's own hypothesis, which, after that succeeds without difficulty, should be literally sealed again. Complicity was aspired to because it was necessary:

"That's just how it is," said the officer. "A phenomenon of the theory of relativity not calculated until now, something like a reverse linkage effect der Vierten Dimension ... Bildlich: Eine Flaschenpost von Überübermorgen ..." Achselzucken noch der begreiflichste Kommentar. Die beiden, von unaussprechbaren Überlegungen absorbiert, sahen zum Fenster hinaus und in die entlaubte Krone einer massigen Kastanie, durchsetzt von schwarzen Gestalten einiger Krähen oder Dohlen, wie ausgestopft reglos, einzeln und ohne Beziehung zueinander, als hätten sie einander schon lange nichts mehr mitzuteilen und ihr einziger Wunsch wäre bloß noch, von allen, auch der eigenen Gattung, in Ruhe gelassen zu werden.

RÜCKBLICK

Dem eignen fremden Leib
entschlüpft
ledig der Last
und aus der Ferne
einen verdorrten Leichnam
einen Kokon
seh ich an meinerstatt
Ein gewisser Tod
hatte sich bei mir angemeldet
erster Vorsitzender der guten
oder sogar besten Gesellschaft
aller denkbaren doch
ich entkam ihm
nordwärts in ein neues Hemd
und in Richtung
Ultima ratio

from the fourth dimension . . . Figuratively, a message in a bottle from the day after the day after tomorrow . . ." A shrug of the shoulders was the most understandable commentary. Both, absorbed in inexpressible reflection, looked out the window and into the leafless crown of a massive chestnut saturated with the black shapes of some crows or jackdaws, motionless as though stuffed, singly and with no connection to one another, as though for a long time they had had nothing more to communicate to one another, and their only wish was to be left in peace, by all things, even their own species.

ALW

RETROSPECT

Slipped
out of my own alien body
rid of this burden
and from afar
I see a withered corpse
a cocoon
in my place
A certain Mr. Death
had called at my house
first chairman of the good
or rather the best
of all possible societies yet
I escaped him
northward into a new shirt
and in the direction of
Ultima ratio

UKG

DER NEUE MENSCH

Sorgfältig umgestülpt
das Innerste nach außen
so daß ich ganz neu erscheine:
Der neue Mensch
sich selber fremd
wie es sich gehört
Mein Mund verzieht sich unsichtbar
während alle Geheimnisse
als verklumpte Arterien
und wirres Nervengeflecht offenliegen:
Nur darum
ist freundlich zu mir jedermann
drückt mir die Hand
daß ich nicht merke
wer ich bin

PLATZWECHSEL

Schmutzig der Stoff
an den Knien: Noch immer trage ich
die Hose so wie ich herkam
Tage gleich Jahreszeit
morgens Sonne mittags Hagel
gehen geschäftig draußen vorüber
indes ich nur
einen Schrank rücke Vorhänge befestige
Kisten öffne in denen mir
die Vergangenheit folgte
bruchsicher verpackt:
Nicht eine Erinnerung
wurde beschädigt
aber keine will mir mehr gehören
nachdem die Holzwolle sie
nicht länger verbirgt

THE NEW MAN

Carefully renovated
turned inside out
so that I appear all new:
The new man
stranger to himself
as is proper
My mouth distorts invisibly
while all my secrets
lie bare like a chaotic tangle of nerves
and clogged arteries:
Only for this reason
is everyone so kind to me
shakes my hand:
I must not notice
who I am

UKG

CHANGE OF ADDRESS

Dirty the knees
of my pants: I am still dressed
the way I arrived here
the days like the season
sun in the morning hail at noon
pass busily by outside
while I merely
move a wardrobe hang curtains
open boxes in which
my past has been following me
packed so as not to break:
Not one of my memories
was done any damage
but not one will belong to me anymore
now that the packing
no longer conceals them

UKG

KENNZEICHEN

Nirgendheim: Da kommen wir her
da fahren wir hin
Zwischen Glücksstadt und Freudenfeld
verhöhnen die Namen den Fremden
und das ist das bessere Los
statt untergehen im südchinesischen Meer:
Keiner versteht deine Sprache
keiner die letzte Botschaft
an die Welt so daß die Welt weitertickt
oder bloß währt

Verkannt
als Geste des Bettelns
deine ausgestreckte Hand eh sie fault:
Nichts bist du und nichts
wirst du: Matter Fleck
verwischte Zahl
stumm unter dem Zierrat kleiner Meldungen

Das Aussichtslose: Du in Person
leer der Blick die Gefäße geschwollen
ohne Kraft des Kopfes
von keiner Hypothese vorgesehen
einer Legende entstammend
in einer anderen sterbend
versehen mit vielen besonderen
Kennzeichen

HALLMARKS

Nowherehome: We come from there
we drive there
Between Glücksstadt and Freudenfeld
the names jeer at the stranger
and that is a better lot
than sinking in the South China Sea:
No one understands your language
no one the ultimate message
to the world so that the world ticks on
or simply lasts

Misread
as a gesture of begging
your outstretched hand before it rots:
You *are* nothing and you'll
be nothing: Faint spot
erased number
mute among ornaments of minor reports

The hopelessness: You in person
empty in the gaze the veins swollen
without power of mind
unforeseen by any hypothesis
emerging from one legend
dying in another
furnished with many special
hallmarks

ALW

SELBSTFINDUNG

Um Jahrtausende gealtert
auf einmal über Nacht:
Meine kannelierten Beine
vom Deckbett halb überwuchert
vermitteln mir nur noch
archäologische Eindrücke
Mein Auge starrt auf die Weite
des musterhaften Vorlegers
in Erwartung der Touristenschwärme
der Kunstfreunde der Altertumsforscher

Die ewige Materie
in Form von zerknüllten Laken
hält mich über dem Abgrund:
ich ahne dort Dunkelheit und Staub
die wahre Substanz der Vergangenheit

An diesen unbeweglichen Kopf
auf meinem marmorfarbenen Kissen
hat die Welt Mühen gewandt
und Hekatomben von Worten—
alles vergebens: es bleibt
der Stein Stein
stets

SELF-DISCOVERY

Aged by thousands of years
all at once overnight:
My fluted legs
half-stifled by the blanket
convey to me only
archaelogical impressions
My eye stares at the distance
of the perfect space rug
expecting swarms of tourists
art lovers archaelogists

Eternal matter
in the form of rumpled sheets
holds me over the abyss:
I sense there darkness and dust
the true substance of the past

Upon this unmoving head
on my marbled-hued pillow
the world has expended toil
and hecatombs of words—
all in vain: stone
always remains
stone

ALW

BEITRAG ZUR GEOLOGIE

Neben der Hülle aus Luft
und Dampf und Gift
umfängt aus Unglück eine
die Kugel

Morgens auf Fensterbrettern
schwarzer Niederschlag
täglicher und nächtlicher Trauer
verlorener Liebesmüh
verschwendet an gierigen Beton

gewesener Hoffnung
wie Papier verbrannt verflogen
millionenfach von den Unzähligen
und Überzähligen und so mißachtet

Ein gemessenes erfasstes Unglück
seiner Zukunft sicher
unstofflich sich verbreitend
und sich verbindend jedem Wort
des Bedauerns
jedem Lächeln wie ein Krampf
jedem Händedruck verräterisch
Gesten Gängen
Atem
der es bis zur Stratosphäre
trägt

ERFAHRUNGEN

Persönliche Erfahrungen in historischen Dimensionen vermögen oft, zumeist sogar, uns auf Dauer nicht zu beeindrucken. Oder wir versenken solche Erfahrungen in unseren tiefsten Schichten, um ihrer Unmittelbarkeit ledig zu sein. Wir wollen nicht wissen, was wir wissen. Freilich wirken sie aus ihrem Versteck heraus stärker auf uns ein als vordem, als wenn wir sie ständig im Bewußtsein parat hielten: als täglichen Maßstab, als permanente

CONTRIBUTION TO GEOLOGY

Next to the hull of air
and steam and poison
the globe surrounds one
with misfortune

Mornings on window sills
black deposits
daily and nightly mourning
for lost pangs of love
wasted on gluttonous concrete

of erstwhile hope
burnt like paper vanished
by the millions from the numberless
and superfluous and so ignored

A measured comprehended misfortune
certain of its future
spreading immaterially
connecting every word
of regret
every smile like a cramp
every handshake traitorously
gestures gaits
breath
that bears it up to the
stratosphere

ALW

EXPERIENCES

Personal experiences within historical dimensions often, for the most part even usually, are unable to impress us in the long run. Or else we sink such experiences into our innermost depths in order to be free of their immediacy. We do not want to know what we know. To be sure, they influence us more strongly from their hiding place than before, as though we had them continually close at hand in our consciousness: as a daily

Warnung, als Indikator, der bei Gefahr aufleuchtet. Ihnen entgegen erfahren wir aus dem absolut Unerheblichen anderes, von dem jedoch eine tiefe und anhaltende Beunruhigung ausgeht, die wir uns nie recht zu erklären verstehen. Ein winziges Stückchen abgeschnittener Haut vom Nagelbett, die einem nach Tagen, vielleicht bloß nach Stunden, zufällig wieder in die Finger gerät, hat für unseren Tastsinn alle Lebendigkeit verloren. Hart geworden, brüchig, fühlt sie sich fremd an, als sei's kein Stück von dir. Etwas Abgestorbenes, Zurückgebliebenes, das du warst und nicht mehr bist: So würde sich der Tod anfassen, könntest du ihn noch berühren, wenn es soweit ist: wie Material, fremd und fremdartig und gänzlich unbekannt.

Warum aber alles von dir Abgetrennte, Haut und Haar, Zähne und Nägel, sogleich diesem prozeß anheimfällt, gehört zu den Rätseln, deren Bestehenbleiben lebensnotwendig ist. Schutzmechanismus zeitweilig und auf besondere Weise belebter Materie, die sich um ihrer selbst Willen gegen solche Selbsterfahrung unbewußt sträubt.

TRAUM

Warum seine Bedeutung geringer sein soll als die des gelebten Lebens, ist unverständlich, denn ebendieses Leben wird nach einer gewissen Weile ihm gleichwertig. Indem der reale Augenblick unaufhaltbar weiter versinkt und dabei seine Intensität und Substantialität mehr und mehr einbüßt, wandelt er sich zum Bild, das, weil es nur erinnert, nicht mehr erneut erfahren werden kann, die Qualität jedes beliebigen Bildes in uns annimmt. Darum wirkt es, wenn wir es nach langer Zeit zufällig aus seinem Gedächtnisfach ziehen, seltsam unwirklich. Hat man tatsächlich erlebt, was einem da einfällt?

Besäße man nicht manchmal Indizien für die persönliche Vergangenheit, etwa Fotos, und allein deswegen hat sich diese Technik auch buschbrandartig verbreitet, es wäre fast unglaublich, daß man es selber gewesen ist, der am 16. Dezember 1972 vom der Spitze des Empire State Building in die Ferne geschaut, den Schmerz der Trennung von einem Freund, den Glauben an Fortschritt durch Regression besessen oder nicht doch alles bloß geträumt hat: Mittels dieser Erläuterung jedenfalls bewahrheitet sich Calderons trauriger Lustspieltitel "Das Leben ein Traum", gegen den eifrige Aufklärer vergebens Sturm gelaufen sind.

standard, as a permanent warning, as an indicator that lights up to signal danger. In the face of these we come to know, through the absolutely trivial, something else from which, however, a deep and constant uneasiness comes that we do not ever completely understand. A tiny piece of skin cut away from the cuticle that after a few days, perhaps only after a few hours, accidentally ends up between the fingers again has lost all sign of life to our sense of touch. Become hard, brittle, it feels strange, as if it were no part of you. Something that has died off, been left behind, that you were but no longer are: Death would feel like this, if you could still touch it when the time comes, like a substance strange and unfamiliar and totally unknown.

But why everything that is severed from you, skin and hair, teeth and nails, immediately falls subject to this process is one of those riddles whose continuing existence is necessary for life. The defense mechanism, temporarily and in a special way, of living matter, which for its own sake unconsciously resists such self-knowledge.

SZ

DREAM

Why its significance should be less than that of lived life is incomprehensible, for this very same life becomes, after a certain amount of time, of equal value to it. While the actual moment sinks inexorably away and, as a result, loses more and more of its intensity and substance, it is transformed into an image that, because it is only a memory and can no longer be experienced anew, takes on the quality of any arbitrary image within us. For this reason it seems, when after a long time we happen to draw it out of its place in our memory, strangely unreal. Did one really experience what then comes to mind?

If we did not sometimes possess evidence of our personal past such as photographs (and solely for this reason did this craft spread like wildfire), it would be practically impossible to believe that we were the ones who on 16 December 1972 looked off into the distance from the top of the Empire State Building, felt the pain of parting from a friend, possessed a belief in progress through regression, or whether we did not simply dream it all. By means of this explanation, in any case, the title of Calderon's tragi-comedy, *Life as a Dream*, which the zealous men of the Enlightenment attacked in vain, proves to be true.

SZ

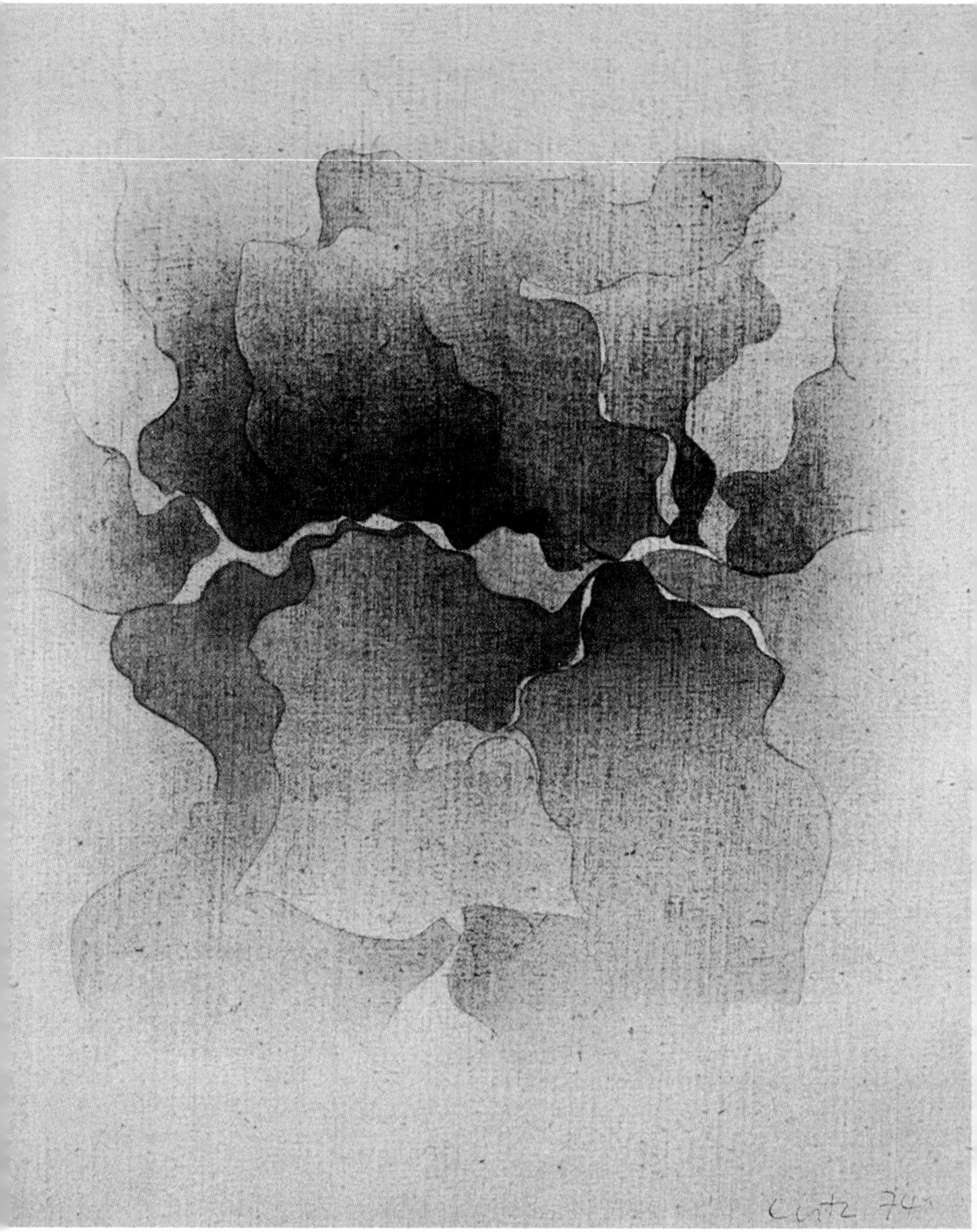

Untitled (1974)

Untitled

Werner Lutz

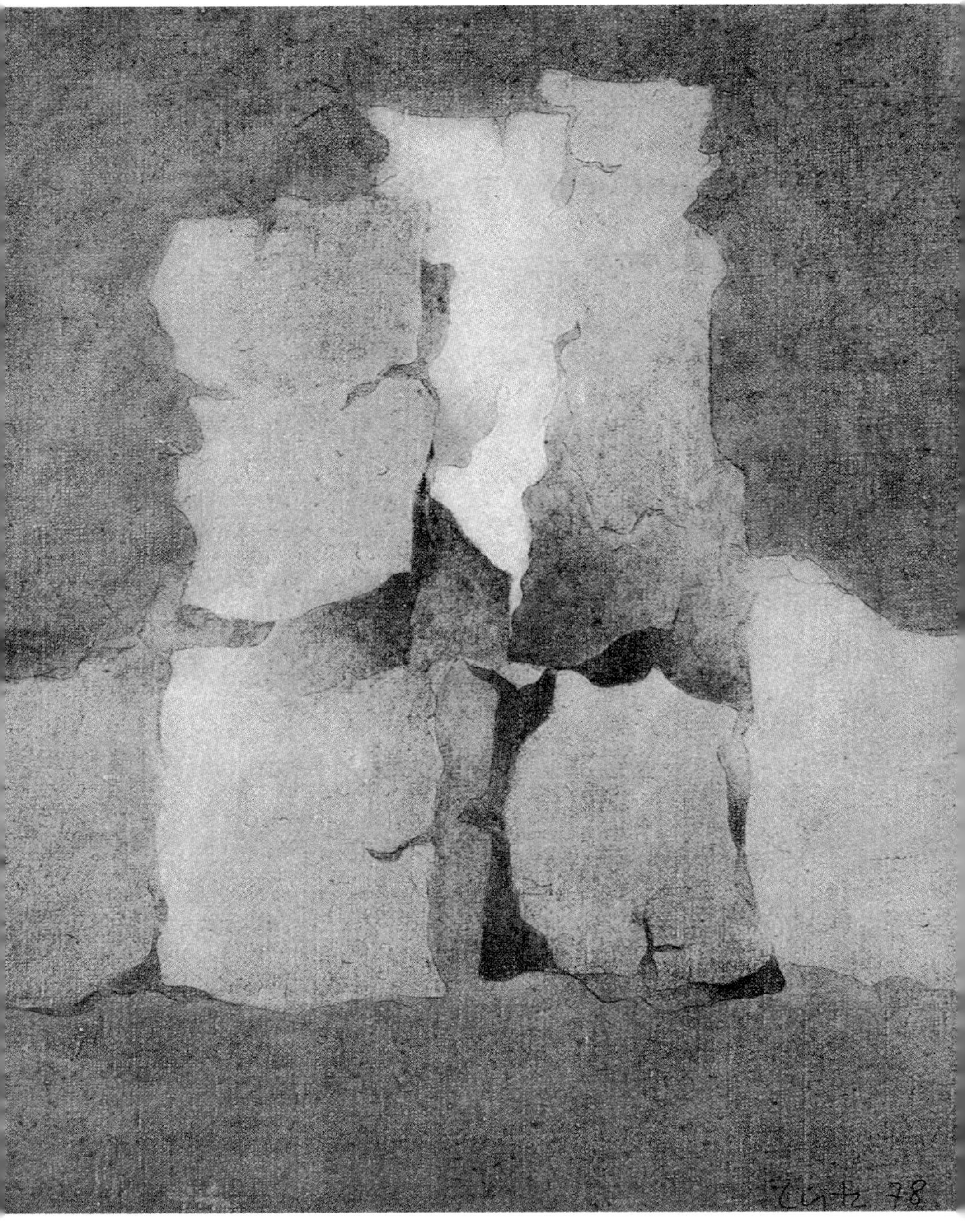

Untitled (1978)

Untitled

ICH BRAUCHE DIESES LEBEN UND ANDERE GEDICHTE

WERNER LUTZ

ICH BRAUCHE DIESES LEBEN

Ich brauche dieses Leben
dieses verlorene Wort in dem ich wohne.
Ich brauche den Schritt aus der Wand
in dieselbe Wand.
Ich taste mich durch meine Blindheit.
Ich brauche sie. Sie ist mein Maß.

Schwebend die Dunkelheit
über die ich gehe
während das Licht den Morgen zeichnet.
Schwebend die Dunkelheit
über die ich gehe
während der Abend seine Kuppel baut.

DIE EBENEN MEINER TAGE

Die Ebenen meiner Tage. Die Hügel
meiner Tage. Die versteinerten Herden.
Das verblühte Licht.
Die Hilflosigkeit, die ich anpflanzte.
Der Regen, der in mir wächst.
Mein unversehrter Glaube. Mein verschüttetes Lachen.
Dieses Leben, dieser Tod
die mir zurufen mit meiner eigenen Stimme
die mir winken mit meiner eigenen Hand.

I NEED THIS LIFE AND OTHER POEMS

WERNER LUTZ
translated by Timothy A. Bonner-Saroff

I NEED THIS LIFE

I need this life
this forlorn word in which I dwell.
I need the step out of the wall—
through the same wall.
I grope through my blindness.
I need it. It is my dimension.

Suspended darkness
past which I go
while the light marks morning.
Suspended darkness
past which I go
while the evening builds its dome.

THE PLAINS OF MY DAYS

The plains of my days. The hills
of my days. The petrified hearths.
The faded light.
The helplessness that I cultivated.
The rain that grows in me.
My undamaged faith. My spilled laugh.
This life, this death
that call to me with my own voice
that beckon to me with my own hand.

Hand, in der sich die Wünsche treffen
um sich zu quälen.
Hand, in der die Traurigkeiten zusammenkommen
um sich zu lieben.
Die Gärten fließen ineinander
in dieser Hand.

AUF MIR WÄCHST DER SOMMER

Auf mir wächst der Sommer.
In mir summt der Honig.
Meine Hände sind Wind und Schwalbe zugleich.
Ich spreche
die verschiedenen Sprachen der Halme.
Ich lache das irre Gelächter der Gerüche.
Ich lebe mein Leben und das der anderen.
Ich trete in die Bilder ein.
Ich schreibe Laub und Schatten
und werde zu Laub und Schatten dabei.

DIE GEFALTETEN HÄNDE UNTER DER ERDE

Die gefalteten Hände unter der Erde.
Die wenigen Augenblicke über der Erde
die zu blühendem Flieder werden.
Die Bäume, wie sie unmerklich weiterziehen.
Die summenden taumelnden Spuren
unserer Wünsche in der Luft.

Ich warte auf etwas, das mich atemlos macht.
Ich beuge mich über verstummte Stimmen.
Ich horche entflogenen Hoffnungen nach.

Hand, in which my desires meet
in order to torment.
Hand, in which my sorrows gather together
in order to love.
The gardens flow into one another
in this hand.

THE SUMMER GROWS UPON ME

The summer grows upon me.
The honey hums in me.
My hands are wind and swallows alike.
I speak
the various languages of blades of grass.
I laugh the crazy laughter of scents.
I live my life and the lives of others.
I step into the pictures.
I write leaves and shadows
and thereby become leaves and shadows.

THE FOLDED HANDS UNDER THE EARTH

The folded hands under the earth.
The few moments upon the earth
which turn into blooming lilacs.
The trees, how they advance unnoticed.
The humming reeling traces
of our desires in the breeze.

I wait for something that takes my breath away.
I humble myself over silenced voices.
I hearken to hopes flown away.

TRIPLET
UND ANDERE BILD-GEDICHTE

FRIEDERIKE MAYRÖCKER

TRIPLET

weeping window

weeping willow

weeping widow

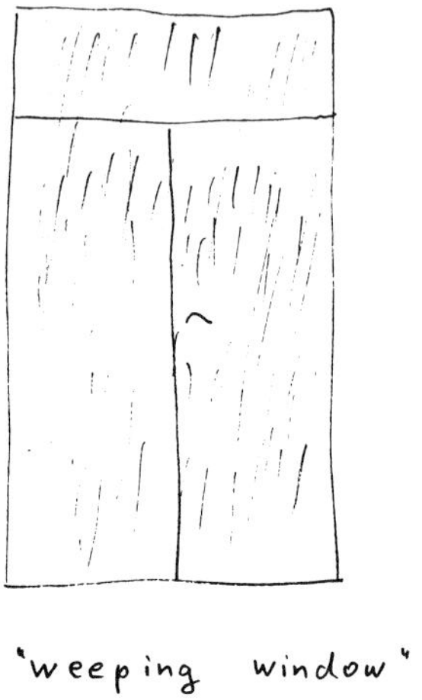

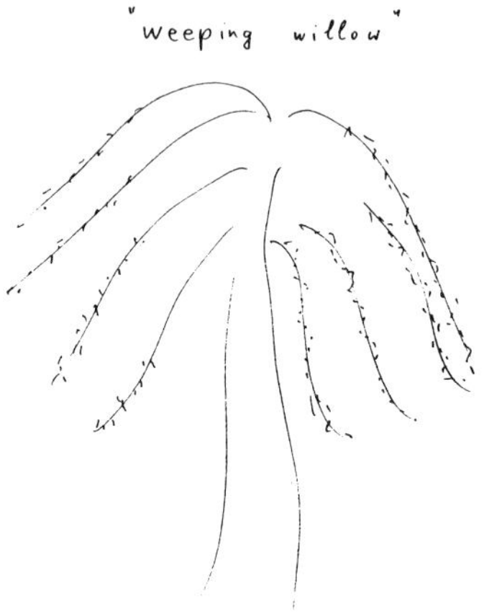

EINE SEKUNDE IN DER EWIGKEIT

1

colombofile seele!

→ tanzungen tanzungen tanzungen
→ huldigung wilhelmsbad
→ tanzungen tanzungen tarnzungen
→ huldigung willibald
→ tarnzungen tarnzungen tarnzungen
→ lob des schwans

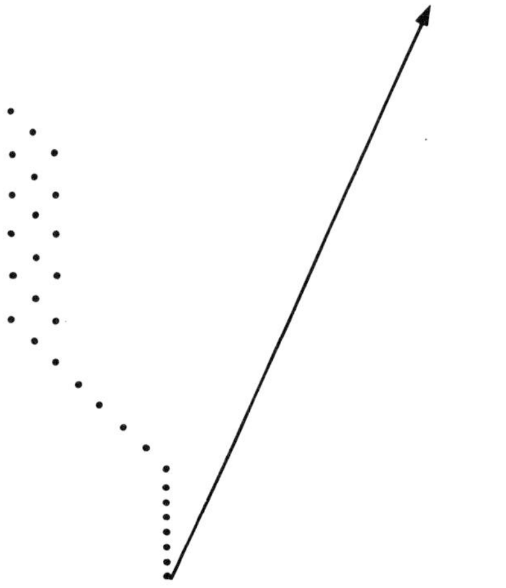

TRIPLET
AND OTHER IMAGE POEMS

FRIEDERIKE MAYRÖCKER
translated by Michael P. Elzay

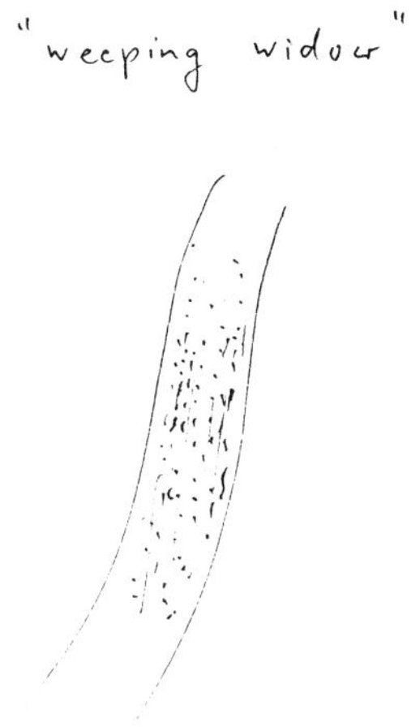

ONE SECOND IN ETERNITY

1

columbine soul!

→ dancings dancings dancings
→ homage to wilhelmsbad
→ dancings dancings maskings
→ homage to willibald
→ maskings maskings maskings
→ praise to the swan

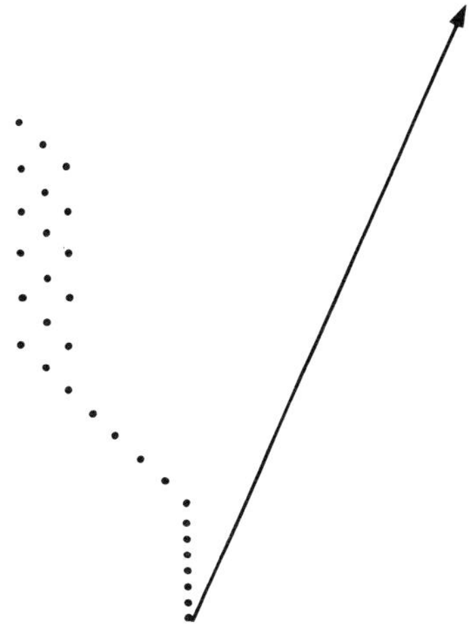

2

3.) ++++++++++ +++

5.) klematis rosen & gehölz

4.) (=himmelsmechanik)

2.) auf der rübenhalde
1.) federbett

LANDMARK

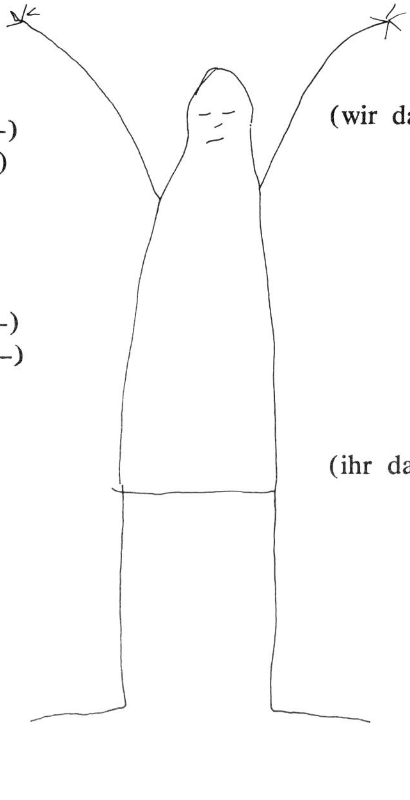

1

(wir da oben —)
(ihr da unten—)

2

(wir da oben —)
(ihr da unten —)

(wir da oben —)

(ihr da unten—)

2

3.) +++++++++++++

5.) clematis roses & copse

4.) (=unearthly contrivance)

2.) on the turnipslope
1.) comforter

LANDMARK

(wir da oben —)

1
(we up here—)
(you down there—)

2
(we up here—)
(you down there—)

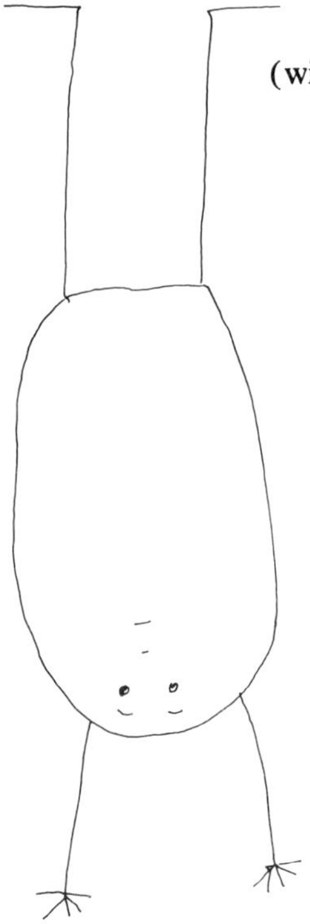

(ihr da unten —)

Christoph Meckel

The thing is there

Das Dings ist da

DAS DINGS DA
Eine Auswahl

CHRISTOPH MECKEL

then it overdoes a little

dann übertreibt es ein bißchen

THE THINGAMAJIG
A Selection

CHRISTOPH MECKEL
translated by Ralph R. Read III

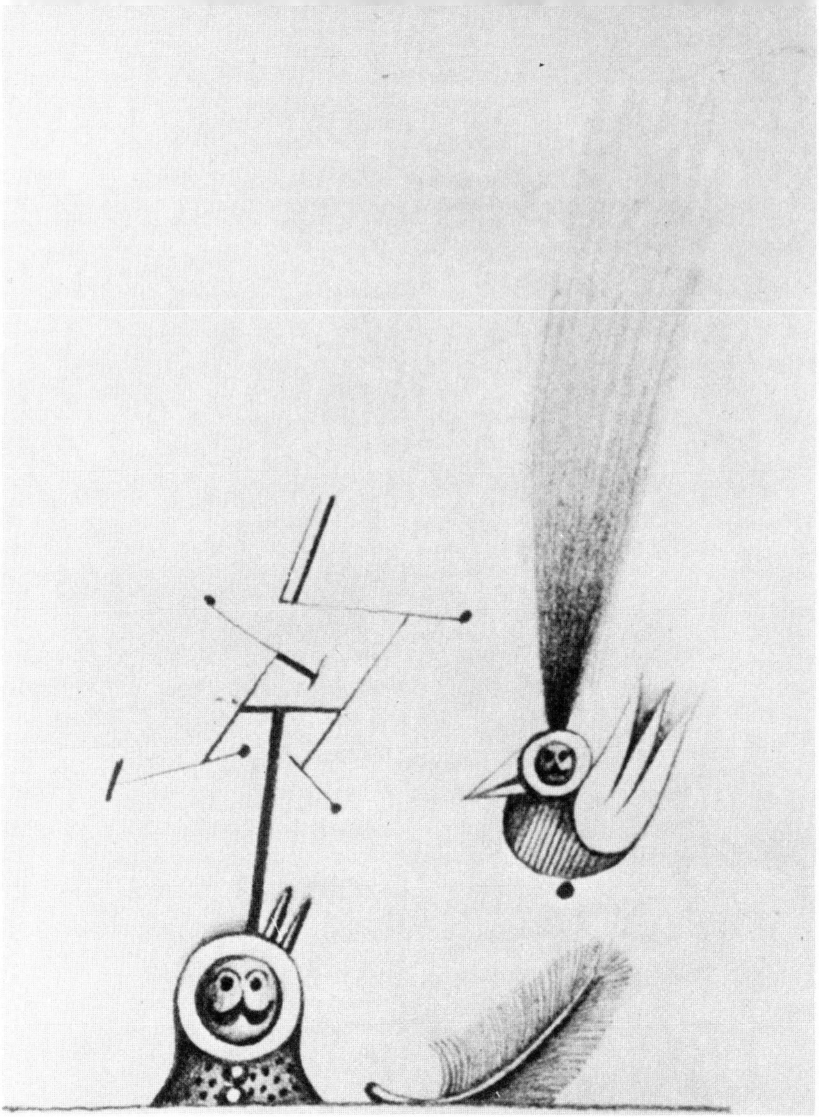

then it overdoes a little more

dann übertreibt es wieder ein bißchen

then it receives a visitor

dann bekommt es Besuch

then it swallows a frog

dann hat es einen Frosch verschluckt

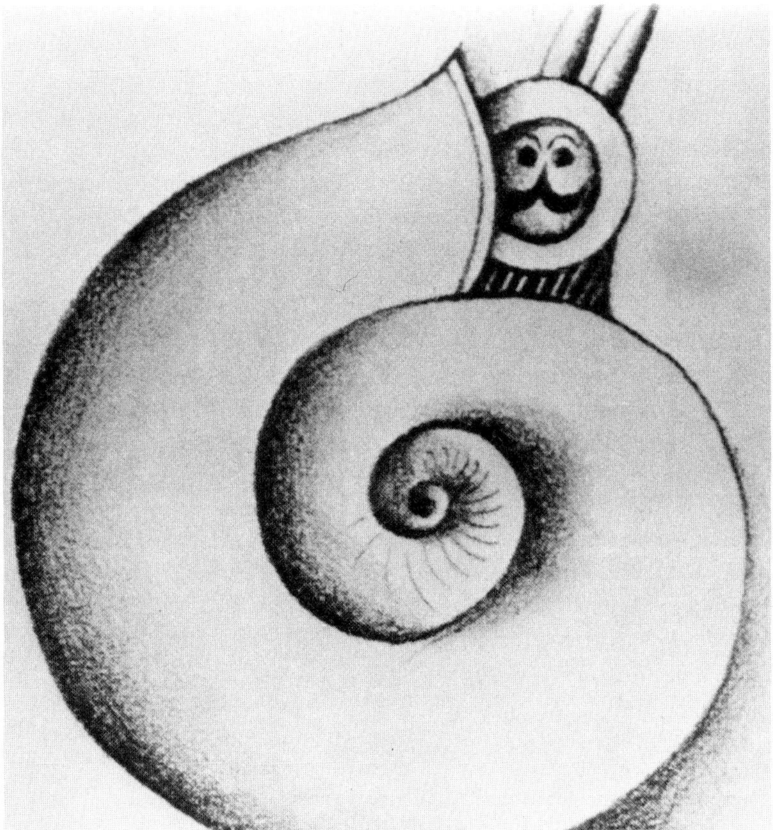

then it feels right at home

dann fühlt es sich wie zuhause

then it expects applause

dann erwartet es Beifall

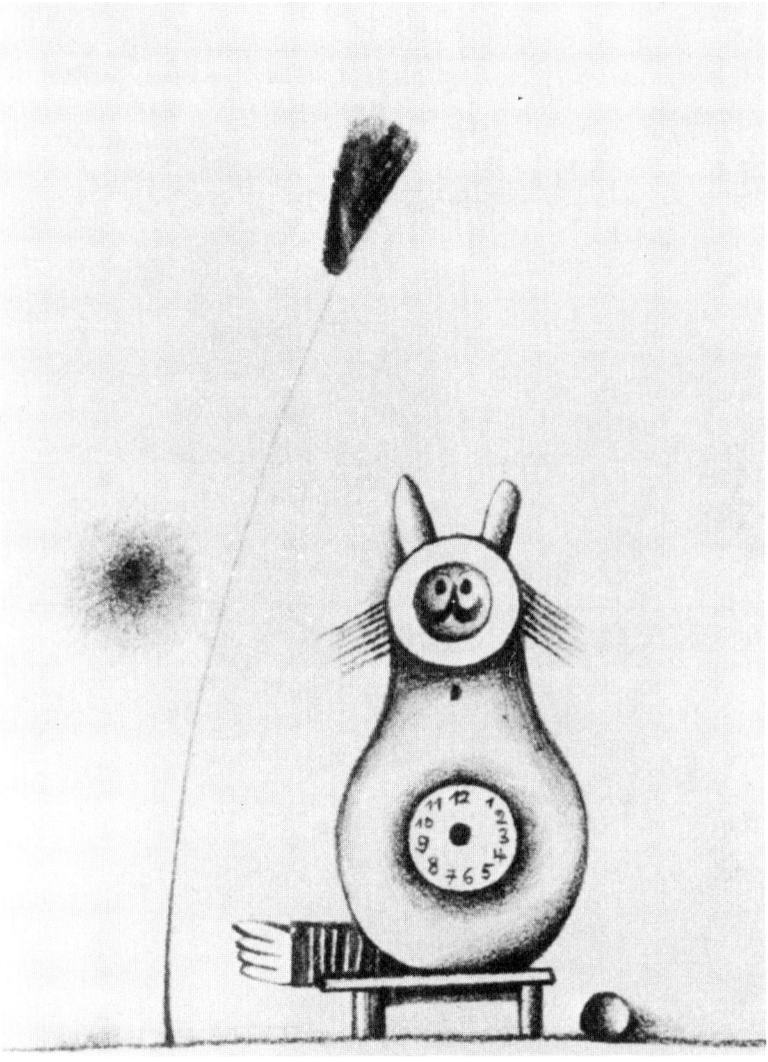

then it swallows a clock

dann hat es eine Uhr verschluckt

dann ist es weg

then it is gone

BERICHT VOM HANDWERK

CHRISTOPH MECKEL

1

Schlaflos, in einer Märznacht, entdeckte ich das Wort Rabe. Ich drehte und wendete, wiederholte das Wort, bis ich die Sache—den Vogel—allmählich vergaß. Ich trainierte vielleicht eine Stunde lang, variierte Lautstärke und Betonung der Silben, bis nichts mehr vom Vogel da war außer dem Wortlaut. Rraabe Rraabe Rraabe. Raab—Raab—Raab—bbe—bee-bbe. Raha Raha—Rahaha. Rrbe Rrbe Rrbe. Ra ra ra. Rabbee Rabbee Rabbee. Brr—raabrr—raabrr—raa. Raberaberaberabera. Rabpe Rabpe Rabpe. Raa—bee Raa—bee Raa—bee. Rabe Rabe Rabe.
Der Wortlaut gehörte keiner Sprache an, hatte nichts mit Sprache oder Musik zu tun, Zweisilbenlaut ohne Sinn in meiner Hypnose, bedeutungslos, eine leere Logik aus Wortlaut. Dann holte ich, ohne an Sprache zu denken, den namenlosen Vogel in mein Gedächtnis, die Leibhaftigkeit des Raben ohne Wortlaut. Ich vergegenwärtigte Flügel, Auge, Gestalt, Bein, Kralle, Schnabel, den fettigen Glanz der Federn und seine Sprache: Krächzen, schnarrender Rachen (ich hatte den Raben morgens im Nebel gehört, das heißt: ein Krächzen gehört und Rabe gedacht). Ich ließ den Namen des Vogels in meiner Sprache, den Wortlaut Rabe, den ausgelaugten Klang, zurück im Bild der schwarzen Gestalt, das mein Tausend-Raben-Gedächtnis verfertigt hatte, federlich, äugig, schnabelig, beinig, rabenkörperliche Suggestion. Ich sah ihn, hörte ihn, sagte ihn: Rabe. Er war da, mein Rabe, nicht länger in Arbeit. Vorausgeflogen in ein Gedicht.

2

Süddeutscher Herbst, Oktobernebel, Nüsse in fauligen Schalen, der Duft neuen Weins. Apfelgeruch in Hausfluren, stürzendes Obst in den Gärten, matschiger Donner—Gewitter für einen Maulwurf. Nasse Abende und leere Straßen. Mit Freunden fuhr ich in ein Gasthaus aufs Land.
Dort wurde gegessen und getrunken bis spät. Ein leeres Glas fiel vom Tisch, rollte zwischen die Schuhe, wurde aufgehoben und eine Stimme

REPORT ON MY CRAFT

CHRISTOPH MECKEL
translated by Ralph R. Read III

1

Sleepless, one night in March, I discovered the word raven. I turned and twisted, repeated the word, until I gradually forgot the thing—the bird. I practiced for perhaps an hour, varied the volume and stress of the syllables, until nothing was left of the bird but the sound pattern. Rraaven rraaven rraaven. Raav—raav—raav—vven—veen—vven. Raha raha—rahaha. Rrven rrven rrven. Ra ra ra. Ravveen ravveen ravveen. Vrr—raavrr—raavrr—raa. Raveraveraveravera. Ravfen ravfen ravfen. Raa—veen raa—veen raa—veen. Raven raven raven.

The sound pattern was not part of any language, had nothing to do with language or music, a two-syllable sound without any sense in my hypnosis, meaningless, an empty logic of sound. Then, without thinking of language, I brought the nameless bird into my memory, the corporeality of the raven without sound. I called to mind wing, eye, shape, leg, claw, beak, the oily gleam of the feathers, and its language: croaking, rasping beak (I had heard the raven in the morning fog, that is: heard a croaking, and thought raven). I allowed the name of the bird to return to my language, the sound-pattern raven, the leached-out tone, in the image of the black shape that my thousand-raven-memory had fashioned, feathered, eyed, beaked, legged, raven-bodied suggestion. I saw it, heard it, said it: raven. It was there, my raven, no longer in the works. Flown on ahead into a poem.

2

Southern German autumn, October fog, nuts in decaying shells, the fragrance of new wine. Smell of apples when you enter a house, fruit tumbling down in gardens, muddy thunder—rainstorm for a mole. Wet evenings and empty streets. I drove to a country inn with friends.

There we ate and drank until late. An empty glass fell from the table, rolled among the shoes, was picked up, and a voice said: MISBEHAVIOR sagte: UNGESCHICKT LÄSST GRÜSSEN! Der Satz—nichts Besonderes, eine alltägliche Wendung—schnitt ins Gehirn und setzte sich fest. Ich folgte noch den Erzählungen, redete selbst, aber der Satz schlug durch alle Gespräche, stellte sich quer und besetzte jeden Gedanken. Der Bodensatz des Gedächtnisses wirbelte hoch. Ich erkannte, noch unscharf, den Anfang eines Gedichts.

UNGESCHICKT LÄSST GRÜSSEN. Gehört und Gedankennerven waren in Aufruhr, bemächtigten sich des eingedrungenen Wortlauts (fremder Körper in einem Ameisenhaufen), belauerten jede Silbe und ihr Geräusch, horchten auf Nebengeräusche und mögliches Echo—sie belagerten den noch uneinnehmbaren Wortlaut. Der Satz war brauchbar, kein Zweifel möglich, aber etwas irritierte noch. LÄSST GRÜSSEN—der zweite Teil des Satzes war brauchbar. Irgendwer oder irgendwas ließ grüßen, der Gruß kam aus Entfernungen, die ich nicht kannte und durchmaß einen Raum, der noch bestimmt werden konnte. Der Gegrüßte (zunächst das vom Wortlaut betroffene, Wein trinkende Ich) konnte im Fortgang der Arbeit umrissen werden. Aber UNGESCHICKT—das war noch zu wenig. Die Silbe UN konnte bleiben—bare Magie. Die schnelle Bewegung der Silbe, das dunkle U, der nasale, schwere schwebende Ausklang N, die in der Silbe enthaltene Negation, schließlich der Charakter der Silbe, archaischer Laut aus Vorwelt, Legende, Traum—das Königreich Unn, der Feuergeist Unn (alter Bekannter des Asmodäus), die Ebenen und Flüsse des Landes Unn, das Gebirge Unn. Die Silbe UN also war verwendbar, das mit ihr verbundene GESCHICKT noch beliebig. Das war nicht umfassend, nicht radikal genug, enthielt mehr Zufall als Notwendigkeit und blieb episodisch. Das schlenkerte im Gefolge des UN und war nicht persönlich genug für meinen Gebrauch. Unfug, Unsinn, Ungestalt, Ungeheuer, Ungemach, Ungeduld oder Unding—das alles traf nicht den Charakter des Worts, das mir fehlte. Vielleicht war im Wortlaut eine Silbe zuviel. Ich war nicht sicher, aber das schien es zu sein. Der Satz und das Wort verlangten nach EINER Silbe. Also, was fehlte noch?

Während der Fahrt durch den Nebel, spät in der Nacht, war die Silbe da. Sie lautete GLÜCK. Also: UNGLÜCK läßt grüßen. War die Silbe—das einzig mögliche Wort—ein blinder, glücklicher, unverdienter oder verdienter Zufall? Hatte ich es erfunden, gefunden, entdeckt? Hatte ich es aus dem Gedächtnis gegraben, erarbeitet, ausgedacht, eingefangen, geködert? War es ein Einfall oder eine Idee? Kam es ans Licht geflogen—aus welcher Versenkung? Hatte ich es aus Soll und Haben errechnet, Ergebnis lyrisch—privater Algebra? Der Satz war vollkommen. UNGLÜCK LÄSST GRÜSSEN. Das war mein Satz, nicht nötig, ihn zu notieren. Er gehörte mir und konnte sich nicht entziehn. Was immer geschah und wo immer ich war—der Satz mußte wiederkommen zu seiner Zeit.

SENDS GREETINGS! The sentence—nothing special, an ordinary expression—cut into my brain and took hold. I kept on listening to the storytelling, talked myself, but the sentence broke through all conversations, thwarted and occupied every thought. The dregs of memory swirled up. I recognized, still vaguely, the beginning of a poem.

MISBEHAVIOR SENDS GREETINGS. Overheard and brain waves were in an uproar, took possession of the intruding sound pattern (foreign body in an ant hill), stalked every syllable and its sound, listened for static and possible echo—they besieged the still unconquerable sound pattern. The sentence was usable, no doubt about it, but something was still irritating. SENDS GREETINGS—the second part of the sentence was usable. Somebody or something sent greetings, the greetings came from distances that I did not know and traversed a space that could still be determined. The one greeted (initially the I who was struck by the sound pattern while drinking wine) could be outlined in the course of the work. But MISBEHAVIOR—that was still too little. The syllable MIS could stay—pure magic. The swift movement of the syllable, the dark S, the nasal, heavy hovering ebbing M, the negation contained in the syllable, finally the character of the syllable, archaic sound from prehistory, legend, dream—the kingdom of Mis, the fire spirit Mis (old acquaintance of Asmodeus), the plains and rivers of the Land of Mis, the mountains of Mis. So the syllable MIS was usable, the BEHAVIOR connected to it still optional. It was not comprehensive, not radical enough, contained more coincidence than necessity, and remained episodic. It shambled along behind the MIS and was not personal enough for my use. Mischief, mistake, misfit, miscreant, mishap, misapprehension, misbegotten—none of those fit the character of the word I was lacking. Perhaps there was one syllable too many in the sound pattern. I was not sure, but that seemed to be it. The sentence and the word demanded only ONE syllable. So what was still missing?

During the drive through the fog, late at night, the syllable was there. It was CHANCE. Thus: MISCHANCE sends greetings. Was the syllable—the sole possible word—a blind, lucky, deserved or undeserved coincidence? Had I invented it, found it, discovered it? Had I dug it out of my memory, extracted it, contrived it, entrapped it, lured it? Was it an inspiration or an idea? Had it come flying into view—out of what hollow? Had I calculated it from my assets and liabilities, lyrical bottom line—from my private algebra? The sentence was perfect. MISCHANCE SENDS GREETINGS. That was my sentence, not necessary to jot it down. It belonged to me and could not escape. Whatever happened and wherever I was—the sentence had to return again in good time.

Die Zeit für den Satz kam in derselben Nacht. Gegen Morgen schrieb ich ein Gedicht, zwei gereimte Strophen, korrigierte wenig und legte es weg. Zusammenhängender Vorgang von einer Stunde. Weder Mühe noch Willensleidenschaft. Ich kann nicht behaupten, die Verse GEMACHT zu haben, ein seltener Fall. Das Gedicht lief durch die Reime wie Wasser durch Gras. Ich schrieb das Gedicht, als befreie es sich, mit meiner Hilfe, aus der Verhaftung durch einen Stoff, den das Gedächtnis versteint hielt. Urelement des Gedächtnisses, älter als ich, elementare Gestaltlosigkeit, überlagert von Schichten der Erinnerung, babylonische Stille, in der sich die Vorformen möglicher Sprache bewegen, Höhle voll Echo auf Nichts, auf Welt und Vorwelt. Unerlöstheit. Sesam. Schlangengrube.
Die Tiefenpsychologie hat dargestellt, daß solche Vorgänge nichts Besonderes sind. Sie sind den Menschen, die SPRACHE MACHEN, gemeinsam, wirbeln durch ihre Träume und unterhöhlen ihr Denken. Sie provozieren Skepsis, Selbstkritik und Verstand, schärfen Gehör und Optik und beunruhigen ihre Neugier. Sie strapazieren ihren Instinkt und ihre Geduld. Sie beschämen ihr Wissen. Wie immer dieser Prozeß erklärt werden kann—als Erfahrung des einzelnen bleibt er ungeheuer. Er erlaubt kein anwendbares System von Handwerk, er ermöglicht oder bestätigt keine Methode. Jeder Wortlaut und jedes Gedicht stellt den homo faber vor eine erstaunlich unvollendete Tatsache. Was in der Nacht und im Wein geschrieben wird, kann sich am folgenden Tag als Klapphorn erweisen. Es kann unleserlich oder unlesbar sein. Schmierpfote, Kauderwelsch, Krakel des Dummen August. Mein Tag war gut, das Gedicht erwies sich als haltbar. Ein Reimpaar schien noch zu flattern, ich tauschte es aus, der Ersatz war Willkür oder Bricolage, bestätigte die Haltbarkeit des ersten, und ich nahm ihn zurück. Das Gedicht war fertig und der Titel—LIED—durch nichts zu ersetzen.

Schlief ich, da nachts vorm Haus
anhielt ein Wagen;
sprang der Kutscher heraus:
Unglück läßt fragen
wenn du was nötig hast
sollst dus ihm sagen,
Unglück wär gern dein Gast
und Wegbereiter,
komm, wenn du Zeit für ihn hast,
Unglück muß weiter.

The time for the sentence came the same night. Towards morning I wrote a poem, two rhymed verses, revised a little and put it aside. Cohesive process of one hour. Neither effort nor willful passion. I cannot claim that I MADE the lines, a rare occurrence. The poem ran through the rhymes like water through grass. I wrote the poem as if it were liberating itself, with my help, from imprisonment in a substance that memory held petrified. Primal element of memory, older than I, elemental formlessness, overlain by strata of recall, Babylonian silence in which the pre-forms of possible language move, cavern full of echoes of nothing, of world and pre-world. Unredeemedness. Sesame. Snake pit.

Psychoanalysis has shown that such processes are nothing special. They are characteristic of people who MAKE LANGUAGE, swirl through their dreams and undermine their thought. They provoke skepticism, self-criticism, and reason, sharpen hearing and vision, and unsettle their curiosity. They strain their instinct and their patience. They put their knowledge to shame. No matter how this process may be explained—as the experience of an individual it remains immense. It allows no applicable system of a craft, it neither makes possible nor confirms any method. Every sound pattern and every poem confronts the homo faber with an astonishingly incomplete fact. What is written at night and in wine can turn out to be doggerel on the following morning. It can be illegible or unreadable. Scribbling, gibberish, squiggles of a clown. My day was good, the poem turned out to be durable. One couplet seemed to wobble, I replaced it, the replacement was arbitrary or a carom, confirmed the durability of the first, and I put it back. The poem was finished and the title—SONG—could not be improved upon.

At night while I slept, a coach
stopped at my doorway;
coachman made his approach:
Mischance would query
if you have a request
tell him before day,
Mischance would be your guest
and your companion,
heed, if you will, his behest,
Mischance must move on.

Sagte ich: "Freund, ich schlief
er wirds wohl wissen,
hab, da ich nicht nach ihm rief
nichts zu vermissen,
hab ja kein Paradies
je zu verbüßen
und käm das Glückstier, dies
trät ich mit Füßen
unter die Erde tief."
Lachte der Kutscher und rief:
"Unglück läßt grüßen!"

Said I: "I slumbered, friend,
surely he knew it,
since for him I did not send
I need not rue it,
I've had no Paradise
to endure even fleeting,
my lucky star I'd entice
trampling and beating
pound it deep in the earth."
Coachman calls out with mirth:
"Mischance sends greeting!"

(*translated by Jeanne R. Willson*)

Untitled

Ernst Meister

Untitled

EINIGE GEDICHTE

ERNST MEISTER

O BLUMEN!
Hier auf dem Balkon
seh ich euch stehn
im Sonnenlicht gegen
das lösliche Gewölbe.

Ihr andern auch
seid gegenwärtig.

(13.6.1979)

Warum erschrecke ich
über Seiendes,
obwohl ich
zu ihm gehöre?

Was ist es
mit dem Unterschied
dessen, das lebt
und das stirbt?
Was, vor allem,
weiß ich schon bald
von Namen noch:

Haus . . . Baum . . .
Blume . . . Ach,
denke nicht,

daß deinen Staub
Nichtsein
qüale.

SOME POEMS

ERNST MEISTER
translated by Georg M. Gugelberger

OH YOU FLOWERS!
I see you standing
there on the balcony
in the sunlight
against the decaying wall.

You others also
be present.

But why am I so terrified
of things that exist
while belonging to them
myself?

What really is it
about the difference
between what lives
and what dies?
Above all what
shall I still know
of names:

House . . . tree . . .
flower . . . Oh,
don't think

that your dust
will be tortured
by non-being.

Es scheint, ich darf
nicht mehr sprechen
von Zusammengehören.

Dein Gesicht
denkt mich nicht mehr,
vielleicht

wegen meiner Gedanken.

Das Wort,
Hand in Hand
mit dem Schmerz,
stülpt es um,

so daß
ein Gewendetes
wäre
durch deutliches Zeigen?

Klarheit
entsteht, was sonst,
die Seele erleichternd.

Nähe des Ursprungs.

Apparently I am
no longer to speak
of what belongs together.

Your face
does not think me anymore,
perhaps

because of my thoughts.

The word
inverts
hand in hand
with the pain,

could a
change occur
through
clear indication?

Clarity
results, what else,
alleviating the soul.

Closeness to the origin.

Das kam
aus einem
Erdenkinderbett,
daß ich die Weile
sagen mußte: Ich.

Hernach, hier-
nach: Ich bin
da durch. Warum
die Blume
farbig steht,
bewußtlos, das

wäre meine Frage,
fragt ich noch.

Der zeichnet Mücken
in die Luft. Der schreibt
die Schwalbe, Fängerin,
mir in die Augen. Der
läßt dich schreiben. Der,
ziemlich hell, streicht durch.
Der streicht den Schreiber durch,
wenn es der Tag ist.

It came
out of an
earthen child-bed
so that I had to
say for a while: I.

After this, here-
after: I had been
through this. Why does
the flower stand
in its colors
unconscious, this

would be my question,
if I were to ask.

This one draws flies
in the air. This one writes
the swallow, the catcher,
into my eyes. This one
lets you write. This one,
rather bright, crosses out.
This one crosses out the writer
when the day comes.

DER ERSTE REGEN
UND ANDERE GEDICHTE

KARL OPPERMANN

DER ERSTE REGEN

Schauer pfeifen über den Hang
im Sturm torkelnde Reben
Die Erde besäuft sich
gurgelt und schluckt
sinnlos quietscht eine Harmonika
aus nassem Balg

THE FIRST RAIN

Showers shiver along the slope
pressing the reeling vines in storm
The earth gets drunk
gurgles and gulps
a wet-bellied accordion
senselessly squeaking

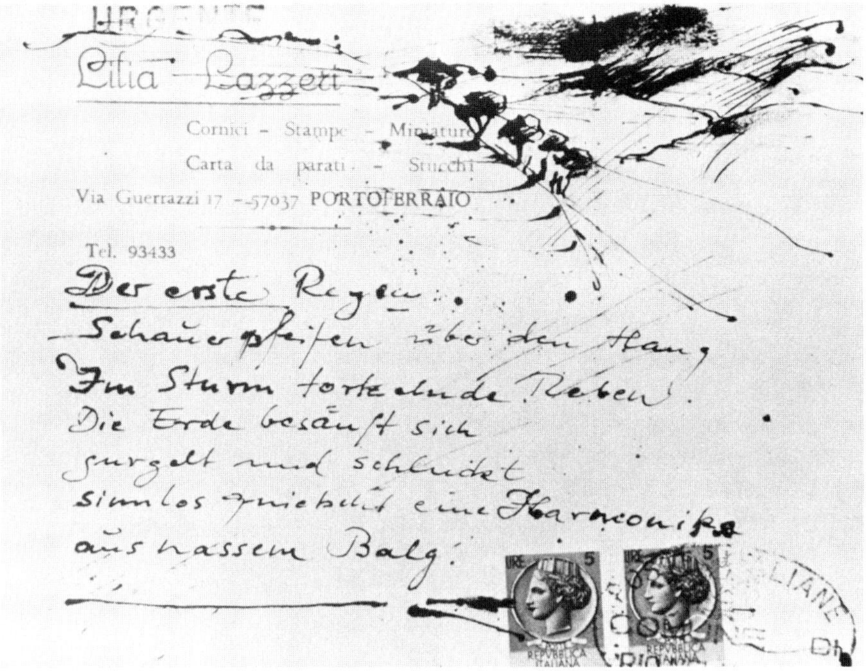
URGENTE

Lilia Lazzeri

Cornici - Stampe - Miniature

Carta da parati - Stucchi

Via Guerrazzi 17 - 57037 PORTOFERRAIO

Tel. 93433

Der erste Regen:

Schauer pfeifen über den Hang
Im Sturm torkelnde Reben!
Die Erde besäuft sich
gurgelt und schluckt
sinnlos quietscht eine Harmonika
aus nassem Balg.

THE FIRST RAIN AND OTHER POEMS

KARL OPPERMANN
translated by Breon Mitchell

ZINNSOLDATEN

Auf unserem Gabentisch
steht noch immer der Generalstab
zur Auseinandersetzung bereit.
Er wiegt dieses und jenes.
Gewichtig und nicht zu übersehen
sendet er Ordonanzen irre,
entdeckt im Fernglas
feindliche Jäger zu Pferd.
Einer brach eine Lanze
man fragt für wen und wo.
Was ritt ihn, obwohl ungespielt
sein Werkzeug zu ruinieren?
Niemanden unter dem Weihnachtsbaum
beschäftigen seine Probleme.

TIN SOLIDERS

On the table for our gifts
the general staff still stands
in readiness for the strategy session.
They weigh this and that.
Forceful and not to be ignored
they send orderlies astray,
discover through the spyglass
enemy riflemen on horseback.
One of them has broken a lance
one wonders in whose cause and where.
What drove him, though not placed in play
to ruin his martial tool?
To those beneath the Christmas tree
his problems are of no concern

was ritt ihn, obwohl ungespielt
sein Werkzeug zu ruinieren?
niemand unter dem Weihnachtsbaum
beschäftigen seine Probleme

RICHARD

Obwohl er den goldenen Daumen hat
fürchtet er die gedeckten Karten
jede einzeln ängstigt ihn.
Wenn sie dann kommen,
bescheinen das Bierglas:
Bube, Dame, König, As
setzt er die harte Miene auf
böse jedem
der seine bunten Bilder sieht.

Er heißt Richard
stammt aus Ostpreußen
wo sie Schnaps destillierten
und Märsche bliesen
Bube, Dame, König, As
Kartoffeln und Eicheln
Ostpreußen war Stichherz
des Reiches.

Richard mischt Karten
er spielt nur mit Blinden
Auge um Auge zählt.

RICHARD

Although he has a thumb of gold
he fears the unturned cards
each one frightens him.
Then when they arrive,
eyeing the beer glass:
Jack, Queen, King, Ace
he puts on a poker face
angry with anyone
who sees his pretty pictures.

He's called Richard
comes from East Prussia
where they distilled schnaps
and blasted out marches
Jack, Queen, King, Ace
potatoes and acorns
East Prussia was trump heart
of the empire.

Richard shuffles the cards
he plays only with the blind
counting an eye for an eye.

Richard
Büße, Dame König As
Er heißt Richard
stammt aus Ostpreussen
Büße, Dame, König, As
Kartoffeln und Eicheln
Ostpreussen war Stiel-Herz des Reiches.
Richard mischt Karten,
er spielt nur mit Blinden

KUNSTSCHULE

Gönnt dem Strich eine Pause,
schwarz muß nicht Trumpf sein
zwischen Stand- und Spielbein
liegt der Hase im Pfeffer

Erwärmt euch am Marmor
an Kriegerdenkmalen
wie schnell kommen Zeiten
mit starkem Bedarf

Übt an wohlpräparierten Schädeln
signiert: made in Germany

SCHOOL OF FINE ARTS

Give line a break for a while,
black doesn't have to be trump
between the free and the supporting leg
you'll find the fly in the ointment

Warm up on marble
on war memorials
how quickly times will come
of heavy demand

Practice on well-prepared skulls
signed: *made in Germany*

Kunstschule

Gönnt dem Strich eine Pause
schwarz muß nicht Trumpf sein
zwischen Stand- und Spielbein
liegt der Hase im Pfeffer.

Erwärmt Euch am Marmor
an Kriegerdenkmalen
wie schnell kommen Zeiten
mit starkem Bedarf.

Übt an wohlpräparierten Schädeln
signiert: Made in Germany.

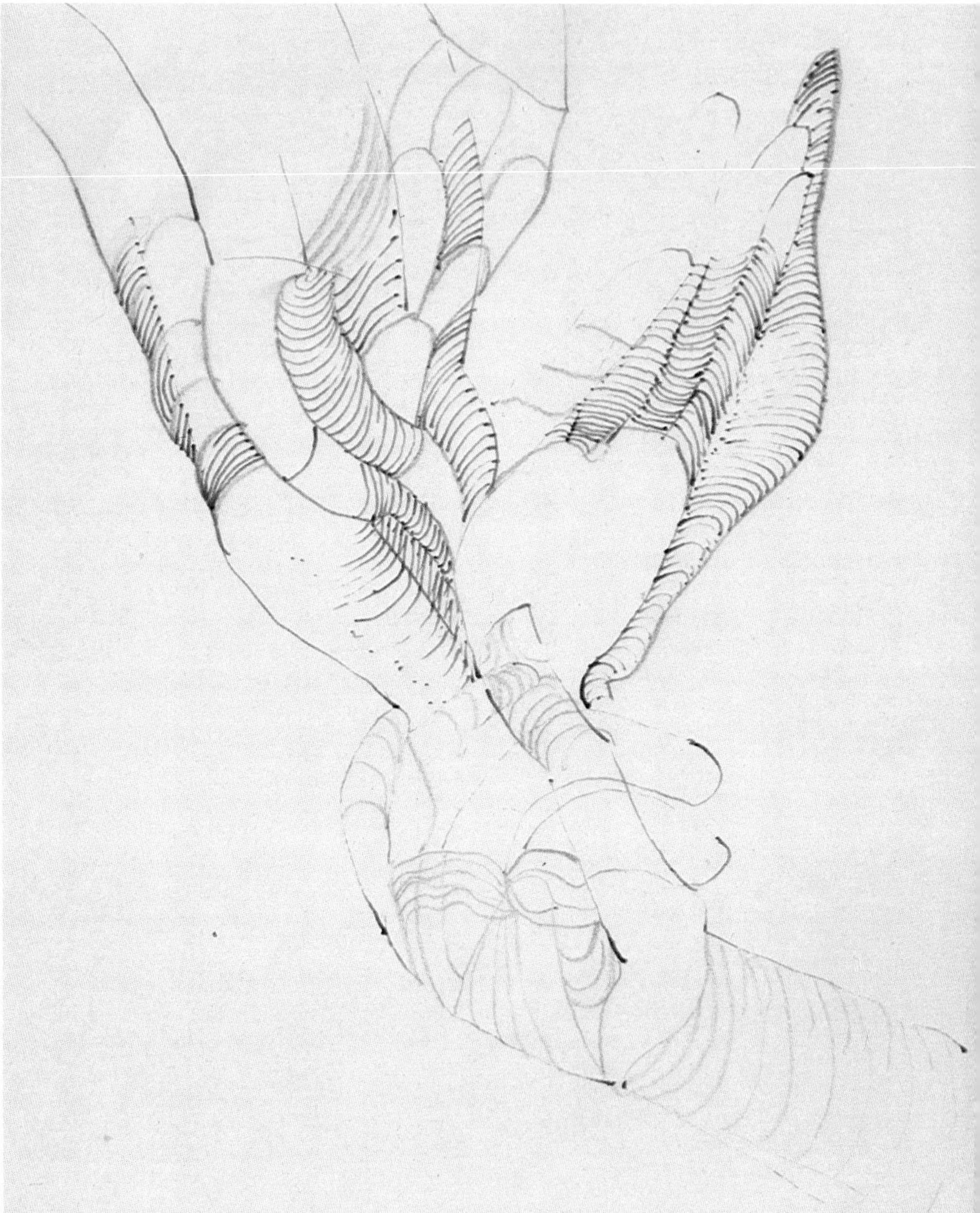

Erica Pedrett

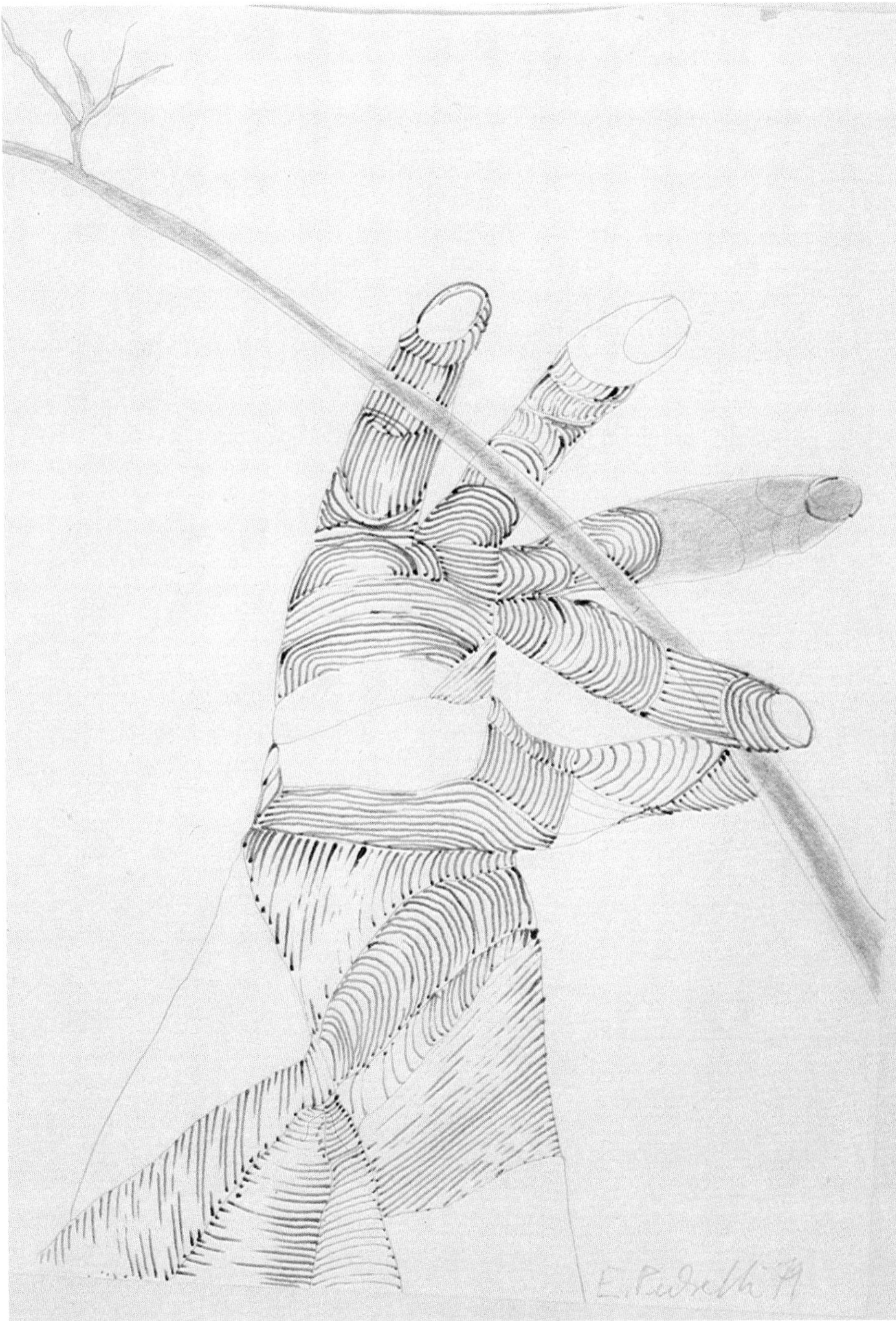

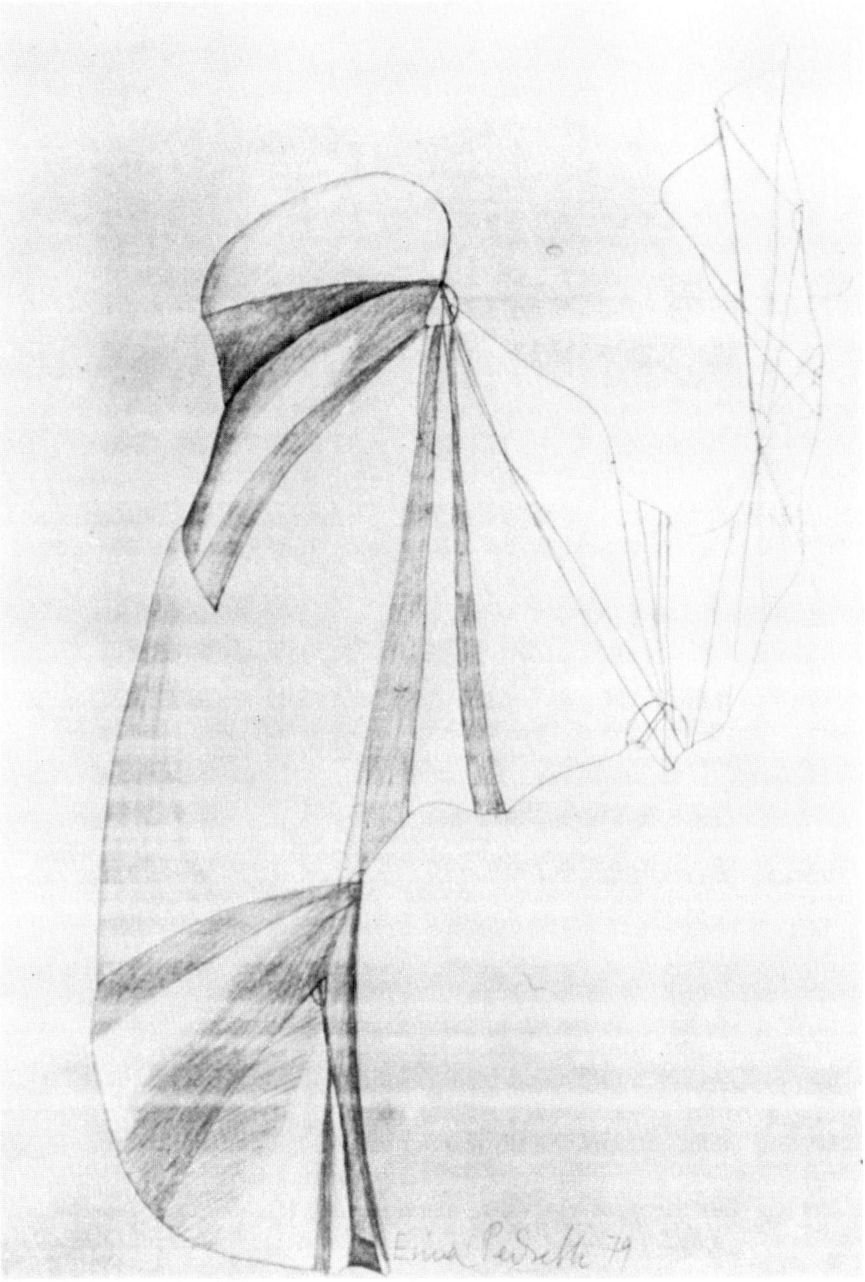

DEPART

ERICA PEDRETTI

DORT KOMMT EINER, WOHER? WOHER ER WILL, SOLL ER NUR KOMMEN mit all seinem Zeug und sich aufstellen, warten, dort stehn oder hin und hergehn oder von einem Fuß auf den andern das Gewicht vertreten und dabei warten, während ich zuschaue wie er nach links schaut, nach rechts schaut, schaue wie einer wartet, wie es scheint, geduldig, so wie ich warte, was er jetzt wohl tun wird, was würde ich in seiner Situation, wenn ich also er wäre, so geduldig wäre, jetzt tun? in dieser mir nur allzu wohlbekannten, nein, nicht wohl-, eher überbekannten Lage, denn warte ich nicht schon lange? wie lange? etwa immer schon? oder zumindest fast immer seit ich mich erinnern kann, wenn auch nicht genauso wie er, sondern irgendwie, auf meine eigene Art anders, indem ich eben jetzt nicht gern stehnbleibe neben diesem Geleise, von dem ich nicht weiß, wohin es führt, ich kann nur hoffen, er weiß es, denn hätte er sich sonst daneben gestellt? und es sieht so aus, als wäre es nicht das erste Mal, als wäre er, was er jetzt anfängt, schon von früheren Malen her gewohnt, nicht, daß es aussähe, als wiederhole er etwas, in dem er geübt wäre, eher so, als kenne er wohl nichts anderes, sei aber auf gewisse Art noch nicht so weit, nicht ganz bereit zu dem, was, vielleicht, auf ihn zukommt, als glaube er nicht wirklich, daß es kommt, als käme es erst nächstes oder übernächstes Mal, das, worauf er wartet, indem er sein Gepäck, mein Gott, wie kommt man nur zu so viel Gepäck? ein Stück ums andre auf den Bahndamm stellt, eine Linie Koffer oder Schachteln an diese Eisenbahnlinie Biel-Rotterdam oder Frankfurt-Irun, an irgendeine dieser Linien, die unser Land durchqueren, den Kontinent zerschneiden, womöglich sogar zu einem Flughafen führen, von dem aus transkontinentale Luftlinien ihn, dich oder mich nach USA, Australien, vielleicht auch nach China bringen, wo immer sein, dein, oder mein Herz, oder was immer in uns der Ausgangspunkt von Sehnsucht sein mag, wer weiß, vielleicht deine Milz, mein Magen, die Augen, Lungen, was immer sich hinsehnt an einen glücklichen ruhigen Ort, Ziel oder neuer Ausgangspunkt? einen Ort mit unerschöpflichen verheißungsvollen weiteren Ausgangspunkten und von ihnen ausgehenden, ausstrahlenden neuen Bahn-, Schiffs- oder Luftlinien an unbekannte, drum unbenützte, noch unbetretene oder kaum betretene reiche Regionen, halt halt wohin willst du? nur nicht so hoch hinaus, warum nicht Bern? oder Lausanne? warum zu den Träumen von Antilopen und Pinguinen, oder wo immer

DEPARTING

ERICA PEDRETTI
translated by Johannes W. Vazulik

THERE'S SOMEBODY COMING, FROM WHERE? FROM WHEREVER HE WANTS, just let him come, bringing all his stuff, and let him find a spot for himself, wait, stand there, or pace back and forth, or shift his weight from one foot to the other as he waits, while I look on as he looks to the left, looks to the right, see somebody, as it appears, patiently waiting, just like I am waiting, wondering what he'll do now, what I would now do in his place if, in fact, I were he, if I were as patient in this situation only all too well known to me, no, not well known, rather, exceedingly well known, for haven't I been waiting a long time? how long? perhaps forever, or at least almost ever since I can remember, even though not exactly like him, but rather, in my own somehow-or-other unique way, inasmuch as I'd rather not stop next to these tracks just now, not knowing where they lead, I can only hope that he knows because why else would he be standing there? and it looks as if it weren't the first time he were doing what he's starting to do now, it looks like something he's used to from before, not that it seems as if he were repeating something in which he were experienced, rather, as if he probably just didn't know what else to do, but in a certain way he is not ready yet, not quite prepared for what might confront him, as if he didn't really believe that it is coming, as if it wouldn't be coming until the next time or the time after next, whatever he's waiting for by placing his baggage, my God, how do you get so much baggage? one piece after the other next to the tracks, a row of suitcases or boxes on this railroad line, Biel-Rotterdam, or Frankfurt-Irun, on any one of these lines that cross the country, cut up the continent, may even lead to an airport from which transcontinental airlines take him, you, or me to the USA, Australia, perhaps even to China, wherever his, your, or my heart or whatever in us may be the point of departure of yearning, who knows, perhaps your spleen, my stomach, the eyes, the lungs, whatever longs for a happy, peaceful place, destination, or new point of departure? a place with inexhaustible, promising, additional departure points and originating and radiating from them new rail-, ship-, or airlines to unknown, therefore unspoiled, still unexplored or hardly explored, lush regions, hold it, hold it, where do you want to go? take it easy, why not Bern? or Lausanne? why to the dreams of antelopes and penguins or wherever someone who is sich einer träumend hinwünscht, auf die Insel, das andere Ufer, in ein anderes Haus, dieses bestimmte Zimmer, zu dieser Liebe oder auch zu einer andern, ihm noch unbekannten an einem noch unbekannten aber doch nur ihm oder mir allein möglichen idealen Ort, Alaska, Nepal, um endlich bei sich selber, im eigenen Herz oder was immer, Milz Leber Lunge, anzulangen mit Schachteln und Koffern? und Zeitung, Transistor. wohin mit dem vielen Gepäck? wie bin ich, wie ist er zu all den Bündeln gekommen, zu all dem, was da drin ist, was ist das? wie konnte sich so viel bei ihm, um ihn herum ansammeln, ein Sammelsurium, das sein eigenes Ausmaß, das Volumen seiner Person um ein Mehrfaches übersteigt, Papiere Geschirr und Kleider, Uhr, Radio und Schreibmaschine, Schuhe und Hüte, ein Schirm, verschiedene Lampen, Seife, Parfum, und so weiter, so daß er jetzt mit dem Aufstellen, dem Ordnen all seines Gepäcks über wer weiß wie lange Zeit vollständig beschäftigt sein wird, wer weiß, ob nicht die Arbeit, alles in eine übersichtliche, planvolle Reihenfolge zu bringen, ihn über eine längere Zeitspanne ablenken, von der aufmerksamen Beobachtung des Geleises, ja eigentlich von jeder Wahrnehmung seiner Umgebung, von allen damit verbundenen Versuchungen abhalten wird? die Vögel und Barbara zwitschern vergeblich, keiner sieht ihre Augenaufschläge, Flügelschläge vollführen ihre Hände und Arme, graziös und vergeblich spaziert sie auf und ab und blinzelt in der strahlenden Sonne oder sie blinzelt ihm, der nichts merkt, zu, und über den Himmel jagen sich, als wären es kleine, übermütige Kinder, weiße Wolken, es könnten auch, warum nicht? Verliebte sein, und er könnte, wäre er nicht so auf seine Dinge bedacht, verschiedenes von ihnen lernen, er müßte nur, was er eben jetzt nicht kann, den Kopf heben und schauen, bevor alles, was gerade noch dramatisch über die Bühne oder den Himmel ging, zerfasert, sich auflöst und Luft wird, und die Bäume verlieren ihre Blätter während Barbaras Parfum vergeht wie das von Veilchen, Rosen, Lilien und Orchideen, von all den Blumen, die für ihn da wären, nur für ihn, da er nach Barbaras Verduften weit und breit der Einzige ist, emsig damit beschäftigt, seine Besitztümer um sich zu ordnen, und so grünt, flirtet, liebt und duftet alles vergebens, nein, keineswegs vergebens, es sei denn für ihn, der alle möglichen Verführungen und Freuden versäumt, es wäre ein Trugschluß zu glauben, Veilchen könnten, ohne wahrgenommen zu werden, nicht duften, es sei denn vergebens, was wäre dann nicht alles vergebens? fast alles, und doch würde es ja genauso weiterbestehen, weitergehen, die Blüten und die Menschen sich entfalten, die Wolken sich zu Ungetümen oder Liebespaaren, Türmen und Schluchten zusammenwälzen, nur Barbara würde weniger, vielleicht gar nicht mehr tanzen, hätte er, was er doch vorhat, diesen Ort erst verlassen, was er aber, dieses Verlassen, Abfahren, dieses Nichtmehrhiersein, kaum denken, sich nicht wirklich vorstellen kann, und dreaming longs to go, to an island, to the other shore, to another house, to this particular room, to this love or else to another, still unknown to him at a still unknown spot but, nevertheless, the only possible one ideal for him or for me, Alaska, Nepal, in order finally to end up by himself, in his own heart or whatever, spleen liver lung, with boxes and suitcases? and newspaper, transistor radio, what's he going to do with all that baggage? how did I, how did he, get all that stuff, everything that's in there, what is it? how could so much pile up next to him, around him, a hodgepodge that exceeds his own size, the volume of his body several times over, papers dishes and clothes, clock, radio, and typewriter, shoes and hats, an umbrella, various lamps, soap, perfume, and so on, so that he'll now be totally occupied for who knows how long a time with the positioning, the putting in order of all his baggage, who knows whether the work of bringing everything into a clearly arranged, systematic sequence won't distract him over a fairly long period of time from the attentive observation of the tracks, yes, in fact, from any perception of his surroundings, from all the temptations connected with it? the birds and Barbara twitter in vain, no one sees her raising her eyes, flapping her hands and arms, gracefully and futilely she walks up and down and blinks into the beaming sun, or she blinks at him, who doesn't notice anything, and white clouds chase across the sky as if they were playful little children, they could also, why not? be lovers, and he could, if he weren't so intent on his possessions, learn different things from them, he would only have to do what he cannot do just now, lift his head and look before everything that just now dramatically crossed the stage or the sky disintegrates, dissolves, and turns into air, and the trees lose their leaves while Barbara's perfume wears off just like that of violets, roses, lilies, and orchids, of all the flowers that would be here for him, only for him, since he, after Barbara's fragrance is gone, is the only one far and wide preoccupied with arranging his possessions around him, and so everything turns green, flirts, loves, and smells sweet in vain, no, by no means in vain, except for him who lets all possible temptations and joys slip by, it would be a misconception to believe violets could not smell sweet without being noticed, unless it were in vain, wouldn't then everything be in vain? almost everything, and still it would keep on existing just the same, keep on going, the flowers and human beings would blossom, the clouds would roll together into monsters or lovers, towers and canyons, only Barbara would dance less, perhaps not at all, if only he had left this place as he after all intends to do, however, this leaving, this departing, this no longer being here, is something he is scarcely able wer könnte das? geht nicht mit mir selber auch alle Welt verloren, indem ich sie nicht mehr sehe, rieche, höre und fühle? und ist sie nicht ohnehin für ihn längst verschwunden? geschrumpft zu diesem winzigen Ausschnitt, den er zur Ausbreitung seiner Güter benötigt und überblickt, den er nun abschreitet mit etwas wie Stolz, während ein Zug unbeachtet eintrifft, wieder abfährt, ja dieses Stück gehört hier-, jenes dorthin, oder besser noch so, den Überseekoffer doch lieber ans Ende, nein lieber, ja doch, jetzt gehts, mit Musik geht es besser, Luxemburg oder Mahler, Ditter von Dittersdorf, nur frag ich mich, was wird er tun, was täte ich, wenn einmal, was jetzt zwar noch nicht abzusehen, aber doch zu erwarten ist, endlich jedes einzelne Stück, der Koffer mit den Schreibereien, den Liebesbriefen, der Wäschekasten, Medikamente und Blumensamensäckchen, alles seinen Platz gefunden hätte, jedes Ding in die richtige Ordnung gebracht, und somit seine selbstauferlegte Aufgabe erfüllt wäre, wenn ich, welch phantastischer, verstiegener Gedanke, einmal alles erledigt hätte, müßte ich, ja könnte ich dann, könnte er wieder warten? und Barbara nicht vergeblich zwitschern, ein Apfelbaum winzige weißrosa Blütenblätter verstreuen, während er hier auf dem Bahndamm der Linie Genf-Amsterdam steht, unter diesen bei zunehmendem Föhn immer schneller und Aufregender sich bewegenden Liebespaaren, und wartet, einmal nach links, einmal nach rechts dem Geleise entlang schaut bis dorthin, wo es sich verliert, oder er könnte, so wie ich, nun von keiner Tätigkeit mehr abgelenkt, die über Hügel, den See, die Wiesen jagenden Wolkenschatten, die unaufhörlich sich verändernde Landschaft ruhig aufmerksam betrachten.

to think of, cannot really imagine, and who could? isn't the whole world lost and me, too, when I no longer see, smell, hear, and feel it? and didn't it long ago disappear for him anyway? shrunk to this tiny section that he needs for spreading out his possessions, and that he surveys, that he now paces off with something like pride while a train arrives unnoticed, departs again, yes, this piece belongs here, that one over there, or better yet this way, preferably the steamer trunk at the end, no, rather, well, yes, now it's all right, it's better done to music, Luxemburg or Mahler, Ditter von Dittersdorf, I only wonder what he will do, what would I do, when sometime what can't yet be conceived of but can nonetheless be expected, finally every single piece, the suitcase with the scribbles, the love letters, the clothes trunk, medications, flower seed packets, all would be in place, every thing put in the right order, and, with that, his self-imposed task be accomplished, if I, what a fantastic, outlandish idea, would one day have taken care of everything, would I have to, even could I then, could he, wait again? and Barbara not twitter in vain, an apple tree strew tiny whitish-pink blossoms while he stands here next to the tracks of the Geneva-Amsterdam line among these lovers who move faster and more excitedly as the wind gets warmer, and waits, looking once to the left, once to the right along the tracks up to where they disappear, or, no longer distracted by any activity, he, the same as I, could now quietly, attentively observe the shadows of the clouds that chase over hills, lake, and meadow, the endlessly changing landscape.

ein ja dazwischen

a yes inbetween

Gerhard Rühm

so sehr

so very much

mehrere Gedanken

several thoughts

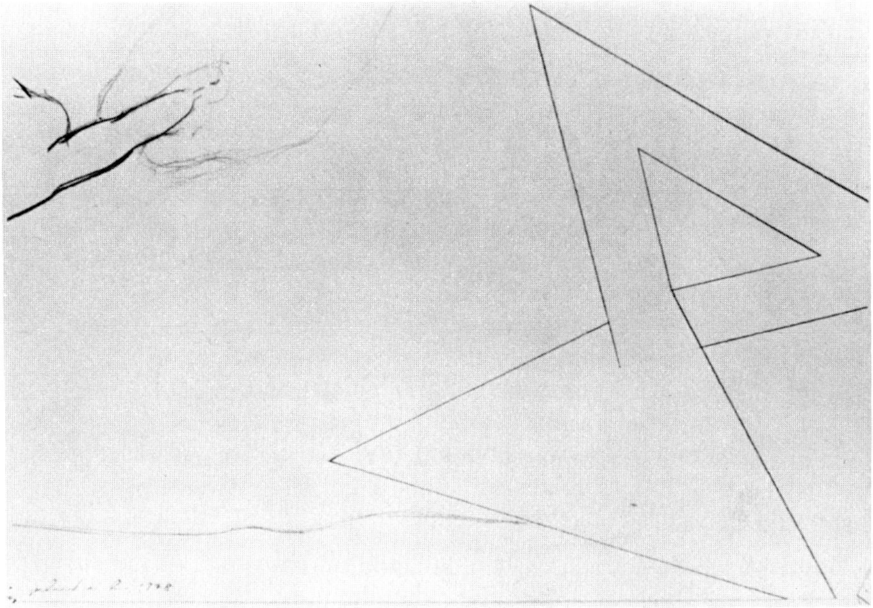

Bleistiftzeichnung

Pencil Drawing

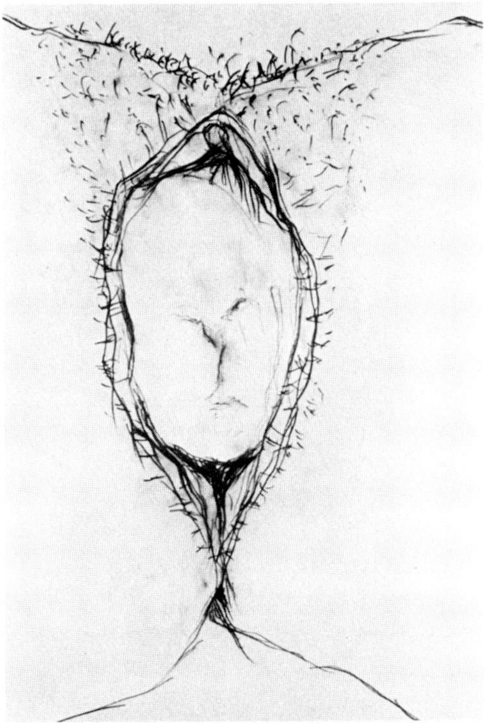

Selbstbildnis

Self-portrait

ABSTEIGENDE GEDICHTE
Eine Auswahl

GERHARD RÜHM

VARIATION EINES BEKANNTEN THEMAS

von zehn fiel eines weg
von neun blieben nur noch acht
von acht nur noch sieben
von sieben nur noch sechs
von sechs nur noch fünf
von fünf nur noch vier
von den vieren, ja du errätst es, nur noch drei
und auch die verringerten sich noch
da wurden aus den restlichen zweien plötzlich
beide
und jedes von den beiden hatte angst
schließlich allein zu sein
denn es schien unvermeidlich
aber auch das würde sicher nicht lange währen

DESCENDING POEMS
A Selection

GERHARD RÜHM
translated by Allen H. Chappel

VARIATION ON A WELL-KNOWN THEME

of ten one fell away
of nine remained only eight
of eight only seven
of seven only six
of six only five
of five only four
of the four, yes, you guessed it, only three
and also they diminished still
then of the remaining two were suddenly
both
and each of the two was afraid
in the end to be alone
for it seemed to be unavoidable
but even that would certainly not last long

AN FRIEDERIKE MAYRÖCKER

im
see
sie
sah
so
suchend
nach
summender
sonne
sacht
sich
sehnend

NATURBESCHREIBUNG

die wolken ziehen sich in falten
die blumen erbleichen
die wiesen wenden sich ab
die wege verkriechen sich
die steine starren vor sich hin
die berge versinken in schweigen
die täler erschauern
ein windstoß entringt sich den lüften
die flüsse treten aus den ufern
die büsche raufen sich die blätter
die bäume schlagen die äste über den wipfeln zusammen

die erde taumelt in die nacht

TO FRIEDERIKE MAYRÖCKER

in the
sea
she
stared
so
searchingly
for the
singing
sun
softly
seeking her-
self

DESCRIPTION OF NATURE

the clouds move in folds
the flowers grow pale
the meadows turn away
the paths sneak off
the stones stare straight ahead
the mountains sink in silence
the valleys give a shudder
a gust of wind is wrested from the breezes
the rivers overflow their banks
the bushes pluck their own leaves
the trees dash their limbs together above their crowns

the earth staggers into night

Robert Wolfgang Schnell

LIEBESKUMMER

ROBERT WOLFGANG SCHNELL

Das Weib ist ein Abgrund mit Blumen.
ARNO HOLZ

ALS ER IM WALD VERSCHAND, BUCHSTÄBLICH VERSCHWUNDEN WAR, BLIEB der Wald unverändert. Was war aus IHM geworden? Konnte der ruhige Wald IHN verschlingen, ohne seine Stämme zu bewegen, sein Laub zu verwirren oder, an einer Stelle wenigstens, Unruhe zu zeigen? Ich war betroffen, denn ich wollte IHN erreichen. Ich war gerührt von SEINEN abfallenden Schultern, von SEINEM Gang, der nicht gerade hinkend war, aber eine Unregelmäßigkeit im Schritt hatte, als suche ER etwas oder prüfe die Sicherheit des Bodens.

Und nun war ER verschwunden. Obwohl ich betroffen war, gab mir SEIN Verschwinden auch Beruhigung. Mich konnte keinerlei Enttäuschung dämpfen, denn hätte ich IHN erreicht, hätte ich mit IHM sprechen müssen. Meine Vorstellung hätte zerstört werden, SEINE abfallenden Schultern keine Weichheit und besondere Sensibilität signalisieren können, sondern es wäre möglich, ich stünde einem gegenüber, der mich auslachte.

Ich wanderte nämlich im Wald, weil ich es nirgend anders aushalten konnte. In der giftigen Sonne zwischen Häusern und Balkons mit Sonnenschirmen, unter denen braungebrannte Faulenzer saßen, dösend in Zeitungen lasen, sah ich Ruinen, zusammengestürztes Gestein, verdeckt von welken Blättern, die auch mich zuregnen wollten. Vor ihnen floh ich in den Wald.

Also von gelben und roten Blättern unter die grünen. Sollte ich darin den Sinn dieser Wanderung suchen? Trotz aller Psychologen: ich verbrachte die fröhlichsten Stunden in schwarzen Zimmern, wofür es sicher auch eine Deutung gibt. Deswegen setze ich gleich hinzu, daß ich allein war und die Tür von außen verschlossen, auch war der Kerzenstummel bald zu Ende. Ich hatte nur mich selbst, einen verwerflichen Narren, den ich nie anerkannt hatte. Es ist zwar so, daß ich immer in mir einen tollen

PANGS OF LOVE

ROBERT WOLFGANG SCHNELL
translated by Ken Fontenot

Woman is an abyss with flowers.
ARNO HOLZ

WHEN HE DISAPPEARED IN THE FOREST, LITERALLY HAD DISAPPEARED, the forest remained unchanged. What had become of HIM? Could the peaceful forest swallow HIM up without moving its tree trunks or entangling its leaves or at least in some place showing a disturbance? I was perplexed, for I wanted to reach HIM. I was moved by HIS sloping shoulders, by HIS walk, which was not exactly a limping walk but had an irregularity of step, as though HE were looking for something or testing to see if the ground would hold him.

And now HE had disappeared. I was stunned by HIS disappearance, but at the same time it gave me comfort. No sort of disappointment could subdue me, for I had reached HIM, I would have had to speak with HIM. My whole conception of HIM could have been destroyed, HIS sloping shoulders could have shown no softness and no special sensitivity, rather it might be possible that I would confront a person who would laugh at me.

You see, I was wandering through the forest because I couldn't stand it anyplace else. In the glaring sun between houses and balconies with sunshades, under which deeply tanned loafers sat drowsily reading their newspapers, I saw ruins, stones collapsed, covered by withered leaves, which were about to deluge me, too. From them I fled into the forest.

So, from yellow and red leaves to green ones. Should I search there for the meaning of this wandering? In spite of all the psychologists: I spent my happiest hours in dark rooms, for which there is surely also an interpretation. Therefore, I'll add right away that I was alone and the door locked from the outside, also the candle stump was soon down to nothing. I had only myself, an abject fool whom I had never acknowledged. Indeed, it is true that I always wanted to see in myself a fine man who remained a

Mann sehen wollte, der im richtigen Maß Knabe geblieben und sein Dasein als Raubritter und gesetzestreuer Steuerbürger in eine Balance zwischen Arbeit und Alkohol brachte, um die ihn jeder beneiden sollte. Aber ehe mich das Glück einer so stolzen Selbstbetrachtung erreichte, erreichte mich stets ein Hieb aus einer furchterweckenden Kiste, aus der ein Springteufel mit Pritsche kam. Und dieser Springteufel hatte alles bei sich: finanziellen Mißerfolg, Entlarvung lebenswichtiger Lügen, Begradigung der schönsten biographischen Kurven, die ich mir zur Erreichung des Lebensglücks gezogen hatte, ja, mit einem Schlag konnte er die Freude an einem schönen Busen zum Haß des weiblichen Objekts verändern, der weiter reichte als die ausgedörrte Stimmung mißglückter Küsse.

ER war jedenfalls verschwunden und vergeblich lauerte ich, ob seine gelbe Gummijacke nicht irgendwo noch einmal durch die Stämme leuchtete. Wie konnte ER, den ich nach SEINEN hilflosen Schultern beurteilte, nur so eine gelbe Jacke tragen! Modische Jünglinge und Mädchen trugen sie, deren Kapuze wie ein kleiner Rucksack Nacken und Schulter verdeckte und verunstaltete. Ich malte mir aus, daß die Entfernung manches nach meinen Wünschen einrichtete. Hätte ich, neben IHM, meinen Arm unter den seinen geschoben, hätte mich SEIN nervös suchender Gang vielleicht abgestoßen. Aber ich ging mit IHM auf andere Art, auf die Art, die mein Kopf erfand, um mein Herz zu befriedigen. So was nennt man wohl intellektuell, und das wirft einen seltsamen Blick auf die Fantasie, als deren Mutter das Gemüt bezeichnet wird. Und ich denke wohl, das *bedrückte* Gemüt war ursprünglich die Mutter dieser gefräßigen Schlange, die normale Zeit und Welt einatmet, um geflügelte Pferde, wandernde Tische, Tarnkappen, Marsmenschen, sprechende Füchse und Traumwelten auszuspeien, denen unten und oben, heute, gestern und die unausdenkbarste Zukunft eins sind.

Ich weiß nicht, ob man in die Fantasie hineinkriechen kann. Ich stelle sie mir als eine riesige befestigte Stadt vor, über deren Mauern nichts hinausragt, von rohen Wächtern geschützt. Die großen Stadttore bleiben stets geschlossen, die besonderen Truppen, die zu ihrem Schutz eingesetzt sind, schlafen. Schlafen seit tausenden von Jahren. Nur durch die kleinen Löcher, mit einem Klappbrett verschlossen, die man früher bei den normalen Stadttoren Nadelöhr nannte, durch das Hunde, Schafe, Ziegen und anderes kleines Getier aus- und einschlüpften, damit die Torwächter nicht für das arme dumme niedrige Volk ein riesiges Tor öffnen mußten—nur durch die Nadelöhr kann man also in die Fantasie hineinkriechen. Auf dem Bauch und man muß selber schlafen, damit die Schlafenden nicht aufwachen von den Bewegungen des Wachen. Innen sind die grellen boy to a proper extent and kept his identity as a robber-knight and a law-abiding citizen in balance between work and alcohol, for which everyone should envy him. But before the good fortune of such a proud self-image came to me, there always reached me a blow out of a frightful box, out of which a jack-in-the-box holding a club jumped. And this jack-in-the-box had everything: financial misfortune, unmasking of lies vital to living, straightening of the most beautiful biographical curves that I had drawn to attain life's happiness, indeed, with one blow, he could change all joy in beautiful breasts into hatred of the feminine object, hatred that reached farther than the dried-up mood of failed kisses.

In any case HE had disappeared and in vain I wanted to see whether his yellow rubber jacket would once again shine somewhere through the trees. How could HE, whom I judged by HIS helpless shoulders, wear just such a yellow jacket? Fashionable guys and girls wore those jackets, whose hoods, like little knapsacks, covered and disfigured their necks and shoulders. I imagined that distance fashioned things according to my wishes. Had I, next to HIM, put my arm under his arm, HIS nervously-searching walk would perhaps have repulsed me. But I walked with HIM in a different way, in a way that my head invented to satisfy my heart. One might call this intellectual, and that throws a peculiar light on fantasy, whose mother is said to be the mind. And I really believe that the *depressed* mind was originally the mother of this insatiable snake, which ingests normal time and world in order to spit out winged horses, wandering tables, cloaks of invisibility, Martians, talking foxes, and dream worlds, to all of which above and below, today, yesterday, and the most impossible future are one.

I don't know if one can crawl into fantasy. I imagine it as a gigantic, fortified city, above whose walls nothing can be seen, protected by barbarous guards. The great city gates are always closed, the special troops mustered to its protection sleep. Have been sleeping for thousands of years. Only through the small holes, closed by a shutter, which at one time in the regular city gates was called the eye of the needle, and through which dogs, sheep, goats, and other small beasts slipped in and out, so that the gate guards did not have to open a gigantic gate for the poor, dumb, inferior folk—only through the eye of the needle can one, therefore, crawl into fantasy. On one's stomach, and one must oneself sleep so that the sleepers don't wake up from the movements of awakening. Inside, the glaring colors are gentle, the tones are parts of the light, and the most

Farben mild, die Töne sind Teile des Lichts, und der schönste Tod ist der Mord, der Messerstich ein glitzerndes Bild, das wie mit einer Seidenleine auf das Kapitol zieht, um dir den Blick zu gönnen in ein Reich ohne Dunst, ohne Wahrheit, ohne Lüge, ohne Bild und Bau und ohne Gleichnis. Ein Reich, in dem niemand verlangt, daß ein Schluß gezogen wird, in dem Anfang und Ergebnis vollkommen gleich sind, wo man kein Alter braucht, um weise zu sein, und keine Jugend, um jung zu sein. Wo eben Fantasie keine besondere Mutter braucht wie Gemüt oder Bewußtsein, wo Fantasie keine Fantasie ist, sondern Atem, wo Atem kein Luftholen ist, sondern Fantasie eben das, was da ist, Sehnsucht, die die Freude der Befriedigung und Befriedigung, die die nächste Sehnsucht ist, ohne Bild und Bau und ohne Gleichnis.

Dahin sehnte ich mich. Ich wollte ja nur IHN in der gelben Gummijacke erreichen, der vor mir herging und dann im Wald verschwand, als seien SEINE rührenden Schultern schon das erste Ducken SEINES Körpers gewesen, mit dem ER sich bereitmachen wollte, um das Nadelöhr nach Fantasie zu durchkriechen.

Da es verschwunden war, brauchte ich mich ja mit SEINEM körperlichen Bild nicht mehr lange aufzuhalten. Ich sprach IHN einfach an.

Ich sagte: Es rührt mich, daß SIE so traurig mit hängenden Schultern durch den Wald gehen.

Wieso mit hängenden Schultern? fragte ER.

Ihre hängenden Schultern rühren mich.

Ich will Ihnen mal etwas sagen, sagte ER und ging weiter, ohne mich anzusehen. Sie können mich ruhig beleidigen, hier im einsamen Wald, ich habe keine Angst. Sie sollten sich alles überlegen, was Sie sprechen, denn ich bin sehr stark und niemand kennt diesen Wald so gut wie ich. Keiner wird Sie hier finden, wenn ich Sie erdrossele und vergrabe.

Und ich überlegte, ob ich SEINE rührenden herabhängenden Schultern nur aus Angst so gesehen hatte. Als ich neben IHM herging, waren sie gar nicht zu bemerken.

Erdrosseln? sagte ich. Sie wollen mir wohl Angst machen?

Ja, Sie haben Angst, ich merke das. Es klang sehr liebenswürdig, wie ER auf mich einging. Die meisten Menschen haben im Wald Angst, weil sie beautiful death is murder, the stab of the knife a glittering image that moves up the capitol as with a silken line, in order to grant you a glimpse into a kingdom without haze, without truth, without lies, without symbol and structure and without parable. A kingdom in which no one demands that a conclusion be drawn, in which cause and effect are perfectly alike, where one needs no age to be wise, and no youth to be young. Just where fantasy needs no special mother like mind or consciousness, where fantasy is no fantasy, but rather breath, where breath is no mere inhaling but rather fantasy, just that which is there, longing, which is the joy of satisfaction, and satisfaction, which is the next longing, without symbol and structure and without parable.

It is that I longed for. Indeed I wanted only to reach HIM in the yellow rubber jacket, who walked ahead of me and then disappeared in the forest as if HIS poignant shoulders were already the first crouching of HIS body with which HE wanted to make himself ready to crawl through the eye of the needle toward fantasy.

Since it had disappeared, I needed no longer concern myself with HIS bodily image. I simply addressed HIM.

I said: it moves me that YOU go through the forest so sadly with sloping shoulders.

Why sloping shoulders? He asked.

Your sloping shoulders are poignant to me.

I want to tell you something, HE said and walked farther without looking at me. You are free to insult me here in the lonesome forest, I'm not afraid. You should consider everything you say, because I'm very strong and no one knows this forest as well as I do. No one will find you here if I strangle and bury you.

And I considered whether I had seen HIS poignant sloping shoulders only out of fear. When I was walking next to HIM, they were not to be noticed at all.

Strangle? I said. Are you trying to frighten me?

Yes, you are afraid, I notice that. It sounded very kind the way HE responded to me. Most people are afraid in the woods because they don't ihn nicht kennen. Sie stürzen sich lieber in den Autoverkehr als zwischen die stillen Stämme. Da sitzt allerdings auch keiner, der das Rauschen der Blätter nach den Bedürfnissen der Wanderer steuern oder anhalten könnte. Das geht durch Mark und Pfennig, ein deutscher Dichter nannte es einmal "donnerdunkles Rauschen." Bei dem, der dieses Bild erfand, kann man schon eine kleine Persönlichkeitsschädigung voraussetzen. Was meinen Sie, warum ich hier herumlaufe?

Ich schätze, Sie wollen einsam sein.

Wenn Sie das annehmen, sagte ER, dann ist es eine Frechheit, daß Sie mich ansprechen.

Das war eine ernste Bemerkung gegen meine Fantasie. Denn ich war ja allein, ich suchte den Mann noch, mit dem ich schon sprach. Niemand hätte mir geglaubt, daß ein Mann mit einer gelben Jacke vor meinen Augen zwischen den Stämmen verschwand, sich aber doch mit mir unterhielt.

Und schon redete ich wieder mit IHM: Es ist natürlich nur eine Phrase gewesen, daß Sie einsam sein sollten. Aber was meinten Sie mit dem Erdrosseln?

Sie haben mich mißverstanden, antwortete ER, ich wollte Sie nicht erdrosseln, ich sagte nur, ich könnte es. Und das ist wahr, ich könnte es wirklich. Sie sprechen von meinen abfallenden Schultern, rührenden abfallenden Schultern, sagten Sie. Solche Schultern sind gerade ein Beweis von Kraft.

Daß ich mit Ihnen über Kraft spreche, das ist komisch, das hätte ich mir niemals denken können. Ich hatte ein ganz anderes Gespräch vor.

Und ich wollte schweigen, sagte ER einfach, ohne weiteres hinzuzusetzen.

Aber das konnte ich mir nicht gefallen lassen, daß ER, der von mir Erdachte, nicht mehr mit mir sprechen wollte. Donnerwetter, sagte ich, Sie nehmen keine Rücksicht auf meine zarte Verfassung—.

Ich dachte, *ich* wäre zart, unterbrach ER mich. Aber Sie brauchen gar nicht soviel zu umschreiben. Sie meinen mit der zarten Verfassung Ihre Angst. Ich hatte eine Geliebte, mit der ich schlief und mich in sie know it. They'd rather rush into traffic than between quiet tree trunks. Certainly there is nobody there who could direct or stop the rustling of the leaves according to the demands of the wanderers. The rustling goes through dime and dollar. A German poet once called it "rustling dark as thunder." As for the one who originated this image, one can already presuppose a slight damage in his personality. Why do you think I'm walking around here?

I suppose you want to be alone.

If that's what you assume, HE said, then you've got some nerve addressing me.

That was a serious remark against my fantasy. For I was, after all, alone, I was still looking for the man with whom I was already speaking. Nobody would have believed me, that a man in a yellow jacket disappeared between the tree trunks before my very eyes but nevertheless was talking with me.

And again I was talking with HIM: Certainly it was only an expression, that you should be lonely. But what did you mean by "strangling"?

You misunderstood me, HE answered, I did not want to strangle you, I only said I *could* do it. And that's true, I could really do it. You talk about my sloping shoulders, poignant, sloping shoulders, you said. Such shoulders are precisely a proof of strength.

That I'm talking with you about strength, that's strange, I would never have been able to think of that. I had a very different conversation in mind.

And I wanted to be silent, HE said simply, without adding anything else.

But I was not willing to accept that HE, whom I had imagined, did not want to speak with me anymore. Well, hell, I said, you have no consideration for my sensitive frame of mind—

I thought *I* was sensitive, HE interrupted me. But you don't need to talk around it so much. By your "sensitive frame of mind" you mean your fear. I had a lover with whom I slept and into whose being I dreamed myself as hineinträumte wie in eine bessere Welt, und eines Tages sagte sie, sie sei nur bei mir geblieben, weil sie Angst gehabt hätte, ich würde sie ermorden.

Der Mord, sagte ich, als die größte Möglichkeit, sich mit dem anderen zu vereinigen, hat mich immer fasziniert.

Faszination, sagte ER trocken, die sollten Sie aus Ihrem Lebenslexikon streichen. Sie ist eine Bindung und keine Verbindung. Eine Bindung, die nur in der Lieblosigkeit und Fahrlässigkeit Ihrer Seele eine Heimat hat. Durch nüchterne Prüfung zur Dauer bestimmt, so müßte die Parole lauten.

Wie sollte Fantasie nüchtern prüfen? warf ich ein.

Wer und was sonst, sagte ER, sollte nüchtern sein? Nur die Fantasie ist es, die aus dem Bekannten das Unbekannte entwickelt und wie sollte das geschehen als durch einen nüchternen Bau, ein Stein zum anderen, ein Grashalm zum anderen und ein Mensch zum anderen; und zwar so, wie Sie ihn denken und sehen, und dann tun Sie dies und das hinzu, bis das brauchbare Bild fertig ist. So wie ich meine Geliebte baute, die mich für einen Mörder hielt.

Das gäbe ja eine schreckliche Welt, sagte ich.

Die einzige, in der Sie sich bewegen können und in der Sie sich ja auch dauernd bewegen. Und wenn das nicht reibungslos läuft, wenn die rührenden Schultern nicht hergeben, was Sie von ihnen haben mochten, na—was soll ich sagen?—na, dann gehen Sie in den Wald, bibbern ein bißchen herum und vertreiben Ihre Angst mit der Vorstellung rührender Schultern. Da haben Sie doch was, das ist doch eine Klammer.

Herrgott, Sie sind doch gar nicht da! schrie ich.

Das möchten Sie gern. ER sprach genau so ruhig wie vorher. Sie finden mich, weil Sie mich finden wollen, und das ist der letzte Rest Gesundheit, der da noch rumort.

Ich ging jetzt sehr viel schneller, um dem Scheusal zu entkommen. Die rührenden Schultern hatte ich vergessen, ich war bereit, diesen verschwundenen Wanderer für eine Kröte zu halten, die wegplumpst und vor lauter Mimikry nicht mehr zu finden ist, wenn man erschreckt vor ihrem feuchten Ruheplatz steht.

in a better world, and one day she said she had only stayed with me because she was afraid I would murder her.

Murder, I said, has always fascinated me as the greatest possibility to unite oneself with another.

Fascination, HE said dryly, you should strike that from the dictionary of your life. It is a commitment and not a connection. A commitment that has a home only in the lovelessness and negligence of your soul. Destined for permanence through sensible examination, that should be the slogan.

How should fantasy examine sensibly? I interjected.

Who and what else, HE said, should be sensible? It's only fantasy that produces the unfamiliar out of the familiar, and how should this happen but through a sensible construction, one stone to another, one blade of grass to another, and one human being to another; and indeed just as you think him and see him, and then you add this and that until a useful image is ready. Just as I had constructed my lover, who took me for a murderer.

That would be a horrible world, I said.

The only one in which you can move around, and in which, in fact, you do move around continuously. And if it doesn't run smoothly, if the poignant shoulders don't yield what you'd like to have, well—what should I say?—well, then you go into the forest, shiver a little, and drive your fears away by imagining my poignant shoulders. There you've got something, that's something to hold on with.

My God, you're not there at all! I screamed.

You'd really like that, HE spoke just as softly as before. You find me because you want to find me, and that is the last remaining bit of sanity that is still left here.

I walked a lot faster now to escape the monster. As for the poignant shoulders, I'd forgotten about them. I was ready to take this vanished wanderer to be a toad that hops away and is no longer to be found because of protective coloration, when you stand aghast in front of its moist resting place.

Sie brauchen nicht zu laufen, sagte ER, was ist in der Fantasie Geschwindigkeit? Ihre Geliebte, mein Lieber, wegen der Sie hier im Wald nach rührenden Schultern suchen, sehnt sich mit ihrem barbarischen Oberteil längst wieder nach Ihnen. Auch der Liebhaber von gestern, dem Sie unterlagen, weil Sie zu feige und zu vornehm waren, ihn mit Fäusten aus dem Haus zu treiben, auch der ist längst weg. Sie wollte nur, daß dieser Herr Sie von Ihrer Sehnsucht nach rührenden Schultern erlöste. Ein derbes Pülverchen, eine spanische Fliege sozusagen, die in Ihnen den alten Adam freimachen sollte, den die Schwachen am meisten lieben, denn sie wollen die Welt an sich ziehen, um ihr mit ihrer Vanillesauce an die Leber zu gehen.

Sie kennen doch meine Geliebte gar nicht, sagte ich.

Sie, Sie selbst gehen doch neben mir, antwortete ER, wie sollte ich Ihre Geliebte da nicht kennen? Ich weiß doch, was Sie sich zusammenbauen, dann bewachen und schließlich vernichten wollen, weil ein Eckchen an ihr nicht stimmt. Ich sah mal meine Mutter, wie sie sich den Rücken am Türpfosten schubberte, weil es sie juckte. Die Bewegung mißfiel mir so, daß ich meine geliebte Mutter jahrelang nicht leiden konnte und sie darauf in eine Trauer verfiel, die sie mir noch mehr entfremdete. Das lag an mir. Ich stand nicht, ich wackelte.

Wenn ich Ihre Reden geahnt hätte, stammelte ich, wäre ich nie in den Wald gegangen.

Dann hätten Sie sich zu Hause von Ihrer Geliebten zerfleischen lassen, und das wäre schön für Sie gewesen. Ein Leben als ohnmächtiger Trauerkloß in sesselgepflegter Umgebung—gibt es etwas Herrlicheres für einen larmoyanten Bürger, der künstlerische Wellen plätschern läßt? Als Eisenbieger in der zehnten Etage eines Hochhauses könnten Sie damit gar nichts anfangen. Nichts, sage ich Ihnen. Und da hätte Ihre Geliebte auch nichts zum Zerfleischen.

Lassen Sie die Geliebte beiseite!

Wenn ich mich mit Ihnen unterhalte, muß ich sie erwähnen. Sie sind nur noch ein Stückchen von ihr. Erst wenn Sie ohne dieses Monstrum existierten, existierten Sie überhaupt. Aber das kann man niemandem beibringen. Ihnen schon gar nicht. Denn Sie glauben, Liebesfähigkeit in erhöhtem Maße zu besitzen, wodurch Sie sich zur Poesie ermächtigt fühlen. Ihr Poetenträumchen, Ihr Ideal, das müssen Sie mal an die

You don't have to run, HE said, what is speed in fantasy? Your lover, my dear sir, because of whom you are looking for poignant shoulders here in the forest, has for a long time been longing for you again with her barbaric upper body. Even yesterday's lover, by whom you were defeated because you were too cowardly and too refined to drive him out of the house with your fists, even he is long gone. She only wanted this man to relieve you of your longing for poignant shoulders. A harsh bit of powder, a bit of Spanish fly, so to speak, that should release in you the old Adam, who is loved most by the weak, for they want to draw the world closer to themselves, in order to get to its liver with their vanilla custard.

But you don't know my lover at all, I said.

But you, you yourself walk next to me, HE answered, why shouldn't I know your lover? Yet I know what you want to construct, then guard, and finally destroy, because a little part of her doesn't fit. I once saw my mother as she rubbed her back against the doorpost because she had an itch. This action displeased me so much that I couldn't stand my beloved mother for years, and thereupon she sank into such sorrow that she alienated me still more. It was my fault. I didn't stand still, I staggered.

If I had foreseen your speech, I stuttered, I would never have entered the forest.

Then you would have let your lover tear you to pieces at home, and that would have been nice for you. Life as a feeble wet blanket in an easy-chair environment—is there anything more splendid for a lachrymose bourgeois who makes artistic waves? As an ironworker on the tenth floor of a high-rise, you couldn't make use of it at all. Not at all, I tell you. And then your lover would have nothing to tear to pieces.

Never mind my lover!

If I talk with you, I have to mention her. You are only a little piece of her. Only if you existed without this monster, would you exist at all. But you can't teach that to anyone. Least of all to you. For you believe you possess the ability to love in the highest degree, through which you feel yourself capable of poetry. Your little poet's dream, your ideal, that is what you have to hang on the clothes line to air out, but where there is

Wäscheleine hängen zum Auslüften, aber da, wo Wind ist, in Ihrem Falle würde ich einen Orkan empfehlen. Etwas, was die rührenden Schultern in die Höhe treibt, damit Sie auch als Kraftsportler Ihr Püppchen mal genießen. Ich hoffe sehr, daß es dann nicht erdrückt wird. Aber Damen sind ja mit Werg gefüllt, der die Jahrhunderte überdauert.

Ich möchte nicht mehr mit Ihnen gehen, sagte ich.

ER ging ungerührt neben mir, und nach und nach merkte ich, daß ich Spaß an dem Mitwanderer fand. Heute abend würde ich alles, was ER zu mir sagte, meiner Geliebten sagen. Ich sah sie aufspringen und hinauslaufen. Mich sah ich nachgehen und die Türen zuschlagen, die sie offen gelassen hatte. Und bei jedem Knall würde ihr Blick härter.

Ich lasse Sie jetzt allein, sagte der Gelbjackige, bog rechts ab und war wieder verschwunden.

Nicht noch einmal werde ich IHN suchen.

Ich drehte um und ging denselben Weg zurück. Ich wußte, daß ich sie jetzt allein zu Hause finden würde mit einem Tuch um den Kopf, im Garten an den Rosen schneidend, einen aufgeklappten Krimi neben der Decke auf dem Rasen. Und sie würde lächeln. Ich würde nicht wissen, worüber, aber der Triumph in ihren Augen würde mich treffen. So, als ob ich IHM mit der gelben Jacke nie begegnet wäre. Ich ging an dem Haus vorbei.

Ich weiß aber nicht, ob meine Vernunft den morgigen Tag überdauern wird.

wind, in your case I'd recommend a hurricane. Something that causes the poignant shoulders to rise so that you can enjoy your little darling for a change as an athlete. I really hope she won't be crushed. But women are filled with stuff that survives for centuries.

I don't want to walk with you anymore, I said.

HE walked next to me unmoved, and little by little I noticed that I was enjoying my fellow wanderer. Tonight I would tell everything that HE told me to my lover. I saw her jump and run out. I saw myself go after her and slam the doors she had left open. And with every bang her look became more stern.

I'll leave you alone now, said the man in the yellow jacket, turned off to the right, and disappeared again.

I will never look for HIM again.

I turned around and walked back the same way. I knew that I would find her now alone at home with a scarf over her head, clipping roses in the garden, an open detective novel lying next to the blanket on the lawn. And she would be smiling. I wouldn't know what about, but the triumph in her eyes would strike me. Just as if I had never met HIM in the yellow jacket. I went past the house.

Yet I don't know if my reason will survive the coming day.

Gerd Sonntag

1.12.71

TOTSEIN IN EINEM WINKEL DER STADT UND ANDERE GEDICHTE

GERD SONNTAG

TOTSEIN IN EINEM WINKEL DER STADT

Sie die mich finden finden Blässe
Das wenige das ich seit jeher trug

Meiner Träume Falter stürzend im Flug
Gleich eines Tags Novembernässe
Träge und taumelnd von Esse zu Esse

Jetzt erst ist alles getan. Es wurde
Die Krankheit beschlossen,
Ihr die Lippen, das Haar benannt und die Augen,
Gezeichnet als zäher Inzest
Muß der Liebenden Bild vorüberziehn.

Jetzt kann jeder sehen
Weißgeblutet der Menschen Reinheit.
Jetzt kann jeder es hören,
Dialoge huschen wie Gestalten
Rasch an Ohren vorbei.

Kein Stimmchen, keine Stimme,
Zu fragen ohne gefragt werden oder
Zu versuchen die bestürzende Antwort:
Wo gehen wir hin? Wo strandet das Ufer,
Da die Wasser sich auflösen?

TO BE DEAD IN A CORNER OF THE CITY AND OTHER POEMS

GERD SONNTAG
translated by George F. Peters

TO BE DEAD IN A CORNER OF THE CITY

Paleness is all those who find me will find
The little I have ever had to wear

Butterfly of my dreams plunging through air
Like a day's drenching of the November wind
From chimney to chimney staggering and blind

Only now is everything done. It was
Determined, her illness,
Described, her lips, her hair, and her eyes,
Labeled as stubborn incest
The image of the beloved must pass on.

Now everyone can see
Bled white the purity of man.
Now everyone can hear it,
Dialogs rush like shapes
Quickly past our ears.

No little voice, no voice,
To ask without being asked or
To attempt the devastating answer:
Where are we going? Where does the shore end,
Now that the waters are dissolving?

Aus den zerfallenden Häusern,
Aus denen Himmel erwächst,
Steigen herab wir, die Keller hinunter,
In die Keller wir,
Eine Kerze auf jedem Finger.

Der Letzte
Schaltet das Licht aus.
Fürchten wir
Manchmal.

KONTROLLPUNKT

Nicht Gültigeres habe ich vorzuweisen
Als den Paß geöffneter Adern,
Deren Abfluß, mein letztes Versteck,
Gespült wird,
Gespült, ehe ich mein Gehirn
In jede Ecke geweint.

Von der Gleichgültigkeit ihrer Wiese
Die Kühe darauf aus Nacht
Fraßen das Lächeln kreiselnder Sonnen.

Alle Schulbänke wurden besetzt
Von Faltern trauriger Augen,
Spielend mit dem Schweigen der Kinder.

Und zur Straße beugten sich meine Möbel,
Zu lieben die Stirn eines Schattens,
Dessen Hochhaus kein Ende nahm.

Rasch kam überein mit der Liebe
Ich, aufzureißen in ihr eine Wunde,
Aus der ich endlich emporwuchs.

Out of the collapsing houses,
Out of which grows the sky,
We climb down, into the basements,
Into the basements with us,
A candle on every finger.

The last one
Turns the light off.
We are afraid
Sometimes.

CHECKPOINT

I have nothing more valid to present
Than this passport of opened arteries,
The flow from which, my last refuge,
Is rinsed away,
Rinsed away, before I have wept
My brain into every corner.

From the indifference of their meadow
The cows on it made of night
Fed on the smile of circling suns.

All the school benches were being taken
By butterflies of sad eyes,
Playing with the silence of the children.

And my furniture bent down to the street,
To love the brow of a shadow,
Whose skyscraper found no end.

Quickly there came at once with love
I, to tear open in it a wound,
Out of which I ultimately rose up.

ZUSTÄNDE
UND ANDERE GEDICHTE

JOACHIM UHLMANN

ZUSTÄNDE

Ich komme aus dem niemandsland
steige die stufen einer knöchernen treppe hoch
seh im vorbeigehn kaum den abgebrannten mann
der ans geländer geklammert seit vielen jahren
seine verkohlten zitate summt.

Wie schön noch einmal die knisternden vögel
als er genau wie jetzt die tür mir öffnet
das wort *logisch* in die luft schreibt
mich auffordert mit geschlossenem mund
einzutreten in die ruine
wo er ein zwitschern eben noch
zur faust geballt verglimmen sah.

Was kann ich dafür daß ich mich nicht erinnere?
Wir nehmen unsere plätze ein
jedenfalls diese nacht an dem schwarzen tisch
der immer leerblieb.
Hier wird ausgezählt! droht mein freund.
Er sitzt mir gegenüber zieht die schublade auf
und beginnt mich zu verhören.

CONDITIONS AND OTHER POEMS

JOACHIM UHLMANN
translated by A. Leslie Willson

CONDITIONS

I come from no-one's-land
climb up the steps of a bony stairs
in passing hardly see the burned-out man
who clasping the bannister for many years
hums his charred quotations.

How nice once again the crackling birds
as just like now he opens the door for me
writes the word *logically* in the air
invites me with his mouth held shut
to step into the ruins
where he even now glimpsed
a dimming twitter clenched into a fist.

How can I help it that I don't remember?
We take our seats
this night anyway at the black table
that always remained empty.
Now for the count-down! threatens my friend.
He sits opposite me pulls out the drawer
and begins to interrogate me.

LANDSCHAFT MIT DEM VOGEL Y

(nach Paul Klee)

Niemand kennt seinen namen.
Jeder hoffte daß der vogel
wenn die erde glüht
wenn alle spuren erlöschen
ihm ins garn geht.

Wie weit war er geflohn
durch die felsensprünge?
Hat er den ort der sonne erreicht
wo im zirkelschlag der tod
als schattenspiel schimmert?

Oder war sein flug der stillstand
zwischen den bäumen des ja und nein
verkündet vom buchstaben ypsilon
dessen zwei wege in einen münden?

Vogel und sonne ja und nein
verschmolzen längst zum lachen
aus dem die vogelleichtmechanik
tropft tönt fällt
und einen leeren schrei hinterläßt
den niemand hört.

LANDSCAPE WITH BIRD Y

(after Paul Klee)

No one knows its name.
Each one hoped that the bird
when the earth glows
when all traces fade out
will go in his own snare.

How far had it flown
through the cliff chasms?
Did it reach the place of the sun
where in the cast circle death
shimmers as a play of shadows?

Or was its flight armistice
between the trees of yea and nay
proclaimed by the letter ypsilon
whose two paths flow into one?

Bird and sun yea and nay
long ago melted into laughter
from which the light mechanic bird
drips drones falls
leaving behind an empty cry
that no one hears.

SCHERENSCHNITT

Wodurch vertraut mein ich dem ich
das zu besuch ist bei der tante hoffnung
die weiße rosen häkelt aber nach verwesung duftet
und wieder nicht den dunklen punkt erklärt
auf den der ausgefranste vater zeigt
bevor er anfängt aufzuhören
weil er die irren maschen nicht versteht?

SILHOUETTE

How can my ego trust the ego
which is on a visit to Aunt Hope
who crochets white roses but has an odor of decay
and again does not explain that shady spot
at which my befringed father points
before he begins to cease because
he does not understand the tricky stitches?

Metamorphose

Metamorphosis

Marionetten

Marionettes

BAHNFAHRT

Vergangenheit singt der zukunft vor
macht schlagzeilen mit stiefmütterchen
in der kälte auf einem balkon
fühlt sich elegant und sicher
läßt ihr graues bewußtsein schlummern
während hinter schmutzigen scheiben
sonnige gräben koppeln kiefern
immer schneller nach hause fliegen
und man sich die gegenwart abgewöhnt.

TRAIN TRIP

The past sings to the future
makes headlines with violets
in the cold air on a balcony
feels quite elegant and assured
lets its graying awareness slumber
while behind the dirty windows
sunny ditches couple pine trees
fly home faster and faster
and one gives up the present.

Schamanentanz

Dance of the Schamans

Vorläufer

Predecessors

Maske

Mask

12 HAIKU ZUM LÖSCHEN DES ICHS

Die mauersegler
kamen wieder und es blüht
der alte himmel.

•

Gehen und warten.
Sonnenwirbel leuchten blau
am rand des umwegs.

•

Mein fenster dunkelt.
Was kann die grille wissen?
Wieder hör ich zu.

•

Auch die amsel glüht
zwischen den vogelbeeren
am sommerband.

•

Ins weisse feuer
flog schimmernd die libella—
ihr schatten wird nacht.

•

Kahltage reisen
nebelsonnen entblättern
krähen weglos ziehn.

•

Zitternd der schatten
des trocknen buchenblattes
im schütteren licht.

12 HAIKUS TO OBLITERATE THE EGO

The purple martins
have again returned and the
old heavens blossom.

•

Walking and waiting.
Sunny whirlpools glisten blue
along the byway.

•

My window darkens.
What is it the cricket knows?
Again I listen.

•

The blackbird glows too
between the rowanberries
on summer's ribbon.

•

Into the white fire
the dragonfly flew shining—
shadow turns to night.

•

Naked days set forth
foggy suns strip off the leaves
crows fly pathless past.

•

Trembling the shadow
of the dried-up beach tree leaf
in the sparser light.

•

Ein gelber kürbis
neben der vogelscheuche—
sie nur tanzt im wind.

•

In regenpfützen
spiegeln die schwarzen äste—
wachsgesichter fliehn.

•

Tote gleise schnee
dazwischen schaukeln birken—
geh auf die reise!

•

Verweht die wege
weit glänzt das weiße schneefeld
hoch steigt die lerche.

•

Rost zerfrißt das rohr
des alten eisenofens—
hör doch das feuer!

•

A yellow pumpkin
by the side of the scarecrow—
only it jigs in the wind.

•

In the rain puddles
the black boughs are reflected—
waxen faces flee.

•

Lifeless rails with snow
between them birches rocking—
go on a journey!

•

The paths are windblown
distant the white snowfield gleams
high ascends the lark.

•

Rust chews up the flue
of the ancient iron stove—
listen to the fire!

Diagnos

Diagnos

Peter Weiss

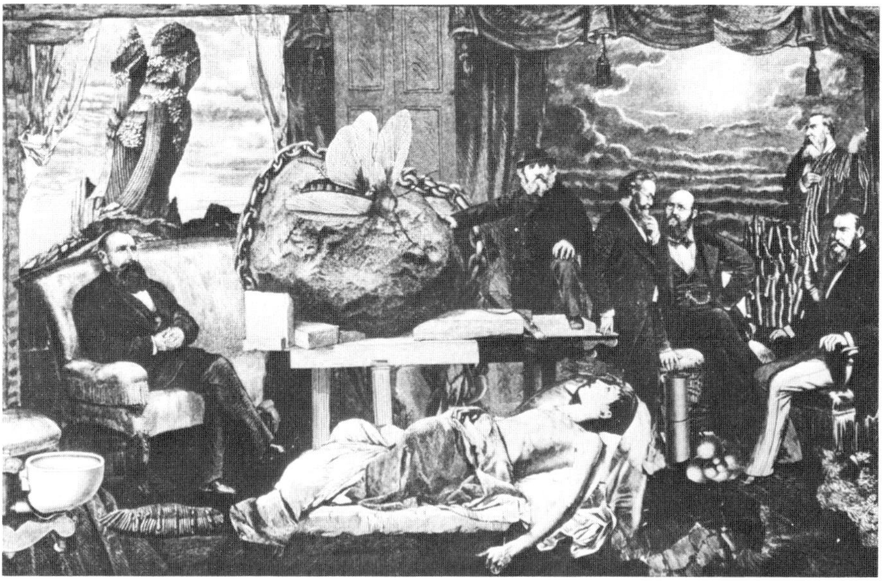

Aus Dem PARISER JOURNAL

PETER WEISS

IN VILARDS LANDHAUS HATTE DAS ZUSAMMENWIRKEN VON INNENRAUM und Garten, das auf dem alten Ateliergrundstück vorbereitet worden war, seine Vollendung gefunden. Der riesenhafte Arbeitsraum nahm durch die gläserne Wand, in der hier und da abgeteilte Flächen nach außen geöffnet waren, den Garten in sich auf. Die hohe, aus groben, weißgetünchten Steinen errichtete Seitenwand setzte sich draußen in der weißen Gartenmauer fort, die ausgerichtet zum Hintergrund verlief und im dichten Laubwerk des Parks untertauchte. Aus dem Gras wuchsen Rhododendronbüsche auf, mit rosafarbenen Blüten, und dazwischen standen Apfelbäume, mit weit um sich greifenden Ästen und hellgrünen Früchten. Das Blaugrün des Himmels, mit goldbraunen Wolkenbänken, legte einen Widerschein auf die Wände, und die untergehende Sonne spann Licht- und Schattenfäden von außen her in den Raum, so daß die Arabesken der Blätter und des Geästs sich auf den Innenflächen regten. Auf einer Reihe von Staffeleien standen die großen Bilder, auf denen dieses Gewebe zu ineinander verschobenen Farbstücken abstrahiert worden war, hier waren, als letzte Ausläufer klassischer Naturgestaltungen, Meditationen über das Aufnehmen und Verarbeiten von Lichterscheinungen in einzelnen Stadien variiert, von Ebenen mit violetten und rötlichen Tönungen bis zu solchen, auf denen nur noch das Schwarz und Weiß hervortrat. Von außen gesehen, als ich durch die Glastür in den Garten gegangen war, und neben mir die langgestreckten ebenmäßigen Blätter des Rhododendron hatte, zeigten sich die Bilder, umspielt von den Schatten, wie Ausschnitte eines organischen Wachstums. Einzelne Gäste bewegten sich hinter der Fensterwand des Ateliers und im Nebenraum, in dem Anne die letzten Vorbereitungen zur Mahlzeit traf. Inez war zu sehen, mit aufleuchtendem Haar, zwischen den Gestalten, die einander umkreisten, und Vilard, hochgewachsen, mit geschorenem silberglänzendem Schädel, trat zu Anne, legte den Arm um sie, und sie entzog sich ihm, mit einer überraschend heftigen Bewegung. Drinnen auf dem gedeckten Tisch waren Kerzen angezündet worden, die den Raum abendlich machten, während zwischen den Bäumen noch klares grünblaues Licht hing. Gläser wurden umhergereicht, gefüllt, ausgetrunken, ich trat wieder ein in das Atelier, in dem jetzt die Schattenwirkungen der Blätter vergangen waren und in dem die Bilder wie barbarische Schilde erschienen, die der Maler um sich

From The PARIS JOURNAL

PETER WEISS
translated by Ralph R. Read III

IN VILARD'S COUNTRY HOUSE THE COMMINGLING OF INTERIOR SPACE AND garden that had been devised on the site of the old atelier had attained perfection. The vast workshop took in the garden through the glass wall in which panels set here and there opened outward. The high side wall, built of rough, white-washed stone, continued outside in the white garden wall that extended and blended into the background and submerged in the dense foliage of the park. Rhododendrons with pink blossoms rose up from the grass, and among them stood apple trees with far-stretching branches and bright green fruit. The blue-green of the sky, with golden-brown cloudbanks, cast its reflection on the walls, and the setting sun spun threads of light and shadow into the room from outside, so that arabesques of leaves and branches stirred on the surfaces inside. On a row of easels rested the large pictures on which this web had been abstracted into pieces of color shifted onto one another; here, as the last offshoots of the classical configuration of nature, meditations on the reception and assimilation of light phenomena were varied at separate stages, from planes with violet and reddish tints to others on which only black and white still stood out. Seen from the outside as I had gone into the garden through the glass door and had the outstretched, symmetrical leaves of the rhododendron beside me, the pictures, played upon by the shadows, showed up like segments of organic growth. Individual guests moved behind the window wall of the atelier and in the adjoining room, in which Anna was finishing preparations for the meal. Inez was visible with her gleaming hair among the circulating figures, and Vilard, standing tall, with his shorn cranium gleaming silver, stepped up to Anna, put his arm around her, and she drew away from him with a surprisingly vigorous movement. Inside, on the readied table, candles had been lit to spread evening in the room while clear, green-bluish light still hung between the trees. Glasses were passed around, were filled and emptied, I stepped back into the atelier, in which the shadow play of the leaves by now had ceased, and in which the pictures seemed like barbaric shields that the painter had set up about aufgestellt hatte, er stand, ein Glas in der Hand, mit einer Gruppe von Gästen in der Mitte des Raums, in einem eifrigen Gespräch, in dem die Worte von der vorschnellenden Zunge aus den aufklaffenden Lippen geworfen und von den zuckenden Bewegungen des Kinns und der Halsmuskeln, von Kopfhebungen und Schulterdrehungen begleitet wurden, in dem die Gesichter sich einander gierig zeigten, mit weitgeöffneten Augen, geblähten Nüstern, ich sah Inez, bei zwei Männern, die vor ihr die weißen Panzer ihrer Hemden aufflammen ließen, die wie Fechter mit der Hüfte zur Seite fuhren, ein Bein zurückschwangen, das andere Bein, im Knie federnd, vorstießen, die blitzenden Gläser hoben, den weißen Docht der Zigarette zum Mund führten, und Inez, am Glas nippend, suchte nach Worten, hörte, aus Ermangelung eigener Worte, dem auf sie eindringenden Schwall von Worten zu, heuchelte mit Lachen und Kopfnicken ein Verstehen, und auch ich geriet in eine Gegenüberstellung, frontal zum Leib einer Frau. Um ihren Torso war ein rotseidenes Tuch gebunden, goldene Schmuckstücke hingen an ihren Ohren, goldene Reifen an ihren nackten Armen, dies war die Frau des jungen Mannes, der uns hierher gebracht hatte und der, wie sich jetzt herausstellte, Lucian hieß, und mir plötzlich als Hersteller von Filmen bekannt war, seine Frau spiegelte den Ruhm, von dem er umgeben war, sie spiegelte die Medaillen, die goldenen Pokale, mit denen seine Werke belohnt worden waren, sie blendete mit ihrem Rot und ihrem Gold, in dem die Ausstrahlung festlicher Premieren lag, sie blendete mit ihrer Stirn, ihren juwelhaft eingefaßten Augen, ihren Schultern, ihren Knien, sie blendete mit ihren Zähnen und mit ihren metallischen Worten, sie polierte mich mit ihrem Strahlenglanz, sie glättete mich, ich reflektierte, ich stand mit einer plötzlich auferlegten Rolle da und strahlte bedeutende Werte zurück, ich widerspiegelte die Gaben, die sie dem Hörensagen nach in mir vermutete, ich hielt mich aufrecht in dieser Ansammlung von Pfeilern der Kultur, bereit, allen Erfolg auf mich zu nehmen, mich zu allen großen Taten zu bekennen, unter dem Windzug von den Schwingen der die Halle durchfliegenden unsterblichen Meister. Das Drama, indem wir uns zusammenfanden, wurde eröffnet mit dem Prolog, wir verschoben uns vom einen zum andern, mit unserm äußersten Aufwand von eroberten und gezügelten Kräften, wir stellten uns voreinander dar, als Träger von Leistungen oder zumindest Gerüchten von Leistungen, obgleich Inez mir im Vorbeigehen anvertraute, daß sie in uns nur die armen Verwandten vom Lande sah, in dieser Versammlung, in der neben Lucian, Anne und Vilard, Größen wie Giacometti, der Regisseur R. und die Schauspielerin Delphine erkannt werden konnten. Während Giacometti sich selbst bestürzend ähnlich war und ganz aufging in seinem eigene, unlöslich mit seinem Werk verbundenen Gesicht, glich Delphine nur von fern der Figur, die sie in den Labyrinthen ihres letzten Films verkörpert himself, he stood, a glass in his hand, in the middle of the room with a group of guests in a lively conversation in which his words were tossed from gaping lips by his darting tongue and accompanied by the twitching movement of his chin and of his neck muscles, by the lifting of his head and the shifting of his shoulders, while greedy faces were displayed with wide-opened eyes, dilated nostrils, I saw Inez with two men, who flashed the white armor of their shirts before her, who moved their hips to the side like fencers, swung one leg back, thrust the other leg forward, flexing at the knee, raised their sparkling glasses, brought the white wick of their cigarettes to their mouths, and Inez, sipping at her glass, searched for words, listened, for want of her own words, to the deluge of words rushing upon her, feigned comprehension by laughing and nodding, and I too found myself positioned facing a woman's body. A red silk cloth was wound about her torso, golden ornaments hung from her ears, golden circlets on her bare arms, this was the wife of the young man who had brought us here, and who, as it now turned out, was named Lucian and was suddenly well known to me as a producer of films; his wife reflected the fame by which he was surrounded, she reflected the medals, the golden trophies with which his work had been rewarded, she dazzled with her red and her gold, in which lay the radiance of festive premières, she dazzled with her forehead, with her eyes set like jewels, her shoulders, her knees, she dazzled with her teeth and with her metallic words, she polished me with her luster, she burnished me, I reflected, I stood there suddenly cast in a role and beamed back significant words, I mirrored the talents that she assumed in me from hearsay, I held my ground in this gathering of the pillars of culture, ready to claim all my success, to admit to all my great deeds, caught in the draft of the pinions of the immortal masters flying through the hall. The drama in which we were met opened with the prologue, we pushed out way from one person to the next with our most extreme display of captured and bridled powers, we presented ourselves to one another as bearers of accomplishments or at least of rumors of accomplishments, although Inez confided to me in passing that she saw in us only poor country cousins in this gathering in which, next to Lucian, Anna, and Vilard, greats like Giacometti, the director R., and the actress Delphine could be recognized. Whereas Giocometti was disconcertingly similar to himself and merged completely in his own face, which was inextricably bound to his works, Delphine resembled only from afar the figure that she had personified in the labyrinths of her last film, she seemed to be a tool hatte, sie schien ein Werkzeug zu sein, das sich verwandeln ließ, das diese Verwandlungen jedoch mit einer eigenen knisternden Aktivität verarbeitete, ich sah sie, einige Augenblicke lang, auf dem nächtlichen Kiesweg des Schloßparks, und zwischen den weißen Straußenfedern in der blendenden Helle des überbelichteten Schlafzimmers auf der Leinwand eines Kinos, dann geriet ich an Anne vorbei, deren Gesicht Spuren von Müdigkeit zeigte, und die sich als Gastgeberin nicht festhalten ließ, ihre Aufmerksamkeit war geteilt an alle Anwesenden, ihr Mund war gespannt und konnte sich während der Sekunden, in denen sie sich unbeobachtet glaubte, an den Winkeln herabziehen wie bei einem enttäuschten Kind, ich sah sie in einem Getriebe von Akteuren, in dem jeder um seine Solistenstimme kämpfte, und dann wandten sich alle Bewegungen dem benachbarten Zimmer zu, alles strömte dem langen Tisch zu, dessen dunkle grobfaserne Platte mit Salaten, Reisschalen, Gewürzen, Pasteten, Käsesorten, Früchten gedeckt war, jeder halb instinktiv, halb von Anne geleitet, seinen Sitzplatz suchend. Vilard ging um die Tafel und füllte dunkelroten Wein in die Gläser, Anne teilte Stücke der Brotstangen aus, reichte Schüsseln umher, ringsum streckten sich Gabeln und Messer, von Händen geführt, in die angerichteten Speisen, zerschnitten sie, zerpflückten sie, zerbrachen ihre Ordnung, höhlten sie aus, sammelten sie zu neuen Kompositionen auf den blauen und grünen Tellern, in einem Zwischenakt, in dem nicht gesprochen wurde, in dem nur die Bestecke klapperten, die Schmuckstücke an den Armen der Frauen klingelten und der Wein aus den Flaschen gluckste, in dem die Hände allein das Spiel übernahmen und sich einander zeigten. Annes Hände waren mager, und unter ihrer dünnen Haut lag das blaue Gewebe der Adern, sie wiesen einen Augenblick lang ihre Verlassenheit auf, sie hingen wie vergessen in der Luft, wußten nicht, wohin sie sich begeben sollten, wurden dann von Vilards kraftvollen eigensinnigen Händen angestoßen, zuckten vor den knotigen Fingern mit den vorgewölbten Nägeln zurück, flatterten aufgescheucht weiter. Giacomettis Hände hatten eben die Werkstatt verlassen, trugen in ihrem Griff noch die Berührungen mit dem Lehm, ihre trockene rissige Haut hatte etwas Eidechsenhaftes, sie hatten auch die Beweglichkeit der Eidechse, hingen aber fest an starken breiten Gelenken, so wie seine Bildwerke, die sich bis zur Verflüchtigung verdünnen können, oft aus gewichtigen klobigen Sockeln hervorwachsen. Lucians Hände zeigten, was sein Gesicht schon gezeigt hatte, sie waren beredt und gewandt, sie ließen nur bei schärfster Beleuchtung ihre Linien erkenne, führten geschwind und ohne zu zögern aus, was von ihnen erwartet wurde, wiesen nach außen hin Sicherheit auf, zeigten in der Innenfläche aber den Schimmer von Feuchtigkeit. Das Auftauchen von Delphines Hand im Kreuzwerk der Hände war beunruhigend, denn diese Hand drohte, mit zusammengeballter nervöser Wildheit über alle that could be transformed but that imbued these transformations with its own crackling activity, I saw her for a few moments on the nocturnal gravel path of the palace park, and between the white ostrich feathers in the dazzling brightness of the overlit bedroom on the screen of a theater, then I drifted past Anna, whose face bore traces of weariness, and who as hostess would not stand still, her attention was divided among all those present, her mouth was tense and, in the moments during which she thought herself unobserved, would pull down at the corners like that of a disappointed child, I saw her in the bustle of actors in which each one was fighting for his soloist's voice, and then all movement turned toward the neighboring room, everyone streamed toward the long table, whose dark, coarse-grained top was covered with salads, dishes of rice, spices, meat pies, cheeses, fruit, everyone seeking out his seat half instinctively, half led by Anna. Vilard moved around the table pouring dark red wine into the glasses, Anna distributed pieces of long loaves of bread, passed bowls around, on all sides knives and forks, guided by hands, reached out to the food that was served up, cut it up, pulled it apart, shattered its order, hollowed it out, rearranged it in new compositions on the blue and green plates, in an interlude during which no one spoke, during which only the silverware clattered, the ornaments on the arms of the women tinkled and the wine gurgled from the bottles, while hands alone took over the game and were displayed to one another. Anna's hands were gaunt and beneath her thin skin lay the blue network of veins, they exhibited their isolation for an instant, they hung in the air as if forgotten, could not decide what to do with themselves, were then nudged by Vilard's powerful, obstinate hands, jerked back from the knotty fingers with the arching nails, fluttered on, startled. Giacometti's hands had just left the workshop, still bore the contact with the clay in their grasp, their dry, cracked skin had something lizardlike about it, they also had the agility of a lizard but hung firmly from strong, broad joints, just as his sculptures, which can be rarefied almost to the sublime, grow up out of heavy, crude pediments. Lucian's hands showed what his face had already shown, they were eloquent and nimble, only under sharpest illumination were their outlines recognizable, swiftly and without hesitation they performed what was expected of them, outwardly they exhibited sureness, but on the inner surface showed the glimmer of dampness. The emergence of Delphine's hand in the gridwork of these hands was unsettling, for this hand, with clenched, nervous wildness, andern Hände herzufallen und sie zu zerreißen, ihre Gefahr lag in ihrer Kleinheit, in ihren kurzen vor Ungeduld und Spannung abgebissenen Fingernägeln, in den hart hervortretenden Knöcheln, ihre Hand war ein lauerendes, sprungbereites, winziges Tier, auch ihre nackten Arme, mit dunklem Flaum, waren tierhaft, und jetzt, da das Sprechen wieder einsetzte, nach dem gemeinsamen Heben der Gläser, überkam mich eine Maßlose Wissensgier, jeder kleinste Abschnitt des Daseins war mit einer ungeheuren Vielfalt erfüllt, die entstehenden Muster waren so kompliziert, daß ich eine Erweiterung meiner Aufnahmefähigkeit herbeiwünschte. Die nackten Hände und Gesichter waren von den Kerzen und vom letzten Licht aus dem Garten beleuchtet, die Körper waren verhüllt und aneinandergereiht, unter der versteckten Haut nahmen die Organismen die Nahrung auf, die von den Mündern zerkaut wurde. Um die gemeinsame Nahrung versammelt, sie in den Mund führend, mit den Zähnen, dem Gaumen, der Zunge zermalmend, den Wein einsaugend, den Wein durch die Kehle in den Magensack fließen lassend, schlossen wir uns zu einer Einheit zusammen, wir waren eine Tafelrunde, mit einem Dutzend Köpfen, zwei Dutzend Händen, und die Gesichter wandten sich hin und her, nahmen Worte auf mit den Trichtern der Ohren, ließen Worte aus den feuchten schleimigen Mündern quellen, und die Worte flossen kreuz und quer ineinander zu einem gemeinsamen Tönen, die Worte vermischten sich mit den verschiedenartigen Geschmackssensationen, der Wein färbte das Gehör, das Sieden des Blutes untermalte die Stimmen, dem Fenster gegenübersitzend, hinter den Köpfen und Leibern an der andern Tischseite den dunkelblauen Garten sehend, vernahm ich Lucians an Inez gerichtete Mitteilungen über seinen Wunsch, Prousts Werk zu verfilmen, während Delphine neben mir von einem Haus an der Place des Vosges sprach, und da wir eine gemeinsame Sprache zur Verständigung gefunden hatten, konnte ich alle Einzelheiten ihrer Eindrücke entgegennehmen, es handelte sich um ein Gebäude aus dem siebzehnten Jahrhundert, das ihr zum Kauf angeboten worden war, ein hohes schmales Haus, in dem die Treppe durch viele Stockwerke bis zu den Turmzimmern führte, und dazwischen hörte ich drüben von Monsieur de Charlus, Swann und Albertine sprechen. Von andern Richtungen her kamen die Erwähnungen von Theaterstücken und Rollen, von Aufführungen und Ausstellungen, von Büchern, von Kunsthändlern, von geplanten und fertiggestellten Werken, Vilard sprach mit Giacometti über Miro und Braque, Anne sprach von einer bevorstehenden Tournee, alle zeigten mit ihren gesättigten Worten, daß sie dem Leben in dieser Stadt angehörten, daß sie zu den Auserwählten gehörten, daß sie unersetzlich waren, sie bildeten eine Familie, und Inez und ich waren die Herbeigereisten, die geduldet wurden, mit ihren mangelhaften Worten, die, im Wohlgefühl der eingenommenen Delikatessen und Gertränke, über ihre threatened to fall upon all the other hands and tear them apart, its danger lay in its smallness, in its fingernails, chewed down in impatience and stress, in the hard, protruding knuckles, her hand was a tiny animal, crouched ready to spring, her bare arms too, with their dark fuzz, were animal, and now, as talking started up again, after the mutual raising of glasses, a boundless thirst for knowledge overcame me, every smallest segment of existence was filled with an enormous variety, the resultant patterns were so complex that I longed for an expansion of my receptivity. The bare hands and faces were illuminated by the candles and the last light from the garden, the bodies were enwrapped and set in a row, beneath the hidden skin the organisms took in the nourishment that was chewed up by the mouths. Assembled around their common nourishment, placing it in their mouths, crushing it with their teeth, their palates, their tongues, sucking in the wine, letting the wine flow through their throats into their stomach sacs, we merged in unity, we were a Round Table with a dozen heads, two dozen hands, and the faces turned back and forth, took in words with the funnels of their ears, let words stream from moist mucous mouths, and the words flowed together from all directions into a collective droning, the words mingled with the various taste sensations, the wine colored their hearing, the simmering of their blood primed their voices; sitting across from the windows, seeing the dark blue garden behind the heads and bodies at the other side of the table, I heard Lucian conveying to Inez his wish to film Proust's work, while next to me Delphine talked about a house on the Place de Vosges, and since we had found a common language for communication, I could receive all the details of her impressions, it was a building from the seventeenth century that had been offered to her for purchase, a tall, narrow house in which the stairs led through many stories up to the tower rooms, and in the midst of this I heard on the other side about Monsieur de Charlus, Swann, and Albertine. From other directions came the mention of plays and roles, of performances and exhibits, of books, of art dealers, of planned and completed works, Vilard spoke with Giacometti about Miro and Braque, Anna was talking about an upcoming tour, all of them showed with their satiated words that they belonged to the life of this city, that they belonged to the elite, that they were irreplaceable, they formed a family, and Inez and I were passersby who were tolerated with our deficient words, who, in the pleasant feeling created by the delicacies and drinks enjoyed, were ques-

Leistungen befragt wurden, und unsere Antworten, die nach etwas Überzeugendem suchten, verloren sich im Gewirr und wurden dort vergessen, so wie alle ausgesprochenen Worte vergessen wurden. Das Blau im Garten wurde zu tiefem Violett, der schwarze Kaffe kam in kleinen Tassen, Flüssigkeiten schwankten in geschliffenen Gläsern, dann saßen wir in Gruppen, in den beiden Räumen verteilt, in kleinen Gesprächswolken, ich versuchte hier und da das Thema zu deuten, das nur selten meinen Vermutungen entsprach, das oft, als ich schon glaubte, dem Sinn auf der Spur zu sein, mich mit jähen Ausfällen in unerwartete Gebiete führte.

An konkreten Unterlagen fand ich Halt, an einer Serie von Federzeichnungen, die Vilard an der atlantischen Küste ausgeführt hatte, und in deren Strichen sich die Bewegungen der Luftmassen, des Wassers und der Strandgewächse erkennen ließen, an den rohen, mit keramischen Farben gebrannten Steinen aus Miros Hand, an einer Mappe mit Photographien, die Giles Ehrmann vorzeigte, und auf denen die Skulpturen, Reliefs und Bauten der französischen Primitiven zu sehen waren. Giles, mit seinem olivfarbenen Gesicht, die Zigarette schief im Mundwinkel, an der Unterlippe festgeklebt, sprach von diesen Kunstwerken, zu deren Ausforschung er Jahre verwendet hatte, seine Worte waren undeutlich, rannen wie ein Gesang unter dem Zigarettenrauch, der ihm die Augen tränen machte, doch die Bilder, mit ihren Detailwirkungen, waren voll von faßbarem Material, es waren die großen unschuldigen Werke, die Werke außerhalb des geschäftigen Marktes, die Werke der Fischer, Bauern und Gärtner, in Büsche geschnitten, in Felsbrocken gehauen, aus Muscheln, Strandgeröll, Glasscherben zusammengesetzt, zu phantastischen Möbeln verwandelt, in die Hauswand eingebacken, gekrönt von der Universalgrotte des Landbriefträgers Cheval, erbaut unter dreiunddreißig Lebensjahren.

Später, in unserm geliehenen Zimmer, in dem jetzt das Dröhnen des Verkehrs vereinzelt auftauchenden und vorbeisausenden Lautstößen gewichen war, machten sich die letzten Stunden geltend, mit dem was verhalten und unausgesprochen gewesen war. Das Fenster zur Straße war geschlossen, das Fenster zum Gelände mit den Hochhäusern stand offen, die zahlreichen Lampen in den gegenüberliegenden Wohnungen erhellten das Schlafzimmer, und auch das Nebenzimmer hinter der offenen Tür lag im Widerschein von Lichtpunkten, die draußen über der Straßentiefe verteilt waren. Stimmen, Gelächter, gedämpfte Tanzmusik drangen mit dem warmen Luftzug ein, die Gardinen regten sich, fremde aufgestapelte Gegenstände lagen im hohen Wandregal, auf den Stühlen lagen unsere Kleidungsstücke, und nebenan stand der riesige Schreibtisch, auf muskulösen Löwenfüßen, mit dem Pergamentschirm der Messinglampe, die Ledersessel standen um den Rauchtisch, die Fotos glänzten an den Wänden, wir waren hier beherbergt, zwischen Dingen, die einem anderen gehörten, und wußten, daß wir hier nicht lange bleiben würden.

tioned about our accomplishments, and our answers, which searched for something convincing, were lost and then forgotten in the jumble, just as all the words spoken were forgotten. The blue in the garden became a deep violet, black coffee came in little cups, liquid swayed in cut glasses, then we sat in groups distributed in both rooms, in small clouds of conversation, here and there I tried to discern the theme, which only seldom coincided with my surmise, which often, when I thought I was already on the track of its meaning, led me with sudden lunges into unexpected territory.

I steadied myself on concrete data, on a series of pen sketches that Vilard had executed on the Atlantic coast, in the strokes of which the movements of air masses, of the water, and of the littoral plants could be recognized, on the stones from Miro's hand, fired in ceramic colors, on a portfolio of photographs that Giles Ehrmann was displaying and on which the sculptures, reliefs, and structures of the French primitives could be seen. Giles, with his olive face, a cigarette dangling from the corner of his mouth, stuck to his lower lip, spoke about these works of art, which he had spent years investigating, his words were unclear, ran like a song beneath the cigarette smoke that made his eyes tear, yet the pictures, effective in their detail, were full of tangible material, these were the great, innocent works, the works outside the busy marketplace, the works of fishers, of peasants, and of gardeners, cut into bushes, carved into boulders, assembled from shells, beach drift, pieces of glass, transformed into fantastic furniture, baked into the house wall, crowned by the universal grotto of Cheval, the country postman, built in the course of thirty-three years of life.

Later, in our borrowed room, in which the droning of the traffic had now given way to isolated blasts of sound rising up and whizzing by, the last hours asserted themselves with whatever had been held back and unexpressed. The window toward the street was shut, the window toward the tract with the high-rise apartments was open, the numerous lamps in the apartments across the way lit up the bedroom, and the next room too, behind the open door, lay in the reflection of points of light that were scattered outside above the depths of the street. Voices, laughter, muffled dance music drifted in with the warm current of air, the drapes stirred, strange objects lay piled up in the tall bookshelves on the wall, our clothes lay on chairs, and in the next room stood the enormous desk, on muscular lion's feet, with the parchment shade of the brass lamp, leather chairs were set around the smoking table, the photos gleamed on the walls, we were sheltered here, among things belonging to someone else, and we knew that we would not remain here for long.

AUTHORS AND TRANSLATORS

HANS BENDER, distinguished short-story author, critic, and editor, has long served as advisory editor for DIMENSION and has contributed critical "Perspective" essays and "Letters from Germany," as well as a short story, "Going Begging," in volume 7. He edits *Akzente* with Michael Krüger. In the spring of 1979 he was feted in Cologne by the Hanser Verlag, publisher and distributor of *Akzente*, on the occasion of the twenty-fifth anniversary of Germany's most prestigious literary magazine, which Bender founded with Walter Höllerer in 1954. The celebration took place at the fabled literary meeting place, Campi's, and was attended by scores of celebrities from the world of publishing. In the fall of 1979 he was guest lecturer at The University of Texas at Austin, following up his first lectureship at that University in 1968.

ALLAN BLUNDEN, who lives in Cornwall in England, previously translated a section of Wolfgang Hildesheimer's *Cornish Times* for DIMENSION in volume 9. Blunden has published translations of stories from Hildesheimer's *Lieblose Legenden* (Loveless Legends). He, as is the case with all translators of Hildesheimer, consulted with the author on his translation of the text related to the biography of the fictional Sir Andrew Marbot.

TIMOTHY A. BONNER-SAROFF studies, with majors in German and political science, at California State University at Fullerton. His translations of poems by Werner Lutz were done in a literary translation class at the Deutsche Sommerschule near Taos, New Mexico. This is his first contribution to DIMENSION.

ALLEN H. CHAPPEL was educated in Virginia and in North Carolina. He is an associate professor of German at the University of New Orleans. He has published translations of works by Gabriele Wohmann, Helga Novak, and Ilse Aichinger in the *New Orleans Review*, the *International Poetry Review*, and *Translation*. His translation of poems by Wohmann appeared in volume 10 of DIMENSION.

FRIEDRICH DÜRRENMATT, world-famous Swiss dramatist and storyteller, is represented on his first appearance in DIMENSION with a focus on aspects of his career little noticed by critics and readers: his paintings. The art works and the essay are reprinted from Dürrenmatt's 1978 volume *Bilder und Zeichnungen* (Pictures and Drawings), published by the Diogenes Verlag in Zurich. Dürrenmatt's postscript to the volume, here published for the first time in translation, reveals the close-knit relationship between his graphic hobby and his genial literary productivity.

Friedrich Dürrenmatt was born in 1921 in Konolfingen in the canton of Bern. After studying philosophy and theology he began writing short prose and in 1947 staged his first drama, *Es steht geschrieben* (It Is Written), followed in 1948 by *Der Blinde* (The Blind Man), neither notable for popular success. His play *Romulus der Große* (1949; *Romulus the Great*, 1964) brought him the first international acclaim. That work was followed by *Die Ehe des Herrn Mississippi* (1952; *The Marriage of Mr. Mississippi*, 1964), *Ein Engel kommt nach Babylon* (1953; *An Angel Comes to Babylon*, 1964), and by his most successful play, *Der Besuch der alten Dame* (1956; *The Visit*, 1958), filmed with a notable performance by Ingrid Bergman. Further works for the stage, all of which continue the "grotesque counterreality" begun quite early, have been *Die Physiker* (1962; *The Physicists*, 1963), *Der Meteor* (1966; *The Meteor*, 1973), *Portrait eines Planeten* (1971; Portrait of a Planet), and *Der Mitmacher* (1973; The Accessory).

In the area of prose Dürrenmatt has written gloomy stories and polished versions of detective fiction with *Der Richter und sein Henker* (1952; *The Judge and His Hangman*, 1954) and its sequel *Das Versprechen* (1957; *The Pledge*, 1959). The former was made into a remarkable film, directed by Maximilian Schell, with the title *The End of the Game*, in which Dürrenmatt himself plays the Writer. A collection of the author's essays and speeches on theater were collected under the title *Theater, Schriften und Reden* in 1966.

MICHAEL P. ELZAY, a successful New York banking executive, has been a frequent contributor to DIMENSION, with translations of works by Friederike Mayröcker in volumes 4, 5, 6, and 8, and by Urs Widmer in volume 12. When not involved in international finance, Elzay resides on Long Island with his wife and small daughter.

ERICH FITZBAUER has appeared with prose in volumes 3 and 5 of DIMENSION and with a long series of poems in volume 8. The watercolors by Fitzbauer published in volume 3 are quite different, not only in technique but in overall atmosphere, from the charcoal drawings in the present issue. The poems in volume 8 were included in his *Zikadenschrei und Eulenruf* (1977; Locust Sounds and Owl's Call). The volume *Die reißende Zeit* (1978; Sundering Time) contains poems that present a critical commentary on the modern age. In 1978 he also published a long story, *Alle Ratten von Bord* (All Rats Abandon Ship), followed in 1979 by a collection of poems, *Kassiopeia*, an essay, *Namenlose Landschaften* (Nameless Landscapes), and a volume of poems and short prose, *Mond im Kleinen Bären* (Moon in the Little Dipper). A further book of poems, *Botschaften* (Harbingers), appeared in 1980. His drawings and watercolors are owned by the Lower Austrian State Museum in Vienna and by private collectors in Austria and abroad.

KEN FONTENOT is a poet and translator who lives in New Orleans. He has translated work by Ilse Aichinger for the *New Orleans Review* and publishes a little magazine himself. His translation of the story by Robert Wolfgang Schnell is his first for DIMENSION.

ULRICH K. GOLDSMITH, born in Germany, and educated in Canada and California, is now professor of German emeritus at the University of Colorado, Boulder. He has published books and articles on Stefan George, Rainer Maria Rilke, Goethe, and Shakespeare. His translations of poems by Günter Kunert are his first for DIMENSION.

GÜNTER GRASS represents the epitome of a combination author and artist, whose themes are inextricably intertwined in the two forms of literature and graphic art. His drawings of the head of an eagle to illustrate the poem "Beobachtet beim Attentat" (Observed in the Assassination Attempt) from the first edition of his first book of poetry, *Die Vorzüge der Windhühner* (1956; The Advantages of Wind Chickens), appeared in an excerpted detail of the eagle's eye on the cover of the first issue of DIMENSION in 1968. In the same issue a drawing by Grass illustrates a poem by Bernd Jentzsch. In volume 2 of DIMENSION a drawing by Grass serves as an enhancing commentary on the excerpt of Ingeborg Bachmann's *Ein Ort für Zufälle* (A Place for Incidents). In 1970 a special issue of DIMENSION recorded and commemorated a symposium on Günter Grass held at The University of Texas at Austin. It contains four scenes from *Davor* (translated as "Uptight" by A. Leslie Willson and published in 1971, in co-translation with Ralph Manheim, as *Max*) and has a cover illustration by Grass, his drawing of a dancing nun that appeared on the limited edition of his aesthetic essay, *Die Ballerina* (1956), published for the first time in English in the present issue. The drawings by Grass that appear in this issue are on the theme of cooks, characters from his play *Die bösen Köche* (1957; *The Wicked Cooks*, 1967), and on the flounder theme related to *Der Butt* (1977; *The Flounder*, 1978).

Works published by Grass since the biobibliographical note in the special issue of DIMENSION in 1970 include *Aus dem Tagebuch einer Schnecke* (1972; *From the Diary of a Snail*, 1973), the aforementioned *Der Butt, Das Treffen in Telgte* (1979; *The Meeting in Telgte*, 1980), and *Kopfgeburten oder die Deutschen sterben aus* (1980; Headbirths or the Germans are Becoming Extinct, to be published in 1981 in a translation by Ralph Manheim). A collection of essays on literature was published in 1980 under the title *Aufsätze zur Literatur*.

Günter Grass has kept his artistic hand at work during the whole span of his literary career. He has illustrated his own three volumes of poetry and has drawn or painted the dust jackets for his novels and other books. A list of available etchings was published in 1980 by Grass and the Andre-Anselm Dreher Gallery in Berlin in an edition of 2000 copies with the title *Werkverzeichnis der Radierungen*. Since 1975 A. Leslie Willson, the editor of DIMENSION, has delivered a lecture on the relationship of the art and literature of Günter Grass, illustrated with forty slides, in Europe and the United States under the title "The Two-Pronged Pen of Günter Grass" (Die doppelspitzige Feder von Günter Grass). Grass himself has mounted an increasing number of exhibitions of his art works in Europe and America.

GEORG M. GUGELBERGER, professor of German and comparative literature at the University of California at Riverside, contributed a long poem by Ingomar von Kieseritzky to volume 4 of DIMENSION. He has published a book of poems by Helmut Maria Soik, *Rimbaud unterm Stahlhelm* (1976; *Rimbaud under the Steel Helmet*, a bilingual edition by the Red Hill Press). At the end of 1980 Gugelberger's translation of selected poems from Ernst Meister's last book of poetry, *Wandloser Raum* (1979; Room without Walls), will be printed by the Red Hill Press.

ALDONA GUSTAS contributed graphics to volume 11 of DIMENSION. She has published seven books of poetry containing her own illustrations, mostly lithographs, with the Verlag Eremiten-Presse in Düsseldorf, the latest being *Eine Welle, eine Muschel, oder Venus persönlich* (1979; A Wave, a Shell, or Venus Herself). In 1977 Gustas edited a bilingual anthology (German and Italian) of work by the group known as the Berliner Malerpoeten (artist/poets), which contains literary texts and art works by fourteen author/artists who live in Berlin. The poems in this issue of DIMENSION are her first literary contribution to the magazine.

WOLFGANG HILDESHEIMER first appeared in DIMENSION in volume 3 with his absurd play *Pastorale.* An excerpt from his novel *Masante,* under the title of "Maxine," was published in volume 5, along with a selection of his drawings. His story "Ich finde mich zurecht" (I Find My Way) appeared in volume 8, and an excerpt from his volume *Zeiten in Cornwall* (Cornish Times) appeared in volume 9. The contribution presented here caused a sensation when it was published in *Die Zeit.* Readers and critics took as absolute fact the commemorative article marking the one-hundred-and-fiftieth anniversary of the death of Sir Andrew Marbot, early-nineteenth-century British art critic, but actually the figment of Hildesheimer's imagination. The reaction surprised the author to such an extent that he carefully points out the fictional provenance of Sir Andrew and his colorful, short life. Graphic art by Hildesheimer is widely distributed in private collections and art galleries.

WALTER HÖLLERER, who appeared in volume 3 of DIMENSION with a selection of poems and in volume 9 with an excerpt from his semiotic novel *Die Elephantenuhr* (The Elephant Clock), makes his debut in the present issue as a whimsical and spirited artist. In 1978 he published a two-act play with bird and nonbird characters, *Alle Vögel alle* (All the Birds, All the Birds), which is the title of a familiar folksong greeting springtime.

IRMGARD ELSNER HUNT, a German-born graduate student at the University of Washington in Seattle, interviewed Günter Grass in Berlin in the summer of 1980.

ERNST JANDL, irrepressible manipulator of language(s), published poetic texts in DIMENSION volume 2 and again in the double issue of volume 8 on Austrian contemporary writing, for which he also served as guest editor. He wrote the "Letter from Vienna" for that double issue. In 1976 Jandl published a volume of essays on the art and practice of literary composition with the title *Die schöne Kunst des Schreibens* (The Fine Art of Writing). A book of poetry, with the new Jandl trend toward extreme, childlike manipulation of language syntax and verb forms mixed with outspoken adult themes, appeared in 1978 with the title *Die Bearbeitung der Mütze* (The Adaptation of Hats). Those trends and innovations were continued in 1980 with a new volume of poetry entitled *Der gelbe Hund* (The Yellow Dog). The year 1980 also marked the publication of a play by Jandl that was greeted with choruses of praise, *Aus der Fremde* (From Abroad). In this issue of DIMENSION he makes his premiere graphic appearance with typical capricious art sketches, along with poems written in English for the occasion.

GÜNTER KUNERT, a valiant and supportive contributor to DIMENSION, has appeared with literary texts in volumes 2, 3, 5, 8, and 10. He contributed an essay to the "Perspective" pages in volume 4, and he guest edited the special issue on writing from East Germany in 1973, for which he drew the cover art, a representation of the Brandenburg Gate. Since his last appearance in DIMENSION Kunert has published *Camera obscura* (1978), a volume of prose, Hanser Verlag; *Ein englisches Tagebuch* (1978; An English Diary), travel impressions, Aufbau Verlag; *Verlangen nach Bomarzo* (1978; Longing for Bomarzo), travel poems with pen-drawings by the author, among them the astronaut planting the Texas flag on the moon that appears in this issue of DIMENSION and was drawn to illustrate the poem "Downtown Manhattan am Sonntagnachmittag" (Downtown Manhattan on Sunday Afternoon), Hanser Verlag; *Ziellose Umtriebe* (Bustling about without Destination), an Aufbau Verlag paperback with cover painting memorializing Kunert's Texas sojourn in 1972, showing a self-portrait of Kunert being photographed on the sands of Padre Island by his wife Marianne; *Die Schreie der Fledermäuse* (1979; The Cries of Bats), a collection of stories, poems, and essays edited by Dieter Zimmer for the Hanser Verlag; and *Abtötungsverfahren* (1980; Process of Mortification), a volume of bitter and revealing poems published by Hanser Verlag after Kunert's departure from his home in Buch on the outskirts of East Berlin to reside in Itzehoe near Hamburg in the early fall of 1979. A volume in appreciation and recognition on the occasion of Kunert's fiftieth birthday, *Kunert lesen* (1979; Reading Kunert), contains commentary and critical examination by twenty-one contributors, none of whom spends more than a single word on the art of Kunert and most of whom remain altogether silent about an activity that has always engaged the author and precipitated his pessimistic and deeply involved viewpoint in visible form. On the walls of his house hang his wry and boldly colorful paintings. A collection of prose published by the Eulenspiegel Verlag of East Berlin in 1975. *Der Mittelpunkt der Erde* (The Midpoint of Earth), is filled with Kunert's graphic commentaries to his prose pieces. Many a friend of Kunert possesses an autographed volume that contains a quick-sketched self-portrait.

The story in this issue of DIMENSION received the short-story prize of the magazine *Westermann's Monatshefte* for 1979; the poems were written in the period immediately after his departure from his home in Buch, as were the two short essays. The happy gardener pencil sketch for Marianne has not been published before.

WERNER LUTZ was born in 1930 in Wolfhalden in Switzerland. Since 1948 he has worked as a commercial artist in Basel, painting and writing poetry on the side. His lyrics have been published in *Basler Texte* and in the Swiss-German anthology, *Gut zum Druck* (Ready for Publication), and his paintings reiterate the blocky but softly contoured abstractions of his poetry.

FRIEDERIKE MAYRÖCKER has been a frequent contributor to DIMENSION with a long poem in volume 4, a story and poetry in volume 6, delightful illustrations to mock-aphoristic guardian-angel wishes in volume 7, and two poems in volume 8, the double issue on Austrian literature. Since 1975 she has continued her literary production with *Heisze Hunde* (1977; Hot Dogs), sensitive lyric prose with illustrations by her ofttimes collaborator Ernst Jandl; *Rot ist unten* (1977; Red Is Below), a volume of short prose, radio-play script, and assorted poems; and *Heiligenanstalt* (1978; Institution for Saints), unorthodox biographies of musicians. Her book of prose, *Die Abschiede* (1980; Farewells), is an oracular life sketch.

CHRISTOPH MECKEL, probably the most inventive and imaginative German writer and graphic artist of today, appeared in volume 1 of DIMENSION with a sampler of prose, poetry, and graphic work. His art and prose and poetry were featured again in volume 4, followed by new prose in volume 6. In 1975 Meckel published a sort of fictional diary in *Die Gestalt am Ende des Grundstücks* (The Figure at the End of the Property). His memoir on the East German poet Johannes Bobrowski, a friend who died prematurely and widely mourned in 1965,

Erinnerung an Johannes Bobrowski (Memoir of Johannes Bobrowski), is a stately memorial to the late poet. In 1979 Meckel published a series of poems, deeply personal and cathartic, under the title of *Säure* (Acid). His contribution to this issue of DIMENSION is an independent essay on the genesis of a poem and drawings from his 1980 volume *Das Dings da* (The Thingamajig).

ERNST MEISTER, distinguished and reclusive poet born in 1911, received the prestigious Büchner Prize of the Darmstadt Academy of Literature posthumously, the first writer in Germany to be so honored, shortly after his death in 1979. Though primarily a poet Meister also published stories, radio plays, and wrote on drama. His first volume of poetry, *Ausstellung* (Exhibition), appeared in 1932. The next volume followed more than twenty years later, *Unter schwarzem Schafspelz* (1953; Under a Black Sheepskin). Then came a series of volumes, *Dem Spiegelkabinett gegenüber* (1954; Opposite the Mirror Cabinet), *Der Südwind sagte mir zu* (1955; The Southwind Suited Me), *Fermate* (1957; Musical Pause), *und Ararat* (1957; and Ararat), *Pythiusa* (1958), *Zahlen und Figuren* (1958; Numbers and Figures), *Lichtes Labyrinth* (1959; The Labyrinth of Light), *Die Formel und die Stätte* (1960; Formula and Places), *Flut und Stein* (1961; Flood and Stone), *Zeichen um Zeichen* (1968; Signs about Signs), *Es kam die Nachricht* (1970; The News Came), *Sage vom Ganzen den Satz* (1972; Say It All), *Im Zeitspalt* (1976; In the Fissure of Time), and *Wandloser Raum* (1979; *Space without Walls*, 1980). A selection of his poetry appeared in 1977, *Ausgewählte Gedichte* (Selected Poems), which was issued in a revised edition after his death, containing poems from later books and from his literary remains. Few people other than his wife Elsie Meister knew that this reticent, visionary, and sensual poet was an artist who splashed and sketched his concentrated abstractions in watercolor and in vibrant, sometimes otherworldly, drawings.

BREON MITCHELL, professor and chairman of the comparative literature program at Indiana University, published translations of texts by Rüdiger Kremer in volumes 5 and 7 of DIMENSION. He is an inspired translator whose work is scheduled to appear in coming issues of the magazine.

KARL OPPERMANN lives and works and paints and writes poetry in Berlin. Since its inception he has been active in the group known as the Berlin poet/painters. He introduced an exhibition of works of the group in Genoa in 1976, an event that resulted in the publication in 1977 of a volume devoted to members of the group, *Berliner Malerpoeten*.

ERICA PEDRETTI was born in 1930 in Sternberg, in North Moravia (Czechoslovakia), and emigrated to Switzerland in 1945. She studied commercial art in Zurich and worked for two years as a gold- and silversmith in New York. She is married to the Swiss artist Gian Pedretti and lives in Celerina in the Engadine. She is the author of a volume of prose, *Harmloses bitte* (1970; Harmless Plea), the novel *Heiliger Sebastian* (1973; St. Sebastian), and a number of radio plays, including *Badekur* (1970; Taking the Waters), *Catch as Katz Can* (1972), and in dialect *Gang in es Inschtitut* (1972; Way to the Institute). A master of the short-prose piece, with a style inimicably her own, Pedretti appears here in DIMENSION for the first time with prose and examples of her art.

JULIA PENN has been a frequent translator for DIMENSION, having translated poems by Christa Reinig, Mathias Schreiber, and Ernst Jandl for volume 2, poems by Gisele Frohlinde-Meyer for volume 5, poems by Kurt Bartsch for the special issue on East German writing in 1973, poems by Lisa Kahn and Hanne F. Juritz in volume 6, poems by Heidi Pataki for the double issue on Austrian writing in 1975, and new poems by Hanne F. Juritz in volume 9. She teaches and is a social worker in Austin, Texas.

GEORGE F. PETERS previously translated prose by Lutz Rathenow for DIMENSION in volume 11. He heads the German section of the Department of Modern Languages at the University of New Mexico in Albuquerque and is co-director, with Peter Pabisch, of the Deutsche Sommerschule near Taos.

RALPH R. READ III, an associate professor in the Department of Germanic Languages at The University of Texas at Austin, has been a frequent translator for DIMENSION. For volume 1 he translated an essay on the radio play by Heinz Schwitzke, a poem by Günter Herburger, and a radio narrative by Paul Schallück. In volume 2 he is represented by the translation of a long poem by Uwe Friesel. Volume 3 contains Read's translations of a television drama by Rolf Hädrich, a "Letter from Germany" by Heinrich Vormweg, and an essay on the new radio play by Heinz Schwitzke. For volume 4 he translated stories by Christa Reinig; for volume 5 a "Letter from Germany" by Hans Mayer, a "Perspective" by Heinrich Vormweg, and a radio play by Karlhans Frank; for volume 6 poems by Fred Viebahn, a sample passage from a novel by Arno Schmidt (translated with Hans-Bernhard Moeller), and an excerpt from Horst Bienek's *Bakunin: An Invention*, later published complete by the Unicorn Press in Read's translation; and for volume 8 poems by Werner Kofler. Volume 9 contains Read's translations of a memoir by Bernhard Blume, an excerpt from his translation of Bienek's novel *The First Polka* (later published in its entirety in England), and his translation of prose by Wolfgang Schiffer. For volume 10 he translated prose by Frank Geerk and by Gertrud Leutenegger and a "Letter from Germany" by Jürgen Theobaldy; for volume 11 an excerpt from a long novel by Peter Weiss and an excerpt from a novel by Walter E. Richartz; and for volume 12 a story by Katrin Hutten and a chapter of Horst Bienek's novel *Septemberlicht* (September Light).

GERHARD RÜHM previously appeared in DIMENSION in volume 4 with a poem. To be added to the selected list of his works noted in that volume are *Gesammelte Gedichte und Visuelle Texte* (1970; Collected Poems and Visual Texts), *Die Frösche und andere Texte* (1971; Frogs and Other Texts), *Ophelia und die Wörter* (1972; Ophelia and Words, theater pieces written between 1954 and 1971), and *Mann und Frau* (1972; Man and Woman). He has published other poems and experimental works and has recorded various readings. He now lives in Cologne and travels weekly to Hamburg, where he is a faculty member of the Art Academy.

HERMAN SALINGER, professor emeritus at Duke University, is a frequent contributor to DIMENSION. His translation of a long poem by Wolfgang Weyrauch appeared in the premiere issue and poems by Karl Krolow have been published in his translation in volumes 1, 2, and 6; poems by Cyrus Atabay in volumes 2 and 4; Peter Henisch's *Hamlet* in volume 3; Rudolf Hagelstange's long poem *A Conversation about Trees* in volume 6; and poems by Erich Fitzbauer in volume 8.

ROBERT WOLFGANG SCHNELL was born in 1916 in Barmen and lives in West Berlin, where he enjoys a career as a writer, painter, and actor. He studied music and has been a director of opera and theater. His literary works include *Mief* (1964; Stale Air), which was republished in 1969 with the title *Die Farce von den Riesenbrüsten* (The Farce of the Gigantic Breasts); the novel *Geisterbahn* (1964; Ghost Ride); poems, stories, and drawings in *Muzes Flöte* (1966; Muze's Flute); the novel *Erziehung durch Dienstmädchen* (1968; Education by Servant Girls, republished in 1978), from which a much discussed television film was made; the children's narrative *Pulle und Pumi* (1969; a collection of stories, *Junggesellenweihnacht* (1970; Bachelors' Christmas); a children's book *Bonko* (1970); a novel for children *Holger wohnt im Zoo* (1971; Holger Lives in the Zoo); a long story *Das verwandelte Testament* (1972; The Transformed Will); and stories in *Vier Väter* (1973; Four Fathers), the story collection *Eine Tüte Himbeerbonbons* (1976; A Sack of Raspberry Candies), and *Die heitere Freiheit und Gleichheit* (1978; Cheerful Freedom and Equality), from which the story and drawing in this issue of DIMENSION are taken.

GERD SONNTAG was born in 1954, has worked as a janitor and stonemason, and served in the East German army. He attended the Art Academy in Leipzig in 1973 and afterwards worked as a stoker. He has published poems in various magazines and has exhibited his art throughout Thuringia.

JOACHIM UHLMANN was born in 1925 in Berlin, where he still lives. He has published four small volumes of sharply hewn verse: *Gemaserte Stille* (1955; Grainy Silence), *Feuer in Würden* (1960; Fire in High Ranks), *Serpentinen* (1967), and *Kernzeit* (1975; Coretime). Between 1968 and 1971 he was co-editor of the yearbook for poetry, *Speichen*. He is an accomplished translator from the English, having done volumes by Djuna Barnes, Percy Bysshe Shelley, and William Blake, among others. His art has the pithy fascination of the poetic haiku form he sometimes employs in his poetic diction. He is a member of the Berlin group of poet/painters.

JOHANNES VAZULIK, who teaches at North Dakota State University in Fargo, contributed an excerpt of a novel by G.F. Jonke to volume 8 of DIMENSION. Since that time he has translated a story by Walter F. Richartz, volume 9, a fairy tale by Beat Brechbühl, volume 10, and a story by Herbert Günther, volume 12.

PETER WEISS, world-renowned author of *Marat/Sade*, made his first appearance with collages and an excerpt from his long novel *Ästhetik des Widerstands* (translated as "The Aesthetics of Revolt," but which he would prefer to have literally translated as "The Aesthetics of Resistance") in DIMENSION 12/1. The third volume of that trilogy is scheduled for completion in 1981. Weiss is preparing *Notizbücher* (Notebooks) in two volumes, which amount to a workshop report on the genesis of the trilogy, with records of sources, sketches, conversations, and with illustrations of artworks, places, and persons portrayed in the novel.

A. LESLIE WILLSON, the editor and founder of DIMENSION, is professor of German at The University of Texas at Austin. He delivered a paper on the short story in Germany with the title "Constancy and Variation" in January, 1980, at the annual symposium on comparative literature sponsored by Texas Tech University in Lubbock. Later in the spring of 1980 he gave the banquet address, "Warum und Wohin and/or Why and Whither," at the annual convention of the Texas Association of German Students at Trinity University in San Antonio. He is completing his second and final term as chairman of the Department of Germanic Languages at The University of Texas at Austin.

JEANNE R. WILLSON is a librarian/archivist at the Barker Texas History Center at The University of Texas at Austin, when not laboring on DIMENSION translation-checking, translating herself, and guiding the magazine through the intricacies of proofreading and paging. As a translator she has been represented in the magazine with a story by Hans Bender in volume 7, a "Letter from Germany" by Hans J. Fröhlich and another by Heinrich Vormweg in volume 11, Karlhans Frank's "Letter from Germany" in the children's issue of volume 12, two "Letters from Germany" by Hans J. Fröhlich and Heinrich Vormweg in the 12/2 issue, and also in volume 12 stories by Hanne F. Juritz, Roderich Feldes, Otto Jägersberg, and Erika Runge, as well as Hans Haid's "Letter from Vienna" in the contemporary dialect poetry issue, 12/3.

STEPHEN ZON is a student at the University of California at Santa Barbara. The translation of essays by Günter Kunert is his first for DIMENSION.

Contents of DIMENSION, Vol. 13, No. 2 (Summer, 1980)

YIDDISH ISSUE

On Contemporary Yiddish Writing — ELIAS SCHULMAN

When Strelisk Burned and other Poems — MEYER SHTIKER
Ven strelisk hot gebrent un andere lider — trans. Stephen H. Garrin

And There Was a Smile and other Poems — MALKE HEIFITZ TUSSMAN
Un a shmeykhl iz geven un andere lider — trans. Daniel Marlin and Jack Hirshman

Not a Poem, but a Prayer, My Child and other Poems — YANKEV (JAKOBO) GLANTZ
Nit a lid, nor a tfile, meyn kind un andere lider — trans. Seth L. Wollitz

Bread for the Birds and other Poems — REYZL ZHIKHLINSKI
Broyt far di feygl un andere lider — trans. Tzipora Baradon

Gravegarden and other Poems — SHLOYME (SELWYN) SCHWARTZ
Kvorim un andere lider — trans. by the author

Autumn Song and other Poems — PERETZ MIRANSKI
Harbst un andere lider — trans. by the author and Adam Fuerstenberg

Jerusalem and other Poems — KHAIM GRADE
Yerushalayim un andere lider — trans. Tzipora Baradon

I'm Talking to Myself and other Poems — RIVKE KOPE
Ikh red tzu mir un andere lider — trans. Stanley N. Werbow

Job and other Poems — ROKHL KORN
Yob un andere lider — trans. Hugh Denman and Dorothy Billik

Before the Cross and other Poems — URI TZVI GREENBERG
Faran tzaylem un andere lider — trans. Sabina Lask-Spinac

Poems from My Diary — AVROHOM SUTZKEVER
Lider fun togbukh — trans. Stephen H. Garrin and Tzipora Baradon

from Other — Y. KH. BILETZKI
fun *Akhayr* — trans. Nathan Goldman

By the Fireside — VULF TAMBUR
Oyfn pripitzhik — trans. Nathan Goldman

The issue will be guest-edited by Stephen H. Garrin and illustrated by Harold A. Liebowitz and Barbara Sturgill.

DIMENSION

Contemporary German Arts and Letters

Volume 13, No. 1, 1980

Department of Germanic Languages / THE UNIVERSITY OF TEXAS AT AUSTIN

DIMENSION

Contemporary German Arts and Letters / Volume 13, No. 2, 1980

Department of Germanic Languages/THE UNIVERSITY OF TEXAS AT AUSTIN

DIMENSION

DIMENSION

Contemporary German Arts and Letters / Volume 13, No. 2, 1980

Department of Germanic Languages / THE UNIVERSITY OF TEXAS AT AUSTIN

STEPHEN H. GARRIN, *Guest Editor*

DIMENSION is published three times yearly at The University of Texas at Austin. Subscription: $12 per year for individuals, $15 per year for institutions in the United States, plus $2 postage and handling; $15 per year for individuals, $20 per year for institutions elsewhere, plus $4 postage and handling. Single copy $6 in the U.S., $8 elsewhere, plus postage and handling. All subscriptions should be sent to DIMENSION, The Department of Germanic Languages, P. O. Box 7939, Austin, TX 78712, USA. All contributions and editorial correspondence should be sent to: The Editor, DIMENSION, P. O. Box 26673, Austin, TX 78755, USA. Unsolicited manuscripts must be accompanied by a stamped, self-addressed envelope.

ISSN 0012–2882
DESIGN AND ART DIRECTION: DAVID PRICE

△ indicates original, previously unpublished contributions in German. All contributions in English appear in print for the first time.

Subscribers to DIMENSION may order microfilm copies or photocopied duplicate issues through University Microfilms, Ann Arbor, Michigan 48106.

CONTENTS

Perspective — STEPHEN H. GARRIN 321
On Contemporary Yiddish Writing — ELIAS SCHULMAN 325
A Note About the Transliteration 341
Ven strelisk hot gebrent — MEYER SHTIKER 342
When Strelisk Burned — *translated by Stephen H. Garrin*
Di sedra veyekhi — MEYER SHTIKER 348
Jacob's Death — *translated by Stephen H. Garrin*
A briv fun gefengenish fun paul verlaine tzu artur rimbaud — MEYER SHTIKER 354
A Letter from Prison from Paul Verlaine to Arthur Rimbaud — *translated by Stephen H. Garrin*
Un a shmeykhl iz geven — MALKA HEIFETZ TUSSMAN 356
And there was a Smile — *translated by Daniel Marlin*
Shalom shulamite — MALKA HEIFETZ TUSSMAN 358
Shalom, Shulammite — *translated by Jack Hirshman*
Tate ziser — MALKA HEIFETZ TUSSMAN 364
Sweet Father — *translated by the author*
Nit a lid, nor a tfile, meyn kind — YANKEV GLANTZ 366
Not a Poem, but a Prayer, My Child — *translated by Seth Wollitz*
Flaterlekh feyer — YANKEV GLANTZ 368
Flickering Flames — *translated by Seth L. Wollitz*
Broyt far di feygl — REYZL ZHIKHLINSKY 372
Bread for the Birds — *translated by Tzipora Baradon*
Ikh kuk areyn in di oygn fun rembrandt — REYZL ZHIKHLINSKI 374
I looked into the Eyes of Rembrandt — *translated by Tzipora Baradon*
Shreybn lider — REYZL ZHIKHLINSKI 376
Writing Poems — *translated by Tzipora Baradon*
Vuhin kumen ahin di reyd? — REYZL ZHIKHLINSKI 378
Where Do the Words Disappear? — *translated by Tzipora Baradon*
Shney — REYZL ZHIKHLINSKY 380
Snow — *translated by David Neale Miller*
Kvorim — SHLOYME SCHWARTZ 382
Gravegarden — *translated by the author*
Hoykhfiberish — SHLOYME SCHWARTZ 384
Thermo High — *translated by the author*
Kindheytsregn — SHLOYME SCHWARTZ 386
The Rain of My Childhood — *translated by the author*
Der geboyren-tog fun meyn balerine — SHLOYME SCHWARTZ 388
Ballerina's Birthday — *translated by the author*
Harbst — PERETZ MIRANSKY 390

Autumn — *translated by the author with Adam Fuerstenberg*
Di zun — PERETZ MIRANSKY 392
Sunset — *translated by the author with Adam Fuerstenberg*
Zey de khakhomim — PERETZ MIRANSKY 394
They the Wise — *translated by the author with Adam Fuerstenberg*
Kine — PERETZ MIRANSKY 396
Envy — *translated by the author with Adam Fuerstenberg*
Tzefat — KHAIM GRADE 402
Safed — *translated by Philip J. Kluhoff*
Ikh red tzu mir — RIVKE KOPE 406
I'm talking to Myself — *translated by Stanley N. Werbow*
Der fidl zeyger — RIVKE KOPE 408
The Violin Clock — *translated by Stanley N. Werbow*
Meyn feder — RIVKE KOPE 410
My Pen — *translated by Stanley N. Werbow*
Oyfn shpitz meser — RIVKE KOPE 412
On the Tip of the Knife — *translated by Stanley N. Werbow*
Trakhtungen — RIVKE KOPE 414
Thoughts — *translated by Stanley N. Werbow*
Yob — ROKHL KORN 416
Job — *translated by Hugh Denman and Dorothy Billik*
Erev regn — ROKHL KORN 422
Before the Rain — *translated by Hugh Denman and Dorothy Billik*
Faran tzaylem — URI TZVI GREENBERG 430
Before the Cross — *translated by Sabina Lask-Spinac*
Fun der poema *"velt-barg-arop"* — URI TZVI GREENBERG 434
From the poem "Downhill World" — *translated by Sabina Lask-Spinac*
Geveyn fun der erd — URI TZVI GREENBERG 440
Lament of the Earth — *translated by Sabina Lask-Spinac*
In melukhe fun tzaylem — URI TZVI GREENBERG 442
In the Kingdom of the Cross — *translated by Sabina Lask-Spinac*
Lider fun togbukh — AVROHOM SUTZKEVER 444
Poems from my Diary — *translated by Stephen H. Garrin*
fun *Akher* — Y. KH. BILETZKI 448
from Other — *translated by Nathan Goldman*
Oyfn pripitzhek — VULF TAMBUR 456
In the Fireplace — *translated by Nathan Goldman*
Ver Ken Heynt Lebn Besholem Mit Zikh? — KHAIM PLOTKIN 458
Who Can Live at Peace With Himself Anymore? — *translated by Marvin Zuckerman*
Authors and Translators 462

PERSPECTIVE

IT BURNS AND BURNS AND YET IS NOT CONSUMED . . .

IN THE JULY 1980 ISSUE OF THE *Saturday Review*, WHICH FEATURED AN INTERVIEW with Nobel Laureate Isaac Bashevis Singer, the interviewer prefaced her article with the following characterization of contemporary Yiddish writing: "Yiddish, which in the nineteenth and early twentieth centuries possessed a flourishing literary tradition, persists today in the work of one man, seventy-six-year-old Isaac Bashevis Singer." To be sure, Singer is the sole Yiddish author to receive the Nobel Prize, and he is the most recognizable figure on the Yiddish literary scene, but he is by no means the only representative of Yiddish writing. Despite the declining numbers of Yiddish readers and speakers since the world war in which the Yiddish language and cultural area of Eastern Europe was decimated, there still appear many fine examples of poetry and prose from the pens of Yiddish authors from South Africa to Australia and from Israel to the United States.

This issue of DIMENSION, the first one dedicated to contemporary Yiddish writing, includes a geographic representation of Yiddish literati. Of course, the centers of Yiddish creativity today are the large metropolitan areas of the United States as well as Tel Aviv, Mexico City, Buenos Aires, Montreal, Toronto, and Moscow. Wherever Jews reside there are likely to be Yiddish speakers, and where there are Yiddish speakers there are readers eager for the Yiddish word.

In place of the Letter that usually prefaces DIMENSION there is an introductory essay, "On Contemporary Yiddish Writing," by Dr. Elias Schulman of the City University of New York. Dr. Schulman was a young "aspirant" of the Jewish scientific Institute (YIVO) in the 1930s when Vilno was a center for Yiddish scholarship and cultural productivity on the eve of the European cataclysm. He brings to the pages of DIMENSION his encyclopedic knowledge of contemporary Yiddish writing and its most significant figures. Even in English there is a distinctive Yiddish coloration to Dr. Schulman's style.

Yiddish is the diaspora tongue of the majority of Jews. There are, to be sure, many other Jewish languages of exile (Judezmo, Judeo-Arabic, Judeo-Persian, etc.), but in Yiddish the height of Jewish exile culture found its literary expression.

Jewish life in almost all the main centers of dispersion is intimately interwoven with Yiddish parlance and its literature. After more than twelve hundred years of homelessness, during which time Jews adopted different languages and served as mediators in the establishment of many a national literature, there sprang up in the medieval ghetto of Germany the first roots of a uniquely Jewish tongue. Into this "ivriteitsch" (Hebrew-German), as it was called, born of a curious mixture of Biblical Hebrew, Middle High German, and some Romance elements, were translated extracts from prayer books, folk songs, Rabbinic writings and responsa, and proverbs of an earthy and universal profundity.

The "Haskala" (Enlightenment) Movement of the nineteenth century witnessed the dawning of a new era in which "Judeo-German" (now referred to as "mame loshn"—mother tongue) proved an effective mouthpiece for the hopes, aspirations, dreams, and disappointments of Europe's Yiddish-speaking Jews.

Previously, the typically nationalistic pseudo-art of the earlier Yiddish writers, with their characteristic folkloric genre art, had been the favorites of those who sought to anthologize Yiddish writing in order to familiarize the world with it. In the late nineteenth century and the early years of the twentieth Yiddish authors chose to march alongside their non-Yiddish counterparts in the procession toward a universal art. No longer bound by parochial themes, these Yiddish poets and novelists, short story writers and dramatists appropriated secular subjects for the first time.

Until about ninety years ago the Jewish muse was all but silent. Even some of the most outstanding poets in that tongue bemoaned their fate. The Russian-Yiddish poet Shimon Frug wrote,

Andersh wolt meyn lid geklungen,
Kh'sol far goyim goyish sungen,
Nisht far yidn, nisht jargon—
S'hot keyn rekhtn klang, keyn ton.

Quite differently my song would sound
Were I to sing it for gentiles in a gentile
tongue,
And not for Jews in their jargon
That has no proper sound or tone.

Fortunately, the Yiddish inferiority complex was overcome and a new wave of stars appeared on the literary horizon, among them Yehoish, Avrom Reisen, and Mani Leyb. They brought to Yiddish a poetry of refinement and sensitivity that earned it a place in world literature. The early years of this century were one of awakened national feeling among Jews: The revolutionary fervor of the Russian Empire, the beginning of Zionist sympathy, and the emergence of the Jewish labor movement all combined to mold Jewish consciousness, and Yiddish was the articulator of that new esprit.

In addition to the enormous influence of the Russian modernizers such as Bergelson there were S. J. Imber and Jacob Mestel in Galizia, who added a dimension to new Yiddish writing through their influence. In America, J. Slonim and the literary group known as "di yunge" (the "Young Ones") bridged the gap between Yiddish poetry and modern western art. The influence of Walt Whitman, the French Parnassians and Impressionists, Nietzsche's Übermensch, and the innovations of Arno Holz reached the European and American ghettos.

In New York a group calling themselves the "Insikhikhsten" (the "Introspectionists") began to exert an enormous power over Yiddish writing. A. Leyeles, Jakob Glatstein, and others were products of that school but later abandoned the narrow strictures of the movement they had set into motion.

As a chronicle of Jewish history, Yiddish has borne witness to the many tribulations of the Jewish people. It was fated to bear witness to yet one more tragedy in that history—the Holocaust. Perhaps more than any other tongue it was Yiddish that was able to capture the essence and meaning of this great tragedy because for the Yiddish writer the Holocaust was, to use the title of Alvin H. Rosenfeld's monograph on Holocaust literature, a "double dying," that is, both genocide and linguistocide.

As a tribute to the indomitable Jewish spirit, Yiddish writing has survived both the loss of its home and its best authors after the war against the Jews and the Stalin purges of the 1950s. Printed poems and short prose pieces prove I. B. Singer's often-quoted assertion that "Yiddish is, indeed, a sick language, but in Jewish history between sick and dead it is a long way."

The selections in this issue of DIMENSION have been printed in transliteration and translation in order to make the original accessible to those who cannot read Yiddish, which is normally written with Hebrew characters.

At this point I would like to express my personal thanks and appreciation to Professor A. Leslie Willson. The Department of Germanic Languages at The University of Texas at Austin has also been most cooperative. Interest in Yiddish language, literature and cultural history among students and faculty here has been most heart-warming and encouraging. In May 1979 Isaac Bashevis Singer spoke to well over a thousand students, faculty, and guests in the auditorium of the L.B.J. Library on the university campus. Thus, in a sense, this special DIMENSION issue marks a culmination and, I hope, the continuation of Yiddish studies at this institution.

STEPHEN H. GARRIN

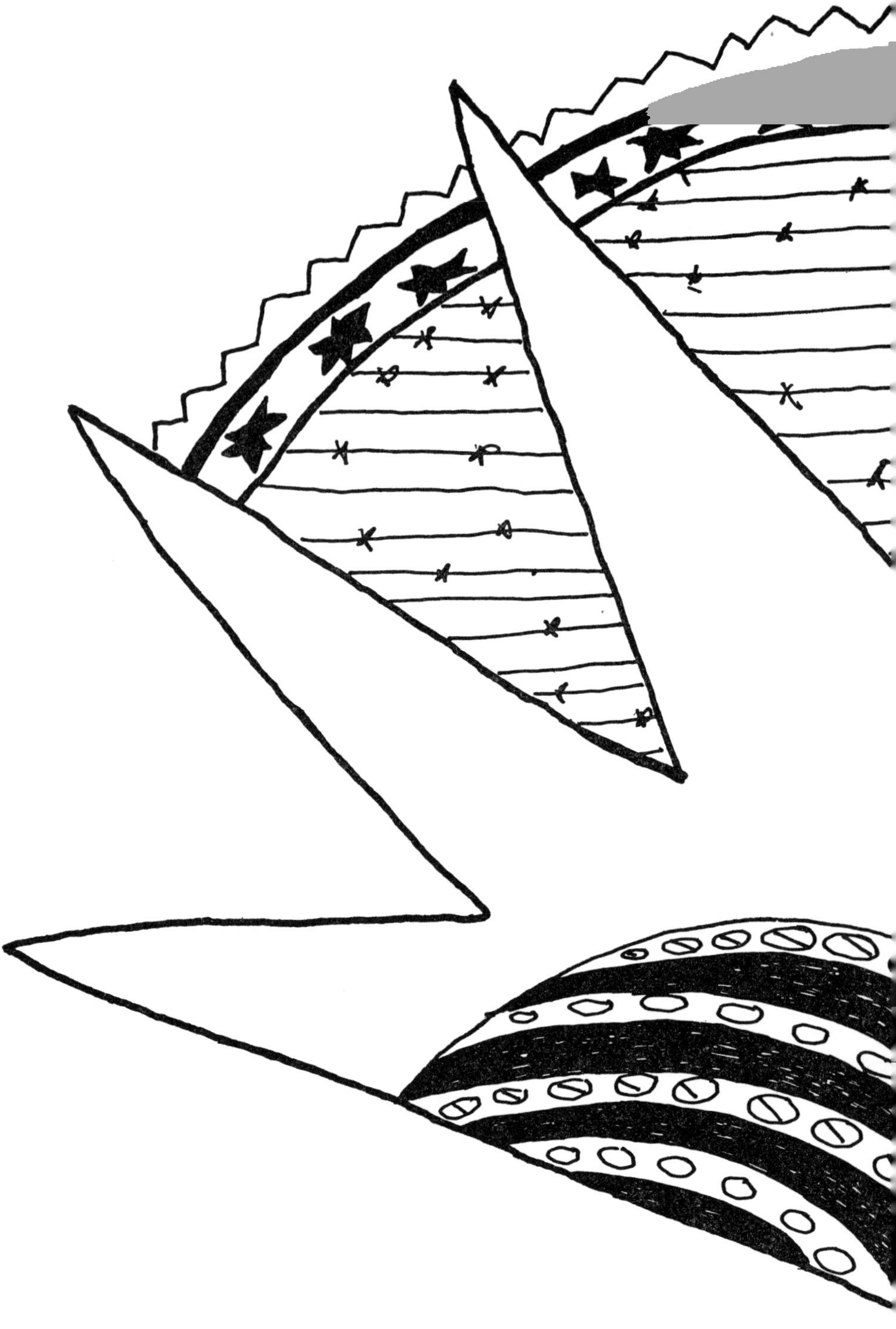

ON CONTEMPORARY YIDDISH WRITING

ELIAS SCHULMAN

HALF A CENTURY AGO A FAVORITE SUBJECT FOR DISCUSSION IN YIDDISH literary circles was: Where is the center of Yiddish literature? Warsaw, Vilno, Moscow, or New York? There were substantial reasons why spokesmen for each city demanded supremacy. In each city Yiddish writers lived, various periodicals were published, and there were publishing houses. There were also Yiddish readers who considered Yiddish literature as their own, and this helped to establish an environment for the writers and a climate for the continuation of Yiddish creativity.

Warsaw and Vilno disappeared from the map of Yiddish literature as the Jewish populations of both cities were destroyed by the Germans during the Holocaust. In Moscow there are some writers who survived; a monthly journal is produced and a general publishing house does offer a few Yiddish books annually.

A small group of writers returned to Warsaw after World War II and tried to maintain a position there for Yiddish writing. A literary monthly was established, a few almanacs were published, and a historical journal appeared regularly. A number of books were printed as well. All literary activity was subsidized by the government, but the writing was not under strict government control as it is in Russia. While no great works were published, much was written about the not–too–distant past of the Holocaust. The small Jewish population supported literary activity, but some writers felt both lonely and restricted and left the country. The official anti-Semitism that accompanied the Six-Day War in 1967 destroyed all Yiddish literary activity. Nearly all the writers left Poland and settled in Israel. At present there is a small Jewish community left, with a weekly newspaper and a few writers and journalists remaining.

In Western Europe, Paris has always constituted a small oasis for Yiddish writers and readers. Before World War I Abraham Reisen, poet, story-teller, and editor, published a fine weekly journal, the *Pariser Journal,* which helped to carve a niche for Yiddish writing in that city. During the two world wars many Jewish writers found a home there, and the emigrants from Poland encouraged those writers. Among those who lived in Paris were Sholem Asch; Ezer Warshavsky; and Zalman Shneur, the Hebrew and Yiddish poet who, previously in Berlin and later in Paris, wrote a series of important novels in Yiddish that describe in a seminal prose Jewish life in Russia in the nineteenth and early twentieth centuries.

After World War II a number of surviving Yiddish writers settled temporarily in Paris, writing and publishing there. Gradually most of them emigrated to Israel, Argentina, and New York. Some do, however, continue to live and work in the French capital today.

New York remains a center for Yiddish literature. It is true that the passing of some of the great personalities in American Yiddish writing in the last decades has contributed to a decline, but with its long tradition of nearly a century of continuous existence it is still a vital factor in Yiddish literature.

In the aforementioned discussion of half a century ago concerning the center of Yiddish productivity, nobody thought of "Eretz Yisroel" (the land of Israel) as having any claim to be a center of Yiddish writing. Ashkenazic Jews spoke and wrote Yiddish in Israel as early as the sixteenth century. A Yiddish periodical appeared in Israel more than a century ago, in 1877. Yiddish writers lived there temporarily or visited the country and wrote about life in what was then Palestine (Sholem Asch, Yehoush, etc.). But literary activity really began after World War I, when a number of authors settled in Palestine and commenced publishing periodicals and books. Hebrew was the official language by then, and Yiddish was not even tolerated. Yiddish gatherings were attacked by the "Defenders of the (Hebrew) Language," and Yiddish publications could not be sold openly. Printing shops of Yiddish journals were destroyed with homemade bombs. Despite the harassment, Yiddish writers displayed courage and carried on with their work. In such an atmosphere no important works could be written, and the results were mediocrity and dilettantism. But these pioneers prepared the soil for a later generation of Yiddish writers in Israel who were to establish that nation as a major location for Yiddish writing and publishing.

The new wave of immigration after World War II brought to the newly founded state many Yiddish readers and authors. This new influx and the destruction of Eastern European Jewry as well as public opinion forced Israeli leaders to alter their stance towards Yiddish. Some Hebrew-Yiddish writers who in "Eretz Yisroel" had written exclusively in Hebrew turned to Yiddish, including I. D. Berkowitch, Jacob Fichtman, and the literary scholar Dov Sadan. Uri Zvi Greenberg's two volumes of Yiddish poetry published by the Hebrew University reveal a Yiddish poet who continued throughout his life to write in a language he had dubbed "a whore's tongue." Together with the writers who came after the Holocaust, with those who came from Poland after World War II and with the immigrants from South America, the new arrivals succeeded in making Israel a creative center for Yiddish writing.

The continued existence of Yiddish literature constitutes nothing less than a miracle. It is a true marvel that, following the destruction of most of the Yiddish speaking Jews and most Yiddish writers in the Soviet Union during the various purges of 1936–1938, the executions of August 12, 1952, and the voluntary linguistic assimilation of the American Jew, Yiddish literature lives, carrying on its mission assigned by a new destiny. It depicts the great Jewish tragedy of that era; it brings comfort to the Jew and gives expression to the great event of our time—the establishment of the State of Israel.

Since the end of World War II, Yiddish writing has been mainly concerned with the Holocaust. A varied literature in numerous languages has emerged dealing with this catastrophe, but in no literature does this tragedy occupy such a central position as in Yiddish. This is understandable, since Yiddish literature concerns itself so much with Eastern European Jewish life. Yiddish writers portrayed the Holocaust in the ghettos, in the various death camps, and on the threshhold of the gas chambers. In the ghettos and camps ordinary people recorded their experiences and composed songs expressing their personal tragedy. Survivors, both poets and common folk, continued writing about what they saw, heard, and experienced. Yiddish writers who were not "there" wrote authentic stories, novels, and poems about the Holocaust. They wrote with deep emotion and with a profound identification with the suffering of the victims. Yiddish literature will concern itself with the Holocaust and its aftermath as long as Yiddish writing survives.

In the last quarter of this century a few great personalities have emerged in Yiddish poetry and prose in the United States. Among them is Isaac Bashevis Singer, who enjoys widespread popularity from his writings both in Yiddish and in translation, and who was awarded the Nobel Prize for Literature in 1978. Singer appeared in Yiddish over half a century ago in 1925, and his stories attracted immediate attention for their style, seminal Yiddish, and character portrayals. His first novel, *Satan in Goray,* was acclaimed for its style and its careful and successful intermingling of modern Yiddish with the Yiddish of the seventeenth century. His European period ended with this novel, and he has resided in New York since then.

The last twenty-five years have been very productive for Singer. He has written many short stories, novels, and personal recollections. All of these have appeared in installments in the *Jewish Daily Forward,* a Yiddish newspaper published in New York, before being translated into English and many other languages.

Chaim Grade was a member of the important literary group "Young Vilno," which was active in the late 1920s and early 1930s. Grade quickly attracted attention with his magnificent poetry, which is replete with vision and genuine Jewishness and reflects the hopelessness of his generation and of the Jewish community of Poland. In my study on Young Vilno (New York, 1946) I pointed out that "as a sensitive poet Chaim Grade realized that tragedy was inevitable, and as a prophet he warned that the apocalyptic time was nearing."

Grade spent the war years in Russia and came to the United States in 1948. He continued to write great poetry and at the same time began writing prose; he has written a number of novellas that place him among the masters of the Yiddish short story. As a prose writer he has developed a personal style that abounds with poetic images and expressions and describes everything with great detail that sometimes interferes with the flow of the narrative. The presence of the author is felt in Grade's prose; both when he comments on the characters and events and when he acts as an observer, his participation is obvious and his intentions are clear.

In his *Di Rebetzin* (The Rabbi's Wife) Grade delves deeply into the psychology of a woman's grief caused by the breaking of her engagement to a rabbi. She ultimately marries a different rabbi, but the insult is unforgettable. *Tzemakh Atlas* is considered one of the most important novels written in the post-Holocaust period. The inner struggles of the hero as well as the Musar (Ethical) Movement are described in this narrative. The disappointment of Tsemakh Atlas after his brief flirtation with secularism and his return to the Yeshiva and the "musar world" are delineated by the master storyteller. *In Beyz Horav* (The Rabbi's House) we again meet some of the best representatives of the rabbinical world and of the struggle between fathers and sons. One son studies philosophy at a Swiss university, where he acquires a doctorate, marries a gentile, becomes the curator of Judaica at the university, and plans to write a book about Maimonides and Spinoza. He conceals his marriage from his parents and remains "a forgotten man in an alien world, whiling [time] away in rooms filled with books from floor to ceiling: books by deceased Jewish scholars, authors of hair-splitting studies of Judaica." In Grade's prose works, as in his poetry, one feels the coming Holocaust and the impossibility of escape from it.

Presently Grade is published a novel in installments in the *Jewish Daily Forward,* entitled *From the Underground,* wherein he recounts the attempts of Holocaust survivors to rebuild their lives in his native Vilno. Their experiences make this endeavor difficult. The struggle for readjustment, flashbacks to their ghetto struggles, and images as partisans in the forest in Russia and Central Asia present a picture of Jewish suffering that penetrates the heart and soul of the reader and evokes compassion for their suffering. In recent years Grade's works have been permeated with Holocaust motifs, as in this novel, but his style and spirit remain as they were in his prewar poetry.

Isaac Metzker has written many stories about life in rural Galicia and in America in which he combines realism and romanticism. His stories about New York are tinged with loneliness, alienation, and a yearning for his former home, which no longer exists. His major achievement is *On Grandfather's Fields,* a novel that depicts the life of Jews living in a village that is surrounded by gentile farmers. Besides depicting the religious Jews, Metzker portrays young people seeking a less traditional life style and presents the non-Jews in their religious beliefs, their behavior and attitude toward the Jews.

Khonon Ayalti acquired his reputation as a prose writer before arriving in the United States. Since then he has written a number of satirical stories and a novel, *Far from Brooklyn,* about life in this country. His latest collection of tales, *The Man from Le Mil* (1974), contains stories about contemporary life and older eras, written with irony, humor, and bitterness and sometimes evoking grotesque images.

L. Treister, in his short story *The Vision at the Vistula* (1971), writes about the Red Army's invasion of Poland in 1920 and the havoc it wrought upon a small Jewish town. In his novel *Near the Rivers of New York* (1978) Treister tells about the lives of several religious families in that city. He recounts his tale in a realistic manner, using the Americanized Yiddish expressions of many New York Jews.

Benjamin Demblin has authored a number of novels and stories dealing with Jewish life in the United States and Europe. He wrote a narrative entitled *West Side* about the depression of the 1930s in which all the characters are non-Jews. In some of his stories he attempts to portray the German-Jewish refugees and their struggle to adjust to life in the New World.

S. L. Schneiderman evokes the memory of his *shtetl* in *When the Vistula spoke Yiddish* and reminisces about the life in his native town with a deep feeling of nostalgia for a world that is no more.

Mordechai Shtrigler emerged as an author from the death camps of Europe. In the years following the Holocaust he wrote several books in a semifictional form about the death factories and his own tragic experiences in the various concentration camps. Since arriving in the United States in the early 1950s Shtrigler has been editing a weekly journal and writing essays and articles about contemporary Jewish problems.

Most of the major American Yiddish poets have passed away during the last two decades, but Yiddish poetry in this country is far from dead. Besides Chaim Grade there is Meyer Shtiker, an important poet who follows the tradition of "di yunge," the group that included Mani-Leyb and Zisha Landau, renovators of Yiddish poetry in America. Shtiker's poems are perfectly formed verses using varied rhyme schemes; they evoke both an emotional and an intellectual response from the reader. His lyrics abound with original images, Jewish allusions, and symbolism. They are filled with the anxiety of the Jew who did not personally experience the Holocaust but identified himself with its martyrs. His childhood home, Boyberik, his parents and grandparents, and the prewar world of eastern Europe form the contours of his verses.

The late Joseph Rubinstein arrived in the United States in 1948, where he wrote vast numbers of short poems and three long narrative poems, "The Scroll of Russia," "The Catastrophe of Poland," and "Exodus from Europe." In thousands of stanzas he describes his personal experiences during the war years as a refugee in Russia, the fear and terror he knew, and his return to Poland where he found only destruction.

Itzig Manger and Aaron Zeitlin were two major Yiddish poets who lived in New York and died within the last twelve years. Zeitlin wrote movingly about the Holocaust, and he authored many deeply religious poems with Kabbalistic overtones and mystical symbolism. He felt that God was silent during the murder of the six million, yet Zeitlin remained a believer.

Manger's verse can be compared to Heine's or Verlaine's in its unique musicality. He was a folk hero popular with, and beloved by, Yiddish readers throughout the world; even in Israel a cult grew up around him. Manger was the inheritor of the bardic tradition of his native Rumania, and he combined folk motives with the most refined elements of modern poetry. Although he was influenced by symbolism and romanticism, he showed his real genius as an ironic balladeer who recharged the old form in his retellings of the classic Biblical tales—Adam and Eve, Cain and Abel, Noah, and others—set in the eastern European landscape.

Among the women writing Yiddish poetry in America are Rachel Veprinsky, who writes in the tradition of "di yunge," and Raizel Zhikhlinsky, who writes in a modern vein. Malke Heifetz Tussman, who resides in Berkeley, represents modernism in Yiddish poetry.

Shloyme Schwartz, M. Olitsky, Khonon Kiel, and Meyer Ziml Tkatch, as well as Gabriel Preil, who writes in both Hebrew and Yiddish, are poets with their own distinct tone, sensibility, and mode of expression.

In Canada, Yiddish literature has carved its own niche. Rokhl Korn continues to write, as do Israel Shtern, Sholem Husid, and octogenarian Haim Leyb Fuks. Fuks' evocation of Lodz and his massive work on Canadian Jewish literature contribute their share to Yiddish writing, as do the works of storyteller I. Zipper and novelist Yehuda Elberg.

Mendel Mann began to write on the eve of World War II. He spent the war years in Russia, first as a refugee and later as a soldier in the Red Army. He fought on battlefields from Moscow to Berlin and was a witness to the heroism of the Russian soldiers, the brutalities of the Nazis, and the murder of the Jews. His novel *People of Tengushy* describes his life among the natives of the far-off Mordovinian Republic. His descriptions of the peasants, landscapes, and nature, and his relationships with the native inhabitants are a novelty in Yiddish literature. The people are primitive, and although their farms are collectives they have not changed their life-styles or traditions; there the Jewish hero finds a temporary home and love. The most important of Mann's stories and novels are those about Poland—about Jewish life there and its tragic end. His most ambitious work is his war trilogy, *At the Gates of Moscow, At the Vistula,* and *The Fall of Berlin.* The trilogy is a portrayal of epic proportions relating an excellent and vivid picture of the war as seen through the eyes of Jewish soldiers.

The author Benjamin Shlevin has been living in Paris since the early 1930s. He served in the French army during the war, was captured, and spent the rest of the war years in prison. Shlevin has written many stories and novels about his former home in Poland and his current life in France. In his youth he wrote in the style of Socialist Realism, later breaking with the movement and the style. He appropriated the method of critical or social realism and has produced a fine body of work.

Itzhak Burstein-Finer is another Parisian novelist and short-story writer. In his lengthy novel *Two Families* he writes realistically about the experiences of a number of Jews in France during the last decades; and in his collection *My Mother,* a portrait of mothers in general, he writes stories which are slightly old fashioned and even sentimental but which are accompanied by a certain charm and genuine empathy.

Abraham Weitz is also a writer of novels and short stories. He has written among others a novel about the Holocaust, which he himself lived through. In his most recent collection, *The Baal Shem Tov Motif and Other Stories,* he tells about the epoch of the Baal Shem Tov, stories that are based on folk tales. Some of them are about life in Poland between the two world wars, about the Holocaust, and about survivors who are so used to suffering that they cannot comprehend their newly found freedom. Weitz' most outstanding work is *Nightmare in a Night of May,* wherein the author writes about the strikes and student rebellions of Paris in 1968.

A number of Yiddish poets live in Paris. One of the important poets of "Young Vilno," Elkhanon Vogler, lived there in the 1960s, where he continued writing his distinguished poems. These poems have been influenced by the Parisian milieu and have the ironic tone of French poetry. The motive of loneliness dominates his Parisian output.

Moishe Shulshtein began as a poet of social protest in the early 1930s, emerging as a bewailer of the Holocaust. He also writes about his experiences in both Poland and France, and in his fine poem "Adam Mickiewicz in Paris" he writes of the attitude of the Polish national poet to the Jews.

Other poets who have made significant contributions to Yiddish poetry are Mishe Waldman, Rivke Kope, and Tania Zisman.

Lazar Aichenrand is a Yiddish poet who lives and writes in Zurich, a poet of twilight and loneliness who writes in the modern idiom. His work is often cerebral and intellectual, and the influence of the "Inzikhist" (Introspective) poets, J. Glatstein and Aaron Leyeles, is very marked. His poems are compact and technically perfect. Aichenrand is a complicated poet, deserving more attention than he has thus far received from the critics.

Yiddish literature in Rumania has its own traditions and style that date back to the last century. The poets wrote their poems to be sung and read in wine cellars. The audience welcomed the troubadours with enthusiasm, and there was a rapport between those who recited and sang and their audience. These bards chose as their subects daily occurrences, and the poems had a folksong quality that made the audience feel at home in the company of the singers. The modern Yiddish poets in Rumania wrote in the traditional forms and the idiom of the early writers, but they perfected and refined their art, which gave rise to such poets as the late Itzik Manger and Jacob Sternberg and contributed to the prose of Moishe Altman, who now lives in the Soviet Union and continues to write at the age of ninety. At this time there are only about thirty-five-thousand Jews in Rumania, and about a dozen Yiddish writers who continue to contribute their share to the world's Yiddish literature. A government publishing house publishes their works, and an annual almanac, *Bukareshter Shriftn,* is produced.

Israel Berkowitch (Israel Bercovici) is a theater historian and poet who writes in the tradition of the folk singers, as he himself states, "in the style of a time long past, as the troubadours." His poems are refined and contain an element of drama. Berkowitch writes with nostalgia about his youth and his *shtetl,* and stresses that he did not avoid the pain he suffered simply for being a Jew. He writes about the Holocaust and the suffering of the Jews in Rumania; however, he expresses faith in humanity and a hope for continued Jewish existence. Israel Berkowitch evokes the names Peretz, Abraham Reisen, Bialik, and other Rumanian Yiddish bards. Berkowitch is a Jewish poet rooted in the tradition of Jewish life and Yiddish poetry.

Wolf Tambur is a prose writer, author of stories and novels. He sought and found new forms of expression that characterize his work; his writings are full of symbolism, mysticism, grotesque imagery, and realism, particularly capturing the local color of the Marmoresh Jews smuggled into the mountains up against the Hungarian border. A clash of styles often occurs, but such contrasts and contradictions help create an original style, introducing something new into Yiddish literature.

In Tambur's novel *The Living Dead* strange things that happen in the other world simply reflect what is happening in the real world. The novel is full of satire about the order of things "there," but the reader can surmise what the author has in mind. In his collection *Beads and Dew* Tambur continues, to a degree, *The Living Dead.* This work also is full of allegories, grotesque hints, and allusions. Some of the stories are about old times but skillfully allude to contemporary events. Many of the stories, miniatures, and homilies surprise us with their originality, courage, and poignancy. In his most recent collection *Autumn with Sun* the author tells about Jewish life in the Rumanian province of Marmoresh. This collection includes artistic descriptions of the local customs and mores as well as scenes pertaining to the dark side of Jewish life. Tambur apologizes for writing about those aspects, especially after Auschwitz.

Tambur believes in the future of the Jewish people. Jewishness, he states, had its origin in fire; it began with a burning bush, and it nearly terminated in the fires of the crematoria; but "fire is eternal" and so is Jewish life. Throughout his stories, whether the subject is contemporary life, Hasidism, the old *shtetl,* or the fantastic world of the Living Dead, there is hope for existence and renewal.

Haim Goldenstein and Iso Schapira are both prose writers who have been influenced by Rumanian and French literatures. Goldenstein is the author of two volumes of short stories and a novel, *The Silent Century.* He displays originality in the short stories and attempts to present the events of the last five decades in a most modern idiom. *The Silent Century* is a modern novel consisting of various episodes with allusions to the Russian Revolution, life in Rumania in the interwar period, the war itself, the Holocaust, and the partisan struggles. From these episodes emerges a novel that tells a great deal about Jewish life and suffering.

Iso Schapira, in his novel *Aleph is an Eagle,* tells about the experiences of Jewish partisans fighting in Rumania against the German army. Previously most of them had participated in the Spanish Civil War. After the collapse of the Loyalist Army they had wandered through France, Palestine (Eretz Yisroel), Africa, and Russia and had arrived in Rumania for the great struggle. Schapira portrays them passing through Jewish towns from which Jews had been deported, painting grim pictures of these empty towns. Through flashbacks the author reproduces scenes of former Jewish life, evoking nostalgia. In this novel, with its contemporary theme, where the heroes are secularized and sometimes revolutionary Jews, there are Biblical allusions, with evocations of the Baal Shem Tov and the romanticism of Hasidism.

In November and December, 1949, and January, 1950, about four hundred Yiddish writers, journalists, scholars, translators, actors, and cultural workers were arrested in Moscow, Kiev, Minsk, and other cities in the Soviet Union. On the twelfth of August, 1952, the most important and talented writers were executed on Stalin's orders; the rest were sent to various labor camps. They were all accused of Jewish nationalism and of spying for the United States and Japan. All Yiddish literary and cultural activity in Russia ceased as a consequence of this liquidation.

After Stalin's death and Khrushchev's "secret" speech, the survivors in the various prisons and camps were released, and Yiddish literary activity resumed on a small scale. In 1959 a few Yiddish books were published, and in 1961 the *Sovetish Heimland,* a bimonthly literary review, appeared in Moscow. Since January, 1965, it has been published monthly. Besides *Sovetish Heimland,* a few Yiddish books appear annually, and in 1979 the journal began publishing a monthly supplement, a booklet of sixty-four pages.

About forty Yiddish writers fell on the battlefields during World War II. The major writers perished during the purges of 1948 through 1953, and in previous purges of 1936 through 1938 some distinguished writers disappeared. In recent years about twenty-five writers migrated to Israel. But despite the losses and the immigration there are still a number of active authors.

As far as we know, there are no dissident Yiddish writers in Soviet Russia at the present time. Those who wished to deviate from the accepted styles left for Israel. The remaining authors write in the style of Socialist Realism; but once in a while we are surprised by the appearance of an original work free, more or less, from the banalities of the Communist Party line.

A recent issue of *Sovetish Heimland* (July, 1980) was devoted to short stories. More than half a dozen writers participated with stories that recalled deeply felt nostalgia for Jewish life in the *shtetlekh,* with references to heroism in Jewish history and to Jewish martyrdom. About fifty or more novels have been published since the inception of the journal. Most of the novels are competent, sometimes factual to the point of photographic representation, and occasionally of surprisingly high literary quality. Some of the writing displays talent, a mastery of form, a genuine expression of Jewish life, and an authentic appreciation of Jewish values. The novels deal with pre-revolutionary times, with the period between the two world wars, and particularly with World War II. In the novels dealing with World War II there are descriptions of the annihilation of the Jews by the German Nazis and of Jewish participation in the partisan struggles in the Red Army.

Hirsch Dobin, Tevye Gen, Haim Melamud, Yekhiel Shraybman, and Buzi Miler, who lives in the Far East in the so-called Jewish autonomous region Biro Bidjan, are all talented writers who occasionally cause a stir with some unorthodox views. In this way Hirsh Dobin caused some consternation by mentioning the unmentionable, the cooperation of the local Belorussian population in the extermination of the Jews, in his novel *Der Koyakh fun Lebn* (The Strength of Life).

The most impressive Soviet Yiddish novel, and one of the major achievements of Yiddish prose in recent years, is Nathan Zabara's *Galgul Hakhoyzer* (The Wheel is Turning). Its separate parts, which were published first in *Sovetish Heimland* and then in book form in Moscow in 1979, are entitled *The Day is Still Young, Under the Hot Sun of Provence,* and *In the Middle of a Clear Day*. Zabara wrote only the first chapter of the fourth part, *Yoel and Menukha,* before he died in 1975. The novel was probably edited and in some parts censored, but there is a complete manuscript in Israel, and hopefully it will be published. The novel aroused a discussion in Moscow, and Zabara was apparently forced to admit that he made some errors in his approach. Before the novel was published it was read in manuscript by the Soviet Jewish historian Hilel Aleksandrov who, quoting Marx and Engels, stated that it was an important historical novel, and with his approval it was published.

Galgul Hakhoyzer gives lavish descriptions of business conditions and the economy during the crusades. Philosophical discussions abound, dealing with the kabbala and religion. Magnificent accounts of entertainments featuring Jewish bars, bartenders, and troubadours are presented. The novel constitutes a great achievement for the late author and for Yiddish literature; it serves as an *apologia pro Judaeis* in stressing the importance of the Jewish community in the medieval world and the pressures that shaped its life and occupations.

The Story of a Love by Note Lurie (*Sovetish Heimland,* 1976 and in book form, Moscow, 1978) recalls the narrator musician's early love for a young girl in a *shtetl* in the former pale. After the war Yokheved, a scientist who lives in Leningrad, decides to visit her former home, where all the Jews were massacred by the Nazis. She finds only the little porch remaining and, determined to plant a tree there, begins to dig. She strikes a bomb left by the Germans; it explodes and she is fatally injured.

Aaron Vergeles, editor of *Sovetish Heimland,* cannot be passed over in silence. His verse recalling the *taign* of Siberia and the experience of living in Biro Bidjan contributes another dimension to Soviet Yiddish poetry; its freshness cannot be denied. His ferocious polemics in defense of the Soviet regime and against Zionism and the "capitalist-imperialist world" have made him the new Litvakoff, the former czar of Yiddish letters in the post-Stalin period.

About one hundred and fifty Yiddish writers live in Israel now. The best two Yiddish journals, *Bay Zikh* and *Di Goldene Keyt,* are published there, as are most of the Yiddish books, including those by writers living in the

Diaspora. Some of the contemporary Israeli Yiddish writers arrived in Israel during the 1920s and 1930s; others arrived after the Holocaust and the establishment of the state. During the late 1960s a number of Yiddish writers remaining in Poland left for Israel as a result of the anti-Semitic campaign after the Six-Day War. Some writers emigrated from South America, and the latest migration is from the Soviet Union.

Of those who settled in mandated Palestine, the poets Yoseph Pupernikov and Jacob Tsvee Shargel are still very active, and their works are imbued with the spirit of the land and the toil of the pioneers.

Uri-Tsvee Greenberg, a major Hebrew poet, wrote a great deal in Yiddish during the 1920s, when he lived in Poland. Greenberg was one of the creators of Yiddish expressionism. For a number of years he did not write in Yiddish, but he renewed his creativity in Yiddish recently, and in 1979 his collected works in Yiddish were published by the Hebrew University in Jerusalem in an academic edition of two volumes.

The late Hebrew-Yiddish writer I. D. Berkowitch, the Hebrew translator of Sholem Aleichem, wrote in Israel his very important recollections, his two novels *Menakhem Mendl in Eretz Yisroel* and *Baginen*, and his wonderful recollections of his youth *Kinder Yorn* (Childhood Years).

The late Arye Shamri, who came to Eretz Yisroel in the 1920s, lived in a kibbutz and mastered Hebrew but wrote his magnificent poetry in Yiddish. Fusing Israeli landscape with religious imagery drawn from the Bible and Hasidic lore, Shamri's poetry transmits the moment of vision into a sense of eternity taking place in the regained Garden of Eden, Israel. His varied lines of free verse in their lyricism parallel *con sordina* the stentorian voice of Uri Zvi evoking beloved Zion.

The Yiddish writers in Israel feel at home in the Jewish state; they are deeply attached to the land and the inhabitants and write about the country, its landscapes, and the toil of the people, at the same time remembering their East European homes and the Holocaust. Both the past and the present are portrayed in their works.

In this essay we can mention only a few writers and their works to give some picture of the state of Yiddish letters in Israel. Among those who came during World War II is Mordecai Tsanin, founder and editor of the first Yiddish Daily in Israel, essayist and novelist. He is at present engaged in the writing of a multivolume historical novel. The first volume, *Artapanos Comes Home,* which has been translated into English, deals with the struggle between the Pharisees and Sadducees and the intervention of Rome. The most recently published volume is the fourth, *The Insurrection in Mezhibozh,* which deals with the development of Hasidism; it is an epic novel of great significance. Recently Tsanin published a collection of stories, *Der Shlisl tsum Himl* (The Key to Heaven), in which fantasy is interwoven with reality, and some of the stories are based on folklore. The superstitions of the *shtetl* are part of the stories.

Elya Schechtman began writing his novel *Erev* (On the Eve) in Russia. It appeared in *Sovetish Heimland* in 1962 and later was published in book form. The novel begins with a description of Jewish life at the turn of the century and follows into the subsequent decades. The writing is in the tradition of Yiddish realism and bears the marked influence of Sholem Asch, Joseph Opatoshu, and particularly David Bergelson. Striking an authentic Ukranian-Jewish note, the author depicts the Boyars, a large Jewish family. The style is vibrant, and its dialogues and inner monologues are both persuasive and characteristic. The milieu and interrelationships are artistically and sensitively described. The novel has its portions of social-realistic banalities, but they are minimal. Schechtman is continuing to write his novel in Israel; he is now free of all restraint, of party lines, of controls, but he has now gone completely in the opposite direction. In parts five and six, published in Tel Aviv in 1979, he continues the family chronicle of the Boyar family, describing their tribulations over a long period of time. He begins with the anti-Jewish pograms, the civil war in the Ukraine in 1919 and 1920, through forced collectivization, the Moscow trials and the purges of the 1930s, through flashbacks of the pre-Revolutionary period. The novel is permeated with Schechtman's present-day ideology, a rapid inversion of Soviet propaganda, and he often expresses his own views and opinions at the expense of his art.

Isaiah Spiegel, author of great stories about the Holocaust, is continuing to write both prose and poetry and has recently published the second volume of his *Geshtaltn un Profiln* (Figures and Profiles) consisting of evaluations of various Yiddish authors.

Yekhiel Granatshtein is the author of *Fremde Velder, eigene Erd* (Stranger's Fields, Our Own Land), a novel depicting life in the interwar period in Poland, the Holocaust, and migration to Israel by a lone survivor.

Itzhak Janasowicz is a creative personality and a man of letters. He is a poet, storyteller, critic, and editor. He has enriched Yiddish literature with excellent stories about Jewish life in Poland, Russia, and South America, all of which he has lived in, and has contributed a volume about his experiences as a refugee during the war in Russia. His *A Shtub in Shtetl* (A House in Shtetl) is an epic poem about the destroyed Jewish life in Poland. His criticism and evaluations of Yiddish writers, all written in the tradition of Yiddish literary criticism with some of the new trends of modern criticism interwoven, constitute a fine appreciation of the state of Yiddish letters.

Abraham Sutzkever, who was known as an important Yiddish poet in his early days in Vilno, continued writing in the forest as a partisan and then wrote in Russia, in Paris, and in Israel, where he is now editing *Di Goldene Keyt.* He writes in the modern idiom, with extraordinary images and metaphors, in a masterly fashion. His description of the landscapes around his native Vilno, of the scenes in Siberia where he spent his early years, of his experiences in the ghetto, later in the forests and still later in Israel, are all written with controlled emotion and highly original technique and are unique in their conception and realization. In recent years he has written some very original stories, imbued with poetic imagination and containing an element of surrealism.

At present there are many talented poets contributing to the growth of Yiddish literature in Israel. Some of these poets are Bunim-Heller, Assia, M. Yungman, Hadassah Rubin, Aleksander Shpigelblat, Rachel Boimwal, Shloyme Roitman, Ephraim Roitman, Joseph Kerler, Haim Maltincky, Yosl Lerner, Shloime Shenhood, Meyer Kharats, M. Sotzkier, Hirsh Osherowitch, Z. Telesin, Rachel Fishman, and Rivka Basman. Among the prose writers are Israel Kaplan, Meyer Yellin, Tsvee Eisenman, Malasha Mali, S. Vorzager, Kobriansky, Yosl Birshtein, a most talented and original storyteller and novelist, and K. Tzetnik (Di Nur), author of numerous works about the Holocaust.

David Sfard, formerly an active participant in the communist Yiddish publishing house *Yidish Bukh* in Warsaw, who left Poland in 1968, is a poet and essayist who distinguished himself in both fields as much for his aesthetic craft as for his political virtuosity.

Leib Rikhman, an author of important novels and stories about the Holocaust, died in 1978. Jacob Friedman, a scion of a Hasidic family, wrote poems imbued with the spirit of genuine Hasidism. Using kabbalistic allusions and Hasidic motifs, Friedman evokes the mystical *Seelenlandschaft* of the true believer, where material representation becomes a metonymy for yet higher world beyond linguistic encoding. He also wrote stories about life in Rumania and Israel. His three volumes of poetry and prose were published posthumously from 1974 through 1979.

Among the literary critics and scholars in Israel are Dov Sadan, L. Podractchik, Simon Kantz, A. Liss, S. H. Shmeruk, Ephraim Shreyer, Ehiel Sheintukh, Khave Turniansky, E. Lipiner, and the previously mentioned Yitzhak Janasowicz and David Sfard.

There are small groups of Yiddish writers in Mexico, Argentina, Brazil, and other South American countries as well as in Australia. Although geographically far away from the main centers of Yiddish writing, Israel and the United States, they contribute their share to world literature.

Yiddish literature is the literature of world Jewry, including those who do not speak the language. It is the language of both the Diaspora and Israel, expressing the hopes and aspirations of all Jews and loyally portraying Jewish life wherever it exists. The condition of Yiddish literature is different now than it was before World War II, and it lacks some of the spirit it had in the interwar years. But the greatest miracle is that after the Holocaust it has come back to itself gradually and is fulfilling its mission—to tell about the past, to portray the present, and to give the Jewish people encouragement for the future. Yiddish authors write for the sake of writing rather than for any material gain. They write with enthusiasm and joy because they are aware that they perform what amounts to a sacred duty and a religious obligation. Yiddish writers must often struggle to have their books published, and they often subsidize the publication of their own works. Therefore Yiddish literature is not a business affair but the sincere and honest expression of each individual writer and of the literature as a whole.

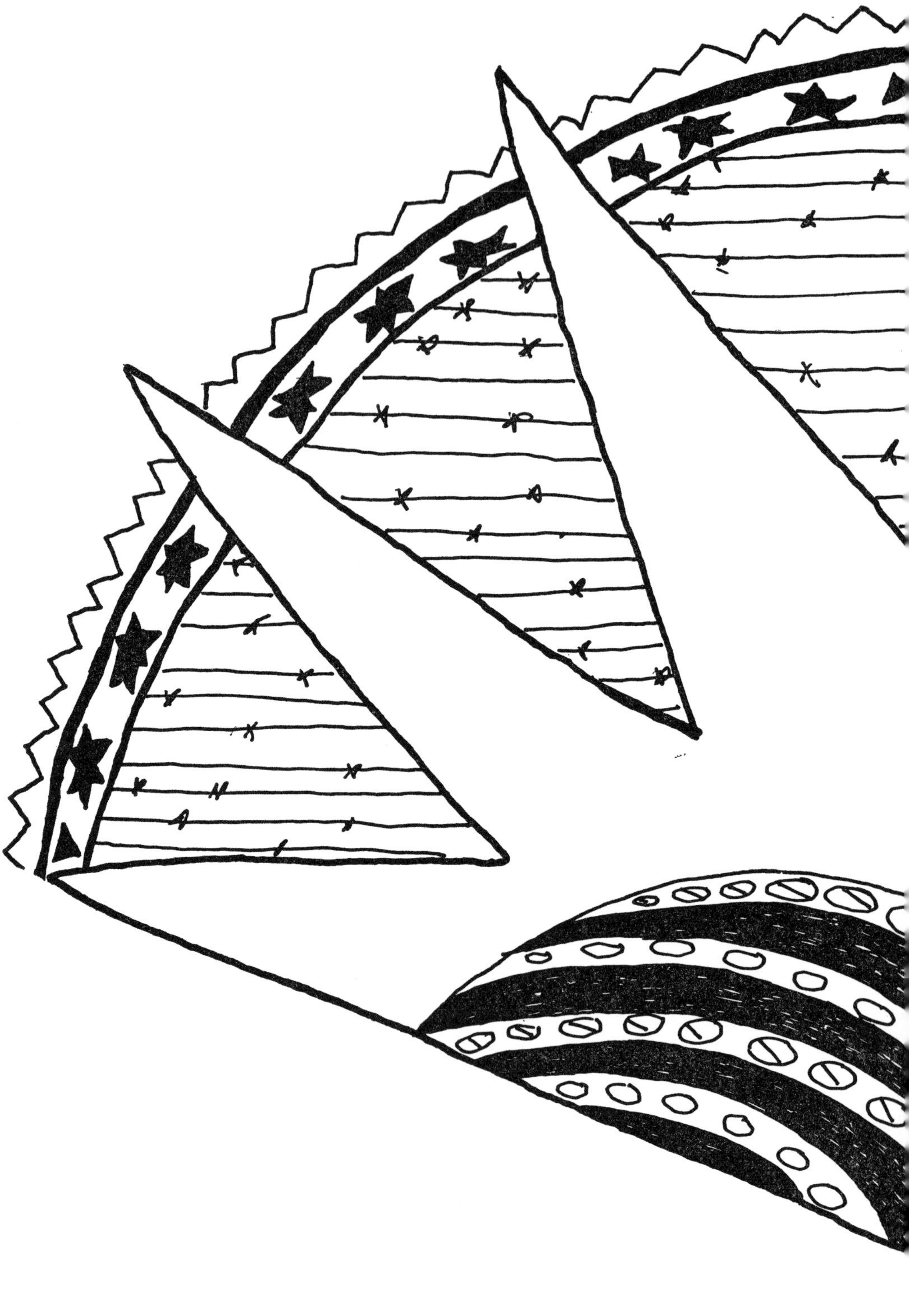

A NOTE ABOUT THE TRANSLITERATION

All the letters are pronounced in Yiddish.

The vowel equivalents in the transliterated texts are as follows:

a = the a in father
e = the e in get
i = the double ee in feet
o = the aw in dawn
u = the double o in moon

Diphthongs:

ey = the i in fine
ay = the ai in pain
oy = the oy in boy

Consonant combinations:

zh = the s in measure
kh = the ch in the German ach

VEN STRELISK HOT GEBRENT

MEYER SHTIKER

(Arum a yor far der ershter velt milkhome iz kemat gantz alt-strelisk, dos galitzishe shtetele etlekhe meyl fun lemberg, avek mit feyer. A sakh yidn fun boyberik, a por meyl avek, hobn zikh aroysgelozt oprateven vos un vemen zey veln nor kenen. Tzvishn yene yidishe geboyrim iz oykh geven meyn zayde noakh paget.)

Tu on dem tizlik, zayde,
Trink oys dem akevit.
Farbeys an eyerkikhl
Un nem dem talis mit.

Es vartn ferd un shlitn
Oyfn shney vos blent,
Tu on dem futerhitl
Un heyde—strelisk brent!

Di feyertzungen shpreytn
Zikh nenter tzu der brik—
Ikh bet dikh, kum besholem
Tzurik keyn boyberik.

Es iz geven a mitvokh
Zibn inderfri,
Ven s'hobn ferd un shlitn
Gelozn zikh in fli.

Di shohn krikhn, krikhn
Areyn in donershtik.
Di bobe klogt un yamert:
Ven kumt er shoyn tzurik?

WHEN STRELISK BURNED

MEYER SHTIKER
translated by Stephen H. Garrin

(About one year before World War I almost all of old Strelisk, a Galician town several miles from Lemberg, was destroyed by fire. Many Jews from Boyberik, a nearby village, attempted to rescue what and whom they could. Among those Jewish heroes was also my grandfather, Noah Paget).

Grandpa, don your weskit,
Drink up your aquavit,
Here, take a bite of biscuit,
And take along your talit.*

Horses and sleighs are ready to go
On the blinding snows.
Put on your fur cap also,
and fast! Strelisk in fire glows.

The tongues of flame are spreading,
Now at the bridge they lick.
Come in peace—I'm begging,
Come back to Boyberik.

It was on a Wednesday
Seven in the morn,
When the horses and the sleighs
Took off in flight that dawn.

The hours they were creeping,
When Thursday soon did come.
Grandma stood there weeping:
"When will he return home?"

* Prayer shawl.

Zi hot geklugt biz freytik,
Ven plutzim, umgerikht,
Er iz tzurikgekumen
A sho far bentshn likht.

Di payes opgesmalet,
Der tizlik opgebrent—
Di bobe khaye sore
Hot im koym derkent.

Er iz arop fun shlitn
Un tzugelofn gikh
Tzu ir un oysgerufn:
—Ikh hob gebrakht mit zikh

A halbn tutz nisrofim,
Biz iber shabes bloyz,
Nor oyb s'iz der nit nikhe,
Fir ikh zey in kloyz.

Di bobe hot geshvign
A rege un nit mer,
Un s'hot zikh in a diment
Farvandelt irs a trer.

Zi hot tzepralt di tiren
Un mit a kol fun freyd
Gevendt zikh tzu di orkhim:
—Meyn shtub far eykh shteyt greyt.

Zey geyen funem shlitn
Arop in veysn shney,
Halb naket un borves
In vintikn zavey.

Di bobe teylt malbushim—
Reklekh, hoyzn, shikh.
Shabesdike rikhes
Shparen fun der kikh.

She complained till Friday,
When suddenly, they tell,
He came back home to stay
Just before the Sabbath fell.

His sidelocks black and singed,
The weskit scorched likewise,
Grandma Chaya Sore looked at him
But could scarcely recognize.

He stepped down from the sleigh
And ran up breathing fast,
To grandma did he say:
"I've brought with me some guests."

A half-a-dozen victims,
Just till the Sabbath's out.
But only if you want them,
I'll show them to the house.

Grandma just stood silent
For a moment there,
Into a sparkling diamond,
Was transformed her single tear.

Standing by the open entry
With a shriek of jubilation,
She turned to the invitees:
"For you my home stands open."

They came down from the sleigh
Onto the glistening snow,
Naked and barefoot were they,
As the winter winds did blow.

Grandma passed out clothing:
Jackets, shoes and slacks.
While Sabbath smells were floating
From the kitchen in the back.

Ikh fil in ale beyner
Di shabesdike vor,
Khotsh s'zeynen shoyn antlofn
Ariber fertzik yor.

I still feel deep inside
That Sabbath atmosphere,
Although with time and tide
Have passed now forty years.

DI SEDRA VEYEKHI

MEYER SHTIKER

VAYIKRA JACOB EL BANOV . . .

A vinter farnakht. Di sedra veyekhi—
Khesed un treyshaft vi seyd un vi samet—
Ikh bin seks yor alt un greykh biz di kni
Fun moishe katzen dem dardikey melamed.

Ikh khazer di parshe mit furkht un ikh veys
Az zeyn linker hant iz iber mir fartzeugen.
Nor zeyn nomen iz oysgeleyzt fun aldos beyz
Un vi bey yakoven tunklen itzt zeyne oygn.

Ikh bin ruven der eltester zun vos hot
Farumvirikt dem voters bet mit zeyn zomen.
Nor zeyn nomen iz mekhtik farn ponim fun got
Un groys in gefekht mit di vaser-shtromen.

Ikh bin shimen ve leyvi, farsholten vi zey
Mit vafn fun royb, mit retzikhe fun mentshn.
Meyn zel iz tzeshpoltn, meyn tzores un vey
Vet keyner nit loybn, vet keyner nit bentshn.

Ikh bin yehudes hant oyfn nakn fun feynt,
Meyne brider tuen zikh tzu mir bukn.
A yunger leyb, mit oygn vi veyn—
Ikh loker oyf felker zey tzu fartzukn.

Ikh voyn vi zevulen bey di bortens fun yam,
Vi dos eyzl yisakher tzvishn shof-gehoyfn,
Der rukn geboygn un mild vi a lam,
Trog ikh di knekhtshaft fun koyfn-farkoyfn.

JACOB'S DEATH

MEYER SHTIKER
translated by Stephen H. Garrin

"AND JACOB CALLED UNTO HIS SON . . ."

A winter eve. The chapter of Veyekhi*—
Righteousness and loyalty, satin and silken—
I'm a six-year-old reaching to the knee,
Of our teacher, Moyshe Katzen.

I repeat the verses with awe, and I know,
That his left hand hovers o'er me,
And his heart is unburdened of all pain and woe,
And like Jacob his eyes see but dimly.

I am Reuben the eldest who defiled the bed
Of my father with my unworthy seed.
But his name remains mighty before the Godhead,
And fearless in battle with the rushing stream.

I am Simon and Levi, cursed as they,
With weapons of plunder and the hatred of men.
My soul is split, my sorrow and pain
No man will praise, nor answer amen.

I am Judah's hand on the enemy's spine.
My brothers bow in homage to me.
A youthful body, eyes red like wine—
In ambush I await my adversary.

I live like Zebulon on the river banks of sand,
The donkey of Issachar where the sheep graze—
My back arched gently as a lamb
I wear the chains of bondage all my days.

* The last chapter of the Book of Genesis.

Ikh bin don vos bafalt vi a shlang dos ferd—
Az dem reyter farkhopt in haldz der otem
Un er falt arunter toyt oyf der erd—
Nor gleykh bin ikh gleykh vi di andere shvotim.

Naftoli bin ikh—meyne reyd hilkhn op
Iber barg un tol, in di tifste tehoymen.
Ikh bin yoysef der pastukh mitn gekroytzeltn kop,
Der fels fun yisroel, der shtrom iber shtromen.

Dos frukhtike beyml beym likhtikn kval,
Vu di tzveygn shtrekn zikh iber di moyer,
Dem foters brokhes vi a vidershtral
Farkleybn mit troyer zikh itzt in meyn oyr.

Nor eyn zakh veys ikh, klor un farvor:
Mit benyomin dem volf vel ikh zikh nit fahern,
Veyl tzum dardike melamed, tzu di yingelshe zeks yor
Vel ikh zikh shoyn keynmol nit umkern.

I am the one who falls like a snake on the horse—
The rider gasps as onward he rides.
And onto the ground is hurled his old corpse—
But I am the same as the other tribes.

I am Naphtali—my words echo on high
Over mountain and dale, in the abyss unseen.
Joseph am I, the shepherd, my curly locks fly.
The coat of Israel, stream of streams.

The fruit-laden tree by the luminous well
Where the branches reach over the wall,
My father's blessings repeat and retell
Of sadness. My ears hear it all.

But one thing I know, clear and true:
Benjamin the wolf I will not disdain.
To the teacher Katzen and the six-year-old Jew,
I will never return again.

Harold A. Liebowitz

A BRIV FUN GEFENGENISH FUN PAUL VERLAINE TZU ARTUR RIMBAUD

MEYER SHTIKER

Veyl dos iz nit di zun, dos iz nit keyn fenster un dos iz nit
keyn moyz untern bet—
Ikh shpir di brudigkeyt fun leylekh unter mir, dos harte
leyvente hemd—
Zeynen es meyne lipn vos shveygn un dos papir vos redt:
Veys, meyn troyeriker kop iz trukn, brudik un nit farkemt.

Vu zeynen deyne finger? Dos kilindike blut unter meyn hoyt
shreyt oys nokh zey,
Un nit nor meyne lipn garn nokh dir, zunik yingl, halbreyfer man.
Ikh veys az ergetz otemst un bizt faran
un veys nit—zeynen di lonkes grin, zeynen di felder
shver gedekt mit shney?

Ikh bin nit shtum nor verter frirn, verter shtarbn in
meyn moyl,
Ikh bin nit toyb—vos vil ikh hern un vos ken ikh hern?
O. got, vi bin ikh shleyferik, o got, vi ikh bin foyl!
Kegn vemen zol ikh zikh shteln, kegn vemen zol ikh zikh vern?

Ikh vart. Es shveygt meyn blut nor meyne shleyfn shpirn:
Es shreyt der tog, di zun blit oyf, di sho dernentert zikh:
O zunik yingl, oyf goldene lonkes vel ikh dikh vider firn.
Vos faln deyne oygn tsu? Badoyerst mikh?

Nor itzt iz shpete nakht. Di shtilkeyt rint. Es drimilt dos
papir.
Dos iz der letzter otemtzug fun likht vos flatert oyf meyn
pen.
Der mider vekhter riglt tzu a skripene tir.
Es benkt nokh dir. . . es benkt nokh dir. . .

Verlaine.

A LETTER FROM PRISON FROM PAUL VERLAINE TO ARTHUR RIMBAUD

MEYER SHTIKER
translated by Stephen H. Garrin

Because this is not the sun, this no window and this is no mouse
beneath my bed—
I feel the filthy bedsheet under me, the
course linen shirt—
Are these my lips that are silent and the paper that said:
You know, my troubled head of hair is dry, coarse, and matted down with dirt.

Where are your fingers? The cooling blood 'neath
my skin calls out from below—
And not only my lips yearn for you, sunny child, half ripened man.
I know that somewhere you breathe and yearn and are there and
don't know—are the lawns green? Are the fields
laden down with snow?

I am not mute but the words freeze; words die
in my mouth,
I am not deaf—what do I want to hear? What can I hear?
Oh God! How weary am I! How lazy am I!
Against whom shall I rise? Against whom draw my spear?

I wait, my blood is silent, only my temples feel now.
The day cries out, the sun blossoms, the hour approaches quickly.
O sunny child, to golden lawns, I'll once again lead thee.
Why do your eyes close? Do you mourn me?

Now, late in the night. Silence flows. The paper
sleeping.
The last breath of light falls gently
on my pen—
The tired watchman locks the door, creaking
I yearn for you—I yearn for you—

Verlaine

UN A SHMEYKHL IZ GEVEN

MALKA HEIFETZ TUSSMAN

Deyn briv—
un a shtilkeyt in meyn hoyz geven
a gantzn tog.

oyf di lipn kh'hob gefilt
di fartifste shtilkeyt.

kh'hob a pips nit geton dem gantzn tog
s'zol oyf ir a dinster klang nit faln.

un a klugshaft iz geven
in der guter shtilkeyt.

un a shmeykhl kh'hob gezen
in der kluger shtilkeyt.

un ikh hob zikh in ir geviklt
vi in meyn mames
          varemer
               terkisher shal
a gantzn tog.

AND THERE WAS A SMILE

MALKA HEIFETZ TUSSMAN
translated by Daniel Marlin

Your letter—
and a silence in my house
the whole day.

on my lips I've felt
the silence deepen.

I haven't made a peep
lest the barest sound shatter it.

and a wisdom was
in the good silence.

and I saw a smile
in the wise silence.

and I have wrapped myself in it
as in my mother's
                    warm
                            turkish shawl
the whole day.

SHALOM SHULAMIT

MALKA HEIFETZ TUSSMAN

Ikh a shprotz oyf tog vos viklt zikh
In shleyrn geheyme,
Oyf der mirpeset, ofn breyt tzum
Tunkl fun geberg
Bin ikh aroys zikh zaygenen mit dir,
Shversterl shulamit

Kh'bin nit gevoynt arumtzugeyen in
Pletzer heylike.
Do bleyb ikh shteyn bey a shteyndele in gas.
Mit erfurkht
Kh'gey dos shteyndele arum
Vi eyner
Tret op an eltern dem veg.

Shulamit,
Kleyninke yorn hobn mikh bayornt,
Kleyninke freydn hobn meyn gedeyikeyt genert
Far der freyd der groyser
Tzu kumen un zingen deyn koved
Fun frier, fun heynt un
fun shpeter.

Ikh hob gekhulemt deyn olive sheynkeyt,
Gekhulemt pastekher, printzn,
Gekhulemt veyngertner un lemelekh veyse.
Itzt veys ikh:
Ven s'vert shoyn mekoyem a khulem
Zukht men nokh altz dem khulem arum.

Altz iz mir do epes kentlekh, epes
Fremdlekh,
Nor altz ometum iz mir heylik
Un ikh veys nit vi in heylikeyt arumgeyn

SHALOM, SHULAMMITE

MALKA HEIFETZ TUSSMAN
translated by Jack Hirshman

In this early dawn winding
In mysterious veils,
On the balcony open to the duskiness
Of the hills
I came to bid you shalom,
Little sister Shulammite.

I'm not accustomed to walking in
Holy places.
I stop here, at a small stone in the street.
In awe,
I walk around it
As one
Encountering an elder.

Shulammite,
Little years have aged me.
Little joys have fed my duration
For the great joy of
Coming to sing your praise
Of the past, the present and
That will be.

I dreamed your olive beauty,
I dreamed shepherds and princes,
Vineyards and white lambs.
Now I know:
Even when a dream comes true
One still is searching for the dream.

Everything here seems familiar, yet
Strange,
Everything here is holy
And I don't know how to walk in

Mit meyn pozlan, iberfuln krug mit libshaft.
Meyn oyn farkukt a- yedn in ponim
Nor se tzindt nit a derkenen
Ub ikh veys nit ven, far vemen efenen meyn tir
Un tzu vemens lipn tzutrogn meyn krug.

Oykh du, shulamit, vos deyn libshaft
Iz gerimt oyf der velt der gorer,
Du host nit ale mol geeylt
Di tir tzu efenen far
Dem printz.
Un du host dokh derkentenish gehat.
Un du host dokh gevust az
"Beser fun veyn iz zeyn libshaft."

In ot der sho
Bistu arumgelofn zukhn dem
Vos deyn zel bagert.
Di shpuren fun deyne trit zeynen nit fargangen.
Efsher du loyfst nokh altz ado arum.
Eybik vet do vidern der viderkol
Fun ruf deynem,
Fun zifst deynem,
Shulamit.

Meyn zilber in di hor
Neygt zikh tzu deyn yungkeyt.
Oykh ikh yung mit a yungkeyt vos
Farshemt mikh un
Vos keyner vet nit rimen.
Ikh hob keynmol gornit nit gehitn:
Nit keyn veyngortn, nit meyne trit
Un oykh meyn tzung opgehitn.
Oft
Ken ikh got fun mentsh untersheydn
Un ver ikh ongerekt tzu zind
Iz dos mir tzu
Avodah gleykh, shulamit.

Un veyl a kuk
Hot gor dos godles mir aroysgeshlogn
Dertzeyl ikh dir do ofn:

Holiness with my brimful jug of love.
My eye, searching every face it meets,
Doesn't flash a recognition
And I don't know who to open my door to,
To whose lips to raise my jug.

You too, Shulammite of the great love,
Glorified all over the world,
Didn't always hurry
To open your door.
To the prince,
You had recognition.
And knew that
"Better than wine was his love."

At such an early hour
You ran around here looking for
The one your soul desired.
The traces of your feet have not vanished.
Perhaps even now you are still lurking, searching.
The echo of your call,
Your sighing will
Forever be resounding here,
Shulammite.

The silver in my hair
Bows to your youth.
I too am young, with a youth that
Shames me and
Gathers no praise.
For I never guarded anything:
Not my vineyard, not my steps
And not my tongue.
Often
I can't distinguish God from man.
I fall into sin
As if it were
Worship, O Shulammite.

Now that one certain short glance has
Knocked out all my pride
I'm here to tell you openly:

S'hot meyn unshuld
Frier shoyn gekhulemt ale zind.

Itzt, oyf der mirpeset,
In der shtilkeyt fun deyn shprotz oyf tog,
Tzu der lobung fun der kikeyt mild vi milkh
Gezegn ikh zikh o, shvesterl kleyne.

Kumen vel ikh nokh tzu dir tzurik ven
Ale meyne leydnshaftn veln zeyn shoyn oysgeleydnt
Un durkhzikhtik kh'vel zeyn azoy
Az s'veln oyfshpiln in mir
Ale vunder fun deyn over, fun deyn hoyve un
deyn osid.

My innocence always dreamed
All the worldly sins.

Here on the balcony
In the stillness of the early Jerusalem hour
Fed by the coolness that is mild as milk,
I bid you shalom, little sister.

I'll come again, I'll return when
All my passions are painless
And as if a mirror
My translucency will play through me
All the wonders of your past, your present, and
what will be.

TATE ZISER

MALKA HEIFETZ TUSSMAN

Un ikh ruf im
Tate siser
Khotsh ikh gedenk nit dem taten.

Dokh epes gedenkt zikh:
A dorn,
A feyer,
A doner,
A barg
Un epes a kol.

Ven mir dakht zikh
Ikh her zeyn kol
Bald shrey ikh:
Do bin ikh!
Do bin ikh, tate ziser!

Az a tate farlozt
Iz er altz nokh a tate
Un ikh vel nit oyfhern benken
Un shreyen
"Do bin ikh"
Biz er vet derhern,
Vet zikh dermonen
Un rufn meyn nomen
Un reydn tzu mir
Durkh likht.

SWEET FATHER

MALKA HEIFETZ TUSSMAN
translated by the author

And I call Him
Sweet Father
Although I don't remember my father.

But I remember
A thorn
A fire
A thunder
A mountain
And something of a voice.

When I think
I hear his voice
I shout at once
Here I am!
Here I am, Sweet Father!

When a father abandons
He is still a father,
And I will not stop longing
And calling
"Here I am"
Until he hears me
And remembers me
And calls my name
And talks to me
Through light.

NIT A LID, NOR A TFILE, MEYN KIND

YANKEV GLANTZ

—"Vi ikh bin a yid!"—meyn tate flegt shvern.
Les-ato nit modne di reyd fun meyn tatn,
Un s'past nit tzi shvern azoy,
Khotsh yidishe trern nokh zeynen vi toy
Oyf di reder, vos forn uns iber.
Un gleyb mir, meyn kind, vi ikh bin a yid!
Nisht leyenen vesto meyn yidishn lid
Fun di shenste un beste afile!—
—Zey moykhl, nisht a lid nor a tfile!
Me hert shoyn nit mer
In di yidishe shtiber
Keyn yidishn nigen, opgeredt—
A vort fun an ekhtn poet.

Un ikh hob far dir
Meyn vort opgevoygn fun itlekhn shir
(Yedn tog oyf der vog)
Un in nekht
Far dir geflokhtn.
    Un vi perl trerl yedern geklibn—
Un vos iz geblibn?
Trukn deyn zefeld, meyn kind,
Vi in midbar dos zamd inem vint,
Ikh veys, a, ikh veys: dir iz liber
A sakh dos gezang funem shokhn!
Un dokh klingt meyn lid fun meyn hartz, vos tzebrokhn
Mit betokhn un gloybn,
    Az got vet derhoybn
Meyn kol nokh a mol funem toy oykh far dir,
    Un meyn shir oyf der erd,
    Vos du host nit derhert.

NOT A POEM, BUT A PRAYER, MY CHILD

JAKOBO GLANTZ
translated by Seth L. Wollitz

"As I'm a Jew!" My father used to swear.
It never sounded strange, my father's talk,
But now, it's out-of-date to swear that way,
Although the tears of Jews still fall like dew
On the wheels which carry us off:
Believe me, my child, as I'm a Jew
You won't read my Yiddish poems —
Not even the very best!
—Excuse me, not a poem but a prayer!
In no more Jewish homes
Are Jewish melodies heard.
The word is stilled —
From an honest poet.

For you,
I weighed my words for every poem
(Each day on a scale)
And at night
I wound them whole for you.
        Each teardrop garnered like a pearl —
What's become of it all?
Barren is your field of vision, my child,
Like sand in the desert wind.
I know all too well you hold much dearer
The song of our neighbor.
Yet my poem rings out from my crumbling heart
In steadfast faith:
        God will again lift
My voice high up from the valley even for you,
        And my song on this Earth
        Is like one you've never heard!

FLATERLEKH FEYER

YANKEV GLANTZ

Ikh gey areyn in meyn lid,
Vi a yid in a tfile far nakht-tzu.
Ikh makh tzu di fentzter
Far klangen farfremde —
Oysyes farshemte fun yidisher shprakh.
Tzi aroyf nor a dakh
Oyf tzelekherter shtub.
Den nekhtn do
Hobn nokh kinder gezungen
Mit yidishe trapn.
Itzt geyt um do a blinder,
Vi okersht aroys fun a grub,
Un zoygt oys mit zeyike finger
Di sheyn, vos farblibn
Fun likhtikn shafn.
Tzeykhns un mufsim,
Vi flaterlekh feyer
In sheyer farbrentn.
Tzi aroyf nor a dakh
Oyf tzelekherte vent do.
Oysyes farshemte
Fun yidisher shprakh.

FLICKERING FLAMES

JAKOBO GLANTZ
translated by Seth L. Wollitz

I enter my poem
Like a Jew into prayer at nightfall.
I latch the windows
From alien sounds—
Shamed alphabet of the Yiddish tongue.
Lift up just a roof top
From the battered house.
Only yesterday
Children still sang
Yiddish syllables here.
Now a blind man shuffles about
Fresh from the grave
And sucks out with insightful fingers
The light which remains
From brilliant works.
Signs and miracles
Like flickering flames
In burnt barns.
Lift up just a roof top
Over battered walls here.
Shamed alphabet
Of the Yiddish tongue.

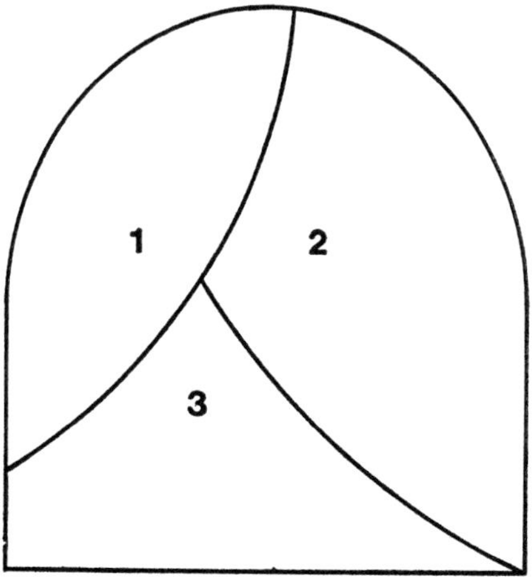

Symbology
tablet shape

1) escape to freedom

2) leaving the old pain—barbed wire

3) floor of the temple.

BROYT FAR DI FEYGL

REYZL ZHIKHLINSKI

Hostu farzukht a mol
Dos broyt,
Vos mentshn varfn far di feygl?
S'hot dem tam
Fun erd,
Fun shteyn,
Fun gelekhter
Un geveyn,
Fun teg un nakht
Blut un zaltz, —
S'hot dem tam fun dir,
Mentsh!
Hostu farzukht a mol
Dos broyt,
Vos mentshn varfn far di feygl?
Es aza broyt —
Un vest zikh oyfheybn
Oyf fligl.

BREAD FOR THE BIRDS

REYZL ZHIKHLINSKI
translated by Tzipora Baradon

Have you ever tasted
The taste of bread
That people throw for the birds?
It has the taste
Of earth,
Of stone,
Of laughter
And moaning,
Of days and nights
Of blood and salt,—
It has the taste of you,
O man! O man!
Have you ever tasted
The bread,
That people throw for the birds?
Eat such bread —
And you will rise
On wings.

IKH KUK AREYN IN DI OYGN FUN REMBRANDT

REYZL ZHIKHLINSKI

Ikh kuk areyn in di oygn fun rembrandt —
Tzvey shvartze tehomen,
Labirintn,
Vos hobn nisht keyn sof
Un nisht keyn nomen.
Zey firn tzurik tzu zikh,
Tvu shvartzer erd.
Nokh lange voglenish
Geyt oyf in mir a sheyn,
Rembrandts sheyn,
Dos likht, vos shtamt nisht fun tog,
Un nisht fun nakht,
Vos loykht fun zikh aleyn.

I LOOKED INTO THE EYES OF REMBRANDT

REYZL ZHIKHLINSKY
translated by Tzipora Baradon

I looked into the eyes of Rembrandt —
Two black depths,
Labyrinths,
Endless
Nameless.
They draw you to themselves—
To dark earth.
I stare and stare
Until overcome by a glow
Rembrandt's glow,
A light that emanates from neither day
Nor night —
Of itself glows this light.

SHREYBN LIDER

REYZL ZHIKHLINSKI

Shreybn lider mit oysyes
Vos muzn dertzeyln fun griber
Mit umgebrengte yidn,
Vos roykhern
Mit di roykhn fun zeks milyonen —
Efsher fargesn dem alef-beys?
Aroysreysn im fun zikoren
Vi a vild-groz?
Un gornisht iz geven,
Gornisht vet zeyn,
Bloyz midber,
Srofedike zun,
Shteyn.

WRITING POEMS

REYZL ZHIKHLINSKI
translated by Tzipora Baradon

Writing poems with letters
That must tell of graves
With exterminated Jews,
Letters smoldering
With the ashes of six million—
Perhaps forget the alphabet?
Weed it out from memory
Like wild grass?
As if nothing had been there,
There will be none
Except desert,
Blazing sun,
Stone.

VUHIN KUMEN AHIN DI REYD?

REYZL ZHIKHLINSKI

Vuhin kumin ahin di reyd
Fun di mentshn
Vos redn tzu zikh aleyn
Oyf di gasn fun der shtot nyu-york?
Faln zey oyfn bruk arop
Bloyz shtoyb?
Oder blondzhn zey arum eybik farloyrn
Tzvishn di planetn—
Kleyne, veyse, elente shtern?

Vuhin kumin ahin di reyd
Fun elente mentshn
Vos redn tzu zikh aleyn
In di groyse shtet fun der velt?

WHERE DO THE WORDS DISAPPEAR?

REYZL ZHIKHLINSKI
translated by Tzipora Baradon

Where do the words disappear?
Of the people
Who talk to themselves
On the streets of New York?
Do they just drop on the pavement
As mere dust?
Or perhaps are they wandering about, forever forlorn
Among the planets—
As white lonely stars?

Where do the words disappear?
Of all the lonely people
Who talk to themselves—
In the large cities of the world?

SHNEY

REYZL ZHIKHLINSKI

S'shneyt,
blaser vern tropns blut
oyfn veysn fartekh fun dem katsef.
Oysyes farlozn di shildn.
Lozn iber meyn zikorn—
a veys, leydik feld.

SNOW

REYZL ZHIKHLINSKI
translated by David Neale Miller

It's snowing,
drops of blood grow paler
on the white apron of the butcher.
Letters leave the signs.
Leave my memory—
a white, empty field.

KVORIM

SHLOYME SHVARTZ

Meyn gortn fun beyner un shteyner
finztert mit gringolenish.
Tate-mame shpatzirn
tzvishn veynendike grozn
mit a tzeblutikte got—
zalbedrit.

Zumer klapt doresdik un
netzokhendik mit kolirn.
Nor in meyn gortn
blit a farshtumter trer
un sharfe nodlen—
vos lebt nit mer.

Unter aza feykhte-tunklshaft
farbrilt mit finzternish
un farbergelt mit tzeyt;
yeder zumer
foylt oyf yeder bletl
beyn hashmoshesdik.
Toyt iz eybik.

In meyn gortn fun beyner un shteyner
altz vakst trukn,
din
un opgeshtorbn.
Tate-mame hobn vider zikh genumen
unter di erdishe shvartze khupe—
ober keyner tantzt nit simkhedik
in tzeflamtn harbstikn veyn-regn.

GRAVEGARDEN

SELWYN SCHWARTZ
English version by the author

My garden of bones and stones
Is dark with green-gripped bitterness.
My parents walk here and there
in the grass
as God between them
bled into the air,

Summer hammers generations and
triumphant with colors.
But in my garden
bleeds a tongue-tied tear
of sharp needles —
that live no more.

Beneath this moist darkness
covered with black
and bandaged by time;
every summer
each leaf decomposes
in the dusk.
Death is eternal.

In my garden of bones and stones
all is dry,
thin
and dead.
My parents walk again
beneath the earthly black canopy—
but no one dances in joy
in the autumnal wine rain.

HOYKHFIBERISH

SHLOYME SHVARTZ

Di blutike zun,
di vund
mit klinishn geruder
geyt oyf
oyf a sakh, a sakh hent,
tzermoniel.

Di vund,
hoykhfiberish,
himlish bloy.
Identish
tzugepast.
Merakhemdik belokhesh.

Vos tut zikh do?
Mir shlofn dokh ale
in a vikher fun vunden
unter dem shirem
fun undzer nakhtikn
khulem.

THERMO HIGH

SELWYN SCHWARTZ
English version by the author

The bleeding sun
a wound
of clinical commotion
of many
many hands
almost ceremonious.

The wound
thermo high
charts your identity
not
altogether heavenly
to suit merciful whispers.

Does it matter much?
We all fall asleep
in a whirl of wounds
under the parasol of
our nocturnal
dreams.

KINDHEYTS REGN

SHLOYME SHVARTZ

Gring kumt di shtilkeyt
eyngezapt in zikh aleyn:
reydloz,
tziterik,
treystloz.

Nokh dem kumt der regn.

Der regn fun meyn kindheyt,
vos ikh hob azoy lib.
Der klang fun di regn-tropns.
Mir hot gefelt di khokhme
tzu visn zeyer vog.

Es farblent di oygn.

Tzvingt aroyf di nakht
in yedn fenzter
in tifn shlumer.
Un in di shpiglen fun meyn shtot
di sheynkeyt fun "leyk mishigen"—
a naketer spektakl.

THE RAIN OF MY CHILDHOOD

SELWYN SCHWARTZ
English version by the author

Silence comes here easily
self-absorbed
unspoken
inverted
inconsolable.

And then the rain.

The rain of my childhood
I used to love.
The sound of raindrops.
And lacked knowledge
of their weight.

It blinds the eyes.

Urging night
in each window
of deep slumber.
In the mirror of blackness
the beauty of Lake Michigan—
a denuded spectacle.

DER GEBOYREN-TOG FUN MEYN BALERINE

SHLOYME SHVARTZ

Zi iz yung, dos lebn iz yinger. . .
Meyn kind veynt vi a tort fun zibn shikhtn.
Un ikh, in khurbn fun bleterfal.
Veyn mit ir in eynem in tempn harbst.

Zi halt meyn hant, un ikh halt ir shmeykhl.
Vos ken ikh ton mit ire frishe trern?
Iber shleferdike landshaftn
Azoyfil gele papirene flishlangen
Hundert meyl hoykh
Firt
Beynakhtike magye oyf goldene banen.

Der kleyne jin. . .
Ir likht tanzt ontkekgn yam
In der umglikhlikhkeyt fun ir khulem.
Asakh yorn vet gedoyrn tzu farnemen
Di tzvishnshtilkeyt,
Di veyse meves,
Di verbildike veln,

Di kseyderike regen-tropns
In zamd,
In tifkeyt fun ir
zkoren
A farlorenem zumer.

BALLERINA'S BIRTHDAY

SELWYN SCHWARTZ
English version by the author

Young as she is, life is still younger.
My child cries like a cake of seven layers;
And I, in a havoc of leaves,
Cry within the bluster of late Fall.

She holds my hand and I her smile.
What to do with her fresh, new tears?
Over sleepy landscapes
So many yellow kites
Fly
A thousand meters high,
The nightly freight to her magic.

The small genie . . .
Her light dances toward the sea.
In the infinite of her small dream
It will take years to comprehend
Interval-silence
White sea gulls
On the rolling waves,

Continual leaping raindrops
On the sand
In the deep
Recollection
A lost season.

HARBST

PERETZ MIRANSKY

Eingedrimlt, oysgetzoygn
Vi a shtorkh,
Tzugemakht di grine oygn
Shtey un horkh . . .

Vi es faln, faln bleter,
Veyn gefarbt;
Vi es shloft, a vint gegleter,
Eyn der harbst.

Kh'volt aleyn zikh veln leygn
Un fargeyn
Mit aza min goldn eygns
In gebeyn.

Zumer-peyres inem sheyer
Eyngehit,
Un a lid fun geln feyer
In gemit.

AUTUMN

PERETZ MIRANSKY
English version by the author with the assistance of Adam Fuerstenberg

Stretched like a stork in slumber,
Not a care,
I stay, while green eyes close,
And I hear

How the wine-red leaves of Autumn
Falling call,
And slipping, wind caressed,
Goes to sleep the Fall.

I too would like to fall asleep,
As he,
With golden riches
Hidden deep in me,

Fruit and grain to my heart's desire
On my way
And a song of golden fire
In my blood.

DI ZUN

PERETZ MIRANSKY

Di zun — a royz an opgerisene —
Farvalgert hot zikh oyfn barg.
Zi ligt un blutikt oyf zeyn lisine
In harbstik-geln bletervarg.

Der vint farbint di royte vunden ir
Mit volkendlekh vi marle din.
Di zun in fibern tzetzundene
Falt niderike. Vu ahin?

Di nakht — a kupershakht a tunkele —
Mit zilbershpritzn un mit kvartz,
Farnemt di zun tzu zikh in zunkeler
Un leygt zi shlofn oyf ir hartz.

Biz van tzvey bloye hent kayorirke
Tsegisn veln veyn a tun
Bey tir fun nakht, der zilberhariker,
Un oyfvekn fun shlof di zun,

Vet zi derveyl mit shotns volene
Fardekt un mit a bloyen rok,
A gantze nakht in shlofn khulemen
Fun blondn morgendikn tog.

SUNSET

PERETZ MIRANSKY

English version by the author with the assistance of Adam Fuerstenberg

The sun, a rose, from sky-bush torn,
Lies on the mountain-top, behold!
She's bleeding and her blood adorns
The autumn leaves of yellow gold.

With little clouds the wind is dressing
Her crimson wounds. And in despair
He is caressing and caressing
The fevered sun that falls down—where?

The night, a silver mine, waits far below
With nickeled stars and moons of quartz.
She brings the sun into her parlor
And rocks her to sleep on her heart.

Until the hands of early morn,
Will paint in red the night's blue lawn,
And with a cloudlet, new-born,
Wake up, from smiling sleep, the sun . . .

That she, with violet shadows covered,
And with the milk-ways hidden gleam,
In meantime, till the night is over,
Of young and purple dawns will dream.

ZEY DI KHAKHOMIM

PERETZ MIRANSKI

Zey di khakhomim, zey gloibn
Az got iz der tog un di nakht.
Un shtern, zey zeynen di toybn
Vos kreyzen ariber zeyn dakh.

Un mir zeynen nor oyf a rege
Tzu lebn un shtarbn geshikt,
Vi shtoyb oyf tzevintikte vegn,
Vos shteygn tzum faln tzurik.

Zey di khakhomin, zey meynen,
Az vint iz der otem fun got
Un mir zeynen grozn oyf fleynen
Vos tzitern in zeyn barot.

Un shturems, gevisers un vinters
Dos iz zeyn beshtrof far der erd,
Un gor unzer zeyn, der tzegrinter,
Iz nor far di kases bashert.

Mir di naronim, mir trakhtn
A khulem vos iz nokh nito:
Az do unzer oylem hatkhosn,
Darf oykh vi der himl zeyn bloy.

Un hoykh in di himlen di shtern,
Vos faln tzetzungn un royt,
Zey zeynen nit toybn, nor trern
Fun got vos baveynt unzer toyt.

THEY THE WISE

PERETZ MIRANSKY
English version by the author with the assistance of Adam Fuerstenberg

They the wise do believe
That God is day and night.
And stars in the sky are pigeons
That circle his roof in their flight.

And we here sent by his motion
To live for a while and to die
Are dust which rises in a storm
To fall again on windy roads nearby.

They the wise do suppose
That winds are the breath of the Lord,
And we but the grass on the prairie
That trembles in the note of his court.

And winters, the storms and the torrents,
They are our fate to await,
And all of our growing and blooming
Is only for sickles and fate.

We the fools are still dreaming
A dream that will sometime come true.
That our black worlds and deserts
Shall be as the heaven's deep blue.

And the stars that are falling from heaven,
Dying while in flight overhead,
Aren't white pigeons but tear drops
From God who bewails our death.

KINE

PERETZ MIRANSKY

Reyzl, reyzele fun gortn,
Hot a hartzele fun gold.
Flaterlekh fun ale sortn,
Hobn reyzlen zeyer holt.

Yeder flierl un flater
Flit fun royz avek, a zater,
Veyl di khibud, vos zi shtelt,
Hot a shem oyf gor der velt:

Honik-kukhn, yash un yayen,
Tzu farzukhn un fardeyen,
Mit gerukhn vos farshmekn,
Mit a tam zikh tzu balekn.

Oykh dos vintele, a gringer,
Kumt tzugast tzu reyzlen oft,
Glet ir mit farlibte finger,
Kusht besod ir, ven zi shloft.

Ale binen rimen, danken,
Loybn reyzlen trey un heys.
Bloyz di kropeve, beym flanken,
Redt oyf royzn aldos beyz.

"Libes firt zi, shtile kushn,
On a khupe, on kedushin,
Past es far der blum fun blumen,
Far dem gortn, far dem frumen?"

Kumt dos vintl un er gist
Zeyn fardros oys, in baginen:
"Sine krigt men far umzist,
Libshaft darf men zikh fardinen. . ."

ENVY: A FABLE

PERETZ MIRANSKY
English version by the author with the assistance of Adam Fuerstenberg

Rose the beautiful, in her garden,
Has a heart of purest gold,
All the insect world regard her
And they love her, young and old.

Every flier and every crawler
Journeys to her to be sated
For the food that she unfolds
Has fame in all their worlds.

Honey cakes, booze, and wine,
To be sampled and digested,
With aromas just divine,
With a heavenly taste invested.

And the winds, cavalier swingers,
Love the rose devoted, deep,
Fondle her with loving fingers,
Kiss her when she goes to sleep.

All the bugs, the bees and beetles,
Wish a myriad blessings on her head!
Only by the fence the nettle
Spreads tales saying she is bad.

"Lovers has she in the hundreds
In the trees and on the ground.
Is it fitting for a flower,
And for our garden, her bestower?"

Comes a wind from off the sea
Whispers in the nettles ear.
"Hatred you may get for free
But love you have to earn. . ."

A rakhmones iz, beym floyt,
Oyf di kropeve, di grine,
Mies iz zi vi der toyt,
Shtekht zi alemen fun kine.

Have pity with your nettles sharp
Even if near fences life is rowdy.
Thus envy grows in nettle's heart
And she is stinging everybody.

Harold A. Liebowitz

TZEFAT

KHAIM GRADE

Men zogt az bey shkies hakhame in tzefat
Derzet men vi s'loykht a yenveltiker khulem,
Dort shpigelt zikh op oykh di yidishe gas
Fun vilne, meyn heymshtot, ole hasholem.

Men zogt, az di menshn vos geyn dort um
Bashteyen nit davke fun baley-emuna,
Nor s'vern di oygn bey alemen frum,
Un lang tzitert tzefat inem hartz vi a strune.

Men geyt dort durkh geslekh aroyf un arop,
Vi yakevs malokhim in gang oyfn leyter.
Un oftmol farnakht ven men dreyt oys dem kop,
Derzet men bafligelte veyse bagleyter.

Di loyterkeyt makht azoy noent di veyt,
Az s'git zikh dos hartz vi der himl an efn,
Un etlikher treft zeyn fargangene tzeyt,
Vos er hot shoyn mer nit gerekhnt tzu trefn.

Oykh dortn iz shabes bloys eyn tog in vokh,
Nor shabesdik zeynen di trit indervokhn.
Un muz shoyn a mentsh geyn ontkegn zeyn brokh,
Iz geyt er ontkegn in shtil, mit bitokhn.

Un ven dort shtelt zikh der freytik farfri,
Gedenkt gantz yisroel: in tzefat iz heynt freytik.
Veyl tzefat iz di shtot fun mekubl ar"i,
Un freytik farnakht vert zeyn frukht-gortn tzeytik.

Der gortn fun epl in zunfargang glit,
Di frukht-beymer zeynen fun oylem-hoemes.

SAFED

KHAIM GRADE
translated by Philip J. Kluhoff

At sunset, it is said
There shines an otherworldly dream;
A mirror of the Jewish street
In Vilna, may she rest in peace, my home.

The people, it is said
Do not consist of men of faith alone,
But all men's eyes become devout,
And Safed's trembling heart reverberates like a string.

They walk her alleys up and down
Like Jacob's angels on the ladder.
And often, in the evening
Feel attended by those winged white companions.

Intimate, no longer is there distance;
Heart and sky lie open to each other.
Everyone confronts his past, a past
He had no longer planned to meet.

In Safed, it is said
Are seven days of Sabbath.
Where one might violate another's law;
His own, the strength of silent faith.

At dawn, all Israel thinks
Today in Safed it is Friday.
For Safed is the city of the mystic Ari;*
In the evening will the orchards ripen.

The orchard glows at sunset,
The fruit trees are of the hereafter.

* Rabbi Isaac Luria, Cabbalist.

Khaval, vos ikh vos ikh hob nit meyn gortn gehit,
Un vild -fremde gertner geloybt in poemes.

Men zogt, az men heylt zikh fun yoesh in tzefat,
Azoy vi dem guf bey di kvaln fun teverya.
Khaval, vos ikh hob nit meyn khurever gas
Gezukht zikh a treyst in di berg fun shveytzarya.

Faran in shveytzarya in tol fun tesin
An azara. Kumen poetn dort shtarbn.
Dort bin ikh gezesn a nakht biz bagin
Un nokhgetrakht ver meyn yerusha vet arben.

O, ver iz der yerush fun yidisher gas?
Khaval, vos ikh hob nit farentfert di sheyle,
Un shpet zikh dervust az di bargike tzefat
Hot erdish geyarshnt meyn vilne shel meyle.

Pity—that I did not attend my garden,
Strange and foreign gardners praise in poems.

It is said, that one is healed of despair in Safed,
Like the body in the waves of Tiberias.
Pity, that I haven't bought my ruined path,
Sought consolation in the mountains of Shveytzaria.

There in a valley, by a lake
Where poets come to die,
One night I sat awake till dawn
And wondered who would inherit my portion.

O, who will inherit the Jewish streets?
Pity—I could not answer.
For only later did I learn, the rising hills of Safed
Were Vilna's earthly heir.

IKH RED TZU MIR

RIVKE KOPE

Gey zog dem hartz,
Es zol nit ariberklapn
Ale zeygers,

Az dervartung
Iz der doyfik oyf berg
Ven du shteygerst. . .

Gey ontkegen mit gleykhgilt
Dem shtral fun freyd,
Pamelekh deyn geloyf. . .
S'kon altz dikh nor trefn
Oyfn letzten trepl
Fun deyn aroyf. . .

I'M TALKING TO MYSELF

RIVKE KOPE
translated by Stanley N. Werbow

Go tell the heart
It should not beat louder
Than all clocks,

That expectation
Is your pulse in the mountains
When you climb . . .

Go toward the ray of joy
With indifference!
Moderate your gait!
It could still happen to you
On the last step
Of your ascent . . .

DER FIDL ZEYGER

RIVKE KOPE

Kh'hob a zeyger in form fun a fidl,
Mit a veyzer vi a smik.
Tzelozt zikh di sho mit a lidl,
Flist oys zikh di tzeyt in muzik.

Er hot an orkester fun shreyflekh
Mit a goldn tirl farshtelt.
Altz iz dort eyngeshtelt seykhlekh,
Farn kapelmeyster der velt. . .

Shpil zeyger mit rod fun der tzeyt,—
Kh'vel troyen dir meyne farlangen
Un bentshn dos hentl vos zeyt—
Di brokhe fun klangen.

THE VIOLIN CLOCK

RIVKE KOPE
translated by Stanley N. Werbow

I have a clock in the shape of a violin
With a hand like a bow.
The hour passes with a song,
Time flows into music.

It has an orchestra of little screws
Closed by a golden door.
Everything is arranged there wisely
For the bandmaster of the world. . .

Play clock with the wheel of time,
I'll entrust my desires to you
And bless the hand that sows,
The blessing of sounds.

MEYN FEDER

RIVKE KOPE

Meyn lid iz nit poshet in tzir,
Oykh nit farshleyert mit herner.
Kh'hob lib fun meyn feder dem hunger,
Vos pikt oyf papir—
Vi a foygl kerner. . . .

Zol zi pikn di kerner
Fun tzevorfene freyd un farlang;
Fun di teg in atraktzie-galop,
Zol zi pikn nokh kerner.
O, feder, meyn shlisl-gesang!

MY PEN

RIVKE KOPE
translated by Stanley N. Werbow

My song is not simply adorned,
Also not veiled with horns.
What I love about my pen is the hunger
That picks at the paper,
Like a bird does kernels.

Let it pick the kernels
Of confused joy and desire;
Of the days in a show-gallop;
Let it pick yet more gladly.
Oh pen, my key-song!

OYFN SHPITZ MESER

RIVKE KOPE

Se lign meyne lider oyf a kishn fun a shotn—
Vi alte besules.
Ikh nem zey teyl mol fun behalt aroys
Un ikh leyen.
Ikh kon ober nit bashteyn,
Az zey zoln tzu keynem nit dergeyen!

A lid muz zikh opsheydn fun bashefer,
Vi a kind aroys fun tate-mame ring,
Nit lign in shotn eyngeknotn
Un varten oyf a feygele,
Vos zol khapn oyf zeyn diapazan
Di notn . . .

ON THE TIP OF THE KNIFE

RIVKE KOPE
translated by Stanley N. Werbow

My songs lie on a pillow of shadow
Like old virgins.
Occasionally I take them out of the hiding place
And I read.
But I cannot stand
That they should go to no one!

A song must depart from its creator,
Like a child from its parent's ring,
Not lie kneaded in a shadow
Waiting for a little bird
To come and catch the notes
In its range.

TRAKHTUNGEN

RIVKE KOPE

Nakht,
Royshik bashefenish fun shtilkeyt!
Der almekhtiger dirigirt a regnkor
Mit mildkeyt—
Un s'klingen di tropns
In meyne gufishe labirintn.

Di gantze velt, dakht,
Ligt hent un fis tzevorfn,
Vi a kind
Un shloft,
Ven ikh bin vakh—
Un vakh in mir iz yede sho,
Vos iz do un—nito.
Meyn gedank geyt zeygerdik
hin un tzurik:
Der zeyger bloyz ahin. . .
Bald vet der frisher tog
Zeyn an oyfgekumene fargangenheyt
Un reysn yugent-blimlekh
Far der elter . . .

Un ikh vel vider a khap ton di zun.
In meyn shpigl farbetn—
Un vel mit ale meyne muskeln,
Der velt a shmeykhl knetn.

THOUGHTS

RIVKE KOPE
translated by Stanley N. Werbow

Night,
Noisy creation of quiet!
The Almighty is conducting a choir of rain
With gentleness,
And the drops sound
In my bodily labyrinth.

The whole world, it seems,
Is lying there, hands and feet awry
Like a child
Sleeping
While I am awake—
And every hour is awake in me
That is present and not present.
My thoughts go like a clock
Back and forth:
The clock merely forward. . .
Soon the fresh day
Will be an arisen past
And pluck young blossoms
Before old age. . .

And I want to catch the sun again.
Invite it into my mirror—
And with my every muscle
Knead a smile for the world.

YOB

ROKHL KORN

Vi s'volt der himl plutzem zikh geefent
Mit a volkenbrokh fun kloles un fun kretz,
Vos hobn ale brokhes opgeshvenkt fun mir,
Kh'zol muzn in meyn gantzn naket shteyn far dir.

Meyn kainigreykh gevorn iz der elent—
Ikh hob gezen mit ekl opvendn di oygn
Fun meyne shkheynem, meyne freynd, meyn veyb
Beym onblik fun meyn yoterdikn, ipishdiken leyb.

Mit besures reyes hostu mikh geshteynikt, got,
Mit besures fun meyn untergang un brokh,
Biz kh'bin geblibn lign unter zey
Mit ponim eyngegrobenem in shtoyb
Un bloyz geshtamelt: vifil, vifil nokh?

Un dokh bin ikh in tifster, biterste ovles
Gevezn reykh nokh in fargleykh mit heynt,
Ven kh'hob tzurik arumgenumen un bagiteret
Mit shof un rinder, veyb un freynd.

Bez es hot geshlogn mikh deyn shverer orem
Bin ikh nokh in meyn lesterung geven deyn treyer knekht.
Du host zikh nokh geshigelt in meyn yeder trer
Un in meyn teyne biterster bistu geven gerekht.

Itzt gistu mit in iberflus mos mir altz tzurik,
Du host fardopelt nokh di tzol fun shof un rinder,
Du gist mir zibn zin un tekhter drey oyfsney,
Kh'zol kenen oysshepn fun fotershaft dos glik.

Vi ken ikh freyen zikh,
Ikh, vos bin reyfer itzt mit drey un zibn gsisos,
Un kh'hob in blut meynem bagrobn toytn tzeyn, tzeyn mises?

JOB

ROKHL KORN
translated by Hugh Denman and Dorothy Billek

As if the heavens had suddenly let loose
A storm of festering curses
That stripped all blessings from me
And left me standing in all my nakedness before you,

My realm became a desolation,
And I saw my neighbours, friends, and wife
Turn their eyes aside in loathing
From my body's fetid stench.

You have heaped tidings of woe upon me, O Lord,
Tidings of my affliction and of my undoing,
Till prostrate beneath the burden,
My face was ground into the dust
And I could only stammer: "How much more, how much?"

Yet in my deepest, most bitter grief
I was richer than now,
When once more I am blessed with sheep and oxen
And surrounded by wife, children, and friends.

While your mighty hand still smote me,
With all my cursing, I was still your faithful slave.
You were mirrored in my every tear
And in my bitterest lament you were still just.

Now in excess measure all is restored to me.
You have doubled the number of my sheep and oxen.
Again you give me three daughters and seven sons,
So that in fatherhood I should once more take joy.

But how shall I rejoice,
I who am riper by three and seven sorrows,
And who have ten times buried my own flesh and blood?

Ikh hob shoyn altz baveynt, vos iz nor vert a trer,
Itzt ken ikh shoyn nisht veynen un nisht lakhn mer.

Un kh'trog meyn nomen, vi a zak mit ash
Tzu shitn im oyf ale shives fun der velt,
Un ikh aleyn, ikh bin gevorn a getzelt
Mit shtendik ofener un freyer tir,
Az vu an umglik, zol es kumen lernen zikh bey mir,
Az vu a brokh, zol men bey mir zikh oysborgn a trer,
Az vu a shtrof, zol ikh der eydes zeyn, der eybiker.

Vi ken ikh gloybn dir, az s'iz nishto in dir
Der gloybn in deyn eygenem bashof?
Vi ken ikh troyen dir, az bloyz tzulib a shpil
Bist eyngegangen mitn sotn a gevet,
Un eyngeshtelt mikh inem kon
oyf pustn, blindn trof?

Iz vintzik dir geven meyn temimesdiker opshey,
Meyn faln koyrem far deyn shtralndikn ongezikht
Bey yedn neyem oyfang fun togs likht?
Ikh bin gevezn gantz un ful in freyd fun meyne teg,
Ikh bin gevezn gantz nokh in meyn peyn un tzar—
Nor itzt bin ikh geshpaltn vi a krug fun leym,
Veyl kh'ze nisht mer keyn zin in rotzn deynem, har.

Volstu geprovet mikh un geshlogn mit deyn tzarn,
Kdey mikh vi pan fun umglik oyfztuheybn,
Dos folk zol dikh in leyd meynem derkenen un derzen,
Zol kumen forkhtigkeyt iber a yedn tzfeyfler
Un oyftrinike zoln ney geboyrn vern inem gloybn—
Volstu mikh khotsh gelozn bey meyn leydn,
Ikh zol fardoplen zikh, fartoyzntfakhn in meyn peyn
Kdey ikh es besheyd fun deyne tuungen banemen un farshteyn.

Nor du, altz arumnemender, groyser har,
Du, vos shteyst iber yeder freyd
Un iber yeden tzar,
Du vilst, as s'zol zikh shpiglen vi amol
In oyg meynem dos blo fun himl un dos groz fun tol
Kh'zol mit a shmeykhl temimesdik un shtil
Frashteln dos gevey in mir, yenem gebril

My tears now are done
And I can neither laugh nor weep.

My name has become like a sack of ashes
To be scattered on all the world's mourners,
And I myself am like a tent
With ever-open door.
Let them who grieve come to me and learn
Let the afflicted come to borrow tears.
Let me be an eternal witness to them that are accursed.

How can I have faith in you,
If you have no faith in your own creature?
How can I trust you, when for idle sport
You wager with Satan,
Staking me in a game
Of blind and empty chance?

Was my guileless awe so little to you,
My bowing down before your radiant countenance
At the dawning of each day so worthless?
I was complete and whole in the joy of my days.
I was whole then even in my pain and in my woe.
Now I am broken like an earthen vessel,
For I see no meaning in your will, O Lord.

Had you but wished to prove me,
striking me in your rage,
So that the people should see you and know you in my pain,
So that the doubter should be filled with trembling
And the faithless should be reborn—
Had you but left me in my suffering,
Though my pain had been increased a thousandfold,
If only I might have apprehended the purpose of your ways.

But, mighty, all-embracing Lord,
You, who are above all joy
And above all sorrow,
You want my eyes to mirror again
The blue of the sky and the green of the valley.
You want me with quiet, artless smile
To silence the scream my body

Ven s'hot meyn leyb geveynt mit eyter un mit kretz—
Vilst kh'zol fargesn altz,
Farknesn zikh oyfsney
Tzu dem, vos shteyt in blinder zikherkeyt
Mikhutz a yedn vey?

Itzt fir ikh oykh a shpil mit dir—
Ikh tu zikh on di shabesdike kleyder,
Ikh tu zikh on dem yontev oyf meyn ponim,
Un bring dir kolerley korbones,
Un reykher veyroykh oyf mizbayakh,
Es zol zikh dakhtn dir fun di ale simonim,
Az kh'bin nokh altz der yob,
Yob fun amol.

Ikh ober bin shoyn tzugekumen tzu dem letztn gvul,
Tzu yener grenitz vu es shteyt keyn vekhter un keyn hiter,
Vu s'hot dos guts un beyzes nisht mer keyn shlite,
Durkh leydn meynem bin ikh tzugekumen tzum yesod—
Nor itz bin ikh nokh oremer, farlozter
Vi in meyn kretzigkeyt un elent fun amol,
Veyl ver ken mir fargitigen meyn grester avayre,
Veyl ver ken mir farbeytn dikh, meyn got?

Wept through suppurating wounds.
You want me to forget all
And betroth myself anew
To a blind faith
Beyond all woe.

Now I sport with you.
I don my Sabbath garments.
I take up my holiday mask.
I make all manner of burnt offerings to you,
Let the smoke of incense rise upon your altar,
So that it should seem
I am the Job of old
Job from before.

But I have reached the final limit,
The unguarded border where there is no watchman.
Where good and evil have no sway.
Through pain I have come to the root of all.
But I am poorer now and more alone
Than in the festering desolation of my past.
For who can make good my greatest loss?
For who can replace you, my God?

EREV REGN

ROKHL KORN

Beymer badekt mit groyem shtoyb,
Vi vanderer, vos ruen oys fun veg,
Hobn mid gedremelt in der mitogdiker zun.

Khmares, vi heyroglifn
Hobn zikh gebundn in tunkele shures
Un gevolt farteytshn dem viln fun himl
Der heyser, durshtiker erd.

Nor eyder s'iz fartik gevorn di shrift
Hot sharfer vint di oysyes tzerisn
Un getzoygn fun mizrekh tzu meyrev
Di stenges fun himl.

Hot a beyzer gerutshet der dembe:
—Shoyn vakhn, vi s'brent undz di hitz
Un khotsh kh'grob meyne vortzlen
Vos tifer in erdishn klem,
Vern gel meyne bleter un vyonen,
Un shmekn fritzeytik mit toyt,
Un der mokh oyf meyn rukn vert trukn un royt
Un krikht oyf meyn guf, vi a flamike grive—

Di bereze, veykhhartzig un mild,
Hot geshepshet shtil tzu dem dembe:
—Du bist groys, du bist shtark,
Un s'kenen afile khadoshim fun dursht
Nisht shvekhn deyn shtam,
Ober ze—
In kreyz fun vortzl-geflekht,
Vos zoygt oys dem markh fun der erd
Vert farsrof't yede flantz, yede blum
Un s'iz kurtz zeyer lebn,
Bloyz gemostn mit teg—

BEFORE THE RAIN

ROKHL KORN
translated by Hugh Denman and Dorothy Billek

Trees covered with gray dust
Dozed wearily in the midday sun
Like travelers resting from the journey.

Storm clouds like hieroglyphs
Gathered into dark lines
Seeking to interpret heaven's will
To the hot, thirsty earth.

But before the writing was done
Mighty winds rent the letters
And chased the tattered clouds
From east to west.

The surly oak grumbled:
"For many weeks the summer's heat has parched us,
And though I extend my roots
Deeper and deeper into the earth's tight crevices,
Still my leaves turn yellow and wither,
And reek of early death.
The moss on my back dries and reddens
And creeps up my body like a flaming mane."

The birch, tenderhearted and gentle,
Whispered to the oak:
"You are tall and strong,
And even months of drought
Do not weaken you.
But look,
Within the matter circle of your roots
That suck out the marrow from the earth
Every plant and flower is scorched.
Their lives are short
And their days are numbered."

Nor der dembe hot gehoybn di tzveygn mit geyve,
Vi er volt zikh geeydust mit himl un zun,
—Vet voynen a groz, tzi a blum,
Vet keynem nisht orn afile,
Vos zenen den zey?
Mist,
Mist, vos makht feter di erd
Far mir un meyn gantzn geshlekht.—

Di topole, vos hot moyre far altz
Un ontloyft mit di bleter far dem mindsten vint,
Hot getzitert, geshtamelt,
Di bleter vi betende hent
Gehoybn mit dlonyes aroyf
Tzu der shtiler bereze.
—Her shoyn oyf, her shoyn oyf,
Vest khalile dertzernen dem dembe, undzer har—

Di kleter-flantz, vos hot zikh tzugerikt vi a shlang
Un gehorkht begeneyve,
Iz gekumen tzu shleykhn tzu di flantzn un grezer
Un gesiket mit sod:
—Sh- sh- sha,
Men shmuest bey di "groyse"
Az s'vet shoyn keyn regn nisht zeyn,
Es iz sof, es iz sof un fargeyn-
Hobn unterteynik zikh geleygt ale grezer
Unter gliyekn seref fun der zun
Un vilik gevart oyfn toyt.

Nor di kropeve,
Di eybik miese un farshemte,
Far khazeyrim der fras,
Durkh fistrit tzugevoynt tzu shveygn un has,
Hot otfgeshtelt di sharfe, veyse her'lekh,
Vi a yeszh, ven er filt di gefar
Un geshtokhn, gevekt mit di reyd
Di mide, viyoynendike leyber fun di blumen:

Ver redt do fun toyt un fun sof?
S'iz a lign—
S'muz kumen der regn!

But the oak disdainfully raised his branches
As if to invoke the sun and the sky:
"If a flower or a blade of grass withers,
Who will even heed it?
What are they then?
Manure
Which fattens the earth
For me and all my kind."

The poplar, ever fearful,
Fleeing every slightest breeze with trembling foliage,
Lifted his leaves palms upward,
As if with suppliant hands,
To the quiet birch
And stuttered:
"No more! No more!
You might, God forbid, offend the oak, our lord."

The climbing vine who had crept up like a serpent
And had listened furtively
Slithered up to the plants and the grasses
And hissed a secret:
"Sh- sh- sh-
The lords of the forest are saying
That there will be no more rain.
It is the end and the passing away of all things."
So the grass fell down in submission
Before the sun's glowing scythe
And waited patiently for death.

But the ever lowly
And degraded nettle,
Fodder for swine,
Trodden underfoot and accustomed to silence and hate,
Bristled with tiny, sharp, white hairs
Like a hedgehog sensing danger
Roused and goaded with his words
The weary, fading blossoms:

"Who speaks of the end and of death?
It's a lie.
The rain must come!

Nokh a tog, nokh a nakht,
S'vet kumen zeyn tzeyt.
Nemt eykh fester tzuzamen,
Zolm untershteln zeyere pleytzes di shtarke
Far di,
Vos mit veykhere kni,
S'tort keyner nisht viyonen, faln far der tzeyt.

Beymer badekt mit groyem shtoyb,
Vi vanderer, vos ruen oys fun weg,
Hobn foyl gedremlt in der mitogdiker zun.
Nisht gehoybn keyn blat,
Nisht gerirt mit keyn tzveyg,
Ven s'hobn di ershte, kleyne khmares
Vi veysinke ketz zikh geshpilt mit der zun,
Vi mit a veykhn, geln beynvlknoyl.
A dek tzu
Un a shprung avek
Mit gehoybenen ek—
Gekukt fun der zeyt,
Vi der knoyl vet zikh rukn tzu mariv.
Un vider gekumen,
Shoyn tzu drey un tzu fir mitamol,
Biz s'zenen tifer gevorn di shotns in tol.

S'hot mit khoshed gekukt di topolye tzum himl
—Men treybt shoyn heynt vider kataves mit undz—
Ober heybt iz dos shoyn nisht geven mer keyn shpas,
S'iz farbeygelofn der ershter farner vint
Vi a hoz,
Un ibergelozt nokh zikh tzvishn groz
A stezhke shmol, vi a shrint.
Shvalbn, vi tunkele blitzn
Hobn tzeakert di luft.
S'hot eyngehaltn dem otem di erd,
Un s'hobn shoyn khayes getrogn in blut
Dem umru fun noentn shturem.

Biz s'zenen gekumen fun hintern vald
Khmares, vi leybn mit oyfgeshtelte grives,
Ven zey geyen nokh nokh dem riekh fun kurbn.
Mit eyn zetz fun der lape farloshn di zun,

One more day, one more night.
Its time will come.
Let us be resolute!
Let those who are stronger shoulder the burden
For those
Who are more frail,
None dare fade nor fall before the time."

Trees covered with gray dust
Dozed lazily in the midday sun,
Like travelers resting from the journey.
Not a leaf stirred,
Not a branch moved,
When the first small clouds
Played with the sun like white kittens
Toying with a ball of soft, yellow cotton.
Leaping forward
Springing back
With lifted tails—
Glancing sideways
As if the ball moved westwards
And back again,
Now three and four at once,
Until the shadows in the valley deepened.

Suspiciously the poplar looked toward the sky,
"We are being fooled yet again."
But there was no more jesting that day.
The first humid rain ran by
Like a hare,
And left behind a narrow path,
Like a line etched among the grasses.
Swallows like dark bolts of lightning
Plowed the air.
The earth held its breath.
The animals already carried in their blood
The unrest of the gathering storm.

Then from behind the forest
Came clouds like lions with erect manes
Moving toward the scent of their prey.
One blow of a paw puts out the sun,

Dan mit di veyse, sharfe tzeyn fun blitzn
In tunkelem kork fun himl zikh eyngebisn
Oyf lebn un toyt.

Shmuesn zikh durkh tzvey hoykhe, shvere berg
Mit brumendikn viderkol fun donern
Vos koylern zikh krekhtzendik un temp,
—hey, bruder, shoyn bald?—
Un als entfer a blitz un a knal un a trask,
Un s'ligt shoyn oyf tzveyen tzesphaltn
Der hekhster, der shtoltzster,
                    der demb.

Shpringt oyf mitamol fun di tzveygn der vint,
Vu r'iz gelegn in a leykhtn driml,
Un makht a veg farn regn,
Vos bindt tzunoyf mit veyse, grobe shtrik
Di erd mitn himl.

Shteln blumen un grezer unter zeyere keplekh,
Un di rukns shoydern mit zisisster dervartung—
Es roysht un es poykt. es zingt un es klingt
Oyf beymer, oyf bleter, oyf grezer, oyf dr'erd,
Un s'lakht shoyn mit grinkeyt di lonke, der vald,
Nor s'kenen di blumen nokh altz nisht banemen—
Iz a soden, a shushken, a shtoynen, a fregn
  —regn?
    regn,
      r-r-r-r-regn

The sharp white teeth of the lightning
Bite into the dark throat of the sky
In a life and death struggle.

With rumbling echoes of rolling thunder,
Moaning and dull,
Two mighty mountains converse—
"O Brother, how soon?"
For answer a flash and a crack and a crash,
And, already split asunder,
The tallest and proudest lies stricken,
            The oak.

Springing all at once from the branches
As if it had been lightly dozing,
The wind makes a path for the rain
That binds together the earth and the sky
With thick white cord.

Grasses and flowers let fall their heads,
Their backs trembling in sweetest anticipation—
Rushing and drumming, sounding and resounding
On trees, on leaves, on grass, on earth,
And the meadow, the wood, are already laughing in their greenness,
But the flowers, still uncomprehending,
Are murmuring, whispering, questioning, amazed—
   "Rain?
   Rain?
      R-r-r-r-rain."

Faran Tzeylem

URI TZVI

I N R I

Lemey bin ikh eyner fun der sheyre tzeveytikte, vos hengt nisht in sheykhes mit dir oyf a dorfishn slup bey a tzeylem-veg, zun trinkt mikh, nakht leygt zikh oyf mir? Deyn bruder, ze, di beyned fun meyn guf. di hut-hasdora fun mir: ikh bin in likht-fun-a velt baginen durkhzikhtig. yesurim leytern. tog iz bronz. nakht iz tint. shtum vi du bin ikh beytog. (ikh ken di meshe bronz oyf kop un oygn nisht trogn). ober beynakht tzit mikh di sugestya fun tife vasern: aruntergeyn, a—biz ibern kop arum zenen vent. a dreygorndike moyer un toyte gasn fun a kloystershtot. kortshe ikh mikh, bruder yeshu, shortshet zikh a yidish hoyt un beyn (atzvey toyzent yor nokh dir. alt!) un meyne lipn vern oyfgerisn: royte vund inem finsternish—s'geyt meyn kol shlangenartik, oyfblitzendik: vey! funem blut aroys—du, reyst zikh funem slup, ven zingendiker regn geyt, beymer varfn bleter op. yomerst oyfn kol. velder shreyen-oyf. velt hengt zikh far dir—un du—far alemens veyen-nekht-shreyst, shreyst yidish-umglik-geshrey—gedenkst du bruder, s'heylike beys-lekhem-dorf? gedenkstu deyn bagegenish mit miryam oyfn galiler felder-veg: akrigele zalbungs-eyl, ire lokn oyf deyne fis, a veyser hibre-er lbervarf oyf deyn guf un [illegible] gevehdt un krekhtzn [illegible]. eyn eyn lama azavtoni? amol ober shney ikh in royzndiker [illegible]-tzeyt, shkiyes hakhama. ekh, der tate meyner tzitert un iber zey a shiker mit a shikerte, foyle gumens hobn zey. farslinerte meyler—ekl mit ekltum. shney, frost shtar. fargliverte hebrayer-tzar. uryidn-vey. gogolte, bruder, zestu nisht. gogolte iz do: arum-arum. pilatus lebt. un in roym tehilimt men in di kloysteres-kh'volt dir gebrakht gliendike koyln in a feyerfan: in an oysgeleydiktn sharbn fun a yidnkop. kdey tzu varemen deyne fis, di farfroyrene—gib ikh ober a trakht: kh'hob brider gekoylete. kh'hob brider in der royter briyonim-armey. un kh'hob brider yingere, vos flantzn in khadores zumpn

ekiliptosn. kedokhes fest zey. shakalnklog. ober a
yam hobn zey. berg hobn zey un der kineret iz
dokh—kineret. nisht veysl—ekh-ekh.
kh'hob brider beym veysl . . . vos
zol ikh dertzeyln fun zey? levone
oyfn veysl. lodkes shteyen geankert
tzum berg. shifn geyn op. nisht
meyne shifn geyn—oyf ale vasern
in der velt firn shifn meyne brider
um—shney. frost. shtar. fargliverte
hebrayer-tzar. uryidnvey. du bist a
domaym gevorn, du host shalve
oyfn kreytz. ikh,—nisht. ikh
nisht—Lemey bin ikh eyner fun
yene teveytikte misbodidim, vos
hengt nisht in shkheynes mit dir oyf
a dirfishn slup bey a tzeylem-veg—

BEFORE THE CROSS

URI TZVI

translated by Sabina Lask-Spinac

I N R I

Why am I not one of the sufferers
who hang next to you on a country
post by a crossroad, the sun desic-
cating me, the night lying down
upon me? Your brother, see, the
bones of my body. This spinal cord
of mine: I am in the transparent
light of a dawning world. Suffer-
ings purify. Day is bronze. Night is
ink. Silent like you I am by day. (I
cannot bear the load of bronze on
my head and eyes). But at night
deep waters draw me: to go under,
ah—till it's over my head. Around
are walls. A three-storied wall and
dead streets of a church town. I
writhe, brother Jesus, Jewish bones
and flesh writhe (two thousand years after
you. Old!) and my lips are torn: red wounds in
the darkness—my voice goes out serpentlike, light-
ning-like: Woe! From the very blood—you tear yourself away from the stake, when the singing rains pour, when the trees shed their leaves. You lament loudly. Worlds cry out. The world hangs itself before you—and you through all the stormy nights—shriek, shriek, Jewish-calamity-scream—Do you remember, brother, the holy town of Bethlehem? Do you remember your walk with Miriam along Galilean country roads: a flask of anointment oil. Her curls at your feet. A white Hebrew mantle on your body and a blue belt girt about your loins? Well, well. It's possible: you no longer remember. So many thousands of bells ringing. So many frenzied praying voices—and a bloody Latin INRI over your forehead. But why do you still glance up to heaven and why do you still moan: My God, my God, why have you foresaken me? Sometimes I stand at rosy Minhah-time of sunset. Ach, my father shakes then in his frock a holy trembling and scoops up with his thirsty eyes the sorrow of a twilight world. My father, though, waits for the stars to

a heap of cut-up Jewish heads, torn tallithim, stabbed parchments. White linen with blood stains. And above them—a drunken man and woman. Foul palates have they. Drooling mouths—horror of horrors. Snow. Frost. Snow-white.

Frozen Hebrew sorrow and Jew pain. Golgotha, brother, Golgotha: everywhere. Pilate lives. And in Rome they sing Psalms in the churches—I would bring you glowing voices in a frying pan: in an empty skull of a Jewish head. To warm your feet, the frozen ones—but I think to myself: I have slaughtered brothers. I have brothers in the red bandit-army. And I have younger brothers, who plant eucalyptus trees in Chadera's swamps. Ague devours them. Jackal wails. But a sea they have. Mountains they have and the Kineret is after all— the Kineret. Not the Vistula—Oh, but I do have brothers at the Vistula . . . What shall I tell of them? Moon upon the Vistula. Boats tied up to the shores. Ships pass by. Not my ships—Upon all the waters of the world ships carry my brothers—Snow. Frost. Snow-white. Frozen Hebrew sorrow and Jew pain. You are now still. You have found peace on the cross.

Not I. Not I

Why am I Not one of those forlorn sufferers who hang next to you on a country post by a crossroad?

Why is there no solar eclipse?

Albatross, Warsaw, 1922

VELT-BARG-AROP
Oystzug

URI TZVI GREENBERG

Mame, mir kumen tzugeyn fun a land, vu s'iz libe nishto
un s'iz got nisht faran.

S'iz mabul in kop un s'iz shkieh in blut.

Di finstere erd iz a blinder planet,
Un vay iz tzu ir, vos zi ligt azoy shvartz
Unter heyzer un fis!

Zi volt oygn geefnt un lipn tzum brum:
Vay iz tzu mir fun berayshis biz heynt!
Un der himl iz shlekht,
Azoy khmarik un shlekht! —:
Er git nisht tzu zeygn der lip fun a boym
Fun zeyn khmariker brust —

Beym tzebrokhenem bok zingt vay a bal-mum
Bizn ovent areyn,
Far di toyzenter fis,
In di pluntern: tog . . .

Mame, di nekht in dem groyzamen land
Zenen sharlikhik-royt.
Di pnimer vern farendert beynakht.
Muter derkent nisht ir eyn-eynzig kind.
Tate derkent nisht zeyn khupedik veyb.
Z-z-z zoynes iz der zhum in der luft fun di nekht.
Mame, deyn zun iz der leydnshaft-shrey in di zoynishe nekht.
Mame, deyn zun iz -er naketer sne in di brandike nekht.
Un a tokhter fun yenem tzezoyntn land,
Vu s'otemet mit sam,
Iz dos veyb fun deyn zun —

DOWNHILL WORLD
Excerpt

URI ZVI GREENBERG
translated by Sabina Lask-Spinac

Mother, we come from a land where there is no love
  and there is no God

There is downpour in the head and sunset in the blood.

The dim earth is a blind planet,
And woe is to her, who lies so black
Under Houses and feet!

She would open eyes and lips to roar:
Woe is to me and the day I was born!
And the sky is foul,
So cloudy and foul!—:
He will not suckle the lip of the tree
From his cloudy breast—

By the shattered idol laments a cripple
Until evening time,
For the thousands of feet,
In the snarl: day . . .

Mother, the nights in this murderous land
Are scarlet-red.
Faces change at night.
Mother does not know her only child.
Father does not know his wedded wife.
Pros-s-s-titution buzzes in the air of the nights.
Mother, your son is suffering outcry in the harlot nights.
Mother, your son is the naked burning bush in the blazing nights.
And a daughter of that whorish land,
Which reeks of poison,
Is wife to your son.

S'hot keyn rov nisht gebentsht,
S'hot keyn galekh geknit
Far di heylike drey —

Aboy tzu di tzarte levone-lid-zinger,
Vos geyen beyikhides in toges fun troyer
Un hobn di bekhore fun takhles-gezangen.

Aboy tzu di kloger oyf khilul hakoydesh
In zeyere ofene geng inem yeshuv.
Aboy — ven zey kumen oyf alte beys-olmens
Dertzeyln di maysim dem khurbn haolem —
Un vay, ven zey kumen in elentn gothoyz
Partzereven risn in samet-parokhes
Un lekn dem shtoyb funem steynernem yeshu.
Mir zenen a khevre fun hefker-brodyages.
Mir hobn di toges di vintn gegebn.
Oyf unzere shterns iz bloyz gevorn
Der tzeykhn fun kin. S'iz hevl bagrobn.
Un velt barg-arop iz tzeshoydert un vundik
Un velt barg-arop iz tzu shkieh gekumen,
Di toyres gelestert.
Nishto keyn kedoshim.
Di libe iz tayve un veyber — pilgoshim!
Un mir zenen hefker-brodyakes. Geverbl.
Un mir zenen zikh fun tzeturemte kroyn-shtet,
Vos shteyen fartoybt funem glokn-klang: dreytzn,
Un mir zene flaker fun veltishe zun-teg,
Un mir zenen sam fun tzezoynte tantz-nekht
Un velt barg-arop — iz tzeshoydert un vundik
Mir zingen fun toyzenter vundn gezang ir:
A shoyder,
A yerbl,
A groyl fun atzmos
Mit zun un levone un shtern in velt-rod.

Yo, yo, es iz emes . . . mir zenen biryonim,
   Mir viln nisht trogn dem kdor haolem
Oyf unzere mat-shoyn-gevornene pleytzes.
Arop mit di kleyder fun shabes un zuntik!
Iz vos — az es zeen di veyber undz naket,
Sey-vi hobn zey undz gekusht ale glider.

No rabbi gave his blessing
No priest knelt down
Before the holy Trinity—

Woe to the gentle minstrels of the moon,
Who roam solitary in gowns of mourning
And have sung heaven's primogeniture.

Woe to the mourners of desecration
On the open roads of their town.
Woe—when they come to the old cemetery
To tell the dead of the world's destruction—
And woe, when they come to the forsaken house of God
To mend rents in the velvet Torah curtain
And lick the dust off the stone Jesus.
We are a band of wanton tramps.
We have flung our gowns to the winds.
On our foreheads there is a vivid mark
The sign of Cain. Abel is buried.
And the downhill world is horrified and wounded
And the downhill world has come to its sunset,
The Torahs blasphemed
There are no saints.
Love is lust and wives—concubines!
And we are wanton tramps. Seething whirl.
We are the sons of impoverished throne-states,
Which stand deafened by bell clangor: thirteen,
And we are the flares of the world sun-days,
And we are the bane of whorish dance nights
And the downhill world is horrified and wounded
We sing its song from thousands of wounds:
A horror,
A jubilee,
A shudder of bones
With sun and moon and stars in the world sphere.

Yes, yes, it is true . . . we are thugs,
Who no longer want to carry the world
Upon our already dulled shoulders.
Down with the Sabbath and Sunday clothes!
So what—if our wives see us naked,
Anyhow, they have kissed each of our limbs.

Yo, yo, es iz emes: mir zenen tzevindte
Biryonim, vos hobn nisht vos tzu farlirn!
Un dos, vos mir hobn — dos shteyt tzum farkoyfn.
Fun untern rukn — far eynmol fargesn
Di velt barg-arop, vi a nide in blutn.
Far eynmol batoybn dos yetushl: elent
Un undzer yerushe: zikhrones, gefiln,
Getlekhe zeung in shpiglen tzebrokhn,
Hishtepakhes-hanefesh, gezetzn un libe —
Mit dem zenen mir mit di vintn gegangen
Tashlekh tzu teykhn . . . un dort hobn mir oykh
Geshrign un blut areyn s'galike sam-vort:
Fun mentsh-barg-arop:
Lehadam!
S'iz tzelofn
Azol vi a sazhlke gal in di nervn . . .

(*Khalyastra*, Warshaw, 1922)

Yes, yes, it is true: we are windswept
hoodlums, who have nothing to lose!
And that which we have—it is up for sale.
Behind our backs—to forget for once
The downhill world, like menses in the blood.
To drown for once that little bug: loneliness
And our inheritance: memories, feelings,
Divine visions in shattered mirrors,
Self-confession, laws and love—
We have taken it all, and with the winds, have gone to the river
To throw away our sins . . . And there we have also
Shrieked into the blood the bitter word of poison:
Of the downhill man:
Ridiculous!
It flowed
Like a pond of bile into the nerves . . .

(*Chaliastre I*, Warsaw, 1922).

GEVEYN FUN DER ERD

URI TZVI GREENBERG

Kumt — veyber akeres, kumt — derner bekhurim, khasene-makhen, oyf
vey-feld
Dem eygenem elent mit undzere leyber tzeveytikte. Midbarishe leyber,
Un undzere gufim, mit viste khatzos-kep, dos zenen di shtangen lekhupe;
Un tzalmim — di slupes mit toyte hebereyer — zey zenen nokh heyliker
efsher;
Un oybn fartziyen mir shofene khmares un khasene hobn mir ale —

Khotsh eynmol, okh, eynmol khotsh shteyn unter khmariker khupe fun
eygenem vey-feld,
Dem eygenem elent tzu zogn oyf altn hebereyish: hare at mekudeshes. . .
Un khotshe keyn hand hot der elent nisht, borgn mir oys undzer hand im,
di viste
Un tuen dem ring on — tebaas-kedushin fun veyen. . .

Sey-vi veln mir shoyn keyn kinder nisht hobn vos lakhn mit glokn bagigens.
Ir — veyber-akeres, mir — derner bekhurim: tzeveytikte leyber: sahares.
Ober fund undzere finstere otems un finstere koyles tzum elent
Veln mir shlangen un soves gebern- vi yezus fun ruekh-hakoydesh —

LAMENT OF THE EARTH

URI TZVI GREENBERG
translated by Sabina Lask-Spinac

Come—barren women, come—fecund lads, to wed upon woe-fields
Each one's desolation with our aching flesh, desert flesh,
And our bodies, with wasted midnight heads, they are the canopy posts;
And crosses—poles with dead Hebrews—they are even holier perhaps;
And we stretch woolly clouds above and we all marry—

But once, oh but once to stand beneath the cloudy canopy of our own
woe-fields,
Our own solitude, to say in Old Hebrew: You are hereby joined unto me. . .
And though solitude has no hands, we lend him, the desolate one, ours
And we put on the ring—wedding band of woe. . .

Anyhow, we'll have no children who will laugh with bells of dawn.
You—barren wives, we—fecund lads: aching flesh: Saharas.
But our dark breaths and dark voices will give birth to
Snakes and Owls—like Jesus of the Holy Spirit.

IN MELUKHE FUN TZAYLEM

URI TZVI GREENBERG

Tut mikh on in a breyter araber-abaye, farvarft oyf meyn aksl a talis,
Flakert oyf mit amol der farloshngevorener mizrekh in oremen blut mir
Un — nat eykh dem frak un dem shnips un di lak-shikh
Vos ikh hob gekoyft in ey-ro-pe.

Zetzt mikh oyf oyf a ferd un befelt: es zol loyfn mikh trogn avek tzu der midber.
Git-mikh-op meyne zamdn. Ikh loz di bulvarn. Ikh vil tzu di zamdn fun midber.
Aza folk iz faranen mit bronzene yungen, mit nakete gufim in zun-brand.
(Keyn glok iz nishto dort, vos hengt iber kep, iber kep geyen bloyz di mazles).
Az a bukher aza fun di bronzene efent zeyn moyl in der rekhoves fun midber
Un glit far ahava, (s'iz tzays hakohavim). . . un shreyt tzu di shtern: ahava.
Dan entfert an oyfshtrom fun bloy-blutik vaser beym zoym fun der midber:
a h a v a .

IN THE KINGDOM OF THE CROSS

URI TZVI GREENBERG
translated by Sabina Lask-Spinac

Dress me in a wide Arabian abaya, throw a tallith across my shoulders,
And the East smothered in my poor blood will flare up at once
And here—have this dress coat and this necktie and these lacquered shoes
Which I have bought in in Eu-ro-pa.

Set me on a horse and command it to carry me off into the desert.
Let me have my sands. I leave behind the boulevards. I wish for the desert.
There is a folk of bronzed youths, their naked bodies in the sun blaze. Sand
(There is no bell there, which hangs over heads. Over heads roam but stars.)
When a lad such as these bronzed ones opens his mouth in the span of the desert
And glows with love (for the stars are rising). . . and calls to the stars: love.
Then answers a gush of blue-blooded water at the edge of the desert:
l o v e .

LIDER FUN TOGBUKH

AVROHOM SUTZKEVER

1974

DEM ONDENKEN FUN ARON TZEYTLIN

Umdoyik bistu, ikh — derveyl umdortn:
Tzvey oysterlishe binshtokn. Bishtike
Bagegenen zikh inem zelbn gortn
Di binen un zey tzien di yenike

Fun khulem. S'volt dokh nit gehat keyn zinen
S'geboyrn vern oyb in gortn voltn
Zikh veyter nit bagegent beydns binen.
Oykh undzer vortkunst volt nit mer gegoltn.

S'bagegenen zikh beydns binen, zeygn
Fun zelbn khulem un dernokh tzesheydte,
Tzurik tzum binshtok vu s'iz heymish-eygn,
Dernerntert zikh an ershte bin, a tzveyte.

A binenzhum in ovent iz der fodem
Fun dir tzu mir. Mir zeen im un hern.
Un s'hert nit oyf ben-odem zeyn ben-odem,
Gebentsht mit ershtn un mit letztn shtern.

POEMS FROM MY DIARY

AVROHOM SUTZKEVER
translated by Stephen H. Garrin

1974

IN MEMORY OF AARON ZEITLIN

You are over there—I, meanwhile, over here:
Two strange beehives. Silently
The bees meet in the same garden, where
They both draw the nectar eagerly

From a dream. It makes no sense
To have been born in the garden
If both our bees would not proceed hence.
Our writing would not be art then.

Both our bees meet, pollinating
Through the same dream, then separate
Back to the honeycomb that's waiting
The first bee, the second, of the nourishment partake.

The bee buzzing in the evening is the band
Tying you to me. We see him and hear from afar.
Man remains never ceasing to be man
Blessed with the first and last star.

Harold A. Liebowitz

FUN *AKHER*

Y. KH. BILETZKI

In karahad
Fun der velt, vi in a farkishuftn
Pshat un remez — in reshus fun mentsh, remez un sod
In reshus fun got.
In geviter —
Di makhshave tzehakt un tzeshplitert.
A meshunediker planter. A velt in tzapl
Fun emuneh un khapire.
Fun sofek un yire.
Oyb iz zikh nokh metapl
Mit zeyne vundn.
Der baran fun der akedeh ergetz-vu farshvundn.
Yitzkhak oyfn sharf fun khalef.
Der tof farplantert in dem alef.
Di aseres hadibros, farkritzt oyf lukhos, droen . . .
Ale neynen un yoen
In feyerdike sh"y olomos knien un veyen.
Vi ken men do a bisl shalve farzayen?
Ver iz do der gloybiker, der zindiker, der lesterer?
Ver iz do der mester
Fun guts un shlekhts un in vemens hent di shliteh
fun d o un d o r t:
Iz der berayshes ongekumen mit vort,
Mit meysim? Un vos dreyt zikh do der sotn
Vi a balebos arum:
Shteyt unter undzer vant, kukt durkh di fentzter,
Blikt durkh di grates.
Yob zitzt nokh altz in zeyne shmates
Un teynet zeyne teynes.
Neyn. Di velt iz nisht keyn ofener sefer mit klorn emes.
Der sod der remez
Nishtert in ale vinkelekh un zukht.

FROM THE POEM *AKHER*

I. KH. BILETSKI
translated by Nathan Goldman

In the circle dance
Of the world, as in an enchanted web,
Literal and hidden in the realm of man,
In the domain of God hidden and secretive.
In a thunderstorm,
The thought chopped up and cracked.
A strange tangle. A world jerking
Between faith and atheism.
Between doubt and awe.
Still burdened
By its wounds.
The ram of the *akedeh*,* of the binding, somewhere disappeared.
Isaac on the edge of the knife.
The end is lost in the beginning.
The decalogue, scratched on tablets, threatens. . .
All agree and disagree
In the fiery 310 worlds kneel and suffer.
How can one foresee a little serenity here?
Who is the believer here, the sinner, the blasphemer?
Who is the master here
Of good and evil; and in whose hands the power
of here and there:
Did the beginning arrive with a word,
With deeds? And what is Satan doing here
Wandering around like a lord?
Stands under our wall, looks through the windows,
Looks through the grating.
Job still sits in rags
And continues his arguing.
No. The world is not an open book with clear truth.
The mystery, the secret
One rummages in all corners and seeks.

* The binding of Isaac.

Nisht shtendik ken der farzeyer areynfirn in sheyer
Mit shalve zeyn frukht.

Ver halt di vokshal fun khokhme in zeyn hant?
In ale frimorgns tzapelt zikh der morgnshtern
Oyfn sharf fun meser.
Got tzu teyvl —
Ver iz hekher, ver iz greser?
Vemens kol fun tehomes un heykhn:
Shel naaleyikh. Tu oys deyne shikh fun deyne fis.

Talmidey khakhomim shteyen mit angst, mit imeh,
Mit ris.

Not from without can the planter bring his fruits
In serenity to the barn.

Who holds the scales of wisdom in his hand?
In all the early mornings the morning star struggles
At the edge of the knife.
God to the Devil—
Who is higher, who greater?
Whose voice from the abyss, the heights.
Sandals. Take the shoes off your feet.

Sages stand in fear, with fright,
With trembling.

FUN *AKHER*

Y. KH. BILETZKI

B.

In di hertzer fun di fir hot gezungen der shir hamales
Tzu got.
In di batey-medrashim hot opgeklungen zeyer omen
Tzu zeyn libn nomen.
Nor in di vakhige nekht hobn zikh tzeshrign sheyles.
Toyzenter sheyles.
Hobn fir khakhomim mitn koyekh fun shemos
(Durkh peyn
Un imes)
Aroyf in himl areyn.
Durkhgeshnitert ale vinkelekh, getrunken fun ale loglen,
Iber di bloye himl shtokhim
Hobn zeyere voglen
Oyfgezamelt ale tehiles fun khruvim, malakhim,
Un zey hobn di shkhineh derzen.
Hot zey got bashtroft un in pardes zey gevrakht.
Der tog hot geloykhtn mit toyzent zunen,
Nor di nakht hot gerisn shtiker fun seyere glider.
Eyner fun zey hot dem veg in pardes gefunen.

Di oyfgeklibene kerner oyf di himlen hot er
Mitn koyekh fun a leyb
Gedroshn
Un di nakht in pardes
Hot nisht farloshn
Zeyn likht.
Nor drey hobn in pardes gevandert tzuzamen
Un in di hertzer: flamen.

Fir zenen ongekumen tzu di reyne mirmelshteyner.
Nor eyner
Iz adurkh.
Di drey

FROM *AKHER*

Y. KH. BILETZKI
translated by Nathan Goldman

B.

The song of ascents sang in the hearts of the four
To God.
In the study house their amen resounded
To the good Lord.
Only in the nights, they screamed out questions,
Thousands of questions.
Four Sages with the strength of Exodus
(Through anguish
And horror)
Reached up to the heavens.
Rummaged through all the little corners, drank from all the vessels,
Above the blue heavenly fields,
Their wanderings assembled
All the blessings of the Cherubim and the other angels,
And they saw the Shkhineh, the Divine Presence.
God punished them and brought them to the Orchard of Wisdom.
The day shone with a thousand suns,
Only the night tore pieces from their limbs.
One of them found the way to the orchard.

The collected kernels of heaven
He threshed
With the strength of his soul
And the night, in paradise
Did not extinguish
His light.
Only three together in paradise they came
And in their hearts: flames.

Four arrived at the pure marble stone,
Only one
Remained.
The three

(Ikh bin geven derbey),
Bey di reyne mirmelshteyner geblibn shteyn
Mit klip un geveyn.

(I was also there)
Remained at the marble, pure
With sobs and tears.

OYFN PRIPITZHEK

VULF TAMBUR

Oyfn pripitzhek gebrent hot a feyerl,
In shtub iz geven heymish un hays;
Rebes un mames gelernt hobn kinderlekh
Dem altn heylikn yidishn alef-bays.

Heynt tliet koym a yidish feyerl,
Un in shtub moyredik eyzn-kalt;
Voyen farvildte sturemvintn
Vi in an oysgedartn khurbn vald.

Nishto mer keyn mames, keyn kinder,
Geblibn koym yidish-dikhter, zaydes;
Ziftzn zey mitn altn aykhe-nign,
Ophentike, vi shtume getreye aydes.

Der pripitzhek, di yidishe kinder,
Un oykh di rebes zenen farbrent;
Dos ash hot der vint fonondergeblozn,
Farsmalete khurbes, di yidish-vent.

Oyfn khurbn golesdikn pripitzhek
Tzanken neshomes vi a ner-tomid;
Aleyn zogn kines di oysyes,
Der alef-bays zogt kadish beym omed.

Gedenkt ir zaydes, gedenkt ir teyere,
Vi azoy amol gelernt hot men do?
Farbrent dem kometz fun unter der alef,
Iz kometz-alef shoyn kmat nisht "o" . . .

Oyfn pripitzhek gebrent hot a feyerl,
In shtub iz geven heymish un hays;
Rebes un mames gelernt hobn kinderlekh
Dem altn heylikn yidish alef-bays. . .

IN THE FIREPLACE

WOLF TAMBUR
translated by Nathan Goldman

In a fireplace, once burned a fire;
The room was homey and warm.
Rabbis and mamas taught the children
The ancient, holy Hebrew A B C's.

Today in the rush of things, there's hardly a Jewish fire,
And the classroom is icy-cold,
And stormwinds outside are howling,
Through a dried-out and perished forest.

There are no more mamas, no more children,
Hardly any Yiddish poets or grandfathers remain.
They sigh with the melody of Lamentations,
Present, as true, mute witnesses.

The fireplace, the Jewish children,
And the rabbis, too, consumed by flames.
The coals are nearly extinguished—
In smoldering ruins, the Jewish walls.

On the ruined exile fireplace
Glow the souls like an eternal lamp;
The letters recite the Lamentations,
The A B C's chant the prayer for the dead.

Remember grandfathers, remember my dear ones,
What was once taught there.
The vowels consumed from beneath the letters.
The vocalics hardly audible.

In a fireplace once burned a fire;
The room was homey and warm.
Rabbis and mamas taught the children
The ancient, holy Hebrew A B C's.

VER KEN HEYNT LEBN BESHOLEM MIT ZIKH?

KHAIM PLOTKIN

1

Nisht mit altz ineynem
Leb ikh besholem
Un nor vintziker
Mit zikh:
Mikh mutshen khaloymes,
Fun vampiren un shaydem;
Zey tantzn un shpotn,
Palmesn meyn ru.
Kh'her zeyere koyles:
—Tzvishn erdishn shaydim,
A shayd bist oykh du!

Funem kushmar
Oyfn shlakhtfeld—
In griber un in heyln
Bizn haldz kh'tu zingn—
Di kanonen koyln,
Inem feyer-mabul,
Di tankn deryogn.
Di zun vert dertrinken
Un funem himl—
Es hert zikh
A yamerdik klogn—
Kh'bin vi in a pastke
Oyfn veg dem veytn,
Vu in di griber
Di verem
kumen
tzum
greytn.—

WHO CAN LIVE AT PEACE WITH HIMSELF ANYMORE?

CHAIM PLOTKIN
translated by Marvin Zuckerman

1

With nothing at all
Do I live at peace.
And even less
With myself:
Dreams torment me,
Dreams of vampires and ghosts;
They dance and mock,
Perform post-mortems on my rest.
I hear their cries:
"Among earthly ghosts,
You too are a ghost!"

From the nightmare
On the battlefield,
In holes and in caves,
I sink to my neck—
The cannon shells
In the fire-flood
Catch up with the tanks.
The sun is drowned
And from the sky—
Is heard
A wailing sound—
I am as if in a trap
On the long road
Where, in the graves,
The worms
Come
To
Ripen.—

Oyb khaloymes kumen funem vakhndikn trakhtn,
Trakht ikh un a shiyur.
Meyne shtilste teg
Zenen oykh gereyte far shlakhtn,
Khotsh tu on tzurik
Dem oysgetrogenem mundir—

11

Meyn hartz iz nisht mit grates,
Nisht bahongen mit shleser.
Kh'hob feynt grentzn
Un has gefelshte peser!
Fun der tzeyt di sholem-toyb
Trogt unter fligl a shverd.
Kh'hob moyre tzu trakhtn
Vos dem morgn iz bashert—
Es buret in mir
Un kh'ken nisht fartrogn
Meyn ikh—
Ikh makh mit meyn hartz nisht keyn sholem:
Ver ken lebn heynt besholem mit zikh?

If dreams come from waking thoughts,
I am never done thinking.
My quietest days
Are ready for battle:
Might just as well put back on
My worn-out uniform.

11

My heart is not barred,
Not shut up with locks.
But I have good borders
And hate false passports!
From now on the peace dove
Carries under its wing a sword.
I am afraid to think
What is fated for tomorrow—
Cold winds whirl in me
And I cannot bear
My "I"—
I make no peace within my own heart:
Who can live at peace with himself anymore?

AUTHORS AND TRANSLATORS

TZIPORA BARADON is a resident of Austin, Texas and is currently pursuing a degree in library science.

Y. KH. BILETZKI was born in 1914 in Kobrin and has lived in Tel Aviv since 1934. He studied at the university in Jerusalem and has published literary criticism, poems in journals in Russia, prior to his emigration, and in Israeli publications. His collections of lyrics include, *Far zikh* (For Myself), 1937; *Shveln* (Thresholds), 1938; *Vey un gloybn* (Pain and Belief), 1944, as well as collections of Hebrew verse.

DOROTHY BILLEK is an assistant professor for Yiddish Language and Literature at the University of Maryland. Her book, *Immigrant Survivors: Post-Holocaust Consciousness in Jewish American Fiction,* will be published by the Wesleyan University Press in 1980.

HUGH DENMAN is a lecturer in German and Yiddish at Queens University in Belfast, Ireland. He is currently working on a monograph about the Soviet-Yiddish writer Dovid Bergelson.

ADAM FUERSTENBERG teaches English at Ryerson Polytechnical Institute in Toronto. He has been researching the writings of Canadian Jewish authors in particular those of A. M. Klein.

STEPHEN GARRIN is an assistant professor in the Department of Germanic Languages and Literatures at The University of Texas at Austin where he coordinates the Yiddish program. His essay on I. B. Singer as a literary translator will appear in a collection of critical essays about the Nobel Laureate to be published by the Cornell University Press.

JAKOBO (YANKEL) GLANTZ was born in 1902 in the Ukraine and currently resides in Mexico City. He received a Jewish and secular education and was a teacher of Yiddish language and literature in Odessa. He began to write poetry in Russian in 1917 and turned to Yiddish in 1927. His first collection of Yiddish verses *Far beginen* (Before the Beginning) was published in Mexico. He was the literary editor of *Der veg* (The Way) from 1936 to 1946.

NATHAN GOLDMAN is an assistant professor of government at The University of Texas at Austin. He has published dozens of poems in various Jewish periodicals and a collection of Holocaust verses in a volume entitled *The Rose of Dachau,* 1977.

CHAIM GRADE was born in 1910 in Vilna, the son of an Enlightenment adherent and teacher of Hebrew. In his youth, until World War I, Grade was involved with the "Workers-Youth" in his native town. He studied in Yeshivas (rabbinical academies) and the Yeshiva world is a frequent setting for his many novels. Grade also became conversant with Hebrew, Yiddish, and world literature. At the age of twenty-two Grade left the Rabbinical Academy and began to write poetry. In 1932 he published his first poems in the *Vilner tog* (Vilna Day). His verses were well received in the literary world. He joined the literary group known as "Young Vilna" and later became one of its principal members. During World War II Grade lived as a refugee in Russia. After the war he returned to his native Poland and after six months left for France.

URI TZVI GREENBERG was born in 1894 in Bialykamien, Eastern Galizia and is decended from Hasidic Rabbis on both his paternal and maternal sides. His earlier poems, both in Hebrew and Yiddish, were published in 1912 in leading periodicals of the day. After World War I Greenberg joined a group of Yiddish expressionist poets and became the editor of the avant-garde journal *Albatros* (1922–23). In 1923 he spent a year in Berlin before immigrating to Palestine. There he ceased publishing in Yiddish and began to write exclusively in Hebrew. Among the collections of his Yiddish works are: *Ergetz oyf felder,* 1915 (Somewhere on the Fields); *Krig oyf der erd,* 1921 (War on the Earth), and *Mefisto,* 1921.

PHILLIP KLUCKOFF is a professor of English at Stockton State College in Pamona, New Jersey, where he offers courses in Yiddish literature.

RIVKE KOPE was born in 1910 in Warsaw. Since 1931 she has resided in Paris. She has published numerous poems, short stories, and essays in Parisian-Yiddish literary journals.

ROKHL KORN was born in 1898 in Podliski, Poland and received the Lamed Award for Yiddish poetry in 1949 for *Kismet,* a collection of poems that appeared in Montreal, where she currently resides. She is also the recipient of the Manager Prize and the H. Leivick Prize for literature. Her lyrics have appeared in English, French, and German translations.

SABINA LASK-SPINAC lives in San Antonio, Texas. She was born in Israel and has studied French and Spanish literature at the City University of New York. At the present time she is preparing a doctoral dissertation on Uri Tzvi Greenberg.

HAROLD LIEBOWITZ is an assistant professor of Biblical Archaeology at The University of Texas at Austin. He supervises the university's dig each summer in Tel Yinam, Israel.

DANIEL MARLIN was born in New York City. He studied at Berkeley, where he became interested in Yiddish under the influence of Malka Heifitz Tussman. He is a poet and painter and has published poetry in English as well as Yiddish.

DAVID NEAL MILLER teaches Yiddish at the Ohio State University. He has published an extensive bibliography of primary and secondary works of Isaac

Bashevis Singer and has edited a volume of essays on the Nobel Laureate that will be published by the Cornell University Press.

PERETZ MIRANSKI was born in Vilna in 1908 and currently resides in Toronto, Canada. His literary debut was in 1934 in the *Vilner Tog* (Vilna Day), where he published two parables. In the same year he became a member of "Young Vilna." Miranski is best known for his parables, which are very popular in Yiddish language schools.

CHAIM PLOTKIN resides in New York. His latest collection of poems, *Oyf meyne vegn* (In My Ways) was published by the Peretz Varlag in Tel Aviv in 1978.

ELIAS SCHULMAN is an adjunct lecturer in Yiddish at the Queens College of the City University of New York. He has published several books on Yiddish literature and contributes literary reviews to the *Jewish Daily Forward,* a Yiddish newspaper printed in New York.

SELWYN (SHLOYME) SCHWARTZ lives in Chicago where he is a businessman. He is the author of ten books. His latest volume, *Brondzener Mabul* (Bronze Flood) will appear soon in the I.L. Peretz Farlag in Tel Aviv.

MEYER SHTIKER was born in 1905 in Galizia and studied in a religious school as well as in a German-language school. From 1914 to 1918 his family lived in Vienna, after which time they moved to Boyberik, Galizia. In the beginning of the 1920's Shtiker came to New York, where he worked on the staff of several Yiddish-language newspapers. His first poems appeared in 1924. His collections include *Lider* (Poems), New York, 1945; *Yidishe landshaft* (Yiddish Landscape), New York, 1958; *Der khulem iz meyn aydus* (The Dream Is My Witness), New York, 1965, and *Yidishe landshaft II,* New York, 1970. Shtiker has translated Hemingway's *Old Man and the Sea* and T.S. Eliot's *Wasteland* into Yiddish.

BARBARA STURGILL is an Austin artist and works at The University of Texas at Austin.

WULF TAMBUR was born in 1910 in Rumania and studied in religious schools. He resides in Bucharest, where he edits and contributes to the Yiddish journal *Bukareshter shriftn* (Bucharest Writings).

REYZL ZHIKHLINSKI was born in 1910 in Poland. She came to the United States in 1951. Her works include *Lieder* (Poems), 1936; *Der regn singt* (The Rain Sings), 1939, and *Shvaigendike Tirn* (The Silent Doors), 1962.

MARVIN S. ZUCKERMAN is associate professor of English and Yiddish at Los Angeles Valley College. His publications include *Words, Words, Words* (MacMillan, 1974), *Yiddish Sayings Mama Never Taught You* (Perivale Press, 1975) and several articles, translations, and book reviews. Although he was born in the Bronx, his mother tongue is Yiddish; he also attended Yiddish secular schools while he was growing up.

Contents of DIMENSION, Vol. 13, No. 3 (Winter, 1980)

Foot in the Net *Der Fuß im Netz*	BARBARA KÖNIG trans. Richard Mills	radio play
Coming of Age *Am Ende der Jugend*	KLAUS SCHLESINGER trans. Von Underwood	story
Time without Bells *Zeit ohne Glocken*	HORST BIENEK trans. Ralph R. Read III	novel excerpt
A Visit on the Veranda *Besuch auf der Veranda*	BERND RACHEL trans. Breon Mitchell	story
The Blue Dragoman *Der blaue Dragoman*	HANNELORE VALENCAK trans. Sandra Celt	story
How Do You Say "Olé" in Hebrew? *Wie heißt "Olé" auf Hebräisch?*	EPHRAIM KISHON trans. Hanna B. Lewis	story
Three Naked Men *Drei nackte Männer*	FRANZ FÜHMANN trans. Esther E. Enns	story

DIMENSION

Contemporary German Arts and Letters / Volume 13, No. 2, 1980

Department of Germanic Languages/THE UNIVERSITY OF TEXAS AT AUSTIN

D I M E N S I O N

Contemporary German Arts and Letters / Volume 13, Number 3, 1980

Department of Germanic Languages/THE UNIVERSITY OF TEXAS AT AUSTIN

DIMENSION

DIMENSION

Contemporary German Arts and Letters / Volume 13, No. 3, 1980

Department of Germanic Languages / THE UNIVERSITY OF TEXAS AT AUSTIN

DIMENSION is published three times yearly at The University of Texas at Austin. Subscription: $12 per year for individuals, $15 per year for institutions in the United States, plus $2 postage and handling; $15 per year for individuals, $20 per year for institutions elsewhere, plus $4 postage and handling. Single copy $6 in the U.S., $8 elsewhere, plus postage and handling. All subscriptions should be sent to DIMENSION, P. O. Box 7032, Austin, TX 78713, USA. All contributions and editorial correspondence should be sent to: The Editor, DIMENSION, P. O. Box 26673, Austin, TX 78755, USA. Unsolicited manuscripts must be accompanied by a stamped, self-addressed envelope.

ISSN 0012–2882

DESIGN AND ART DIRECTION: DAVID PRICE

EDITORIAL ASSISTANTS: JULIE CARTER, INGMAR STOMBERG

ACKNOWLEDGMENTS

"Der Fuß im Netz" by Barbara König is published with the permission of the author.

"Am Ende der Jugend" by Klaus Schlesinger is from his volume *Berliner Traum* © 1977 by VEB Hinstorff Verlag, Rostock, and is reprinted with the permission of the author and the publisher.

"Zeit ohne Glocken" by Horst Beinek is from his novel of the same name, © 1979 by the Carl Hanser Verlag, Munich, and is reprinted with the permission of the author and the publisher.

"Besuch auf der Veranda" by Bernd Rachel is published with the permission of the author.

The funny animals drawn by Lilo Fromm are from *Der Papagei Die Mamagei* by Mascha Kaléko, © 1979 by Verlag Eremiten-Presse, Düsseldorf, and are reprinted with the permission of Friedolin Reschke.

"Der blaue Dragoman" by Hannelore Valencak is reprinted with the permission of the author.

"Wie heißt 'Olé' auf Hebräisch" by Ephraim Kishon is from his volume of satires *Salamos Urteil—Zweite Instanz,* © 1972 by Langen-Müller/Herbig Verlag, and is reprinted with the permission of the author and the publisher.

"Drei nackte Männer" by Franz Fühmann is from his volume *Bagatelle, rundum positiv,* © 1978 by the Suhrkamp Verlag, Frankfurt am Main, and is reprinted with the permission of the author and the publisher.

△ indicates original, previously unpublished contributions in German. All contributions in English appear in print for the first time.

Subscribers to DIMENSION may order microfilm copies or photocopied duplicate issues through University Microfilms, Ann Arbor, Michigan 48106.

CONTENTS

Perspective	A. LESLIE WILLSON	473
Der Fuß im Netz Foot in the Net	BARABARA KÖNIG *translated by Richard Mills*	476
Am Ende der Jugend Coming of Age	KLAUS SCHLESINGER *translated by Von Underwood*	500
Zeit ohne Glocken Time without Bells	HORST BIENEK *translated by Ralph R. Read III*	524
Besuch auf der Veranda A Visit on the Veranda	BERND RACHEL *translated by Breon Mitchell*	542
Der blaue Dragoman The Blue Dragoman	HANNELORE VALENCAK *translated by Sandra Celt*	554
Wie heißt "Olé" auf Hebräisch? How Do You Say "Olé" in Hebrew?	EPHRAIM KISHON *translated by Hanna B. Lewis*	562
Drei nackte Männer Three Naked Men	FRANZ FÜHMANN *translated by Esther E. Enns*	584
Authors and Translators		614

PERSPECTIVE

WHAT'S GOING ON?

A lot. DIMENSION, like any magazine, plans its issues long before they appear. Manuscripts that arrive from authors, submissions by translators, and miscellaneous suggestions that come to the editor are reviewed and selections made. After the actual process of translation, the manuscript is combed and groomed (that is, reviewed in exquisite detail) by the editor, assisted always by his staunch supporter Jeanne R. Willson and occasionally by a helpful apprentice translator or editor, before it is prepared finally for publication. In the past that meant sending the manuscript to the University of Texas Printing Division for typesetting, a long procedure that involved repeated readings (galley proofs, page proofs, often second and third times) before the issue finally was ready to mail to subscribers. Beginning with volume 14 that procedure will change drastically. Using his dedicated Exxon Office Systems word processor, the editor will himself in effect do the typesetting of DIMENSION, sending the resultant "manuscript" on a magnetic disk to an electronic typesetting machine via modem and telephone. The entire manuscript will be formated on the word processor—instructions about indentations, lines, spaces, typeface and type size, running heads, titles, accents are all encoded. The makeup of the magazine then will take place in the editor's study, where he will paste up the issue. The printing that then follows from the pasted up "boards" will produce an issue of DIMENSION that is in no way different from those that have preceded. The whole procedure should expedite the publication of the magazine and bring it more readily into the hands of subscribers in a more timely manner.

Volume 14 will be a test of both editor and machine. The volume has already been three years in production—that is, selections were made, translations assigned and delivered and checked, short biobibliographical accounts of authors and translators written, permissions secured, and so on, over that period of time. The issue will be a DIMENSION first: a whole volume (three issues) in one number, in this instance a volume of lyric poetry by scores of contemporary German-language poets between two covers. Represented in this issue-volume of more than 500 pages will be poets ranging from Ilse Aichinger to Frank Zwillinger, familiar names such as H.C. Artmann, Jürgen Becker, Horst Bienek, the late Nicolas Born, Volker Braun, Hans Magnus Enzensberger, Walter Helmut Fritz, Günter Grass, Hans-Jürgen Heise and others, to lesser known poets such as Clemens Eich, Thomas Erwin, Hans Kroliczak, and Peter Pabisch. It is a rich assortment, with themes as varied as the lyric modes chosen by the poets. It will be representative of German-language poetic voices of lyric talents young and old, known and unknown, tried and untried. They are defiant, lulling, observant, prophetic, lamenting, joyous. They epitomize the exuberance and vitality of German poetry today.

Coming issues of DIMENSION will increasingly feature topics: the radio play, dramas for the stage, first chapters of assorted novels, younger writers, German-language writers from Rumania, women writers, stories. A series of interviews with writers is planned as are profiles of publishers. All this adds up to exciting issues ahead. The editor hopes that readers of DIMENSION will find something riveting, something enthralling, something notable in each. He invites readers to send suggestions of writers and/or works to consider, but requests that they keep in mind the DIMENSION editorial policy of publishing only contemporary German-language authors who have some kind of publication in Europe (it need not be in book form) and of the text not having appeared in English translation before. Send suggestions to: The Editor, DIMENSION, P.O. Box 26673, Austin, TX 78755.

A. LESLIE WILLSON

DER FUSS IM NETZ
Hörspiel

BARBARA KÖNIG

Personen

Monnsen
Nina
Reporter (weiblich und männlich)
Gratulanten (dito)
Redner I
Redner II

Redner I: Heute vor fünfunddreißig Jahren opferte der Feldgeistliche Johann Schorr sein Leben, um einen zum Tode Verurteilten vor der Hinrichtung durch ein Militärkommando zu bewahren.

(Streichquartett einige Takte)

Wir ehren einen *Menschen.*

(Streichquartett einige Takte)

Redner II: Der Verurteilte, ein junger Soldat, hat den Kreig überlebt. Wir dürfen ihn zu dieser Feier begrüßen.

(Streichquartett Schlußtakte)

Redner I: Wir danken Ihnen.

Redner II: Wir danken Ihnen.

Redner I: Wir danken Ihnen, daß Sie gekommen sind.

Reporter: Wenn Sie uns ein paar Fragen gestatten . . .

Da sind noch einige Fragen . . .

Wir hätten gern gewußt—

(entschlossen) Was hat diese Feier für Sie bedeutet?

Was diese Tat, das *Opfer?*

Was die Person des Paters Johann Schorr?

Und Sie waren nicht besonders befreundet mit ihm? Sie waren nicht sein Schützling, sein Vertrauter?

Aber die drei Kameraden in Ihrer Zelle, die sterben mußten, weil keiner da war, der sich für sie geopfert hätte—die kannten Sie?

Gemeinsam hatten Sie beschlossen, im April 1945 die Sprengung einer Straßenbrücke zu verhindern, gemeinsam wurden Sie dabei ertappt

FOOT IN THE NET
Radio Play

BARBARA KÖNIG
translated by Richard Mills

Characters

Monnsen
Nina
Reporters (male and female)
Well-wishers (ditto)
Speaker I
Speaker II

Speaker I: Thirty-five years ago today the Army Chaplain Johann Schorr sacrificed his life to keep a man condemned to death from being executed by a firing squad.

(a few measures of a string quartet)

We honor a *human being.*

(a few measures of a string quartet)

Speaker II: The condemned man, a young soldier, survived the war. We take pleasure in welcoming him to this ceremony.

(concluding measures of the string quartet)

Speaker I: We thank you.
Speaker II: We thank you.
Speaker I: We thank you for coming.
Reporters: Would you allow us to ask a few questions . . .

There are still a few questions . . .

We would like to know—

(firmly) What is the significance of this ceremony to you?

Of this deed, the *sacrifice*?

Of the man, Father Johann Schorr?

And you weren't a good friend of his? You weren't his protégé, his confidant?

But the three comrades in your cell who had to die because no one would sacrifice himself for them—you knew them?

Together in April 1945 you decided to prevent a bridge from being demolished, together you were caught doing so, and together were con-

und gemeinsam von einem Militärgericht zum Tode verurteilt—ist das richtig?

Doch am Morgen der Hinrichtung wurden Sie nicht gemeinsam aus der Zelle geführt, sondern an Ihrer Stelle ging der Feldgeistliche Schorr, den Sie kaum kannten. Und Sie fragten nicht, warum, Sie ließen es einfach geschehen?

Sie hörten die Schüsse des Hinrichtungskommandos. Sie setzten sich auf Ihrer Pritsche auf und sahen sich um; alle anderen waren fort, auch der Feldgeistliche. Sie waren allein, und Sie wußten, was die Schüsse bedeuteten. Mußten diese Schüsse Ihnen nicht im Ohr bleiben, auch Jahre später noch, bis heute?

Wie haben Sie es fertiggebracht, fünfunddreißig Jahre lang mit dem Bewußtsein zu existieren, daß Sie im Grunde nicht Ihr eigenes Leben, sondern das eines anderen lebten?

Vielmehr: wie haben Sie es fertiggebracht, fünfunddreißig Jahre lang *ohne* dieses Bewußtsein zu existieren?

Sie haben sich nie mit dem Gedanken befaßt, welche Erwartungen der Pater in Sie gesetzt haben mag? Sie hätten sich auch weiterhin nicht damit befaßt, wenn dieser Mensch nicht für seine Opfertat ausgezeichnet worden wäre?

Und wenn der Feldgeistliche Schorr plötzlich vor Ihnen stünde und fragte: Ich habe dir fünfunddreißig Jahre geschenkt, was hast du damit angefangen? Wie würden Sie ihm antworten?

Sie haben das Ereignis zu einem Glücksfall erklärt und es dabei bewenden lassen? Sie haben sich nicht bemüht, ihm irgendwie gerecht zu werden?

Und Sie nennen sich trotzdem einen zufriedenen Menschen? Nur weil Ihnen ein bequemes Leben geschieden war?

Sie sagen, daß Sie tief und traumlos schlafen?

Wie bringen Sie das fertig?

Nina: Du hast Angst gehabt, ich möchte wissen, warum. Als ob du das nötig hättest! Schon deine Verlegenheit, dort auf dem Podium, als der Bischof sein Rede hielt, und der Bürgermeister. Dabei könntest du stolz sein! Denk doch, wie sie gezittert haben müssen, das Kirchenkomitee und die Stadtverordneten, als sie deinen Namen kannten, aber noch nicht wußten, wer du warst; und die Erleichterung, als sie dich kennenlernten! Er hätte ja ein ganz übler Typ sein können, dieser Gerettete, ein Trinker, ein Krimineller, ein gewissenloser Lump—und sie hätten sich nicht drücken können, die Feier war beschlossen, sie hätten ihn herholen müssen, zumindest seinen Namen nennen, die Presse hätte alles aufgedeckt.

Aber du warst verlegen, und nachher, vor den Reportern, da hast du beinahe gezittert; du hast dagestanden wie vor Gericht.

demned to death by a military court—is that correct?

But on the morning of your execution you were not led together out of your cell, but instead Army Chaplain Schorr, whom you hardly knew, went in your place. And you didn't ask why, you simply let it happen?

You heard the shots of the execution squad. You sat up on your cot and looked around; all the others were gone, the army chaplain too. You were alone, and you knew what the shots meant. Didn't these shots keep on ringing in your ears, even years later, until today?

How have you managed to exist for thirty-five years with the knowledge that you didn't really live your own life, but instead lived someone else's?

In fact, how have you managed to exist for thirty-five years *without* this knowledge?

You never bothered to think about the expectations the priest might have had for you? You wouldn't have thought about it, if this person hadn't been honored for his noble deed?

And if Army Chaplain Schorr were suddenly to stand before you and ask: I gave you thirty-five years, what did you do with them? How would you answer him?

You called the event a lucky accident and left it at that? You haven't tried to be somehow worthy of it?

And in spite of this you call yourself a contented man? Just because you were fated to have an easy life?

You say that you sleep soundly and without dreaming?

How do you manage that?

Nina: You were afraid, I'd like to know why. As if you had any reason to be! Your embarrassment was bad enough, up there on the podium, when the bishop made his speech, and the mayor. And you could have been proud of yourself! Just think how they must have trembled, the church committee and the city officials, when they learned your name but still didn't know who you were; and their relief when they met you! After all, he could have been a really bad sort, this man who was saved—a drunkard, a criminal, an unscrupulous rascal. And they couldn't have gotten around it, the ceremony had been announced, they would have had to put him on stage, or at least release his name, the press would have revealed everything.

But you were embarrassed, and afterwards, in front of the reporters, you almost trembled; you stood there as though you were on trial.

Sieh doch die Zeitungen, in allen steht deine Geschichte. Daß du dich emporgearbeitet hast, praktisch aus dem Nichts. Weißt du nicht mehr, wie du geschuftet hast, die ersten Jahre? Hier steht es: ". . . und heute Mitinhaber einer gutgehenden Maklerfirma ist . . ."

Monnsen: Zeitungen, Zeitungen. Überall mein Name. Der lang Gesuchte. Ein Bankräuber, der Jahrzehnte von den gestohlenen Millionen gelebt hat. Nun zerrt man ihn ans Licht, und mehr: man zwingt ihn, sich zu fragen, ob es sich auch gelohnt hat.

Nina: Du bist mein Mann, und ich bin stolz auf dich. Ich werde nicht zulassen, daß du dich kleiner machst, auch nicht vor diesem Pater.

Monnsen: Überall mein Bild: verlegen lächelnd neben dem neugotischen Pult in dem neugotischen Saal, den Hut in der Hand, mit gesenktem Kopf, ein eher—belangloser Mann. Darunter steht: "Ein Mann hat Glück." Ein beschämter Beschenkter, dort neben dem Rednerpult, sehr allein, wie übriggeblieben. Der Arme Sünder; wehrlos der Güte ausgeliefert. Daneben, immer wieder das Gesicht des Paters.

Nina: Natürlich war er etwas Besonderes, ein Held, ein Märtyrer. Nur: er wurde alles erst durch dich. Dadurch, daß er sich für dich geopfert hat. Vorher hat nie jemand von ihm gehört, jetzt kennt ihn die ganze Welt. Das darfst du nicht vergessen. Er brauchte dich für seine Heldentat, so wie du ihn zum Weiterleben brauchtest.

Monnsen: Das Gesicht des Paters ist still und freundlich. Bekümmert, ja, aber doch auch wieder sehr unbekümmert, als wollte er sagen: Sterben ist schlimm, aber so schlimm auch wieder nicht; es gibt Schlimmeres. Sterben mit ansehen müssen, zum Beispiel, ist schlimmer.—Er hat große dunkle Augen, die ein wenig vorstehen, sodaß es aussieht, als wollen sie dem anderen entgegengehen, den er gerade ansieht, und ihn stützen. In diesem Falle, mich.

Er wird mein Weggenosse sein, ab jetzt, falls ein Gesicht ein Weggenosse sein kann, aber mehr als dieses Gesicht ist nicht da, und es genügt vollkommen.

Nina: Nur gut, daß du dich beruhigt hast, ich hatte mir schon Sorgen gemacht. Nicht erst bei der Pressekonferenz, schon im Hotel, im Frühstückssaal, als die beiden Herren kamen. Da bist du zusammengezuckt; ich habe es gemerkt. Als ob du verhaften werden solltest. Wahrscheinlich steckt es noch immer in dir, der Schock von damals, und jetzt kommt alles wieder hoch. Sie muten dir einiges zu, nicht wahr? —Doch, doch, du *bist* erschrokken. Ich kenne dich besser.

Monnsen: Sie kennt mich besser. Ich *bin* erschrocken.

Zwei Herren in der Tür. Sie sehen sich unauffällig um, sie entdecken mich. Daß sie in Hut und Mantel sind, macht sie so fürchterlich, und zu zweit. Die Schergen. So ein altmodisches Wort. Das hat es schon immer

Just look at the newspapers, your story's in all of them. That you worked your way up, practically from nothing. Don't you remember how you had to slave those first few years? Here it says: ". . . and is now co-owner of a successful brokerage firm . . ."
Monnsen: Newspapers, newspapers. My name in all of them. The man they were all looking for. A bankrobber who lived for decades on the stolen millions. Now he's dragged into the light of day, and what's more, he's forced to ask himself if it was worth it.
Nina: You're my husband, and I'm proud of you. I won't let you humble yourself, not even on account of this priest.
Monnsen: My picture's everywhere: me, standing with an embarrassed smile next to the neo-Gothic lectern in the neo-Gothic hall, hat in hand, with bowed head, a rather—insignificant human being. Under it the caption: "A lucky man." Mortified by fate's favor, next to the speaker's lectern, quite alone, as though left over. The Poor Sinner; exposed to goodness, defenseless. And the priest's face always next to it.
Nina: Of course, he was something special, a hero, a martyr. But he became that only because of you. Because he sacrificed himself for you. Nobody had heard of him before, now the whole world knows who he is. You mustn't forget that. He needed you for his heroic deed, just as you needed him to keep on living.
Monnsen: The priest's face is calm and friendly. Troubled, yes, but then again quite untroubled, as though he were about to say: Dying is sad, but not all that sad; there are worse things. To watch someone else die, for example, is worse. —He has large, dark eyes that bulge a little, so that it seems as though they are about to approach the person he's looking at, in support. In this case, me.

He will be my companion from now on, assuming a face can be a companion, but there's nothing besides this face, and that's more than enough.
Nina: It's a good thing that you've calmed down, I was getting worried. And not just during the press conference, but even before then, in the hotel, at breakfast, when the two gentlemen came. You winced then, I saw it. As though you were going to be arrested. I guess the shock of those days has always stayed with you and now it's surfacing again. They're asking a lot of you, aren't they? —Yes, yes, you *are* frightened. I know you better than that.
Monnsen: She knows me better than that. I *am* frightened.

Two gentlemen at the door. They look around inconspicuously, they discover me. The fact that they are wearing hats and coats makes them so dreadful, and there's two of them. Constables. Such an old-fashioned gebeben, die Boten einer anonymen Macht. So auffällig unauffällig. Durch die Leere in ihren Gesichtern fließt ungehindert die Gewalt und preßt mich auf meinen Stuhl. Dabei, gelacht, ist der Saal voller Menschen, sie sitzen an kleinen Tischen und trinken ihren Grapefruitsaft, sie legen den Kopf zurück und entblößen ihre Kehlen, ohne an Würgegriff und Messer zu denken, sie sind stumpf geworden gegen jede Art von Gefahr, zum Untergang bereit.

Vor allem: sie sind kein Schutz. Es sind die selben Leute, die stumm in der Bahn sitzen und zusehen, wie einer von ihnen hochgezerrt und niedergeschlagen wird. Und wenn sie selber vom Sitz gerissen und niedergeboxt werden, dann finden sie es in Ordnung, daß keiner der anderen ihnen hilft, sie erdulden mit offenem Mund die Gewalt, staunend: nicht darüber, daß es sie gibt, nur, daß sie ausgerechnet ihn gewählt hat: warum gerade mich? Und auch dies nur so lange, bis ein Stiefel an ihrer Schläfe ihnen das Vergessen gestattet, das geliebte Dunkel.

Ich wage nicht, mir die Stirn zu trocknen in diesem Frühstückssaal, unter Ninas Augen, also betupfe ich beiläufig mit der Serviette die feuchte Stelle zwischen Mund und Nase, die Herren treten lächelnd auf mich zu, sie verbeugen sich sogar, und während mich beim Aufstehen die Schwäche in meinen Knieen verwirrt, stellen sie sich vor: ein Stadtrat und ein Kirchenreferent, sie holen mich zur Feier ab, sie dürfen mich herzlich begrüßen.

Nina: Ein wenig bist du immer noch verstört, ein wenig. Es wird sich geben.

Monnsen: Nina. Auf einmal kann ich sie kaum noch ertragen, ihren aufmerksamen Blick, ihre ständige Wachsamkeit: Wie geht es ihm? Ist er heiter, mürrisch, deprimiert? Hat er schlecht geträumt? Und woher kommen solche Träume? —Wie sie unzählige feine Sonden in meine Person hineinläßt, meinen Hirn-, Herz- und Blutstrom mißt, wie sie die Resultate mit dem Klang meiner Stimme, der Farbe meiner Haut, dem Tempo meiner Bewegungen kombiniert, mit dem Niveau meines Allgemeinbefindens und dem Zustand am Tage zuvor vergleicht, in computerhafter Geschwindigkeit ein Urteil fällt und dann ganz nebenbei, am Mittagstisch etwa, die Augen hebt: "Ein wenig bist du noch verstört, ein wenig; es wird sich geben."

(*Pause*)

Es wird sich geben. Sie ist eine warmherzige Frau, ich weiß nicht, was ich ohne sie täte. Sie weiß mehr von mir als ich selber. Ich habe mich sinken lassen, sie hat mich aufgefangen; sie trägt mich.

Gratulanten: . . . dürfen wir Sie von ganzem Herzen beglückwünschen. Sie sind ein Auserwählter! Sie sind—

Geben Sie mir die Hand! Bei uns zuhause sagt man: es bringt Glück, einen Glücklichen zu berühren!

Da haben Sie so lange in unserer Nachbarschaft gewohnt, und wir haben nicht geahnt, was für ein berühmter Mann Sie sind . . .

word. They're nothing new, the heralds of an anonymous power. So conspicuously inconspicuous. Violence flows unhindered through the emptiness of their faces and presses me onto my chair. Meanwhile, what a joke, the room is full of people, they are sitting at small tables, drinking their grapefruit juice; they tilt their heads back and expose their throats without thinking about strangleholds and knives, they've been dulled to any kind of danger, ready for the end.

Above all: they're no protection. They're the same people who sit dumbly in the subway and watch as one of them is grabbed and beaten. And when they themselves are torn from their seats and struck down, they aren't at all surprised that none of the others helps them, they endure the violence with open mouths, amazed, not by the fact that violence exists but because it happened to choose them: Why did it happen to me? And even this lasts only until a boot on their temple grants them forgetfulness, the beloved darkness.

I don't dare wipe my forehead in this dining room, since Nina is watching, so I casually dab the wet spot between my mouth and nose with a napkin, the gentlemen come smiling up to me, they even bow, and while the weakness in my knees confuses me as I stand up, they introduce themselves: a city council member, a religious liaison, they're escorting me to the ceremony, they take great pleasure in welcoming me.

Nina: You're still a little upset, just a little. It'll pass.

Monnsen: Nina. All at once I can hardly stand her anymore, her observant gaze, her perpetual vigilance. How is he feeling? Is he cheerful, sullen, depressed? Did he have bad dreams? And what causes those dreams? —The way she inserts countless tiny probes into my body, measuring my brain, my heart, and blood pressure, the way she combines the results with the timbre of my voice, the color of my skin, the tempo of my movements, comparing them with the way I feel today and my condition the day before, reaching a conclusion with the swiftness of a computer, and then quite casually, over lunch, for example, raises her eyes: "You're still a little upset, just a little; it'll pass." (*pause*)

It'll pass. She's a warmhearted woman, I don't know what I'd do without her. She knows more about me than I do myself. I let myself fall, she caught me; she supports me.

Well-wishers: . . . we'd like to offer you our heartfelt congratulations. You're one of the chosen few. You're . . .

Let me shake your hand! Back home we always say it's good luck to touch a lucky person!

You've lived in our neighborhood for so long, and we never suspected that you were such a famous man . . .

. . . ein Autogramm bitten, für meinen Enkel, der ist Lehrling in einer Gärtnerei, und alles, was er will, sind Autogramme, Autogramme . . .

Habe Sie in der Abendschau gesehen: Donnerwetter, sage ich zu meiner Frau, wenn das nicht der Herr Monnsen ist! Was denn, sagt sie, immer nur mit halbem Ohr dabei, ist der jetzt in die Politik gegangen? (*lacht*)

Ich habe Sie gleich erkannt, nach dem Bild in der Zeitung. Ich möchte nur sagen, daß ich Sie bewundere: das muß doch gar nicht so einfach sein, das Leben eines anderen zu führen, das kann doch direkt zur Last werden, oder nicht.

Nina: So viele Gratulanten! Und alle meinen es ehrlich. Eigentlich erstaunlich: da bekommt einer das Wertvollste geschenkt, was überhaupt zu verschenken ist, und keiner neidet es ihm. Wo doch sonst schon ein Lottogewinn, ein neuer Pelz, eine Beförderung . . .

Aber vielleicht ist es gar nicht so erstaunlich: warum sollen sie dich beneiden um etwas, das sie doch alle selber haben?

Monnsen: Ich gehe durch die Stadt; auf mein Büro zu und daran vorbei. Die Tausende von Malen, die ich darauf zugegangen bin, und keinmal, bis heute, vorbei.

Merkwürdig, wie gut es sich mit einem so winzigen Bruchteil von Bewußtsein leben läßt, wie schwerelos.

Reporter: Wie fühlen Sie sich als ein Mensch, welcher: einen Sprung vom Eiffelturm überlebt hat, über Nacht zum drittreichsten Mann von Cincinnati wurde, das Große Los gewann und verlor? Wie fühlen Sie sich als ein solcher?

Monnsen: Ich kann nur immer wieder sagen, wie unendlich dankbar ich bin.

Nein, ich weiß es nicht. Ich weiß nicht, warum er ausgerechnet mich gewählt hat.

Ich war sprachlos, erschüttert. Völlig durcheinander. Der Unterschied zwischen ihm und uns? Wir fürchteten den Tod, und er fürchtete ihn nicht, das war der Unterschied.

Reporter: Bitte versuchen Sie, sich zu erinnern: der Krieg, das Ende, der Anfang. Bitte versuchen Sie es.

Monnsen: Das ist so lange her, das ist schon nicht mehr wahr. Fragt sich, was jetzt noch wahr ist.

Mein Beruf füllt mich aus. Mein Tageslauf ist geregelt, meine Mahlzeiten, meine Freizeit. Meine Frau ist mir liebevoll zugetan. Mein Haus ist glatt und neu, mein Garten gepflegt. Mein Blick ist stumpf.

Reporter: Sie gehen und gehen. Wie einer, der versucht, müde zu werden, weil er hofft, daß er dann schlafen kann. Dabei, sehen Sie doch, ist es

. . . ask you for an autograph, for my grandson, he's working in a greenhouse, and all he wants are autographs, autographs . . .

Saw you on the evening news. Look at that, I said to my wife, if that's not Mr. Monnsen! What's that, she says, just listening with one ear like always, has he gone into politics now? (*laughs*)

I recognized you right away, from the picture in the newspaper. I'd just like to say that I admire you. After all, it's not so easy to live somebody else's life, that could become a real burden, don't you think?

Nina: So many well-wishers! And they all really mean it. Actually, it's amazing: Somebody is given the most precious thing in the world and no one envies him. But when you win in the lottery, get a new fur coat, or a promotion . . .

But maybe there's nothing amazing about it at all. Why should they envy you for something that they all have themselves?

Monnsen: I go through the city, toward my office and past it. The thousands of times I've gone to it and never, until today, gone by it.

Strange, how easy it is to live with such a tiny bit of knowledge, like floating.

Reporter: How does it feel to be a person who: survived a leap off the Eiffel Tower, became the third richest man in Cincinnati overnight, hit the jackpot, and lost it? How does it feel to be a man like that?

Monnsen: I can only repeat how eternally grateful I am.

No, I don't know. I don't know why he chose me of all people.

I was speechless, devastated. Completely confused. The difference between him and us? We feared death, and he didn't, that was the difference.

Reporter: Please try to remember the war, the end, the beginning. Please try.

Monnsen: That was so long ago, it's not even real anymore. The question is, what is still real now.

My job keeps me busy. The course of my day is set, my meals, my leisure time. My wife is affectionately devoted to me. My house is bright and new, my yard well groomed. My gaze is dull.

Reporter: You walk on and on. Like someone who is trying to tire himself in the hope that then he'll be able to sleep. But, as you can see, it's still

immer noch Tag: die Sonne scheint.
Monnsen: Plötzlich die Furcht, daß mich, bevor ich die Stadtbahn erreiche, mein Ziel loslassen könnte, vielmehr der Wille, zur Bahn zu gehen, nach Hause oder sonstwohin zu fahren . . .

Etwas hat sich geändert: Was? Die Dinge sind ja noch da, auch die Menschen, ich brauche nur die Hand auszustrecken. Doch wenn ich die Hand ausstrecke, ziehen sie sich zurück. —Nina?
Nina: Was hat sich dann geändert? Nichts hat sich geändert. Du lebst so weiter wie bisher. Kein Mensch hat dir etwas genommen, keiner dich verletzt, im Gegenteil: man sieht in dir den Glückspilz, den Beschenkten.

Allerdings—
Monnsen: Wir haben alles so glatt gemacht, wir rutschen überall ab, wir finden nirgends mehr Halt. Und ausgerechnet damit haben wir Jahrzehnte verbracht: mit Glätten und Polieren, mit Abstimmen. Wir sind wie Glas in Glas, wir haben keine Sprünge. Wir sind der Gleichklang ohne Dissonanz, unhörbar. Um uns ist Wasser ohne Widerstand, Luft ohne Atem, Stille.
Nina: Allerdings fange ich an, mich zu fragen . . .
Reporter: Ein Minimum an Biografie müßte sich beschaffen lassen, das hat doch jeder.
Monnsen: Ich möchte Ihnen gerne helfen, aber ich weiß nicht, wie. Ich habe keine Erinnerungen und keine Gefühle. Ich könnte höchstens, Ihnen zuliebe, welche erfinden.

Sie vergessen, daß ich ein Durchschnittsmensch bin; an mir geht vieles folgenlos vorbei.

Nein, ich bemühe mich nicht einmal, aus dieser Mittelmäßigkeit herauszukommen. Es ist leichter so: der Ablauf des Lebens läßt sich besser vorhersehen, schon weil er in hunderttausend Fällen ähnlich war. Ausgenommen, natürlich, Überraschungen wie diese.

Danke; im ganzen gesehen, bin ich zufrieden. Ich kann mich nicht beklagen
Reporter: Die Frage ist: Könnte sich der Pater beklagen? Wäre es nicht denkbar, daß er, wenn er Ihnen heute gegenüberstünde, seinen damaligen Entschluß, ich will nicht sagen: bereute, aber vielleicht doch, sagen wir, in Zweifel stellte. Denn darüber sind wir uns doch im klaren: daß sein Opfer dem Familienvater galt. Ob er Sie irrtümlich dafür hielt oder einfach damit rechnete, daß Sie einer werden würden—es bleibt das einzig einleuchtende Motiv, nicht wahr? Eine Tat für den Fortbestand der Welt, sozusagen.
Nina: Mein Leben ist mein Leben, ich kann damit machen, was ich will. Und wenn ich nichts damit mache, dann ist das auch meine Sache. Bei dir ist das etwas anderes, oder? Oder etwa nicht.
Monnsen: Es wäre so einfach gewesen: ein Haus voller Kinder, ein ausgefülltes Leben. Oder: man häuft sich einen Berg Steine vor die Tür und

daylight; the sun is shining.
Monnsen: Suddenly the fear that my goal could abandon me before I reach the subway, or more exactly, the desire to go to the subway, to go home or anywhere else . . .

Something has changed: What? Everything is still there, people too, I only need to hold out my hand. But when I hold out my hand, they retreat.—Nina?
Nina: But what's changed then? Nothing's changed. You're living just like you always did. No one's taken anything from you, nobody's hurt you, on the contrary; they think you're a lucky fellow, a privileged man.

Nevertheless . . .
Monnsen: We've made everything so smooth, we're slipping off everywhere, there's nothing for us to hold onto anymore. And we've spent decades that way: smoothing and polishing, adjusting. We're like glass inside glass, there are no cracks in us. We're harmony without dissonance, inaudible. We are surrounded by water without resistance, air without breath, stillness.
Nina: Nevertheless, I'm beginning to wonder . . .
Reporter: You must be able to come up with some sort of biography, everybody has one.
Monnsen: I would like to help you, but I don't know how. I have no memories and no feelings. The most I could do is invent some, to please you.

You forget that I'm an ordinary man, a lot of things that happen don't make any impression on me.

No, I haven't even tried to get out of my complacency. It's easier this way; the course of life can be predicted better, simply because it was that way a hundred thousand times before. Except, of course, for surprises like this.

Thank you; all in all, I'm satisfied. I can't complain.

Reporter: The question is: Could the priest complain? Isn't it possible, if he were here to see you today, that he would, I won't say regret, but perhaps, let's say, have misgivings about his decision? After all, I think we agree that his sacrifice was for the head of a family. Whether he mistakenly thought you were one, or simply assumed that you would become one—there isn't any other convincing reason, is there? A contribution to the continuation of the world, so to speak.
Nina: My life is my life, I can do what I want with it. And if I do nothing with it, then that's my problem. That's not what you think, is it? Or isn't it?

Monnsen: It would have been so easy: a houseful of children, a full life. Or: you pile a mountain of stones in front of your door and spend a useful verbringt ein nützliches Dasein damit, ihn wieder wegzuschaufeln. Verrückt! Andererseits: war da nicht eine Instanz, die sagte: ein Berg Steine gehört vor jede Tür? Und: wohl dem, der viel zu schaufeln hat? Aber was war das für eine Instanz, und inwieweit hatte sie *recht*?

Gratulant (Junge, Brief lesend): . . . haben wir Sie als Thema Nummer Eins auf unsere Diskussionsliste gesetzt und möchten wir Sie um Beantwortung folgender Fragen bitten: Was hat die Ehrung des Feldgeistlichen Schorr für Sie bedeutet? Eine Änderung Ihres bisherigen Lebens? Einen Aufbruch ins Neue? Wohin? Glauben Sie, daß der Feldgeistliche Schorr den Wunsch hatte, ein Märtyrer zu werden, und glauben Sie, daß ein Märtyrer für die heutige Jugend noch ein Leitbild sein kann? Was bedeutet Ihnen der hinterlassene Wahlspruch des Feldgeistlichen Schorr: "Meine Augen sind auf den Herrn gerichtet, Er wird meinen Fuß aus dem Netz ziehen"?

Monnsen: Was andere ein- oder zweimal im Jahr tun, am Geburtstag oder an Silvester, und auch dann nur zehn Minuten lang, mit dem Sektglas in der Hand, das ist mein tägliches Programm: dieses Umschauen, sich-Orientieren, die Selbstbefragung: wo stehst du? Wie weit bist du gekommen? Was hast du getan, um deinem Leben einen Sinn zu geben? Was tust du, wirst du noch tun? —Und keine Möglichkeit, das Glas hinzustellen und zur Tagesordnung überzugehen, denn was auch immer auf meiner Tagesordnung stehen mag—es genügt nicht.

Nina: Richard wäre neunzehn jetzt, und Viktoria siebzehn. Du erinnerst dich? Wir hatten schon die Namen ausgesucht. Das erste sollte ein Junge sein, und das zweite ein Mädchen; wie üblich, Richard wäre im Dezember geboren worden, ein Schütze; im Januar darauf hast du dich an der Firma beteiligt. Zwei Jahre danach haben wir das Haus gebaut; Viktoria wäre ein Widdermädchen, eigenwillig, willensstark. Ein Schütze und ein Widder —sie hätten sich gut verstanden.

Monnsen: Immer diese Furcht, die wird mich von jetzt an begleiten, die Furcht, daß ich etwas unterlassen könnte, was ich eigentlich tun müßte, ohne wirklich zu wissen, was das eigentlich ist, das ist das Schlimmste daran, dieser Nebel: da ist ja nichts, woran man sich halten kann, nichts.

Dann denke ich: ganz sicher ist da etwas, das genau richtig wäre für einen Menschen wie mich, in meiner ganz bestimmten Situation, etwas, das er tun müßte, um die Hoffnung zu erfüllen, die in ihn gesetzt wurde, denn wozu sonst sollte das alles geschehen sein, und dann sehe ich mich um und finde nichts, wieder nichts, mir fehlt vielleicht nur die Fantasie, ich kann mir einfach nicht vorstellen, was ich tun müßte in meiner ganz bestimmten Situation: soll ich mein Leben ändern? Und wie? Und ich fürchte mich vor dem Tag, an dem es zum zweiten Mal und endgültig zuende sein wird, und wie ich dann zurückblicke und sagen muß: Pech. Was immer

life in shoveling it away. That's crazy! On the other hand, wasn't there some official who said a mountain of stones belongs in front of every door? And, count your blessings, if you have a lot to shovel? But what sort of official was that, and to what extent was he *right*?
Well-wisher (boy, reading a letter): . . . we made you topic number one on our discussion list, and we would like to ask you to answer the following questions: What did the commemoration of Army Chaplain Schorr mean to you? A change in your previous lifestyle? A departure into something new? Into what? Do you think that Army Chaplain Schorr wanted to become a martyr, and do you think that a martyr can still be a model for today's youth? The army chaplain's posthumous motto was: "My eyes are turned toward the Lord, He will take my foot out of the net." What does that mean to you?

Monnsen: What other people would do once or twice a year, on their birthday or on New Year's Eve, and even then only for ten minutes, with a champagne glass in their hand, is a daily event for me: this looking around, orienting myself, questioning myself: Where do you stand? How far have you come? What have you done to give your life a meaning? What are you doing, what are you planning to do? —And no chance to set the glass down and move on to the daily agenda, because regardless of what's on my daily agenda—it's not enough.
Nina: Richard would be nineteen now, and Victoria seventeen. Do you remember? We already had the names picked out. The first one was to be a boy, and the second one a girl; the usual. Richard would have been born in December, a Sagittarius; the following year you joined the firm. Two years after that we built the house; Victoria would have been an Aries, self-confident, strong-minded. A Sagittarius and an Aries—they would have gotten along well together.
Monnsen: Always this fear, it will be with me from now on, the fear that I might neglect something that I should really do, without actually knowing what it really is, that's the worst part of it, this fog: There's nothing you can hold onto, nothing.

Then I think: Undoubtedly there's something that would be just right for a person like me, in my particular situation, something that he would have to do in order to fulfill the hopes that were placed in him, otherwise why did all of this happen, and then I look around and find nothing, nothing at all, maybe I'm only lacking in imagination, I simply can't figure out what I'm supposed to do in my particular situation: Should I change my life? And how? And I'm afraid of the day when it'll be all over for the second and final time, and how I'll look back and have to say:

da gewesen sein mag in der Absicht, im Entwurf: ich habe es nicht erreicht; ich habe mich verfehlt.

Reporter: Was mich an Ihrer Situation fasziniert, das ist ihre Ausweglosigkeit, die läßt sich in Ihrem Fall geradezu mathematisch nachweisen. Denn in dem Augenblick, in dem Sie das Opfer angenommen, beziehungsweise es sich bewußt gemacht haben, gehen rings um Sie alle Türen zu. Erstens: Sie können nicht weiterleben wie bisher, denn der Anspruch des Opfers fordert mehr. Zweitens: Sie können kein heiligmäßiges Leben führen, denn dazu reichen, verzeihen Sie, Ihre Gaben nicht. Drittens: Sie können sich nicht für einen anderen hinopfern, denn damit wäre die Schuld nicht beglichen, nur weitergegeben. Viertens: Sie können sich nicht das Leben nehmen, denn damit wäre die Tat des Paters ad absurdum geführt. Fünftens—tja, Sie können natürlich resignieren, aber gerade das können Sie sich am allerwenigsten leisten.

Monnsen: Damals waren wir ganz einer Meinung, Nina und ich. Ich habe es ihr weder eingeredet, noch habe ich sie in eine Lage gebracht, in der sie nicht anders konnte. Wenn ich gesagt hätte: gut, krieg du das Kind und sieh zu, woher wir die nächste Miete nehmen—aber nein, darum ging es längst nicht mehr, es ging nur noch darum, daß wir alles verplant hatten, das nächste Jahr und unsere Ausgaben . . . Wir sagten: jetzt im Aufbau hätten wir sowieso nicht genug Zeit für ein Kind, ein Kind wird es bei uns besser haben, wenn wir erst aus dem Gröbsten heraus sind. Das geschah einmal, und dann noch einmal, und dann wurde auch nicht mehr davon gesprochen, jahrelang nicht. Bis wir wußten, daß sie keine Kinder mehr bekommen konnte. Da sprachen wir noch einmal davon, in einem Klinikzimmer, kurz, bedauernd, so wie man sich von einer lieben Vorstellung trennt; am Ende Achselzucken: es hat nicht sollen sein.

Nina: So eine Ausnahme bist du nun auch wieder nicht! Jeder Krieg ist voll von edlen Taten, da opfern sich Freunde für den Freund, Kompanieführer für ihre Kompanie, Partisanen für ihren Chef . . . Die meisten kennt man gar nicht, oft weiß es nicht einmal der Gerettete . . .

Nur, daß sie alle Männer sind. Wann wäre je ein Mann für eine Frau gestorben? Wenn er sich aus unglücklicher Liebe vom Kirchturm stürzt: dann ist es seine Liebe und nicht ihre! Und die Aberhunderte, die sich im Morgengrauen duellierten, angeblich um die “Ehre einer Frau”: wofür sie starben, war ihre eigene Eitelkeit, sonst nichts.

Monnsen: Ein aktives Leben, das wäre die Rettung. Noch einmal sich in Arbeit stürzen können, gefesselt sein, berauscht. Vergessen, daß die Zeit vergeht. Bedauern, wenn man unterbrechen muß, weil Abend ist, oder Wochenende. Süchtig sein. Wenn Sie mich fragen, wann ich glücklich war: da war ichs.

Nein, nein; es ist mir alles entglitten. Ich gehe nicht mehr gerne ins

Too bad. Whatever I may have intended or planned to do, I didn't accomplish it; I failed.
Reporter: What fascinates me about your situation is your helplessness, which in your case can be demonstrated almost mathematically. For in the moment when you accepted, or shall we say became aware of, the sacrifice, all the doors around you closed. First, you can't keep on living like before, because the sacrifice demands more than that. Second, you can't lead the life of a saint, because you aren't, if you'll excuse me for saying so, gifted enough for that. Third, you can't sacrifice yourself for someone else, because that wouldn't negate your guilt but would simply pass it on. Fourth, you can't take your own life, because that would lead the priest's deed on ad absurdum. Fifth—well, of course, you could give up, but that's the very thing you can least afford to do.

Monnsen: At that time we both felt the same way, Nina and I. I neither talked her into it nor did I put her into a position where she had no choice. If I had said: Fine, go on, have the baby, and we'll see where next month's rent comes from—but no, that had long since ceased to be a problem, it was simply because we had already planned our expenditures for the next year . . . We said, now that we're getting started we wouldn't have enough time for a child anyway, it'll be better for the child once we've got the worst behind us. That happened once, then once more, and then it wasn't even talked about, not for years. Until we realized that she couldn't have children anymore. We talked about it once again then, in a hospital room, briefly, regretfully, the way you do when you part with a favorite idea; in the end a shrug of the shoulders: It wasn't meant to be.

Nina: What happened to you wasn't all that unusual! Every war is full of noble deeds, friends sacrifice themselves for their friend, squad commanders for their squads, partisans for their leader . . . We don't even know about most of them, often even the people who were saved don't . . .

However, they're always men. When did a man ever die for a woman? When he jumps off a church steeple because of a broken heart: then that's his love, and not hers! And the hundreds and hundreds of men who duelled at the break of dawn, supposedly because of a "woman's honor." They were dying for their own vanity, nothing else.
Monnsen: An active life, that would be the solution. Being able to immerse yourself in work once again, be captivated, intoxicated. Forgetting that time's passing. Sorry that you have to stop because it's evening, or the weekend. Being addicted. If you ask me when I was happy: I was then.

No, no, it's all slipped away from me. I don't like going to my busi-

Geschäft, es ist auch nicht wirklich nötig, es läuft auch so. Beruf, nicht wahr, ist ein Ort, an dem man mehrere Stunden des Tages verbringt, eine gewisse Quantität an Intelligenz und Tatkraft investiert, im Austausch dafür sein Leben, oder was man dafür hält, erhält. Schade.

Nina: Jetzt, wenn ich dich so ansehe, und wenn ich sehe, wie du dich windest und nach Ausflüchten suchst, und wie du immer noch hoffst, daß du *bestehen* könntest—womit denn, frage ich dich, womit bloß—da fange ich auch an, mich zu fragen, was ich überhaupt jemals an dir gesehen habe und wie das gekommen ist, und ich frage mich weiter, was denn der Pater damals in dir gesehen haben mag: wie du ihn wohl getäuscht hast mit welchen Augen und welchen stillen Versprechungen, und ob es nicht die gleichen waren, die später mich so getäuscht haben, ja, das frage ich mich.

Monnsen: Nina und ich, wir schlafen jetzt getrennt. Es ist besser so, denn um vier Uhr früh ist die Nacht für mich zuende, da sitze ich aufrecht im Bett, schweißbedeckt und mit flatterndem Puls. Und immer wieder ist es die *Katastrophe,* die mich aus dem Schlaf wirft, die letzten Schritte auf dem letzten Hof, das Füsilierkommando. Ich weiß, dieser Abgrund wartet auf mich, und daß kein Weg daran vorüberfährt; kein Zweifel, ich muß da hinunter.

Ich stehe auf und öffne die Vorhänge und falle dann wieder in meine eigene, unruhige Dämmerung zurück, in diesem wie mit Spinnweben verhängten Raum, den ich bei mir das Halbschlafzimmer nenne.

Reporter: Der Feldgeistliche in der Todeszelle: Ein König unter Bettlern. Der Tod, für ihn, war keine Katastrophe, nicht wahr?

Und die anderen: wenn sie gewußt hätten, daß er für Sie sterben wollte—was hätten sie getan? Hätten sie nicht gerufen: nimm mich! Nimm mich?

Monnsen: Ich gehe über einen zugefrorenen See, und die Eisdecke wird immer dünner; am Ende ist es, als ginge ich auf dem Wasser, das schenkt mir ein ungeheures Selbstgefühl, ein, zwei, drei Schritte lang, bevor ich zu sinken beginne.

Gratulanten (Geschäftsfrau): Und immer so bescheiden! Das habe ich auch dem Fräulein von der Presse gesagt: der Herr Monnsen kauft doch schon Jahre bei mir ein, aber er hat sich nie anmerken lassen, daß er nicht ist wie unsereiner, daß er etwas Besonderes ist . . .

(Mädchen, andächtig) Das muß ein wunderbares Gefühl sein, zu wissen, daß man ausersehen wurde . . . So ein Mann des Geistes, der gibt doch nicht für irgendwen sein Leben hin, der sieht sich doch genau an, für wen er sich da opfert . . .

(Mann, freundlich-nüchtern) Im Grunde müssen wir nicht Ihnen gratulieren, sondern uns: Sie haben uns da allerhand erspart, nicht wahr? Die ganzen Fragen und die Grübelei . . . *(lacht gutmütig)* Und wenn Sie

ness anymore, and it's not really necessary, they manage without me. A job, don't you agree, is a place where you spend many hours every day, investing a certain amount of intelligence and energy, and that in turn supports whatever kind of life you've chosen. Too bad.
Nina: Now, when I look at you, and when I see how you squirm and look for excuses, and how you keep on hoping that you'll manage to *survive*—how will you do it, I ask you, just how will you do it—that's when I also start wondering what in God's name did I ever see in you and how did it happen, and I also wonder what it was that the priest saw in you then: With what kind of eyes and what kind of quiet promises did you manage to fool him, and were those not the same ones you so fooled me with later on, yes, that's what I wonder about.
Monnsen: Nina and I, we now sleep in separate bedrooms. It's better this way, because night is over at four in the morning for me, I sit upright in bed, covered with sweat and my heart quaking. And it's always the *catastrophe* that yanks me out of my sleep, the final steps on the final courtyard, the firing squad. I know this abyss is waiting for me and that no path leads around it; no doubt about it, I have to go into it.

I get up and open the curtains and then fall back into my own restless twilight, in this room I call my dozing room that seems to be draped with cobwebs.
Reporter: The army chaplain on death row—a king among beggars. Death was no catastrophe for him, was it?

And the others: If they had known that he wanted to die for you—what would they have done? Wouldn't they have cried out: Take me! Take me?
Monnsen: I'm walking on a frozen lake, and the ice is getting thinner and thinner; in the end it's as though I were walking on water, that gives me an unbelievable feeling of self-confidence, one, two three steps long, before I start to sink.
Well-wishers (shopkeeper, female): And always so modest! I said that to the lady from the newspaper too: Mr. Monnsen's been a customer for years, but he never acted like he wasn't one of us, like he's someone special.

(girl, reverently): That must be a wonderful feeling, knowing that you were selected . . . A religious man like that wouldn't lay down his life for just anybody, he'd take a good look at the person he's sacrificing himself for . . .

(man, friendly, soberly): Basically we shouldn't congratulate you, but ourselves instead: You saved us from all sorts of things, didn't you? All the questions and the brooding . . . *(laughs good-naturedly)* And if

einmal doch den Fuß aus dem Netz kriegen sollten—das ist dann sozusagen auch *unser* Fuß, nicht wahr?
Monnsen: Unten sind die Piranhas; ich schwimme inmitten eines Schwarms, und als einer von ihnen meinem Gesicht so nahe kommt, daß er mich hören kann, klage ich ihm: "Sie fressen mich! Sie werden mich auffressen!" —Das ist schlimm, sagt der Fisch, aber vor mir mußt du keine Angst haben, ich bin nicht so, ich will nur einen winzigen Bissen von dir! Und schon schnappt er mir die Nase weg, und die anderen strömen herbei und nehmen jeder seinen winzigen Bissen, und schwupp bin ich ein Skelett und weine salzige Tränen ins Meer und weiß, daß ich Jahre brauchen werde, um wieder Fleisch anzusetzen.
Nina: Und so frage ich mich heute, nach allem, was wir mitgemacht haben: Hat denn der Pater wirklich *gewußt*, was das Gute ist, als er sich für dich erschießen ließ, oder hat er es nur für das Gute *gehalten?* Denn schließlich sollte man das Gute an seinen Früchten erkennen, und die Frucht seiner Tat, das wäre, nach so vielen Jahren, du, hier, heute, so vor mir, und da frage ich mich, nicht nur, weil du dich selber fragst, sondern ganz objektiv, so objektiv wie möglich: war es tatsächlich so ein großes Gutes?
Reporter: Und die Jahre danach? Die fünfmal sieben Jahre? Sonderbar, daß Sie sich nicht erinnern. Als ob Sie sich gar nicht erinnern wollten.
Nina: Wenn du doch glaubst, daß Kinder deine einzige Rechtfertigung wären, dein Alibi: warum läßt du dich nicht scheiden und fängst noch einmal von vorne an? Oder hast du Angst, daß du plötzlich dastehst, und siehst: es reicht nicht? Auch Kinder ändern nichts, der Mangel bleibt; ich habe es mir zu einfach gemacht?
Monnsen: Endlich geht die Sonne auf, ungewöhnlich schnell, wie mir scheint, und in Sprüngen. So wie im Flugzeug auf dem Weg nach Osten: jedesmal, wenn ich hinsehe, steht sie schon ein Stück höher.
Reporter: Sie fühlen sich nicht verantwortlich für die Entscheidung eines anderen, das wollten Sie doch sagen.
Monnsen: Das wirklich Böse habe ich immer nur meinem Gewissen zuliebe getan. Vater, verzeih mir, ich habe dich nicht sterben lassen. —Noch einen Tropf? fragte der Arzt, nun schon selber zweifelnd, das bringt ihn auf jeden Fall über die nächste Woche; danach ist nichts mehr zu hoffen. Und ich sah seine nach oben gedrehten Augen, weiß in dem weißen Gesicht, ich dachte: er fleht, aber *worum* fleht er? Ich fragte: Vater! Du willst doch leben? Will nicht ein jeder leben? Ich weiß nicht, ob er mich hörte.

Ich dachte an mein Gewissen. Das böse Tier: es wird über mich herfallen, wenn ich ihn sterben lasse, es wird mich des Vatermords bezichtigen. Dunkle Erinnerung an frühe Verwünschungen: der Teufel soll dich holen! Ich kann es mir nicht leisten, ihn sterben zu lassen, ich muß ihn weiterschleppen. Noch eine Woche, sagte ich, die schenken wir ihm. Brav,

someday you do manage to get your foot out of the net—then in a manner of speaking that's *our* foot too, isn't it?
Monnsen: The piranhas are below me; I'm swimming in the middle of a swarm, and when one of them comes so close to my face that he can hear me, I cry out to it: "They're eating me! They'll eat me up!" —That's terrible, the fish says, but you don't need to be afraid of me, I'm not like that, I only want a tiny bite of you! And he's already snapped my nose off, and the others stream by and each one takes a tiny bite, and presto, I'm a skeleton and weep salty tears into the sea, knowing that it'll take me years to put on flesh again.

Nina: And so now I ask myself, after everything that we've gone through: Did the priest really *know* what's right when he decided to be shot in your place, or did he only *think* it was right? After all, you should be able to recognize goodness by the fruit it bears, and the fruit of his deed, it would be, after all these years, you, here, today, as I see you, and so I ask myself, not only because you are asking yourself, but quite objectively, as objectively as possible: Was it really such a good deed?
Reporter: And the years after that? The five times seven years? Strange that you don't remember. As though you don't even want to remember.
Nina: If you really think that children would be your only excuse, your alibi: Why don't you get a divorce and start all over again? Or are you afraid that suddenly you'd stand there and see it wasn't enough? Even children don't change anything, something's still missing; did I make it too easy on myself?
Monnsen: At last the sun is rising, surprisingly fast, it seems to me, and in leaps. Like in an airplane flying east: Every time I look down it's risen a little.
Reporter: You don't feel responsible for someone else's decision, that's what you wanted to say?
Monnsen: Only because of my conscience did I ever do anything really evil. Father, forgive me, I didn't let you die. —One more drop? the doctor asked, also starting to doubt, that'll last at least through next week; after that there's no more hope. And I saw his eyes turn upward, white in his white face, I thought: He's begging, but *what* is he begging for? I asked: Father! You want to live, don't you? Doesn't everyone want to live? I don't know whether he heard me.

I thought about my conscience. That evil animal: It will leap on me if I let him die, it will accuse me of patricide. Vague memories of early curses: The devil take you! I can't afford to let him die, I have to keep dragging him along. One more week, I said, we'll give him that. Good, my sagte mein Gewissen, wer seinen Vater liebt, der verlängert sein Leben. Ich weiß jetzt, daß du gern gestorben wärst, du hast um deinen Tod gefleht und ich wollte es nicht hören. Ich wollte mein Gewissen schonen; ich schonte mein Gewissen.

Nina: Schon möglich, daß ich dir unrecht tue; wenn du nicht bist, wofür ich dich gehalten habe, so ist das höchstens meine Schuld; ich habe mir ein Bild gemacht, wie ich dich haben wollte. Ich habe Schwäche mit Sanftmut verwechselt.

Monnsen: Ich hätte so gern ein Hobby gehabt; ich beneide die Menschen, die am Abend ihre Briefmarken und Münzen hervorholen, oder zu ihrem Kegelclub, ihrem Reitverein, ihrer Schützengilde gehen. Ich habe umsonst versucht, mich zu interessieren, für Golf, Kakteen, Amphoren. Ein noch so schmales Gebiet hätte mir genügt, wenn ich es nur *beherrschte*. Es hätte mir den Punkt außerhalb verschafft, von dem aus ich das Wirrwarr von Geschehnissen betrachten und mir sagen konnte: so wie hier, in meinem kleinen Bereich, so wird es auch dort irgendwie zusammenhängen. Es hätte mir die Welt, in einem winzigen Ausschnitt zumindest, überschaubar gemacht.

Reporter: Sie fühlen sich in die Ecke gedrängt. Er hat Ihnen die Möglichkeit genommen, sich unbefangen zu bewegen. Er hat Sie zu einem Ausstellungsstück gemacht, das heißt, jeder, der Sie ansieht, und zur Zeit sehen alle Sie an, verlangt von Ihnen, daß Sie sich wie ein Ausstellungsstück benehmen: mustergültig, fehlerlos.

Monnsen: Will laufen, kann nicht. Mein Fuß hängt im Netz. Und weiß nicht, wohin ich meine Augen richten soll. Versuche, zu springen und schlage lang hin, den Mund voller Steine, Sand.

Genug. Ich will nicht mehr. Ich habe es satt, der ewig Schuldige zu sein: daran, daß ich aus einem Leben nichts gemacht hätte, das mir geschenkt worden ist. Nicht einmal, sondern zweimal geschenkt. Ich habe beide Male nicht darum gebeten.

Reporter: Halten wir das einmal fest: Geborenwerden verpflichtet zu nichts. Es gibt keine Instanz, der wir ein erfülltes Leben schulden. Wenn überhaupt, dann verpflichtet ein unverlangtes Geschenk zu einem freundlichen Dank, weiter nichts. Das meinten Sie doch?

Monnsen: Wenn Sie es hören wollen: dieses kostbare Leben, von dem Sie immer sprechen, interessiert mich nicht. Ihre Fragen haben mir gezeigt, daß ich nie wirklich gelebt habe. Nun haben Sie es: ich bin einverstanden damit, wir sind uns einig.

Von rechts wegen war ich mit Zwanzig ein Toter; ich bin es immer noch. Ja und? Andere sterben auch. Wofür dann soll ich mich bedanken? Was mir wirklich geschenkt wurde, das waren: eine furchtbare Schuld, ein gequältes Gewissen, die Pflicht, einen Sinn zu finden, wo keiner zu finden ist, ein später Tod anstelle eines frühen mit allen, was er einschließt:

conscience said, whoever loves his father will lengthen his life. I know now that you wanted to die, you begged to die, and that's what I didn't want to hear. I wanted to spare my conscience; I spared my conscience.

Nina: Could be that I'm not being fair to you; if you're not what I thought you were, then at worst that's my fault; I pictured you the way I wanted you to be. I mistook weakness for gentleness.

Monnsen: A hobby would have been so nice; I envy people who take out their stamps and coins in the evening, or go to their bowling league, their horse club, or their shooting range. I tried in vain to get interested in golf, cacti, amphoras. Any subject, be it ever so small, would have been enough, as long as I *mastered* it. It would have given me a point outside, from which I could view the hodgepodge of events and say to myself: Just like here, in my little domain, out there it'll somehow make sense as well. It would have made the world, or at least a little part of it, comprehensible to me.

Reporter: You feel you're being driven into a corner. He took away your chance to move freely. He turned you into a museum piece, I mean, anyone who looks at you, and right now everyone's looking at you, demands that you behave like a museum piece: exemplary, flawless.

Monnsen: Want to run, but can't. My foot's caught in the net. And I don't know where I should turn my eyes. I try to leap and fall on my face, my mouth full of stones, sand.

Enough, I've had it. I'm sick of always being the person in the wrong: because I didn't do anything with the life that was given to me. And not just once, but twice. I didn't ask for any favors either time.

Reporter: Let's get this straight: Being born doesn't obligate us to anything. We don't owe a fulfilled life to any authority. At most, presents that we don't ask for simply oblige us to say thank you in a friendly manner, nothing more. That's what you meant, isn't it?
Monnsen: If you want to know: This precious life that you're always talking about doesn't interest me. Your questions have shown me that I've never really lived. There you have it: I agree with you; we're unanimous!

By rights I was a dead man when I was twenty; I still am one. So what? Other people die too. What should I be grateful for? What I was really given was a terrible guilt, a tormented conscience, the duty to find a meaning where there's none to be found, a late death, instead of an early one, along with everything that includes: old age, sickness and decrepitude,

Alter, Krankheit und Verfall, die tödliche Langeweile . . .

Ich hätte ein Genie sein müssen, um diesem Anspruch zu genügen, und selbst dann—(*achselzuckend*) Wir haben beide versagt, der Pater genau so wie ich. Er hat sich geirrt, er ist für den Falschen gestorben.

Reporter: Womit Sie jedenfalls zugeben, daß Ihre so oft beteuerte Dankbarkeit nichts als Heuchelei war, der vorübergehend geglückte Versuch, Ihr Scheitern zu bemänteln. "Ich bin unendlich dankbar"—das habe ich an vierzehn Stellen notiert.

Monnsen: Und Sie? Fragen Sie sich doch selber! Sie sind doch Christ, oder nicht. Dann ist auch für Sie einer gestorben, nicht wahr. Und was tun *Sie* dafür? Was sind *Ihre* Konsequenzen? Geben Sies zu, Sie drücken sich. Sie sagen: er hat ja nicht mich im besonderen gemeint, sondern *alle*. Sie verstecken sich in der Menge. Als ob Menge je ein Versteck gewesen wäre!

Nina: Langsam mache ich mir Sorgen. Du schläfst zu wenig, und du ißt kaum noch. Wenn du so weitermachst, brichst du zusammen.

Monnsen: Vielleicht war ich auch nicht persönlich gemeint? Vielleicht ging es dem Pater gar nicht darum, das Leben eines anderen zu retten, sondern nur, sein eigenes zu vollenden? Und ist auf meine Kosten zum Märtyrer geworden? Der allernobelste der Egoisten?

Reporter: Sie haben ihn beneidet, schon damals: er hatte alles, und Sie hatten nichts.

Nina: Langsam läßt es nach, der Rummel verläuft sich. Bald werden sie dich ganz in Ruhe lassen.

Monnsen: Er sieht mich an mit seinen leicht vorquellenden Augen und fragt: Warum betest du nicht? Ich habe es nicht gelernt, sage ich, oder auch nur vergessen. Esel, sagt er, warum ziehst du es vor, im dunklen Zimmer herumzutappen, dich an den Möbeln zu stoßen, die Tür nicht zu finden, nur weil du zu dumm und zu bequem bist, den Stecker an das große Stromnetz anzuschließen? Dann wäre auf einmal Licht. —Das kommt, sage ich, weil ich im Dunkeln den Anschluß nicht finde. Das bringt ihn zum Lächeln. Gut, sagt er, dann gestatte mir, daß ich ein kleines Licht für dich anzünde, nur gerade soviel, daß du dich hintasten kannst, und ein paar andere mit dir, vielleicht, im besten Falle.

Nina: Du bist nicht deines Bruders Hüter, du bist der behütete Bruder. An den denkt ja keiner, wie der sich fühlt. Muß er dem großen Bruder dankbar sein? Oder nimmt er es für selbstverständlich, daß er behütet wird? Vielleicht will er es auch gar nicht, vielleicht will er lieber, unbehütet, sterben?

Monnsen: Bald werden sie mich ganz in Ruhe lassen.

deadly boredom . . .

I would have had to be a genius to fulfill these demands, and even then—(*shrugging his shoulders*) We both failed, the priest as well as I. He made a mistake, he died for the wrong person.

Reporter: Which means you're really admitting that the gratitude you've so often professed was nothing but hypocrisy, the temporarily successful attempt to disguise your failure. "I'm eternally grateful"—I wrote that down fourteen times . . .

Monnsen: And you? Why don't you look at yourself? After all, you're a Christian, aren't you? Then someone died for you too, isn't that right? And what are *you* doing about that? What consequences do *you* draw from that? Admit it, you're avoiding the issue. You say: But he didn't single me out in particular, rather *everyone*. You're hiding in the crowd. As though a crowd were ever a hiding place.

Nina: I'm beginning to worry about you. You don't get enough sleep, and you eat next to nothing. If you keep on this way, you're going to collapse.

Monnsen: Maybe he didn't mean me personally either? Maybe the priest wasn't even trying to save someone else's life, but was simply trying to bring his own to a fitting conclusion? And became a martyr at my expense? The noblest of all egoists?

Reporter: You envied him, even then; he had everything, and you had nothing.

Nina: It's slowly starting to let up, the hubbub is dying down. Soon they'll leave you in peace.

Monnsen: He looks at me with eyes that protrude slightly and asks: Why aren't you praying? I don't know how, I say, or just forgot how to. Fool, he says, why do you choose to grope around in a dark room banging into the furniture, unable to find the door, just because you're too stupid and too lazy to plug into the universal current? You'd have light instantly. —The reason, I say, is because I can't find the outlet in the dark. That makes him smile. Good, he says, then permit me to light a small candle for you, just big enough to help you feel your way, a couple of others along with you, perhaps, at best.

Nina: You're not your brother's keeper, you're kept by your brother. No one thinks about him, how he feels. Does he have to be grateful to his big brother? Or does he expect to be protected? Maybe he doesn't even want it, maybe he would rather not be protected, and die?

Monnsen: Soon they'll leave me in peace.

AM ENDE DER JUGEND

KLAUS SCHLESINGER

1

Kurz bevor ich aufwachte, hatte ich einen Traum. Ich sah mich im Zimmer meiner Eltern, auf dem Bett sitzend, jemand hämmerte gegen die Wohnungstür, und eine Stimme, die mir bekannt vorkam, rief meinen Namen. Ich wollte zur Tür, war aber wie gelähmt. Angst befiel mich, ganz plötzlich, ohne daß ich hatte sagen können, worauf sie sich bezog: Ich hatte Mühe, Luft zu holen, fiel irgendwann durch eine lilaschwarze Leere und stand in einem Raum, der mir wie ein Schulzimmer vorkam. Ich saß auf einer Bank, flankiert von zwei Wächtern. Hinter dem Katheder stand eine Frau in schwarzem Kostüm, sah mit ernstem, fast strengem Blick zu mir herüber und fragte mich, wer ich sei.

—Ich heiße Gottfried, sagte ich, indem ich aufstand, bin vierundzwanzig Jahre alt und technischer Assistent am Institut für Serologie.

—Setzen Sie sich, sagte die Frau, in der ich nun meine frühere Englischlehrerin erkannte.

Dann entdeckte ich Martin. Er stand im Gespräch mit ein paar Leuten und tat sehr entschlossen. Als er sah, daß ich ihn beobachtete, senkte er seine Stimme und kam zu mir herüber. Er beugte sich über die unbeteiligt ins Leere blickenden Wächter und sagte, daß jeder im Raum es hören konnte: Mach dir keine Sorgen! Ich werde auf jeden Fall bezeugen, daß du in der fraglichen Zeit bei mir warst!—Alle sahen auf Martin, der nun, über die Wächter hinweg, die Hand nach mir ausstreckte und sie auf meine linke Schulter legte. Im ersten Moment spürte ich Erleichterung, die aber sofort einer Bestürzung wich, wie wenn etwas verletzt wäre in mir, ein sehr großes, ehrliches Gefühl, aber da war wieder das Klopfen, und ich wachte auf, wußte, daß ich geträumt hatte, rollte mich seitwärts aus dem Bett und stand taumelnd im Zimmer. Marie schlief noch. Wenn ich sie je um etwas beneidet hatte, dann um ihren Schlaf. Ich schleppte mich zur Wohnungstür, sah durch die Vorhänge, daß heller Tag war, dachte, daß draußen eigentlich nur Martin stehen konnte, war aber nicht überrascht, als es Rosenberg war.

—Sei bitte still, sagte ich, Marie schläft noch.

—Was denn, flüsterte er, es ist gleich Mittag, ihr versäumt ja das Wichtigste, oder wißt ihr noch garnichts?

—Komm rein, sagte ich, aber sieh dich nicht um.

COMING OF AGE

KLAUS SCHLESINGER
translated by Von Underwood

1

Just before I woke up, I had a dream. I saw myself in my parents' room, sitting on the bed. Someone was hammering at the front door and a voice that seemed familiar to me was calling my name. I wanted to answer the door but was as if paralyzed. Fear came over me, all at once, without my being able to say what it was about. I had trouble getting my breath, fell at some point through a dark lilac emptiness, and was in a place that seemed to me like a classroom. I was sitting on a bench, flanked by two guards. Behind the teacher's desk stood a woman wearing black, who looked over at me with an earnest, almost severe look and asked me who I was.

—My name is Gottfried, I said as I stood up. I'm twenty-four years old and am a technical assistant at the Institute for Serology.

—Take a seat, said the woman, whom I then recognized to be my former English teacher.

Then I made out Martin. He was in conversation with a couple of people and was behaving in a very determined way. When he noticed that I was watching him, he lowered his voice and came over to me. He leaned over the disinterested guards, who were staring off into space, and said, so that everyone in the room could hear it: Don't worry! No matter what happens, I will testify that at the time in question you were at my place! —Everyone was looking at Martin, who reached out over the heads of the guards toward me and placed his hand on my left shoulder. In that first instant I felt relieved, but it immediately gave way to consternation, as though something in me were wounded, a very intense, sincere feeling, but then there was the knocking again and I woke up, knew that I had been dreaming, rolled to one side out of bed and stood dizzily in the room. Marie was still sleeping. If I had ever envied her for anything, it was for her sleep. I dragged myself to the apartment door, saw from the curtains it was broad daylight, thought that it had to be Martin outside, but was not surprised when it turned out to be Rosenberg.

—Please keep it down, I said, Marie is still asleep.

—Asleep, he whispered, but it's almost noon, you're neglecting the most important things, or haven't you heard anything yet?

—Come in, I said, but don't look around.

In meinem Kopf war ein dumpfer Druck, ich kam mir wie ausgelaugt vor, nur dieser Traum war da, verschwommen zwar, aber wie auf der Lauer, bereit, mich jederzeit anzuspringen. Rosenberg stand da und wechselte periodisch das Standbein. In seiner massigen Gestalt steckte eine Unruhe, die ich sonst nur an ihm bemerkt hatte, wenn er an einem neuen Arbeitsthema saß.

—Willst du einen Kaffee, fragte ich.

—Nein, danke, sagte er, ich bin nur auf einen Sprung hier. Ich habe Bereitschaft im Institut.

—Wieso Bereitschaft, fragte ich und zog die Vorhänge vom Fenster zurück.

Draußen zog eine Wolkenfront über den Himmel und färbte die Hauswand gegenüber grau.

—Du weißt also noch nichts?

—Nein, sagte ich, was ist denn nur los?

—Die Grenzen sind zu. Heut früh ging's los. Um eins.

Ich ging an Maries Bett und schüttelte sie. Sie setzte sich auf und war sofort wach.

—Hallo, sagte sie und nickte Rosenberg ohne Verwunderung zu.

—Ich wollte eigentlich nur sehen, ob ihr noch da seid, sagte Rosenberg, nicht ohne Ironie.

—Ach Gott, sagte ich, ich dachte, wir kennen uns besser.

—Ich hab schon Pferde kotzen sehn, sagte er.

—Was ist denn los, fragte Marie endlich.

—Halten Sie sich fest, sagte Rosenberg, die Grenzen sind zu.

Marie sah mich an, und ich hatte das Gefühl, sie war erleichtert. Der Teekessel begann zu pfeifen, ich ging in die Küche und goß Wasser auf den Kaffee. Seit Marie schwanger war, machte ich das Frühstück. Ich deckte den Tisch, bekam plötzlich einen starken Widerwillen, etwas zu essen, und goß Kaffee in die Tassen. Rosenberg sagte—Nur einen Schluck, ich muß wirklich weiter.

Ich sagte: Wir kommen auch gleich mit!

Marie stöhnte und sagte: Du, ich fühl mich nicht so, ich hör's mir im Radio an.

Wir tranken die Tassen leer, ich küßte Marie auf die Wange, dann gingen wir hinunter. Die Treppen zitterten unter Rosenbergs schwerem Körper. Er lief vor mir, und ich sah den spärlichen Haarwuchs auf seinem Hinterkopf. Rosenberg war im Mai vierunddreißig geworden. Wir hatten im Institut gefeiert, und jemand hatte mir seine Geschichte erzählt: Halbjude, die letzten zwei Jahre unter Hitler illegal gelebt, dann Polizeidienst, ABF, Biologiestudium und mit zweiunddreißig das Diplom. Rosenberg war eigentlich der erste, zu dem ich—Martin natürlich ausgenommen—Kontakt

There was a dull pressure in my head. I felt drained. Just this dream was there, hazily to be sure, but as if lurking, ready to pounce on me at any moment. Rosenberg stood there periodically shifting his weight from one foot to the other. There was a restlessness in his bulky figure I had seen in him only when he sat down to a new project.

—Would you like coffee, I asked.

—No thanks, he said, I just dropped in here for a minute. I'm on call at the Institute.

—How so on call, I asked and drew back the curtains at the window.

Outside a cloudfront was drawing over the sky and coloring the wall of the building opposite gray.

—Then you don't know anything yet.

—No, I said, what's going on?

—The borders have been closed. It started early this morning. Around one.

I stepped over to Marie's bed and shook her. She sat up and was immediately awake.

—Hello, she said, and nodded to Rosenberg without surprise.

—I just wanted to see if you were still here, said Rosenberg, not without irony.

—Good Lord, I said, I thought we knew each other better.

—I've seen pigs fly, he said.

—What on earth is going on, Marie asked finally.

—Brace yourself, said Rosenberg, the borders are closed.

Marie looked at me and I had the feeling she was relieved. The kettle began to whistle and I went into the kitchen and poured water over the coffee. Since Marie had become pregnant, I made the breakfast. I set the table, suddenly felt a strong aversion to eating, and poured coffee into the cups. Rosenberg said: —Just a little, I really have to go.

I said: Hold on a second and we'll come with you!

Marie groaned and said: You go, I don't feel so well. I'll listen to it on the radio.

We drank down the coffee, I kissed Marie on the cheek, then we went out. The stairs shook under Rosenberg's heavy body. He went ahead of me and I saw the thinning hair at the back of his head. Rosenberg had turned thirty-four in May. We had celebrated in the Institute and someone had told me his history: A half Jew, the last two years under Hitler lived illegally, then police service, ABF, course of study in biology, and at thirty-two, a degree. Rosenberg was actually the first person, except, of course, for Martin, with whom I had had any contact at the Institute. There was bekam im Institut. Es war etwas in seinem Wesen, das diese Distanz, wie sie Doktor Weiß oder der Professor hatten, als unnatürlich empfand. In gewissen Momenten hatte er sogar etwas Brüderliches.

Auf dem letzten Treppenabsatz blieb Rosenberg stehen, wandte sich um und sagte: Und dein Freund Martin?

Ich sagte: Der wird zu Hause sein.

—Na, sagte Rosenberg, hoffentlich!

Im Hausflur verabschiedeten wir uns.

—Sehen wir uns noch, fragte er

—Vielleicht, sagte ich und gab ihm die Hand.

Ich nahm die Zeitung aus dem Briefkasten, warf einen Blick auf die Titelseite, las BESCHLUSS DES MINISTERRATES DER DEUTSCHEN DEMOKRATISCHEN REPUBLIK in großen schwarzen Buchstaben, schlug die nächste Seite auf, DEM FEIND KEINEN FUSSBREIT BODEN, faltete die Zeitung zusammen und steckte sie zurück in den Kasten.

2

Ich weiß nicht, ob ich die Stadt jemals wieder so gesehen habe wie an diesem Tag. Dabei hätte ich nicht sagen können, woran es lag; es war alles unverändert, diese graue, lange Straße, die stummen, mächtigen Häuser mit ihren bröckligen Fassaden—alles unverändert und doch auf eine schwer faßbare Weise anders, nicht nur weil ich, außer an Staatsfeiertagen, noch nie so viele Menschen auf den Straßen gesehen habe, die eilig und meist in Gruppen in Richtung der Grenze liefen: Ehepaare, fest untergehakt, als könnten sie sich verlieren, ganze Familien, Großeltern, Eltern, Kindern, in den Gesichtern—ob sie nun Zorn oder Triumph zeigten—etwas Einendes, allen Gemeinsames, ja es war die gleiche Ungläubigkeit in den Gesichtern der Menschen, die an mir vorbei zur Grenze zogen.

Mein Herz klopfte, und obgleich ich mir sagte, daß ich im Grunde mit der ganzen Sache nichts zu tun hätte, war in mir ein ähnliches Gefühl wie damals, vor drei, vier Jahren, als ich von zu Hause, aus Neustrelitz, hier ankam, mit zwei Koffern in der Hand auf dem Bahnhofsvorplatz stand, vergeblich nach Martin Ausschau hielt, der versprochen hatte, mich abzuholen, und immer wieder den Brief des Professors las, daß meine Bewerbung akzeptiert sei, mir Arbeitsplatz und Wohngenehmigung zur Verfügung stünden und daß er sich persönlich sehr auf meine Mitarbeit freue.

Auch ich freute mich, schon wegen Martin, der ein halbes Jahr vor mir nach Berlin gegangen war und auf dessen Empfehlung sich der Brief des Professors bezog, fühlte mich aber dennoch fremd und unbehaglich, als ich auf dem Bahnhofsvorplatz stand, vor diesen Straßen, vor diesen Häusern, die something in his nature that made the distance, such as Doctor Weiss and the professor maintained, seem unnatural. At certain moments there was something even brotherly about him.

On the last landing Rosenberg came to a halt, turned, and said: And your friend Martin?

I said: He should be at home.

—Well, said Rosenberg, let's hope so.

We took our leave of each other in the hallway.

—Will we see each other later, he asked.

—Perhaps, I said, and offered him a hand to shake.

I took the newspaper out of the mailbox, glanced at the front page, read RESOLUTION OF THE COUNCIL OF MINISTERS OF THE GERMAN DEMOCRATIC REPUBLIC in large block letters, hurriedly turned to the next page, TO THE ENEMY NOT ONE SQUARE INCH OF SOIL, folded the paper, and stuck it back in the box.

2

I don't know if I ever again saw the city as I did on that day. For all that, I could not have said exactly what the difference was; everything was unchanged, this gray, long street, the silent, immense buildings with their crumbly facades—all unchanged, and yet, in a way that was difficult to grasp, different. Not only because, except for on public holidays, I have never seen so many people on the street, in a hurry and mostly in groups headed in the direction of the border: married couples, arm firmly in arm, as if they might lose each other, whole families, grandparents, parents, children, in their faces—whether they showed anger or triumph—something unifying, common to all of them; there was the same disbelief in the faces of the people who drew past me on their way to the border.

My heart was pounding, and, although I told myself that I had basically nothing to do with the whole matter, I had a feeling inside like the one I had on the day three, four years earlier, when I arrived here from home, from Neustrelitz, with two suitcases in hand and kept watch in front of the train station in vain for Martin, who had promised to pick me up, and read again and again in the letter from the professor that my application had been accepted, that work space and a residence permit were waiting for me, and that he was personally looking forward very much to working with me.

I, too, was pleased, if for no other reason than because of Martin, who had gone to Berlin six months ahead of me, and to whose recommendations the letter referred. Yet I felt out of place and ill at ease as I stood in front of the station, before these streets, these buildings, which had a gray grau und bedrückend auf mich wirkten, fast feindlich, ein Gefühl, das erst verschwand, als Martin auftauchte, verspätet, wie immer, und mit einem Taxi, aber er stieg so ruhig aus, als käme er lange vor der Zeit.

Ich stieg an der Ecke in die Straßenbahn, fuhr bis Pankow und ging durch baumbestandene Straßen mit Vorgärten und kleinen Häusern, die mich in dieser Stadt noch am ehesten an Neustrelitz erinnerten. Eine halbe Stunde später stand ich vor Martins Wohnungstür. Ich klingelte, aber niemand öffnete, dann entdeckte ich den kleinen Zettel, der hinter das Namensschild gesteckt war. Mit Mühe konnte ich entziffern, daß Martin in der HÜTTE war.

Ich lief hinunter, traf im Hausflur Frau Erlwein, Martins Nachbarin, eine freundliche alte Frau, die uns manchmal mit Tee oder Zucker aushalf.

—Guten Tag, Frau Erlwein! rief ich, haben Sie meinen Freund gesehen?

Sie blickte mich an, als würde sie mich nicht kennen.

—Meinen Freund Martin, wiederholte ich.

—Soldaten, sagte sie flüsternd, überall Soldaten.

—Ich bin Martins Freund, Frau Erlwein, sagte ich.

—'s kommt Krieg, flüsterte sie drohend, zog die verschlissene Tasche an ihren Körper und ging hinauf.

Ich fuhr zurück, stieg am Bahnhof Schönhauser aus und lief die paar Schritte bis zur HÜTTE, die nachmittags Kaffeebetrieb und abends Tanz hatte, aber die Jalousien waren herabgelassen, und mir fiel ein, daß es sonntags ja Ruhetag war und Martins Zettel sich auf den gestrigen Abend bezogen haben mußte.

Gegenüber stand eine Telefonzelle. Ich ging hinein und wählte die Nummer von Gerhard Schwager.

Schwager war Filmschauspieler, ich kannte ihn aus der HÜTTE, wo er manchmal auftauchte, meist nach den Dreharbeiten und immer mit ein paar Mädchen am Arm. Zwei- oder dreimal waren Martin und ich nachts mit zu ihm nach Hause gegangen.

—Hallo, sagte eine matte Stimme.

—Frau Schwager, sagte ich, hier ist Gottfried . . .

—Herr Gottfried, sagte Frau Schwager schnell, gut, daß Sie anrufen. Haben Sie eine Ahnung, wo mein Mann ist?

—Ihr Mann? sagte ich verwirrt.

—Ja, sagte sie, er wollte noch nachts zurückkommen vom Drehen, aber bis jetzt hat er sich nicht gemeldet.

—Keine Ahnung, sagte ich, ich bin auch gerade raus aus dem Haus.

—Herr Gottfried, sagte Frau Schwager, ich bitte Sie um eins! Gehen Sie bei Kauffeld vorbei und sehen Sie nach, ob er dort ist.

—Frau Schwager, sagte ich, ich kenne ja keinen Kauffeld.

and depressing, almost hostile effect on me, a feeling that went away only when Martin showed up, late as usual, and in a taxi. Yet he got out just as calmly as if he had come well ahead of time.

I caught a streetcar at the corner, rode to Pankow, and walked down the tree-lined streets with front gardens and small houses that reminded me more than anything else in this city of Neustrelitz. A half hour later I was standing in front of the door to Martin's apartment. I rang the doorbell, but no one answered. Then I discovered the small note stuck behind the name-plate. With difficulty I was able to decipher that Martin was at The Hut.

I ran down the stairs, met Frau Erlwein, Martin's neighbor, in the hallway. She was a friendly old woman who sometimes helped us out, lending us tea or sugar.

—Hello, Frau Erlwein, I called, have you seen my friend Martin?

She looked at me as if she didn't recognize me.

—My friend Martin, I repeated.

—Soldiers, she said in a whisper, everywhere, soldiers.

—I am Martin's friend, Frau Erlwein, I said.

—War's coming, she whispered threateningly, clutched her worn purse to her body and went upstairs.

I rode back, got out at Schönhauser Station and walked the short distance to The Hut, which normally served coffee in the afternoons and had dancing at night, but the blinds were down, and it occurred to me that they were closed Sundays, and that Martin's note must have been for the night before.

There was a telephone booth across the street. I went in and dialed Gerhard Schwager's number.

Schwager was a film actor. I knew him from The Hut, where he sometimes turned up, for the most part after filming sessions and always with a couple of girls on his arm. Two or three times Martin and I had gone home with him at night.

—Hello, said a feeble voice.

—Frau Schwager, I said, this is Gottfried . . .

—Herr Gottfried, Frau Schwager said quickly, good that you called. Do you have any idea where my husband is?

—Your husband, I said confused.

—Yes, he said he was going to come home at night after the filming, but he hasn't checked in.

—I have no idea, I said, I just came out of the house myself.

—Herr Gottfried, Frau Schwager said, do something for me! Go by the Kauffelds' and check for me, see if he's there.

—Frau Schwager, I said, I don't know anyone named Kauffeld.

—Der Regisseur, sagte sie ungläubig, der Regisseur Kauffeld!

—Nein, sagte ich, kenne ich nicht.

Ihre Stimme wurde ganz hoffnungslos.

—Was soll ich denn machen, sagte sie. Ich trau mich ja gar nicht vom Telefon weg.

—Er wird sich schon melden, sagte ich, bestimmt!

Durch den Hörer drang ein merkwürdiges fauchendes Geräusch, und ich rief erschrocken: Frau Schwager! und merkte erst an ihrer erstickten Stimme, daß sie weinte.

—Wenn ihm was passiert ist, sagte sie und schluchzte, mein Gott, die Kinder!

Es war klar, was sie befürchtete, und ich war mir nicht sicher, ob sie nicht recht hatte, aber wir irrten uns beide. Ein halbes Jahr später spielte Schwager einen Kampfgruppenmann, der seine Freundin hindert, über die Grenze zu gehen.

—Was soll ihm denn passieren, sagte ich ins Telefon und gab meiner Stimme einen möglichst unbesorgten Klang, vielleicht versucht er gerade jetzt anzurufen.

—Meinen Sie, fragte sie unsicher.

—Bestimmt, sagte ich, aber sie hatte schon aufgelegt.

Ich ging die Schönhauser hinunter, ließ mich, ohne festes Ziel, durch das Menschengewühl treiben, wechselte unter den Trakt der Hochbahn, die sich grau und fest über die Straße wölbte. Straßenbahnen fuhren vorbei, olivgrüne Militärlastwagen, auf denen Uniformierte saßen mit eisernen Mienen. An der Dimitroff sprang mir ein Transparent ins Auge, das weiß auf rot ALLE KRAFT ZUR LÖSUNG DER ÖKONOMISCHEN HAUPTAUFGABE forderte, und ich bog rechts ab, die Eberswalder hinunter, vorbei an der Post und am Stadion. Überall dasselbe Bild, Sperrketten bewaffneter Kampfgruppen und auf beiden Seiten Menschen.

Ich spürte eine körperliche Sehnsucht nach Marie, schlug die Richtung nach Hause ein, lief instinktiv die Straßen in Grenznähe entlang, Kremmener, Rheinsberger, Anklamer, überall Menschen vor bröckelnden Fassaden, Kopfschütteln und heftige Armbewegungen. An einer Ecke standen Frauen und sahen hinüber auf die andere Seite. Eine rief: Verwandte ersten Grades dürfen immer, Verwandte zweiten Grades nur auf Genehmigung!, während eine andere wölfische Blicke um sich warf und gezwungen zu lachen begann.

—Nee, nee, sagte eine dritte, im Radio habe ich gehört . . .

Sie dämpfte ihre Stimme, als ich vorüberging.

Ich lief zur nächsten Straßenbahnhaltestelle und fuhr drei Stationen bis nach Hause. Als ich um die Ecke ging, griff jemand nach meinem Arm und hielt mich fest. Ich riß ihn aus der Umklammerung, sprang instinktiv zur Seite, als ich sah, daß es Martin war, der neben mir stand.

—The director, she said in disbelief, the director, Kauffeld!

—No, I said, I don't know him.

Her voice became completely desperate.

—Then what can I do, she said. I don't dare leave the phone for a second.

—He'll call in soon, I said, for sure!

A peculiar sputtering sound came out of the receiver and I shouted in alarm: Frau Schwager! and realized only then, from her choking voice, that she was crying.

—If something has happened to him, she said and sobbed, my God, the children!

It was clear what she was afraid of, and I was not sure she wasn't justified, but we were both wrong. Six months later Schwager played a member of a combat group who stops his girl friend from crossing over the border.

—Oh, what could happen to him, I said into the phone, and gave my voice as unconcerned a tone as possible, he might be trying to call right now.

—Do you think so, she asked uncertainly.

—Of course, I said, but she had already hung up.

I walked down Schönhauser, drifted without any particular destination through the throngs of people, crossed under a section of overhead tramway that arched sturdy and gray across the street. Streetcars passed by, olive-green military trucks on which uniformed men sat with stony expressions. On Dimitroff a banner caught my eye, demanding, white on red: STRENGTH TO MEET OUR CENTRAL ECONOMIC TASK, and I turned off to the right, down Eberswalder, past the post office and the stadium. Everywhere the same picture: cordons of armed combat troops and on both sides of them, people.

I felt a physical longing to be with Marie, set out in the direction of home, going instinctively along the streets close to the border, Kremmener, Rheinsberger, Anklamer, people in front of crumbling facades, shaking of hands and violent movements of the arms. Women stood on one corner and were looking over to the other side. One shouted: Immediate family can cross anytime, other relatives only with official approval, while another cast wolfish glances in all directions and started to laugh.

—No, no, said a third, on the radio I heard . . .

She lowered her voice as I passed by.

I walked to the next streetcar stop and rode the three stations home. As I went around the corner, someone grabbed my arm and held me firmly. I tore my arm out of his grip, sprang instinctively to one side, and I saw that it was Martin standing beside me.

3

Wir gingen in eine Kneipe gegenüber. Der Raum war überfüllt, es war laut und heiß, Rauch stand über den Köpfen. Wir zwängten uns an einen Tisch, an dem gerade zwei Plätze frei wurden, hatten dann Bier vor uns stehen und tranken uns zu.

Es war merkwürdig, aber seit ich Martin getroffen hatte, war meine Spannung gleich Null, das Bedürfnis zu reden verschwunden, wie wenn es nichts mehr gäbe, was problematisch sein konnte, sogar der dumpfe Druck in meinem Kopf hatte nachgelassen.

—Du warst in der Hütte, fragte ich Martin.

—Gestern abend. Aber wir sind noch weitergezogen. Ich hab woanders geschlafen, aber frag mich nicht, wo.

—Und Gret, fragte ich.

—Schluß, sagte er, seit gestern. Es ging ein halbes Jahr gut, aber jetzt ist es einfach zu Ende.

Er schien eher bedrückt als erleichtert, trank sein Bier aus und winkte dem Kellner. Mein Glas war noch halb voll.

—Wir haben bis mittags geschlafen. Rosenberg kam und hat es uns gesagt.

—Hör auf, sagte er und winkte ab, ich hab's aus dem Radio erfahren. Ein beschissener Tag!

Er rief wieder nach dem Kellner, und ich lehnte mich für einen Moment zurück, wischte mir den Schweiß von der Stirn, als mir jemand die Hand auf die Schulter legte. Neben mir stand ein älterer, hagerer Mann und sah mit Augen, wie sie Betrunkene haben, auf mich herab. Sein Hemd war durchgeschwitzt und hing an seinem Körper herunter.

—Die machen was mit uns, wa? sagte er mit einer schleppenden, aber kräftigen Stimme.

Mir war nach allem anderen zumute als nach einem Gespräch, schon gar nicht in einer Kneipe und mit einem Angetrunkenen. Ich zog meine Schulter weg, brummte so etwas wie jaja, du hast schon recht und drehte mich ein wenig herum. Der Mann zögerte einen Augenblick, lief dann aber weiter, und ich dachte schon, wir wären ihn los, als er Martin erblickte und leicht schwankend auf ihn zuging.

—Dreiundzwanzig Jahre, sagte der Mann, dreiundzwanzig Jahre war ich da. Fritz Lenk, Bauunternehmen, Charlottenburg, kennste sicher.

Martin schüttelte den Kopf. Ich dachte noch, das war ein Fehler!

—Polier war ich, sagte der Mann. Stunde viersiebzig.

Martin blieb stumm, sah dem Mann aber in die Augen.

—Kongreßhalle, kennste doch, ja? Hab ich gebaut, sagte der Mann und stieß seinen Zeigefinger auf das schweißnasse Hemd.

3

We went into a pub across the street. The room was overcrowded; it was loud and hot, and smoke hung in the air. We squeezed through to a table at which two seats had just become free, had beer set in front of us, and drank to each other.

It was strange, but since I had run into Martin my tension was immediately nil. My desire to talk had vanished, as though there were nothing more that could be a problem. Even the dull pressure in my head had eased up.

—You were at The Hut, I asked Martin.

—Yesterday evening. But we went on from there. I slept somewhere else, don't ask me where.

—And Gret, I asked.

—Finished, he said, since yesterday. It went fine for six months, but now it's simply over.

He seemed more depressed than relieved, drained his beer, and beckoned the waiter. My glass was still half full.

—We slept past noon. Rosenberg came and told us.

—Hold it, he said with a wave of his hand, I got it from the radio. What a lousy day!

He called again for the waiter, and I leaned back for a moment and was wiping the sweat from my forehead when someone laid a hand on my shoulder. Beside me stood an elderly, thin-faced man, looking down at me with eyes like drunken people have. His shirt was soaked with sweat and hung down on his body.

—They've really done it to us this time, huh? he said in a sluggish but powerful voice.

The last thing in the world I wanted was a conversation and especially not in a pub with somebody who was drunk. I pulled my shoulder away, growled something like, yeah, yeah, you said it, and turned a little away from him. The man hesitated for an instant and then went on by, but just as I thought we were rid of him, he caught sight of Martin and, staggering a little, walked up to him.

—Twenty-three years, said the man, twenty-three years I was there. Fritz Lenk Building Contractors, in Charlottenburg, I'm sure you've heard of it.

Martin shook his head. That, I thought, was a mistake!

—I was foreman, said the man. Four-seventy an hour.

Martin stayed silent, but looked the man in the eye.

—Congress Hall, now that you've heard of, right? I built it, said the man, and prodded with his index finger at his sweat-soaked shirt.

Martin nickte.

—Ach, sagte der Mann und ließ seinen hageren, sonnengebräunten Arm durch die Luft sausen: Ich sag dir, alles Verbrecher.

—Wen meinen Sie denn? fragte Martin.

Ich verstand ihn nicht. Was hatte es für einen Zweck, in einer Kneipe ein Gespräch anzufangen, und dann noch mit einem Angetrunkenen?

—Na, du machst mir Spaß, sagte der Mann und schüttelte den Kopf.

—Hör auf! sagte ich zu Martin, das hat doch keinen Zweck. Du kannst doch jetzt keine Diskussion anfangen.

Martin hörte nicht. Er sah aufmerksam auf den Mann. Ich hatte das Gefühl, er nahm ihn ernst.

—Polier war ich, verstehst du. Dreiundzwanzig Jahre. Und jetzt zerhaun die die Stadt.

—Hören Sie, sagte Martin, so können Sie das nicht sehen . . .

Der Mann fiel ihm ins Wort.

—Wo kommste denn her, Mann, wo biste denn her. Bist du denn überhaupt Berliner, du, bist du Berliner!

—Das hat doch nichts mit der Sache zu tun, sagte Martin, ob ich Berliner bin.

—Doch, schrie der Mann, doch!

—Aber diese Stadt, sagte Martin eindringlich und ernst, ist schon seit fünfzehn Jahren geteilt, seit wir diesen beschissenen Krieg verloren haben und . . .

—Hör mir auf mit dem Krieg! sagte der Mann laut. Ich hab dich gefragt, ob du Berliner bist.

—Nein, sagte Martin, wenn Sie es genau wissen wollen, ich bin kein Berliner.

—Dann halt die Fresse, sagte der Mann. Die haben die Stadt zerhaun, die Verbrecher, und wenn du wissen willst, wen ich meine, dann kann ich's dir auch sagen. Das sag ich ganz laut, hörst du, das ist mir scheißegal. Dreiundzwanzig Jahre war ich bei Lenk, hörst du, mir kannst du nischt weismachen.

—Hör uff, Kalle, sagte eine Stimme am Nebentisch. Du redst dir um Kopp und Kragen!

—Quatsch, sagte der Mann, der Kalle hieß, das kann jeder hören. Den Spitzbart meine ich, den Spitzbart!

In der Kneipe war es ganz still. Alle sahen zu uns herüber. Der Mann stand jetzt kerzengerade vor Martin, und ich fand, er sah gar nicht mehr betrunken aus. Schweiß schoß mir ins Gesicht. Ich wünschte, wir kämen so schnell wie möglich aus dieser Kneipe hinaus, aber Martin schien nichts von allen zu bemerken.

—So können Sie die Sache nicht sehen, sagte er. Aber wenn wir uns

Martin nodded.

—Oh, said the man and snapped his lean, suntanned arm up into the air: I tell you, they're all crooks.

—Who do you mean, asked Martin.

I did not understand him. What was the point of starting up a conversation in a pub, and on top of that, with somebody who was drunk.

—C'mon, you gotta be kidding, the man said and shook his head.

—Stop it! I said to Martin, there's no point in this. You really can't start a discussion right now.

Martin did not listen. He was looking intently at the man. I had the feeling he took him seriously.

—I was foreman, understand. Twenty-three years. And now they're hacking the city to pieces.

—Listen, said Martin, you can't look at it that way . . .

The man cut him off.

—Are you from around here, man, where do you come from? Are you even a Berliner, you, are you a Berliner?

—That's got nothing to do with it, said Martin, whether I'm a Berliner or not.

—Oh yes it does, shouted the man, yes it does.

—But this city, said Martin insistently and earnestly, has already been divided now for fifteen years, since we lost that lousy war and . . .

—Leave the war out of this! said the man loudly. I asked you if you were a Berliner.

—No, said Martin, if you want to know the truth, I'm not a Berliner.

—Then shut your trap, said the man. They've hacked up the city, those crooks, and if you want to know who I mean I can tell you. I'll say it nice and loud, y' hear, I don't give a shit who hears it. Twenty-three years I was at Lenk, y' hear, you can't fool me.

—Lay off, Kalle, said a man at the next table. You'll talk yourself into a neck stretching.

—Bull, said the man who was called Kalle, everybody can listen. That goatee, I mean, that little goatee, Ulbricht!

The pub fell completely silent. Everyone was looking over at us. The man stood straight as a nail in front of Martin, and I found that he no longer looked drunk. Sweat broke out on my face. I wished that we could get out of this pub as fast as possible, but Martin seemed not to notice any of it.

—You can't look at it that way, he said. But if we're going to talk unterhalten wollen, dann müssen wir schon sachlich bleiben.

Er sagte das ohne die geringste Spur von Erregung, ja mit beinahe freundlichem Ton, und der Mann schien zu stutzen, seine Schultern senkten sich unmerklich und sein Gesicht, das eben noch verkrampft und wie von Haß erfüllt war, nahm einen interessierten Ausdruck an. Wahrscheinlich wäre alles noch gut gegangen, hätte nicht die Stimme am Nebentisch gesagt: Paß uff, Kalle, das isn'n Hundertfufzichprozentiger! und der Mann, irritiert durch den Einwurf, plötzlich abwinkte und: Ach, leck mir die Bollen! schrie und ein anderer, ich weiß nicht wer, Martin, der gerade zum Glas griff, anstieß, so daß das Bier sich breit und gelb über den Tisch ergoß und das Glas herabfiel und mit klirrendem Geräusch zersprang. Wir standen auf, sahen uns im gleichen Moment umringt, wütende, haßerfüllte Gesichter, die bedrohlich näherrückten, jemand stieß mich von hinten, ich fiel gegen Martin, der sich nur mit Mühe aufrecht halten konnte, aber dann rief eine Stimme: Hört auf, verdammt! Es war der Wirt, der nun vor uns stand und raus hier! sagte, wenn ihr Streit anfangen wollt, dann nicht in meinem Lokal, und jetzt wird gezahlt und dann ab! Ich zog Geld aus der Tasche, reichte es dem Wirt und schob Martin, der nur widerstrebend ging, zur Tür. Ich wußte, es hatte keinen Zweck, und war im Grunde froh, daß es so glimpflich verlaufen war, und erst auf der Straße sah ich, daß Martin verletzt war.

—Mensch, du blutest ja! sagte ich erschrocken, aber als ich ihm mein Taschentuch hinhielt, lachte er, erstickte fast vor Lachen, aber es war ein unnatürliches, gezwungenes Lachen, so daß ich manchmal nicht wußte, ob er weinte, wenngleich ich mir einen weinenden Martin einfach nicht vorstellen konnte. Schließlich nahm er das Taschentuch, das ich noch immer in der Hand hielt, lehnte sich gegen eine Hauswand, seine Schultern zuckten leicht und arhythmisch, und dann drehte er sich herum und war wieder ganz normal.

4

Gegen vier Uhr waren wir am Institut. Das Klinikgelände war von Kampfgruppenleuten bewacht, aber ich kannte einen von der Gewerkschaft, und wir kamen unbeanstandet durch das Tor. Auf der Treppe begegnete uns Grombal. Er habe es eilig, müsse zur Anleitung, aber wir sollten unbedingt bei ihm vorbeischauen, unbedingt! rief er uns zu. Grombal war mit Martin ganz gut bekannt.

Oben stand Rosenberg; man sah ihm an, er freute sich, daß wir gekommen waren. Es seien außer uns noch drei Kollegen gekommen, spontan, sagte er bedeutungsvoll, sah Martin dabei an, entdeckte die Wunde:

this over, we'll really have to remain objective.

He said that without the slightest trace of excitement, in an almost friendly tone, and the man seemed to be startled, his shoulders sank imperceptibly, and his face, which had still been tense and as if filled with hate, took on an interested expression. Everything would probably have gone well, had the voice at the next table not said: Look out, Kalle, that's a hunnert-fifty-per-center! And the man, irritated by the remark, suddenly, with a dismissing sweep of his arm, shouted: Ah, kiss off! and another, I don't know who, gave Martin, who was just reaching for his glass, a shove, so that his beer spilled broad and yellow over the table, and the glass fell and shattered with a crash. We stood up and in the same instant found ourselves surrounded, raging hate-filled faces that moved threateningly nearer. Someone shoved me from behind. I fell against Martin, who had trouble keeping his feet, but then a voice yelled: Knock it off, damn it! It was the pub owner who stood suddenly in front of us and said: Get out of here! If you want to start a fight, don't do it in my place, now pay up and beat it! I pulled money out of my pocket, paid the man, and shoved Martin, who came only reluctantly, to the door. I knew that it was pointless and was basically glad that it had come off as lightly as it had, and it was only in the street that I noticed that Martin was hurt.

—Man, you're bleeding, I said in fright, but when I held out my handkerchief to him, he laughed, almost suffocated with laughter, but it was an unnatural, forced laughter, so that I was sometimes uncertain whether or not he was crying, although I simply could not imagine a crying Martin. Finally he took the handkerchief, which I was still holding in my hand, propped himself against the wall of a building, his shoulders twitched slightly and arhythmically, and then he turned around and was completely normal again.

4

At about four o'clock we were at the Institute. The clinic grounds were guarded by people from the combat groups, but I knew one of them from the union and we got through the entrance way without being stopped. On the steps we ran into Grombal. He was in a hurry, on his way to Instruction to find out how the official party position was going to run, but he said that no matter what, we should check with him later. No matter what! he called to us. Grombal and Martin knew each other very well.

Rosenberg was at the top of the stairs. You could tell that he was glad we had come. He said three other colleagues had come in addition to us, instinctively, he added meaningfully and looked at Martin, discovering his

Was ist denn mit Ihnen los? Martin winkte ab und ging zum Apothekenkasten. Doktor Schnabel kam aus dem Assistentenzimmer, hinter ihm einer der Doktoranden und Messemer, ein blasser, aufgeschossener Laborant, der nebenher Gedichte schrieb.

—Was ist denn passiert, fragte Rosenberg noch einmal, und ich erzählte ganz kurz unser Erlebnis und bemerkte dabei Martins verzogenes Gesicht, als Doktor Schnabel die Wunde auswusch.

—Es ist nur ein Hautriß, sagte er.

In meinem Labor stand alles so, wie ich es gestern verlassen hatte. Ich weiß noch, daß ich so etwas wie Befriedigung empfand, wie wenn man etwas entdeckt, das sich als unverrückbarer, absolut sicherer Wert herausstellt. Unter mir lag der Park zwischen der Chirurgie und der Neurologie. Der Rasen wirkte verstaubt, die Blätter der Bäume waren gelb an den Spitzen. Auf dem Weg stapfte eine Kolonne Grenzsoldaten in Richtung des S-Bahn-Traktes, der das Klinikgelände westlich abschloß und auch Grenzlinie war.

Ich wischte ein Fädchen vom Dach der Analysenwaage und ging wieder zu den anderen. Messemer hatte Tee gekocht, auch ich nahm mir ein Glas und goß es voll. Rosenberg, der eine Vorliebe für bedeutungsvolle Sätze hatte, hob sein Glas und sagte: Ich glaube, dieser Tag ist der wichtigste, seit dieser Staat gegründet wurde, ja vielleicht ist er sogar die wirkliche Geburtsstunde des deutschen sozialistischen Staates.

Niemand widersprach. Doktor Schnabel war, wie wir, durch die Stadt gelaufen, seit dem frühen Morgen schon, war die ganze Grenze abgelaufen, von Wilhelmsruh bis zum Potsdamer Platz. In Pankow hatte er gesehen, daß man vergessen hatte, ein Eckhaus zu besetzen, und die Leute eine ganze Stunde lang durch die Tür auf unserer Seite hinein und durch die andere Tür drüben wieder hinausgegangen waren.

Der Doktorand hatte gehört, daß in der Bernauer, in der die Häuserfront der einen Straßenseite noch zu uns, der Gehsteig davor aber schon zum Westen gehörte, Leute aus dem Fenster gesprungen waren, auf Matratzen und Federbetten, einer sogar aus dem vierten Stock.

—Mein Gott, sagte Doktor Schnabel und griff sich an die Stirn, er hat fünfzehn Jahre Zeit gehabt, über die Straße zu gehen, und hat es nicht getan, und dann springt er aus dem vierten Stock!

—Es ist einfach Panik, sagte ich, sicher ist es Panik.

—Dabei hat man sich an den fünf Fingern abzählen können, daß über kurz oder lang dicht gemacht wird, sagte Rosenberg. Kein vernünftiger Mensch hat doch geglaubt, daß wir das noch lange mit ansehen.

—Die letzte Zeit waren es täglich dreitausend, sagte der Doktorand, und die Kurve stieg noch an.

—Ach, sagte Doktor Schnabel, trauen Sie nicht der Statistik.

—Na, jetzt ist die Kurve jedenfalls auf Null, sagte Rosenberg trokwound: What on earth happened to you? Martin waved the question off and walked to the medicine cabinet. Doctor Schnabel came out of the assistants' room, behind him one of the graduate students and Messemer, a pale, lanky lab technician who wrote poems on the side.

—What on earth happened, asked Rosenberg a second time. I told him briefly of our experience, in the meanwhile noticing Martin's contorted face as Doctor Schnabel washed out the wound.

—It's just a scratch, he said.

In my laboratory everything was just as I had left it the day before. I remember that I felt something like satisfaction, as if I'd found something that turned out to be of unshakable and absolutely certain value. Below my window lay the park between Surgery and Neurology. The grass had a dusty look. The leaves of the trees were yellow at the tips. A column of border troops trudged along the walk in the direction of the stretch of S-Bahn tracks that bounded the Clinic grounds to the west and was also now the border.

I brushed a thread from the cover of the analytical scales and went back to the others. Messemer had made tea. I got myself a glass and poured it full. Rosenberg, who had a penchant for meaningful phrases, raised his glass and said: I believe this day is the most important day since the founding of this state, yes, it may even be the virtual hour of birth for the German Socialist State.

No one contradicted him. Doctor Schnabel had walked through the city, as we had, but beginning early in the morning, and he had walked the entire border, from Wilhelmsruh to Potsdamer Platz. In Pankow he had noticed that someone had forgotten to secure a house on a corner, and for a full hour people had gone in through the door on our side and walked out through the other door, on the other side of the border.

The graduate student had heard that on Bernauer, where the houses on one side of the street still belonged to us but the sidewalk in front of them was already in Western territory, people had jumped from the windows onto mattresses and eiderdowns, one had even jumped from the fifth floor!

—My God, said Doctor Schnabel and put his hand to his forehead, he had fifteen years' time to cross that street and didn't do it, and now he jumps from the fifth floor!

—It's simply panic, I said, it's definitely panic.

—As far as that's concerned, it was as plain as the nose on your face that things would be sealed up sooner or later, said Rosenberg. No one in his right mind really believed we could tolerate it for much longer.

—The last few weeks three thousand a day were leaving, said the graduate student, and the curve was still rising.

—Pah, said Doctor Schnabel, don't trust statistics.

—Well, in any case, the curve is on zero now, said Rosenberg drily.

ken. Wir lachten, bis auf Martin und den Laboranten.

—Ich weiß nicht, sagte Messemer leise, wie Sie darüber lachen können. Verstehen Sie, ich bin ja nicht dagegen. Ich meine nur, hinter jedem Menschen, der weggeht oder sogar aus dem Fenster springt, da steckt doch ein Schicksal. Ich meine, jeder ist doch was und hier . . . naja . . . hat gewisse Rechte . . . ja . . . über sich und sein Leben, meine ich.

Messemer kam ins Stocken.

—Kommen Sie mir nicht mit diesem bürgerlichen Kram, sagte Rosenberg. Freizügigkeit und ähnliche Sachen, wenn ich das höre! Die haben uns systematisch kaputt machen wollen! Das war Klassenkampf, und da hört der Spaß auf!

Messemer wurde rot und brachte kein Wort mehr heraus.

—Versteh doch, sagte Doktor Schnabel zu Rosenberg, er ist doch im Prinzip dafür, er meint doch nur das Individuelle und das Gesellschaftliche, und daß da ein Widerspruch . . .

Rosenberg ließ ihn nicht ausreden. Er sah auf Martin, der bisher geschwiegen hatte.

—Und was meinen Sie? fragte Rosenberg.

Martin sah ihn an. Sein Gesicht hatte einen merkwürdig traurigen Ausdruck.

—Bitte, sagte Rosenberg, Ihre Meinung interessiert mich.

—Komm, hör doch auf, sagte Schnabel besänftigend, aber Rosenberg reagierte nicht, hielt seine blaßblauen runden Augen weiterhin auf Martin geheftet, als glaubte er, er müsse ihn zwingen zu sprechen, in diesem Moment und in keinem anderen.

Rosenberg und Martin musterten sich. Martin griff in die Tasche, zog eine Zigarette heraus und zündete sie sich in aller Ruhe an.

—Ich glaube, sagte er zwischen zwei Zügen, es gibt Alternativen, vor die ein Mensch nicht gestellt werden sollte.

Rosenberg zog seinen massigen Körper voll Luft und stieß sie, eher empört als befriedigt, wieder aus.

—Na, und weiter? sagte er.

—Nichts weiter, sagte Martin.

—Das ist ausgesprochen wenig, sagte Rosenberg.

Das Telefon im Gang klingelte. Doktor Schnabel ging hinaus und nahm den Hörer ab, kam wenige Momente später wieder und sagte zu Martin: Herr Grombal hat angerufen, er will jetzt gleich rübergehen.

—Danke, sagte Martin, und ich stand auf.

We all laughed, except for Martin and the lab technician.

—I don't know how you can laugh about it, said Messemer quietly. You understand, I'm not against it. I just mean, behind every person who leaves, or for that matter who jumps out of a window, there is a destiny. I mean, each of them counts and here has . . . well . . . has certain rights . . . yes . . . in regard to himself and to his life, in my opinion.

Messemer faltered.

—Don't come at me with that bourgeois rubbish, said Rosenberg. Freedom of movement and settlement and such things, when I hear that stuff! They wanted to systematically break us down! That was a class struggle, and that's where the fun stops!

Messemer turned red and did not say another word.

—Try to understand, said Doctor Schnabel to Rosenberg, he's for it in principle. He just means the individual and the societal, and that a contradiction . . .

Rosenberg did not let him finish. He looked at Martin, who had been silent up to then.

—And what do you think, asked Rosenberg.

Martin looked at him. His face bore a strangely sad expression.

—Please, said Rosenberg, your opinion interests me.

—Come on, you could ease up a little, said Schnabel placatingly, but Rosenberg did not respond, kept his round blue eyes still fastened on Martin, as if he believed he had to force him to speak, in this moment and in no other.

Rosenberg and Martin eyed one another. Martin reached in his pocket, took out a cigarette, and lit it calmly, taking his time.

—I think, said Martin between two draws on his cigarette, that there are alternatives a person should never be confronted with.

Rosenberg drew a deep breath into his bulky body, more with indignation than satisfaction, and forced it out again.

—Well, and what else, he asked.

—That's all, said Martin.

—That's certainly not very much, said Rosenberg.

The telephone in the corridor rang. Doctor Schnabel went out and picked up the receiver, came back a few minutes later, and said to Martin: Herr Grombal called. He'll be going over right away.

—Thanks, said Martin, and I stood up.

5

Wir gingen hinüber in die Radiologie, die im nordwestlichen Teil des Klinikgeländes lag, unmittelbar an der Grenze. Grombal hatte sein Zimmer im Erdgeschoß, war aber noch nicht dort, und so liefen wir im Flur auf und ab, er mußte ja gleich kommen.

Wir gingen an den elfenbeinfarbenen Bänken, auf denen an Sprechtagen die Patienten saßen, vorbei, rauchten und schnippten die Asche in die kastenförmigen Behälter, die an der Wand angebracht waren, standen dann im hinteren Teil des Ganges, genau vor der Tür, die auf die Straße führte. Ich drückte auf die Klinke, die hart war und kühl. Ich weiß bis heute nicht, was mich dazu veranlaßte. Jeder wußte doch, die Tür war versperrt. So wie jeder wußte, daß es von dort nur wenige Schritte bis zur Grenze waren. Heute frage ich mich oft, ob ich die Klinke heruntergedrückt hätte, wenn mir klar gewesen wäre, was dann folgte.

Ich drückte also auf die Klinke und öffnete die Tür. Sonnenlicht traf mich so überraschend, daß ich die Augen zusammenkniff. Ich spürte Martins Hand in meinem Rücken, die mich sanft nach vorne schob, trat hinaus, stockte aber schon nach wenigen Schritten, so daß Martin an meine Seite kam, mich überholte, die zwei Stufen, die auf das Straßenpflaster führten, hinabschritt und dort stehenblieb. Ich folgte ihm zögernd und begriff erst jetzt, in welcher Situation wir uns befanden. Ich sah rechts von uns, vielleicht sechs oder sieben Meter entfernt, die stahlgrauen Uniformen der Kampfgruppenleute, die geschulterten Maschinenpistolen, den LKW, der mit dem schwarzen Schlund seiner Hinterfront uns zugewandt war und von dem einige Männer Gitterzäune abluden und sie quer über die Straße aufzustellen begannen, genau zwischen sich und der Menge schauender Menschen; ich sah links von uns die Brücke, die über den trüben, ölschlierigen Kanal führte, sah eine Gruppe grünuniformierter Polizisten, einen französischen Jeep und lässig herumstehende Reporter, denen Fotoapparate vor der Brust und an den Handgelenken baumelten, und vor uns, hoch und grau, die Seitenfront eines Amtsgebäudes, und, gelbgrün und spärlich belaubt, die Bäume davor und die Menschen hinter dem Gitterzaun, der sich langsam komplettierte, ein frischgelackter Metallzaun, grasgrüner Strich auf steingrauer Straße, und der Geruch nach Staub, Kanalwasser und Spätsommer, der mich so plötzlich traf wie die Ahnung, ich stünde an einem Platz, den einzunehmen ich gar nicht in der Lage war, gezwungen etwas zu tun, nach links zu gehen oder nach rechts, ein Zwang, der sich von selbst ergab und dem nachzukommen es nur ein paar Bewegungen des Körpers bedurfte, zehn oder zwölf Schritte vielleicht, nicht mehr. Wir standen dazwischen, standen genau zwischen den stahlgrauen Uniformen der Kampfgruppenleute auf dieser und den grasgrünen Uniformen der Polizisten auf der anderen

5

We walked over into Radiology, which was in the northwestern part of the Clinic complex, and right on the border. Grombal's room was on the ground floor, but he was not there yet, so we walked up and down in the corridor; he would surely come soon.

We walked past the ivory-colored benches on which the patients sat on the days the Clinic was open, smoked, and flicked our ashes into the box-like receptacles fastened to the walls, then, in the back part of the hallway, stood right in front of the door that opened onto the street. I pressed the door handle down. It was hard and cool. I don't know to this day what made me do it. Everyone knew the door was locked. Just as everyone knew that it was only a few steps from there to the border. Today I often wonder if I would have pressed the door handle down, if it had been clear to me what would follow.

So I pressed down the handle and opened the door. Sunlight struck me so unexpectedly that I flinched and squinted my eyes. I felt Martin's hand on my back, gently pushing me forward, stepped out, but hesitated after only a few steps, so that Martin came to my side, passed me, stepped down the two steps to the street, and there came to a halt. I followed him hesitantly, and only then began to grasp the situation we were in. I saw to our right, perhaps six or seven meters away, the steel-gray uniforms of the people from the combat groups, the shouldered submachine guns, the truck turned with its back to us, a gaping pit from which several men were unloading chainlink fence and beginning to set it up straight across the street, right between themselves and the crowd of watching people. I saw to our left the bridge that led over the murky, oil-streaked canal, saw a group of green-uniformed policemen, a French jeep, and reporters standing around casually, cameras dangling at their chests or from their wrists, and in front of us, high and gray, the side of an office building and the yellow-green, sparsely leaved trees in front of it, and the people behind the fence that was slowly being completed, a freshly painted metal fence, a grass-green stroke on the stone-gray street, and the smell of dust, canal water, and late summer, which struck me suddenly as the realization that I was in a position impossible for me to hold, compelled to do something, to move to the left or to the right, a compulsion that was resolving itself, that required only a few movements of the body to be satisfied, ten or twelve paces perhaps, nothing more. We were standing in the middle, exactly in the middle, between the steel-gray uniforms of the combat groups on this side and the grass-green uniforms of the policemen on the other! It was a position, or better, a situation that I

Seite! Es war ein Platz oder besser: eine Situation, bei der ich instinktiv wußte, sie war so gewaltig für mich, daß ich ihr nicht in gleicher Größe gegenübertreten konnte, ja ich empfand ein körperliches Gefühl der Kleinheit, und es traf mich mit einer solchen Heftigkeit, daß ich mich sekundenlang nicht bewegen konnte, als der uns nächststehende Kampfgruppenmann den Kopf drehte, uns bemerkte und eher erschrocken als drohend, aber nichtsdestoweniger mit scharfer Stimme rief: Treten Sie zurück, Bürger!, wodurch er sofort die Aufmerksamkeit der Menschengruppe links von uns erregte, und ich spürte die Blicke der Grünuniformierten, wache, gespannte, beinahe suggestive Blicke, während die Reporter ihre Kameras vor die Augen rissen, und auch rechterhand starrten drei, vier Dutzend Augenpaare auf uns, mit ebenso wachen, ebenso gespannten, ebenso suggestiven Blicken.

Ich weiß nicht, wie lange das alles dauerte, sicher nicht länger als ein paar Sekunden; ich war mir sicher, daß alles gleich zu Ende sein würde, meine Lähmung, dieses merkwürdige Gefühl der Nichtigkeit, sicher war das alles gleich vorbei, dachte ich, und konnte schon meine Schultern bewegen, als Martin losging. Er ging einfach los! Erst langsam, als zögere er, dann schneller und entschlossen. Ich stand und begann zu schrumpfen. Etwas Unbekanntes, Fremdes legte sich über meine Haut, sog meinen Kopf leer, schlug auf meinen Magen, riß an den Därmen und zog die Hoden unerträglich schmerzhaft zusammen. Ich stand, schnappte nach Luft und sah Martins Rücken sich entfernen, hatte den Gedanken, daß ich jetzt meine Beine bewegen müßte, ganz mechanisch ihm folgen, wie ich es immer getan hatte, sah plötzlich Marie und ihren berghohen Bauch, hörte Rosenbergs polternden Triumpf und das schnarrende Schnappen der Objektivverschlüsse wie hundertfach verstärktes Maschinengewehrhämmern; vor mir das Amtsgebäude wuchs mitsamt seinen spärlich belaubten Bäumen ins Riesenhafte, und tatsächlich schien mich niemand zu bemerken, alle standen und starrten auf Martin, die einen auf seinen Rücken, die anderen auf sein Gesicht, alle auf Martin, als wäre ich nicht vorhanden, so daß ich, meiner Glieder wieder mächtig, langsam mich rückwärts zu bewegen begann, im Krebsgang schlich ich, hob vorsichtig, als ich den Widerstand der ersten Stufe an meinem Hacken spürte, erst das rechte, dann das linke Bein, und weiter zurück, zur zweiten Stufe, ließ meinen Kopf unbewegt, nur meine Augen schossen nach links und nach rechts, jetzt war ich ganz wach, und noch immer sah keiner zu mir hin, und als ich die Tür in meinem Rücken spürte, hinter mich griff und tastend die Klinke erreichte, wagte ich meinen Kopf nach links zu drehen, sah Martin die Brücke überqueren und sich umdrehen, suchte seine Augen, aber da war er schon umringt von Reportern und Polizisten und versank in einem Gewühl heftig gestikulierender Menschen, während ich mich unbemerkt durch die Tür schob, im langen Gang der Klinik stand und wie betäubt und ohne etwas zu bemerken hinauslief.

knew instinctively was so overwhelming for me that I could not contend with it on equal terms. I felt a sensation of physical smallness, and it seized me with such violence that for a few moments I could not move as the man standing nearest to us in the combat group turned his head, noticed us, and more in alarm than threateningly, but nonetheless with a sharp voice, shouted: Step back there, citizens! which immediately attracted the attention of the group of people to the left of us, and I felt the eyes of those in the green uniforms, alert, tense, almost suggestive gazes, while the reporters whipped their cameras up in front of their eyes, and on the righthand side as well, three, four dozen pairs of eyes stared at us with gazes just as alert, just as intense, just as suggestive.

I don't know how long that all lasted, certainly not longer than a few seconds; I was certain that everything would be over soon, my paralysis, this strange feeling of total hollowness, certainly that all would be over quickly, I thought, and could already move my shoulders as Martin took off. He just went! First slowly as if he was hesitating, then more quickly and decisively. I stood there and began to shrink. Something unknown, foreign, lay over my skin, sucked my head empty, pounded at my stomach, tore at my gut, and pulled my testicles unbearably painfully together. I stood there, gasped for breath, and saw Martin's back moving away, had the thought that I must move my legs, completely mechanically follow him as I had always done, suddenly saw Marie and her belly, big as a mountain, heard Rosenberg's blustering triumph and the whirring snap of the shutters, like the hammer of a machine gun a hundred times amplified; in front of me the office building and its trees with meager leaves grew enormous, and in fact no one seemed to be noticing me, everyone was standing and staring at Martin, on the one side at his back and on the other at his face, all of them at Martin, as if I did not exist, so that I, in control of my limbs again, slowly began to move backwards, in a crab-like motion I crept back, carefully, as I felt the resistance of the first step against my heel, lifted first the right, then the left leg, and farther back, to the second step, kept my head unmoving, only my eyes shot to the left and to the right, I was totally alert, and still no one looked over at me. And when I felt the door at my back, I reached behind me and gropingly found the door handle, I risked turning my head to the left, saw Martin cross over the bridge and turn around, sought his eyes, but he was already surrounded by reporters and policemen, and he sank down into a throng of violently gesturing people, while I crept unnoticed through the door into the long hallway of the Clinic, and, as if in a daze and without noticing anything, ran out.

ZEIT OHNE GLOCKEN
Auszug

HORST BIENEK

SIE GINGEN WEITER IN RICHTUNG ZUR BADEANSTALT, JETZT SCHNELLER ALS vorher. Als ob sie es nicht erwarten konnten, mit den Evangelischen zusammenzustoßen.

Der Hannes, entschied Andi, fängt an. Er wirft die ersten Steine!

Er würde schon darauf achten, daß er tatsächlich anfinge, und damit würden auch seine letzten Zweifel ausgeräumt sein.

Damit kannst du dich in unsrer *Ferajna* bewähren, sagte Wonzak. Er konnte es sich bis heute nicht eingestehen, daß es die *Ferajna* nicht mehr geben sollte. Vielleicht waren zwei, drei Jungs, wenn sie nur fest entschlossen waren, auch schon eine *Ferajna*.

Also, ich bin dabei. Und ich fange auch an, wenn ihr wollt! sagt Hannes. Er hätte sich lieber woanders bewährt. Aber vielleicht würde er dadurch einen Freund gewinnen, das würde ihm dieser Einsatz wert sein. Für den Wonzak allein hätte er das niemals getan. Er mußte sich ganz schön ranhalten, um mit den andern Schritt zu halten. Außer Atem brachte er hervor: Andi, was du da vorhin gesagt hast, ich meine über die Evangelischen, das stimmt so nicht . . .

Willst du nicht mehr mitmachen? unterbrach Andi mißtrauisch.

Nein, drum geht es nicht, sagte Hannes. Ich mach mit, das hab ich erklärt. Ich mein was anderes, unabhängig davon, also ich mein . . . Er mußte seinen Schritt wechseln, weil ihm der Ossadnick ein Stück voraus war . . . die sind nicht anders als du und ich—wenn sie glauben. Natürlich nur, wenn sie glauben. Sie haben das gleiche Vaterunser, sie beten den gekreuzigten Christus an wie wir, sie glauben an die Auferstehung wie wir, und sie . . .

Noch einmal unterbrach Andi: Woher weißt du das alles so genau? Es war nicht allein der alte Verdacht, der in ihm aufstieg, ihn störte auch, daß Hannes sich widersetzte, bevor ihre Freundschaft besiegelt war. Schmeißt du nun als erster die Steine oder nicht? Die Stimme schnitt wie ein Messer.

Ja doch, sagte Hannes. Tu ich. Wenn du es verlangst.

Ich denke, das sind zwei verschiedene Sachen, sagte Andi. Jetzt geht es darum, ob du zu uns gehörst, dann mußt du das machen, was wir von dir verlangen, und das ist erst der Anfang. Es werden noch andere Dinge auf dich zukommen!

TIME WITHOUT BELLS
Excerpt

HORST BIENEK
translated by Ralph R. Read III

THEY WALKED ALONG IN THE DIRECTION OF THE PUBLIC BATH, FASTER NOW than before. As if they could not wait to clash with the Lutherans.

Hannes, decided Andi, will start it. He'll throw the first stones!

He would see to it that he actually did start it, and this would clear away his last doubts, too.

You can prove yourself in our ferajna that way, Wonzak said. To this day he could not admit to himself that there would be no ferajna anymore. Maybe two or three guys together, if only they were very determined, constituted a ferajna.

Well, I'm with you. And I'll be the one to start, if you want me to, Hannes said. He would rather have proven himself some other way. But maybe this would win him a friend, that would make the investment worth it. He would never have done it for Wonzak alone. It was all he could do to keep pace with the other two. Out of breath, he gasped: Andi, what you were saying before, I mean about the Lutherans, that's not the way it is . . .

Don't you want to go along with us? Andi asked, mistrustful.

No, that's not what it's about, Hannes said. I'll go along, just like I said. I mean something else, something different, well, I mean . . . He had to lengthen his stride, Ossadnik was getting ahead of him again. . . . They're no different than you and me—if they believe. Naturally, only if they believe. They have the same Pater Noster, they pray to Christ on the Cross, like we do, they believe in the Resurrection like we do, and they . . .

Andi interrupted him again: How do you know all that so well? It was not merely the old suspicion rising in him again, it bothered him that Hannes was resisting before their friendship was sealed. Are you going to be the first one to throw the stones, or not? His voice cut like a knife.

Yes, I will, Hannes said. I'll do it if you want me to.

I think that's two different things, Andi said. What matters is whether you're going with us, then you have to do what we tell you to, and that's just the beginning. There are other things in store for you!

Hannes Stein antwortete nicht, aber sein Blick, den er Ossadnik zuwarf, verriet mehr von seiner Bereitschaft, als jedes Wort es hätte ausdrücken können.

Hinter dem alten Schützenhaus fingen sie an, Steine zu sammeln, weiße und graue Kiesel, die sie in einem ausgetrockneten Bachbett neben der Straße fanden. Sie füllten damit ihre Hosensäcke, die immer voller und schwerer wurden. Andi mußte seine mit den Händen festhalten, damit sie nicht durchrissen. Als sie sich an der Ecke Neue-Welt und Passon-Straße—man konnte schon die Richtersdorfer Badeanstalt und den Friedhof sehen—den Baracken des KLV-Lagers näherten, merkten sie, daß sie alle drei bereits eine Weile geschwiegen hatten. Sie spürten jetzt die Stille des Vormittags beinahe körperlich. In der Entfernung sahen sie ein paar Jungen zwischen den Baracken, vernahmen aber kein Geräusch. Es war wie in einem Theaterstück, nachdem der Vorhang aufgegangen war und Schauspieler wie Publikum auf das erste Stichwort warteten. Sie näherten sich die Einfahrt, die durch einen heruntergelassenen Schlagbaum versperrt war, aber links und rechts davon führten Fußwege in das Lager hinein. Den Schlagbaum empfanden sie—unausgesprochen—als eine Barriere, als eine Grenze, die sie nicht überschreiten wollten, obwohl sie keiner daran gehindert hätte. Auf der linken Seite wuchsen Ginstersträucher, die schon im Verblühen waren. Dahinter versteckten sie sich. Nein, verstecken konnte man das nicht nennen, das hätte wohl auch ihrer Absicht widersprochen. Sie wollten die Überraschung nur etwas vergrößern.

Wenn es aber keine Evangelischen sind, flüsterte Hannes. Er hätte ruhig laut sprechen können.

Es sind Evangelen, log Andi Ossadnick. Ich bin ganz schön aufgeregt. Und ihr?

Um die Wahrheit zu sagen, er war von allen dreien der aufgeregteste. Für die andern war es ein Abenteuer, ein Jungenstreich, ein Nervenkitzel, für ihn war es mehr. Für ihn war es die Geißelung.

Und nicht auf die Fensterscheiben, sagte Andi leise, sonst machen sie hinterher Sabotage draus. Nur auf die Dächer einen Steinregen. Und dann abtrimoo!

Sie knieten sich hin, entleerten ihre Hosensäcke und schichteten die Steine zu kleinen Häufchen. Nur ganz wenige ließen sie in den Taschen zurück, damit sie bei der Flucht Munition hatten. Sie sprachen jetzt kaum noch ein Wort.

Andi forderte Hannes mit einer Kopfbewegung auf, zu beginnen, und Hannes warf den ersten Stein. Sie hörten einen leisen Anprall auf das Dach der Baracke. Zu leise, um ihre Herzen höher schlagen zu lassen oder gar das Blut in den Kopf zu treiben, wie sie es sich eigentlich gewünscht hatten. Und vielleicht noch etwas mehr, wobei sie nicht wußten, was dieses

Hannes Stein did not answer, but the look he gave Ossadnik conveyed his readiness better than any words could have expressed.

Behind the old rifle club they began to collect stones, white and gray pebbles that they found in a dry creek bed next to the road. They filled their pockets with them, which kept getting fuller and heavier. Andi had to hold his up with his hands to keep them from tearing. When they were approaching the barracks of the Children's Evacuee Camp at the corner of Neue Welt and Passonstrasse—the Richtersdorf public bath and the cemetery were already in sight—they noticed that all three of them had been silent for quite some time. They felt the morning's silence almost physically now. In the distance they saw a few boys between the barracks, but they did not hear a sound. It was like a drama, after the curtain has risen, and the actors as well as the spectators are waiting for the first cue. They approached the entry, which was blocked by a lowered crossing gate, but to the right and left of it footpaths led into the camp. They sensed the crossing gate—unconsciously—to be a barricade, a border that they did not want to cross although no one would have stopped them. Gorse bushes with already fading blossoms were growing off to the left. They hid behind them. No, they were not really hiding, that would have contradicted their intention. They just wanted to intensify the surprise.

But what if they're not Lutherans? Hannes whispered. It would not have mattered if he had spoken out loud.

Those are Lutherans, Andi Ossadnik lied. Am I ever excited. How about you?

To tell the truth, he was the most excited of the three. For the others it was an adventure, a prank, a thrill; for him it was more. For him it was the scourging.

And not at the windows, Andi said softly, otherwise they'll call it sabotage afterwards. Just at the roofs, a rain of stones. And then hit the road!

They kneeled down, emptied their pockets, and arranged the stones in little piles. They left only a few in their pockets so they would have some ammunition for their retreat. They spoke hardly a word.

With a nod, Andi directed Hannes to begin, and Hannes cast the first stone. They heard a soft thump on a barracks roof. Too soft to make their hearts beat faster, let alone drive the blood to their heads, which is what they were hoping for. And perhaps for something more, without

Mehr bedeuten würde. Aber es würde ihren öden, langweiligen, grauen Vormittag verändern.

Und Hannes, von den Blicken der anderen ermuntert, warf noch einen Stein, und ein dritter Wurf folgte nach. Das war für die andern beiden das Signal, jetzt ihre Steine in das Lager zu schleudern. Sie hatten kein genaues Ziel, sie ließen die Steine einfach auf die Baracken regnen. Sie warfen und warfen. Und lauschten. Auf einmal das Klirren einer Fensterscheibe.

Andi fühlte, das war das Geräusch, auf das er die ganze Zeit gewartet hatte. Nun stieg ihm die Hitze ins Gesicht und veranlaßte ihn, noch schneller die Steine hinüberzuschleudern. Er sah nichts, er hörte nur. Er hörte Stimmengewirr, Türenschlagen, Schritte auf Holz, einen Schrei. Jedes Geräusch machte sein Gesicht ein Stück heller.

Im Lager stürzten die Jungen aus den Baracken und wirbelten eine Weile hin und her, ehe sie begriffen, was los war. Der erste, der die Angreifer hinter dem Ginsterstrauch entdeckte, zeigte mit beiden Händen auf sie, aber stumm und ratlos, und es dauerte eine Zeit, bis die andern ihre Überraschung überwanden und auf sie losstürzten. Im Laufen fingen sie an zu schreien, um sich gegenseitig anzustacheln, im Laufen sammelten sie Erdklumpen auf oder Holzstücke, einer schwenkte eine Zaunlatte.

Pjerunnische Evangelen! Reformierte!

Heiden! Lutheraner! Freigeister!

Protestanten! Schweine!

Andi konnte sich später nicht erinnern, wer mit den Beschimpfungen angefangen hatte. Sie warfen den jetzt heranstürmenden Jungen die letzten Steine entgegen und begannen wegzurennen. Andi rannte in die Richtung der Schießstände. Er vernahm das Geschrei seiner Verfolger hinter sich, aber da sie alle drei in verschiedenen Richtungen weggelaufen waren, wurde es bald schwächer. Er blickte sich im Laufen um und sah etwa fünf oder sechs Jungen, die hinter ihm her waren und aus der Entfernung Steine nach ihm warfen; einer hatte ihn am Rücken getroffen, ein anderer am Kopf, er hatte nur einen dumpfen Prall, keinen richtigen Schmerz gespürt. Andi sprang über den versiegten Bach und drehte sich noch einmal um, als ihn ein Stein direkt ins Gesicht traf und seine Brille herunterriß, er konnte sie gerade noch festhalten, wobei er merkte, daß ein Glas zersplittert war. Er rannte und keuchte, keuchte, rannte. Das Auge war nicht verletzt, aber Splitter mußten seine Haut geritzt haben. Er spürte keinen Schmerz, nur den Geschmack von Blut auf den Lippen. Er rannte weiter und dachte daran, daß ihn beim Geräusch der splitternden Fensterscheibe eine seltsame Erregung erfaßt hatte. Es war ein Erschrecken dabeigewesen, auch über sich selbst, so wie jetzt das Erschrecken über knowing what this more would mean. But it would change their dreary, boring, gray morning.

And Hannes, encouraged by the glances of the others, threw another stone, and a third followed. That was the signal for the other two to hurl their stones into the camp. They had no exact target, they simply rained the stones down on the barracks. They threw and threw. And listened. All at once the shattering of a window.

Andi felt that was the sound he had been waiting for the whole time. Now the heat rose to his face and made him hurl the stones even faster. He saw nothing, he only heard. He heard the babble of voices, door slamming, steps on wood, a shout. Every sound made his face a shade brighter.

In the camp the boys tumbled out of the barracks and milled around for a while before they realized what was happening. The first to spot the attackers behind the gorse bushes pointed at them with both hands, but silent and stymied, and it took a while for the rest to recover from their surprise and dash towards them. They began to yell as they ran, to goad each other on, they picked up clumps of dirt or pieces of wood as they ran, one of them was brandishing a fence picket.

Pjerunnish Lutherans! Reformers!

Heathens! Evangelicals! Free-thinkers!

Protestants! Swine!

Afterwards Andi could not remember who had begun the name-calling. They threw their last stones at the boys storming towards them and began to flee. Andi ran in the direction of the rifle range. He heard the yelling of his pursuers behind him, but since all three of them had run off in different directions, it soon grew weaker. He looked back as he ran and saw about five or six boys chasing him, throwing stones at him from a distance; one of them had hit him in the back, another on the head; he had felt only a dull thud, no pain, really. Andi leaped over the creek bed, and as he turned around again, a stone hit him directly in the face and knocked his glasses loose; he was just barely able to catch them, noticing that one lens was shattered. He ran and gasped, gasped, ran. His eye was not injured, but slivers of glass must have cut his skin. He did not feel any pain, just the taste of blood on his lips. He ran on, thinking about how a strange excitement had seized him at the sound of the shattering window pane. There had been fear there, fright at himself too, just as now fright at his seine Verfolger, zusammen mit einer unerklärbaren Sehnsucht, von ihnen gefangen zu werden.

Was würde geschehen, wenn er jetzt stehenbliebe? Sie würden über ihn herfallen, auch wenn er sich wehrte, es würde nichts nützen, sie waren in der Überzahl. Sie würden ihn zusammenschlagen und liegenlassen. Oder sie würden ihn zurückjagen ins Lager und ihn der Wut der andern ausliefern. Oder sie würden ihn krankenhausreif schlagen und ihn der Polizei ausliefern, wegen der Fensterscheibe.

Sollten sie ihn schlagen, quälen, erniedrigen, ja, er verdiente eine solche Bestrafung, nicht für das Steinewerfen, nicht für die blöde Fensterscheibe, natürlich nicht, für etwas anderes, für eine Schuld, für seine Schuld, und er dachte nicht an etwas Bestimmtes, er dachte an die Schuld, die jeder vor IHM hatte, und die nicht aufhören würde. Er dachte daran, wie sie IHN gegeißelt und mit Dornen gekrönt hatten. Wie SEINE Hände und Füße von Nägeln durchbohrt wurden.

Plötzlich blieb er stehen, er stoppte so rasch, daß er sich an einem Birkenstamm festhalten mußte, um nicht zu stürzen. Er drehte sich um, schob seinen Hals nach vorn und sah ihnen entgegen. Er spürte das Herz so laut, daß er die Schläge gar nicht hätte zählen können. Als ER gegeißelt wurde, hat ER sich nicht gewehrt. Die Verfolger waren überrascht, sie verlangsamten ihren Lauf. Der ihm am nächsten war, machte noch einige Schritte, dann blieb auch er stehen. Sie sahen sich an, über ein Dutzend Meter hinweg, als wollten sie sich mit den Blicken festhalten. Die andern Jungen rückten bis zu ihrem ersten Mann auf und scharten sich um ihn, als ob dort eine unsichtbare Linie verliefe, die nicht überschritten werden durfte. Ihre Energien, die in den letzten Minuten einzig und allein darauf gerichtet waren, den Fremden, den Angreifer, einzuholen und zu fassen, waren jetzt, wo sie ihr Ziel erreicht hatten, wie verflogen, jetzt, wo sie nichts anderes zu tun brauchten, als die wenigen Schritte weiterzugehen und ihn festzunehmen. Jetzt könnte er ihnen nicht mehr entkommen. Statt dessen verharrten sie wie festgenagelt, und wenn er jetzt auf sie zuginge, würden sie vielleicht sogar zurückweichen.

Andi Ossadnik rührte sich nicht. Er fühlte eine dumpfe, wohlige Schwäche, die langsam den Körper überflutete, seine Arme schwach machte und herunterhängen ließ, seinem Gesicht ein hartes Lächeln aufsetzte und auf der Zunge den Geschmack von Metall hinterließ. Er wünschte sich, die andern mögen näher kommen, ihn stoßen, puffen, boxen, schlagen, sich auf ihn werfen und mit den Füßen treten. Ganz willenlos war er, nur noch dazu da, zu empfangen, sonst nichts. Er würde sich nicht wehren. Jetzt sah er die andern auf sich zukommen, ein großer Schatten, der sich auf ihn zubewegte, beinahe zeitlupenhaft. Keine Stimmen, kein Schrei. Er wartete auf den ersten Schlag.

pursuers, along with an inexplicable yearning to be caught by them.

What would happen if he stopped right there? They would overwhelm him, even if he resisted, it would not make any difference, they outnumbered him. They would beat him up and leave him lying there. Or they would chase him back to the camp and deliver him up to the fury of the others. Or they would beat him to a pulp and hand him over to the police, because of the window pane.

Let them beat him, torture him, humiliate him, yes, he deserved such punishment, not for throwing the stones, not for the stupid window pane, naturally not for that, for something else, for guilt, for his guilt, and he was not thinking of anything particular, he was thinking of the guilt that everyone has in the face of HIM and that would not stop. He thought about how they had scourged HIM and crowned HIM with thorns. How HIS hands and feet were pierced by nails.

All at once he stopped, he braked so suddenly that he had to hold onto a birch tree to keep from falling. He turned around, craning his neck, and looked towards them. His heart pounded so loud and fast that he could not have counted the beats. When HE was being scourged, HE did not resist at all. His pursuers were surprised, they slowed their pace. The one closest to him took a few more steps, then he stopped. They looked at each other, a dozen meters apart, as if trying to hold one another with their eyes. The other boys moved up as far as their leader and grouped themselves around him, as if up against an invisible line that must not be crossed. Their energy, which in the last few minutes had been directed solely to catching up with and capturing the stranger, the attacker, was as if evaporated now that they had reached their goal, now when they had nothing more to do than take a few steps and grab him. He could not escape them now. Instead they stood there as if nailed in place, and if he walked toward them now, they might even give ground.

Andi Ossadnik did not move. He felt a dull, pleasant weakness slowly saturating his body, making his arms weaken and dangle, placing a hard smile on his face, and leaving the taste of metal on his tongue. He wished the others would come closer, whack him, punch him, slug him, hit him, throw themselves at him, and kick him. He was entirely without will, he existed only to receive, for nothing else. He would not resist. Now he saw them advancing towards him, a large shadow moving towards him, almost in slow motion. No voices, no shouting. He waited for the first blow.

Sein Vater hatte ihn nie geschlagen. Solange er sich erinnern konnte, hatte er nicht erlebt, daß sein Vater eines seiner Kinder schlug. Er war einfach nicht der Typ dafür, seine Kinder zu schlagen. Obwohl er oft genug dazu Veranlassung gehabt hätte, bei fünf Jungen und einem Mädchen. Nicht bei dem Mädchen, aber gewiß bei allen fünf Jungen. Aber das gab es nicht, daß sein Vater einmal eines seiner Kinder geschlagen hätte. Vor einem Monat gab es die einzige Ausnahme: sein Vater hatte ihn geschlagen. Sonst war es Tonik, der ihn schlug. Tonik schlug alle seine Brüder. Tonik war der älteste. Wenn irgend jemand etwas ausgefressen hatte, was nur durch Schläge gesöhnt werden konnte, sagte sein Vater nur: Tonik! Oder wenn der Tonik nicht da war: Warte nur, bis Tonik kommt. Und wenn Tonik kam, sagte er: Tonik. Und zeigte auf den Jungen. Tonik fragte nicht, er wußte schon, was er zu tun hatte, und an dem Gesicht des Vaters, an seinem Kopfnicken, an einer Geste erkannte er, ob er leicht oder heftig zuschlagen mußte, ob er den Stock oder den Ochsenziemer nehmen, ob er auf die Finger oder auf den Hintern schlagen sollte, oder ob eine saftige Ohrfeige genügte. Eine Kopfnuß gab der Vater schon mal selbst. Aber nur eine Kopfnuß. Niemals Schläge! Tonik entledigte sich die Schläge wie einer ganz gewöhnlichen Arbeit. Man konnte nicht sagen, daß es ihm Vergnügen bereitete, aber auch nicht, daß es ihm unangenehm oder lästig war. Er unterzog sich dem wie eine notwendige Pflicht. Er war der Älteste, er kam gleich nach dem Vater, und da der es nicht tat, mußte er es eben tun. Es war ein Auftrag, den er sorgfältig ausführte. Wenn der Vater die Hand zum Einhalt hob, hörte Tonik auf. Mutter dagegen konnte jammern oder heulen, das nützte nichts. Das schien der Tonik überhaupt nicht wahrzunehmen.

Vor einem Monat hatte der Vater ihn geschlagen. Das würde er nie vergessen. Da hatte etwas angefangen. Alle Schläge, alle furchtbaren Schläge Toniks waren vergessen. Diesen einen Schlag ins Gesicht von seinem Vater würde er nie vergessen. Er war allein mit ihm in der Küche. Er hatte sich schon lange gewünscht, mit seinem Vater einmal allein zu sein. Er wollte mit ihm über ein paar Sachen sprechen, über die ein Junge von sechzehn Jahren mit seinem Vater schon immer sprechen will, und dann, wenn es soweit ist, doch nicht darüber sprechen kann, und so haben sie über allerlei Nebensächlichkeiten gesprochen, und das Allernebensächlichste schien ihm die Politik, auf die sie dann aber doch am Schluß gekommen waren, und er hatte seinen Vater gefragt, ob er denn auch glaube, daß der Krieg verloren sei, und der Vater hatte ihn lange zugesehen und geschwiegen; und dann hatte er seinen Vater gefragt, warum er denn in die Partei eingetreten sei, und der Vater hatte ihm mehr als eine Antwort darauf gegeben; und dann hatte er seinem Vater gesagt, im Büro in der Knappschaft erzählte man sich, daß bei einem verlorenen Krieg alle

His father had never beaten him. As long as he could remember, he had never seen his father strike one of his children. He simply was not the type to beat his children. Although he had occasion to often enough, with five boys and a girl. Not with the girl, but certainly with all five of the boys. But it never happened that his father hit any of his children. The only exception occurred a month ago: His father had hit him. Otherwise it was Tonik who hit him. Tonik hit all of his brothers. Tonik was the oldest. If any of them had done something that had to be paid for in blows, then his father just said: Tonik! Or if Tonik was not there: Wait until Tonik gets here. And when Tonik got there, he said: Tonik. And pointed at the boy. Tonik did not ask questions, he knew what to do, and by his father's face, by the nod of his head or a gesture, he would tell whether to hit lightly or hard, whether he was supposed to take the stick or the strap, whether he was to hit him on the fingers or the hind end, or whether a healthy slap on the side of the head was enough. His father would occasionally administer a rap on the head himself. But only a rap on the head. Never blows! Tonik took care of them like any other job. You could not say that it afforded him pleasure, but also not that it was unpleasant or offensive to him. He performed it like a necessary duty. He was the oldest, he came right after the father, and since his father did not do it, Tonik had to. It was a task that he carried out conscientiously. When his father raised his hand to check him, Tonik stopped. Mother could wail and blubber, but to no avail. Tonik seemed not even to notice.

A month ago his father had hit him. He would never forget it. That was the start of something. All the blows, all of Tonik's frightening blows were forgotten. He would never forget his father punching him in the face. He was alone with him in the kitchen. For a long time he had been wishing he could be alone with his father for once. He wanted to talk with him about a few things that a boy of sixteen always wants to talk about with his father, and then, when the time comes, can't talk about, and so they talked about trivial things, and to him the most trivial seemed politics, which they had wound up talking about at the end, and he had asked his father whether he thought that the war was lost, and his father had looked at him for a long time without speaking; and then he had asked his father why he had joined the Party, and his father had given him more than one answer to that; and then he had told his father that in the office at the miners' association they said if the war was lost, all the Party members

Parteigenossen in Ghettos eingesperrt würden, so wie man es jetzt mit den Juden machte. Und der sonst so ruhige Vater hatte angefangen zu schreien und wollte wissen, wer denn so etwas gesagt habe, damit er den Mann an die richtige Stelle bringen könne, denn so etwas sei *Greuelpropaganda*; und er hätte beinahe den Namen genannt, wenn Vater nicht Greuelpropaganda gesagt hätte, denn das war es, weshalb sie den Kaplan Mikas ins Kazett eingesperrt hatten, aus dem er erst nach 1½ Jahren wieder herausgekommen war. Als er das seinem Vater gesagt hatte, war der aufgestanden und hatte ihm die Faust ins Gesicht gestoßen. Ohne ein Wort zu sagen, hatte er sich gleich danach abgewandt und war hinausgegangen, als ob er sich dieser Handlung schämte. Am Abend, als sie alle zusammen am Tisch saßen, merkte er, daß der Vater ihm mit den Augen auswich. Und überhaupt dachte er manchmal, wenn er seinen Vater beobachtete, und er beobachtete ihn jetzt aufmerksamer als früher, daß da ein anderer Mensch in seinem Vater gewesen sein muß, der ihn geschlagen hatte. Noch nie hatte ihn ein Schlag so geschmerzt, noch nie hatte er sich so erniedrigt gefühlt, noch nie war er so verwundet gewesen. Es war schon einen Monat her. Seitdem hatten sie sich nicht mehr in die Augen gesehen.

Jetzt müßte er sein Gesicht schützen. Aber seine Arme hingen so schwer herunter, er würde sie nicht mehr heben können. Er wartete auf die Schläge. Vielleicht hatte er sich den Überfall nur ausgedacht, um diese Schläge zu empfangen. Aber die Schläge kamen nicht. Statt dessen eine Stimme, ganz nah an seinem Gesicht: Warum hast du das gemacht?

Andi spürte langsam die Kraft zurückfluten, zuerst in den Beinen, dann in seinem Leib, zuletzt in seinem Kopf. Er sah den Jungen an, der ganz dicht vor ihm stand, sah ihm aber nicht in die Augen. Er sammelte Speichel in seinem Mund. Er hörte den Atem des andern, kurz und schnaufend, und das Geräusch mischte sich mit dem Geräusch seines eigenen Atems. Er sah in das runde weiße Gesicht, öffnete langsam seine Lippen, schob den Speichel nach vorn und schnellte ihn von der Zunge, direkt in das runde, weiße Gesicht hinein.

Unter Stöhnen und Schreien prasselten jetzt die Schläge und Hiebe auf ihn ein, Andi stürzte zu Boden und drückte sein Gesicht ins Gras. Der Schmerz, der von allen Stellen seines Körpers ausgehend in seinem Kopf zusammenfloß, ließ erst nach, als die Schreie leiser wurden und sich entfernten.

Wer die Jungen vom KLV-Lager auf dem Heimweg gesehen hätte, hätte meinen können, daß da eine Gruppe von jungen Leuten eine ganz besonders exotische Art von Gymnastik ausführte. Sie zeigten sich gegenseitig und immer wieder, wie und mit welchen Schlägen sie es dem fremden Jungen gegeben hatten. Und als sie vor ihrem Lager angekommen waren, would be locked up in ghettos, like what was happening to the Jews right now. And his father, usually so calm, had begun to yell, and wanted to know who had said such stuff, so he could report the guy; that amounted to *atrocity propaganda*; and he would have given him the name, if his father had not said atrocity propaganda, for that was the reason why they had thrown Chaplain Mikas into the concentration camp, where they kept him for a year and a half. When he told his father that, he had stood up and punched him in the face. Without saying a word, he then turned around and walked out, as if he were ashamed of what he had done. That evening, when they were all sitting at the table together, he noticed that his father was avoiding his eyes. And when he observed his father, and he observed him more closely than before, sometimes he thought that inside of his father there must have been a different person who hit him. Never had a blow hurt so much, never had he felt so humiliated, never had he been so wounded. It had been already a month ago. Since then they had not looked each other in the face.

Now he should protect his face. But his arms hung down so heavily, he would not be able to lift them again. He waited for the blows. Maybe he had devised the attack only so as to receive these blows. But the blows did not come. Instead, a voice, very close to his face: Why did you do that?

Slowly Andi felt his strength flowing back, first into his legs, then into his body, finally into his head. He looked at the boy, who was standing right in front of him, but did not look into his eyes. He collected saliva in his mouth. He heard the boy's breath, short and panting, and the sound mixed in with the sound of his own breathing. He looked into the round, white face, slowly opened his lips, rolled the saliva forwards, and shot it off his tongue, straight into the round, white face.

Yelling and grunting, they slammed into him. Andi was knocked to the ground, and he pressed his face into the grass. The pain, issuing from all over his body and flowing together in his head, did not diminish until the shouts grew quieter and more distant.

If anyone had seen the boys from the Evacuee Camp on their way home, he might have thought that a group of young people was performing some exotic gymnastics. Again and again they demonstrated to one another how they had polished off the stranger. And by the time they got back to waren sie sich nach lebhaftem Wortwechsel darüber einig geworden, daß es sich nur um einen Polenjungen gehandelt haben konnte.

Typisch, sagte der eine, er hat kein Wort gesprochen, nicht ein einziges Wort, er wollte sich nicht verraten.

Und der andere: Feige war er, hat sich nicht mal gewehrt. Feiger Polenjunge!

Auch denen, die im Lager zurückgeblieben waren, erzählten sie, was sie mit dem Jungen gemacht hatten. Am Ende bekamen sie Vorwürfe, warum sie ihn nicht zurück ins Lager geschleppt hatten. Die beiden andern Jungen waren ihnen nämlich entwischt.

Andi ist liegengeblieben. Er hätte nicht sagen können, wie lange. Der Himmel über ihm ist weiß, gleißendes Weiß, das ihn blendet, ein weißer Wolkenschleier, vor die Sonne gehängt, an manchen Stellen schon dünn und abgewetzt, läßt die ersten Sonnenstrahlen hindurch. Andi blickt auf die rosafarbene Haut seiner Hand, sieht das saftige Grün eines Grasbüschels, betrachtet die Zacken eines Löwenzahnblattes. Er fühlt Schmerz und spürt Durst.

Er ist allein unter dem Himmel. Jedenfalls fühlt er so. Die Sonne wärmt ihn. Die Erde trägt ihn. Der Schmerz bündelt sich jetzt an einigen Stellen seines Körpers. Überm linken Auge, am Hinterkopf links oben, an der linken Schulter, an den Knien, am stärksten an der linken Braue. Er wischt mit zwei Fingern darüber und sieht, daß die Finger blutig sind. Da er kein Taschentuch hat, streift er das Hemd hoch und drückt es aufs Gesicht. Als er es herunternimmt, kann er darin den Abdruck seiner Wunden sehen. Es ist vor allem die linke Augenbraue, die noch heftig blutet. Andi reißt ein Blatt heraus, feuchtet es mit Spucke an und klebt es auf die Braue. Das wird das Blut vielleicht stillen.

Er würde gern wütend sein. Aber weiß nicht, auf wen. Auf die, die ihn gejagt haben, kann er es jedenfalls nicht sein.

Er dreht sich langsam um und bewegt vorsichtig seine Gliedmaßen. Zunächst rutschen seine Füße mehr durchs Gras als daß sie gehen. Er ist jedenfalls froh, daß die Jungs ihm die Schuhe gelassen haben. Mit der Zeit bewegen sich jedoch alle Glieder wieder, er kann es an seinem Schatten beobachten, der schräg neben ihn auf die Landstraße fällt. Auf der Straße geht es sich auch viel besser als auf der buckligen Wiese. Er empfindet seinen Schatten als etwas Fremdes. Vielleicht, weil er früher nie auf seinen Schatten geachtet hat. Als ob es der Schatten eines andern wäre. Und als er näher an die Stadt kommt und in der Eichendorff-Allee ihm die ersten Leute begegnen, nimmt er ihre Verwunderung über ihn als die Verwunderung über einen andern, ihr Erschrecken als ein Erschrecken über einen andern, ihre Zurufe als die Zurufe an einen andern. Er fühlt sich jetzt ganz in Ordnung. Wenn nur die Augenbraue aufhören würde zu bluten. Er wird camp they had come to the opinion, after a lively debate, that the boy must have been a Pole.

Typical, one of them said, he didn't say a word, not a single word, he didn't want to give himself away.

And another: He was a coward, he didn't even put up a fight. Chicken of a Pole!

They told the boys who had remained at the camp how they had taken care of the stranger. But they were finally blamed for not dragging him back to camp. The other two boys had gotten away from them.

Andi lay there. He did not know for how long. The sky above him is white, a glistening white that blinds him, a veil of white clouds hanging in front of the sun, thin and worn through in some places, letting the first rays of sunshine through. Andi looks at the pink skin of his hand, sees the juicy green of a tuft of grass, studies the zigzags of a dandelion leaf. He feels pain, senses thirst.

He is alone beneath the sky. At least he feels that way. The sun warms him. The earth bears him up. The pain is focusing at a few places in his body. Above his left eye, at the back of his head to the upper left, in his left shoulder, in his knees, worst at his left eyebrow. He wipes at it with two fingers and sees that the fingers are bloody. Since he doesn't have a handkerchief, he pulls his shirt up and presses it to his face. When he takes it away, he can see the impressions of his wounds on it. The left eyebrow is the worst, still bleeding freely. Andi pulls off a leaf, moistens it with spit, and sticks it to the eyebrow. Maybe that will staunch the bleeding.

He would like to be furious. But he does not know at whom. He cannot be at the boys who were chasing him, at any rate.

He turns around slowly and moves his limbs cautiously. At first his feet stumble through the grass more than they walk. He is glad that they left him his shoes, at least. In time, though, all his limbs move again, he can watch this in his shadow, which falls on the road at an angle to him. Walking on the road is a lot easier, too, than across the rough field. He senses his shadow as something foreign. Perhaps because he has never paid any attention to his shadow before. As though it were the shadow of somebody else. And when he gets closer to town and meets the first people on Eichendorff Avenue he takes their amazement at him for an amazement at somebody else, their shock as shock at somebody else, their shouts as shouts at somebody else. He feels in good shape now. If only his eyebrow would nach Hause gehen und sich waschen, ein sauberes Hemd anziehn, das Gesicht mit Nivea einfetten und auf die Augenbraue ein Pflaster tun.

Erst als er in das Gesicht von Felix Bronder sah, der ihm am Preußenplatz entgegenkam, wußte er, daß er selbst der andere war. Der diesen blöden Überfall auf das KLV-Lager organisiert hatte, der weggerannt war, der von den Jungen bestellt und zusammengeschlagen worden war. Jetzt sah er das alles viel nüchterner. Der Wolkenschleier war zerrissen, nur hin und wieder schoben sich kleine weiße Wölkchen vor die Sonne und warfen flüchtige Schatten.

Mein Gott, Schielok, sagte Bronder halb erschreckt, halb schadenfroh, du siehst ja aus, als ob du gerade von der Teufelsinsel entsprungen wärst! Was ist denn passiert?

Nischte nichts, sagte Andi trotzig.

Das müssen aber drei gewesen sein, die dich so zugerichtet haben, einer hätt's bestimmt nicht geschafft, dir so 'ne Landkarte ins Gesicht zu malen.

Bronder stellte sich etwas zur Seite, weil er fürchtete, Schielok würde ihm trotz seines Zustands eine runterhauen.

Andi konnte ihm ja nicht sagen, daß es fünf gewesen waren. Vielleicht auch mehr. Er wußte überhaupt nicht, wie er jemand die ganze Geschichte klarmachen könnte. Jetzt wollte er auf dem schnellsten Weg nach Haus.

Hast du Wonzak irgendwo in der Stadt gesehen oder den Jungen, der bei Dolezich Papierwaren verkauft, du weißt, wen ich meine?

Bronder wußte nicht, wen er meinte. Und Wonzak hatte er seit Tagen nicht mehr gesehn. Der war auch in einem andern Fähnlein. Tut mir leid, Schielok, sagte er, weil er nicht wußte, was er sonst sagen sollte. Er suchte nach einem Taschentuch und fand schließlich auch eines, ganz unten im Hosensack, und er freute sich, ihm damit wenigstens die Wunde an der Augenbraue abtupfen zu können. Aber als er sah, wie schmutzig es war, steckte er es beschämt wieder ein.

Mitleid war das wenigste, was Andi jetzt ertragen konnte. Er war niemals ein Feigling gewesen. Er hatte sich immer gewehrt. Aber heute war es etwas anderes gewesen. Vielleicht wollte er einmal erleben, wie das ist, wenn man unterliegt. Wenn man der Geprügelte ist. Wenn man unten liegt und getreten wird. Er lächelte Bronder an, dabei verzerrte sich sein Gesicht.

Bronder wußte nicht, ob Andi sein Gesicht vor Schmerz verzerrte oder ob das ein Lächeln sein sollte.

Weißt, was los ist?! Die holen die Glocken vom Turm der Peter-Paul-Kirche, sagte Bronder und wischte sich aufgeregt die Haare aus dem Gesicht.

stop bleeding. He'll go home and wash, put on a clean shirt, rub some Nivea cream on his face, and put a bandage on his eyebrow.

Not until he looked into the face of Felix Bronder coming toward him at Preußenplatz did he know that he himself was the somebody else. Who had thought up the stupid attack on the Evacuee Camp, who had run away, who got himself cornered and beaten up. He saw it all much more soberly now. The veil of clouds had torn, only now and then did little white clouds intrude in front of the sun to cast fleeting shadows.

My God, Squintok, Bronder said, half scared and half malicious, you look as if you'd just escaped from Devil's Island! What on earth happened?

Nothing much, Andi said stubbornly.

There must have been three of them, by the shape you're in it took more than one guy to work you over like that.

Bronder edged away a little, he was afraid that Squintok would slug him, in spite of the shape he was in.

Andi could not tell him, after all, that there had been five of them. Maybe even more. He did not at all know how to explain the whole story to anybody. He wanted to get home as fast as possible now.

Have you seen Wonzak anywhere around town, or the boy who sells stationery at Dolezich's, you know who I mean?

Bronder did not know whom he meant. And he had not seen Wonzak for days. He was in a different troop, too. Sorry, Squintok, he said, because he did not know what else to say. He was searching for a handkerchief and finally found one, too, at the very bottom of his pocket, and he was glad that he could at least mop the wound on his forehead for him. But when he saw how dirty it was, he put it back in his pocket, embarrassed.

Pity was the last thing Andi needed now. He had never been a coward. He had always fought back. But today it had been different. Perhaps he had wanted to experience how it is to be defeated. To be beaten up. To be kicked when you're down. He smiled at Bronder, his face a grimace.

Bronder did not know whether Andi was grimacing in pain or whether that was supposed to be a smile.

Know what's going on?! They're taking down the bells from the tower of Peter-Paul Church, Bronder said, excitedly brushing the hair out of his eyes.

Andi begriff nicht, was der Junge meinte. Nur die fahrigen Gesten verrieten ihm, daß etwas Ungewöhnliches geschehen sein mußte. So wiederholte er mechanisch: Sie holen die Glocken von Peter und Paul? Warum denn das?

Da hört sich doch alles auf, sagte Bronder ungeduldig. Die machen Kanonen draus. Weißt du das nicht? Wir haben doch auch für die *Hajott* Buntmetalle gesammelt. Jetzt reicht das nicht mehr. Jetzt kommen die Glocken dran. Überall!

Andi did not understand what he meant. Only the nervous gestures indicated that something unusual must have happened. So he repeated mechanically: They're taking down the bells from Peter and Paul? Why are they doing that?

That's the height of something, Bronder said impatiently. They're making artillery out of them. Didn't you know that? We've been collecting nonferrous metals for the Hitler Youth. That's no longer enough. So now they're taking the bells. Everywhere!

BESUCH AUF DER VERANDA

BERND RACHEL

SEIN AUGE WAR HINTER DUNKLEN BRILLENGLÄSERN VERBORGEN. ER HATTE die abgewetze Lederjacke an und die irische Wollmütze auf dem Kopf; dabei saß er auf der Terrasse mitten in der Nachmittagssonne. Die Sonne war rot und warm.

"Großvater", fragte ich ihn, "ist das in Kalifornien auch der Indianersommer?"

Er räusperte sich unwillig, als wäre er gerade aufgewacht, streckte seine langen dünnen Beine in die Sonne und sah mich an. Hinter der Sonnenbrille war nicht auszumachen, welches das Glasauge war.

"Aber Großvater", ich drehte meinen Kopf zu den kahlen Bergen hinter seinem Haus, "wie nennt man es denn, wenn im Oktober noch die Sonne so kräftig scheint, daß man genausogut nackt rumlaufen könnte! Und im Pullover kommt man trotzdem nicht ins Schwitzen. Hörst du, Großvater, verstehst du mich?"

Hinter den dunklen Brillengläsern zuckten die Wimpern um sein richtiges Auge, ich glaube, es war das linke.

"Im Osten", krächzte er und zeigte mit dem Finger hinter das Haus, "in den Staaten im Osten, wenn die Sonne rot wird und es Zeit wäre für die Büffel, das ist dort der Indianersommer. Im letzten Monat, bevor die Schneestürme kommen. —Lege dir den Jug auf den Ellbogen, so, und den Daumen mit dem Henkel hoch, ja, sonst läuft dir der ganze Brandy aufs Hemd."

Ich mußte mich in einem fort räuspern beim Zuhören. Meine Stimme kam mir jetzt auch belegt vor: "Das saftige Gras treibt noch einmal neu für die Büffelherden. Ich habe das in den Filmen gesehen. Und die rote Sonne, Großvater, genau wie hier, die ganze letzte Woche schon."

"Mein Sohn", sagte er und strich umständlich seine Hose glatt, "ein Europäer hat kein Auge mehr dafür. Es ist das Licht. Das Licht ist anders drüben in Vermont, weil im nächsten Monat der Schnee kommt."

Sein Hund war aufgestanden und an den Rand der Terrasse in den Schatten eines Eukalyptusbaums gezottelt. So konnte ich mich jetzt auf die Wolldecke zu seinen Füßen setzen. "Wie war das eigentlich im Winter mit den Indianern? Ich habe mich oft gefragt, wenn ich die Indianerfilme gesehen habe, wie das war im Winter. Die nackten Indianer in den Zelten."

"Geh", sagte er, "hol dir den Schaukelstuhl aus dem Haus. Sag der Großmutter, daß ich dir erlaubt habe, in dem alten Schaukelstuhl zu sitzen."

A VISIT ON THE VERANDA

BERND RACHEL
translated by Breon Mitchell

HIS EYE WAS HIDDEN BEHIND DARK GLASSES. HE WAS WEARING HIS SCUFFED-up leather jacket and the woolen Irish beret, yet he sat on the porch in the middle of the afternoon sun. The sun was red and warm.

"Grandfather," I asked him, "is this called Indian Summer in California too?"

He cleared his throat involuntarily, as if he had just awakened, stretched his long thin legs in the sun, and looked at me. With the sunglasses on you couldn't tell which one was the glass eye.

"Well, Grandfather," I turned my head toward the bare mountains behind his house, "what do they call it then, when the sunshine is so strong in October that you could go without clothes, but you don't even get hot in a sweater? Do you hear, Grandfather, do you know what I mean?"

Behind the dark glasses lashes of his good eye twitched, I think it was the left one.

"Back East," he croaked, and pointed back behind the house, "in the Eastern states, when the sun gets red and it would be time for the buffalo, that's Indian Summer. The last month before the snow storms arrive. —Here, lay the jug on your elbow like this, with your thumb hooked through the handle, that's right, otherwise you'll have brandy all over your shirt."

I had to keep clearing my throat while I was listening. My voice sounded husky to me too now. "The thick grass springs up again for the buffalo herds. I saw that in the movies. And the red sun, Grandfather, just like here, for the whole past week."

"My boy," he said, and carefully smoothed his trousers, "a European lacks an eye for such things these days. It's the light. There's a different light back there in Vermont, because the next month the snows arrive."

His dog got up and shuffled along the edge of the terrace in the shadow of the eucalyptus tree. Now I could sit on the wool blanket at his feet. "What was it really like in winter for the Indians? I always wondered when I saw cowboy and Indian movies, what it was like in winter. The naked Indians in their teepees."

"Go on," he said, "get the rocking chair from the house. Tell Grandmother that I said you could sit in the old rocking chair."

Ich holte den Schaukelstuhl und stellte ihn vor den Terrassenrand, daß ich beim Sitzen meine Füße gegen die Holzbalken stemmen konnte.
Der alte Mann hatte inzwischen sein leinernes Tabaksbeutelchen gezogen und streute die Krümel auf ein Zigarettenpapier, vor seiner linken Gesichtshälfte.
"Hier", sagte er, und warf mir den Beutel herüber, "aber geh sparsam damit um, man bekommt nirgends mehr den Tabak dafür. Bald gibt es gar nichts mehr zu rauchen."
Erst als er eine lange Glut geraucht hatte und die Zigarette schon ganz faltig und braun geworden war, sprach er weiter. "Im Mittleren Westen hat es in den Wintern Schneemassen gegeben, daß die großen Überlandbusse steckenblieben bis zur Schmelze. Daß man die Schulkinder mit Hubschraubern herausholen mußte.
Die Indianer hatten Mützen aus Eichhörnchenpelzen, Fußsäcke aus Biberfellen, Pulswärmer und Kragen vom Waschbär, und Umhänge aus so feinem Hirschleder, wie man es heute nicht mehr so weich gerben kann. Ihre Kinder steckten sie bis zum Hals in Säcke aus Otterfellen, den glatten Pelz nach außen und innen wettiert mit Schwandaunen.
Die Indianer haben an den Wolkenkratzern in New York als Fensterputzer gearbeitet, weil sie schwindelfrei waren; fünfunddreißig, vierzig, sechzig Stockwerke hoch, die hockten auf einem Brettchen an einem Kran, wie auf einer Schaukel. Gebaut haben sie die Wolkenkratzer auch, und die Hochbrücken. Keiner hat dabei je die Balance verloren, sie waren schwindelfrei.
Über den St. Lorenz haben sie eine Stahlbrücke gebaut, droben in Kanada. Vierzig Yards hoch sollte die Brücke über den Fluß gehen. Die Arbeiter auf der Brücke waren alles Mohawks; bei den Mohawks waren die Männer so schwindelfrei wie die Adler."
"Sind die Mohawks auch ausgestorben?"
"Damals gab es den Stamm noch. An einem Nachmittag ist die Brückenkonstruktion über dem St. Lorenz in sich zusammengebrochen, der Bau war noch nicht halb fertig. Mitsamt den Eisenträgern und den Kränen und Gerüsten sind die Indianer in den Fluß gestürzt. Die meisten Männer waren gleich tot. Erschlagen von den Stahlplatten oder ertrunken oder einfach gestorben, weil sie abgestürzt waren. Die schwindelfreien Mohawks.
Ein gutes Dutzend Indianer lebte noch, eingeklemmt zwischen den Eisenträgern. Sie lagen im flachen Wasser des St. Lorenz, es war Ebbe an dem Nachmittag. Einzelne starben bald, die, denen der Bauch zerquetscht war. Manche hatten nur die Beine eingeklemmt oder nur einen Fuß. Die hielten die Köpfe über Wasser. Und abends kam die Flut."
"Haben sie den Sterbegesang gesungen?"
"Ich weiß nicht, das ist nicht überliefert. Natürlich haben sie gesungen. die Indianer haben immer ihr Lied gesungen, wenn sie starben. Oder es hat

I brought out the rocking chair and placed it in front of the porch railing, so I could prop my feet on the wooden slats while I sat. The old man meanwhile had pulled out his linen tobacco pouch and was sprinkling the shreds of tobacco along a cigarette paper, which he held in front of the left half of his face.

"Here," he said, and threw me the pouch, "but go easy with it, you can't get tobacco for it anywhere anymore. Before long there won't be anything left to smoke."

Not until he had taken a long draw and the cigarette had already turned brown and crinkly did he continue. "In the Middle West such great masses of snow piled up in winter that the big transcontinental buses were stuck till it thawed. They had to haul the school kids out with helicopters.

"The Indians had caps of squirrel fur, slippers of beaver skin, muffs and mufflers of raccoon, and cloaks of fine deerskin—no one can tan that soft anymore. They stuck their kids up to their necks in sacks made out of otter skin, the smooth coat turned outward and the inside lined with swansdown.

"The Indians were hired as window washers for New York skyscrapers because they never got dizzy; thirty-five, forty, sixty stories high, they squatted on a narrow board on a crane like they were on a swing. They built the skyscrapers, too, and the great bridges. Not a one ever lost his balance, they never got dizzy.

"They built a steel bridge across the St. Lawrence, up in Canada. The bridge had to be built forty yards over the river. The workers on the bridge were all Mohawks; Mohawk men never got dizzy, they were like eagles."

"Have the Mohawks all died out?"

"The tribe was still in existence back then. One afternoon the bridgework over the St. Lawrence collapsed, it wasn't even half finished. The Indians all fell into the river, along with the iron girders and the cranes and the framework. Most of them died instantly. Smashed by the steel beams or drowned or just from the fall. The Mohawks who never got dizzy.

"A good dozen were still alive, caught between the iron girders. They were lying in shallow water in the St. Lawrence; it was low tide in the afternoon. A few died quickly, the ones who had been squashed in the middle. Some were only caught by the legs, or by one foot. They held their heads above the water. And the evening tide came in."

"Did they sing their deathsong?"

"I don't know, that hasn't come down to us. Of course they sang it, the Indians always sang their deathsong when they died. Or a priest had

sich ein Priester an die Unglückstelle zu den eingeklemmten Männern rudern lassen. In Kanada waren viele Indianer katholisch geworden."
"Ein Pfarrer?"
"Das Boot steigt mit der Flut. Die Indianer im Wasser sehen den Priester aufrecht im Boot stehen, das Sakrament hält er hoch vor seinen Kopf, die große Hostie. Zwei Ministranten rudern aus Leibeskräften, damit das Boot auf der Stelle bleibt. Bei Flut zieht es den ganzen St. Lorenz hinauf, als hätte sich der Strom umgekehrt.
Der Priester beugt seinen Kopf vor der Hostie, er betet.
Wie das Wasser ansteigt und dabei das Boot hebt mit dem Priester und den rudernden Ministranten, geht es den Indianern über die Brust und an den Hals und sie recken die Köpfe nach dem Priester im Boot und sie spüren kaum mehr ihre eingeklemmten Beine zwischen den Stahlträgern im Flußbett. Der St. Lorenz hat da einen Tidenhub von zwölf Yards, das sind fast elf Meter."
"Mein Gott, du meinst, sie haben da in der steigenden Flut gelegen und einfach auf den Pfarrer gesehen?"
"Nein, sie haben bestimmt ihren Sterbegesang gesungen. Es waren sechsunddreißig Mohawks. Ihr Vorarbeiter war der Unterhäuptling Massasoit, die Weißen nannten ihn Quiet Man; aber der war schon tot, als da am Abend die Flut kam."
"Man hat sie nicht retten können?"
"Aus Europa kamen bessere Bauzeichnungen. Zwei Jahre später war die Eisenbahnbrücke über den St. Lorenz fertig. Es ist alles eine Frage der Statik. Die Brücke steht heute noch, nach über 70 Jahren."
Ich nickte und sah ihn nicht an. Die Eisenbahnbrücke war immerhin dreizehn Jahre jünger als er. Er hielt den Kopf geradewegs in die Sonne, ich sah zwei kleine Sonnen auf seinen Brillengläsern.
"Und die ganzen amerikanischen Brückenkonstruktionen? Golden Gate, das haben doch Amerikaner entworfen."
"Ja heute. Wir lernen schnell. Was haben wir schon alles den Japanern nachgemacht, Autos, Kameras. Die neue Mayo-Klinik, habe ich jetzt gelesen, wurde bis aufs Haar der Berliner Charité nachgebaut. Dir fällt das vielleicht gar nicht auf, aber wer von uns soll sich da noch zurechtfinden?"
Ich schob meine Baskenmütze in die Stirn, hielt die Schuhe gegen die Terrassenbrüstung gestemmt und schaukelte lässig mit dem Stuhl. "Aber die neuen Automodelle heißen alle nach ausgestorbenen Indianern: Dakota, Pontiac, Cherokee, Pawnee, Huron. Und immerhin fährt der Präsident einen Lincoln. Bei uns denkt kein Mensch daran, ein Auto 'Bismarck' zu taufen."
"Komm, Sohn", sagte er, "hier kann auch niemand von der Tradition allein leben. Wenn du mich trägst, gehen wir auf die Jagd. Bis zum Abend könnten wir draußen sein."

himself rowed to the scene of the accident. A lot of Indians in Canada had turned Catholic."

"A clergyman?"

"The boat rises up with the tide. The Indians in the water see the priest standing upright in the boat; he's holding the sacrament high above his head, the consecrated host. Two acolytes are rowing for all they're worth to keep the boat in place. At high tide the whole St. Lawrence flows upriver, as if it had changed directions.

"The priest bows his head before the host, he prays.

"As the water rises, lifting the boat with the priest and the rowing acolytes, it covers the chest and reaches the throats of the men, and they crane their heads toward the priest in the boat, and they scarcely feel their legs anymore, trapped between the steel girders in the river bed. The St. Lawrence has a tidal shift of twelve yards at that point, that's almost eleven meters."

"My God, you mean they were trapped in the rising tide and just stared at the priest?"

"No, they definitely sang their deathsong. There were thirty-six Mohawks. Their foreman was chief Massasoit, the white man called him Le Silencieux; but he was already dead when the tide rose that evening."

"They couldn't be saved?"

"Better engineering plans were sent from Europe. Two years later the railroad bridge over the St. Lawrence was finished. It's all a question of statics. The bridge is still standing today, after almost seventy years."

I nodded and didn't look at him. Even so, the railroad bridge was thirteen years younger than he was. He held his head straight toward the sun; I saw two small suns on his glasses.

"And what about American bridge construction? Surely Golden Gate was designed by Americans."

"Yes, nowadays. We learn quickly. Look at everything we've copied from the Japanese, cars, cameras. Now I read that the new clinic at Mayo's is a detailed copy of the Berlin Charity Hospital. You might not notice in particular, but there's nothing to be satisfied with in that."

I pushed my basque beret down on my forehead, propped my shoes against the porch railing, and rocked lazily in the chair. "But all the new cars are named after Indian tribes that have died out: Dakota, Pontiac, Cherokee, Pawnee, Huron. And the President still drives a Lincoln. No one would think of naming an automobile a 'Bismarck' back home."

"Come on, son," he said, "we can't just live on tradition here either. If you'll carry me, we'll go hunting. We can stay out till evening."

Er blieb sitzen und gab mir die nötigen Anweisungen. Ich holte die beiden Gewehre über dem Kamin; nein, nicht die, sagte er, nimm die Jagdkarabiner aus dem Schrank. Dazu drei Schachteln Munition .30–.30, in den Ledergurten steckte noch genug der Munition für die Schrotläufe. Dörrfleisch, ordnete er an, Kaffee, Kaffeekanne und Tassen aus Emailleblech, ein kleiner Vorrat Tabak. Ich trug alles auf der Terrasse zusammen, holte noch schnell ein paar Wolldecken von dem Feldbett in seinem Zimmer und verschnürte sie mit den anderen Sachen zu einem Bündel.

“Hol dir noch einen Hut”, sagte er, “links in meinem Schrank, der dunkelblaue mit dem Riß in der Krempe, der hat schon deinem Vater gepaßt.”

Ich holte mir noch den Hut, das Schweißband war so durchgeschwärzt, als wäre es noch naß von meinem Vater.

Es ging leichter, als ich mir gedacht hatte. Der alte Mann auf dem Rücken hielt sich an meinem Jackenkragen fest, vor der Brust trug ich an einem Riemen das Bündel, ein Gewehr hatte ich in der Hand behalten als Stütze. Den dunkelblauen Hut wagte ich noch nicht aufzusetzen, ich hängte ihn an den anderen Gewehrlauf, der aus dem Deckenbündel ragte. Ich sah nach dem Hund, er war uns schon vorausgelaufen.

Der Weg ging ziemlich steil schräg am Berghang hinauf, er war asphaltiert, aber es war seit Jahren Lehm und Geröll auf die Fahrbahn geschwemmt; der Asphalt war nur noch in den ausgewaschenen Rinne zu sehen.

Obwohl der alte Mann gut einen Kopf größer war als ich, war er nicht allzu schwer auf meinem Rücken; das ging, ich hätte ihn auch den steilsten Berg huckepack hinaufgetragen. Er machte sich so leicht wie möglich, er achtete darauf, daß er seine Hände nicht vor meinem Hals verschlang; er gab sich Mühe, hielt sich geschickt an meiner Jacke fest, dann wechselte er den Griff an meinen Gürtel, daß es mich mehr emporhob, als daß ich ihn schleppen mußte. Es war bestimmt nicht das erste Mal für ihn, auf die Jagd getragen zu werden mit seinen Raucherbeinen. Ich glaube, er strengte sich dabei mehr an als der Träger.

In einem Comic mit Daniel Düsentrieb hatte ich einmal gesehen, wie die Panzerknacker eine neue Erfindung gestohlen haben, Rucksäcke mit Raketenrückstoß. D.D. hatte die Rucksackraketen eigentlich für die Boyscouts erfunden, damit sie verunglückten Bergwanderern helfen konnten. Fast bis zum Ende des Comics schwebten die Panzerknacker über die Wolkenkratzer von Entenhausen, mit Düsentriebs Erfindung auf dem Rücken, schalteten das gesamte Stromnetz der Stadt aus, die Alarmanlagen waren lahmgelegt, die Neonreklamen erloschen, nur die Augen der Panzerknacker leuchteten hinter ihren Gangstermasken wie bösartige Glühwürmer. Beinahe hätten sie in dieser Nacht Onkel Dagoberts Tresor gesprengt. Ich wollte Großvater danach fragen, aber er hustete bei jedem meiner Schritte, wenn er mir die Geschichte hätte erzählen wollen, hätten wir umkehren müssen.

He stayed seated and gave me the necessary directions. I brought both guns from above the fireplace; no, not them, he said, take the hunting rifles from the gun cabinet. Three boxes of .30-.30 shells, too; there was still enough number 4 ammunition in the leather belts for the shotgun. He ordered up dried meat, coffee, an enameled tin coffee pot and coffee cups, and a small supply of tobacco. I brought everything out onto the porch, grabbed a couple of wool blankts from the cot in his room, and tied them together with the other things into a single bundle.

"Get a hat for yourself, too," he said, "in my closet on the left, the dark-blue one with the rip in the brim, it fit your father before you."

I got the hat out; the sweatband was so dark it might still have been damp from my father's head.

It turned out to be easier than I thought. The old man held on piggyback by my jacket collar. I carried the bundle on a string in front of me, keeping a gun in one hand as support. I didn't yet dare to put on the dark-blue hat; I hung it on the barrel of the other gun, which protruded from the blanket bundle. I looked around for the dog. He had already run ahead.

The road climbed fairly steeply up the side of the mountain. It was asphalt, but clay and gravel had flooded it for years. The asphalt was only visible in the washed-out ruts.

Although the old man was a good head taller than me, he wasn't all that heavy on my back; it was all right, I could have carried him piggyback up even the steepest mountain. He made himself as light as possible; he was careful not to wrap his arms around my neck; he held onto my jacket with tight dexterity, then he would shift his grip to my belt so that it was more like he was lifting me than I was carrying him. It certainly wasn't the first time he'd been carried hunting, with his smokers legs. I think he worked harder at it than I did.

In a comic book with Gyro Gearloose I once saw how the Beagle Boys had stolen a new invention, backpacks with rockets on them. Gyro had actually invented the rocket-powered backpacks for the Boy Scouts, so that they could rescue mountain climbers in trouble. Near the end of the comic book the safecrackers were floating over the skyscrapers of Duckville with the invention on their backs, they had cut off the entire city's electricity, the burglar alarms were useless, the neon lights had gone out, and only the Beagle Boys' eyes still shone behind their gangster masks like evil glowworms. They almost broke into Uncle Scrooge's treasure that night. I wanted to ask Grandfather about it, but he was coughing at every step; if he had wanted to tell me the story, we would have had to go back.

Der Hund kam angerannt mit einer zerschossenen Tontaube in der Schnauze.
"Laß mich ab", sagte der alte Mann, er keuchte vor Anstrengung. Ich setzte mich vorsichtig vor einen Blaugrashügel, daß er sich bequem darauf niederlassen konnte. Aber er drehte sich gleich herum zu dem Hund, packte ihn am Nackenfell und zerrte mit der anderen Hand die Tontaube aus seinem Maul.
"Guter Kerl, guter Kerl", lobte er den Hund und klopfte ihm das Fell. Dann rieb er die Tontaube an seiner Hose, spuckte noch einmal darauf und warf das Ding mit einem großen Schwung den Berg hinunter in einen Akazienhain.
Der Hund riß seinen Kopf herum und jagte dem hellen Gipsbrocken nach, ich hörte ihn im Gestrüpp unten herumstöbern, er jaulte, dann kam er suchend heraus auf die Grasfläche, ohne Tontaube; der alte Mann schlug sich herrisch auf die Schenkel, darauf verschwand der Hund wieder unter den Bäumen.
"Großvater", sagte ich, "stimmt es, daß ihr jedes Jahr im Frühling die Jagdhündinnen draußen in der Prärie angepflockt habt, damit sie sich nachts mit den Wölfen paaren?"
Er rutschte hinauf auf den Grashügel und pfiff mit aufgestülpten Lippen zum Akazienhain hin. Dann drehte er den Kopf zu mir, ich sah sein totes Auge unter der Brille, als blickte es scharf an meinem Gesicht vorbei in die Bäume, während er nickte ging die Glaspupille auf und ab. "Schau dir Rover genau an. Den buschigen Schwanz und die gelben schmalen Augen, die hat er vom Wolf. Alle meine Hunde waren Kinder vom Wolf."
Der Hund kam jetzt wieder den Berg heraufgerannt, ich achtete auf seine gelben Augen und den buschigen Schwanz. Vor uns beiden legte der Hund eine leere Flasche Moet & Chandon ins Gras.
"Als ich mein Haus baute", er wies mit dem Finger bis zum Pazifik, "war hier schon alles Wüste. Unten in der Stadt gab es noch überall die Leuchtreklamen und die Gangsterautos hatten natürlich noch Weißwandreifen. Aber hier oben war Wüste. Wir wohnten zuerst im Hotel. Wenn ich mich abends rasierte in unserem Hotelzimmer, leuchtete die Neonreklame durch die Jalousien, immer einen Strich mit dem Rasiermesser lang, an, aus, an, im Spiegel war mein Unterhemd lila für den kurzen Moment und die Hosenträger dunkelblau, an, aus; ich hatte mich daran gewöhnt, mich so zu rasieren.
Die Frauen hatten noch dicken Lippenstift, daß man nach jedem Kuß das weiße Seidentuch aus der Brusttasche holen mußte und sich den Mund abwischte.
Als ich mein Haus gebaut hatte, den Kamin aus unbehauenen Felsbrocken, ist meine erste Frau im Wochenbett gestorben."
Er kickte mühsam die Flasche beiseite. Der Hund zuckte mit seinem buschigen Wolfsschwanz und schaute nervös zu seinem Herrn. Aber der achtete

The dog came running up with a broken clay pigeon in his mouth.

"Set me down," said the old man; he was gasping from exertion. I sat down carefully in front of a bluegrass mound, so that he could let himself down comfortably on it. But he turned around immediately to the dog, grabbed him by the scruff of the neck, and pulled the clay pigeon out of his mouth with the other hand.

"Good boy, good boy," he praised the dog and patted him on the back. Then he wiped off the clay pigeon on his trousers, spit on it again, and threw it in a great arc down the mountain into a grove of acacias.

The dog jerked his head around and chased after the bright piece of clay; I heard him blundering about in the brush; he whined, then came out searching onto the flat grass, without the clay pigeon; the old man slapped his thigh imperiously, and the dog disappeared again among the trees.

"Grandfather," I said, "did you really use to tether the bitches in heat out on the prairie each year in the springtime so that they would pair with the wolves at night?"

He pulled himself up on the grassy mound and whistled with pursed lips toward the acacia grove. Then he turned his head to me; I saw his dead eye under the glasses as he peered sharply past my face into the trees; the glass pupil went up and down as he nodded. "Look closely at Rover. He got that bushy tail and the narrow yellow eyes from the wolves. All my dogs were wolf pups."

Now the dog came running up the mountain again; I looked over his yellow eyes and the bushy tail. The dog laid down an empty bottle of Moet & Chandon in the grass in front of us.

"When I built my house," he pointed towards the Pacific, "there was nothing but wilderness here. Down below in the city there were neon lights everywhere and, of course, the mobsters' cars still had wide white-sidewall tires. But everything up here was wilderness. At first we lived in a hotel. When I shaved at night in our room, the neon lights shone in through the blinds, always in time with the strokes of the razor, on, off, on; for each short moment my undershirt was violet in the mirror and my suspenders dark blue, on, off; I got used to shaving that way.

"The women still wore thick lipstick, so that you had to pull out your white silk handkerchief from your breastpocket and wipe your mouth after every kiss.

"Just when I had finished building my house and the rough fieldstone fireplace, my first wife died in childbirth."

He kicked the bottle aside laboriously. The dog wagged his bushy nicht darauf, breitete seine mageren Arme aus, legte den Kopf zurück und schloß sein linkes Auge.

"Schieß", sagte er nach einer Weile leise. Ich sah zu dem Hund, der blieb genauso angespannt liegen, nicht einmal mit dem Schwanz wedelte er mehr.

"Schieß doch", sagte der Mann drängend. Ich nahm das Gewehr und hielt es ihm hin. "Dort", zischte er, "der braune Fleck neben der sechsten Akazie. Du mußt knapp unter den ersten Ast zielen. Schieß!"

Ich zog das Gewehr wieder herüber und zielte auf den braunen Fleck, knapp unter den Akazienast.

"Ruhig zielen. Einatmen."

Ich drückte ab. Der Hund sprang auf und stürzte zum Akazienwäldchen.

Langsam ließ der alte Mann seine Arme sinken, er saß nun ganz ruhig da, seine Schultern hingen schlaff, sein Auge war noch geschlossen. Er sprach wieder in gewöhnlichem Ton. "Damals, als wir hierherkamen, war schon Wüste überall. Jahre vorher, vielleicht hundert Jahre vorher, bevor die Europäer über die Berge kamen, haben die Arapahos Feuer in ihren Bibliotheksturm gelegt, die Brücken haben sie abgerissen, ihre Gräber eingeebnet und ihre ganze Stadt niedergebrannt. Und dann hat der letzte von ihnen einen mächtigen Wasserfall über die Trümmer geleitet. Hast du den Film davon gesehen?"

Der Hund winselte und bellte in dem Wäldchen und ereiferte sich immer mehr, seine Stimme überschlug sich. Ich konnte ihn nicht sehen; der alte Mann lauschte auch hinüber, und als der Hund zu knurren begann, knurrte mit jedem Atemzug und man hörte, wie seine Zähne aneinander rieben, da stand der Großvater auf, rückte seine Sonnenbrille zurecht und sagte:

"Trag mich jetzt nach Hause. Du hast eben den letzten amerikanischen Berglöwen erlegt."

wolf's tail and eyed his master nervously. But he paid no attention, spread out his thin arms, leaned his head back, and closed his left eye.

"Shoot," he said softly after a moment. I looked at the dog, who was still lying in tense readiness, not even wagging his tail now.

"Go ahead and shoot," he said insistently. I took the gun and held it out to him. "There," he whispered, "the brown patch by the sixth acacia. Aim just under the first branch. Shoot!"

I took the gun back and aimed at the brown patch, just under the branch of the acacia.

"Aim carefully. Draw a breath.'

I pressed the trigger. The dog leaped up and raced toward the acacia grove.

Slowly the old man let his arms sink; now he sat there perfectly quietly, his shoulders slumped, his eye still closed. He spoke again in a normal voice. "Back then, when we arrived here, everything was after all wilderness. Years before, maybe a hundred years earlier, before the Europeans came over the mountains, the Arapahos set fire to their library in the tower, they tore down their bridges, leveled their burial ground, and burned their whole city. And then the last survivor diverted a mighty waterfall across the rubble. Did you see the film they made of that?"

The dog whined and barked in the grove and became increasingly excited, his voice cracking. I couldn't see him; the old man was listening, too, and as the dog began to growl, growling with every breath, and you could hear his teeth grinding, then Grandfather stood up, adjusted his sunglasses, and said:

"Carry me home now. You just bagged the last American mountain lion."

Lilo Fromm

Komische Tiere / Funny Animals

Die Schnecke/*The Snail*

DER BLAUE DRAGOMAN

HANNELORE VALENCAK

ICH WOLLTE MIR KEINEN DRAGOMAN MIETEN. WENN ICH AUF REISEN WAR, war ich lieber allein. An diesem Morgen wollte ich Luxor entdecken. Ja, eine Entdeckung und keine Besichtigung sollte es sein, das hatte ich mir vorgenommen. Für die Fahrt hatte ich eine Pferdekutsche gemietet und mir einen Fliegenwedel aus Hanf gekauft.

Der Morgen war noch kühl und ließ mich in Frieden. Dafür umschwärmten mich Kinder, hüpften vor mir auf und ab und forderten kreischend von mir: "Bakschisch! Bakschisch!" Ich teilte mein Kleingeld aus und hoffte, nun Ruhe zu haben. Aber die Kinder bestanden mit größerem Nachdruck auf Geld. Sie flitzten neben der Kutsche her und stießen jedesmal, wenn der Kutscher sie anschrie und seine Peitschenschnur in das Rudel hineinschnalzen ließ, ein rachedurstiges Klagen und Heulen aus. Da ich ihnen keine Münzen mehr geben konnte, bewarfen sie mich mit Steinen und Straßenkot, verloren Zeit mit dem Suchen, Bücken und Zielen, schrien auf, als wir ihnen entwischten, und trollten sich mißgestimmt.

Es war Mai. Im Niltal war schon Getreideernte. Die Straße führte an Stoppelfeldern vorbei. Mir fiel ein Druschplatz auf, der im Schatten eines niedrigen Baumes mit einer breiten und flachen Schaumkrone lag. Das Getreide war auf den Boden geschüttet, zwei Rinder im Joch gingen darauf im Kreis herum und zogen einen Schlitten mit hölzernen Kufen, den ein Mann mit dem Gewicht seines Körpers beschwerte. Der Schlitten zerhäckselte die Getreidehalme. Die beiden Rinder traten die Körner heraus. Diese geruhsame, archaische Arbeitsweise—wahrscheinlich die gleiche wie in der Pharaonenzeit—gefiel mir, und ich bat den Kutscher zu halten. Er lenkte sein Gefährt in den Schattenbereich. Über dem Druschplatz lag eine summende Hochsommerstille. Ich glaubte im Trotten der Rinderhufe das Platzen der Hülsen und das Rieseln der Körner zu hören. Es war nicht Gegenwart, nicht Vergangenheit, es war ein Augenblick im Sothisjahr.

Ich wäre gerne noch länger in diesem Schatten, in dieser rieselnden, summenden Stille geblieben, doch war schon wieder ein bettelnder Knirps bei mir. Er wollte eine Zigarette haben und war nicht gesonnen, auf meinen Wink zu verschwinden. Ich hatte keine Zigarette mehr—nur die eine, die ich soeben rauchte. In diesem Moment hatte ich sie erst angezündet. Damit mich der Knirps in Ruhe ließ, gab ich sie ihm. Er nahm sie und rannte über das Feld. Schon schickte ich mich an, ihn zu vergessen, doch in diesem

THE BLUE DRAGOMAN

HANNELORE VALENCAK
translated by Sandra Celt

I HAD NO WISH TO HIRE A DRAGOMAN, I PREFERRED TO TRAVEL ALONE. THIS morning I wanted to discover Luxor and had definitely decided to make it a discovery instead of a sightseeing tour. For the trip I had rented a horse and carriage and bought myself a hemp fly-whisk.

The morning was still cool and did not bother me; the children, however, did, hopping up and down in front of me, squawking and demanding "Bakshish! Bakshish!" I distributed my change, hoping to buy some peace and quiet, but their insistence upon money became even more imperious. They scurried alongside the carriage, bursting into vindictive cries and yowls whenever the coachman yelled at them and snapped his whip into the pack of predators. Since I ran out of coins, they pelted me with stones and dung, wasted time searching, bending over, and aiming, screeched when we escaped, and then milled around in bad-tempered listlessness.

It was May, already harvest time in the Nile valley. The road wound through fields of grain stubble. I noticed a threshing operation in the shadow of a squat tree topped by a broad, flat crown of foam. The grain had been poured onto the ground; two yoked oxen plodded in circles pulling a sledge with wooden skids that a man was weighting with his own body. The sledge chopped up the stalks. The oxen trampled out the grain. I liked this relaxed, archaic way of working, probably the same as in pharaonic times, and asked the driver to stop. He guided his coach into the shade. A buzzing midsummer stillness hovered over the workplace. I thought I could hear the bursting husks and slithering kernels under the treading hooves. It was neither past nor present, only a moment in the Sothic year.

I would like to have stayed a while in the shade, in this buzzing percolating peace, but a tiny beggar appeared, demanding a cigarette; he was not about to disappear when I waved him off. I had no more cigarettes, except for the one I was smoking—I had just lit it and gave it to the kid, hoping to be left alone. He grabbed it and ran across the field. I had barely decided to put him out of my mind when I saw a young man standing on the

Moment stand ein junger Mann auf dem Trittbrett. Ich hatte ihn nicht kommen sehen. Plötzlich war er da und erschreckte mich. Sein unverhofftes Erscheinen war wie ein Angriff auf mich, und auch das Gesicht des Mannes war angriffslustig. Es war ein intelligentes, hübsches Gesicht, ein schmales Semitengesicht mit tabakbrauner Haut, mit schwarzen, geraden Augenbrauen und einem kräftigen, gutgeschnittenen Mund. Auch das kleine, glatte Lippenbärtchen, das zu solchen Männergesichtern gehört, war da. Ich schaute in ein Gesicht, das nicht auffiel, aber stimmte. Ich hätte es gern sympathisch gefunden, doch es verwahrte sich gegen mein freundliches Urteil, indem es geradezu vor hämischer Bosheit glühte. "Do you like a cigarette?" fragte der junge Mann und gab mir meine Zigarette zurück. Ich erkannte sie an ihrem geschwärzten Ende. Als mir endlich die passende Antwort einfiel, nämlich die, er möge lieber darauf achten, daß der Knirps, als dessen Anwalt er auftrat, nicht bettelte und den Leuten lästig fiel, war er schon wieder fort und hatte nach Punkten gesiegt.

Ich ließ mich zu den Ruinen von Karnak bringen, ging eine Weile zwischen ihnen umher, sagte mir vor, daß sie groß und gewaltig seien, fühlte mich irritiert und fuhr bald wieder ins Hotel.

Am nächsten Morgen ging ich zur Rezeption und äußerte den Wunsch, einen Fremdenführer zu mieten. Ich redete mit demselben Mann, der mich gestern gefragt hatte, ob ich nicht einen Dragoman wünschte, und dem ich gesagt hatte: "Nein. Diese Leute stören mich nur." Er blickte mich kurz und verständnisvoll an und lächelte mit den Augen, als er mich um Geduld bat, in einer Stunde werde ein Dragoman da sein.

Ich saß in der Halle, als er kam, und sah ihn im Gegenlicht durch die Glastür treten. Er war sehr groß und trug ein langes, blaues Gewand. Mir fiel auf, daß dieses Blau sehr schön und ganz rein war, eine kühle, traumhafte Farbe von großer Intensität. Als der Dragoman sich in der offenen Tür bewegte, entfaltete sich sein Gewand und umwehte ihn und war einen Augenblick wie vom Licht gebläht. Er kam leuchtend herein und erlosch im Zwielicht der Halle. Ich schaute in sein Gesicht. Es war tabakbraun und schmal, ein Semitengesicht mit schwarzen geraden Brauen. Die Gesichter dieses Menschenschlags ähneln einander sehr, und trotzdem erkannte ich dieses eine wieder. Ich erschrak. Wahrscheinlich errötete ich sogar. Mein erster Impuls war, diesen Dragoman abzulehnen. Dann begegnete ich seinem höflichen, ruhigen Blick und wußte, daß er mich nicht wiedererkannte. Er grüßte und nannte mir seinen Namen, und ich ging wortlos und entwaffnet mit ihm.

Der blaue Dragoman lieferte mir ein erstaunliches Beispiel, wie ein Mensch sich durch seine Kleidung verändern kann. Gestern mit seinem offenen Hemd und den achtlos aufgekrempelten Ärmeln, hatte er sehr ungestüm und sehr jung gewirkt. Heute, in seinem wehenden blauen Gewand, sah er footboard. I had not seen him coming, suddenly he was there and startled me. His unexpected appearance was like an assault, and even his face was aggressive. It was an intelligent, handsome face, a narrow Semitic face with tobacco-colored skin, straight black eyebrows, and a strong, well-shaped mouth. Not even the neat little moustache that belongs to the faces of such men was missing. I looked at the inconspicuous but appropriate face and would like to have found it pleasant, but it rejected my friendly inclination by fairly glittering with spiteful glee. "Do you like a cigarette?" the young man asked, handing me my own; I recognized its blackened tip. By the time the right response finally occurred to me—he should make sure that the twirp he was representing didn't beg and bother people—he was already gone and had scored a point victory.

I had myself carted to the ruins at Karnak, meandered among them for a while, recited to myself how huge and majestic they were, felt irritated and soon returned to the hotel.

The next morning I went to the reception desk and expressed my wish to hire a tour guide. I spoke with the same man who had asked me yesterday whether I didn't want a dragoman, and whom I had told, "No. Those people only bother me." He gave me a quick, understanding glance; his eyes smiled at me as he requested patience on my part, a dragoman would be there in an hour.

When he arrived, I was sitting in the lobby and saw his backlighted frame walking through the glass door. He was very tall and wore a long blue robe. I noticed the beauty and total purity of this blue, a cool, dreamy color of great intensity. His motions on the threshold caused the robe to unfold in breezy waves around him; for a moment it looked like it was puffed up with light. He entered, shining, and dimmed in the dusky lobby. I looked at his face. It was narrow and tobacco-colored, a Semitic face with straight black brows. Even though the members of this particular race seem to resemble each other very much, I recognized this face and was startled. I probably even blushed. My first impulse was to refuse to accept this dragoman, but then I met his calm, polite gaze and knew he did not recognize me. He said hello and gave me his name, and I went with him, disarmed and silent.

The blue dragoman furnished me with an astonishing example of how clothes can change a person. Yesterday, with his open shirt and carelessly rolled-up sleeves, he had given the impression of being impetuous and extremely young. Today, in his flowing blue robe, he looked as unreal as a

unwirklich aus wie ein Tempelpriester. Er ging mit gemessenen Schritten neben mir her, winkte eine Kutsche herbei und bot mir, als diese beim Einsteigen schwankte, den Arm.
Er hatte mir seinen Namen genannt, doch mir war nur sein Vorname, Hassan, im Gedächtnis geblieben. Das war ein einschüchternd männlicher Name, scharf wie ein Messerschnitt und unerhört stolz. Mein Dragoman fragte mich, ob ich Karnak besuchen wollte, und ich hätte beinahe gesagt: "Dort war ich schon gestern." Doch dann fiel mir rechtzeitig ein, daß das Gestern vergessen sein sollte, und ich stimmte mit einem Kopfnicken zu: nach Karnak.
Heute sah ich in Luxor keine Kinder. Keine bettelnde, kreischende Horde lief neben uns her. Und auch der Tempel von Karnak war nicht der gleiche wie gestern. An diesem Morgen stürmte er auf mich ein und zerschlug meinen Maßstab samt den Wortmarken: "groß" und "gewaltig." Was gestern nur eine Ruinenstätte, wenn auch eine eindrucksvolle, gewesen war, stand heute als Tempel des Reichsgottes Amun da. Mein Dragoman führte mich durch ihn und war kein Schulmeister, sondern ein Märchenerzähler.
Von Menschen geschaffene Räume umgaben uns. Sie waren weit und klar und nach oben hin offen. Die Riesensäulen erreichten und trugen den Himmel—ein tiefblau leuchtendes Tempeldach. Eine einzeln stehende Säule nahe beim Eingang verdeckte die Sonne mit ihrem Kapitell, das breit und wie eine Opferschale geformt war, und das Feuer der Sonnenkorona brannte drin. Ich horchte auf meinen Märchenerzähler. Er redete—und was er sagte, geschah. Thutmosis der Dritte erwachte zum Leben und haßte seine Stiefschwester Hatschepsut, seine Gemahlin, die Königin. Er riß die Macht an sich und beseitigte Hatschepsut, ließ jedes Bildnis zerstören, auf dem sie zu sehen war, und tötete sie damit zum zweitenmal und für immer. Amenophis der Dritte lebte und nahm die bürgerliche Teje zur Frau, König Ramses der Zweite ließ seine Statuen meißeln, so überlebensgroß, wie er sich fühlte. —Männer und Frauen, leben und weiterleben, ein Haß, der noch eine tote Königin schändet—und wahrscheinlich auch Liebe, die kein Chronist überliefert hat.
Am Nachmittag fuhren wir zu den Königsgräbern. Sie lagen westlich des Nils, im Totenbezirk. Auf der Hinfahrt, bei der es nichts zu erzählen gab, saß Hassan still neben mir und schaute mich nicht einmal an. Ich ermunterte ihn, mir von sich zu erzählen, und fragte ihn, wo er sein fließendes Deutsch gelernt habe. Er gab kurz und höflich Antwort, er habe Sprachen studiert und verdinge sich zuweilen als Dragoman, um seine Kenntnisse in Schwung zu halten. Ich schaute ihn von der Seite an und dachte: Hassan, der Mann mit dem schönen, gefährlichen Namen. Wer ist er? Wie lebt er? —Er sagte es mir nicht.
Die Straße führte durch eine Schlucht in das Thebanische Gebirge hinein.

temple priest. He accompanied me with measured stride, beckoned to a carriage, and offered me his arm for steadiness to enter the swaying coach.

He had mentioned his Semitic surname, but only his given name, Hassan, had remained in my memory. That was an intimidatingly masculine name, sharp as a knife and unbelievably proud. My dragoman asked whether I wanted to visit Karnak; I was about to retort "I was there yesterday," when I remembered that I wanted to forget yesterday, and I nodded my assent: to Karnak.

Today I saw no children in Luxor. No begging, screeching horde surrounded us. Not even the Karnak temple was the same as yesterday. This morning it crashed in upon me and destroyed my standard of weights and measures, including denominations such as "huge" and "majestic." What had been ruins yesterday, albeit impressive ones, now had the stature of a temple: that of the imperial god Amun. My dragoman guided me around and was no schoolmaster, but rather a weaver of fairy tales.

Rooms created by human beings surrounded us, wide and bright and open at the top. Gigantic pillars grazed and carried the heavens—a luminous, deep-blue skyroof. The capital of a solitary pillar near the entrance eclipsed the sun with its breadth, its shape that of a sacrificial bowl, with the solar corona burning within. I listened to my storyteller—whatever he narrated occurred. Tuthmosis III was resurrected hating his stepsister Hatshepsut, his wife, the queen. He usurped royal power and rid himself of her, had every portrait destroyed on which she could be seen and killed her thus for the second time, and forever. Amenhotep III lived and took the commoner Tiy as his wife; King Ramses II had statues sculpted larger than life, just the way he felt. —Men and women, living and living on, a hate that would degrade an already-dead queen—and probably a love as well, undocumented by chroniclers.

In the afternoon we traveled to the royal tombs in the necropolis west of the Nile. During the uneventful trip—there were no stories to be told —Hassan sat next to me quietly and did not even look at me. I encouraged him to tell me about himself and asked where he had learned my language so fluently. His response was concise and polite: he had studied languages and worked now and then as a dragoman in order to avoid becoming rusty. I studied him from the side and thought: Hassan, the man with the beautiful, dangerous name. Who is he? How does he live? —He did not tell me.

The road led through a gully into the Theban mountainside. The

Die Sonne war weiß und gab ein brennendes Licht. Erst in den Königsgräbern war es kühl. Osiris warb mit Milde um jeden, der bei ihm eintrat.

Das Leben, das die Abgeschiedenen führten, war aus dem Raum in die Fläche zurückgekehrt. In reinen Farben leuchtete es von den Wänden: das Totengericht, der Horusfalke, der hundeköpfige Totenbestatter Anubis.

Hier unter der Erde, in der Stille, dem Dämmerlicht, kam mir das Alleinsein mit einem fremden Mann zu Bewußtsein. Die Enge der Grabstollen übte einen Zwang auf mich aus. Der natürliche Abstand zwischen Hassan und mir war schwerer einzuhalten als draußen unter dem Himmel. Ich wehrte mich gegen diese Annäherung. Ich empfand sie als störend und unstatthaft, obwohl sie nur ein Vorgang in meinem Gefühl war und nichts Entsprechendes geschah. Hassan ging neben mir, sprach erklärende Worte, war sogar höflicher als am Vormittag, so höflich, daß er fast steif und förmlich wirkte —und trotzdem war die Distanz zwischen uns verringert. Er spürte das sicherlich auch und kämpfte dagegen an. Ob er redete, ob er schwieg, in allem war Übertreibung. Seine Stimme stockte zuweilen. Ein brüchiger Klang war in ihr. Das waren die Zeichen der Befangenheit—zweifellos. Ich nützte den Vorteil, nicht reden zu müßen, aus und machte seinen Nachteil damit noch größer. Es war seine Aufgabe, nicht aus der Rolle zu fallen. Ich war nur sein Publikum—wohlwollend, aber wachsam. Ich fand meine Sicherheit wieder, indem ich schwieg, und ihm kam sein fließendes Deutsch immer mehr abhanden. Ich verstand, daß darin eine Huldigung für mich lag, und faßte den Entschluß, sie anzunehmen. Sie sollte eine Entschädigung sein, die Buße für meine Demütigung von gestern.

Was unter der Erde begonnen hatte, konnte draußen im Licht nicht mehr völlig eingedämmt werden. Die Spannung, die mich zu Hassan, hinzog, blieb, doch war sie nicht stark genug, um gefährlich zu werden. Sie war angenehm und erhöhte mein Selbstgefühl. Hassan war weiterhin um Distanz bemüht, nur streifte mich manchmal sein Arm, wenn wir nebeneinandergingen.

Wir fuhren nach Deir el Bahari, zum Totentempel der Hatschepsut, der in einem heißen, rotbraunen Felskessel stand. Ich wunderte mich über seine Klarheit und Unversehrtheit. Vollzählig und in genau bemessenem Abstand, zwischen langen, ungebrochenen Parallelen verankert, waren die Tempelsäulen zu Hallen gereiht, standen Rampen kantig und festgefügt da und erstreckten sich breit von einer Terrasse zur nächsten. Mit großen horizontalen Flächen war dieser Stufentempel in die Landschaft gefügt, die ihn felsig, mit schroffen, lotrechten Klüften in einem bizarren und theatralischen Halbrund umfing. Nichts war weich oder weiblich an diesem herrlichen Bau, an dem die Zeit sich vergeblich gescheuert hatte und der nach fast viertausend Jahren so alterslos dastand, als wäre er erst ein Entwurf auf dem Zeichenbrett.

sun was white and gave off a burning light; not until we reached the royal tombs was it cool. Osiris courted every entrant with his mildness.

The life led by the departed had reverted from solids to planes. Pure colors illuminated the walls: the judgment of the dead; the Horus falcon; Anubis, the dog-faced burier of the dead.

Here, beneath the ground, in the quiet twilight, I became aware of the fact that I was alone with a strange man. The narrow tombs transmitted a feeling of compulsion. The natural distance between Hassan and myself was more difficult to maintain here than under the open skies. I resisted this incipient closeness, perceiving it as annoying and impermissible, although it was a mere subjective procedure with no basis in reality. Hassan walked along next to me, spoke explanations, was even more polite than during the morning, so polite that he seemed almost stiff and formal—but the distance between us was diminished nevertheless. He must have noticed that and fought against it. His words and his silences contained an element of exaggeration; his voice occasionally faltered, it had a brittle timbre. Without a doubt, those were the signs of embarrassment. I made use of my advantage —not having to speak—and thereby increased his disadvantage. It was his job to remain in character. I was his audience, benevolent but watchful. I regained my composure in the security of silence, whereas his fluency deteriorated progressively. I realized that this was a type of homage to me and decided to accept it—as compensation and penitence for yesterday's humiliation.

What had begun underground could not be fully subdued in the bright outside light. The tension that drew me to Hassan remained, but it was not strong enough to become dangerous. It was pleasant and flattered my ego. Hassan was still anxious to retain his reserve, except that his arm occasionally brushed against mine while we walked side by side.

We drove to Deir el Bahari, to Hatshepsut's temple-tomb, which was situated within a kettle of hot, reddish-brown cliffs. I wondered at its clarity and intactness. Complete in number, separated by exactly calculated intervals, anchored between long and unbroken parallels, the temple pillars had been arranged into halls; angular, immovable platforms stretched broadly from one terrace to the next. Great graduated horizontals fit this temple into the landscape, whose cliffs and abrupt vertical ravines embraced it in a bizarre, theatrical semicircle. There was nothing soft or feminine about this magnificent building, which time had tried to scour in vain; after almost four thousand years it was still as ageless as a sketch on a drawing board.

Ich bat Hassan, mir mehr von Hatschepsut zu erzählen. Er sagte, sie habe ihr Land zu Frieden und Wohlstand geführt, und zeigte mir Zeichnungen an den Tempelwänden, die von dem Leben unter ihrer Regentschaft erzählten. Kein Krieg, kein Gemetzel, sondern friedliche Expeditionen, die Fahrt nach Somaliland—in das Weihrauchland Punt. Bienenkorbähnliche Hütten, Palmen, ein ruhendes Rind, die fette Fürstin von Somaliland. Wir standen vor einem steinernen Bilderbuch, lächelten und wendeten plötzlich einander den Blick zu—in einem Moment, in dem ich mich schlecht bewachte. Als ich zuließ, daß Hassan mir in die Augen schaute, war es mir klar, daß ich mir eine Blöße gab. Er überbrückte die Distanz, die ich sorgfältig zwischen uns einhielt, auf einem geraden und abgesicherten Weg und befand sich im innersten Kreis, bevor ich ihn abwehren konnte. Ein freier, uneingeschränkt bewundernder Blick, der eine Frage stellte und eine Antwort erhoffte, traf mich, und ich erschrak. Ich dachte: Keinen Schritt weiter! Das war nun kein Spiel mehr. Das war schon ein Kräftemessen. Ich äußerte eilig den Wunsch, nach Hause zu fahren. Dies war meine Antwort—und meine Errettung um Haaresbreite.

Am anderen Morgen, als ich wiederkam, schlug Hassan mir vor, in das Dorf der Töpfer zu fahren. Als ich zustimmte, war das wieder ein Schritt zu ihm hin. Das Töpferdorf, in das er mich führte, war ein Schock aus Hitze, Armseligkeit und Gestank. Die Wege waren staubig und schmal und von mannshohen Lehmmauern eingesäumt, die die gespeicherte Sonnenglut widerstrahlten und keinen Schatten warfen, in den man sich flüchten konnte. Kadaver von Katzen und Hunden lagen herum, halb verwest, halb mumifiziert, und verströmten Miasmen. Die Lehmmauern waren von Toröffnungen unterbrochen. Vor einer Toröffnung blieb der Dragoman stehen und forderte mich zum Eintreten auf. Ich betrat einen kleinen ummauerten Hof, in dem eine fensterlose Lehmhütte stand. Den Großteil des übrigen, unverbauten Hofraums nahm ein Haufen aus Kehricht und Tierexkrementen ein, auf dem schmutzige, krank aussehende Hühner hockten. Vor der Tür zur Lehmhütte stand eine junge Frau mit einem entsetzlich leeren, fast toten Gesicht. Sie trug ein schwarzes Gewand und war hochschwanger. In ihren Händen, die sie mechanisch bewegte, hielt sie ein langes, formloses Strickzeug aus schwarzem Garn. Hassan richtete ein paar Worte an sie, da trat sie gleichgültig ein paar Schritte beiseite und gab mir Gelegenheit, in die Hütte zu schauen. Sogleich stob mir gackernd und kreischend ein Huhn entgegen. Staub und Federn flogen um mein Gesicht. Dann hüllten mich Schwaden von schlechter Luft, von scharfer, menschlicher Ausdünstung ein, und ich hatte Mühe, meine Übelkeit zu bezwingen. Das Wohnloch, in das ich schaute, war zuerst vollkommen schwarz und erhellte sich langsam im Streulicht, das durch die Tür fiel. Ich gewahrte im Winkel am Boden etwas wie eine Bettstatt, sah ein paar aufgehängte Kleiderfetzen und machte erschrocken

I asked Hassan to tell me more about Hatshepsut. He said that she had led her nation into peace and prosperity and pointed out pictures on the temple walls describing life under her regency. No war, no slaughter, just peaceable expeditions, the trip to Somaliland—into Punt, the incense country. Beehive huts, palm trees, placid cattle, the fat Somali princess. We were standing before a stone picture book and smiling when we suddenly glanced at one another, at a moment when my guard was down. As I allowed Hassan to look into my eyes, I realized that I was exposing myself. He bridged the distance between us, which I had been so careful to maintain, via a straight, secured path and was in the inner circle before I had time to repulse him. He hit me with a free, unreservedly admiring look that asked a question and hoped for an answer. Taken aback I thought: Not another step! This was no longer a game. It was a test of strength. I hurriedly expressed the desire to go back home—my answer, and my hairbreadth salvation.

When I returned the next morning, Hassan suggested that we drive to the potters' village. My assent was a step in his direction again. The potters' village he showed me was a shock consisting of heat, stench, and misery. The paths were dusty and narrow and lined with man-high mud walls that stored and reflected the incandescent sun and provided no merciful shadow to flee into. Cat and dog corpses, half rotten and half mummified, were strewn around, exuding vapors. The mud walls were pocked with gate entrances; the dragoman stopped before one of them and invited me to enter. I stepped into a small enclosed courtyard containing a windowless mud hut; the greatest part of the remaining unused space in the courtyard was taken up by piles of rubbish and animal excrement on which dirty, sick-looking chickens squatted. A young woman with a horribly empty, almost dead face was standing before the door to the hut. She was wearing a black robe and was far along in pregnancy. Her mechanically moving hands held some long, shapeless knitting of black yarn. Hassan said something to her, and she stepped aside indifferently so as to allow me a look inside the hut. I was immediately assailed by a squawking, screeching hen; dust and feathers enveloped my face, followed by the stench of musty air and of acrid human excretions. I suppressed my nausea with great difficulty. The hovel before me was completely black at first, only slowly did the scattered light illuminate it through the doorway. I perceived something like a bed on the floor in the corner, saw a few ragged clothes hanging about, and beat a frightened re-kehrt, als der Brechreiz wiederkam. Ich flüchtete aus der Hütte und aus dem Hof und hatte das Gefühl, auch vor Hassan fliehen zu müssen, damit er mir nicht noch einmal so etwas zeigte.

Er führte mich aus dem Dorf, an den Gruben vorbei, in denen die Töpfer saßen und ihr Handwerk ausübten. Eine böse Hitze lag über dieser lehmgelben Welt. Hassan fragte mich, ob ich eine Erfrischung wünschte, und brachte mich, als ich bejahte, zu unserer Kutsche zurück. Wir gelangten nach kurzer Zeit zu einem Gutshof, einem großen Hof mit Bäumen und weißen Gebäuden, der nirgends durch Mauern eingeengt und trotzdem etwas völlig Geschlossenes war. Auf der Erde lagen hohe Getreidehügel. Aus einem Baumschatten trat mir ein Mann entgegen, ein kleiner, hagerer Mann im weißen Gewand. Er war vielleicht sechzig Jahre alt und hatte ein stilles Lächeln, das mich für ihn einnahm. Er bat mich, im Schatten Platz zu nehmen, und begann ein kluges weitläufiges Gespräch, an dem ich, erschöpft von der Hitze, nur lustlos teilnahm. Sofort bemerkte er es und sagte: “Sie können nicht zuhören, weil Sie an Wasser denken. Ich werde veranlassen, daß man Ihnen etwas zu trinken bringt.”

Ich fand, daß er die Höflichkeit eines weltabgekehrten Weisen hatte, der alles verstehen und billigen kann, aber auch alle seine Gedanken schonungslos ausspricht.

Man brachte mir Wasser in einem irdenen Krug, das kalt und frisch war und wie Quellwasser schmeckte. Nachher kam in einer Kupferkanne Kaffee. Nun wurde mir auch gesagt, wer mein Gastgeber war: Hassans Vater. Und dies hier war sein Besitztum. Mittlerweile war noch eine Schar von Leuten dazugekommen, Familienmitglieder, Gesinde, und alle begrüßten sie mich. Hassan hielt sich im Hintergrund. Er trug auch heute sein blaues Mantelgewand, das sein Berufsgewand als Dragoman war, und somit trat er nicht als mein Gastgeber auf. Er hatte mir nur das Gegenteil jener Fellachenhütte gezeigt und damit ein unvollständiges Bild, das Bild von der Welt, in der er lebte, ergänzt.

Hassan zwang mich, über ihn nachzudenken, und übte dadurch einen Einfluß auf mich aus, den ich als störend und zugleich als erregend empfand. Es wurde also Zeit, daß ich Luxor verließ und weiter nach Süden fuhr—am besten gleich morgen. So sagte ich Hassan am Nachmittag, daß ich nur noch heute seine Dienste beanspruchen werde. Meine Stimme reicherte ich mit künstlichem Hochmut an. Ich bemerkte, als es gesagt war, das Kopfrucken Hassans. Er schaute mich an, sehr lange und sehr intensiv, und forderte mich damit auf, seinen Blick zu erwidern. Ich blieb aus Schwäche standhaft und schaute geradeaus.

Wir standen in einem der thebanischen Gräber. Die Wände der Grabkammer waren mit duftigen, zarten, doch unglaublich dichten Bildern geschmückt, die nicht starr und schematisch waren, sondern lebten. Ich sah treat when I again felt the need to vomit. I fled both hut and courtyard with the feeling that I would have to flee Hassan as well so he would not show me anything like that again.

He led me out of the village, past the potters plying their trade in the pits. A nasty heat engulfed this mud-yellow world. When Hassan asked me if I wanted refreshments, I said yes, and he took me back to the coach. We soon arrived at a manorial estate, a great courtyard with trees and white buildings, self-enclosed even in the absence of any constricting walls. Grain lay piled on the ground. A man emerged from the shadow of a tree and walked toward me, a small, gaunt man wearing a white robe. He appeared to be about sixty years old and had a quiet smile that disposed me in his favor. He invited me to sit in the shade and started a wise and lengthy conversation; exhausted by the heat, I participated only listlessly. He noticed immediately and said, "You cannot listen because you are thinking of water. I will have them bring something for you to drink."

I found that he had the politeness of a world-renouncing sage who understood and tolerated everything, but who also expressed all his thoughts unsparingly.

They brought me water in an earthenware jug, fresh and cold and tasting like spring water. Coffee followed in a copper pot. I was also told that my host was Hassan's father. And this was his property. A crowd of people had joined us in the meantime, family members, domestic servants, and everybody greeted me. Hassan remained in the background. He was wearing his cloaklike blue robe today also, his dragoman's working vestment, and therefore did not act as host. He had only shown me the opposite of that fellahim hut, thus complementing an incomplete picture, the picture of the world in which he lived.

Hassan forced me to think about him, thus exerting an influence over me that I perceived as both irritating and exciting. It was time for me to leave Luxor and travel farther to the south—it would be best to leave tomorrow. So I told Hassan that afternoon that I would be needing his services only today, enriching my voice with artificial arrogance. I noticed his head jerk when I finished speaking. He looked at me for a long time and very intensely, challenging me to return his gaze. I remained steadfast in my weakness, staring straight ahead.

We were standing in one of the Theban tombs. The chamber walls were decorated with hazy, delicate, yet unbelievably dense pictures that were alive, not stiff and schematic. I saw a bird-hunt in the papyrus thicket, the eine Vogeljagd im Papyrusdickicht, den Grabherrn, sein Wurfholz schwingend, auf einem Floß, ein Gewimmel von Fischen im Wasser, ein Vogelgeschwirr in der Luft—blaue Vögel und rotbraune Schmetterlinge, eine Wildkatze, in den Leib eines Vogels verkrallt, flüchtig dies alles und zeitlos —das Leben im Tod. Blau entfaltete sich ein Papyrusfächer. Blau war der Halsschmuck, den der Grabherr trug. Ich war hier, um dieses bezaubernde Bild und nicht einen jungen Ägypter anzuschauen, dessen Aufgabe darin bestand, mir das Bild zu erklären. Er tat es, indem er einen Spiegel schwenkte, den Lichtschwall, der durch den Grabeingang kam, durch den dunklen Innenraum wandern ließ und Szene um Szene darin zum Aufleuchten brachte.

Und dann war vor meinen Augen plötzlich ein anderes Bild. Hassan hatte den Spiegel geschwenkt und hielt ihn nun so, daß ich mich selbst darin sah und an meiner Seite, halb hell, halb verschattet, ihn. Ehe ich mich gegen den Überfall absichern konnte, war mein Blick von dem seinen gefangen und klar befragt. Es wurde kein Wort gesprochen, doch ich begriff. Ich sah Hassans dunkles, ernstes Gesicht und, alles überstrahlend, das Blau seines Mantels märchenblau und dem wirklichen Leben entrückt—ein Zauber, dem ich nicht anheimfallen durfte. Mein ganzer abendländischer Hochmut stand auf und gebot mir, den Kopf zu schütteln: Undenkbar! —Diese Gemeinsamkeit, die Hassan hergestellt hatte, war nur ein Traum in einem blauen Papyrusdickicht, die blauen Vögel flogen darüber hin—doch ein rotbrauner Mann schwang sein Wurfholz und tötete sie.

Ich wünschte Hassan nie mehr widerzusehen und glaubte mir diesen Wunsch bis zum nächsten Tag. Dann aber, als ich auf dem Bahnhof stand und Hassan plötzlich auf mich zukommen sah, wurde mir der wahre Sachverhalt klar.

Hassan trug nicht mehr sein blaues Märchengewand, sondern einen gestreiften Anzug und ein offenes Hemd. Sehr jung sah er aus, und sehr stark zog es mich zu ihm hin. Auch seine Stimme war anders als in den Tagen vorher. Sie klang freundlich und unbefangen, als er mir sagte, er hätte ebenfalls in Assuan zu tun. Er stieg mit mir ein. Es war alles alltäglich und harmlos. Ich hatte keine Handhabe gegen ihn.

Da nun ein weiterer Schutzwall durchbrochen war und ich darauf vertraute, daß der innerste hielt, bewilligte ich mir eine kleine Romanze. Ich sagte mir, daß ab einem bestimmten Stadium der Verliebtheit jedes Ankämpfen gegen die Leidenschaft dieser nur förderlich sei. Dies zu vermeiden, mußte ab nun meine Taktik sein.

Die Bahnfahrt ging zwischen fahlgelben Bergen dahin, Kieswüste wechselte mit Schwemmland, die Zeit verstrich. Hassan, der mir gegenüber saß, redete unverfängliche Worte mit mir, und alles, was sich ereignete, war erlaubt. Das Gefühl des Bedrohtseins von gestern war einer Erwartung, ja fast einer angenehmen Neugier gewichen. Plötzlich, erschreckend unmittelbar, bot lord of the tomb swinging his throwing-stick aboard his raft, water teeming with fishes, birds whirring and chirping in the air—blue birds and reddish-brown butterflies, a wildcat clawing at a bird's body, everything fleeting and timeless—life within death. Blue was the papyrus fan unfolding; blue was the jewelry the lord of the tomb wore around his neck. I was here to contemplate this delightful picture, not a young Egyptian whose job it was to explain the picture to me. He did this by reflecting the light coming through the entrance, using a mirror to illuminate one scene after another within the dark interior.

Then, suddenly, another picture appeared before my eyes. Hassan had turned the mirror to such an angle that it now contained my own reflection; next to mine, half light and half shadowed, was his. Before I could protect myself against this surprise attack, my gaze was caught and clearly interrogated by his. Not a word was spoken, but I understood. I saw Hassan's dark, serious face and, eclipsing everything, the blue of his robe, a fairy-tale blue removed from real life—a spell to which I must not succumb. My entire Western haughtiness reared up and ordered me to shake my head; Unthinkable! —This togetherness Hassan had created was only a dream in a blue papyrus thicket with blue birds flying above—but a reddish-brown man swung his throwing-stick and killed them.

I didn't want to see Hassan again, ever, and actually believed this wish of mine until the next day. But when I saw him coming toward me at the train station, I realized what the true circumstances were.

Hassan was wearing a striped suit and an open shirt instead of his fairy-tale blue outfit. He looked very young, and I felt strongly attracted to him. Even his voice was different from the previous days—friendly and relaxed—when he told me that he had some business in Aswan too. He got into the train with me. It was so everyday and so harmless. I had no handle to use against him.

Since another protective wall had been successfully stormed and I was confident that the innermost one would hold, I granted myself the luxury of a little romance. After a certain stage of infatuation, I told myself, fighting the passion only serves to increase it. My strategy must now be directed toward avoiding such an outcome.

The train wound among ash-yellow mountains, gravel desert alternating with flooded farmland, time passed. Hassan chatted innocuously, sitting across from me; nothing occurred that was not permissible. Yesterday's threatening feeling had given way to expectation, almost pleasant curiosity. Then suddenly, with frightening immediacy, Hassan offered me a

Hassan mir eine Zigarette an. Er entnahm sie der Packung und hielt sie mir hin, mit der gleichen Gebärde wie vor einigen Tagen, und sagte mit ernster Stimme: "Bitte, verzeihen Sie mir!" Und ich sagte nichts, holte nur mein Erröten nach. Ich nahm die Zigarette und rauchte sie. Die Aschenkuppe wuchs zwischen meinen Fingern. Durch den Rauch sah ich Hassan an, jung, mit offenem Hemd und mit Ungestüm in den Augen—wie vor Tagen.

In Assuan kam er am Nachmittag in mein Hotel und lud mich zu einer Bootsfahrt ein. Er wollte mir die Nilkatarakte zeigen. Meine Bereitschaft, eine Romanze zu erleben, war nicht mehr zu widerrufen—so fuhr ich mit ihm.

Der Nil floß jung und grün zwischen Grauwacken und Granit. Aus dem Wasser ragten Steine wie Elefantenrücken oder wie Herden badender Flußpferde auf, braun oder grau oder von einem trockenen Olivgrün. Das Wasser war manchmal seidig und glatt, rann manchmal strähnig und schnell zwischen engen Passagen dahin oder war narbig und quaddelig, wo es verborgene Wirbel und Strudel in ihm gab.

Hassan war heiter, selbstsicher und gesprächig. Zum erstenmal wollte er wissen, woher ich kam, wer ich war, wie ich lebte, und ich erzählte es ihm. Ich sagte ihm, daß ich Geographin war und eben mein Studium beendet hatte, daß ich das Herumzigeunern liebte und mit einem Frachtschiff nach Ägypten gekommen war. Für das nächste Frühjahr war mir eine Stelle als Hochschulassistentin in Aussicht gestellt, und bis dahin war ich frei. Ich betonte das letzte Wort. Ich war frei und wollte es bleiben—das mußte zwischen uns klar sein. Hassan schaute mich an und widerlegte mich wortlos.

Ein Leuchten war in der Luft. Das Wasser war jung und rein. Unser Segelboot schwebte von Ufer zu Ufer. Auf der Höhe der Nilkatarakte liegt die Insel Sehel. Dort stiegen wir aus und gingen ein Stück landeinwärts. Unser Bootsmann suchte sich einen Schatten und legte sich schlafen. Unmittelbar war ich wieder mit Hassan allein. Wir gingen über weißen, muldigen Sand. Niedrige Sanddünen warfen uns ein grelles Streulicht entgegen. Eine Gruppe von Palmen war in der Nachmittagshitze erstarrt, die aus dem prallen, platzenden Sonnenball ausrann. Wir gingen auf einen Felsen zu, und ich sah, daß in Steinplatten Bilder eingeritzt waren: Hieroglyphen, Gott Chnum mit dem Widderkopf, ein König mit der Krone von Oberägypten.

Ein eckiger Fußpfad führte auf den Felskopf hinauf. Hassan stieg mir voran, machte große Schritte, fand Griffe, schwang sich an ihnen höher hinauf und stand oben, dunkel in einem grellweißen Blickfeld. Ich stieg durch Hitzeschwaden, die quälend waren. Mir schien, als käme das Brennen auf meiner Haut von einer heißen Substanz, mit der ich gepanzert war, von einer erstarrenden Schmelze, die sich über mich ergoß. Oben bei Hassan fand ich in einem Felsspalt Schatten. Ich lehnte mich eine Weile fest und flach an den Stein, damit mich der Glutschwall der Sonne nicht mehr erreichte. Dann cigarette. He removed it from the pack and held it in my direction with the same gesture as a few days ago and earnestly said, "Please forgive me!" I did not answer, merely recovered from blushing; I took the cigarette and smoked it. The ashhead grew between my fingers. I looked at Hassan through the smoke, young and openshirted and vehement-eyed—as he had been before.

That afternoon he came to my hotel in Aswan and invited me on a boat trip. He wanted to show me the Nile cataract. Since my willingness to experience a romance could no longer be revoked, I went with him.

The Nile threaded young and green through graywacke and granite. Rocks towered out of the water like elephant backs or herds of bathing hippopotamuses, brown or gray or a dry olive-green. Sometimes the water was silky and smooth; sometimes it ran in strands and rapidly through narrow passes or was scarred and swollen where there were hidden whirlpools and maelstroms.

Hassan was cheerful, self-confident, and talkative. For the first time he wanted to know where I came from, who I was, how I lived, and I told him: that I was a geographer and had just finished my studies, that I loved the gypsy life and had come to Egypt on a freighter, that I had been offered a university assistantship next spring but was free till then. I emphasized that word. I was free and wanted to stay that way—that must be very clear between us. Hassan looked at me, refuting my words in silence.

The air was glowing, the water was young and pure. Our sailboat floated from one riverbank to the other. The island of Sehel is located at the level of the Nile cataract; we got off there and walked inland for a while. Our boatman found shade and went to sleep. I was suddenly alone with Hassan again. We trudged over troughs of white sand; squat dunes scattered glare in our direction. A group of palm trees had frozen in the afternoon heat exuding from the swollen bursting sunball. We walked toward a cliff, and I saw that pictures had been engraved into the monoliths: hieroglyphics, the ram-headed god Chnum, a king with the crown of Upper Egypt.

An angular footpath wound up the cliff. Hassan preceded me, took long steps, found footholds, swung higher, and stood above, dark in a glaring white environment. I climbed through unbearable streams of heat; it felt as though the burning sensation on my skin emanated from some armor I was trapped within, molten stultification pouring over me. When I reached Hassan, I found a bit of shade in a crevice and leaned firm and flat against the rock for awhile to escape the solar deluge. Then I bent down to look at schaute ich vorgebeugt in das Niltal hinunter, sah flußabwärts kühles, flutendes Grün und flußaufwärts die steinerne Landschaft der Katarakte, ausgewaschene Rinnen und zackige Wände, wirr zernarbt wie abgenagte Maiskolben. Und noch weiter oben, im flirrenden Lichtdunst, der Staudamm. Und neben mir Hassan, unentwegt gegenwärtig. Er hatte sich zwischen mich und die Sonne gestellt und schenkte mir, mit der Hand an den Felsen gestützt, seinen Schatten. Ich fühlte den Schatten nicht, wohl aber Hassans Wärme, einen starken, ununterbrochenen Strom, den ich nicht mit dem Körper, sondern auf andere Weise wahrnahm und von der Sonnenwärme deutlich unterschied. Hassan blickte auf mich nieder und sagte: "Heute bin ich nicht mehr Ihr gemieteter Dragoman." —Ich wurde matt und verlor mein Raumgefühl, sah flirrendes, kreisendes Licht und als Ruhepol Hassans Blick—den dunklen Glanz seiner Augen, befehlsgewohnt— und fühlte, daß man vor Begehren eiskalt werden kann. Gefahr war im Spiel —eine klar erkannte Gefahr. Wenn ich nur die flüchtigste körperliche Berührung zuließ, in diesem Moment, da mir Hassan so nahe war, daß in meinem Ohr schon die Katarakte des Hinstürzens tosten, würde dies meine völlige Unterwerfung sein. Ich gab zur Antwort: "Nein, heute bin ich Ihr Gast." Und damit war meine Widerstandskraft verausgabt. Wenn Hassans Augen auf ihren Wünschen, die auch die meinen waren, so stark, so leicht erfüllbar—ja, was dann? Er aber trat zurück und sagte: "Das weiß ich." Die schaukelnde, flirrende Welt bewegte sich wieder ins Lot, und ich fühlte, als intensiven Schmerz, ihr Erstarren.

Wir fuhren zurück, und der Abend kam. In Assuan nahm ich von Hassan zum zweitenmal Abschied.

Die Nacht, die heranschlich, wurde beklemmend und lang. Ich hatte Träume, die beängstigend waren, da ich sie von der Wirklichkeit nicht unterscheiden konnte und nur eine kleine Verschiebung erlebte, breit genug, um das Bedrohliche einzulassen. Ich hatte im Traum die Augen offen—wenigstens glaubte und fühlte ich das—und sah, daß ich in meinem Hotelzimmer lag. Alles Mobiliar war an seinem Ort und klar zu identifizieren. Doch an meinem Bettrand saß Hassan und schaute mich an, grinste, war seiner Beute sicher und machte obszöne Bewegungen, die mich entsetzten. Dann wieder war er voll nobler Resignation, saß da und schützte mich vor der Bedrohung durch ihn. Und ich floh, einmal zu ihm hin, einmal von ihm fort, wollte um Hilfe schreien und konnte es nicht, lag stimmlos auf dem Schlammgrund meines Erschöpfungsschlafes und fühlte die Schreie in meiner Kehle vergurgeln. Vor dem offenen Fenster nahm ich eine Bewegung wahr, ein Zischeln und Sausen zuerst, dann ein Rütteln und Dröhnen. Dämonen führten ihren entfesselten Tanz auf, lauerten, daß ich starb und meine Seele hinausflog, schrien, brüllten und stritten schon jetzt und erprobten das Reißen der Beute, die ihnen gewiß war. Immer tiefer sackte ich in den Sog einer Schwärze the Nile valley, saw a cool surge of green downriver and the cataract stonescape upriver, eroded trenches and jagged walls, scarred chaotically like gnawed-off corncobs. And the dam higher up, flickering in the hazy light. And Hassan next to me, unflinchingly present. He had placed himself between the sun and me and was making me a gift of his shadow, one hand braced against the cliff. Although I couldn't feel the shadow, I did perceive Hassan's warmth through some extra-corporeal way, a strong and steady stream distinctly different from that of the sun. Hassan looked down at me and said, "Today I am no longer your hired dragoman." —I felt faint and spatially confused, saw light flicker and circle about; Hassan's eyes were the eye of this hurricane, dark, shiny, and accustomed to giving orders. I learned that desire can turn a person ice-cold. Danger came into the picture, a clear and distinct danger. If I allowed even the most fleeting physical contact in this moment—Hassan was so near that my own cataracts were roaring in my ears—that would be my complete surrender. I answered, "No, today I'm your guest." With that my resistance was exhausted. If Hassan's eyes insisted on their wishes—wishes that were mine as well, strong and so easy to satisfy —then what? But he took a step backward and said "I know that." The swaying, flickering world regained its equilibrium and caused me intense pain when it congealed.

We went back, evening came. In Aswan I said goodbye to Hassan for the second time.

A long, oppressive and anxious night crept upon me. My dreams were fearful, since I could not distinguish them from reality; only a small shift was needed, just wide enough to let the threat inside. My eyes were open during this dream (at least I felt and believed this): I was in my hotel room, the furniture was in place and clearly identifiable. But Hassan was sitting on the side of my bed staring at me and grinning, sure of his prey, and making obscene gestures that horrified me. Then suddenly he was full of noble resignation, sat there protecting me from the threat that was himself. I fled alternately toward and away from him, tried to call for help but could not, tripped in the muddy swamp that was my exhausted torpor, and felt the screams gurgle away, voiceless. I perceived a movement in the open window, first accompanied by hissing, whirring whispers, then by rumbling jolts: demons performed a wild and uninhibited dance, lay in wait for my death, shrieked and squabbled and fought for my ambushed soul, sure of their prey.

hinein, versuchte mich aufzubäumen und wollte noch leben, wollte zu Hassan, der hoch oben zurückblieb und mich anschaute—doppelseitig und doppelgesichtig.

Noch war es ein Schlaf, doch jetzt gleich würde es der Tod sein—da schrie ich mit letzter, verzweifelter Kraft und erwachte.

Eine fahlgelbe Morgendämmerung war vor dem Fenster, und das Sausen und Rütteln hielt an. Ein Sandsturm war ausgebrochen. Eine mehlig getrübte Luft war im Raum, hatte überall Staub abgelagert und hemmte den Atem. Immer noch wurde Staub durch das Fenster gepeitscht, ich schloß es, gegen den Anprall des Sturmes kämpfend. Papierfetzen stoben in reißendem Flug vorbei, ein großes Stück Wellpappe stieg in einem Sturmwirbel senkrecht nach oben, die Palmwedel waren straff in die Horizontale gebogen, schlugen um sich, und die Palmstämme knarrten.

Ich legte mich wieder auf mein staubiges Bett, bemüht, nicht mehr einzuschlafen, und atmete freier. Nein, es war keine Bleibe in diesem Land. Je eher ich wieder nach Norden fuhr, desto besser. Durch den rachsüchtig heulenden Sandsturm fuhr ich zum Bahnhof, stieg aus dem Taxi, wurde schwefelgelb angefaucht, mein Haar wurde wild um den Kopf gefetzt, und mein Kleid stieg aufgebauscht an mir in die Höhe. Erst als ich im Zug saß, fühlte ich mich halbwegs außer Gefahr. Ein Blick in den Handspiegel zeigte mir, daß mein Gesicht mit Staub überkrustet war. Ich sah eine Maske aus Gips und darüber zottiges Hanfhaar. Mir grauste vor meinem Anblick, ich suchte den Waschraum auf und verließ ihn zwar nicht gepflegt, aber menschenähnlich. Ich lehnte mich in den Fensterwinkel, genoß das Gefühl der Erfrischung, der Sicherheit, den Geruch nach Juchtenwasser auf meiner Haut, wollte die Augen schließen und—sah Hassan.

Er saß ein paar Bankreihen von mir entfernt, eingestäubt und verkrustet, doch unbekümmert, saß ruhig auf seinem Platz, mit dem Rücken zu mir, und ließ mir die Möglichkeit, ihn nicht zu bemerken. Nun gut, er war da und fuhr, so wie ich, nach Hause. Nur war ich woanders daheim als er—ganz woanders. Ich bekräftigte diesen Gedanken, indem ich aufstand und mich so hinsetzte, daß ich Hassan nicht mehr sah. Starrsinnig schaute ich in die Sturmwelt hinaus, die von den fliegenden Sandfahnen schräg gestriemt war.

Wir fuhren. Im Waggon herrschte schläfriges Schweigen. Auf einer der Sitzbänke hockte ein betender Moslem. Ernst und gesammelt verneigte er sich gegen Mekka, richtete sich auf und verneigte sich abermals und hielt, als der Zug sich durch die Bergschluchten wand, mechanisch und instinktiv die Richtung nach Osten. Meine Himmelsrichtung war Norden, doch fühlte ich nicht, wo das war. Hassan, der Fremdling, zog meine Gedanken an sich.

Der Sturm zerrüttete und zerstäubte das Land, bog wühlend die Wedel der Palmen, zerschliß ihr Gefieder und züchtigte geduckte Fellachenfrauen, die

I sank deeper into black quicksand, tried to struggle, wanted to live—tried to reach Hassan standing high above and looking at me, double-faceted and double-faced.

In a moment it would be death, not sleep—I screamed in final desperation and awoke.

A sallow, ash-yellow sun rose in the window; the hissing jolts had not stopped, for a sandstorm had broken out. A flourlike substance had muddied the air, depositing dust throughout the room and inhibiting respiration. More dust was being whipped in through the window; I fought against the impact of the storm to close it. Snips of paper tore past, a large piece of corrugated cardboard ascended in a vertical pirouette, the stiffly horizontal palm fronds thrashed above the creaking trunks.

I returned to my dusty bed, tried not to fall asleep again, and breathed more freely. No, there was no shelter in this land; the sooner I traveled north, the better. I took a taxi to the train station through the vindictive howling sandstorm; a gust of sulphurous yellow spat upon me as I got out of the cab, shredding my hair wildly and whipping my clothes up all around me. I did not feel halfway safe until I was sitting in the train. A glance into the hand mirror showed that my face was encrusted with dust, I looked like a plaster mask with a shaggy, matted hemp wig. My own appearance horrified me. I found the washroom and left it looking humanoid, if not exactly well-groomed. I leaned into the window corner, savored a feeling of security and freshness, smelled the Russian-leather cologne on my skin and was just about to close my eyes when I saw—Hassan.

He was sitting a few benches away, full of dust and crust, but unconcerned nonetheless; he sat quietly with his back to me, giving me the option of not noticing him. Very well then, there he was, going home like me—except that my home was not near his, nowhere near. I reinforced this thought by standing up and moving into a position from which I could no longer see Hassan. I stared obstinately into the stormy world, striated diagonally by flying flags of sand.

The train proceeded. The car was dominated by a sleepy silence. A praying Muslim crouched on one of the benches: solemn and collected, he bowed in the direction of Mecca, straightened up and bowed again; as the train wound through the mountains and ravines, he continued facing east mechanically and instinctively. My direction was north, but I could not feel where that was. Hassan the stranger had magnetized my thoughts.

The storm disordered and scattered the land, bent and tattered the palm fronds, castigating stooped and swathed fellahim women on the field eingemummt über die Feldwege gingen. Ein neidisches Gelb fraß die Welt. Sie würde nie wieder blau sein. Und ich verließ meinen blauen Dragoman. Ich trug dazu bei, daß das Häßliche, Fahlgelbe siegte, indem ich etwas grausam Vernünftiges tat. Ich tat das Notwendige, Richtige, einzig Erlaubte. Ich tat es. Es mußte sein, ich konnte gar nicht anders. Ich stand auf, tat ein paar Schritte und setzte mich neben Hassan und wußte, daß er die ganze Zeit, seit Beginn meiner Flucht vor ihm, vielleicht schon seit Tagen, insgeheim zuversichtlich gelächelt hatte.

paths. An envious yellow devoured the world. I would never be blue again. And I left my blue dragoman. I contributed to the victory of this horrid sallow yellow by doing something cruelly sensible, the only thing that was necessary, right, and permitted. I did it. It had to be, there was no other way. I got up, took a few steps, and sat down next to Hassan, knowing that all this time, possibly for days, ever since I had begun my flight, he had secretly been wearing a very confident smile.

WIE HEISST "OLÉ" AUF HEBRÄISCH?

EPHRAIM KISHON

Soweit wir über die Geschichte des Stierkampfs informiert sind, hat noch niemand versucht, die Meinung der Minorität einzuholen. Offenbar interessiert es keinen Menschen, wie der Stier über das alles denkt. Es mußte erst ein hebräischer Schriftsteller kommen, um eine diesbezügliche Bresche zu schlagen.

In Spanien ist der Stierkampf eine nationale Einrichtung, ähnlich wie in Texas das Verzehren von Steaks. Es besteht sogar eine gewisse Ähnlichkeit zwischen den beiderseitigen Materialien, nur bevorzugen die Spanier ihr Steak auf den Hufen. Stier und Stierkampf gehören, wenn man so sagen darf, zu ihrem täglichen Brot. Ohne Stierkampf kein Spanien. Ohne Spanien kein Stierkampf.

Infolgedessen fragte ich sofort nach meiner Landung in Barcelona den erstbesten Zollbeamten:

"Kann ich einen Stierkampf sehen?"

"Sí," lautete die Antwort. "Den letzten in diesem Jahr. Sie haben Glück."

Wie sich herausstellte, gewährt man den spanischen Stieren mit dem Beginn der kalten Jahreszeit eine Atempause. Ich war kurz vor Schließung der Arenatore angekommen.

In den nächsten Tagen bekam ich von den feuerigen Söhnen Kataloniens immer wieder zu hören, was für ein Glückspilz ich sei. Und als Trumpf fügten sie noch hinzu: "Miguel wird kämpfen!"

Es klang verheißungsvoll und aufregend.

Mein Gastgeber, einer der bekanntesten Rechtsanwälte Barcelonas, erwarb im Vorverkauf zwei sehr gute Sitze, direkt unter der reichgeschmückten Loge des Ehrenpräsidenten, der Miguel mit einem Wink seines Taschentuches das Signal zur Tötung des Stiers geben würde.

Etwa 60,000 Sport- und Fleischliebhaber füllten das riesige Stadion. Die Hälfte von ihnen waren amerikanische Touristen, einer war ein verwirrter Israeli. In der Luft knisterte elektrische Spannung. Jedermann wußte, daß es unweigerlich zu einem Zusammenstoß zwischen Miguel und dem Stier kommen würde. Schwarzhaarige Senoritas fächelten sich lässig Kühlung zu. In ihren dunklen Augen glitzerte die Mordgier. Ich

HOW DO YOU SAY "OLÉ" IN HEBREW?

EPHRAIM KISHON
translated by Hanna B. Lewis

As far as we know or are informed about the history of bullfighting, no one has ever tried to get the opinion of the minority. Obviously no one is interested in what the bull thinks about the whole matter. A Hebrew writer had to come along to fill this breech.

In Spain bullfighting is a national institution similar to the devouring of steaks in Texas. There is even a certain similarity between the materials on both sides, but Spaniards prefer their steaks on the hoof. Bulls and bull-fighting are part, if one may say so, of their daily bread. Without bullfighting, no Spain; without Spain, no bullfighting.

As a consequence, I aked the first customs official I met, immediately after my landing in Barcelona:

"Can I see a bullfight?"

"Sí" the answer came. "The last one this year; you're lucky."

As it turned out, the Spanish bulls get a pause for breath at the beginning of the cold season. I had arrived shortly before the closing of the arena gates.

In the next few days I heard again and again from the fiery sons of Catalonia about what a lucky fellow I was. And as a trump they added: "Miguel is going to fight!"

It sounded promising and exciting.

My host, who was one of the best known lawyers of Barcelona, had in the advance sale obtained two very good places directly under the richly decorated box of the honorary president, who with a wave of his handkerchief would give Miguel the signal for the killing of the bull.

Approximately 60,000 sport and meat lovers filled the giant stadium. Half of them were American tourists, one was a confused Israeli. Electrical tension sparked through the air. Everyone knew that it would come unavoidably to a conflict between Miguel and the bull. Black-haired senoritas lazily fanned up a cooling breeze, and in their dark eyes glistened the lust meinerseits begnügte mich damit, an meinem Kaugummi zu kauen.

Plötzlich stieß mich mein Freund aufgeregt an.

"Achtung! Da kommt Miguel!"

In der Arena erschien eine Kavalleriebrigade mit leichten Waffen, gefolgt von den persönlichen Adjutanten des Matadors. Und dann kam er selbst, ein wenig mager zwar, aber in einer kostbar bestickten Uniform von leuchtender Seide. Er verbeugte sich vor der Loge des Präsidenten, und da er dabei den Blick auch in meine Richtung lenken mußte, erwiderte ich seinen Gruß, indem ich den Daumen abwärts drehte. Mein Gastgeber konnte das zum Glück nicht sehen. Er war gerade mit der Lektüre des Programms beschäftigt und studierte die List der heute beschäftigten Stiere: Name, Größe, Gewicht, Zivilstand, Vorstrafen.

"Lauter gefährliche Exemplare," murmelte er. "Miguel muß sich in acht nehmen."

Ich fragte ihn, ob er die Stiere haßte.

Nein, sagte er nach kurzem Nachdenken, er haßte sie nicht, er verüble ihnen nur ihre heimtückische Einstellung zu den Toreros.

Ich fragte weiter, was mit einem Stier geschähe, der nicht kämpfen wollte, und erfuhr, daß er sofort aller bürgerlichen Rechte verlustig ginge; eine gutaussehende Kuh würde in die Arena geschickt und lockte den unglückseligen Pazifisten hinaus. Er müßte dann monatelang warten, ob er vielleicht noch eine Chance bekäme, sich zerfleischen zu lassen.

Zum Glück war unser Stier aus anderem, härterem Material. Er kam in die Arena gesaust und stürzte sich sofort auf die roten Tücher, die von den Picadores—oder wie man das nennt—eifrig geschwenkt wurden. Auch als er sie immer wütender attackierte, bewahrten die Helden kühles Blut, stoben auseinander und schwangen sich elegant über die Brüstung, um den drohenden Hörnern zu entgehen.

Ein Sturm des Protestes erhob sich. Männer sprangen auf und schüttelten ihre Fäuste gegen die blutgierige Bestie, Frauen warfen zierliche Kußhändchen nach den unschuldig verfolgten Picadores.

"Renn nicht so idiotisch herum!" Es war mein Gastgeber, der dem Stier diese Worte zuschrie. "Was glaubst du eigentlich, wer du bist?"

Der Stier hielt erschrocken inne und blinzelte zu uns herauf.

"Was stehst du da und glotzt?" brüllte mein Freund. "Greif endlich an, zum Teufel!"

Der Stier senkte die Hörner und stürmte auf einen uniformierten Platzanweiser los.

"Aufhalten!" Die Stimme des Rechtsanwalts überschlug sich. "Aufhalten den Mörder!"

In der Tat: Es ist kein schöner Anblick, einen Stier zu beobachten, der seiner Abneigung gegen die Menschen freien Lauf läßt, nur weil man for murder. As for me, I was satisfied just chewing my gum.

Suddenly my friend poked me excitedly.

"Look! Here comes Miguel!"

In the arena appeared a cavalry brigade with light weapons, followed by the personal adjutants of the matador. And then he himself came, a little thin perhaps, but in a gorgeously embroidered uniform of gleaming silk. He bowed before the president's box and, since he had to turn his gaze in my direction at this point, I answered his greeting by turning down my thumb. Luckily my host was unable to see that. He was at that moment occupied with reading the program and studying the list of the bulls being used today: name, size, weight, citizenship, and previous convictions.

"A lot of dangerous specimens," he murmured. "Miguel must be careful."

I asked him if he hated the bulls.

No, he said after a short consideration, he only held their underhanded attitude toward the bullfighters against them.

I later asked what would happen to a bull that didn't want to fight and learned that he immediately lost all of his civil rights. A good-looking cow would be sent into the arena to lure the unfortunate pacifist out. He then had to wait for months to see if he perhaps would get another chance to let himself be disemboweled.

Luckily, our bull was made of other, sterner stuff. He came rushing into the arena and immediately hurled himself upon the red cloths enthusiastically waved by the picadors, or whatever they are called. Even when he attacked more and more furiously, the heroes kept their composure, scattered, and swung themselves elegantly over the barricades to escape the threatening horns.

A storm of protest arose. Men sprang up and shook their fists at the bloodthirsty beast. Women threw dainty kisses to the innocently persecuted picadors.

"Don't run around like such an idiot!" It was my host who screamed these words at the bull. "Who do you think you are anyway?"

The bull, frightened, stopped and looked up at us.

"What are you standing there for and staring?" screamed my friend. "Attack, damn it, attack!"

The bull lowered his horns and stormed down upon a uniformed usher.

"Stop!" The voice of the lawyer broke. "Stop that murderer!"

Actually, it's no pretty sight to watch a bull who lets his revulsion against human beings run a free course—only because they attack him with ihm mit kleinen Harpunen zusetzt und ihm ein paar Speere, Widerhaken und Eisenstäbchen mit Nationalflaggen ins Fleisch bohrt.

Die Zuschauer dampfen von Haß und Rachegelüsten. Kein Zweifel: Wenn sie nicht so diszipliniert wären, würden sie den Stier lynchen.

Verstärkungen werden in die Arena geworfen, zwei Züge eines Panzerbataillons mit automatischen Waffen. Die ersten Helikopter kreuzen auf, um im Notfall Bodenraketen einzusetzen.

Der Stier hat an der Brüstung haltgemacht und atmet schwer. Zornbebend beugt sich mein Freund gegen ihn vor.

"Du Feigling! Ist das die Art, wie du kämpfen willst?"

Der müde Blick des Stiers scheint zu sagen:

"Wer will hier kämpfen?"

Mein tobender Freund wendet sich an die Bewaffneten in der Arena.

"Macht ihn fertig, den Bastard! Tötet ihn! Aber schnell! Sonst—bei der heiligen Jungfrau von Guadalajara—komm ich selbst hinunter und zeig's euch!"

Er setzte zum Sprung an, besann sich aber rechtzeitig auf die Würde seines Standes und blieb.

Fanfarenstöße erklangen. Auf gepanzertem Schlachtroß hielt ein Ritter in strahlender Rüstung seinen Einzug.

"Miguel?" fragte ich.

"Noch nicht", belehrten mich die Umsitzenden. "Der Stier muß erst richtig müde werden." Und sie überhäuften ihn aufs neue mit Schmähungen: "Los, du lächerliche Kuh! Wir wollen sehen, was du kannst!"

Das ließ sich der Stier nicht zweimal sagen. Er nahm Anlauf und rannte das Pferd nieder, so daß es auf seinen Reiter zu liegen kam.

Ein Aufschrei ging durch die Menge.

"Polizei! Guardia civil! Bändigt die reißende Bestie!"

Wieder war es mein Freund, der Anwalt, der mit seiner Äußerung ins Schwarze traf.

"Unschuldige Pferde attackieren, was?! Das wird dir noch leid tun, du Abschaum!"

Der Stier sah ihn kaum an; offenbar konnte er Rechtsanwälte nicht leiden. Auch hatte er jetzt schon große Mühe, sich auf den Füßen zu halten.

Ich überdachte die Situation von seinem Standpunkt aus und fand sie eher deprimierend: auf fremdem Boden einer feindseligen Menge ausgesetzt, die ihm zahlenmäßig stark überlegen war—wie sollte er sich da durchsetzen?

Während ich noch so vor mich hin philosophierte, gerieten die Frauen ringsum plötzlich in Ekstase. Zu schmetternder Orchesterbegleitung betrat Miguel die Arena, in der Hand ein überdimensionales Schwert, um die Schultern ein golddurchwirktes Cape. Seine ganze Erscheinung atmete little harpoons and stick a few spears, barbs, and little steel spikes holding national flags into his flesh.

The spectators steam with hate and desire for revenge. Without a doubt, if they weren't so disciplined, they would lynch the steer.

Reinforcements are thrown into the arena. Two platoons of an armored batallion with automatic weapons. The first helicopters cross over in order to utilize ground rockets in case of emergency.

The bull has stopped at the barricade and breathes heavily. Quivering with rage, my friend bends down over him.

"You coward! Is that the way you want to fight?"

The weary look of the bull seems to say:

"Who wants to fight?"

My raging friend turns to the bearers of arms in the arena.

"Kill him, the bastard, finish him. But quickly! Otherwise, by the Holy Virgin of Guadalajara, I'll come down myself and show you how!"

He prepared himself for the leap, but considered the dignity of his profession just in time, and stayed.

Fanfares sounded and a knight in shining armor on an armored battle charger made his entrance.

"Miguel?" I asked.

"Not yet," the people around me informed me. "The bull must be quite worn out first." And they heaped more and more insults upon him. "Go ahead, you silly cow, we want to see what you can do!"

The bull didn't have to be told that twice. He took a running start and ran the horse down, so that it fell on its rider.

An uproar went through the crowd.

"Police! Civil Guard! Restrain the ravening beast!"

Again it was my friend, the lawyer, who hit the mark with his utterances.

"Attack innocent horses, huh! You'll be sorry for that, you scum."

The bull hardly looked up at him. Obviously he could not stand lawyers; besides, he was now having great difficulty keeping on his feet.

I thought over the situation from his point of view and found it rather depressing: exposed on unfamiliar ground and to a hostile crowd, which was vastly superior to him in number, how could he win here?

While I philosophized to myself this way, the women around me suddenly went into ecstasy. To clashing orchestral accompaniment Miguel entered the arena, in his hand a tremendous sword, around his shoulders a gold embroidered cape. His whole appearance breathed power, compo-

Kraft, Gelassenheit und Ruhe.

Unter Zuhilfenahme seines roten Tuchs produzierte er als erstes eine Reihe klassischer Ballettposen, die vom Publikum mit lustvollem Stöhnen aufgenommen wurden. Im übrigen war er hauptsächlich damit beschäftigt, dem Stier auszuweichen, und rief jedesmal, wenn dessen Hörner ins Leere stießen: "Olé!"

Zwischendurch reizte er seinen Gegner durch hämische Sticheleien etwa folgenden Wortlauts:

"Na so komm doch, mein Stierchen, komm zum Onkel Miguel, er wartet auf dich . . . Hopp, Stierli-Stierli . . . Ja was war denn das . . . Nur nicht frech werden, sonst wirst du zu Hackfleisch verarbeitet, olé!"

Aus zarten Frauenhänden ging ein Blumenregen auf ihn nieder. Schon hob er das Schwert zur rituellen Schlachtung.

"Er muß ihm die Lunge, das Herz, die Leber und sämtliche Eingeweide durchbohren," informierte mich, vor Aufregung keuchend, mein Freund. "Mit einem einzigen, virtuos geführten Streich!"

Miguel hatte sich auf die Zehenspitzen gestellt und stieß zu. Aber er schien nicht alle Ziele getroffen zu haben, denn der Stier brach in keiner Weise zusammen. Im Gegenteil, es sah ganz danach aus, als ob er sich erholt hätte.

"Was ist los mit dir?!" johlte mein Rechtsanwalt und meinte den Stier. "Möchtest du nicht endlich tot umfallen?!"

Der Stier schüttelte unwillig den Kopf und galoppierte zur Loge des Präsidenten.

"Senor!" rief er hinauf. "Befreien Sie mich von diesem Idioten auf meinem Rücken, oder ich spiele nicht weiter!"

Der Präsident winkte ab.

"Mit Stieren rede ich nicht. Man töte ihn!"

Abermals hob Miguel, zu voller Größe aufgereckt, das Schwert und gab damit seinen Adjutanten das Zeichen, ihm letzte Hilfe zu leisten. Etwa 20 Mann stürzten herbei und bearbeiteten den Stier mit spitzen Lanzen, vergifteten Pfeilen und einer Ladung Tränengas. Denn es ist schwer, eines blutrünstigen Monstrums Herr zu werden, solange es noch auf vier Beinen steht.

"Das ist das Ende!" jauchzte dicht neben mir der Rechtsanwalt. "Jetzt bekommt er, was ihm gebührt!"

Wenn es dem Torero gelingt, seinem Widersacher ein besonders schönes, stilvolles Ende zu bereiten, macht ihm der Präsident ein Ohr des Stiers zum Geschenk. Erfolgt die Tötung mit unvergleichlicher, noch nicht dagewesener Perfektion, darf er auch den Schweif behalten. Und dieses seltene Ereignis schien sich anzubahnen.

"Passen Sie auf!", raunte mein Freund mir zu. "Sie sehen jetzt sure, and calmness.

With the aid of his red cloth, he produced the first in a series of classical ballet positions, which were accepted by the public with happy groans. In addition to that, he was primarily busy escaping the bull and cried out "Olé!" each time the latter's horns struck empty air.

In the meantime he provoked his opponent by malicious taunts of approximately the following content:

"So come on now, little bull, come to Uncle Miguel, he's waiting for you. Quick, bully, bully. Now, what was that? Don't be imprudent, else we'll turn you into hamburger. Olé!"

From the tender hands of the women, flower blossoms showered him. He was already lifting his sword for the ritual slaughter.

"He must bore through his lungs, his heart, and intestines," my friend informed me, panting with excitement, "with a single masterly stroke."

Miguel had risen to his tiptoes and thrust. He didn't seem to have hit all of his targets, because the bull in no way collapsed. On the contrary, he really looked as though he had recovered.

"What's the matter with you?!" yelled my lawyer, meaning the bull. "Why don't you drop dead?"

The bull shook his head stubbornly and galloped to the president's box.

"Senor!" he cried. "Please get this idiot off my back, or I'm not going to play anymore."

The president dismissed him with a gesture.

"I don't talk to bulls. Kill him!"

Again Miguel stretched to his fullest height, raised his sword, and with it gave his adjutants the sign to give him some last aid. Approximately twenty men rushed to his side and worked on the bull with pointed lances, poisoned arrows, and a blast of tear gas, because it's very difficult to master such a blood-thirsty monster as long as he is still standing on four legs.

"That's the end!" the lawyer rejoiced next to me. "Now he's going to get what he deserves!"

If the bullfighter succeeds in giving his opponent a particularly beautiful, stylish end, the president presents him with the ear of the bull. If the killing is accomplished with an incomparable perfection never before achieved, he is also given the tail. And this rare experience was about to happen.

"Pay attention!" whispered my friend to me. "Now we'll see some-etwas Einmaliges. Miguel wird in die Knie gehen und den Stier mit einer sogenannten Veronica erledigen. Er wird sich im allerletzten Augenblick seitwärts biegen und wird der wütenden Bestie, die auf ihn zugeschossen kommt, den Stahl ins Herz bohren . . ."

Die schneidige Marschmelodie des Orchesters wurde durch einen dumpfen Trommelwirbel abgelöst. Miguel ging in die Knie, der Stier kam planmäßig auf ihn zugeschossen, Miguel rückte ein wenig zur Seite, auch der Stier änderte seine Laufrichtung—und in der nächsten Sekunde segelte Miguel durch die Luft, vollzog eine Bauchlandung und blieb reglos im heißen Sand liegen.

Ringsum herrschte Totenstille, die nur da und dort von schwachen Rufen nach einem Arzt durchbrochen wurde.

Der Stier machte kehrt, trottete an den unverändert daliegenden Miguel heran, beschnupperte ihn, rollte ihn behutsam vor sich her, senkte die Hörner, schleuderte ihn abermals in die Luft.

Jetzt hielt es mich nicht länger.

"Olé" rief ich zu und sprang begeistert auf. "Hopp, Stierli-Stierli! Zeig's ihm! Bravo!" Auch der haßerfüllte Blick des Rechtsanwalts konnte meinen schmetternden Jubelrufen nichts anhaben. "Olé und nochmals Olé!"

Als Miguel zum drittenmal durch die Luft segelte, kannte mein Enthusiasmus keine Grenzen. Ich warf dem Stier Kußhändchen zu, ließ meine Krawatte folgen, zerriß mein Programmheft in viele kleine Stückchen, streute sie wild um mich und begann sogar eine passende Melodie aus 'Carmen' zu singen, die allerdings im jählings einsetzenden Lärm unterging. Der Lärm kam zum Teil von den Panzerwagen, die jetzt in die Arena rollten und das Feuer eröffneten, zum Teil von den Schmährufen der Menge, die gegen mich Stellung nahm.

Mit knapper Not gelang mir die Flucht. Als draußen unter den Kolonnaden trunkenes Siegesgeheul an mein Ohr drang, wußte ich, daß es um den tapferen Stier geschehen war. Der Anblick eines Rettungsautos, das den legendären Nationalhelden Miguel aufnahm, tröstete mich ein wenig.

Noch trostreicher war die Gewißheit, daß aus meinem Sohn Amir niemals ein Stierkämpfer werden kann, weil er rote Haare hat.

thing extraordinary. Miguel will kneel and finish off the bull with a so-called veronica. He will bend sideways at the very last moment and will thrust his sword into the heart of the raging beast as it comes rushing toward him."

The sharp march melody of the orchestra was replaced by a leaden drumroll. Miguel went to his knees, the bull rushed him according to plan, Miguel moved a little to the side, the bull changed his direction too—and in the next second Miguel was sailing through the air, made a belly landing, and lay motionless on the hot sand.

Around him was the silence of death. Only here and there a weak call for a doctor broke through.

The bull turned around, trotted to the recumbent figure of Miguel, sniffed him, rolled him over carefully, lowered its horns, and hurled him into the air again.

Now I couldn't restrain myself any longer.

"Olé!" I called and sprang up enthusiastically. "Come, bully, bully! Show him! Bravo!" Even the hate-filled look of the lawyer couldn't stop my ringing cry of exultation. "Olé and olé again!"

When Miguel sailed through the air for the third time, my enthusiasm knew no bounds. I threw kisses at the bull, let my tie follow, tore my program up into little pieces, strew them wildly around, and began to sing a suitable melody from *Carmen,* which unfortunately was drowned out by the suddenly beginning uproar. The uproar came partially from the armored cars, which now rolled into the arena and opened fire, and partially from the abusive cries of the crowd expressing their views against me.

I just barely got away. When a drunken howl of victory came to my ears, as I stood outside under the colonnades, I knew what had happened to the brave bull. The sight of an ambulance collecting the legendary national hero, Miguel, gave me some comfort.

Still more consoling was the certainty that my son Amir will never become a bullfighter, because he has red hair.

DREI NACKTE MÄNNER

FRANZ FÜHMANN

SIE WAREN NICHT OFT IN DER SAUNA, ICH GLAUBTE IM GANZEN VIER- ODER fünfmal, doch ich bin durchaus in der Lage, sie genau zu beschreiben. Sie kamen und gingen und bewegten sich zwischen Kommen und Gehen stets in der gleichen Weise, und ich bin fest überzeugt, daß, kämen sie auch erst nach Jahren wieder, sie sich genau so aufführen würden wie das erste Mal, selbst wenn es denn gar nicht dieselben drei nackten Männer mehr wären.

Zwei waren von durchschnittlicher Größe, der eine ein wenig länger, der andere ein klein wenig kürzer als mittleres Mittelmaß, und auch ihr Gewicht mochte noch dem Normalen entsprechen, wenngleich ein Anflug von Schwammigkeit, vor allem in den Gesichtern, darauf hinwies, daß sie, jetzt Anfang der Vierzig, sicher bald Mühe haben würden, es zu halten. Der Mann in ihrer Mitte war voll im Fleisch. Er war einen ganzen Kopf kleiner, gedrungen, feist, doch erstaunlich gelenkig, und über und über mit einer grauschwarzen kräusligen Wolle bewachsen, auch über die Schultern und rund ums Knie. Wenn er in Schweiß geriet, glänzte er silbrig. Auch sein Haupthaar war dicht, wiewohl er Mitte der Fünfzig sein mußte; es war graubraun, ein wenig gewellt und, zurückgekämmt, recht kurz gehalten; er trug auch weder Bart noch Koteletten und sah stets aus, als habe er sich soeben rasiert. Vielleicht aber war sein Bartwuchs schwach, was ja bei Leibbepelzten häufig vorkommt, denn die Haut zeigte vom Kinn bis zu den Schläfen nicht jenes lästige Violett, wie es nach vielem Rasieren auftritt. So leuchteten die Backen nacktweiß und voll über dem Moos der Schulter; der Hals war sehr kurz, das Gesicht fast faltenlos, auch die—nicht sehr hohe—Stirn beinah glatt, nur das Kinn von einer herzförmigen Delle gezeichnet, deren Spitze sich in den Kiefergrund zog. Kleiner Mund, kleine Ohren, der Nacken fest; auf die Augen komme ich noch zu sprechen. Seine Hände wirkten, trotz der stumpfen Fingerkappen, zart, die Nägel, auch die Zehennägel, waren glatt, gleichmäßig rund gefeilt, ohne Einriß, rosig, mit deutlichen Halbmonden, und die Hand- und Fußsohlen ohne Hornhaut weich, ja fast weiberhaft. Peinlichste Sauberkeit; kaum merkbare Spuren von Parfüm oder sehr guter Seife. Breite Brust, durchaus ein Bauch, bedeutend sogar, aber fleischig, nicht fett, und gewölbt, statt hängend, gedrungene Beine, gedrungener Geschlechtsteil, das Schamhaar von der Wolle des Bauchs und der Brust kaum abgehoben. Massiver Trauring, das Gebiß kräftig, und Gold auch hier; der Atem rein, keine Brille. Man sieht

THREE NAKED MEN

FRANZ FÜHMANN
translated by Esther E. Enns

THEY WERE NOT AT THE SAUNA OFTEN—IT SEEMED I HAD SEEN THEM A total of four or five times—but I am nevertheless in a position to give an accurate description of them. They came and went, and their movements between coming and going were always identical, and I am firmly convinced that even if they were not to return until years later, they would still act just as they had the first time, even if they were no longer the same three naked men.

Two were of average height—the one a little above, the other a little below mid-average—and their weight was also still within the range of normal, even though a touch of flabbiness, especially in the faces, indicated that now in their early forties they would surely soon have trouble keeping their weight down. The man between them was fleshy. He was a whole head smaller, squat, thickset yet surprisingly agile, and overgrown with an iron-gray sort of frizz that covered even his shoulders and grew right around his knees. When he perspired, he shone with a silvery luster. The hair on his head was also thick, although he already seemed to be in his mid-fifties; it was grayish brown, slightly waved, combed back from the forehead, and kept quite short. He had neither beard nor sideburns, and he always looked freshly shaven. But perhaps he had sparse facial hair, which is often the case with furry men, for from chin to temples the skin showed no trace of that bothersome purplish tinge that develops after years of shaving. And so the cheeks glowed moonwhite and full above the mossy shoulders. His neck was very short, the face had next to no wrinkles, the not-so-high forehead was nearly smooth as well; only the chin was marked by a heart-shaped dimple that pointed right down to the lower jaw. Small mouth, small ears, the neck firm; the eyes I shall come to. His hands had a delicate look despite the blunt fingertips, the nails—the toenails as well—were smooth, filed uniformly to an oval, without nicks, rosy, with well-defined half-moons, and the palms of his hands and soles of his feet were without callouses and soft, almost womanish. Scrupulously clean; bare traces of perfume or fine soap. Broad chest, most definitely a potbelly, and a substantial one at that, but fleshy, not fat, and nicely rounded rather than droopy; legs stocky, genitals compact, and little contrast between the pubic hair and the wool covering the potbelly and chest. Massive wedding band, strong set of teeth with gold displayed there as well; fresh breath, no glasses. So so viel Gesundheit in diesem Alter nicht oft.

Nun seine Augen. Sie waren hellbraun und kugelrund, und auch die Lidrandung rund, und sie waren, wenn er sprach, auf seine Art in Bewegung, von der man versucht ist zu sagen "sie wanderten", wäre diese Bewegung ruhig, und "mausartig", wäre sie scheu gewesen. Es war ein Mustern, doch auch dieser Ausdruck ist ungenau, denn dies Mustern geschah nicht durch prüfendes Hingleiten übers Objekt, sondern durch ruckhafte Sprünge zuerst des Kopfs und hernach der Blicke; es war eine Summe von Momentaufnahmen genau fixierter Partien, Facettenbilder eines in die Zeit gekästelten Insektenauges, und zwar seltsamerweise immer um die Pole ihres Gegenstandes. So betrachtete er von einem Menschen nur den Kopf und die Füße, immer nur Kopf und Füße, von jedem, und dies mit einer so ungeheuerlich ungenierten, sich also so selbstverständliches Recht gebenden Sicherheit, daß sie schon nicht mehr als Flegelei empfunden wurde, ja man hätte es vielleicht sogar hingenommen, wenn er solcherart die Penisse gemustert hätte. Nie verheimlichte er einen Blick, nie wandte er ihn verlegen ab, wenn man aufsah, und nie hätte er sich stören lassen—; mir ist allerdings dazu auch kein Versuch bewußt.

Obwohl ich mir vornahm, seine Bekleidung zu erkunden, versäumte ich jedesmal die Gelegenheit. Man kommt ja von außen, von der Straße oder den medizinischen Bädern in die Sauna herauf, geht in die Umkleideräume, drei enge Gänge zwischen vier Wänden schmaler Blechspinde, und betritt dann nackt durch eine selbsttätig schließende Glastür den Vorderraum mit dem kalten Becken und den Duschen, von dem rechter Hand die Tür in die eigentliche Sauna und linker Hand die in den Ruheraum führt. Nun sind die Badezeiten, in vier Schichten zwischen Mittag und Abend festgelegt, äußerst knapp bemessen, man will seine Zeit nicht beim Umziehen vertun, und da die drei immer etwas später kamen und stets etwas früher gingen, sah ich sie eben erst, wenn sie den Vorraum betraten, und da waren sie natürlich schon kleiderlos. Ihr Eintritt vollzog sich jedesmal im gleichen Gänsemarsch. Über den Kopf des Wolligen zurück überwies, durch ein Nachstoßen mit den Fingerspitzen, der vorangehende Längere die zur Garderobe hin aufgezogene, schon wieder ins Schloß schwingende Tür dem beschließenden Kürzeren, dessen vorschnellende Hand sie überm Kopf des Wolligen auffing und nochmals zurückriß; ein kompliziert zu beschreibendes Entrée, das jedoch kein Aufsehen erregte, auch wenn es sich, mit zweckgebotenen Abweichungen natürlich, bei jeder Tür wiederholte: Zur Sauna, aus der Sauna, zum Ruheraum, aus dem Ruheraum, und dies dreimal, und zum Schluß in den Umkleideraum zurück, und so bei jedem der fünf Besuche. Nie brauchte der Wollige eine Tür anzufassen, aber auch nie wurde sie vor ihm devot aufgetan; nie betrat er anmaßend einen Raum als Erster, doch stets tat nach dem Passieren der Tür der much health is seldom seen at this age.

Now his eyes. They were light-brown and round as balls, and their rims also formed a circle, and when he spoke, these eyes moved in a manner that would almost have produced the effect of a "wandering gaze," had this movement been smooth and "mouselike," it would have been of a bashful nature. It was a scrutinizing stare, but this term, too, is inexact, for this scrutiny did not involve a searching perusal of the object, but rather abrupt shifts first of the head and then of the gaze; it was a sum of instantaneous impressions of firmly fixed parts, faceted images of an insect eye that perceives chronological blocks, and it strangely enough always focused around the two poles of the object. And so he viewed the head and feet of a person, always only head and feet, of everyone, and this with such shocking, unabashed matter-of-factly legitimate assurance that it did not fit into the category of boorishness. It might perhaps even have been tolerable had he scrutinized their penises in this way. Never did he conceal a glance, never did he bashfully look away when someone noticed him staring, and never would he have let himself be disturbed—I must admit that I am unaware of any such attempt ever having been made either.

Although I intended to find out what kind of clothes he wore, I missed the chance each time. You see, you enter from the street or from the medical baths downstairs, come up to the sauna, go into the changing rooms—three cramped aisles between four walls of narrow metal lockers—and, naked, you pass through a self-closing glass door and then set foot in the anteroom with the cold-water tank and the showers—a room from which the door on the right leads into the sauna itself and the door on the left into the resting room. Saunas are offered in four extremely brief shifts during the afternoon, so nobody wants to waste time changing, and since the threesome always came a little late and left a little early, I did not see them until they set foot in the anteroom, and then of course they were already undressed. They always filed in like geese. Over the top of the wooly man's head, with a tap of his fingertips, the one in front—the taller man—left the door, which had been pulled open in the changing room and was already swinging shut, for the end man to take—the shorter man—whose eager hand grabbed the door over the top of the wooly man's head and pulled it open again. An entrance procedure that is hard to describe but that attracted no attention, even though it was repeated, with appropriate modifications of course, at each and every door: into the sauna chamber, out of the sauna chamber into the resting room, out of the resting room, this circuit three times, and finally back into the changing room, and so it went on each of the five visits. Never did the wooly one have to touch a door, but then again, never was one opened up before him fawningly; never did he presumptuously lead the way into a room, but having passed

Vorausgehende einen Spreizschritt zur Seite, der Letzte schloß auf, und die beiden wahrten ihren halben Schritt Abstand hinter dem solcherart an die Spitze gekommenen Mittleren auch beim Langsamerwerden und Stehenbleiben. Das alles sah völlig natürlich aus und lief ab, als sei es lang eingeübt, obwohl solche Riten gewiß nicht exerziert werden können, ja wahrscheinlich nicht einmal einer Weisung entspringen. Sie ergeben sich; sie sind einfach die Form, die ein Vorgang von einiger Wichtigkeit annehmen muß, und also sind sie doch natürlich: die Natur der Gesellschaft drückt sich darin aus. Zu dieser Zeit gerade in ästhetisch-theoretische Grübeleien um eine Apologie der Form versponnen, nahm ich diese Erkenntnis mit Genugtuung auf.

In der Tat: den Unterschied zwischen lebendiger und erstarrter Form, den ich bei meiner Arbeit durch einen Vergleich zweier Sonette—Texte verwandter Thematik von Gryphius und Emanuel Geibel etwa—oder auch was allerdings schwieriger, aber auch eindrucksvoller gewesen wäre, durch einen Vergleich zweier Termine analoger Autoren herauszuarbeiten gedachte, ich hätte ihn, was die lebendige Form anlangte, kaum besser studieren können als eben hier, und besonders dann, wenn die drei den Saunaraum betraten. Gegen ein Zeremoniell feierlichen Eintritts würden wir uns empört haben, denn das hätte die Tür ungebührlich lang offengehalten, und da waren wir alle sehr empfindlich. Mit Recht: die Ofenleistung war mit einem Maximum von fünfundsiebzig Grad durchaus unzulänglich, und wir hatten uns kurz zuvor sogar mit einer Bande von Rowdys angelegt, die eine Kraftprobe versuchten und die Tür für ihren Einzug sperrangelweit aufstießen—da hatten wir kräftige Worte gefunden, und da wären wir auch einer Prügelei nicht aus dem Weg gegangen, doch die drei gaben uns kein Ärgernis. Kaum hatte der Längere die Tür aufgeklinkt, war auch der Wollige schon hindurch und der Kürzere schloß: schneller hätten sie auch auf andere Weise nicht passieren können. Sie hielten sich überhaupt strikt an die Regeln. Daß sie die Badezeiten nicht überschritten, sagte ich schon; daß sie weder lärmten noch rauchten noch Alkohol tranken, war selbstverständlich, und als der Wollige—es geschah dies nur beim ersten Besuch—eine Handbürste mit in die Schwitzstube brachte, ließ er sie nach einem Blick auf eines der Verbotsschilder unbenutzt, wiewohl nur wenige Badegäste auf den Bänken saßen und keiner davon unmittelbar neben ihm. Er sprang—gegen welche Anstandsregel sonst sehr viele sündigten—auch niemals ins Kaltwasserbecken, wenn jemand in der Nähe stand, den er hätte bespritzen können, und selbstverständlich duschte er vorher, was auch nicht jeder tat.—Ins Kaltbecken sprang er stets in der Hocke, mit hochgezogenen Knien, aber nie die Beine mit den Armen umfaßt, was in solcher Unvollkommenheit etwas Rührendes hatte. Von seinen Begleitern folgte ihm keiner. Hasenherzigkeit? Je nun—die zwei standen mit solch wacher through a door, the one in front always took a step sideways, the end man opened the door, and even during slowdown and standstill the two of them kept their half-step distance behind the center man, who had thus come out in front. All of this looked completely natural and was performed as if preceded by long rehearsal, although such rites could most certainly not be drilled and could probably not even stem from any directive. They just happen; they are simply the form that a procedure of any importance whatsoever must take on, and so they are natural after all: They are an expression of the nature of society. Wrapped up as I was at that time in esthetic and theoretic brooding in search of a justification for form, I was most receptive to this insight.

Indeed, the difference between living and petrified form, which I intended to work out through a comparison of two sonnets—thematically related texts by Gryphius and Emanuel Geibel* perhaps—or else through something more difficult, but also more impressive: through a comparison of two terms from analogous authors. And as far as living form is concerned, I could hardly have found better occasion to study it than right here, and especially at those times when the threesome entered the sauna. A ceremony of solemn entry would have upset us, because then the door would have had to remain open for an indecently long period of time, and that was a sore subject with everyone. And rightly so: The stove's maximum heating capacity of seventy-five degrees was totally unsatisfactory, and just beforehand we had quarreled with a gang of rowdies who had wanted to test their strength and had almost pushed the door off its hinges as they barged in—we made our verbal attack, and in this case we would not have shied from a physical attack either, but the threesome gave us no trouble. The taller man had barely unlatched the door and already the wooly one had slipped through and the shorter one closed it again. They could not have gone about it any more quickly. But it was like them to stick firmly to rules. That they did not stay overtime in the sauna I have already mentioned; that they made no noise and neither smoked nor drank alcoholic beverages goes without saying, and when the wooly one brought a handbrush—but this happened only on the first visit—into the sauna chamber, he made no use of it after spotting the sign prohibiting brushes, even though only a few people were inside on the benches and nobody was sitting immediately beside him. He was considerate enough never to jump—a sin most of the others were guilty of—into the cold tank when someone whom he could have splashed was standing nearby—and of course he always took a shower first, which is another thing that not everyone did. He always jumped into the cold tank in a crouching position with knees pulled up towards the chest, but never with the arms embracing the legs—the artlessness was touching. Neither one of his companions followed

Lässigkeit vor den beiden zugänglichen Beckenumrandungen (die beiden anderen gingen in die rechten hinteren Eckwände des Vorraums über), daß jeder einen Bogen ums Becken machte, doch sie ließen mich anstandslos die Stufen in die Kälte hinab, als sich einmal der Wollige noch darin tummelte. Es lag mir natürlich fern, sie zu erproben; ich hatte geschwitzt, geduscht und wollte mich abkühlen, das war alles, und da ich wußte, daß der Wollige länger als wir alle im Becken aushielt, wich ich von meiner Gewohnheit ab und stieg zu ihm. Sonst warte ich nämlich stets, bis das Becken frei ist; ich pflege nur rasch einzutunken und mich dabei am Stufengeländer festzuhalten, und da man im kalten Wasser im Nu bis ins Mark friert, will ich niemand den Rückweg versperren und warte eben. Beim Wolligen aber wußte ich, daß er verweilte: Nach dem Einsprung (in der Hocke, man erinnert sich) blieb er stets einen Augenblick untergetaucht, dann schwoll er, sich kräftig vom Grund abstoßend, senkrecht bis über die Leisten herauf, warf die Arme über den Kopf und fiel aufplatschend nieder und hüpfte in diesem Auf und Ab prüstend und um sich schlagend das Becken hindurch bis zum armdick einschießenden Frischwasserstrahl, unter dem er gehöhlten Kreuzes die Schultern dehnte und renkte, bis die Lippen blau anliefen, um dann, immer noch hoch- und niederfahrend, der Wuschlichkeit des gelb-weißen Flauschtuchs entgegenzueilen mit dem ihn der Längere zu seiten des Einstiegs erwartete. Nun stand er vorm Wasserstrahl und schien nichts als Behagen zu empfinden: Er plantschte wie ein Kind; das Glück des Leibs strahlte unverdrängt und ungebrochen von seinen Backen, und da es mir ebenso ging, geschah es, daß ich ihn für einen Badegast gleich uns hielt und mit irgendeiner der Floskeln ansprechen wollte, die man bei dieser Gelegenheit äußert und die, wenn sie auch nicht mehr besagen als ein gemeinsames Lächeln oder Schmunzeln zufällig zusammengeführter Alltagsgefährten, eben doch einem gemeinsamen Erlebnis entspringen und Ausdruck dieser Gemeinsamkeit sind. Ein Wohlgefühl, und daraus ein naiver, kaum artikulierbarer Mitteilungsdrang, mehr Geste als Wort, und so stieg ich nach dem Unterducken nicht gleich die Stufen wieder hinauf, sondern wandte mich dem nun auch mir sich Zuwendenden zu, um ihn anzureden, da spürte ich den Blick im Nacken und ließ es sein. Es war einer der Blicke, die durch jede Arglosigkeit unter die Haut dringen; ich fuhr herum, und da stand der Kürzere lässig zwischen dem Beckenrand und den Steinbänken, darauf man die Badesachen ablegt; er stand lässiger als sonst, das Gewicht ganz aufs linke Bein verlagert, die rechte Ferse auf der Steinbank, die Hände überm Gesäß, den Unterkiefer vorgeschoben und den Blick gleichmütig zwischen mir und dem Wolligen auf him. Chicken-heartedness? Whatever the reason, they occupied the two accessible approaches to the tank—the two inaccessible edges were part of the back, right-corner walls of the anteroom—with such wary lassitude that everyone steered clear of it. But they let me descend the steps into the icy water without raising an eyebrow one time when the wooly one was still busy romping around. Of course, it was not like me to challenge them; I had perspired, showered, and had then wanted to cool off—that was all. And since I knew that the wooly one could endure the cold water longer than any of us, I broke with my usual custom and joined him in the water. As a rule I like to wait until the tank is empty. I generally hold on to the railing and take just a quick dip, and since the cold water instantly chills a person to the bone, I do not want to block the way for anyone wanting to climb out, and for this reason I wait. But I knew that the wooly one would linger. After the big jump (in crouching position, you will remember) he would always stay submerged for a moment, and then, having vigorously pushed off from the bottom, he would rise upwards, up over the haunches, throw his hands over his head, and splash back down. Bobbing up and down and sputtering and thrashing about in this way, he would cross the tank to where a jet of fresh water as thick as an arm came gushing in. Erect, with chest high, he would stand in the stream of water, stretching and writhing his shoulders until his lips turned blue, and—still bobbing up and down—hurry towards the snuggly softness of the yellowy-white, fleecy towel awaiting him in the hands of the taller man at the side of the steps leading into the tank. And so he stood in the stream of water seeming to feel nothing but contentment. He splashed around like a child; the sensuous thrill of it was obvious in the steady glow of his cheeks. And since I shared that feeling, it so happened that I took him to be one of us—one of the sauna crowd—and wanted to toss him one of those phrases often used in this sort of context. And even though they involve no more than a smile or chuckle shared by everyday associates brought together by chance, they still do stem from a shared experience and express this fellowship. A feeling of well-being, and, arising from that, a naive, barely expressible urge to communicate—gesture rather than words. And so I did not go right back up the steps after my dip, but with the intention of saying something, I turned to him as he was also turning towards me. But then I felt a stare at the back of my neck and changed my mind. It was one of those all-seeing stares that penetrates all traces of innocence whatsoever. I spun around and saw the shorter man standing casually between the edge of the tank and the stone benches where people leave their bathing things. His stance was more lax than usual, all weight was on the left leg, the right heel on the stone bench, hands behind his back, jowl set, the gaze calmly fixed on a spot in the greenish water somewhere between me and the wooly dem grünen Wasser. Er rührte sich nicht, doch in diesem Augenblick fühlte ich von der Steinbank aus einen körperlosen Schatten zwischen mich und den Wolligen springen; lautloses Aufklatschen; Eiseskälte; ich tat fröstelnd einen Schritt zurück ins Becken und sah den Wolligen über die Stufen steigen, ins Tuch sich hüllen und, vom Kürzeren gefolgt, in den Ruheraum treten, dessen Tür der Längere vor ihm aufstieß.

Im Ruheraum ruhte er wie immer konzentriert, doch hier war, wie ebenfalls immer, die Ruhe schon nicht mehr Genuß: Er versuchte angestrengt, sich zu entspannen, und so ruhte er ohne auszuruhn. Er lag— (man konnte durch die Glastür alle fünf Pritschen beschauen), er lag zwar unbewegt auf dem Rücken, die Knie durchgedrückt, die Hände unter dem Nacken verschränkt und die Augen geschlossen, allein er lag wie in einer Schablone vollkommen symmetrisch, und spätestens nach einer Minute begann er im grübelnden Selbstgespräch die Lippen zu bewegen und die Stirn zu runzeln, dann schien er sich bei diesem unerlaubten Nicht-Ruhn zu ertappen und kniff den Mund zu und lag die nächste Minute vollkommen steif. —In den Ruheraum begleitete ihn meist nur der Längere; der Kürzere seifte sich in dieser Zeit ab, was der Längere selten und der Wollige nie tat. Das Glück, das der Wollige im Kaltbecken erlebte, geschah dem Kürzeren unter der warmen Dusche: Er ließ, träg sich rekelnd, den körnigen Strahl minutenlang auf sich niedersausen, dann seifte er sich von der Stirnglatze bis zu den Knöcheln ab, brauste, seifte sich abermals schaumig, rieb mit dem Waschlappen herunter, wusch, im Kauern, die Füße und seifte ein drittes Mal die Partien, die er besonders zu säubern gedachte: das Gesicht, den Nacken, die Leistenbeuge, den Penis und die Afterspalte, und die, in breiter Grätsche gebückt, noch ein viertes Mal. Nach dem Abseifen drehte er die Dusche, so heiß er's ertrug, und stand wohlig schnaufend, dann packte er, aus allen Poren dampfend, die rosa Seife ins Schälchen, und dann kam meist auch der Wollige mit dem Längeren zurück, und sie gingen schwitzen. Diesmal, wie gesagt, waren sie zu dritt im Ruheraum: der Längere dösend, der Wollige angespannt sich entspannend, der Kürzere mit seitlich von der Pritsche herabhängenden Armen und Beinen, und als sie wieder den Vorraum betraten, pfiff er, der Kürzere, vor sich hin.

Und dann geschah das Unerwartete.

Im Schwitzraum (ich war gleich nach den dreien hineingeschlüpft) lud der Wollige noch, wie üblich, seine Begleiter, die wie immer eine Bank unter ihm Platz genommen hatten, durch ermunterndes Nicken und mehrmaliges Hochrucken der seitwärts der Hüften abgewinkelten und nach oben geöffneten Hände zu sich herauf, und wie üblich tat er dies, nachdem er schon die ersten Worte eines Gespräches begonnen, will sagen, ihnen mit one. He did not move, but right at that instant I felt a bodiless shadow jump between me and the wooly one from the direction of the stone bench: a noiseless flop, icy coldness. Shivering, I took a step backwards into the tank and saw the wooly one climb up the steps, wrap himself in the towel, and, followed by the shorter one, enter the resting room through the door that the taller one had pushed open in front of him.

In the resting room he rested, as usual, conscientiously. But here, again as usual, the rest was pleasure no more. He made a laborious attempt to relax, and so he rested without resting. He was lying—(all five cots were visible through the glass door) he was indeed lying still on his back, eyes closed, hands folded under his head, and legs straight, but at the same time he was lying as if molded in perfect symmetry, and after one minute at the most he began to move his lips in brooding monologue and wrinkle his brow. Then he seemed to catch himself at this forbidden restlessness, and he clamped his mouth shut and lay totally still for the next minute. Usually only the taller one accompanied him to the resting room; during this interval the shorter one lathered up—something done only seldom by the taller one and never by the wooly one. The thrill that the wooly one experienced in the cold tank, the shorter man felt in the hot shower. Lolling languidly, he let the water pellets beat down upon his skin for several minutes. Then he scrubbed with soap everywhere, from bald forehead right down to the ankles, showered, lathered up once more, rinsed it all off using a cloth, washed—in a crouching position—his feet, and for a third time lathered up the areas he was especially intent on cleansing thoroughly: face, neck, groin, penis, and the rear cleavage. And, stooped over with legs spread wide, he washed the latter yet a fourth time. After the soap treatment he turned the shower on as hot as he could bear it and stood there gasping with pleasure. Then, his whole body steaming, he placed the pink soap neatly into its little dish, and by then the wooly one was usually already returning with the taller one, and they all left for the sweatroom. As already mentioned, the entire threesome was in the resting room this time, the taller one dozing, the wooly one resting restlessly, the shorter one dangling arms and legs off the sides of the cot. And when they came back into the anteroom he was whistling—the shorter one that is—merrily to himself.

And then the unexpected happened.

In the sauna chamber (I had slipped in right after the threesome), by nodding coaxingly and repeated gesturing with his hands, palms up, bent from beside his hips up towards himself, the wooly one once again invited his companions, who had seated themselves as they always did on a bench one level beneath him, to join him up there. And once again he did this after having uttered the first few words of a conversation—or rather, after verhaltener Stimme einige uns Umsitzenden unverstehbare, von den beiden Emporlauschenden aber mit beflissenem Nicken oder Schmunzeln quittierte Worte zugesprochen hatte, und wie immer glitt nach dieser Erhebung ein Lächeln begnadeter Freude über ihre Züge, beglückter beim Längeren, genugtuungsvoller beim Kürzeren, doch bei beiden ans Erstaunen von Söhnen des hohen Nordens erinnernd, die jedesmal neu überwältigt die Sonne nach langer Winterhaft aufgehen sehen. Bis dahin also auch diesmal wie je: Eintrittsritual, Platznahme nach Rang, Anrede, Erhöhung, und zwei gesetzte Männer schnellten fast rücklings nach oben, da fragte, statt sein Sich-Mitteilen fortzusetzen, der Wollige laut als wie unsereins, wieviel Grad es denn habe, und auf die gedämpfte Entgegnung des Längeren, es habe vierundsiebzig Grad, fragte, und weiterhin so, daß ihn jeder vernehmen konnte, der Wollige weiter, ob das vierundsiebzig Grad Reaumur oder Fahrenheit wären, und setzte, zum Längeren gewandt, doch uns alle meinend, seine Fragen mit der Erkundigung fort, ob der Witz von dem Mann, der zur Leipziger Messe fahre, bekannt sei, und das war einfach unerhört. Unerhört natürlich nicht der Witz, sondern daß er uns einbezog. Sonst hatte er, wie gesagt, nur zu den beiden geredet, leise, bedeutend, mit leisen und bedeutenden Gesten und großen Pausen zwischen den einzelnen Worten, die er wie Sigel von Unabdingbarem setzte, verhalten, eindringlich, letztinstanzlich, und manchmal auch mit dem hintergründigen Lächeln für Eingeweihte, das über Wohl und Wehe Dritter entschied und das die beiden mit einer Gebärde empfingen, die der Übergang vom Nicken einer Vollzugsbereitschaft zur Verneigung vor schicksalhaft Waltendem war. Jedenfalls sah es so aus, und nie hatten wir mehr als ein unerschließbares Raunen vernommen; nie hätten wir von seinen Lippen zu lesen vermocht; nie hatten die beiden um ihn durch ein Mienenspiel etwas von dem Mitgeteilten verraten—und nun an uns alle, und nun gar ein Witz! Natürlich wartete er nicht auf ein Ja oder Nein zu seiner Frage, sondern fuhr—nach einer Pause, in der sich sein Mund schon auftat und sein Blick uns noch einmal überflog, ehe er sich, wie bei jedem Lehrenden, auf einen imaginären Punkt im Fernsten richtete—, fuhr also, ein wenig vornübergebeugt, in kurzen, durch öfteres Händeöffnen weit voneinander abgesetzten Passagen zu reden fort, daß eines Morgens zwei Männer auf eine Dienstreise nach Leipzig zur Messe gegangen seien und am Fahrkartenschalter zwei Fahrkarten nach Leipzig verlangt hätten, wobei—und nun erhob er Kopf wie Stimme—, having expressed in a low voice a few words incomprehensible to those of us sitting around him, but acknowledged with eager nods or smiles by the two who were attentively listening to the sounds coming from above. And as it always happened after this sign of favor, their faces lit up with the joy of having been blessed in this special way. The smile of the taller one revealed his rejoicing, while for the shorter one it was one of satisfaction. But both their smiles were reminiscent of the smiles of Arctic people who marvel each year anew when, after a long winter's bondage, they see the sun rise. Up to this point the customary routine had also been followed on this particular day: the entrance ritual, the seating arrangement by rank, the first words, the uplift, and the leap of two sedate men upwards and almost over backwards. But then, instead of continuing his whispered remarks, the wooly man asked, in a tone of voice as loud as any of ours, what the temperature reading was. And when the taller one replied in a hushed voice that it was seventy-four degrees, the wooly one asked—and still loud enough for everyone to hear—whether that was seventy-four degrees Rankine scale or Fahrenheit. And still facing the taller man, but meaning all of us, he continued his queries by asking if anyone had heard the joke about the man who had gone to Leipzig to see the doctor for his annual physical checkup—and all of this was simply unheard of. Of course, it was not the joke that was unheard of, but rather the fact that he was including all of us. Before, as already indicated, he had addressed only the two others, quietly, meaningfully, with quiet and meaningful gestures and long pauses between the individual words. And these he set as if they were symbols for the ultimate—in a subdued, insistent, final manner, and sometimes with that unfathomable smile, intended only for a chosen few, that determined the weal and woe of outsiders—a smile approved by the two men with a gesture that was no longer a nod of acceptance but almost a submissive bow to the hand of Fate. At least that is what it looked like, and never had we perceived more than inscrutable rumblings; never would we have been able to read his lips; never had the changing facial expressions of the two companions revealed any part of the message—and now he was addressing all of us, and with a joke at that! Naturally he did not wait for anyone to answer with a yes or no, but rather continued—after a pause during which his mouth opened and his eyes scanned us once more before he focused them, as do all who teach, on an imaginary spot on a distant back wall—continued, as he leaned slightly forward, with his speech. And hand motions were interspersed among the words marking the long breaks between the phrases that made up his story, which told of a man who had just been to Leipzig to see the doctor for a checkup. After the doctor's appointment, a colleague had asked him about his state of health, whereupon—and at that point he raised both head and wobei der eine der Reisenden erklärt habe, sie reaumierten heute zur Messe (wörtlich: "Mir reaumieren nämlich heute zur Messe—"), bei welcher Wendung der Längere wie der Kürzere ins glucksende Lachen ungläubiger Erheiterung ausbrechen, worauf der Wollige, mit jovial-genußhaftem Blick in unsre noch stumme Gesichtsrunde zurückkehrend, das soeben berichtete Verbum unter neuem Aufglucksen der beiden bestätigend wiederholte, um dann, nach einer kunstvollen Pause, in der die Vorfreude auf die eigne Pointe und mit der unverhohlenen Erwartung, in wenigen Augenblicken eine Runde begeisterten Lachens um sich versammelt zu sehen, ihm die Augenbrauen hochzog und Lippen samt Backen erzittern machte, um also endlich mit ihr, der Pointe, herauszurücken: Man sei, so der zweite seiner Messebesucher zur Fahrkartenverkäuferin, man sei jetzt im Fernstudium nämlich gerade beim Physikkapitel, und da verwechsele der Kollege doch jedesmal Fahrenheit und Reaumur; er habe sagen wollen: "Mir fahrenheit zur Leipziger Mes—", und da platzte der Kürzere heraus, eine schallende Lache, in die der Längere erst einstimmte, als der Wollige mit triumphierendem Ton die Pointe halb wiederholend vollendet hatte: "—mir fahrenheit nach Leipzig zur Messe—fahren heut, ja?", und nun lachte er selbst im breiten Gelächter der beiden mit, und der Längere schlug sich auf den Schenkel: "reaumiehrn—"; und der Kürzere, trockener, kopfschüttelnd zwischen kargeren Lachstößen: "—so einer; na!", und in den braunen, den wasserhellen klaren freudengeweiteten runden Augen des Wolligen schimmerte wieder die kindhafte Lust wie im Frischwasserbecken; und er hob schon, den Mund breitbehaglich verziehend, die Hände, seine Knie statt des Wassers zu schlagen, da war das Lachen der zwei in der Stille des Schweigens zerbröckelt, denn es blieb still ringsum, eine unbeteiligte Stille, auf allen Bänken, ganz still, und der Wollige, hilflos, erläuterte noch: "Das hat der verwechselt", dann ging sein Blick für einen Moment wieder in die Ferne und kam gleich zurück auf seine Zehen, und im Ofen knisterte ein Stein. Knistern im Ofen; natürlich, wir waren ja in der Sauna mit ihrer trockenen heißen Luft und dem trockenen heißen Holz und dem gnadenlos ausgeleuchteten trockenen heißen saharafarbenen Innen, in dem man jedes Haar und jede Fiber und jeden auf der Maserung verdampfenden Schweißtropfen sieht; hätte er diesen Witz im Dampfbad erzählt, in den wallenden Schwaden, wo auch die Phantasie und das Wohlwollen wallen, in den treibenden, ineinander sich wälzenden Wolken, aus denen Gesichter tauchen und Bäuche und Hände und Worte und Gutmütigkeiten, Vages im zischenden Nebel, zersprühende lindernde Kühle, Gelöstheit, Gemüt und Genüge, vielleicht hätte es dort, wo *alles* Volk war, ein Lachengegeben, heiteres Gebrüll aus den kochenden Schwaden, Herzlichkeit aus allen Poren;

voice—whereupon he had told him how the doctor had thought he was underweight but at the proper rank in scale. And after this phrase had been uttered, both the taller and the shorter man, out of incredulous delight, burst out chortling. And on that, the wooly one threw a jovial, gratified look into our blank-faced midst and, with the two men chortling anew, repeated this phrase in case we thought we had not heard correctly. After an artful pause, in which the undisguised anticipation of hearing his own punch line together with the expectation of being surrounded by enthusiastic laughter in a few moments time had made his eyebrows rise and his lips and cheeks tremble, he could finally come out with it—with the punch line. It so happened that the two colleagues were taking a correspondence course in physics, and since the one had just been working on the chapter dealing with thermodynamics, he was always confusing Fahrenheit with the Rankine scale of temperature. He had intended to quote the words of the doctor: "You are fair in height, but low in . . ." It was then that the shorter man broke into his next fit of laughter—a reverberating bellow—and the taller one did not join in until the wooly one, in a triumphant tone of voice, had had another go at the punch line and completed it: "You are fair in height, but low in weight—Fahrenheit, get it?" And then he himself laughed uproariously along with the other two, and the taller one slapped his knees, "rank in scale—" and the shorter one, more aloofly and shaking his head between the more restrained outbreaks of laughter: "He's really something!" And round with delight, the brown, the crystal-clear eyes of the wooly man shone once again with childlike enthusiasm, just as earlier in the cold tank. And with a Cheshire-cat grin, he was already lifting his hands, this time to slap his knees instead of the surface of the water. And then the laughter of the other two fizzled out in the still of the silence, for all around everyone remained silent—an apathetic silence, on every bench, total silence—and helplessly the wooly one proceeded to spell it out: "He confused the two, you see." Then his gaze once more wandered off into the distance, but right away became fixed on his toes again; and in the stove the crackle of a stone. Crackling in the stove—but of course, we were, after all, in a sauna bath, what with its dry, hot air and the dry, hot wood and the unmercifully burning, dry, hot, Sahara-colored interior, where every hair and every fiber and every bead of perspiration evaporating on the wood grain is visible. If he had told this joke in the steambath, in the wallowing vapors where fantasy and well-wishing wallow as well, within the drifting clouds that billow over and under each other and from which faces and bellies and hands and words and goodwill emerge—vague images in the seething mist, diffusing soothing cool, abandon, affect, and abundance—perhaps there, where *all* were common, there would have been some laughter, some rollicking howls emerging from the surging steam, good cheer aber er ging ja nicht dorthin, und hier? Gnadenlos alles: gnadenlos die Luft, gnadenlos die Hitze, gnadenlos die Trockenheit, gnadenlos die Sonderung, ein gnadenlos vertaner Moment kaum möglichen Zusammenfindens, doch da sah der Wollige schon den Längeren an und sagte, beiläufig, uns grade noch hörbar, doch ganz zu dem Angesprochnen gerichtet: "Ach, ihr kanntet den schon", und dann, nach dem Nicken der beiden, doch ohne ihr Nicken erwartet zu haben und so, wie wenn nie etwas geschehen wäre—und es *war* ja auch gar nichts geschehen—, begann er wie je seine Worte zu setzen: unhörbar, bedeutend, mit sehr langen Pausen und sicherbeschließenden strichhaften Gesten, und dann schlug er noch einmal die Augen zu uns auf, die wir alle geblieben waren und dies und das sprachen, was man in der Sauna so spricht: Belangloses, Nichtiges, Halblautes, Silben, Partikel, und er sah uns alle in *einem* Blick an, gleichgültig, in lässiger Nichtbeachtung des einzelnen uns insgesamt abtuend; dann stand er, ein Wort zum Kürzeren äußernd, auf, wiewohl es noch nicht seine Zeit war (er blieb immer genau zwölf Minuten im Schwitzraum, eine Zeit, deren Dauer dem recht schnell ins Perlen geratenden Längeren offensichtlich nicht sehr angenehm war, doch er hielt natürlich jedesmal durch), stand also noch nicht triefend auf und ging, indes der Längere hautnah vor ihm durch die Tür glitt, in den Vorraum, und der Kürzere folgte ihm hautnah und schloß. Draußen dann machte der Wollige, nach dem Duschen natürlich, Kniebeugen; es waren, wobei er lautlos mitzählte, ihrer zwanzig, dann spritzte er Knie und Unterschenkel mit dem Kaltwasserschlauch ab, den ihm, da er danach griff, der Längere schon entgegenstreckte, und dann verließ er die Sauna endgültig, eine Viertelstunde zu früh und stets ohne Gruß.

Ich dachte, er käme nicht mehr, doch schon zum nächsten Turnus trat er, und verspätet, ein wie immer, dann aber duschte er kürzer als sonst, ging sofort in den Schwitzraum, wiewohl es dort voll war, setzte sich ohne Zögern in eine Lücke der Mittelreihe, und seine Begleiter nahmen unten bei den Neulingen Platz. Fast eine Minute saßen sie so in völligem Schweigen, dann sagte der Wollige zwei unverstehbare Worte, und der Kürzere sprang auf, eilte ans Thermometer, schaute, ein wenig ins Knie gehend, lange die Skala, und als er dann, zurückgekehrt, Meldung erstattete, drehte der Wollige den Kopf sehr langsam vom Gradaus nach ganz rechts, von dort nach ganz links and von dort zur Mitte zurück, fixierte dann, die Augen zum Thermometer erhoben, die von seinem Platz aus unablesbaren Ziffern, um schließlich ein den Umsitzenden deutlich vernehmbares "das ist wieder zuwenig" zu sagen, und zwar in einem Ton der Mißbilligung, in oozing out of every pore. But that is not where he went. And here? It was all merciless: merciless the air, merciless the heat, merciless the dryness, merciless the isolation, a mercilessly wasted moment of an almost impossible convergence. But right away, in a casual manner and in a tone of voice just loud enough for us to barely understand, but addressing only the taller man directly, the wooly one looked at him and said: "Oh, you already heard that one." And then, after the two had nodded, but without having expected them to nod, and acting as if nothing had happened—in fact, nothing had—he began to speak the same way as before: inaudibly, meaningfully, with very long pauses and assuring, underscoring gestures. And then he once again raised his eyes to look at all of us, who had stayed and were busy chatting about this and that, the sort of thing you chat about in the sauna—unimportant things, trifling matters, subdued words, syllables, particles—and in one sweeping glance he looked at us all—indifferently, lazily disregarding each individual and thereby snubbing all of us. And then, while saying something to the shorter one, he stood up, even though his time was not up yet (he always stayed in the sauna chamber for exactly twelve minutes—a period of time that was obviously unpleasant for the taller one, who was very quickly covered with beads of perspiration, but endured nevertheless, naturally). So he entered the anteroom without being soaking wet, while the taller man glided through the door a hair's-breadth ahead of him and the shorter one trailed by only a hair's-breadth and shut the door. Outside then, but only after showering, of course, the wooly one did deep-knee bends. He did some twenty of them and kept track by counting along silently. Then he sprayed off his knees and calves with cold water coming from a hose that the taller one was holding for him to take as soon as he reached for it. And then he left the sauna for good—fifteen minutes early and, as always, without saying goodbye.

I thought he would not be back, but the very next time he walked in—late, as usual. However, his shower was shorter than usual. He then went straight into the sauna chamber, even though it was full in there, sat down without any hesitation in a space in the middle row, and his companions joined the newcomers on the bottom bench. About one minute elapsed in total silence, and then the wooly one uttered two incomprehensible words. The shorter man jumped up, rushed over to the thermometer, and, bending his knees slightly, he examined the scale at great length. After he had gone back and given a report, the wooly one turned his head very slowly from a straight-ahead position to the far right, from there to the far left, and from there back to center position. With his eyes raised towards the thermometer, he stared at the numbers that could not be deciphered from where he sat, and finally voiced his clearly comprehensible complaint ("It's too low again") to his neighbors. And this he did in a tone of disapdie sich sowohl Genugtuung über den Eintritt eines sicher vorausgewußten Ereignisses wie ehrliches Staunen darüber mischte, daß dieses Ereignis doch eingetreten—sein Timbre rührte ans Rätsel der Prädestination. In diesem Augenblick sah alles zum Thermometer: es zeigte wie stets vierundsiebzig Grad, und wir hörten den Wolligen noch einmal und nun nur noch mißbilligend sagen, daß dies für eine Sauna zuwenig sei, da aber war er schon aufgestanden und ging in den Duschraum und gab noch in der Tür, die dadurch ein wenig länger als sonst offenblieb, dem beschließenden Kürzeren eine uns unhörbare Weisung, die dieser mit lebhaftem Nicken entgegennahm. Dann ging er, und am nächsten Tag war die Sauna geschlossen; ein Windschutz würde eingebaut, hieß es, und als die Anstalt nach neun Wochen wieder geöffnet wurde, war ein Lederschirm um die Tür gebaut und das Thermometer hielt genau bei achtzig Grad. Jetzt war wohl jeder gespannt auf des Wolligen Rückkunft, und ich war zudem auch neugierig, einmal seine Reaktion auf ein gänzlich überraschendes, schon im Ansatz und nicht nur im Ziel unvorhergesehenes Ereignis zu erfahren, und ich nahm mir vor, es das nächste Mal so einzurichten, daß ich mich zwischen ihn und einen seiner Begleiter auf die oberste Saunabank drängte, doch da erschien er nicht mehr bei uns. Oder besser gesagt: erst nachdem er längere Zeit nicht mehr erschienen war, kam ich auf jenen Gedanken. Es fiel mir dann noch vieles ein, ihn herauszufordern, so etwa, ihn einfach anzusprechen oder ihn, wenn er mich musterte, zu fragen, ob er etwas von mir wünsche, doch ich kam, wie gesagt, nicht mehr dazu, und sollte er noch einmal erscheinen, werde ich es wahrscheinlich doch nicht tun.

Übrigens traf ich ihn kürzlich auf der Straße. Ich ging zu einer Sitzung des Verbandes der Freunde ästhetischer Forschung, um meine erwähnte Schrift über Formnotwendigkeiten zu verteidigen (was mir, nebenbei gesagt, gar nicht gelang: ich wurde zu meiner Verblüffung, ich hatte wirklich nicht damit gerechnet, als Träger einer recht bedenklichen Fehleinschätzung der deutschen Barockdichtung verurteilt), da fuhr er in einer schwarzen Limousine die Allee herunter, die ich hinaufging. Ich erkannte ihn sofort: Der Längere fuhr, der Kürzere saß auf dem Beifahrerplatz, und der Wollige wie in der Sauna hinter den Beiden, und die Blicke der kugelrunden Augen sprangen musternd über den Bürgersteig. Nun fielen sie auch auf mich, und er schien mich tatsächlich zu erkennen; er lächelte ein wenig, ganz flüchtig, natürlich, der Anflug eines Lächelns nur, aber doch eines Lächelns, und dann nickte er mir auch wohlwollend zu, doch da hob sich der Wagen schon vom Straßenbelag und fuhr, in eine leichte Serpentine schwenkend, in langsam stetigem Steigen direkt durch proval in which were mixed satisfaction at seeing something occur as confidently expected, but also honest surprise at the expectation actually having materialized—a tone that in itself came close to the enigma of predestination. Instantaneously all eyes turned toward the thermometer. As always, it read seventy-four degrees, and then we heard the wooly one repeat, but this time merely in a disapproving tone, that this was too low for a sauna. But by then he had already stood up and gone to the shower room, and in passing through the door, which for this reason stayed open a little longer than usual, he conveyed an order to the trailing shorter man, not loud enough for us to hear, but which this man acknowledged, nodding vigorously. Then he left, and the following day the sauna was closed. Rumor had it that a screen to protect against drafts was being installed, and when they reopened after nine weeks, a leather screen was built up around the door, and the thermometer held a steady eighty degrees. Presumably everyone was now eagerly waiting the day of the wooly one's return, and besides that, I was curious for once to see his reaction to a totally surprising occurrence—unpredictable not only from the point of view of the end result but also from the point of view of its very conception. And I decided that the next time I would somehow manage to squeeze in between him and one of his companions up on the top bench, but he never showed himself in our midst again. Or rather, only after his not having appeared for quite some time, did this idea occur to me. Then other ones occurred to me as well: to challenge him either by simply speaking to him, or by asking him when he scrutinized me, if there was something he wanted from me. But, as I said, I never did get to do these things, and even if he should still turn up someday, I probably will not follow through anyway.

And by the way, I did just happen to meet him on the street the other day. I was on my way to a meeting of the Association of Friends of Esthetic Research to defend my aforementioned paper on the need for form (at which, while on the topic, I was unsuccessful: to my amazement I was criticized—I really had not counted on this happening—as being guilty of a rather serious misinterpretation of German Baroque poetry), when I spotted him in a black limousine that was driving down the avenue that I happened to be walking up. I recognized him right away. The taller man was driving, the shorter one was sitting in the passenger seat, and, just as in the sauna, the wooly one was sitting behind them both, and the eyes that were round as balls darted about, casting critical glances up and down the sidewalk. Then these eyes met mine, and he actually seemed to recognize me. He smiled slightly—very briefly of course, only a trace of a smile, but a smile nevertheless—and then he gave me a well-wishing nod. But already the car was leaving the pavement and, following a gentle spiral, was climbing slowly, steadily, right through the air into a silently and out-die Luft in ein lautlos von innen sich öffnendes Fenster eines fünften oder sechsten Stockes des Hochhauses am Markte, das sich lautlos und leicht wie ein Schmetterlingsflügel hinter dem Entrückten wieder schloß.

wards opening fifth- or sixth-story window of the highrise by the market-place— a window that then drew shut silently and as softly as the wings of a butterfly behind the man who had disappeared.

* Andreas Gryphius was one of the most eminent German poets of the seventeenth century, comparable to the English John Milton. By contrast, Emanuel Geibel, whose poetry is of lesser literary value, was a poet of the nineteenth century, comparable to his English contemporary, Alfred Lord Tennyson. *Translator's Note.*

AUTHORS AND TRANSLATORS

HORST BIENEK has appeared several times in DIMENSION with poetry and novel excerpts. The novel chapter here is from the most recent volume of his tetralogy called informally The Gleiwitz Chronicle. A chapter from *The First Polka* appeared in DIMENSION 9/2.

SANDRA CELT, who edits the *ATA Chronicle*, is a graduate with an M.A. in translation theory from the City University of New York.

ESTHER E. ENNS has translated three stories from Franz Fürmann's book *Bagatelle, rundum positiv*, including the one in this issue of DIMENSION. She lives in Toronto, Canada.

LILO FROMM is a painter who has distinguished herself particularly as an illustrator of children's books, with pictures vibrant with color and characterized by meticulously fine brush strokes. She works often with acrylic paints. Her illustrations in this issue of DIMENSION are representative of the humorous feature many of them have, fed by an inventive and playful imagination.

FRANZ FÜHMANN was born in Rokytnice, Czechoslovakia in 1922. He was a prisoner of war in Russia until 1949, after which he went to Berlin as a journalist in 1950. His earlier writings concentrate heavily on German fascism. This is his first appearance in DIMENSION.

BARBARA KÖNIG was born in 1925 in Reichenberg/North Bohemia. After spending two years in protective custody by the Gestapo, she moved briefly to the United States in 1950. She joined the Gruppe 47 in the same year. She became a full-time author upon her return to Germany and has published novels and stories, among which are *Kies* (1961, Gravel), *Das Kind und sein Schatten* (1958, The Child and Its Shadow), *Die Personenperson* (1965, The Personperson). She was awarded the Federal Association of Industry Literature Prize in 1962. In the spring of 1975 she was a visiting writer in the Department of Germanic Languages at the University of Texas at Austin. She lives in a lakeshore village near Munich with her physician husband and her daughter. The publication of the radio play in this issue of DIMENSION marks her first appearance here.

EPHRIAM KISHON was born in Hungary in 1924 and moved to Israel in 1949. He has held many jobs in his life but wrote plays as a hobby. He resides in Tel Aviv with his wife and their children. He has gained popularity in Germany through his satirical view of contemporary mores, which he describes with broad humor.

HANNA B. LEWIS is a faculty member of the Foreign Language Department at Sam Houston State University in Huntsville, Texas.

RICHARD MILLS, a graduate of the University of Texas at Austin with an MA in German, works in Austin.

BREON MITCHELL teaches comparative literature and German at Indiana University.

BERND RACHEL appeared in DIMENSION 11/3 with a selection of poems. He continues to write poetry principally, but also writes radio plays, such as the recent *Geld oder Leben* (Your Money or Your Life).

RALPH R. READ III, a prolific translator, is a popular professor in the Department of Germanic Languages at The University of Texas at Austin.

KLAUS SCHLESINGER was born in Berlin in 1937. He is the author of the novel *Michael* (1971), a repertorial essay *Hotel oder Hospital* (1973), and two collections of stories, *Alte Filme* (Old Films) (1976) and *Berliner Traum* (Berlin Dream, 1977).

VON UNDERWOOD is studying currently in Berlin on a fellowship. He is a graduate student at Boston University.

HANNELORE VALENCAK was born in the Steiermark in 1929. She studied physics at the University of Graz and worked in a metallurgical laboratory in a steel plant. She has devoted her time exclusively to writing since 1975. Among her works are the collection of stories *Morgen werden wir es wissen* (1961, Tomorrow We'll Know), and several novels, *Die Höhlen Noahs* (1961, Noah's Caves), *Ein fremder Garten* (1964, A Strange Garden), *Zuflucht hinter der Zeit* (1967, Flight beyond Time), and *Vorhof der Wirklichkeit* (1972, Vestibule of Reality). She is also a poet, with *Nur dieses eine Leben* (1966, Just This One Life), and the author of children's books, such as *Ich bin Barbara* (1974, *When Half-Gods Go*) and *Regenzauber* (1976, *A Tangled Web*). She resides in Vienna and appears for the first time in DIMENSION.

STANLEY N. WERBOW, a graduate of The Johns Hopkins University, is a longtime professor of Germanic Languages at The University of Texas at Austin, a past-chairman, and innovative past-dean of the now defunct College of Humanities*

SETH WOLLITZ holds a professorship in Hebrew Studies at The University of Texas at Austin*

A. LESLIE WILLSON is editor of DIMENSION.

* His name was omitted inadvertently from the Authors and Translators section of DIMENSION'S Yiddish issue, 13/2.

* His name was omitted inadvertently from the Authors and Translators section of DIMENSION'S Yiddish issue, 13/2.

DIMENSION : INDEX : VOLUME 13, 1980

BENDER, HANS	Letter from Germany	11
BIENEK, HORST	*Zeit ohne Glocken* Time without Bells	524
BILETZKI, Y. KH.	fun *"Akher"* from "Other"	448
DÜRRENMATT, FRIEDRICH	*Persönliche Anmerkung* Personal Notes Paintings	15
FITZBAUER, ERICH	*Syrakus und andere Gedichte* Syracuse and other Poems Drawings	40
FROMM, LILO	Drawings: *Komische Tiere/* Funny Animals	554
FÜHMANN, FRANZ	*Drei nackte Männer* Three Naked Men	594
GARRIN, STEPHEN	Perspective: It Burns and Burns and Yet Is not Consumed . . .	321
GLANTZ, YANKEV	*Nit a lid, nor a tfile, meyn kind* Not a Poem, but a Prayer, My Child	366
	Flaterlekh feyer Flickering Flames	368
GRADE, KHAIM	*Tzefat* Safed	402
GRASS, GÜNTER	*Die Linkshänder* The Left-Handers	52
	Die Ballerina The Ballerina Graphics	68
GREENBERG, URI TZVI	*Faran tzaylem* Before the Cross	430
	Fun der poema *"velt-bargarop"* From the Poem "Downhill World"	434

GREENBERG, URI TZVI		*Geveyn fun der erd* Lament of the Earth	440
		In melukhe fun tzaylem In the Kingdom of the Cross	442
GUSTAS, ALDONA	△	*Sechs Gedichte* Six Poems Graphics	144
HILDESHEIMER, WOLFGANG		*Leben und Tod von Sir Andrew Marbot* The Life and Death of Sir Andrew Marbot Graphics	92
HÖLLERER, WALTER		*Steinbruch-Morgenbuch* Stone-Quarry Morning Diary Drawing	122
HUNT, IRMGARD ELSNER		An Interview with Günter Grass	84
JANDL, ERNST	△	from: *Schittelbecker's Holiday* (illustrated)	154
KISHON, EPHRAIM		*Wie heißt "Olé" auf Hebräisch?* How Do You Say "Olé" in Hebrew?	584
KÖNIG, BARBARA	△	*Der Fuß im Netz* Foot in the Net	476
KOPE, RIVKE		*Ikh red tzu mir* I'm Talking to Myself	406
		Der fidl zeyger The Violin Clock	408
		Meyn feder My Pen	410
		Oyfn shpitz meser On the Tip of the Knife	412
		Trakhtungen Thoughts	414
KORN, ROKHL		*Yob* Job	416
		Erev regn Before the Rain	422

KUNERT, GÜNTER		*Prosa, Gedichte, Kleine Essays* Prose, Poems, Mini-Essays Graphics	158
LUTZ, WERNER	△	*Ich brauche dieses Leben und andere Gedichte* I Need This Life and other Poems Paintings	190
MAYRÖCKER, FRIEDERIKE	△	*Triplet und andere Bild-Gedichte* Triplet and other Picture Poems	196
MECKEL, CHRISTOPH		*Das Dings Da* (illustrated) The Thingamajig	200
MECKEL, CHRISTOPH		*Bericht vom Handwerk* Report on My Craft	208
MEISTER, ERNST		*Einige Gedichte* Some Poems Paintings	218
MIRANSKY, PERETZ		*Harbst* Fall	390
		Di zun Sunset	392
		Zey de khakhomim They the Wise	394
		Kine Envy	396
OPPERMANN, KARL		*Der erste Regen und andere Gedichte* The First Rain and other Poems (with graphics)	226
PEDRETTI, ERICA		*Depart* Departing Graphics	234
PLOTKIN, KHAIM		*Ver Ken Heynt Lebn Besholem Mit Zikh?* Who Can Live at Peace with Himself Anymore?	458
RACHEL, BERND		*Besuch auf der Veranda* Visit on the Veranda	542

RÜHM, GERHARD	*Absteigende Gedichte* Descending Poems Graphics	244
SCHLESINGER, KLAUS	*Am Ende der Jugend* Coming of Age	500
SCHNELL, ROBERT WOLFGANG	*Liebeskummer* (illustrated) Pangs of Love	252
SCHULMAN, ELIAS	On Contemporary Yiddish Writing	326
SCHWARTZ, SHLOYME	*Kvorim* Gravegarden	382
	Hoykhfiberish Thermo High	384
	Kindheytsregn The Rain of My Childhood	386
	Der geboyren-tog fun meyn balerine Ballerina's Birthday	388
SHTIKER, MEYER	*Ven strelisk hot gebrent* When Strelisk Burned	342
	Di sedra veyekhi Jacob's Death	348
	A briv fun gefengenish fun paul verlaine tzu artur rimbaud A Letter from Prison from Paul Verlaine to Arthur Rimbaud	354
SONNTAG, GERD	*Totsein in einem Winkel der Stadt und andere Gedichte* To Be Dead in a Corner of the City and other Poems Paintings	268
SUTZKEVER, AVROHOM	*Lider vun togbukh* Poems from My Diary	444
TAMBUR, VULF	*Oyin pripitzhek* In the Fireplace	456
TUSSMAN, MALKA HEIFETZ	*Un a schmeykhl iz geven* And There was a Smile	356

TUSSMAN, MALKA HEIFETZ	*Shalom shulamite* Shalom, Shulammite	358
	Tate ziser Sweet Father	364
UHLMANN, JOACHIM	*Zustände und andere Gedichte* Conditions and other Poems Paintings	274
VALENCAK, HANNELORE	*Der blaue Dragoman* The Blue Dragoman	562
WEISS, PETER	*Aus dem Pariser Journal* From the Paris Journal Collages	288
WILLSON, A. LESLIE	Perspective: Author/Artists	9
	Perspective: What's Going On?	473
ZHIKHLINSKY, REYZL	*Bryt far di feygl* Bread for the Birds	372
	Ikh kuk areyn in die oygn fun rembrandt I Looked into the Eyes of Rembrandt	374
	Shreybn lider Writing Poems	376
	Vuhin kumen ahin di reyd? Where Do the Words Disappear?	378
	Shney Snow	380

Translators contributing to Volume 13 are: Tzipora Baradon, Dorothy Billik, Allen Blunden, Timothy A. Bonner-Saroff, Sandra Celt, Allen H. Chappel, Hugh Denman, Michael P. Elzay, Esther E. Enns, Ken Fontenot, Adam Fuerstenberg, Stephen H. Garrin, Nathan Goldman, Ulrich K. Goldsmith, Georg M. Gugelberger, Jack Hirshman, Philip J. Kluhoff, Sabina Lask-Spinac, Hanna B. Lewis, Daniel Marlin, David Neale Miller, Richard Mills, Peretz Miransky, Breon Mitchell, Julia Penn, George F. Peters, Ralph R. Read III, Herman Salinger, Sholyme Schwartz, Malka Heifetz Tussman, Von Underwood, Johannes Vazulik, Stanley N. Werbow, A. Leslie Willson, Jeanne R. Willson, Seth Wollitz, Stephen Zon, and Marvin Zuckerman.

The volume will feature scores of lyric poets, almost 150 in 500 pages. It will be a triple-issue volume.

DIMENSION

Contemporary German Arts and Letters / Volume 13, Number 3, 1980

Department of Germanic Languages/THE UNIVERSITY OF TEXAS AT AUSTIN

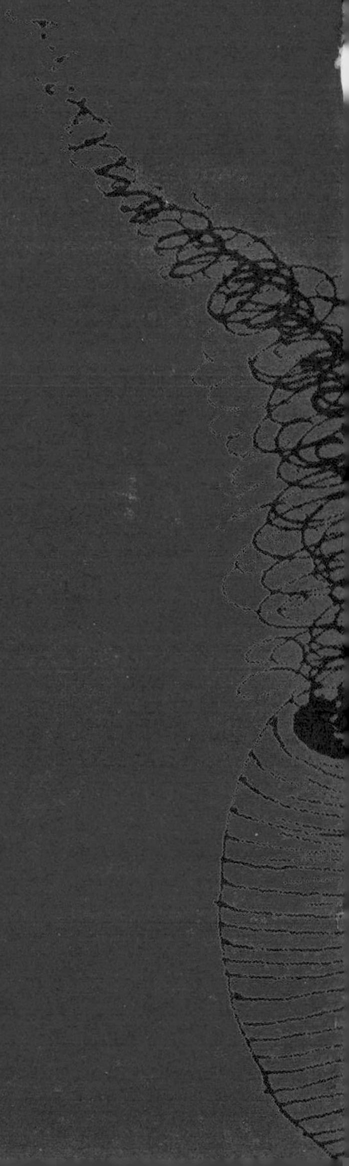